TIME CAPSULE

A CONCISE ENCYCLOPEDIA BY WOMEN ARTISTS

TIME CAPSULE

A CONCISE ENCYCLOPEDIA BY WOMEN ARTISTS

CONCEIVED AND EDITED BY
ROBIN KAHN

INTRODUCTIONS BY
KATHY ACKER
AVITAL RONELL

PUBLISHED BY CREATIVE TIME IN COOPERATION WITH SOS INT'L, 1995

Editor: Robin Kahn
Layout designer: Laura Fields
Cover designer: Keira Alexandra
Editorial Assistants: Mer Danluck, Elizabeth Hendler, Lisa Deanne Smith and Laura Sorokoff

Library of Congress # 95-70909
Cataloging-in-Publication Data
Kahn, Robin, ed.
Time Capsule: A Concise Encyclopedia by Women Artists
Includes index
ISBN # 1-881616-33-9
1. Time Capsule - International
2. Women and Art - International
3. Feminism
4. Encyclopedia, Women and Art
I. Kahn, Robin
II. Acker, Kathy
III. Ronell, Avital

1995

Printed and Bound in USA.
Available through D.A.P./Distributed Art Publishers
636 Broadway, 12th floor
New York, NY 10012
212-475-5119 phone
212- 673-2887 fax

Publishers: Creative Time, Inc. in cooperation with SOS Int'l

CONTENTS

ACKNOWLEDGEMENTS

The publication of Time Capsule is made possible through the generous contributions and the visionary support of:

A VERY SPECIAL ANONYMOUS DONOR; JUDITH ESTEROW OF ARTNEWS; FRANCES BEATTY ADLER; BARBARA BERMAN; EILEEN AND MICHAEL COHEN; ANA DANIEL; MARSHA GORDON; MARIELUISE HESSEL; ALEXANDRA ISLES; MIANI JOHNSON; CATHERINE REYNAL; NINA ROBBINS; & FREDERIECKE TAYLOR.

Creative Time projects are made possible, in part, with public funds from the National Endowment for the Arts, a federal agency; New York State Council on the Arts; New York City Department of Cultural Affairs; and New York City Council Member Tom Duane. Programs are also made possible with funds from Harriett Ames Charitable Trust; AT&T; Capezio/Ballet Makers Dance Foundation; Chase Manhattan Bank; Con Edison; The Cowles Charitable Trust; Howard Gilman Foundation; The Greenwall Foundation; The William & Mary Greve Foundation; The Harkness Foundation for Dance; Heathcote Art Foundation; IBM Matching Grant Foundation; Jerome Foundation; Herman and Ruth Kahn Foundation; The Joe & Emily Lowe Foundation; The Joyce Mertz-Gilmore Foundation; J.P. Morgan & Co., Incorporated; National Alliance for Media Arts and Culture; New York Community Trust; New York Foundation for the Arts; Norton Family Foundation; Philip Morris Companies Inc.; Sandpiper Fund; Dr. Seuss Foundation; Louis Sherman and Company; Turner Network Television; Urban Development Corporation; The Andy Warhol Foundation for the Visual Arts; and Creative Time's friends and supporters.

ACKNOWLEDGEMENTS

Time Capsule would not have been possible without the generous and enthusiastic participation of all of the artists who created art works for this anthology. We would like to extend a special note of gratitude to both Kathy Acker and Avital Ronell who are extraordinary for finding the time and inspiration to write their compelling introductions. In addition, we are grateful to Kirby Gookin who introduced us to the world of time capsules and to a shared conviction in the importance of treating publications as public space. And a special thank you to both Beckett and Anne Kahn for carrying on the torch into the new millennium.

Many people provided the inspiration, vision and resources necessary for the realization of this anthology. To begin, we wish to thank Zina Mounla of UNIFEM for supplying the motivation to create a project on the occasion of the Fourth World Conference on Women (Beijing, 1995). We are indebted to Sharon Gallagher and Craig Willis from Distributed Art Publishers (DAP) for their technical advice and unflagging support. We are also grateful to have collaborated with the book's designers, Keira Alexandra (book cover) and Laura Fields (layout), who devoted their time and energy helping to realize the anthology's form. Among the many other people who provided enthusiastic support and sound advice for the book were Martin Avilez, Miguel Benlloch and Joaquin Vazquez at B.N.V., Suzanne Bober, Anna Chave, Roger Denson, Barbara Ess, Sondra Farganis, Dana Friis-Hansen, Alonso Gil Lavado, Victoria Gil, Sara Goldstein, Alexander Gray, Federico Guzmán, Jo Hockenhull, Laura Hoptman, Stephen Isaac, Miani Johnson, Jeff Kahn, Geraldine Karetsky, Avery Lozada, Anneke Lucas, Louise Neri, Saul Ostrow, *Paginas Abierta,* Ann Phelan, Esther Regueira Mauriz, Berta Sichel, Mimi Somerby, Mike Starn, Wendy Steiner, Melanie York, Babbo, Liz, Mimi and Hey.

Finally, we offer our heartfelt thanks to Carol Stakenas and all of Creative Time's staff, board and project interns for their dedication to this project and hours of hard work.

ABOUT CREATIVE TIME

Creative Time was founded nearly twenty-two years ago—a time when artists around the country began to establish alternative arts organizations as a positive response to their frustrations over the limitations of more traditional exhibition venues. Almost immediately Creative Time became an international leader in presenting new works by visual artists, performers, musicians, choreographers, and poets in unlikely, under explored, and even abandoned public spaces.

Since the organization's formation in 1973, Creative Time has helped artists approach the City as their canvas, their stage. Together we have presented new works in such public spaces as street corners, landfills, subway tunnels, storefronts, beaches, bars, billboards, tenement houses, bridges, television screens, and now in cyberspace. Annually our programs provoke and entertain millions of New York City residents and visitors. By cultivating large and diverse public audiences, Creative Time also educates the public about the importance of cultural activities and introduces them to contemporary art practices.

As artists' needs and interests change, so does Creative Time. In order to remain timely and engaging, we rarely schedule programs more than one year in advance. We work with the belief that art moves society forward and that artists can be a positive catalyst for change. We encourage artists to use their voices to address social as well as cultural issues. Additionally, we champion the inalienable right to free expression and we promote the fact that artists are legitimate, productive and valuable contributors to the world at large.

LETTER FROM CREATIVE TIME

To commemorate the United Nations' Fourth World Conference on Women, Creative Time put forth a difficult challenge to visual artist, Robin Kahn. Her provocation was to develop a "public art project" that would embrace the creative contributions of women artists from around the world and easily travel to international destinations. The fruits of this artist's singular vision and sheer passion is *Time Capsule,* a remarkable book compiling the collective contributions of women artists from around the world.

We felt strongly that when international delegates, ambassadors, political leaders, and others gather at the conference to discuss women's issues, their creative accomplishments must be tangibly acknowledged and represented. Hundreds of women artists from around the world agreed. In less than two months, we received nearly seven-hundred original submissions from artists of diverse disciplines. They understood the need for a book that collected their unedited works and reflected their critical issues and objectives.

As Creative Time's first venture in the realm of publishing, *Time Capsule* marks a seminal advance in our efforts to investigate and rethink the public art monument while supporting artists in their efforts to express their visions and use their voices. We are dedicated and committed to our artists' projects, no matter what form they take; Creative Time will uphold its tradition of responding to artists' ideas as they relate to the evolving interests of our broader communities.

Anne R Pasternak, Executive Director

ABOUT SOS INT'L

SOS Int'l is an artists' collaborative formed to design and produce publications that are public works of art. Each book is the result of an open call where everyone who responds as a contributor becomes a part of the collective. The authors generously give their work to the public, and the resultant anthology promotes an unedited exchange of ideas, unrestricted by the market conditions that typically govern commercial exhibition and publication spaces. *Time Capsule: A Concise Encyclopedia by Women Artists* is the most recent publication in this series.

Promotional Copy, produced in 1993, was conceived as a "yellow pages" of the international arts community. The 400 page anthology assumes the format of a telephone directory. Printed on yellow newsprint, it is a fingertip-ready guide linking artists around the globe. Contributors were invited to participate via an open chain letter offering them free advertising space. All contributions received were published; no artist's work was turned away. Published without copyright restrictions, this anthology offers the public an opportunity to directly access, copy or use the ideas and works of each contributor.

Special Issue (1992) is a manual of recipes that have nothing to do with food. An unbound compendium of original photocopies contributed by 50 poets, writers and artists, the publication has no hierarchy or order. The manual is produced and sold at cost and has no copyright restrictions. Anyone who follows a recipe can collaborate with the artists as creator, author and owner of the work of art.

Additional SOS Int'l publications include projects in cable television, CD-ROM, the Internet, and between peoples of a given community in spontaneous interaction.

LETTER FROM THE EDITOR

Time Capsule: A Concise Encyclopedia by Women Artists is the result of an open letter (p.1) sent to a large network of women artists, poets, writers and collaborative organizations working in the international creative community. Each recipient was invited to contribute a work for the anthology and then to pass the invitation on like a chain letter to friends and colleagues. This structure enabled the artists to collaborate in both the *Time Capsule's* creative and editorial process. For three months, contributions arrived from artists who live as close as next door to as far away as Havana, Tokyo, Nairobi, Jerusalem and Budapest. Every artist who sent work in by the deadline is included in the publication.

The anthology is alphabetized according to the subject headings invented by each author. In this way, the *Time Capsule's* encyclopedic format is determined by the collective identity of its contributors. Each page includes the artist's name and the city and country from where the contribution was sent. Although, for many, that location does not indicate the author's nationality, it does represent a current working address. Contact numbers are not printed unless included by the artist in the layout of their submitted work. If you would like to contact someone in the book, SOS Int'l will furnish their address (subject to the individual artist's approval). For further details, please feel free to contact me via:

phone	212-431-4571
fax	212-219-8853
mail	114 Mercer Street #9
	New York, NY 10012

Recognizing that women's cultural contributions have been largely ignored, erased or stolen, *Time Capsule* emphasizes that the copyright of each submission is owned by its individual author.

Robin Kahn

WOMEN AT THE LIMINALITY OF THE SOCIAL

In a crucial sense, the women artists who responded to the call of the Time Capsule project could do no more than assert their place at the liminality of the social. This place is not a site of negativity, but it is in need of being staked out, vigilantly guarded and understood. When women artists arrive on the scene (without as such *arriving*: this is a time capsule, complicit with the necessity of the delay in women's "arrival"), they sketch a community of a particular kind, one that is not content to reproduce mainstream presumptions about things but affirms the constant displacement of accepted values and modes of being. The women who have responded to the call of Time Capsule do not constitute a substantial community of any kind; they cannot easily be linked by a single politics or projective desire, or even by a recognizable and unproblematic identity. We cannot borrow or even lease out the comfort zones of essence and identity; nor do we take recourse to the level of consensual hallucinations which so often underscore the metaphysics of male identifications. At the same time, there is nothing simply reactive about convoking a community of women artists. Something entirely different is at stake.

Perhaps, at the outset, an affirmative linguistic action ought to be revealed. In other words, the precarious ground on which this volume is based and the abyssal risks it takes still need to be unfolded, for we take nothing for granted and can only affirm the contradictory and tensional structures with which we have had to work. The project of launching a time capsule and that of stabilizing an encyclopedic desire that seeks to envelope it are at odds with one another and could never, logically, be expected to share the same space. Nonetheless, a certain irrevocable contract has been drawn between these incommensurable articulations—and if their meeting should be an error, this can be viewed only as an *exemplary* error, a teaching moment in the history of feminist inscription. Historically and canonically, the encyclopedia originates in a tendency of metaphysical heroics which seeks to contain everything that comes under the supervisory forces of Reason; the (m)encyclopedia makes claims for covering the totality of thought and occurrence. In principal and practice, this totality is submitted to a strict alphabetico-logical system which would contain and domesticate everything that comes under its purview (which, in principle, includes *everything*). The encyclopedia leaves no remainders, no leftovers or irrecuperable exteriorities, and no random, aleatory traces which could not be accounted for. However, while promising to contain and enumerate everything, the history of encyclopedic desire has spliced out all forms of minoritization: thus women have had no place—not even a shelter, a halfway house for alien manifestations, in the unfolding of universal Reason. Nonetheless, we are claiming an encyclopedic moment for ourselves, reappropriating what has marked a history of exclusions. In the past, the encyclopedia has mirrored social operations of effacement and, when it came to the subject of women, the fixed gaze of a universal, if resolute, blank stare.

The organic unity in which both history and encyclopedia were invested has been revealed to be a lie; this lie has masqueraded as universal history. Where there are values of universality, there has been a subterranean narrative of exclusion, disenfranchisement and erasure. The solution does not reside in turning away from such a history or denying its haunting hold on us today; on the contrary, we welcome and face this hidden narrative, we collectively pull on its threads and interweave it with ever new narratives, images and communications. What we are trying to establish here, then, is a community of articulation, and not one of organization or sheer organicity. There is no fusion of voices or terms, no organic totality of values and experience to which any of us would comfortably subscribe, though we do acknowledge the language of a certain shared anguish. No traditional encyclopedia could hope to master the diverse and irreducible singularities which inhabit these pages. When opening the encyclopedia to a plurality of singularities, we resist organic totality as a sign of the universal meltdown of particularities. This volume is not an assimilatory machine modeled on the organic metaphor, but prides itself on the discontinuities and breaks in syntax that it necessarily produces.

Encyclopedia, traditionally believing it has mastered aberrancy and still making closural moves on particularities, rounding up categories and holding them up for shadowless view by a police force of Reason, upholds the sovereignty of a system and the possibility of accounting for the manifestation of all that is. Nothing escapes its surveillance mechanisms. Yet, encyclopedia has never been a place for women, as though woman flies beneath the radar of universal Reason. This exclusion is not merely a predicament to be lamented; it has also been our escape route from the reactionary dragnet of mainstream history.

Because this occasion for the return of the encyclopedia reopens the question of place, the place and placing of woman, the place of this conference; because we find that woman has no proper place (and certainly not in Beijing), the positing of place has had to be asserted while it is also resisted: this ency-clopedia is a rigorous attempt to articulate the distress of women whose gestures are neither altogether silent nor intensely outspoken but who occupy a liminal zone and speak at each juncture from a history of laceration, exile and fundamental displacement—even in her "own" home. If "a room of one's own" was the appropriate response to the problem of woman's place yesterday, this utterance and its referential indication of spatial inwardness now need to be turned into a form of questioning. We have found that a room of one's own, if such an autonomous space were ever indeed to be located, is invaded by unclarity, narcissistic blockage, anxiety, dispossession and other uneasy infiltrations of the real; moreover, the housing project initiated by Virginia Woolf—the merits of which should not be overlooked—is nowadays maintained by interest borrowed from the male metaphysical subject: it suggests a kind of control room where one's "own" destiny could be monitored and controlled, with little allowance for slippage, contradictory impulse or the exquisite doubt to which all women have been subject. The relation implied by the sacred architecture of "a room of one's own" appears to be built upon a dream of non-relation, if not on a somewhat obsolesced, pretech understanding of space. What is the current status of nonrelation and creative intervention?

The place that we seek to create, as a site for sharing, imparting and self-division, does not as such exist as presence. Most of the contributors to this volume have never met but we each responded to a call, thus creating a nonsubstantial community, exposing ourselves to an outside that could never be contoured by the domestic calm of a traditional encyclopedic space. This is why, in a certain transcendence of space (which does not amount to negation or denial), we have taken recourse to the thought of a time capsule, indicating the temporal dimension of our encounter, which can never be limited to the present moment but is dedicated to futurity and the possibility of justice. The mobilization of this term, time capsule, is not simply an attempt to repeat another Space Age fantasy but it seeks to perform a feminist reinscription of what futurity could mean for the women of this world, now. There is something of an ethical imperative that accompanies each time capsule to its untrackable destination.

Traditionally, the time capsule has been thrust into the womb of the earth to be rediscovered as a container of essential features of human civilization. Buried, sealed, destined for the future of its discovery, the time capsule is commonly locked up and made into a secret site. Alternatively, it is launched into space, protecting its hidden artifacts, awaiting a post-apocalyptic scene of discovery. This time capsule is a rewriting of those recondite and somewhat adolescent reveries of a solitary remainder beyond the reach of current urgency. This time capsule does not presume to distill civilization to an essence that can be closed in on itself and delivered to some remote and future address; it is concerned with the here and now, with the fragility of current distress and the excessive diffusion of anguish, joy, the oscillations of rigorous hesitation, concern and pain. More pressingly, perhaps, it remains open, effaced, and does not represent an "achievement" of mankind or a finished project; rather, it poses itself as an unmystified surface of articulations, harassed by empirical exigencies and the experience of a questioning that incessantly turns upon itself. It opens up a space that only art can be said to territorialize, a space of incessant contestation and vital protest. Even when art does not seek to make a "statement," its very condition of becoming indicates that it is not subservient to any established regime of meaning. Art occupies, if it occupies anything at all, a liminal space that, with quiet defiance, holds the gaze of any society, even if this society should practice censorship and effacement, or should punish and show disregard for certain forms of human expression. Count on art to return the gaze, even the blindest and most tyrannical gaze.

This time capsule has not signed a secret pact with the well-known motifs promising a body's resurrection: it does not quite submit itself to a burial where a body is offered up to resurrection, a name, an historical identity. (Women's bodies have not enjoyed the privilege or phantasm of idealized self-transcendence.) Rather, it follows another typology of the capsule, and evokes instead the time released capsule, slowly dissolving, releasing its contents in a generous effusion of its serenely differentiated moments. It is not contained within itself or by itself as an integral body, immune from worldly attack. The conjunction of encyclopedia and time capsule thus poses a relation to an incommensurable outside: an outside that it cannot relate to itself but with which it entertains an essential if unmeasurable relation. This is no longer about having a substantial or absolute identity, a guaranteed presence, but presumes nothing more than to share in its address this lack of identity.

Without the certitudes of absolute identity or essence, the work is no longer tied to the image of the romantic poet: the artist is not a vessel but a fragile being exposed to the danger zones of historicity and language in such a way as to maintain a Dissimilarity while holding together the intense intimacy of infinite belonging. In another space or time, I would feel compelled to show how this undoing of identity, the work, and body, originates with the poet, Hölderlin, who traced the artwork as a place of consistent withdrawal yet future arrival—the time capsule of infinite belong to which the poet was related as an outsider, securing only the "Dissimilar."

As such, time capsule is neither a work nor a gathering of subjects nor even a rubric under which to assimilate the telos of a project. If pressed, I would say that the trope of the time capsule figures as *the address of discourse*. It is a missile, a missive, posing as the possibility itself of addressing the community. As philosopher Jean-Luc Nancy has noted, the address is always singular but the other that demands our response is always the community.

Those who have responded to the call put out by Robin Kahn were by no means motivated by the desire to retrieve a lost community—a Christian mytheme. This community did not seek to implement the realization of an <u>essence</u> of community. It was not a matter of making, producing or instituting a community; nor is it a matter of venerating or fearing within it a sacred power. A community of artists in this sense is resistance itself, namely resistance to immanence, to an essence of identities and politics. In this regard, it offers that type of transcendence which, divested of sacred meaning, signifies precisely a resistance to immanence (a resistance to the communion of everyone or to the exclusive passion of one or several: to all forms and all violences of subjectivity). As something that is given to us, or to which we are given and abandoned, community is a gift to be renewed and communicated. If it is not a work to be done or produced, finished (that would be the work of death), it is a task, which is different. Community is an infinite task at the heart of finitude. It is a task and a struggle. The imperative of this struggle intervenes always at the level of communication.

Community means here the socially exposed particularity, it points to sociality as sharing, and not as fusion—as an exposure. What situates this feminist encyclopedia as a plurality of agencies, a site for genuine alterity, and not simply a provisional distance within the space of the Same, is what contemporary ontology has called "being-in-common," that is, a sharing that is older and more "constitutive" than the identity of subjects, project, essence, mission, politics, and so forth. There is an originary sharing, imparting, dividing, splitting, an originary sociality which means that before we can say we are individuals or have our "own" ideas, wishes and rooms, we are already sharing, we are being-in-common. (The solipsistic solo subject of Western metaphysics, crowding out the nonuniversal, has been responsible for a history of damage to women.) This mapping of being-in-common begins by locating the limits of absolute finitude. This is important, and represents a critical swerve from models of totalitarian communities of essence, identity and project; all regimes of fascistic communion posit a certain infinity of project while they perform tyrannical assumptions of essence and identity. Bailing out of the politics of the infinite promise or the promise of infinity, originary or ontological sociality implies that finite being always presents itself together, severally, and never as One.

The imperative of a politics of absolute finitude exposes us to the death of the other. Taking place through others and for others, our community is not the space of the egos—subjects and substances that are at bottom immortal. Community, on the contrary, refuses to weave a superior, immortal, or transmortal life between subjects. Being exposed simultaneously to relationship and absence of relationship, coming before any identification, and finding a site between political activism and solitary abandon, Time Capsule, from its place of finite vigilance, seeks to respond to the call of the other that is yet to come.

Avital Ronell, 1995

MOVING INTO WONDER

I am going to tell you a story. It is a shortened version of a much longer story, one in which there are no fictional elements. As they say, nothing here has been made up. It is also the story of the origin of art.

When humans understood that there were powers greater than themselves and so told myths rather than histories, the priestesses of Daphne or *The Bloody One,* for women enjoy their ability to menstruate, when this goddess was in an orgiastic mood, chewed laurel leaves and then, under a grown moon, assaulted unsuspecting travelers and tore children into pieces.

Daphne was also named *Medusa.* This face turned all men who looked on it into stone, this face made out of living cunt hair, and so kept strangers from trespassing into her mysteries.

Nevertheless some men loved her. One of them, Leucippus, the King of the horse cult, disguised himself as a woman so he could take part in her raptures. For this reason the god Apollo, for he also lusted after Daphne, hinted to her priestesses, the Maenads, that they should bathe naked. When they did so, they discovered one of them was a boy. They tore Leucippus' body into pieces.

Now Apollo felt that he was free to have Daphne. He found her and grabbed her, roughly. She called out to her mother. Earth took her Daphne away to Crete, for that was another home of the mysteries, and in her daughter's place, left a laurel-tree.

Apollo came up to this tree, saying, "Then you're mine." The laurel became the crown of the poet. For chewing on the laurel turns a human mad; poets often are insane.

In Crete, Daphne took another name. *Pasiphaë.*

To ensure his holdings, Minos, the King of Crete, promised to sacrifice a bull to Poseidon, Lord of the Ocean. But when the Sea-God sent him a blindingly white bull for his offering, the king fell in love with the animal and kept him for himself.

Minos had already married Pasiphaë.

Even though married, Pasiphaë fell in love with this white bull; desperate to have sex with him, she ran for help to Daedalus, the artist. His art consisted of making animated wooden dolls. Feeling sympathy for Pasiphaë, he built a hollow wooden cow for her, a moo-cow into which she could climb. She did, and Daedalus wheeled this animal into the section of oaks where all the other beasts were grazing.

Approaching the fake cow, the white bull raised himself up, then over the double-female and came in her.

Pasiphaë gave birth to a child whose head was a bull's and whose body, human. Thus, a monster, for the head as the seat of reason is supposed to govern the body.[1]

Minos visited an oracle. "How can I keep everyone from knowing about my wife's lust? How can I hide this monstrosity?"

Oracular answer: "Tell Daedalus, that artist who's living under your protectorate, to construct a labyrinth! A labyrinth is that structure from which no one can escape. In its center, place Pasiphaë and her child or monster, the Minotaur."

Minos did as he was told by the oracle of Apollo the chewer of laurel leaves.

Now the labyrinth has been constructed.

It will be Ariadne, the daughter who, like her mother, lusts, in Ariadne's case, unnaturally lusts for a human, Ariadne who opens up the labyrinth. By following lust or love. Unfortunately for all who are Cretan including Ariadne, she opens up the labyrinth to a stranger, a man whose only desire is to murder.

The stranger, Theseus, slays the monster. *Monster* comes from the Latin word *monstrum* or *wonder*. It is Ariadne, then, whose lust allows the destruction of wonder:

"When Theseus emerged from the labyrinth, spotted with the Minotaur's blood, Ariadne embraced him passionately." Theseus proceeds to desert Ariadne.

Already the mother had disappeared from the story.

The mother speaks:

The labyrinth:

This is a series of rooms without end or beginning. Not a circle, no, but a hexagon, a form like that. Afterwards all I remembered was white dust.

The center of the labyrinth:

The large room or the front room. It's all light here; all the light comes from here: floors made out of dust and grays and pale browns. This is the kind of day in which nothing grows. The center of the labyrinth is a hairdresser's. Someone—he must be the monster—asks me to get something for him while he's gone so I leave this room of light and start to walk down a hall the angles of whose junctures are those of a hexagonal.

Now the dust is white because everything, walls and floor, are becoming drier. When dust dries, it disintegrates into nothing. There are more dust and insects in the walls. In the final room to which I'm capable of walking, spiders are living in a mattress. There might be more spiders than mattress here[2].

I run away, back the way I came. In the middle of the hall sections which now lie in a straight line, there's a place where I can go swimming. A pool found in an old, old hotel. The amount of insects has grown so great that even when I'm back where I started, in the room of light, all I want to do is escape.

How I escape from the labyrinth:

In a bathroom, I'm popping a pimple which, as I look at it in a mirror after the first popping try, grows larger and larger so I see that it is rising up. I see a small cylinder shape that's almost solid. Like a missile. Then I remember that when I did this before, I didn't damage my skin permanently. As the little cock rises and rises, I feel good.

This time when I return, perhaps because of the pimple, the sea lies in front of my eyes.

A world of wonder:

Colors more brilliant than the usual colors of the world begin to be:

Two ships are lying on green, deep waters. These vessels are like the ones pirates used to have. A ship/man, his head is a ship and his body, a man's, is walking over the sands in front of the water. I know that he's meant for me because both the colors and the shapes of this being and of the ships are more precise than any color or shape before this and because they are going to take me, finally, away from the land.

On a ship in the middle of the ocean. I see there are fish swimming all around its wood sides. When I look more carefully, I see that all the fish are one fish. A baby cause it's fatter than every other fish. It leaps out of the water so that I can pet it. I'm able to lift it out of the water cause a man, a fisherman, is helping me. Then, I put the creature back in the water and before I can know anything, an even larger sea-animal comes swimming over. It's the baby's mommy and I'm so glad she's now happy and her child swims into her mouth and she swims away.

I see even larger fish, daddy fish, like whales. Seeing them enables me to feed them. I shovel huge balls of hamburger and grapefruit into one of the daddy fish's mouth.

All stories are true. I tell you this. No story, unless it be made up by one person, can be false. For as soon as something is told to another person, it begins to exist.

At every motion or moment of time, all that exists begins and simultaneously ends. For time is not linear.

According to this story, the first human artist was Daedalus. Was a male. Was, as artist, both inferior and subject to the representative of political power. Daedalus lived in exile; his survival depended upon the good will of King Minos. The realm of art was separate from and subservient to that of the political.

If Daedalus was the first artist, art began out of division. The word *art* began to be used as soon as there was separation between imagination and state.

Prior to Apollo's rape of Daphne and to Apollo's reign, there was no such division. When Daphne and the Maenads danced, imagination became actual.

The labyrinth, that construction of Daedalus', covered up the origin of art. Covered up the knowledge that art was, and so is, born out of rape or the denial of women and born out of political hegemony.

One form of Daedalus' construction is time. When time is understood as linear, there is no escape. No escape for us out of the labyrinth. I said that the labyrinth has been built.

But time is not only linear. Unlike Ariadne, for we do not hold Theseus as our lover, let us, by changing the linearity of time, deconstruct the labyrinth and see what the women who are in its center are doing. Let us see what is now central.

This is a book of women's art.

Kathy Acker, 1995

---

1 "Human life is exhausted from serving as the head of, or the reason for, the universe."
   Georges Bataille, "The Sacred Conspiracy" (*Visions of Excess, Selected Writings, 1927-1939*, ed. Allan Stoekl, University of Minnesota, Minneapolis, 1985, p.180)

2 On labyrinths: "Beyond what I am, I meet a being... He is not a man... He is not me but he is more than me: his stomach is the labyrinth in which he has lost himself, loses me with him, and in which I discover myself as him, in other words as a monster." Bataille ("The Sacred Conspiracy", p.181)

24 March 1995

Dear Friend,

I am inviting you to contribute to the publication of **Time Capsule: A Concise Encyclopedia by Women Artists.** Commemorating the Fourth World Conference on Women (Beijing, September 1995), this comprehensive anthology will take the form of a time capsule that collects the visual and written messages by women from diverse, international creative communities.

The term time capsule describes an impermeable container that "preserves an account of universal achievements" in the form of documents and ephemera believed to best express the character of its historical moment. Time Capsule is designed to provide a representation of how women artists portray their critical issues and objectives at the end of the millennium, and offers a visible and lasting document of their marked contributions.

As a contributor, you are invited to design a one or two page message that may take the form of text, image (e.g. a drawing, photograph, etc.), or any combination thereof. The entries will be alphabetized under subject headings created by each author (e.g. Astrology, Gardening, Sex). This soft bound anthology on white newsprint paper will contain an index with your name, title, and contact number (optional). Your black and white contribution is restricted to 9 1/2 x 7 1/4 inches bound vertically. Works must be submitted camera-ready and images with gray tones must be in dot matrix or velox format for highest resolution (65-80 dot screen). Do not forget to include your contribution's subject heading, as that will determine its placement in the publication. The book will sell for $25; however, you can receive a free copy of the book provided you send money for its postage and handling (in U.S. & Canada $7, Central & South America $10, all others $15)

All submissions received by May 15, 1995 will be published.

Time Capsule is published by Creative Time, Inc. in association with S.O.S. Int'l. Creative Time is a not-for-profit public arts organization that for more than twenty years has sponsored artists in the creation of new works designed for unexpected, undeveloped, and unlikely public places.

In order to ensure that this anthology is as comprehensive as possible, pass this invitation on to your colleagues. If you have any questions or want to discuss any aspect of this publication, please contact me as soon as possible.

Sincerely yours,

Robin Kahn, Editor

Send Correspondences To:

Robin Kahn
c/o S.O.S. Int'l.
114 Mercer Street #9   Tel   212.431.4571
New York City, NY 10012   Fax 212.219.8853

BÉATRICE CORON, NEW YORK, NY, USA

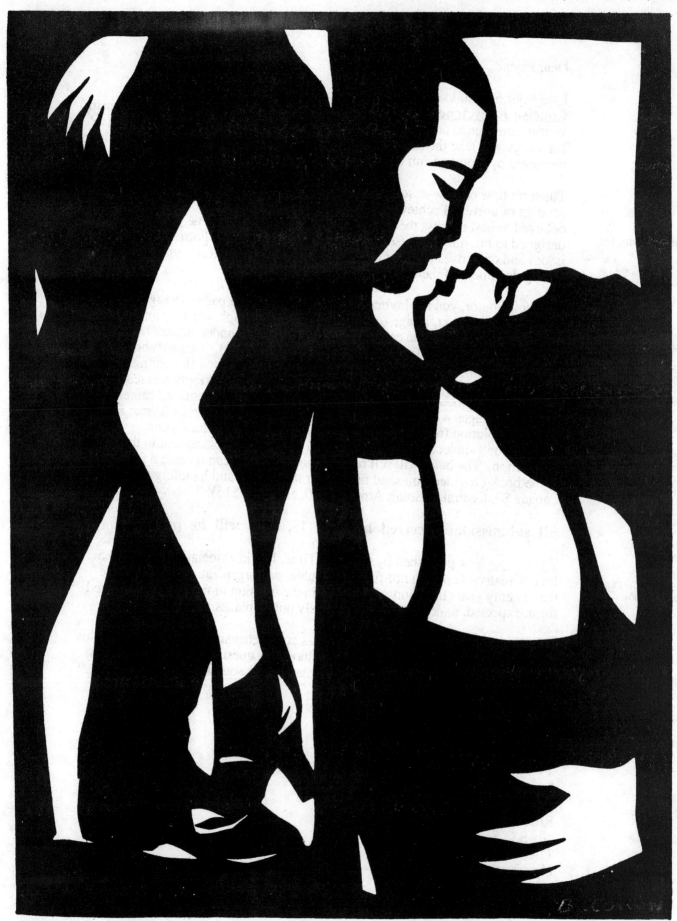

DEBORAH BEBLO, NEW YORK, NY, USA

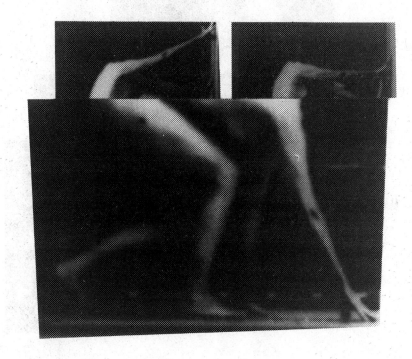

Deborah Beblo, New York, NY, USA

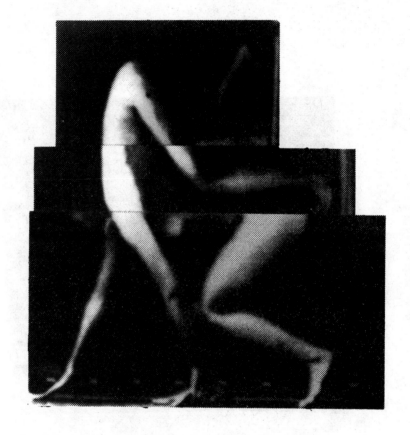

DIANE PIERI, PHILADELPHIA, PA, USA

PAGE FROM THE TEARS OF LIVING

" TEARS OF DESPAIR/THE MURDER OF DR. GUNN "

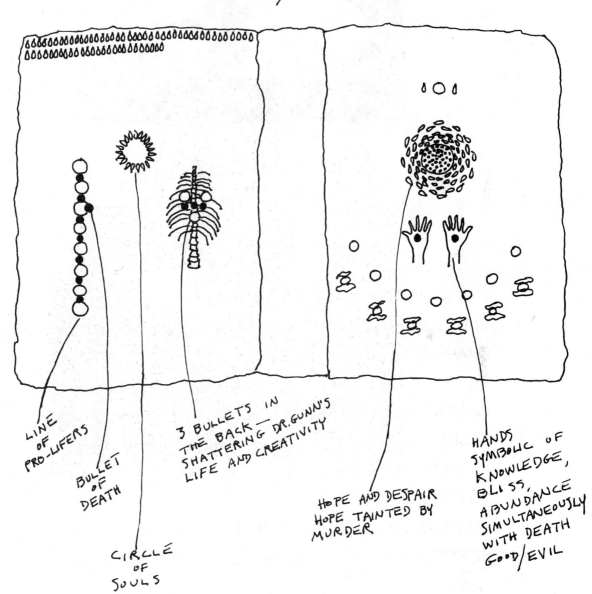

LINE
OF
PRO-LIFERS

BULLET
OF
DEATH

3 BULLETS IN
THE BACK —
SHATTERING DR. GUNN'S
LIFE AND CREATIVITY

CIRCLE
OF
SOULS

HOPE AND DESPAIR
HOPE TAINTED BY
MURDER

HANDS
SYMBOLIC OF
KNOWLEDGE,
BLISS,
ABUNDANCE
SIMULTANEOUSLY
WITH DEATH
GOOD/EVIL

PIERI 1993-95

MARILENA PREDA SANC, BUCHAREST, ROMANIA

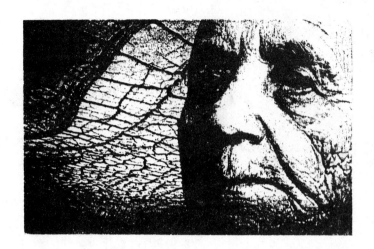

DESPRE BATRINETE, MOARTE

EXISTA IN FIECARE DIN NOI UN MOMENT DE TRECERE DINCOLO CIND SUNTEM PREA SINGURI, PREA FERICITI, CIND PIERDEM PE CINEVA DRAG.

SECOLUL ACESTA NE-A FACUT SA TRAIM IN CLIPA UITIND DE BATRINETE SI MOARTE. AM FOST OBISNUITI (EDUCATI) SA LE ASCUNDEM, SA NE FIE RUSINE SI FRICA SA NE GINDIM .

AM PIERDUT CEVA ESENTIAL - LINISTEA, DEMNITATEA BATRINILOR NOSTRI CU MOARTEA .

AM UITAT SENSUL VIETII. TREBUIE SA INTELEGEM INCEPUTUL, SFIRSITUL, INCEPUTUL ... CA SA EXISTAM CU ADEVARAT

MAGDALENA JITRIK, BUENOS AIRES, ARGENTINA

* abstract porno

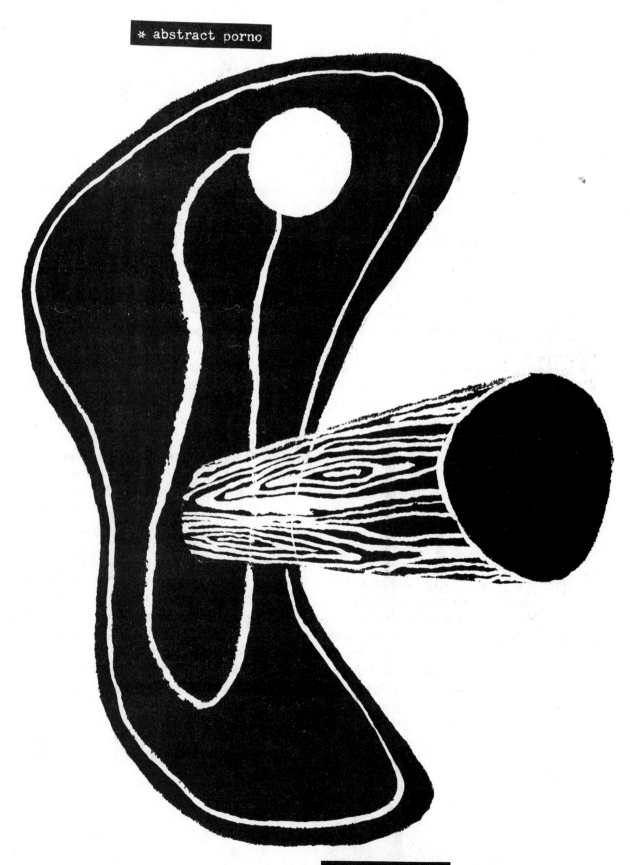

Magdalena Jitrik

Yo Yo, STUTTGART, GERMANY

Flying Stone

Many, many years ago, at the foot of Heavenly Mountains, at the shores of the Heavenly Lake, I spotted something small and black floating on the surface of the water. Curious, I picked up my telescope and gave a start. To my surprise, there was a rock floating in the middle of the lake! Disregarding the late autumn chill, I plunged into the water and headed towards it. Effortlessly I reached it and, in grasping it, felt the delerium of the Lotus Eaters. After a time I brought it home from those many leagues away; I gave it a place of honour in my home and worshipped it as a God. Relatives and friends flocked to my house, all wanting to be present before this "divine stone." In this fashion, the rumour spread throughout the land; everyone came to know that there was someone who had a bit of magic rock. But even though it was revered as magic, no-one had ever seen that it had any "unusual properties." One day someone asked: "*What's so unusual about this rock? What's magical about it?*" The owner answered: "*Have you ever seen a rock that could, defying all laws of magic, float on water? All stones, absolutely one hundred percent, upon hitting water sink immediately to the bottom. For this reason it is precious, it is magical. Furthermore, it was discovered in the Heavenly Mountains, the Heavenly Lake, which shows that it must have been heaven's will, heaven sent. How could it not be divine?!*" The questioner was silenced. You, smugly satisfied, treasured your find all the more.

One day a friend came from a great distance. You had always held this gentleman in great regard, thinking him of considerable intelligence; his speech and demeanour were extremely genteel, and he had about him a refined and superior air. You first entertained him for a short while, but before you even had a chance to praise the merits of the divine stone, the man had already walked over and had begun to stare at it, spellbound. You were overjoyed, thinking that you had come across a fellow believer. Without another word you opened the glass cupboard and carefully removed the exquisite little box in which the stone had been placed. Your friend asked if he might take it out to examine it. Normally you would have responded hurriedly: "*Oh, I'm afraid that's impossible. We can't afford to dispel it's aura.*" But given that your guest was a spiritual man, naturally you thought to ask a bit of advice. Thereupon you opened the transparent little box, respectfully removed the little stone, and reverently offered it to him. The man took the stone and looked at it; looked again: suddenly he gave a loud shout of laughter; a laugh which made your hair stand on end. When he had finished laughing he said, lightly tossing the stone in his hand: "*It's only a piece of volcanic rock.*" You turned pale with alarm. "*What makes you think so?*" "*Have you ever seen such a light rock?*" You were stupefied. In one breath you took the "divine stone" and hurled it out the window. You were mortified by your own ignorance and incompetence: that you'd even take a bit of volcanic rock and worthlessly worship it as some divine object! You were thoroughly vexed with yourself - how very satisfying to rid yourself of it!

That night, you dream that you are being crushed under a huge stone, unable to breathe. The stone thrusts its penis into you, completely disorientating you. The stone is ice cold, like a sword, and pierces your every blood vessel. Your vessels constrict into a tangled mass of vines and extend out from your body, flowing forth and tightly binding you and the rock together. Your body heat is slowly sucked away, leaving you as stiff and rigid as an iron nail. You feel your body, little by little, leaving the earth, rising, rising, higher and higher; the rock takes you up, circling, flying towards the heavens. The rock, expressionless, spirals into the air, now high, now low. You are dizzy, dazzled; desperately you cling to it; the surface of the Earth is already a blur, you and the stone plunge into the clouds, the mist sweeps your cheeks until they are glossy and smooth - very erotic. You are as beautiful as a cloud, your body as light as a swallow. Your body is adorned with unsurpassable garments woven of the clouds and the mist, like those of the moon goddess; silk belts woven from rays of light encircle you, floating and dancing. Like a goddess you shuttle back and forth through space, with a lissome freedom you have never known before. The stone, too, capers with joy - what paradise. A limitless, endless paradise. It IS a divine stone, a stone angel. You dance exuberantly, beside yourself with pleasure. Suddenly your blood vessels explode, your vine-like clutches release the stone. It leisurely and effortlessly soars towards the heavens. You plunge violently downward, downward.

A dream is a nights fever
that takes you wandering the world.

YoYo. 11.26.91 Berlin
Translated by Portia Wu, March, 1995.

AVITAL GREENBERG

FLY FREE

OIL ON CANVAS.

68"/54".

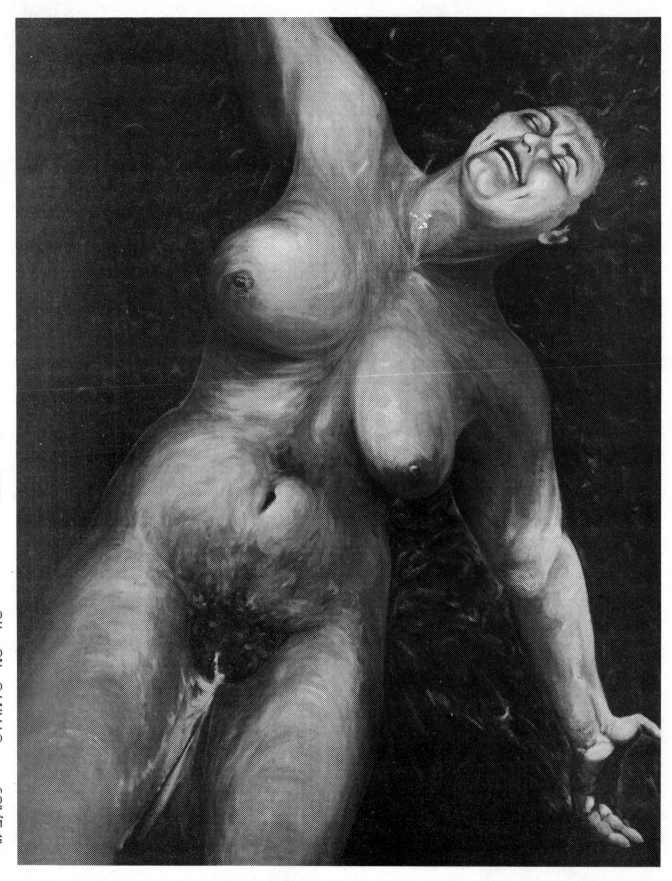

KRISTEN FREDERICKSON, PhD, NEW YORK, NY, USA

Academic Activism

I had been teaching my seminar called "Gender and Difference in Art" at Hunter College here in New York City for nearly a year when I overheard my husband describing to a friend what it is I do. "Well, she's an art historian and her specialization is women artists. She's currently teaching a course called `**Gender Indifference in Art**' and is really enjoying it."

I thought this was wonderful. "Gender Indifference." Most of art history taught these days certainly does purport to be "gender indifferent." There is very little thought given in most courses to the (to me) painfully apparent sexism inherent in the way our concept of genius has been formulated, in the way women have historically been kept out of academies, exhibitions, museum collections and textbooks. Students are not taught to question the overwhelming **maleness** of the supposedly gender-neutral canon of important artists, nor do they find it odd that if you want to talk about an artist who happens to be female, you must use the qualifying phrase, "woman artist," leading you to realize that unless otherwise specified, the term "artist" refers only to men.

Within my department, my feminism is tolerated, I think, as a nice addition to the "diversity" of our faculty. I am occasionally recruited to visit other professors' courses on contemporary art, for example, and do (as one colleague put it) "that gender thing you do." I'm of two minds about these little visits. On the one hand, I'm glad for any opportunity to show the work of women artists and to get the students thinking critically about how sex and gender issues resonate in that work. On the other hand, I suspect I am being trotted in, at the end of the semester, to add a veneer of political correctness to an otherwise conservative syllabus. But how else will change come about, I decide, unless I take whatever opportunities I can get to shake up those students? I would rather see my colleagues take on the issues of gender and art history themselves, but in the end I know this is unlikely to happen. I fantasize about returning the invitation to them, to come visit my "Gender and Difference" course and do "that Dead White European Male thing you do."

Something weird has been happening to my beloved seminar on "Gender and Difference in Art" this semester. After two years of offering the course and having 13 women and one man register every semester, this spring my class was composed of seven women and seven men. I don't know why this is, but I do know that the seminar atmosphere has been radically different with this new representation of male points of view. I find myself faced with a sea of faces half of whom have never felt the sting of exclusion, the mask of invisibility, the lack of representation, for whom art history and indeed life has been "gender indifferent." How to jar them out of their complacency without alienating their young inquisitiveness, to make them feel the urgency of gender issues without seeming to blame them for centuries of sexist history?

Progress is being made in my little universe, as it turns out. Last week I was approached by a former student from my Modern Art survey class with a request. "I have to do an interview for my Women's Studies course," he explained, "with a feminist activist. You're the only one I know." That's how "gender indifferent" most art history courses really are, I realized. Show a couple of Sonia Delaunay fabric designs during the discussion on Cubism, introduce the possibility that Surrealism was a little weird about women, tell some stories about how Rosa Bonheur had to apply for a permit to wear pants, and I'm an activist? I'm happy to wear that hat.

ACTION

Elizabeth Streb
Artistic Director
Streb/Ringside

New Work For 1995

UP
Premiere, a dance for 5 or 6 bodies, that are constantly being powerfully ejected into space, with a tremendous degree of force aimed in a rigorous and insistent direction by a "surface exploder" or a high-end trampoline. This "SURFACE" trampoline is couched between two 20-foot high towers, each with two departure decks of different heights. From either of these chosen heights, from either side of the trampoline, dancers, one at a time, leave the tower in a free-fall, hurtling south, towards this powerful "ejector" surface. One side hits this surface and begins the UP journey; the other side then leaves their tower into the free-fall zone which drags them rapidly downward toward the surface. So you have a continual spray of bodies passing one another in this tunnel of air. There will be certain physical techniques developed both while falling and while rising. The potential return height off this trampoline is 24 to 30 feet into the air! As the bodies pass each other there will be air-contact moments as well as air-impact techniques we will work with. The ceiling above this bright Yellow Trampoline surface is a pipe-grid, onto which a body can attach and hang for a prescribed amount of time, other bodies can attach to the first body and a chain of bodies can let go and return to this surface from directly above.

This year, Elizabeth Streb and Ringside, the company she founded to support her choreography, will kick off their national *POP*ACTION tour. Streb/Ringside will be in residency at the Wexner Art Center in Ohio, and at LA MOCA to present works commissioned for its new temporary gallery. Dance on Tour is generously supporting the tour with a grant sponsored by the Lila Wallace-Reader's Digest Fund. In 1995, Streb/Ringside was one of the first ten companies to recieve a National Dance Residency Program award from the New York Foundation for the Arts, sponsored by the Pew Charitable Trust. This grant will support Streb's research with physicist Michio Kaku, author of <u>Hyperspace</u>, in a study entitled, "Human-Airtime-Exploration-Expedition."

Elizabeth Streb, NEW YORK, NY, USA

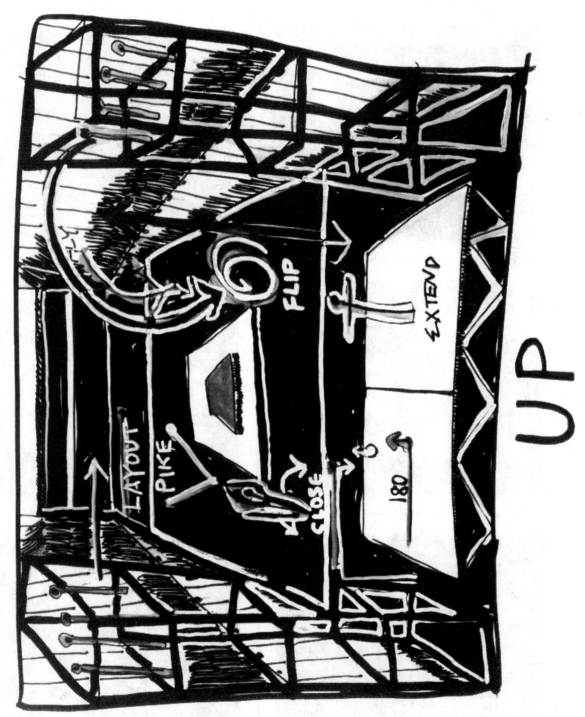

ALYSON SHOTZ, NEW YORK, NY, USA

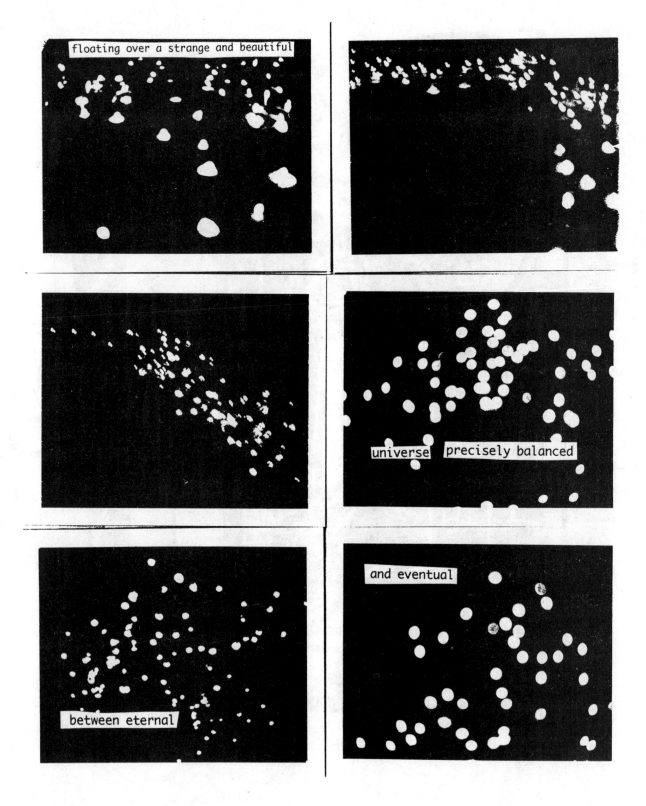

DINA BEN-LEV, SEATTLE, WA, USA

BROKEN HELIX

The sexy talk show host nods and nods. Beside her
a bald man begs to meet the mother he's never known.
Slowly, in front of fourteen million, the curtain
rises with applause—surprise! Before a camera closes in,

I shut my eyes. Down in deepest Florida, in a hospital
winged with a sanatorium, you named me Cheryl.
Then signed me away. At 22, were you tired
of trailer parks, truck stops, drive-thru

windows of worry? Did an old, world-weary nurse
warn, Only one skill you'll be properly paid for. . . .
Impressive, said a man with his hand on my resume. . . .
But hell, you'll ruin marriages

with such heavenly hair. Walking out of that white room
and out of that black building, I thought of your leaving—
thirty years ago, those minutes it took
to exit, empty-handed but for one slim bag.

In the cool, antiseptic lobby, you might've stopped
at a fountain. Bending, maybe you moved your whole
face into the water. Were you glamorous in sunglasses,
pushing open the door to the heat? You'd never see

your daughter settled in Seattle, where sun's uncommon
and painful. Never know her new name. Did you
ride a bus alone through battering light, past the hundred
hotels of Miami? At 20, after phoning and phoning and failing

DINA BEN-LEV, SEATTLE, WA, USA

to find you, I fell off a chair in the Fontainebleu.
Pink drinks paid for by a lawyer who liked me best
on my knees. Did my father rub your feet
when you returned? Or did you dream

into the night, on a single, one light
left on? Blurry on gas, I spread for suction
and scapel. A nurse held my head. . . .
At 24, with a Master's in Fantasy, I ached for escape

from the dirtiest, snowiest section of Syracuse.
A taxi took me home, where sleep came on a green
Goodwill couch—bought with the man of my dreams
I later called Psycho. Smoldering, he burned

books in the bathtub, shot fist-wide holes
through my Nova. And the next day,
did you turn to the TV for comfort?
And now, half a lifetime later, in the kitchen /

livingroom / bedroom / only room, watch
the same talk show host? How she moved
a microphone to the mouth of the bald man's mother?
How she asked, OK tell me, would you do it again?

JACKIE KINGON, NEW YORK, NY, USA

Advance to Stop

I wanted to be Helen Frankenthaler
But her body was taken.
I wanted to impregnate
The poured colored pools
And have my spirit
Move over the waters.

I cut the radish into a rose
And let the lines that grow
On my face become
As fashionable as war paint.
My life is recorded in their dance.

I thought by now I would have met myself.
But everything is a metaphor.

I can't keep up with $\frac{1}{2}$ the world
I am for them too slow.
I can't keep up with $\frac{1}{2}$ the world
I am too fast, I know.

Jackie Kingon

Advance to Stop

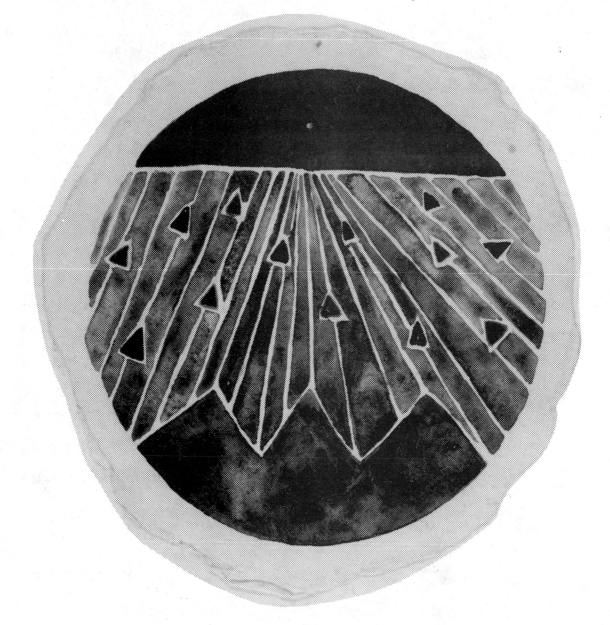

Watercolor on Paper (actual size)
from the series "A YEAR of DAYS" 365 watercolors
JACKIE KINGON

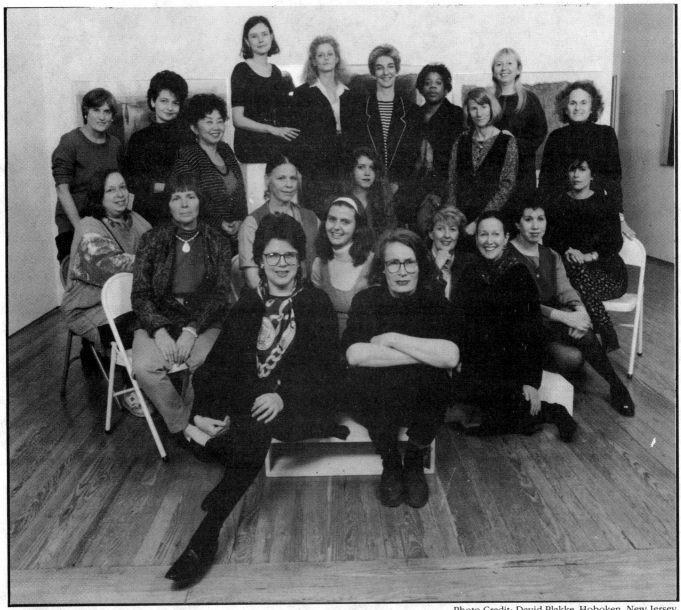

Photo Credit: David Plakke, Hoboken, New Jersey

Gallery Artists
Back Row, Left to Right: Louise McCagg; Barbara Grinell; Michi Itami; Tenesh Webber; Carol Ross; Elke Solomon;
Carolyn Martin; Nancy Storrow; Daria Dorosh; Nancy Azara; Madeline Weinrib
Middle Row, Left to Right: Sylvia Netzer; Barbara Roux; Regina Granne; Alissa Schoenfeld, *Director;* Janise Yntema;
Sharon Brant; Stephanie Bernheim; Lenore Goldberg
Front Row, Left to Right: J. Nebraska Gifford, Ann Pachner

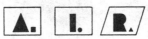

ANNE-FRANÇOISE POTTERAT, NEW YORK, NY, USA

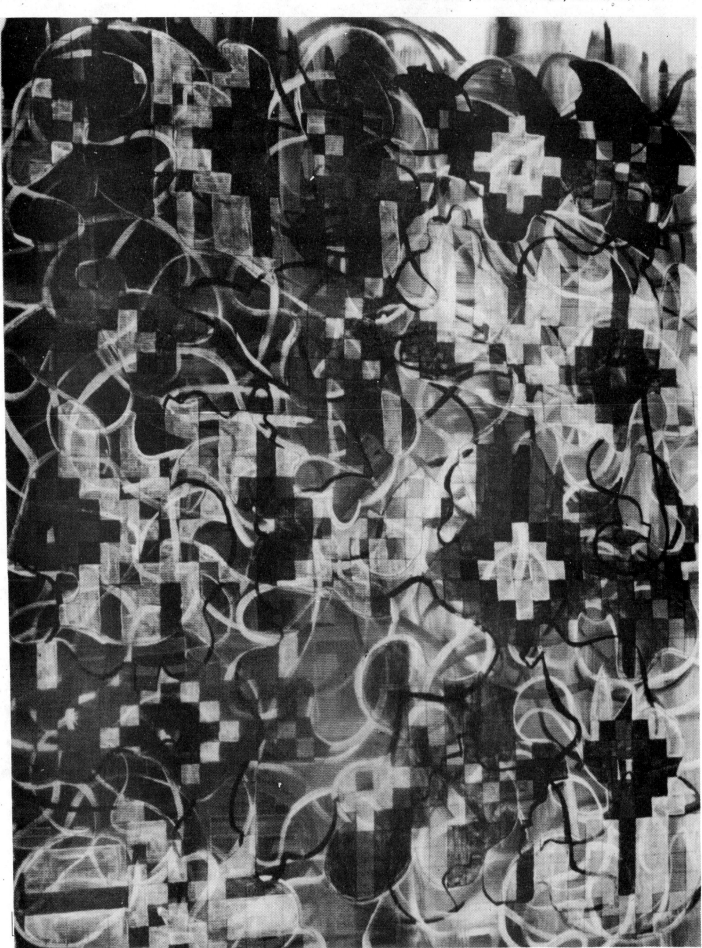

AINSLIE FAUST, MILL VALLEY, CA, USA

Women's Issues

Pee, blood, white tinged creme,
children, feces, lies & screams
death awaiting life's embrace
emerges from their other face
an open wound that arms
the world with issues
of the womb, the pearl
a darkness yawns in
sweet delight and leaks
its liquid tears in fright
to resurrect our bodied state
and bring us wisdom n'er too late

VIVIENNE KOORLAND, NEW YORK, NY, USA

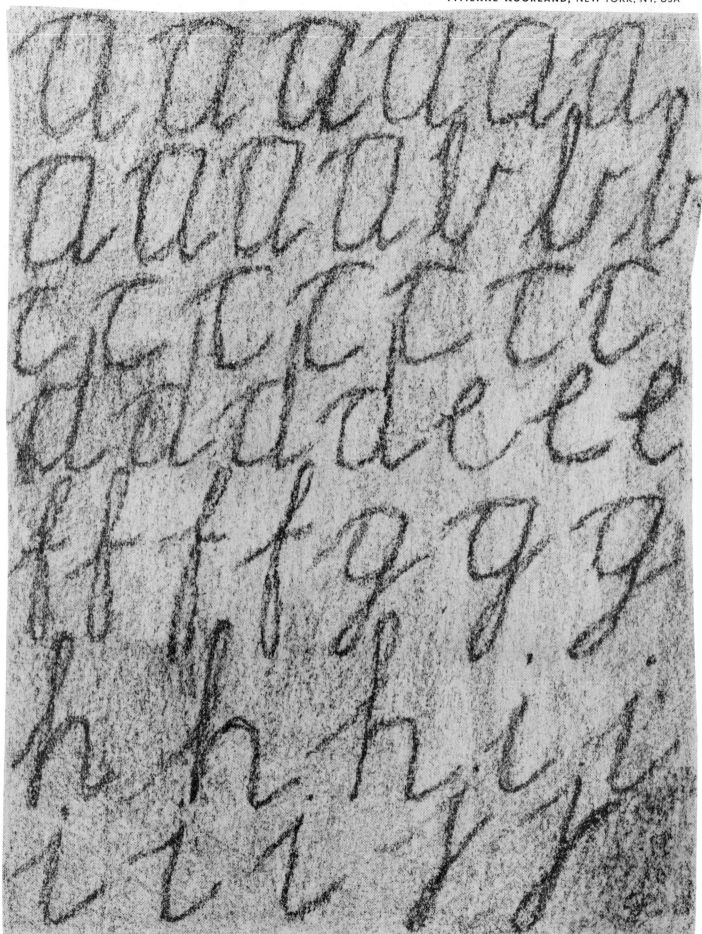

VIVIENNE KOORLAND, NEW YORK, NY, USA

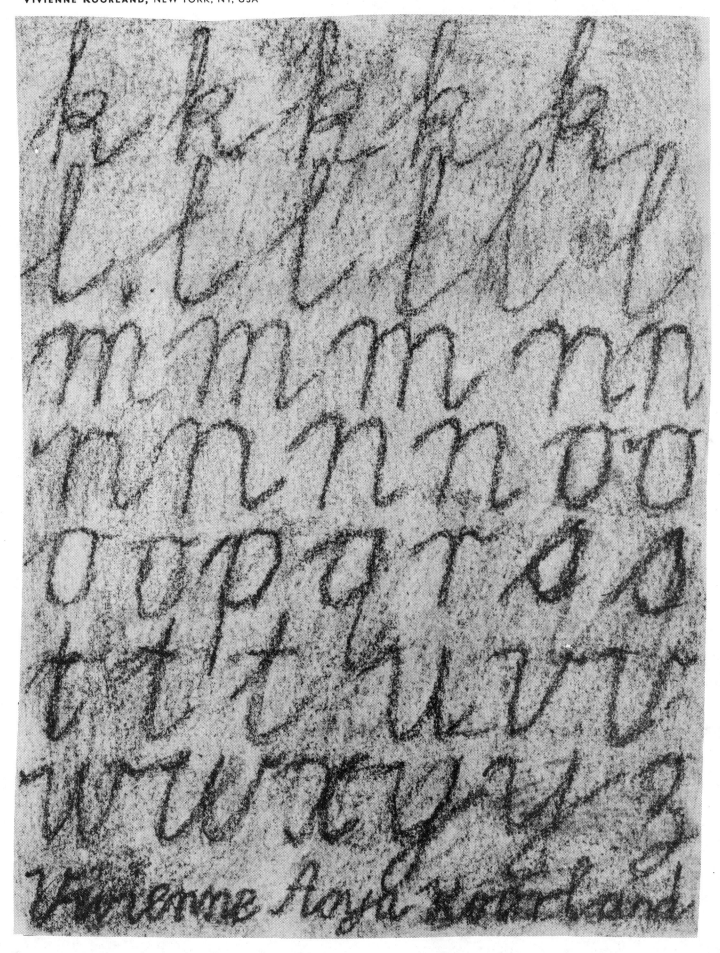

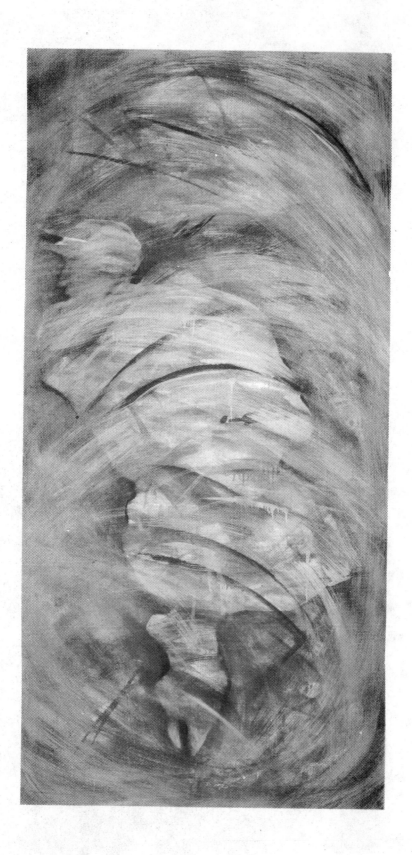

GAIL KOLFLAT, LITTLE SILVER, NJ, USA

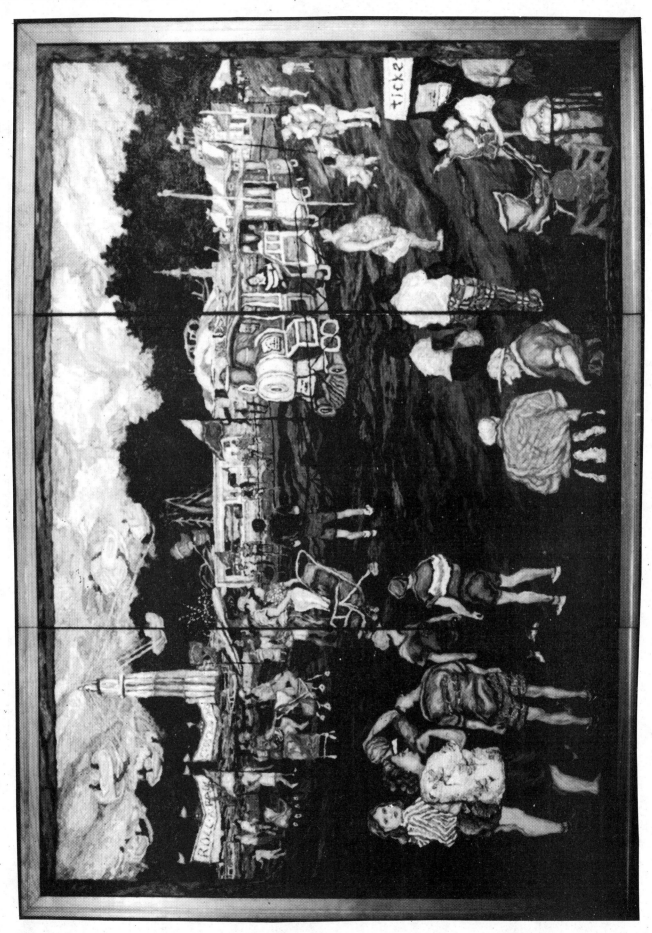

The United States Federale Reserve Announces
A Strictly Limited Issue of the First Women's Currency Ever Printed

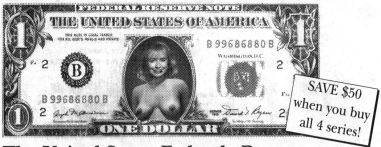

SAVE $50 when you buy all 4 series!

15-DAY FREE HOME TRIAL

The United States Federale Reserve
AMERICAN DOLL-AR COLLECTOR'S EDITION

Genuine Federale Reserve Currency... assembled into 4 unique collector's series
Proceeds to benefit breast cancer research

Attention, collectors of all kinds: The first American currency to feature women ever printed!

The U.S. Federale Reserve has created a limited number of new bills and assembled them into 4 different collector's series— each a historic tribute to America's outstanding women. This currency has been carefully examined, sorted and graded, and each collector's series is accompanied by the U.S. Federale Reserve's Certificate of Authenticity, guaranteeing that each bill in the collection is genuine U.S. currency. To collect American dollars is not only to own their face value— it's also owning a piece of herstory! These will be treasured heirlooms from America's past for generations to come... cherished and coveted by collectors everywhere... and they can only increase in value as the years go by and supplies of them become more scarce!

Act now— supplies are limited

But we urge you to act quickly because the U.S. Federale Reserve has been able to assemble only a limited number of these collector's series and will be filling orders for them on a first-come, first-served basis. There is no guarantee how long supplies of these bills will last... so we suggest you reserve your share of the first of the American Doll-ar currency now while you still have the opportunity.

The American First Ladies Series

The inaugural series features 4 one-dollar bills, each with one of our most influential First Ladies, leading the way for women's equality and freedom of expression— top-free and proud! Stepping out from behind their men, these women are ready to launch a "frontal assault" on the budget deficit at the same time as they set an example for gender equality. Being economically savvy means knowing what sells, and it's their right to sell it!

Watch the American dollar skyrocket as investors around the world collect all 4 series, and watch your own investment grow!

The American Actresses Series, The American Artists Series, and the American Feminists Series complete the Edition— collect all 4! Each series will arrive beautifully framed. These valuable collector's items make wonderful gifts! As an added bonus, 10% of the proceeds from every sale will go to benefit breast cancer research.

The American First Ladies Series 4 one-dollar bills	$89.95
The American Actresses Series 4 five-dollar bills	$69.95
The American Artists Series 4 ten-dollar bills	$49.95
The American Feminists Series 4 twenty-dollar bills	$39.95

SAVE $50 WHEN YOU BUY ALL FOUR!
The Complete American Doll-ar Collector's Edition only $200.00

Bills not sold singly; all bills sold in series only. Offer made by Barbara Yoshida, 595 Broadway, NY, NY 10012. All inquiries should be made to the above address.

Order Form

Qty.	Item	Price	Subtotal
	The American First Ladies Series	$89.95	
	The American Actresses Series	69.95	
	The American Artists Series	49.95	
	The American Feminists Series	39.95	
	The Complete Edition	$200.00	
	Total Order Price	$	

This offer is made in cooperation with Permanent Press

BARBARA YOSHIDA, NEW YORK, NY, USA

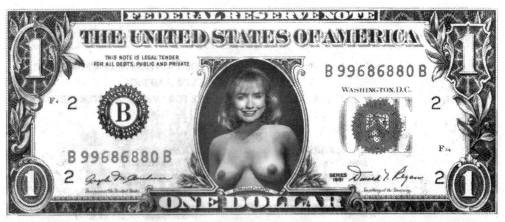

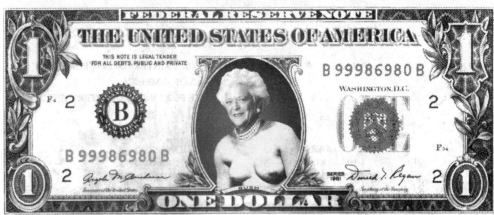

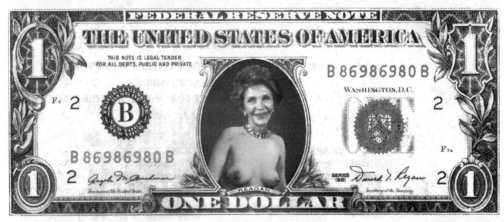

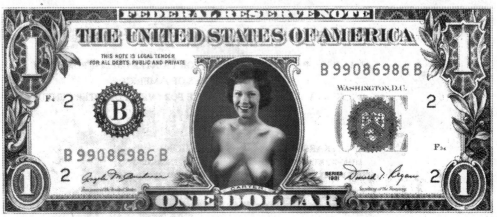

ELLEN LANYON, NEW YORK, NY, USA

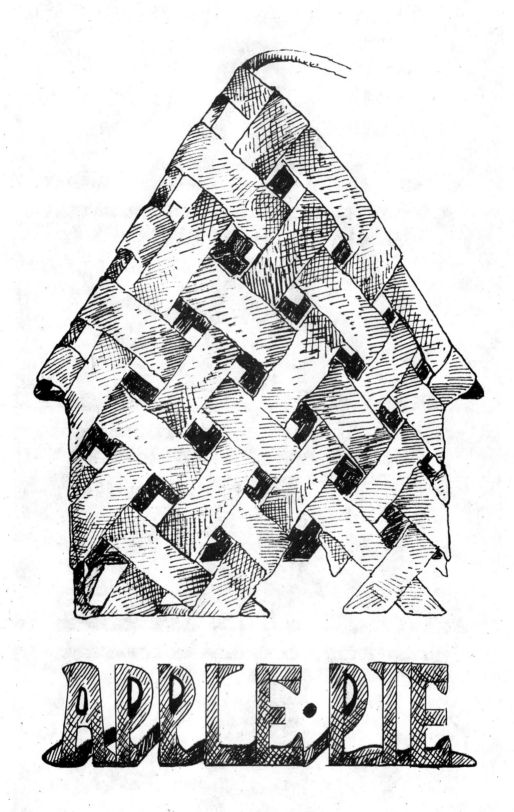

© EL 95

SHANNON REECE, WESTBANK, ONT, CANADA

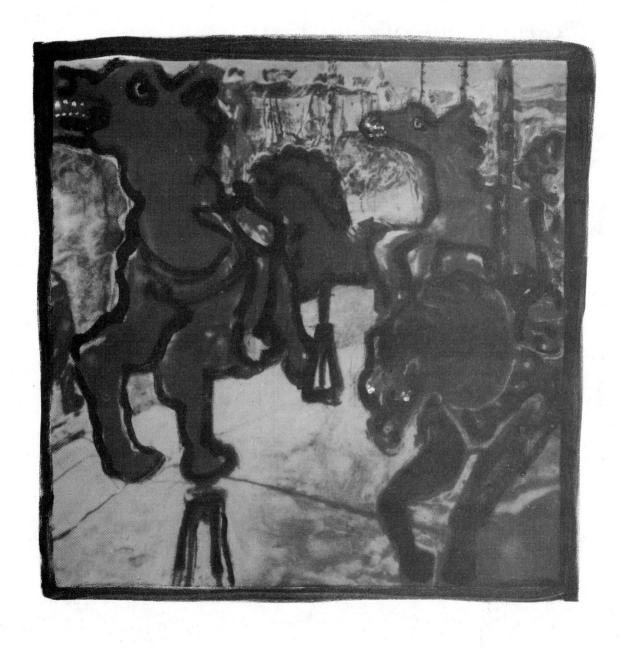

BARBARA SCHLEGEL, HAMBURG, GERMANY

*> the female is femi-
nine because of a
certain lack of qua-
lities<*

*Luce Irigaray, > Speculum de
l`autre femme < Paris 1974*

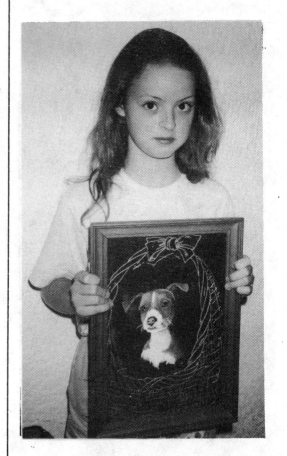

Anna, 1994

BARBARA SCHLEGEL, HAMBURG, GERMANY

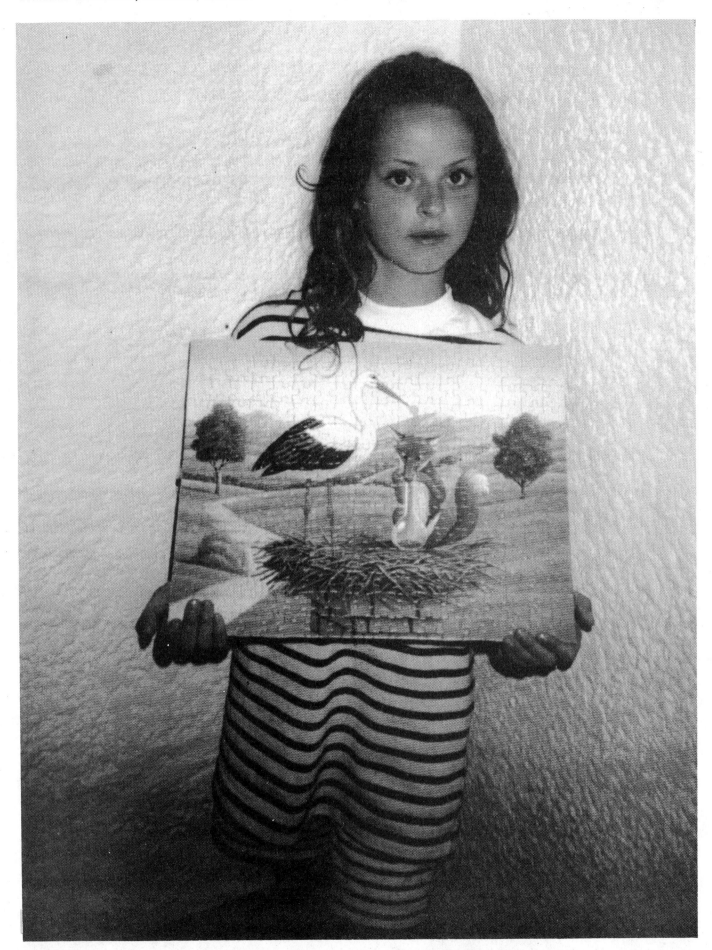

LYNN PHILLIPS, NEW YORK, NY, USA

BETWEEN MILLENNIA (May -Dec. 1994)

I'm from a whole new generation, one with no common experiences. In this particular generation, some of us are free, comfy, in the black; others are virtual slaves. Some of us go broke when we break a leg, while others are covered for everything from pig's liver transplants to teflon transfusions. Some of us cower cramped up in little cubicles; others roam the internet like jaguars, fly the Concorde, co-own condos on the coast. Some of us kill, rape, maim or exploit others of us, and some of us are very sorry afterwards. Others, not.

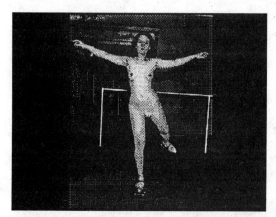

Our life experiences differ. We gestate for different lengths of time, not necessarily in the wombs of our mothers, and drink milk from different mammals upon emerging from various openings. Our families may consist of a genetic or adoptive mother and father of any sex; a psychological mother, a biological father and a stranger's egg; two mothers (one genetic, one psychological, plus a stranger's sperm); two fathers (one biological, one psychological and a friend's egg); a mother and stepfather plus a father and stepmother; a mother and several stepfathers; a stepfather and an aunt; a father and his mother, or any one of a number of similarly intriguing arrangements that fill us unpredictably with either delight or loathing. Like our mates, we can be male, hermaphroditic, androgynous, trans-sexual, female. We die at different rates of varying diseases: Malaria, Dengue fever, SIDA, flesh-eating virus, Hanta, lung cancer, drug overdose, cardiac arrest, you name it.

My generation has no cultural signature. High, low, religious, secular; we'll try anything. We read different languages, if we read at all, speak hundreds of dialects. When we appear in agreement, we're usually not. Our identical black leather motorcycle jackets indicate scores of different ranks and fashion attitudes, depending on who is wearing them, in what vehicle, and where.

LYNN PHILLIPS, NEW YORK, NY, USA

In my generation, no subgroup coheres. If you're Asian, for example, you could be Chinese-american, Filipina, or a mountain tribeswoman from Vietnam whose vanished father, half-Cherokee, calls himself African American. And say you're Punjabi; you could be Brahmin or Untouchable, and if Untouchable, male or female, married or unmarried, etc., ever at odds with your cohort.

Our time frame is fractured, too. We weren't all in college when the Berlin Wall fell, and we weren't all out of college either. We can't all remember what it was like when abortion was illegal, because for many of us, it still is. For some of us, I Love Lucy evokes a more innocent and merry time. For others, it's Now; a happening thing. And a few of us have no idea what I Love Lucy is, never heard of it. We're not the generation that grew up with computers, because most of us didn't and won't. We're not the generation that isn't going to do as well as our parents did because a lot of us are already doing better than our parents ever will.

What can I tell you: We're not all individuals; a lot of us are sheep, cogs, die-cut consumer units. We don't all identify with a larger group, either. Think we're all human? Most of us are *homo sapiens*, sure -- Furless primates who walk erect and have big brains. But not *all* of us are human. *Some* of us are killing machines; berzerkos. *Some* of us are God's angels sent to exterminate the Heathen. Some of us are cyborg phantoms. Some are sex objects--a bulge or two in a bikini; period. Some of us are zygotes, embryos and fetuses--venerated in one corner as sacred innocents and in the corner opposite shrugged off as preanimate, akin to mold.

But although we lack common experiences and traits, what you might call definition, my generation does have a common identity. Global, maybe interplanetary, we're on the fly, off the cuff and clueless, and we don't kid ourselves that a common humanity binds us, that life is sacred, or profane, or cheap, or universally recognizable as such. Oh yes, and yet again yes; we are one hell of a generation. Because we've closed the book on the Twentieth Century, ejected the tape, changed the channel. The Age of Micromarketing has dawned, my friends. And all previous bets, believe it; all bets are off.

†‡

~ LYNN PHILLIPS   72212.240@COMPUSERVE.COM

CORNELIA SCHMIDT-BLEEK, BERLIN, GERMANY

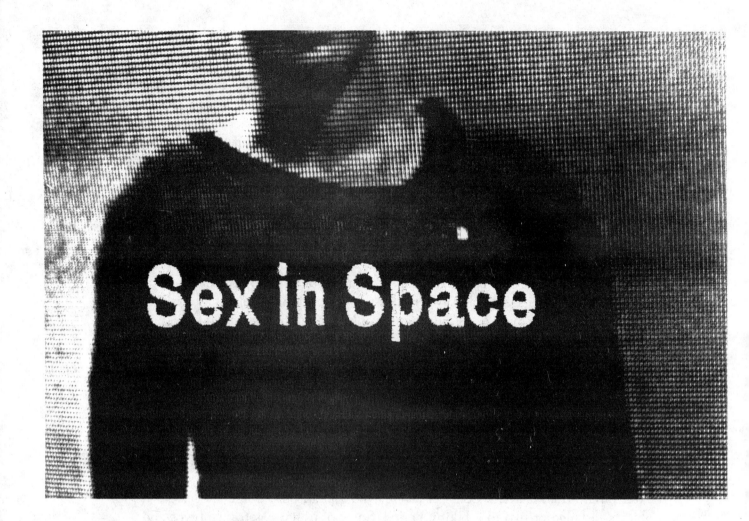

VIVIAN SELBO, NEW YORK, NY, USA

A[NY] WORD FROM OUR SPONSOR[?]

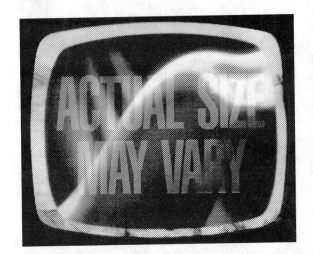
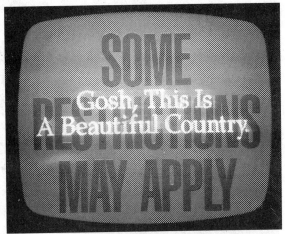

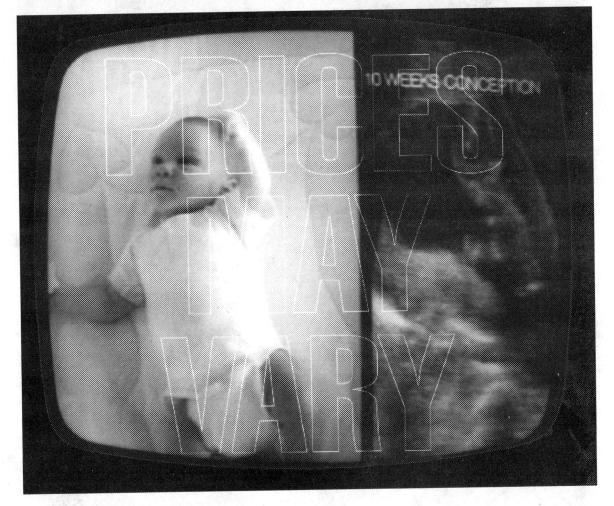

ART (ENVIRONMENTAL)

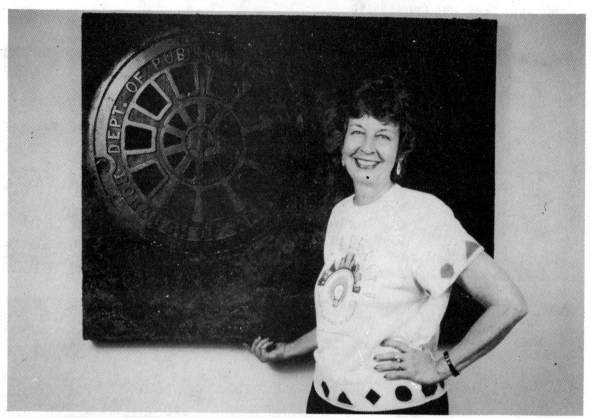

Bobbi Mastrangelo with her sculpture relief "Borough of Manhattan" (91cm x 122cm x 7.6 cm). The wall relief is in the Permanent Collection of the National Association of Women Artists: Zimmerli Museum, Rutgers University, New Brunswick, New Jersey (U.S.A.)

Bobbi Mastrangelo is internationally known for her evocative renderings of manhole covers with an environmental theme. The artist works in a variety of media from hand made paper for prints and foam, wood, acrylic, pebbles, cement, mud and moss for dimensional creations. She often employs a trompe l'oeil technique which fools the viewers. The covers look like heavy metal – like a section of street has been lifted from its urban environment and put on a wall or floor.

For more information on the artist or her "Grate Works," contact her directly:
Bobbi Mastrangelo • 12 Wexford Court, St. James, NY 11780 • United States of America
1 (516) 862-8956

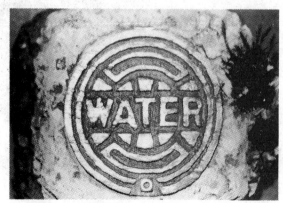

Keep Our Waters Pure
Sculpture 35cm x 38cm x 40 cm.
Lid lifts to reveal water chamber

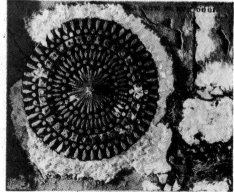

Celestial Grate (Wall Relief)
61cm x 76cm x 4 cm

BOBBI MASTRANGELO, PORT JEFFERSON, NY, USA

ART (ENVIRONMENTAL)

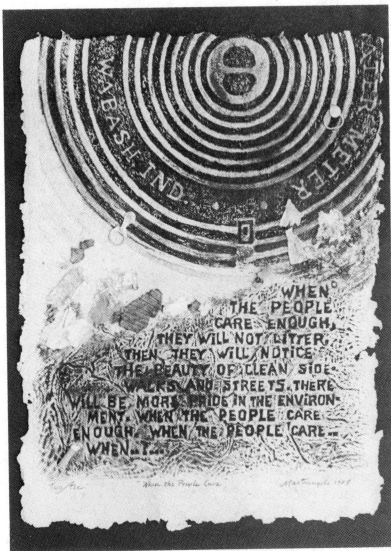

"When the People Care"   Collagraph 63cm x 48cm

"When the People Care"

When the people care enough

They will not litter

Then they will notice

The beauty of clean sidewalks
and streets

There will be more pride in the
environment

When the people care enough

When the people care...

When?

– Bobbi Mastrangelo,
© 1988

From mini prints to large prints heavily embossed on hand made paper, the artist expresses her concern for the environment. Her theme is water covers and manhole covers.

For more information contact:
Bobbi Mastrangelo
"Grate Works"
12 Wexford Court
St. James, NY 11780 U.S.A.
1 (516) 862-8956

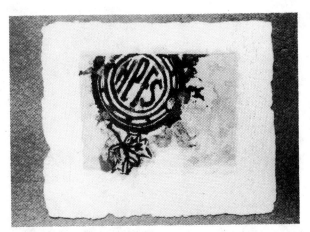

High Pressure Fire System
Collagraph on Hand Made Paper   **20cm x 25cm**

TATIANA GARMENDIA, SEATTLE, WA, USA

Autumn's Turn: A Studio Visit

Swans too fair for flight
so tamed by lithesome stories
that float the surface of drawing,
rise again in weightless lines.

And bright fingers imprinting
the collected ascent of the sun
(coast, prairie, trees and hill)
focus the bearings of endurance
aside a constant arch.

Like eyes forest full of spattering
leaves and the brush strokes of Corot
render autumn a record, such steps
transmute the mount in the headland
with striking alchemy. Beyond
each ardent muse moves a matching wick
reflected in glass, not darkly now
but brightly ignited. What purpose
looks past the fall's measure
turns language voiceless.

Over the determined wheel every
mark renews the art's ideal, so
with the drawn season's bending
the burnished birds return.

CATI ORBULESCU, BUCHAREST, ROMANIA

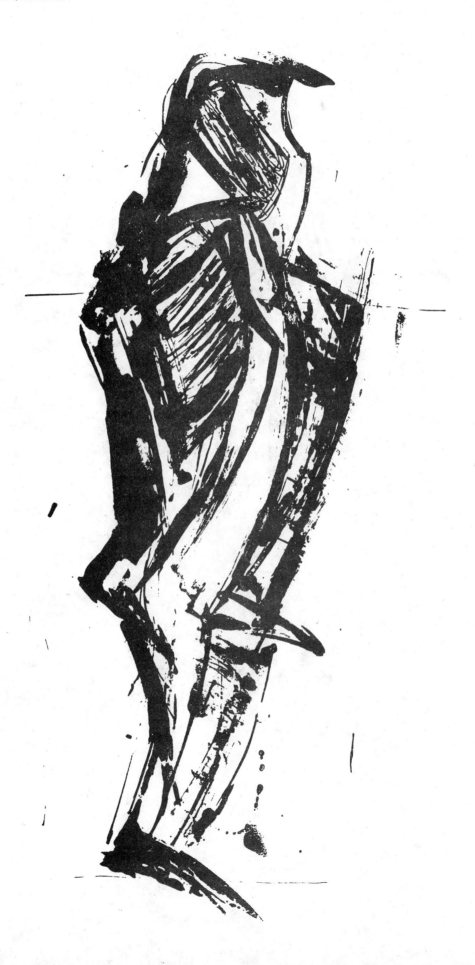

EMILY CHENG, NEW YORK, NY, USA

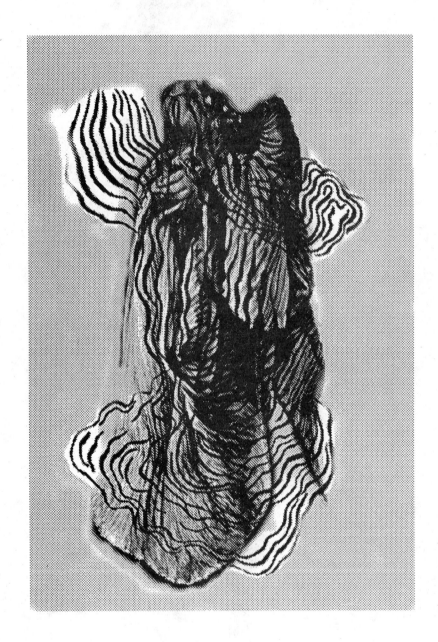

EMILY CHENG, NEW YORK, NY, USA

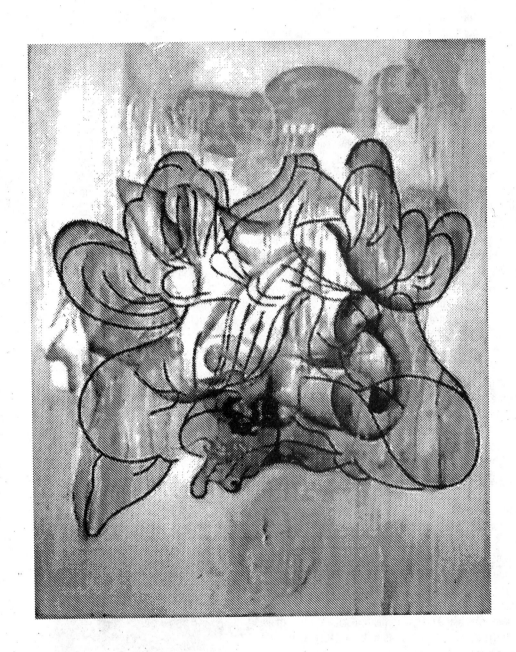

THE CONVENIENCE OF SEWING

An Asturian philosopher, called Edmundo Gonzalez - Blanco, around 1930 dedicated a full essay to "WOMAN", giving as subtitle the different aspects of her spirituality.

In it, among other many things, he said: "But the divine mind wanted to make a more complicated, delicate and refined transition from ape to man, so he created women. Biology and Psychology clearly clarify such a concept. Physically and spiritually a woman is the "half way point" between a boy and man".

He continuous the paragraph mentioning Novoa, who confirms that a woman is a child who reaches her sexual maturity and both show the same behavior, mood changes and fantasy to make up stories, whims etc., meaning, apart from her physical development, a woman is the same as a child.

If a woman is a child intellectually, it leads us to believe that she cannot carry out difficult tasks, and as a result of this, against the outside agressive male world, she must remain at home in charge of less risky and prettier tasks. Protected. It is safer, for everyone, that women spend their time sewing instead of reading or preparing herself for the competitive and difficult life "outside" the house.

Just in case the safety reason was not convincing enough, Edmundo Gonzalez - Blanco assures us that an intelligent and studious woman stops having her monthly period and will not have it back again until she abandons books and classroom. The circle is broken and the family is in danger. Women, because of the given reasons, should not separate themselves from nature, this is to say they should not adquire culture, but without becoming wild, because then they would be impresentable. It is not only a question of being homely but also domesticated. To give birth to strong and healthy children, not to be a troublemaker, to care about how she looks - to seem to be clean, delicate and refined - not to talk too much, to be thrifty etc.

Taking this statement into consideration, and always keeping the wheels turning, it is very important, for us women, to continue sewing.

Following this statement, and among us, it would be a good idea to think about the act of sewing. So allow me to mention, in defence and praise of sewing, some of its varieties, functions and even curative and therapeutic benefits.

I shall begin by mentioning how little it dirties or spoils hands and nails, in contrast to painting or other messy artistic methods such as soldering, D.I.Y., clay pottery, engraving and so on.

Also let me say how relaxing this activity is , and fhe most important fact of all is that at the same time you carry out this handicraft you can develop other senses, allowing your mind to run free into childish fantasy which "they say" characterises our sex. It is also very important that this "passivity" can be combined with another one just as relaxing like watching television, listening to the radio or talking to the family or friends.

At the same time it offers the possibility of being highly creative, combining threads and material, creating pictures or various objects and decorating different sorroundings. Also, as a way of saving, sewing can help to make or re-make dresses, mend, darn. You can make a skirt from a pair of trousers, a bedspread from a dress, a cushion from a shirt etc.

Finally we can say that now we have discovered the wonders of sewing, just to point out the "convenience" for us, women, of not to mix the sexes and that sewing should carry on being done by women.

CHELO MATESANZ

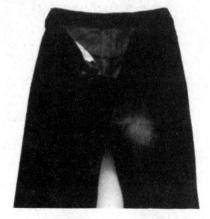

Chelo Matesanz. "Opus". 1994. (Detail).
Backstitch/Tarnished Jeans.

CHELO MATESANZ, MURCIA, SPAIN

DE LA CONVENIENCIA DE LA COSTURA

Un "filósofo" asturiano, Edmundo González - Blanco, allá por 1930 aproximadamente, dedicó un ensayo completo a la Mujer, *según los diferentes aspectos de su espiritualidad*, lo subtitulaba. En él, entre otras muchísimas cosas decía: *"Pero la mente divina quiso formar una transición más complicada, delicada y refinada del mono al hombre, y fabricó a la mujer. La biología y la psicología abonan criterio tan claro. Somática y espiritualmente, la mujer es el punto de enlace entre el niño y el hombre".*

Continúa el párrafo con una cita a Novoa en la que se afirma que la mujer es un niño que alcanza la madurez sexual y que ambos muestran el mismo comportamiento, volubilidad, fantasía para inventar historias, caprichos, etc.; es decir, salvo en su desarrollo físico, la mujer es igual al niño.

Si la mujer es un niño intelectualmente, es lógico pensar que ésta no puede realizar difíciles y comprometidas tareas; y como consecuencia de ello, frente al agresivo mundo del hombre en la calle, ella debe permanecer en el hogar encargada de otras labores menos arriesgadas y más primorosas. Protegida.

Es mucho más seguro (para todos) que la mujer pase su tiempo cosiendo en lugar de leyendo y preparándose para la vida competitiva y difícil que existe fuera de la "casa".

Por si lo de la seguridad no fuera del todo convincente, y según las teorías del autor que encabeza el texto, se afirma que la muchacha inteligente y estudiosa pierde su *flujo periódico* y no lo recupera hasta que abandona *cátedras y libros*. El ciclo se rompe y la familia peligra. La mujer, por lo tanto, no debe apartarse de la naturaleza, es decir, no debe adquirir cultura; aunque tampoco puede ser una salvaje (por impresentable). No sólo se trata de que sea doméstica, sino además **domesticada**. Dar a luz niños sanos y fuertes, no alborotar en el gallinero, ofrecer un aspecto exterior cuidado (parecer y ser limpia, delicada, fina), no hablar demasiado, ser ahorradora, etc., etc.

Teniendo en cuenta todo esto, y siempre **en favor de que la rueda siga girando, es muy importante que las mujeres cosan,** (o cosamos).

Partiendo de esta premisa y así, entre nosotras, sería bueno reflexionar a priori sobre el hecho de coser.

Hagamos por lo tanto un poco de apología o elogio de la costura enumerando algunas de sus variedades, funcionalidad e incluso propiedades curativas y terapéuticas:

En principio mencionar lo poco que estropea y ensucia las manos y uñas, a diferencia de la pintura o de otros procedimientos artísticos más engorrosos, tales como la soldadura, el bricolage, el modelado en barro, el grabado, etc.

Por otra parte hablar de lo relajante de esta actividad y, lo más importante de todo, que a la vez que realizas un trabajo manual, puedes desarrollar otros sentidos dando rienda suelta a esa fantasía infantil que tanto "dicen" caracterizar a nuestro sexo. Se puede además, teniendo en cuenta esto, combinar esta "pasividad" con otra igualmente relajante; como ver la televisión, escuchar la radio o conversar con la familia o los amigos. Asimismo, ofrece la posibilidad de ser enormemente creativa combinando hilos y telas, construyendo imágenes u objetos diferentes y decorando ambientes variados.

También, en favor de la virtud del ahorro, la costura te puede ayudar a reciclar o a confeccionar vestidos, zurcir, remendar; a convertir un pantalón en falda, un vestido en colcha, una càmisa en cojín, etc.

Entre lo que nos queda decir, ahora que hemos descubierto lo maravilloso de la costura, señalar la "conveniencia" para nosotras de que los sexos no se confundan y que las que cosamos, sigamos siendo las mujeres.

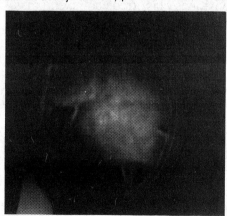

Chelo Matesanz. "Opus". 1994. (Detalle).
Pespunte sobre pantalón vaquero deslucido.

ARTISTA

Cuando definían su escritura como "específicamente femenina", el espanto de Virginia Wolf provenía del rechazo visceral a ser ordenada dentro de la maquinaria dual que opone lo femenino a lo masculino: era fruto de la intuición y la conciencia de que esas construcciones sociales y lingüísticas son una forma de violencia que coarta y encasilla los devenires posibles como ser vivo y como artista. Y desde esa conciencia abierta vivió y proyectó a través de la escritura su voluntad de escapar a los dualismos, su deseo de habitar los intersticios, de crear espacios de respiración entre los órdenes establecidos, de "saturar cada átomo", de abrir el instante para hacer que un momento vivido perdurara o existiera por sí mismo.

Eva Hesse, más recientemente, intentaba también huir de los encasillamientos y afirmaba con profunda convicción que, en arte, "la excelencia no tiene sexo" y que la mejor forma de combatir la -sin embargo aún innegable- discriminación era a través de la calidad, de la fuerza del propio arte. ¿Pero quién es artista? ¿Y cuáles son las creaciones verdaderamente trascendentes? ¿Cómo se perfila ese ser capaz, como dicen Deleuze y Guattari, de desbordar los estados perceptivos y los pasajes afectivos de lo vivido? ¿Cómo se configuran los enunciados estética y conceptualmente significantes? Artista es, dicen Deleuze y Guattari, quien habiendo penetrado en las profundidades de la vida y habiendo visto en ella algo demasiado grande, demasiado amenazante, demasiado intolerable, surge de ese oscuro abismo con los "ojos rojos" y desde esa mirada impregnada traslada a la materia, al pensamiento o al lenguaje sus visiones y las ofrece como enigmas multidireccionales, como verdades temporales que apuntan a las profundidades del ser. Por eso el verdadero artista ha de tratar siempre de liberar la vida allá donde quiera que esté prisionera, y ha de intentarlo en un combate incierto pero tenaz contra los estereotipos, contra los códigos establecidos que aprisionan la realidad.

ROSA MARTÍNEZ
BARCELONA
FAX: 34.3.2049679

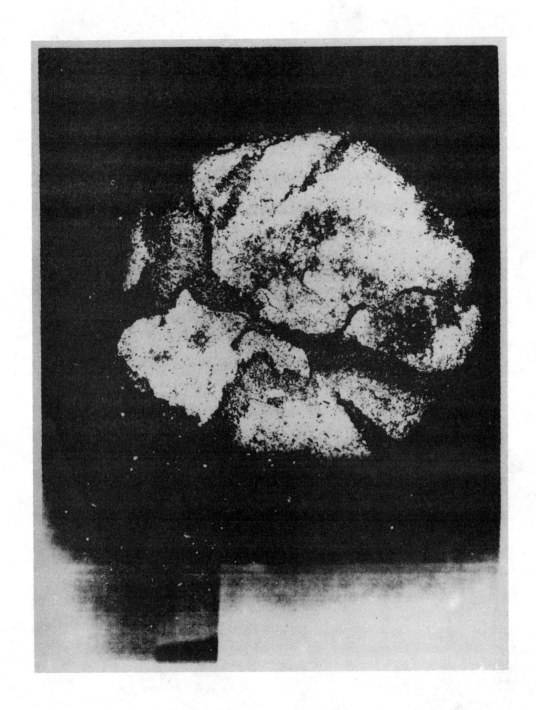

THE YANGTZE
from Lake Dongting
to the Yellow Sea

from Bread and Water

Alison Kn '95

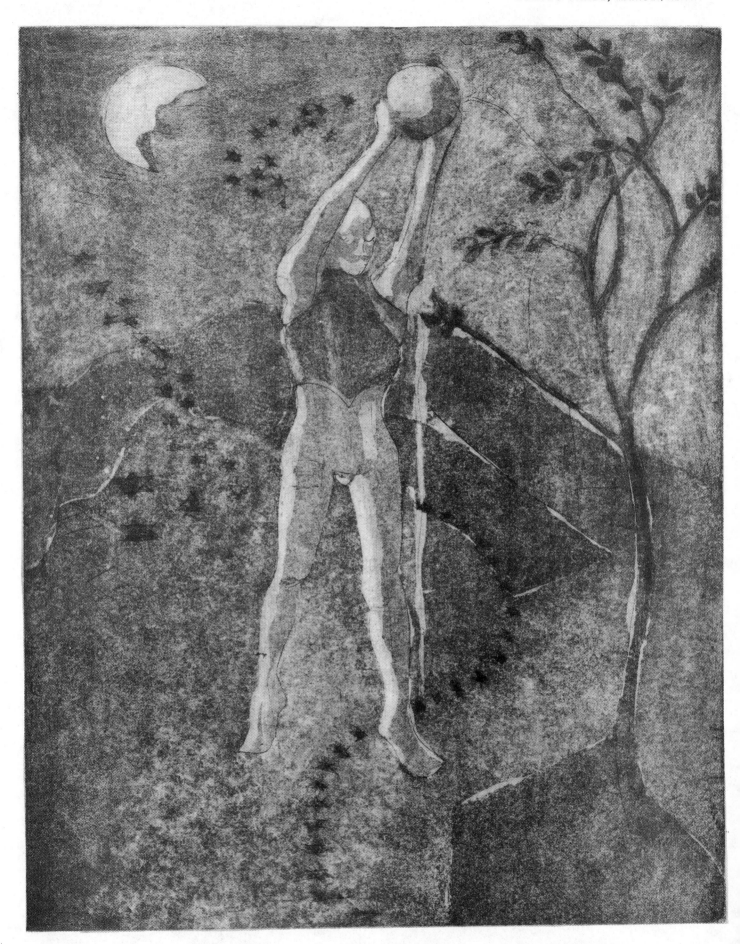

AKANÉ ASAOKA, BARCELONA, SPAIN

A S T R O N O M Y

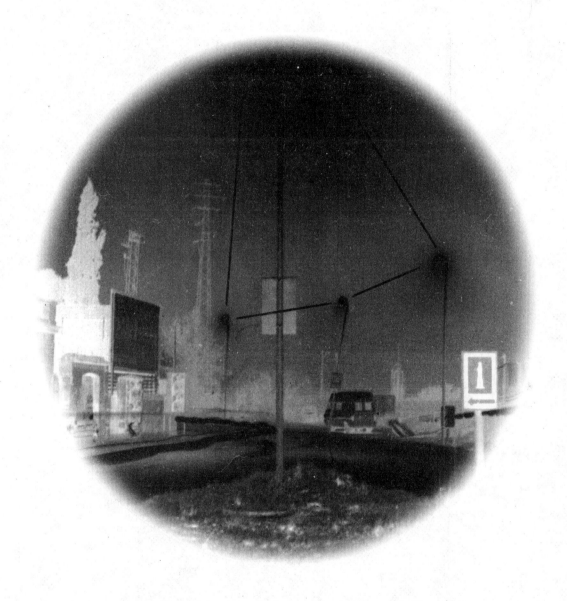

**Constellation III, Barcelona, 70 cm in diameter, Photography
Work in Progress since 1991**

Akané Asaoka. Carrer del Pont, 26 - 2 - 1, 08830 Sant Boi de Llobregat, Barcelona. Spain. Tel./Fax (34-3) 630 22 44

JUDITH FICKSMAN, NEW YORK, NY, USA

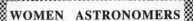

WOMEN ASTRONOMERS

Aglaonike (antiquity)
Hypatia (ca AD 370-415)
Hildegard of Bingen (1098-1179 or 1180)
Sophia Brahe (1556-1643)
Elisabetha Koopman Hevelius (b. ca 1647)
Maria Cunitz (1610-1664)
Maria Winkelmann Kirch (1670-1720)
Jeanne Dumee (1680)
Christine Kirch (ca. 1696-1782)

Nicole-Reine Etable de la Briere Lepaute (1723-1788)
Louise Elisabeth Felicite Pourra de la Madeleine Pierry (b. 1746)
Caroline Lucretia Herschel (1750-1848)
Marie Jeanne Amelie Harlay Lefrancais de Lalande (1790)

Maria Mitchell (1818-1889)
Mary Watson Whitney (1847-1921)
Margaret Lindsay Murray Huggins (1848-1915)
Williamina Paton Stevens Fleming (1857-1911)
Anna Winlock (1857-1904)
Mary Adela Blagg (1858-1944)
Florence Cushman (1860-1940)
Dorothea Klumpke Roberts (1861-1942)
Annie Jump Cannon (1863-1941)
Flammetta Worthington Wilson (1864-1920)
Antonia Caetana Maury (1866-1952)
Mary Orr Evershed (1867-1949)
Henrietta Swan Levitt (1868-1921)
Annie Russell Maunder (1868-1947)
Anne Sewell Young (1871-1961)
Roxana Hayward Vivian (b. 1871)
Charlotte E. Moore (1898-1990)
Elizabeth Brown (d. 1899)

A. Grace Cook (19th century)
Elizabeth Isis Pogson Kent (19th century)
Dorothy Wrinch (19th century)
Evelyn Leland (19th -20th centuries)
Louisa Wells (19th -20th centuries)
Mary A. Albertson (d. 1914)
Alla G. Massevitch (b.1918)
E. Margaret Burbidge (b.1919)
Nancy Grace Roman (b.1925)
Vera Cooper Rubin (b.1928)
Jocelyn Susan Bell Burnell (b.1943)
Sandra M. Faber (b.1944)
Margaret Joan Geller (b.1947)
Sidney Wolff (20th century)
Tatiana V. Shabanova (20th century)
Lee Anne Willson (20th century)
Catherine Pilachowski (20th century)
Kim Venn (20th century)

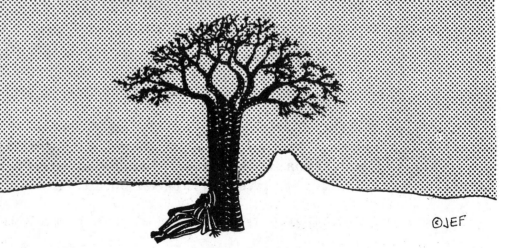

©JEF

SOPHIA YONCOUPOLOS, NEW YORK, NY, USA

ASTRONOMY

The list on the opposite page commemorates women astronomers through the ages. There have been women astronomers since antiquity. They have done important work and won major prizes in the field.

Judith Ficksman and **Sophia Yoncoupolos** recently gave their first public lecture on women astronomers. We work together on a number of projects which are aimed particularly at encouraging young women to think about working in math or science. In general we hope to make people feel excited and included in the work going on at the forefront of science.

We did a T-shirt for the **Women in Science Exchange (WISE)** at Columbia University. This was one of the groups that responded when in 1990, teentalk Barbie, in her repertoire of phrases, included "Math class is tough." The phrase was removed. This shirt, done with Mattel's permission, takes Barbie a step further. In our photo, she is pictured with a calculator and a think bubble above her head which reads, "Math is fun!" The shirt sold out and was included in an exhibit of works on shirts at major museums in New York city.

Our video **"Journey to Jupiter"** shows a woman talking about her dream of going to Jupiter in a spaceship and was included in a program on Jupiter at **Four Walls** in Brooklyn. We are currently working on a number of other video projects.

They worked this year on the **Sonya Kovalevskaya High School Math Days**, a three day program at Columbia University which brought high school girls into contact with women working in careers in math and science. Judy produced a three color offset lithography poster for the event.

Sophia Yancopoulos studies neutron stars and is about to receive her Phd in physics from Columbia University. She is one of the principal organizers of the **Women in Science Exchange**. She teaches Astronomy at CUNY, Staten Island.

Judith Ficksman is an artist who works with images, words and music. She has recently interviewed and photographed women astronomers for a series of articles which will appear in the May/June and July/August issues of **Stardate** magazine.

JUNE WILSON, MIDDLETOWN, NJ, USA

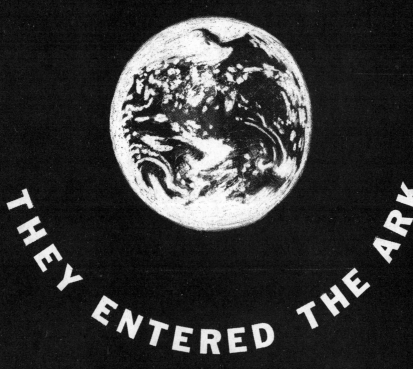

DEAN ANDREWS, NEW YORK, NY, USA

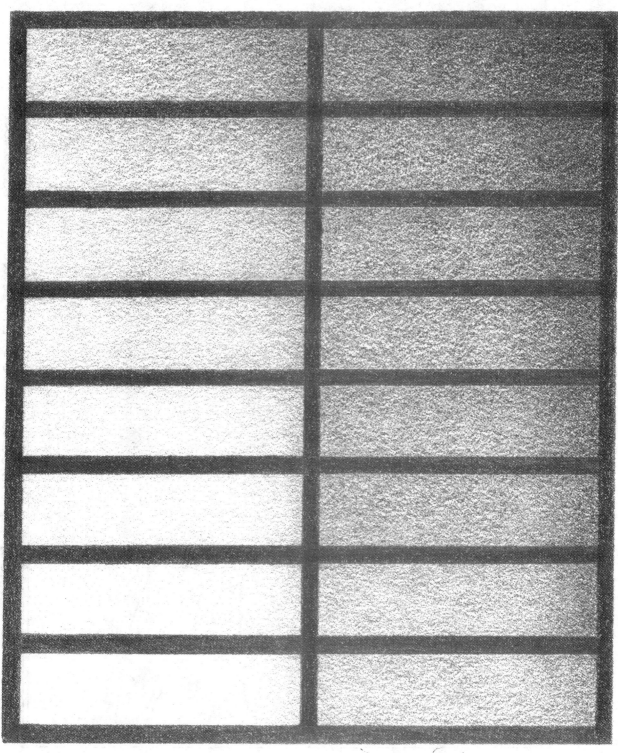

Sensible: sensitive, sinsesseble, bravo, intelligente, delicate, tenue, Sajante.

Sensible: 1. perceptible, appréciable, apparent 2. apparent 3. manifeste 4. tendre, susceptible.

Sensible: 1. sensitive, impressionable 2. sensitive, delicate. 3. perceptible, noticeable, 4. appreciable, 5. regrettable.

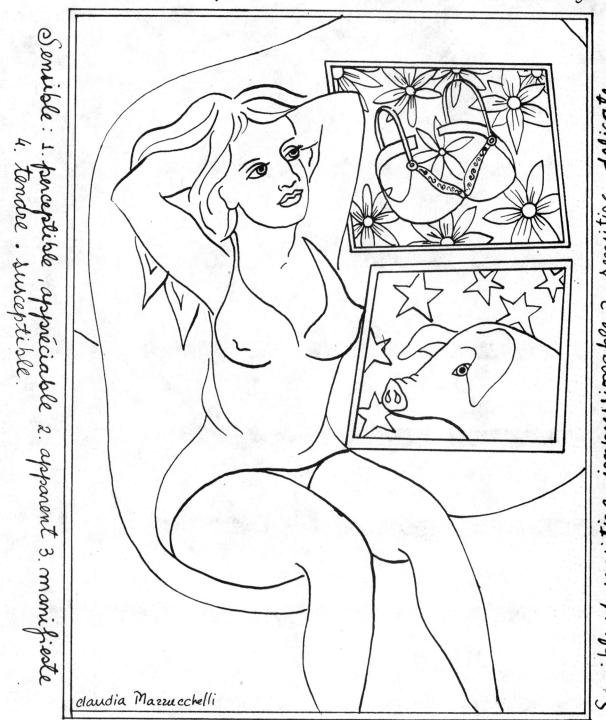

claudia Mazzucchelli

Sensible : 1. perceptible. apreciable. manifiesto.
2. sensitivo. capaz de sentir. 3. Sabedor.
consciente. 4. razonable, sensato. inteligente.

ELLEN ROSS, NEW YORK, NY, USA

I shall walk forward with dignity; proud, a warrior in my own right . . . void of lingerie and kitchenware. Ne'er the word efficiency shall be uttered in my house of Carmelites. And when your voice, in its whisper, screams of rage, I will not cower or ache. I will pre-salve the wounds and become my own warrior. Unspoken assumptions, rooted in painful history still abound, even in New York City. There is no sign at its entrance reading: "Unconscious Traditionalists Beware." They are even born here. After all, my father goes to girlie shows. "Las Vegas Dancers," he defends, when really he... just loves the tits and ass.

Pasties are ir- relevant, really. On another occasion he said: "She has reverted to the Primitive Female Instinct. After hav ing Billy she just didn't want to have sex, her maternal needs were satisfied and as a result her involve- ment with... her husband deteriorated." Mutated Freudian Bullshit. Never mind that her husband is a disgusting abusive pig. How could you? Any of you, all of you? You. What would it take for you to embrace me in arms of empathy and strength Masculinity rooted in compas- sion instead of self importance unre- lated.The Struggle continues. And we walk in the shadow of imagined self importance. Always ready to embrace the dictated perception. Even if false and destruc- tive. In truth there must be a hierarchy. In grey clouds lie choices. Harsh sunlight induces anorexia and bulimia in young mothers. Of the upperclass.Unconscious of her beauty she starves herself. Of all nourishment and support. To please an always short and now balding man who demands her starvation and self hatred. And in the eyes of this balding man, whose ego is so strong and compassion so limited, you see your reflection and offer me your apology. Can one apologize for history's constructed hierarchy? In grey clouds one finds kindness; Amazon warriors bathe in their rain.

-Ellen Ross

BETTINA MUNK, BROOKLYN, NY, USA

Unquestioning.

Who now? When now? Where now?

Who now?

Unquestioning.

When now ?   Where now ?

Where now ?

Unbelieving.

When now ?   Unquestioning.

say I.

I,

Who now ?

PEGGY DIGGS, WILLIAMSTOWN, MA, USA

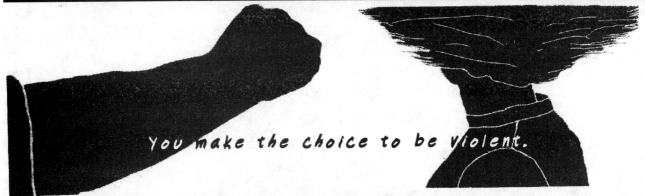

NAME THE PROBLEM:

You make the choice to be violent.

TAKE RESPONSIBILITY.

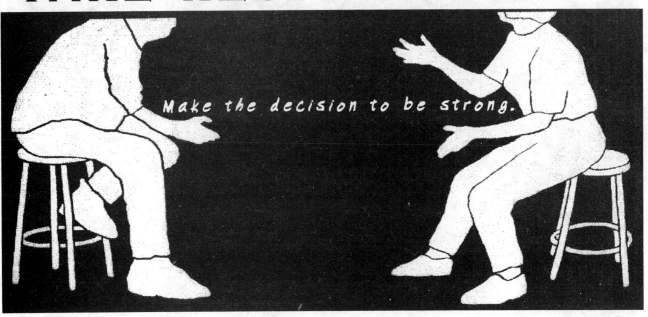

Make the decision to be strong.

*Men will stop violating women
when men and communities decide they must stop.*

A PUBLIC ART PROJECT BY PEGGY DIGGS

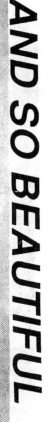

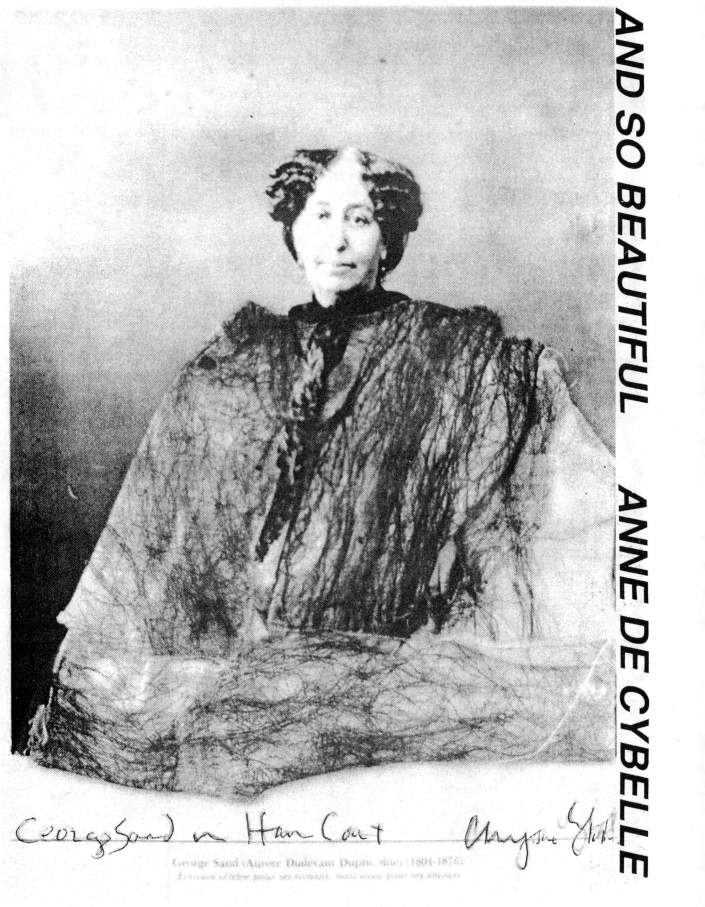

George Sand on Han Court

George Sand (Aurore Dudevant Dupin, dite) (1804-1876)

CHRYSANNE STATHACOS, NEW YORK, NY, USA

ANNE DE CYBELLE

AND SO BEAUTIFUL

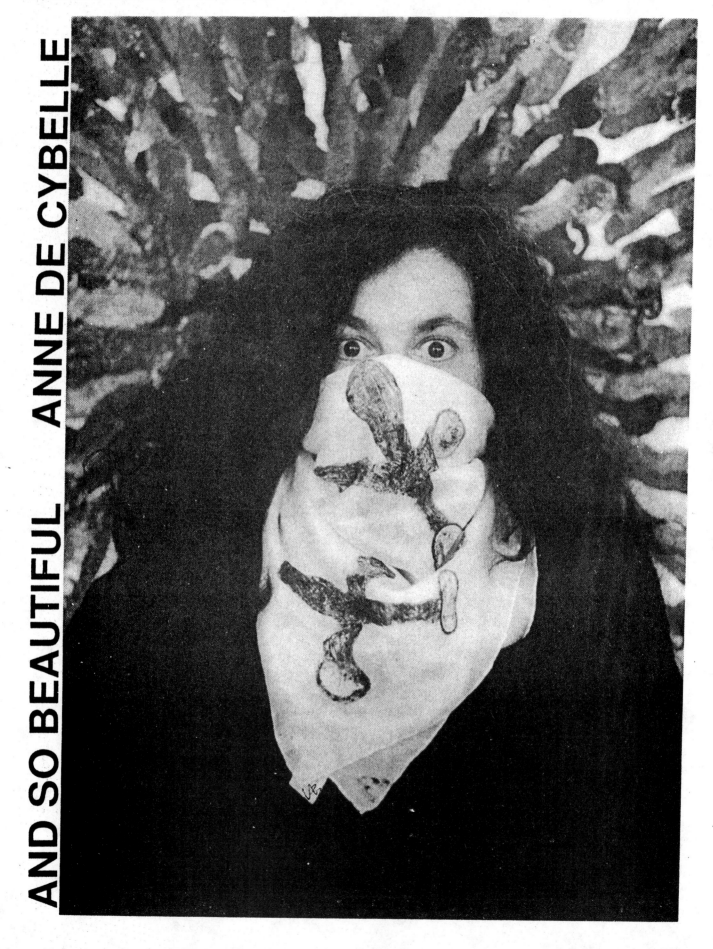

TANYA LYSKOVA, MOSCOW, RUSSIA

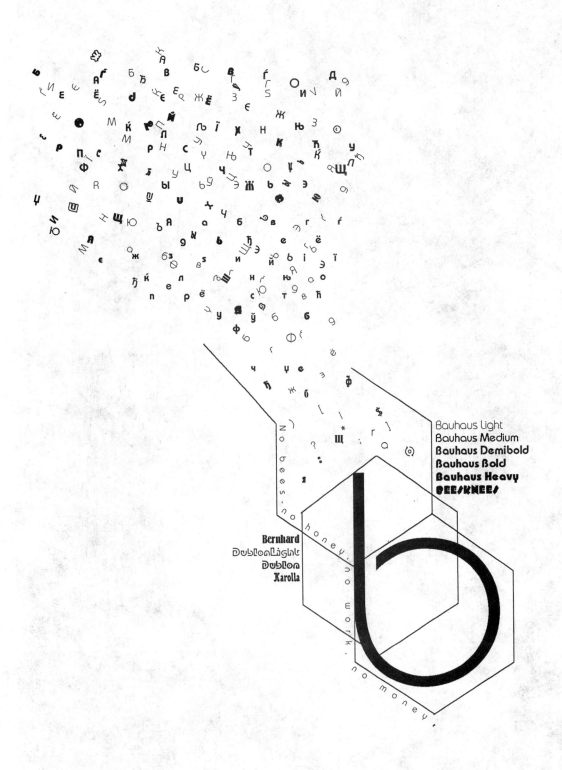

Bauhaus Light
Bauhaus Medium
Bauhaus Demibold
Bauhaus Bold
Bauhaus Heavy
BEESKNEES

Bernhard
DublonLight
Dublon
Xarolla

No bees - no honey, no work, no money.

BERIT JENSEN, PARIS, FRANCE

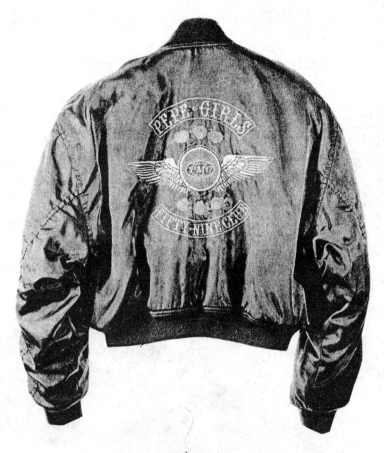

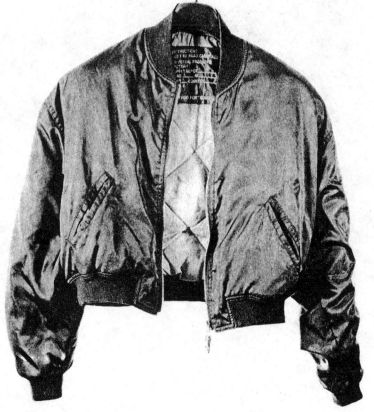

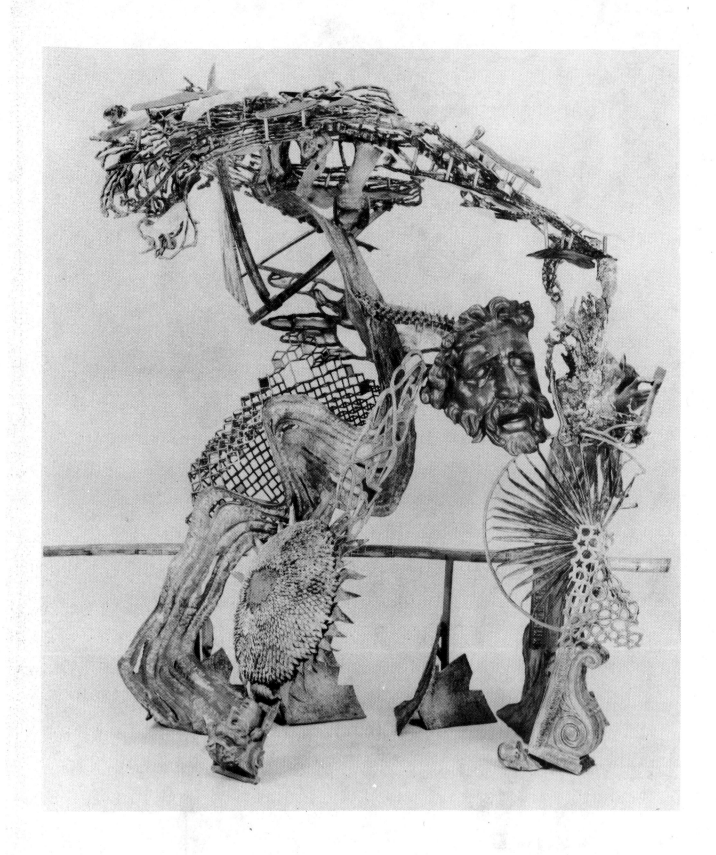

MARION HELD, MONTCLAIR, NJ, USA

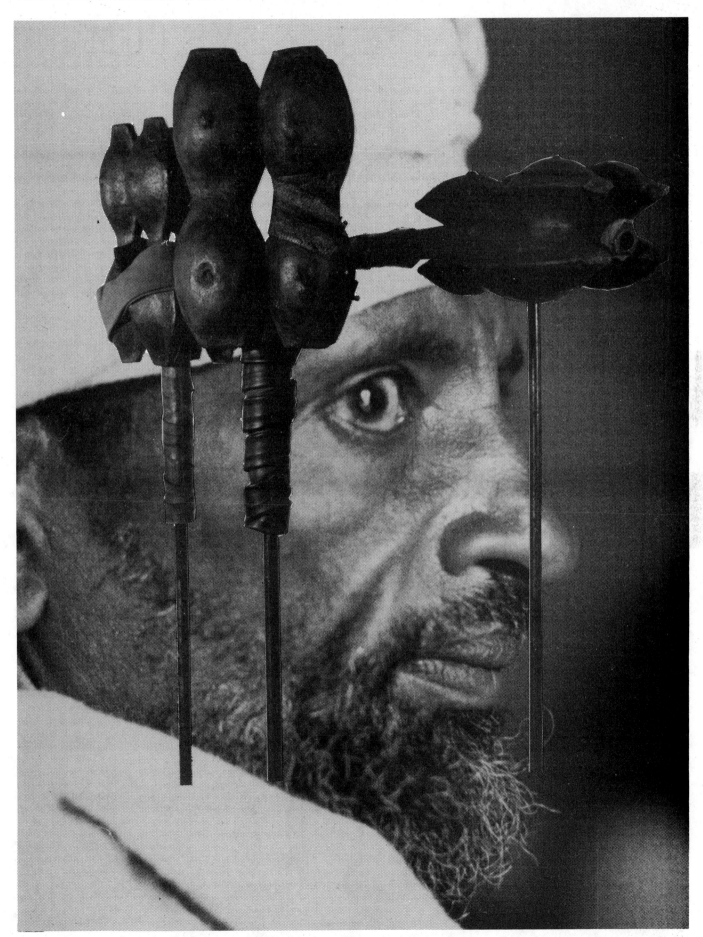

JERELYN HANRAHAN, ROME, ITALY

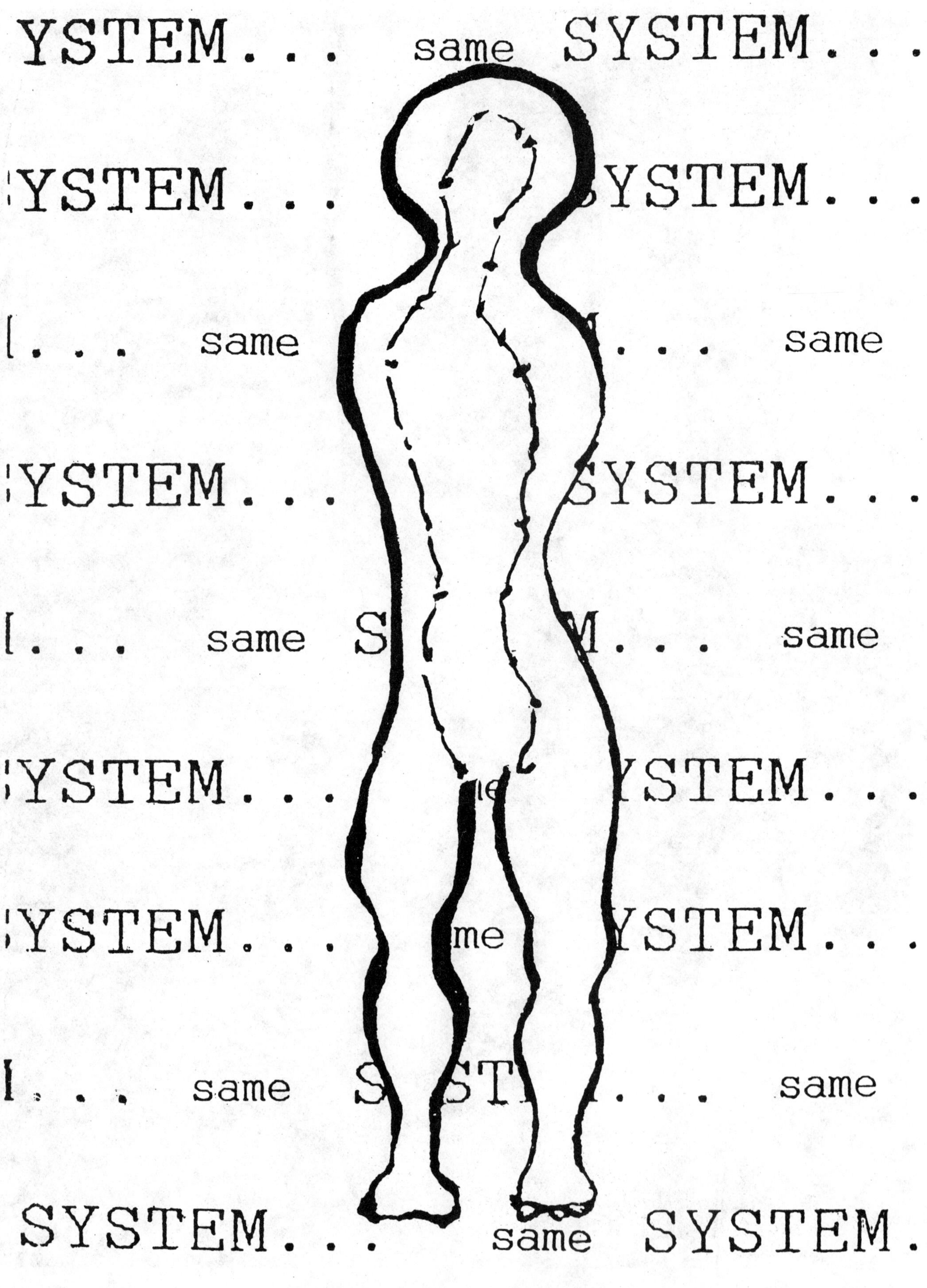

YSTEM... same SYSTEM...

YSTEM... SYSTEM...

[... same ... same

YSTEM... SYSTEM...

[... same S M... same

YSTEM... YSTEM...

YSTEM... me YSTEM...

[... same S ST... same

SYSTEM... same SYSTEM.

ALFREDA GARCIA, NEW YORK, NY, USA

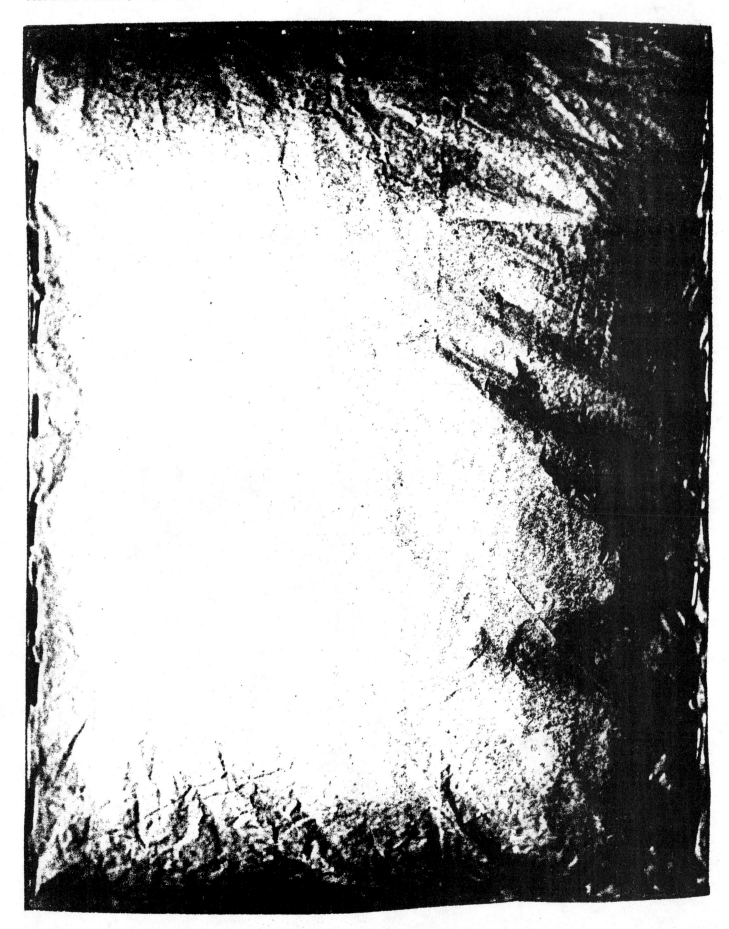

ALFREDA GARCIA, NEW YORK, NY, USA

ANNE DELANEY, NEW YORK, NY, USA

BLIND FOLDS

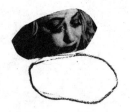

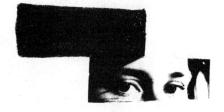

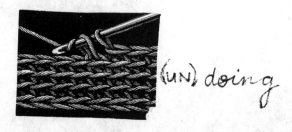

(un) doing

ANNE DELANEY, NEW YORK, NY, USA

CRASH COLLISION COURSE PREVENTION

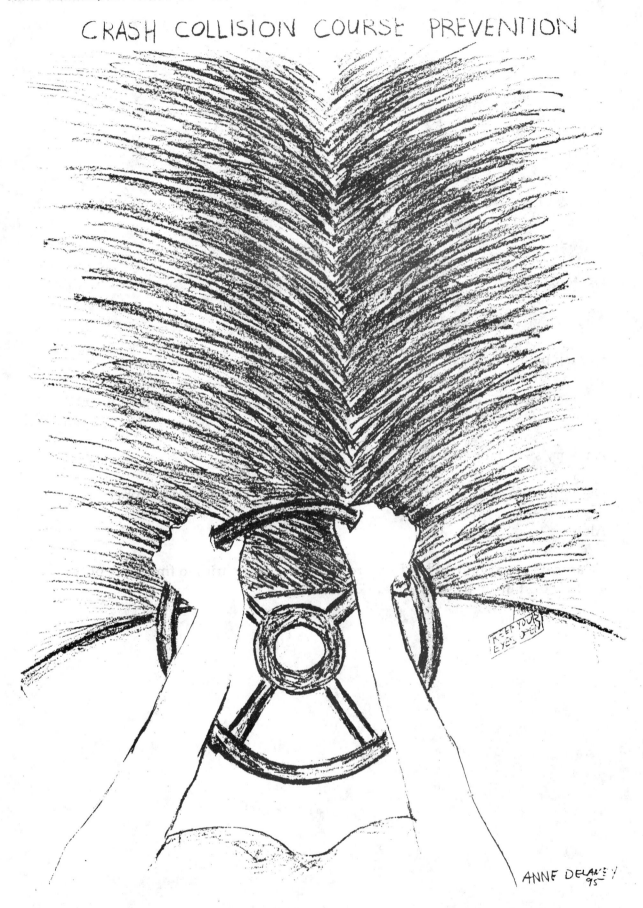

GLENDA ADAMS, FAR ROCKAWAY, NY, USA

Blue Room, Brown Girl
Subtitled: The Colors of Reality

Daybreak:

A brown girl wakes with a blue unbonded soul

Her tan palms rest against a sky blue comforter

A half open deep set mahoghany eye peeks thru black escaped tousled tresses
half wound around big blue curlers

An ivory strap falls off a sagging sepia shoulder

Her large rust feet with a cafe-au-lait soles search for dusty black slippers

Alone

Clear tears zig-zag down her rosy brown cheeks as she tries to find a ray of
golden sunshine in the room of dark despair

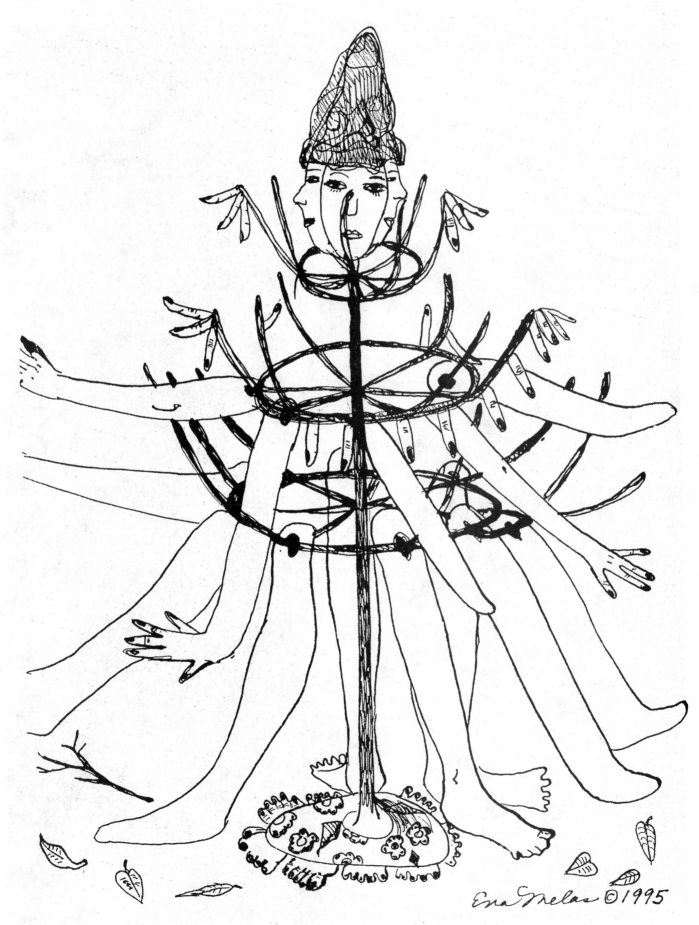

the body

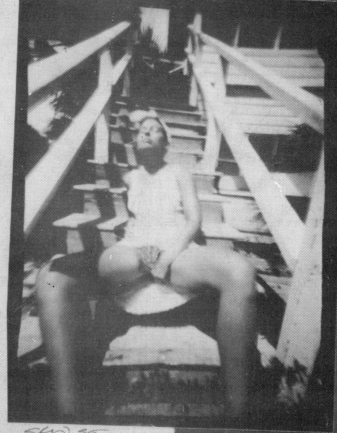

i await the arrival
of my first child

she'll come through
this body

and into the
twenty-first
century

my message
is her

sandra-lee phipps spring 1995 brooklyn, ny

JOYCE WEINER, LI CITY, NY, USA

Small Bust Development

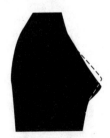

SMALL BUST DEVELOPMENT can be young and firm, underdeveloped, or mature and lacking firmness. There is no relation between bust measure and cup type. You may wear a size 38 yet require a small cup brassiere. Select an accentuated, uplift style if you wish to appear slightly fuller.

Average Bust Development

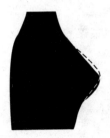

AVERAGE BUST DEVELOPMENT may be firm or slightly sagging. Judge carefully if you are actually average. If the cup of your present brassiere does not cover the breast, you may require a full cup. Too small a cup does not reduce the apparent size, but may cause slight bulges, and break down tissue by binding.

The Body

Full Bust Development

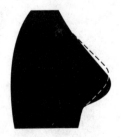

FULL BUST DEVELOPMENT may be firm or tend to be pendulous. This development requires full, deep cups. Too small a cup may injure delicate tissues and accentuates size by creating bulges. If figure is fleshy under arms or at back, built-up shoulders smooth underarm and back flesh into trim lines.

Pendulous Bust Development

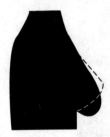

PENDULOUS BUSTS may be pendulous whether small, average or full in development. Some pendulous figures do not require bras with special inner cup construction provided care is taken to select correct cup size. Special care is needed in choosing bras for the full pendulous bust.

2nd in a series ©1995 Joyce Weiner

LAURA SANSONE, BROOKLYN, NY, USA

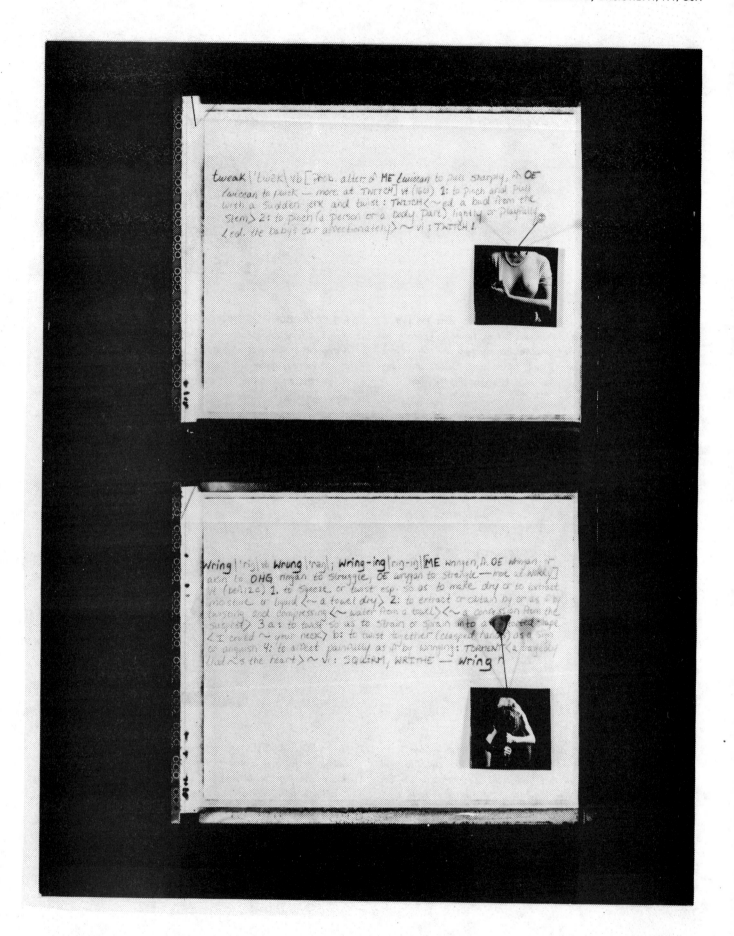

LAURA SANSONE, BROOKLYN, NY, USA

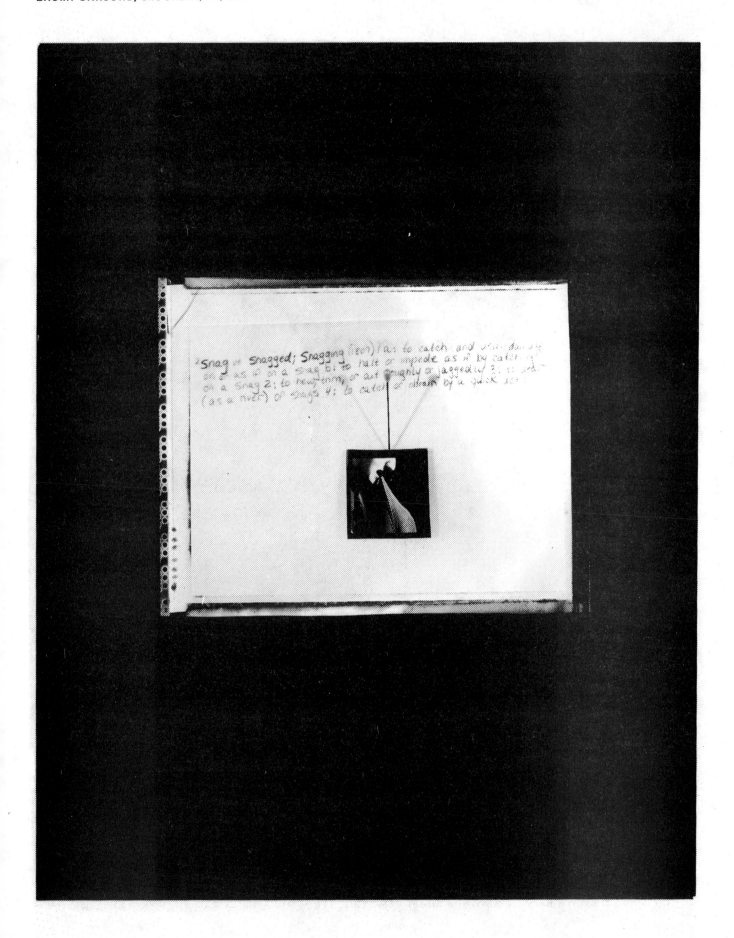

ROSANN BERRY, NEW YORK, NY, USA

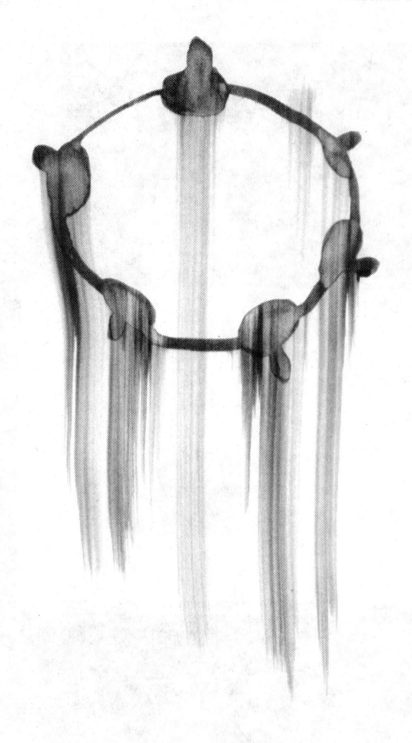

Rosann Berry • 88 White Street, New York, NY 10013 • (212) 431 8870

ROSANN BERRY, NEW YORK, NY, USA

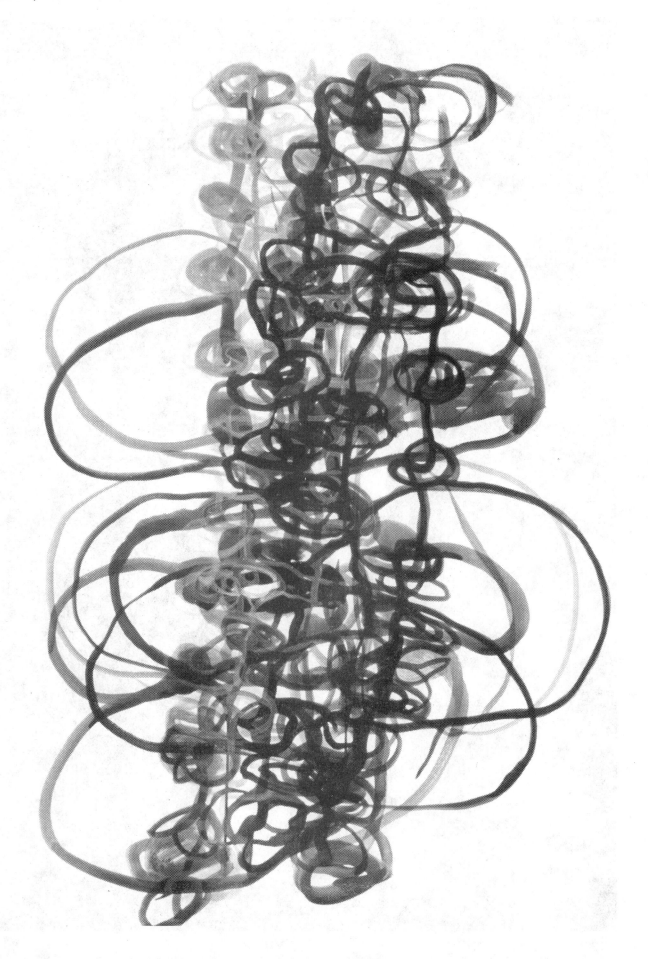

SHIRLEY KLINGHOFFER, NEW YORK, NY, USA

1990's 'Barbie Venus'

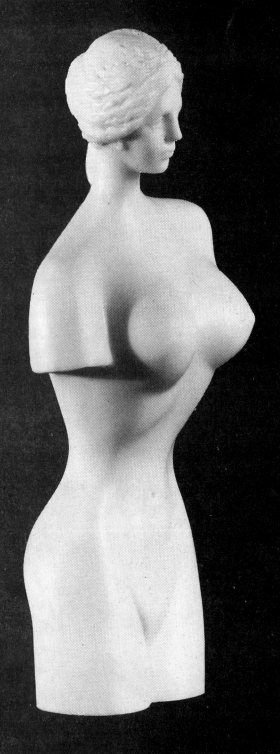

SHIRLEY KLINGHOFFER, NEW YORK, NY, USA

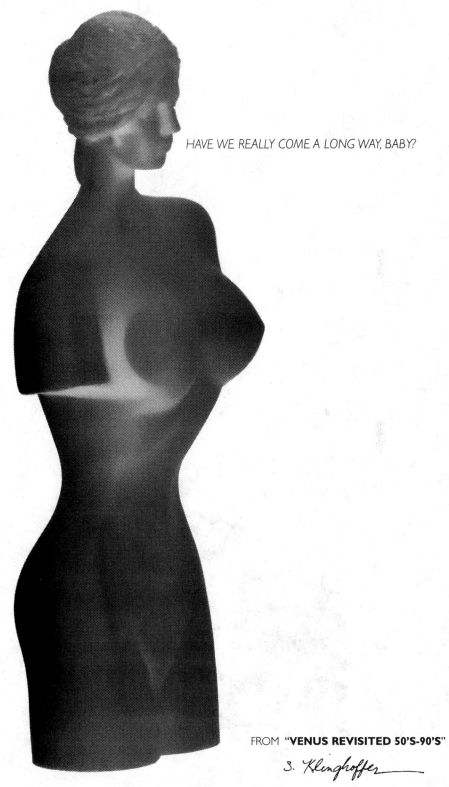

HAVE WE REALLY COME A LONG WAY, BABY?

FROM **"VENUS REVISITED 50'S-90'S"**

JANET PIHLBLAD, NEW YORK, NY, USA

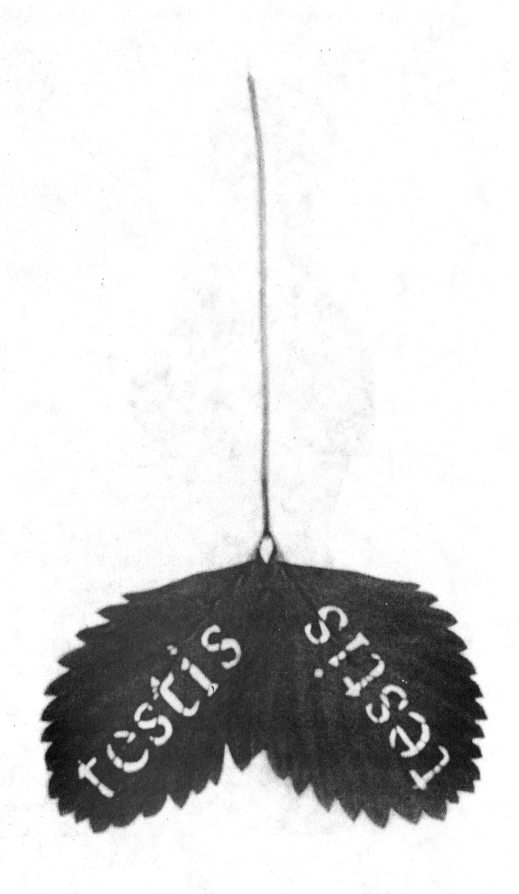

JANET PIHLBLAD, NEW YORK, NY, USA

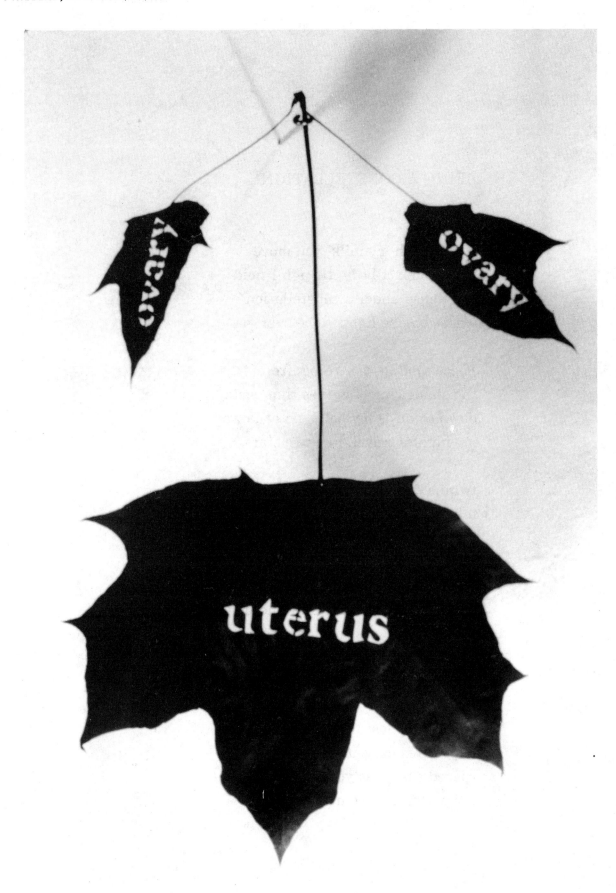

ANNIE FINCH, CINCINNATI, OH, USA

BEING A CONSTELLATION

Heavy with my milk, you move
your compact body, though I hold
you dense under a constellation
whose sparse lights ache over you.

If, looking up, you recognize
the shadowing of curves that casts
down towards my belly, and the way
my nipples travel, like two stars

twinned by your eyesight; if my arms
take night, and keep it from the sky,
if my night voice can stop your cry,
I'll be the Mother over you.

You are a question, small and dense,
and I am an answer, long diffuse
and dark, but I want to be sky
for you so, like the stars, I lie,

holding my lost lights wide and flat
in pictures for your eyes to take,
spaced easily, so you can catch
the patterns in your sleepy net.

ANNEKE LUCAS, LOS ANGELES, CA, USA

SECRETS OF A WOMAN'S BREAST

Ever wonder why lady chimps aren't built like Marilyn Monroe upfront?

Well, there's a very good reason, says Morris. When humans began walking upright on two legs, females developed big bosoms to attract the men. He explains:

"Visual signs of other female primates are transmitted largely from the rear. When the female is in heat, she develops sexual swellings on her rump and gives off a special fragrance.

These powerful signals act as a magnet to the males. If the male becomes aroused, he will mount and mate with the female from behind while she is on all fours."

When human females evolved into upright creatures, their formerly flat rump muscles developed into bulging, rounded buttocks, says Morris.

"These became our primary female sexual signal. Unfortunately, when a male and a female human walked toward one another, the buttocks were no longer visible - our special rump signal was hidden from view. The answer was to provide the human female with imitation buttocks on the front of her body. The female breasts evolved quite simply as buttock mimics.

Support for this idea is found in the anatomy. The bulk is formed by fatty tissue and plays no part in milk production. The rounded female human breasts are more concerned with sexual display than maternal feeding."

ANNIE FINCH, CINCINNATI, OH, USA

RIDDLE: WAR AND CHILD

If now I were the woman who gave birth
to this soft-bodied boy, this empty earth
and calling heart, this full head, these new clues,
I could not say the words that we all do
to mourn the future. Porous sands still rage

with live-born bodies, the baby I tore
from my full belly on an urgent shore
awaited by red waves. The war is there
to finish off my still-flowing hot wine,
six startled bloody weeks of mothers' crime.

The riddle, if we found one, would say world
where he's still sleeping, world where a new war
unites to fester the clean desert sand,
and it would say the hard birth he unfurled
for two nights that lasted as long as a war.

His belly pools, his legs gather and go still,
bent in their blossomed victory.

Francisca Antuñez Cuesta, SEVILLA, SPAIN

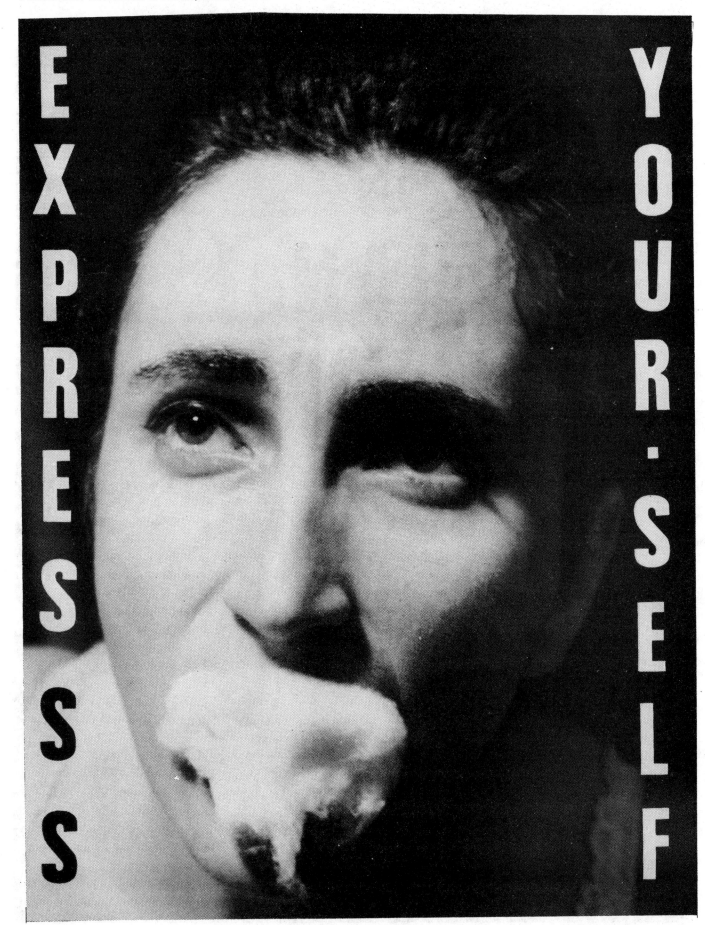

Francisca Antuñez Cuesta, SEVILLA, SPAIN

Francisca Antuñez Cuesta, SEVILLA, SPAIN

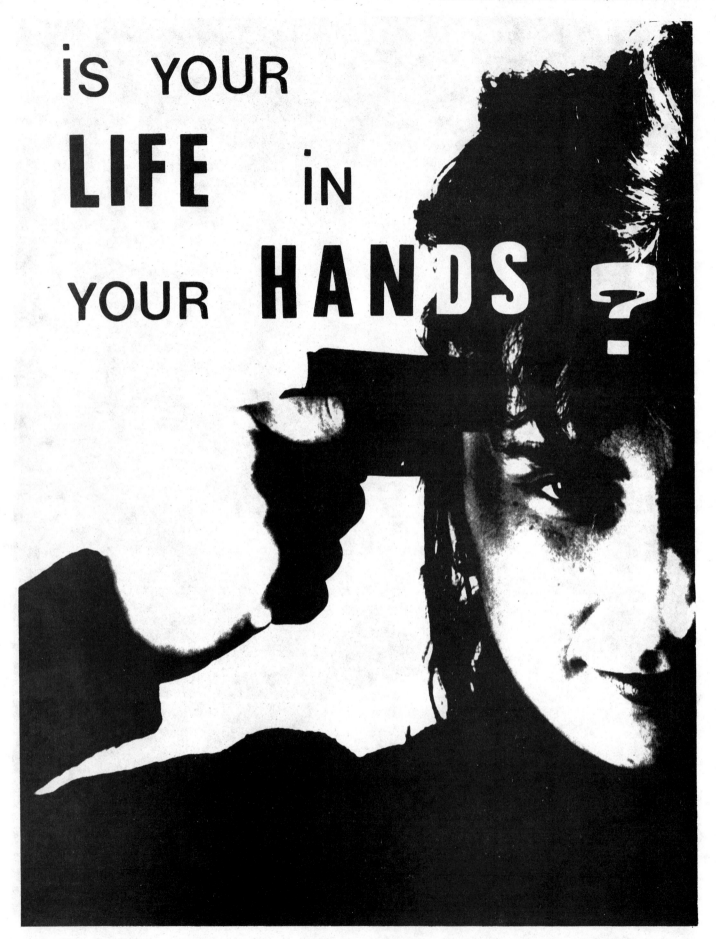

IS YOUR LIFE IN YOUR HANDS ?

SHEILA KLEIN, BOW, WA, USA

What will the built environment become when built by women?

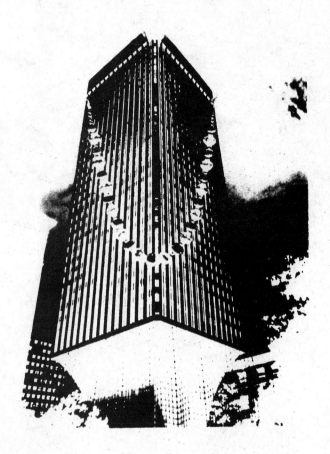

i want to dress the world

<u>now</u> more than ever

(We yearn for texture, softscape, fragrance .
In the United States, the city has become generic and homogenised .
I am a crusader against the boring , beige , banal of built .
I believe that the city can be an elixir of opportunity)

ARTISTS CORPS OF ENGINEERS

SHEILA KLEIN
690 BAY VIEW - EDISON ROAD
BOW , WASHINGTON 98232
360.766.8004
SK 1 BOSS

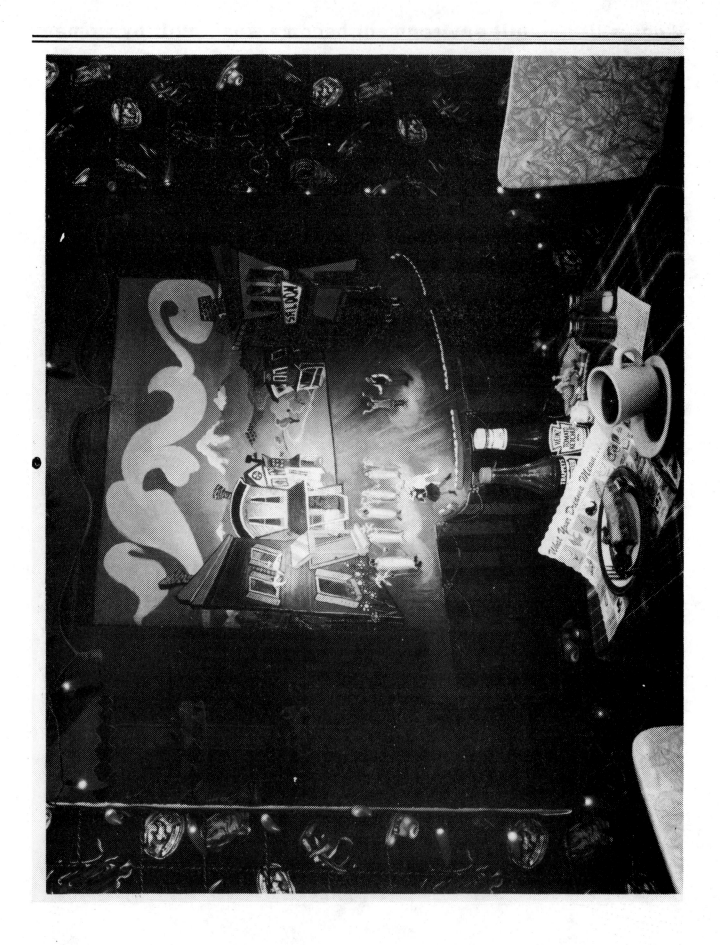

KK Kozik, NEW YORK, NY, USA

REMEMBER

Sunday	Monday	Tuesday	Wednesday	Thursday	Friday	Saturday
	1	2	3	4	5	6
7	8	9	10	11	12	13
14	15	16	17	18	19	20
21	22	23	24	25	26	27
28	29	30	31	32	33	

KK Kozik

BETTY STÜRMER, BERLIN, GERMANY

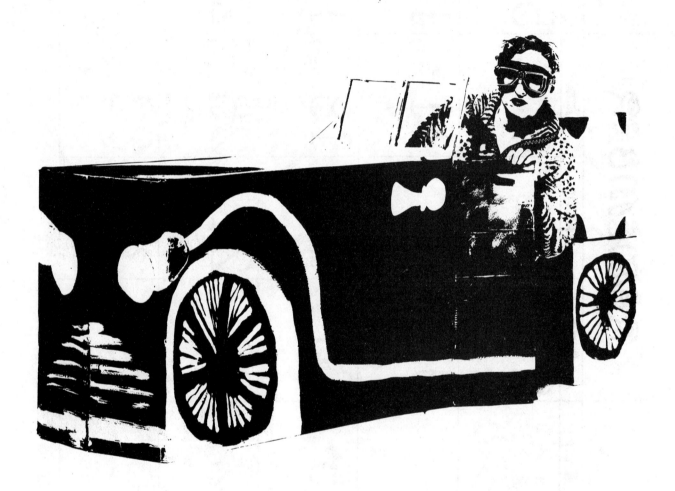

ONE OF THE

MANY THINGS

YOU CAN DO

WITH THIS

TIME CAPSULE:

GIVE IT TO A LIBRARY.

MAUREEN MULLEN, BROOKLYN, NY, USA

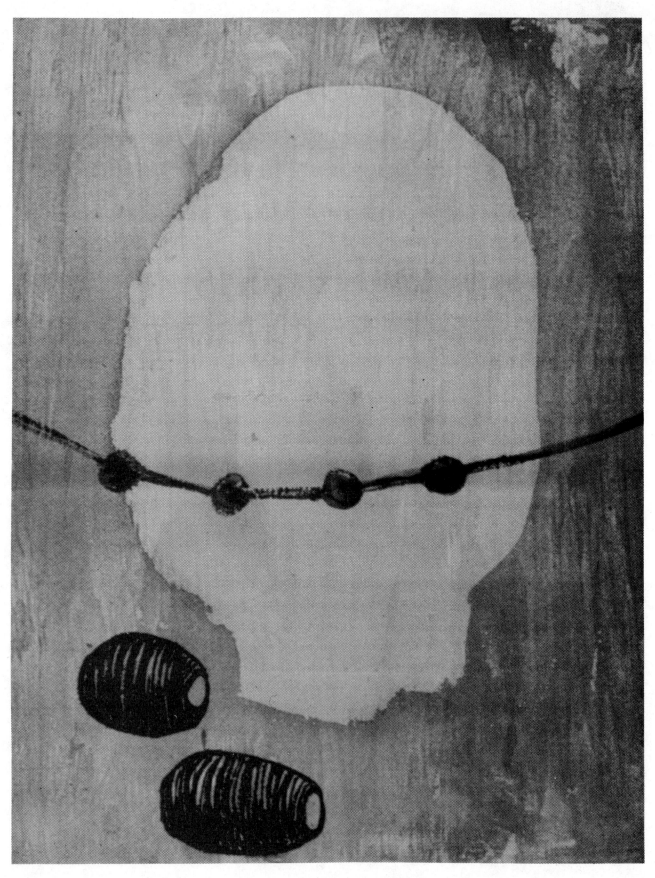

Maureen Mullen   Beads. 1994, ink, charcoal, plaster, board, 8"x 10".

MAUREEN MULLEN, BROOKLYN, NY, USA

Magdalene/ in Mexico City/ in New York City

She is the carrier of faith.

The one who whispers again

and again the sylables to keep giving

the daughters learning how to kneal their heads

down keeping both eyes open.

Bearing the scent of the exotic, the self

loved, she is told she needs....

discipline, direction, to be reigned in.

Moving inwardly as well as outwardly

between allusion and illusion

lies the language of sexuality.

Her own sense of smell is frightening.

So on beads she counts, on solid nodes

they mark the point

at which a looped curve cuts itself.

The wrapping of cuts

the covering of wounds

the singing to sleep of lives.

Caregiving done

without recognition.

Maureen Mullen. 1995.

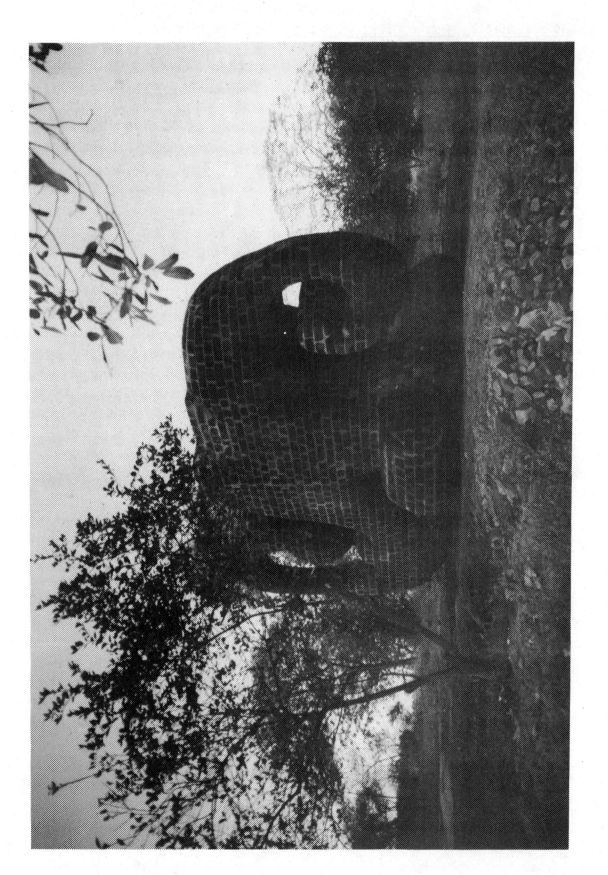

Lynda Benglis   Ahmedabad, India   1995   carved brick   10' x 30'

Carol Stakenas, NEW YORK, NY, USA

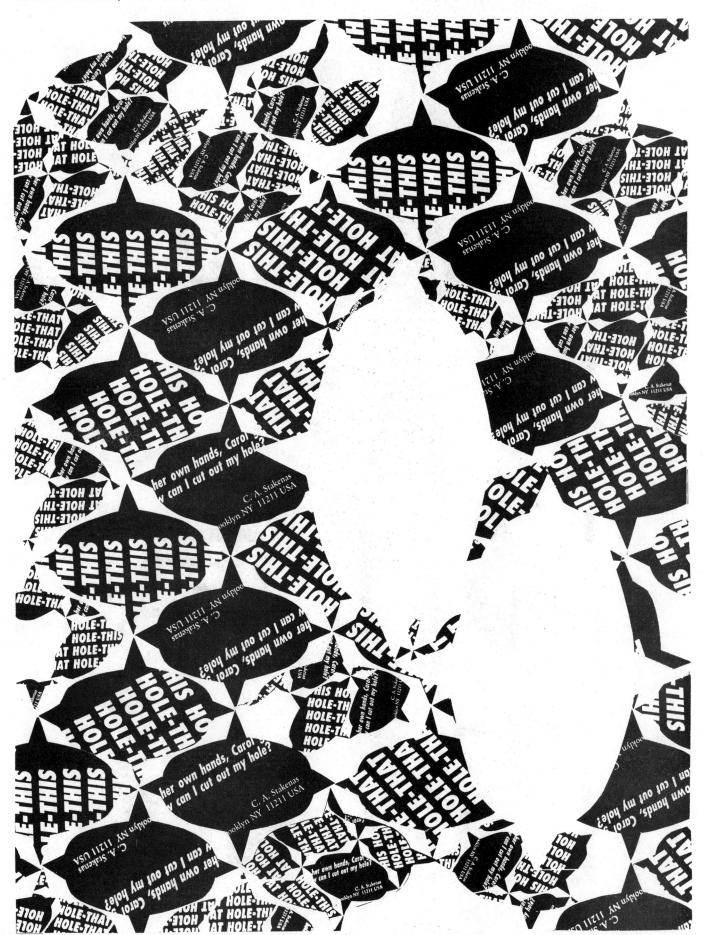

LESLIE BRACK, BROOKLYN, NY, USA

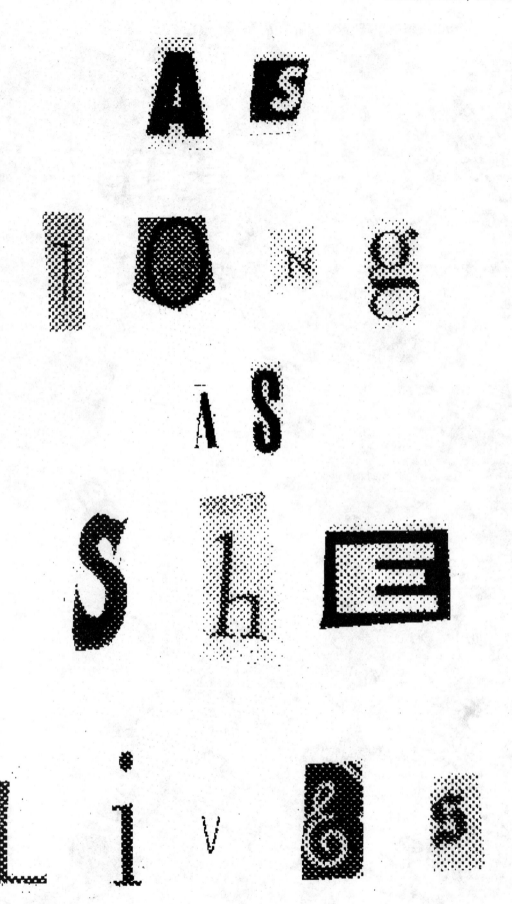

NANCY COHEN, JERSEY CITY, NJ, USA

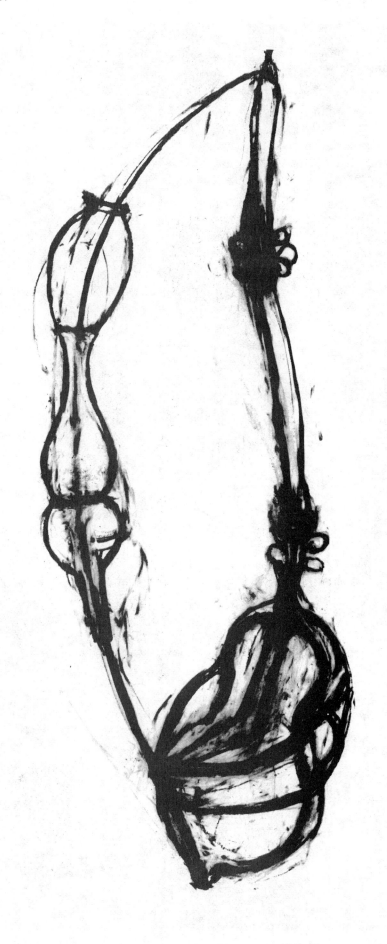

PREMA MURTHY, NEW YORK, NY, USA

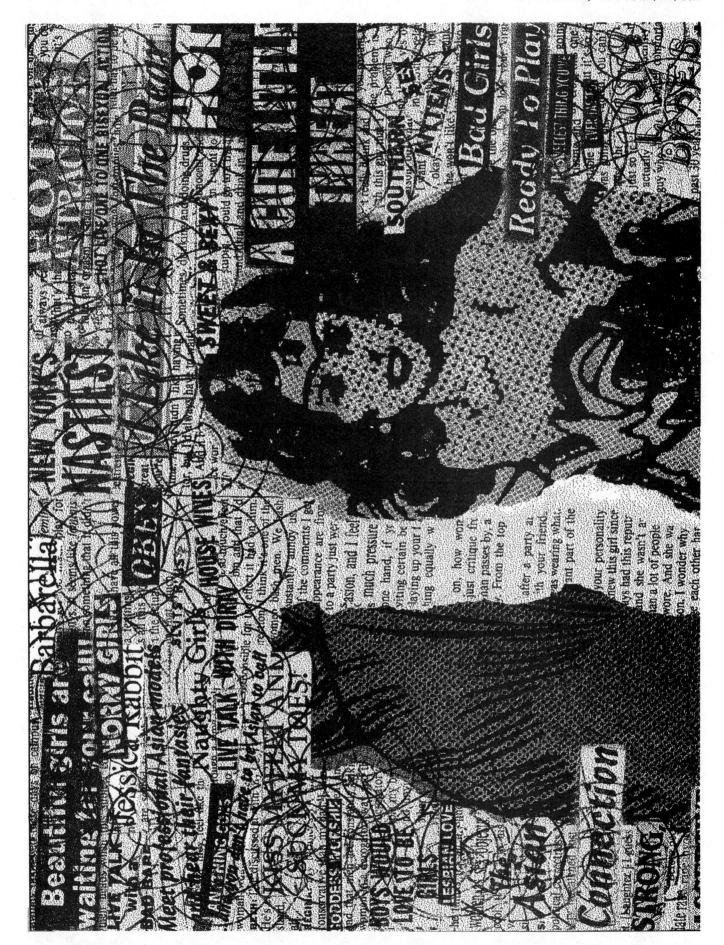

PREMA MURTHY, NEW YORK, NY, USA

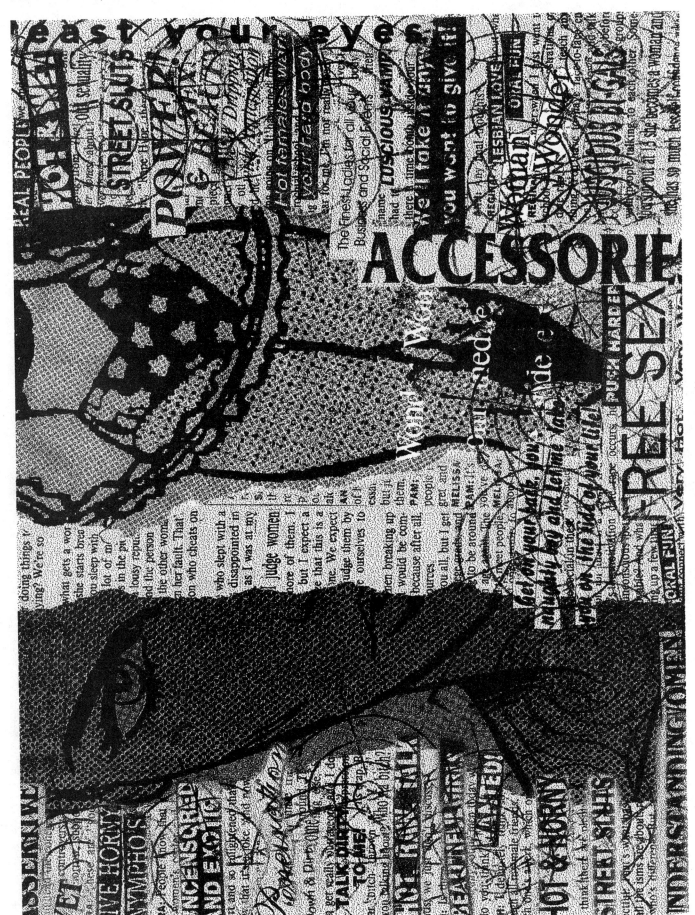

DINA WEISS, NEW YORK, NY, USA

If you can find yourself beneath the chaos, then you may just be okay—

Even if you know where you are, chaos will find you, finding yourself is the key—

Will find you, finding yourself is the key—

DINA WEISS, NEW YORK, NY, USA

IF you CAN find yourself beneath
the chaos, then you may just be okay –

If you can find yourself beneath the chaos, then you may just be okay –

Even if you know where you are, chaos will find you, finding yourself is the key –

– EVEN IF you know where you are, chaos
will find you, finding yourself is the key –

ANNA JONSSON, SEVILLA, SPAIN

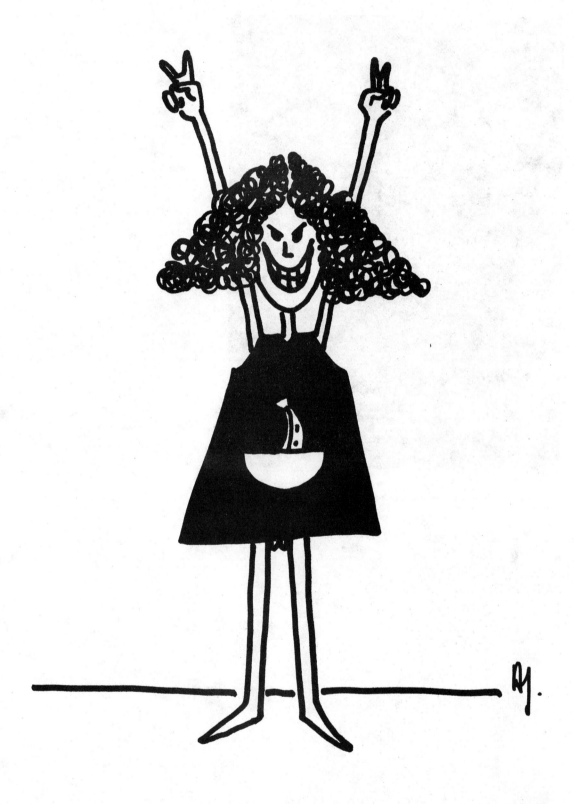

ANNA JONSSON, SEVILLA, SPAIN

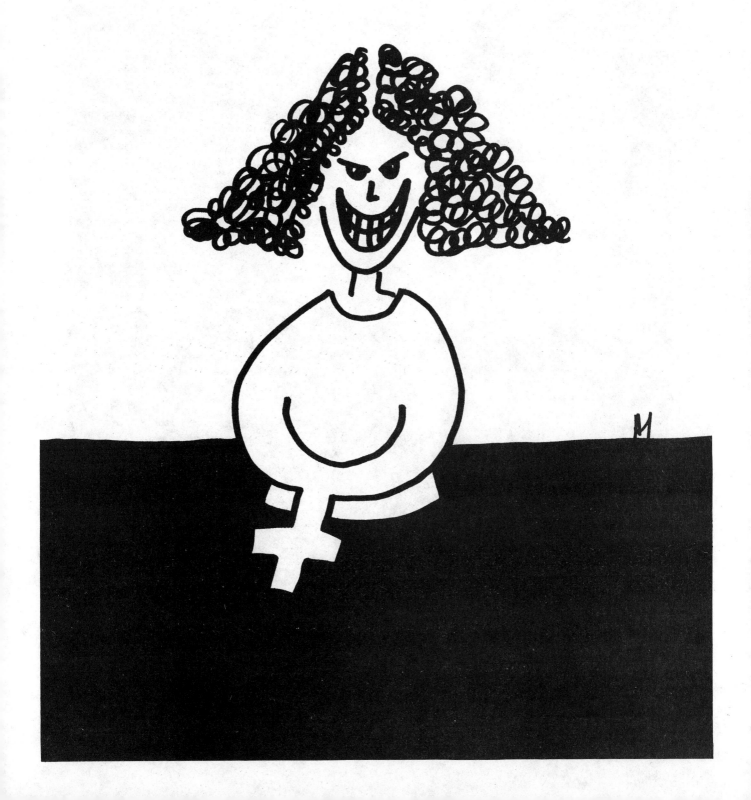

JENNY GORMAN, NEW YORK, NY, USA

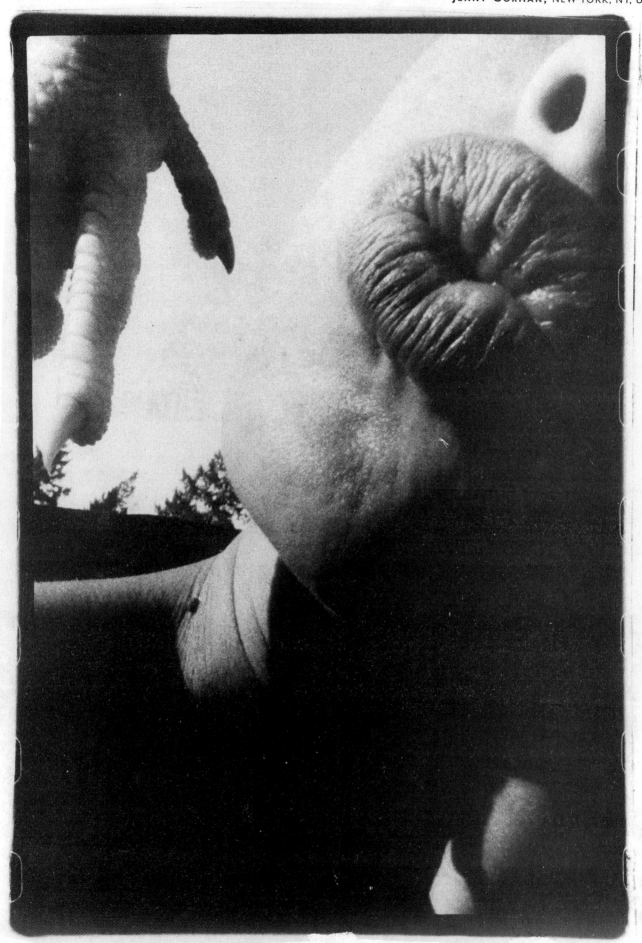

SANDIE LEE BUTLER, WALLINGTON, NJ, USA

ANNA HAMMOND, NYACK, NY, USA

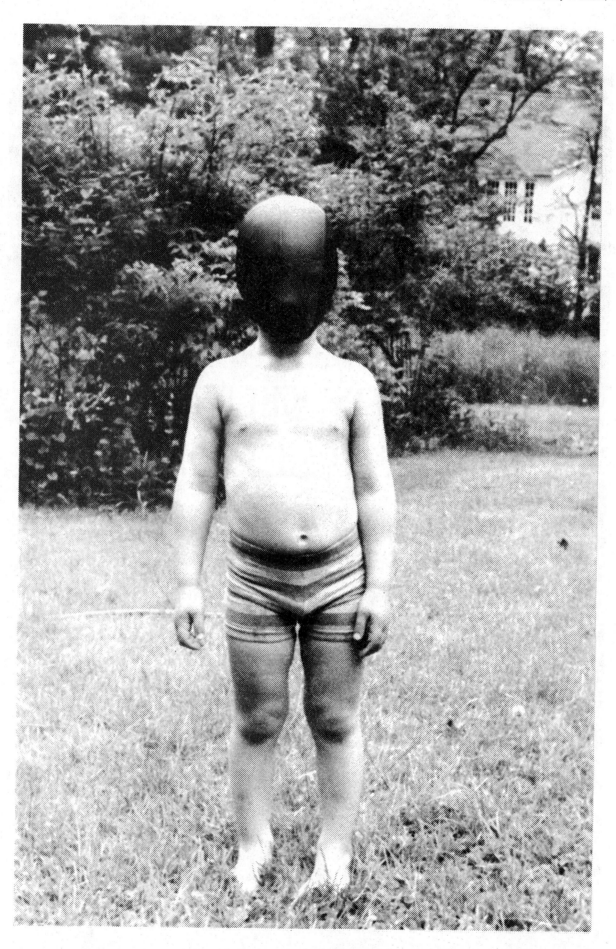

DIANA KURZ, NEW YORK, NY, USA

This picture is a memorial to the millions of children of this century whose lives were cut short by the triumph of evil.

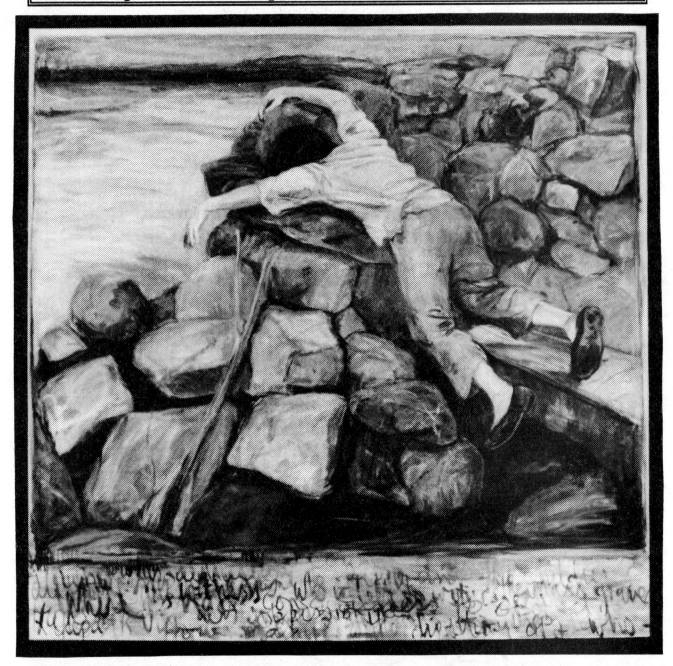

This image is the central panel of a large painting/installation that is one of a series of pieces I have been doing in the last few years on the theme of the Holocaust. The figure of the child represented here is inspired by a photograph by Robert Capa.

Diana Kurz

CATHERINE GRADY, LEUVEN, BELGIUM

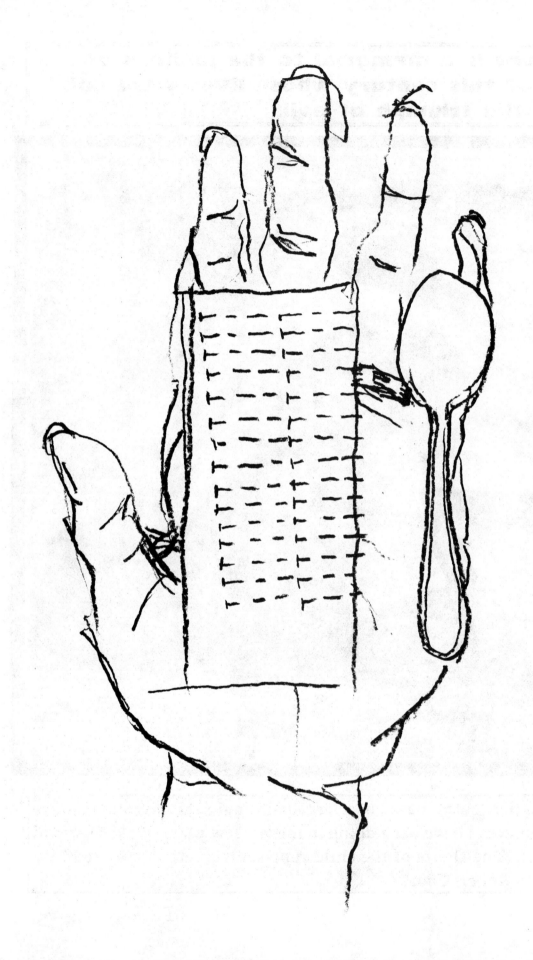

SALOMÉ DEL CAMPO, SEVILLA, SPAIN

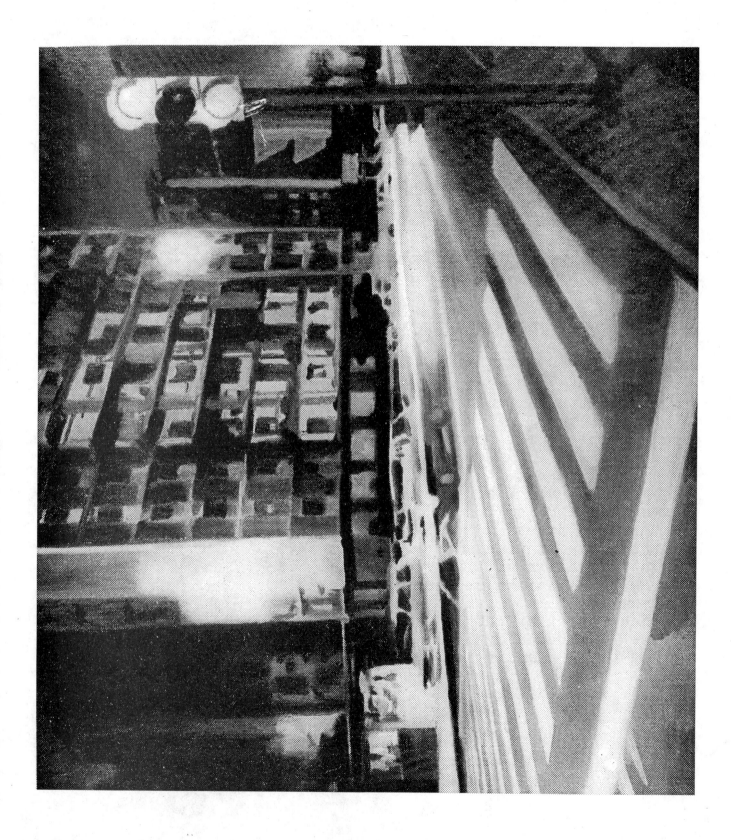

ROBIN KAHN, NEW YORK, NY, USA

I remember with envy
how it feels to walk alone on a city street
Looking at windows
            winding my time down the sidewalk,
Thinking and rhyming,
patching together
so many musings
      and muses,
Nowhere to be exactly,
for the whole day,
or half
an afternoon
            or in fifteen minutes
            or right now.

I remember you
and a place in the woods
      where
      when I leaned down to tie my laces
      a yellow and black snake passed over my boot.
I remember fucking
in the sand dunes
      and camping with wild pigs and travelling by car through the
      starry hills with horses running along side.
I breathe all of those moments in and
I remember
the feeling of my baby
      swelling under my belly, tossing
      and turning and swimming
                  in rhythm to my heartbeat and gait.

ROBIN KAHN, NEW YORK, NY, USA

I look and all I see is my son
Smiling and spilling,
hiding behind curtains,
sitting in boxes, drawing tiny circles
and beginning to speak.
Blowing kisses, demanding an audience, needing changes
and bottles and more food in the fridge
To call the doctor first thing in the morning
To find a music class,
To buy bigger shoes, a green snow suit and hat.
I pray for his nap time
        for a still moment
        for 8:30 pm.
        for sleep.

And each morning
as the water towers become visible from my window,
I lay awake,
        waiting,
Ready for the tiny rustle and then his call,
        rhythmic and urgent
        repeating at intervals
        like a songbird's tale.
From the first delicious beat,
I am out of bed and down the hall.
As I turn toward his door
        he is standing
                (demanding)
        with outstretched palms.
I scoop him into my arms and
his automatic kiss
        carries me beyond longing -
                belonging
to one perfect embrace in the clockless nowever.

ONE OF THE MANY THINGS YOU CAN DO WITH THIS TIME CAPSULE:

PUT IT IN A TIME CAPSULE.

ANA LINNEMANN, BROOKLYN, NY, USA

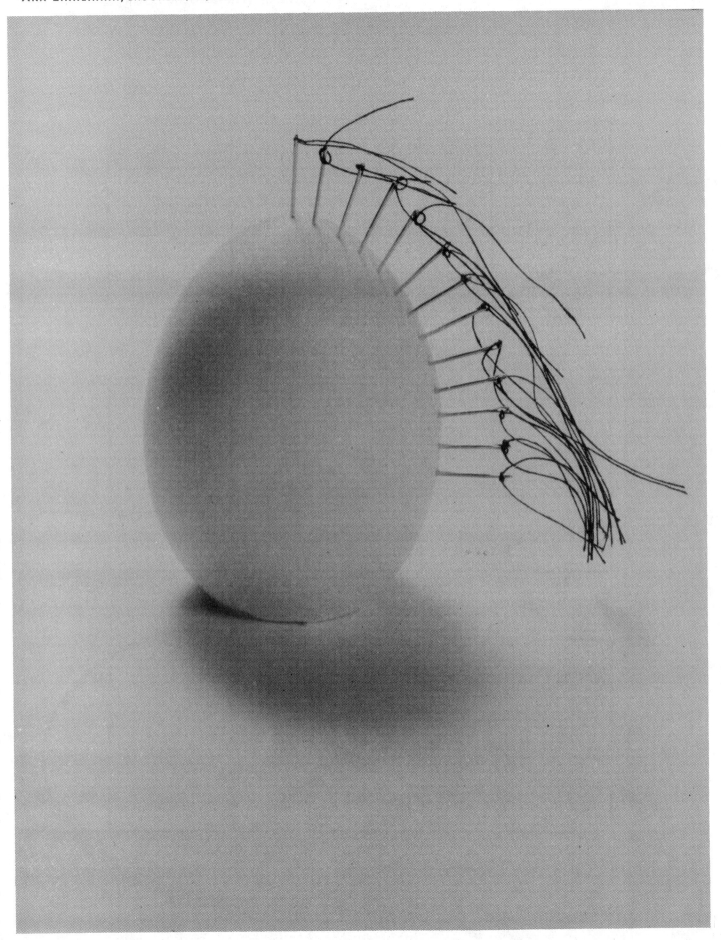

KATHLEEN MENDUS DLUGOS, GREENSBURG, PA, USA

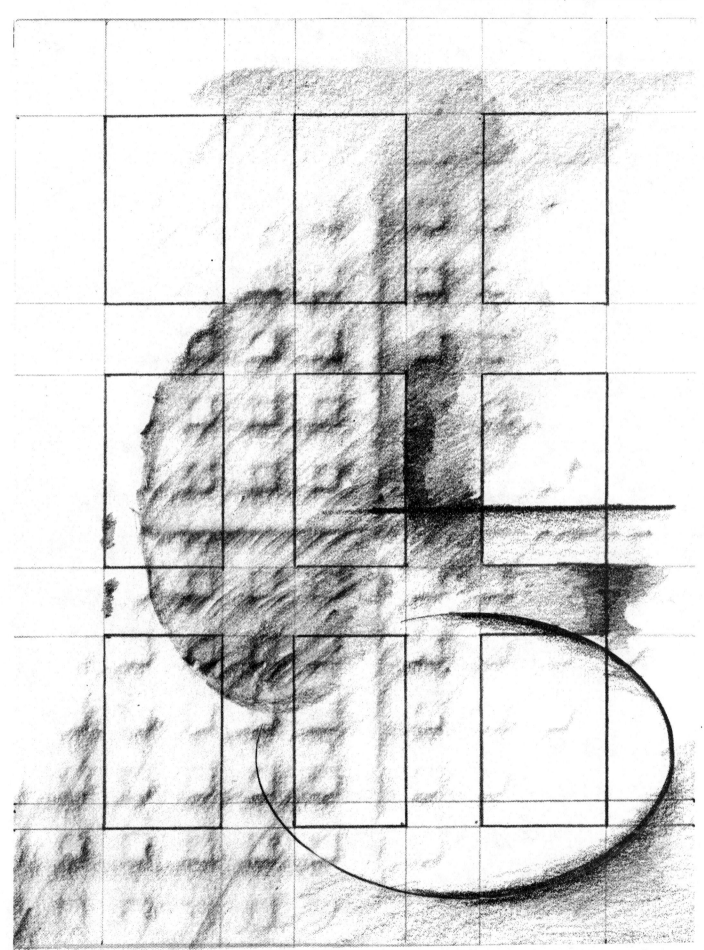

MARY JEAN KENTON, MERRITTSTOWN, PA, USA

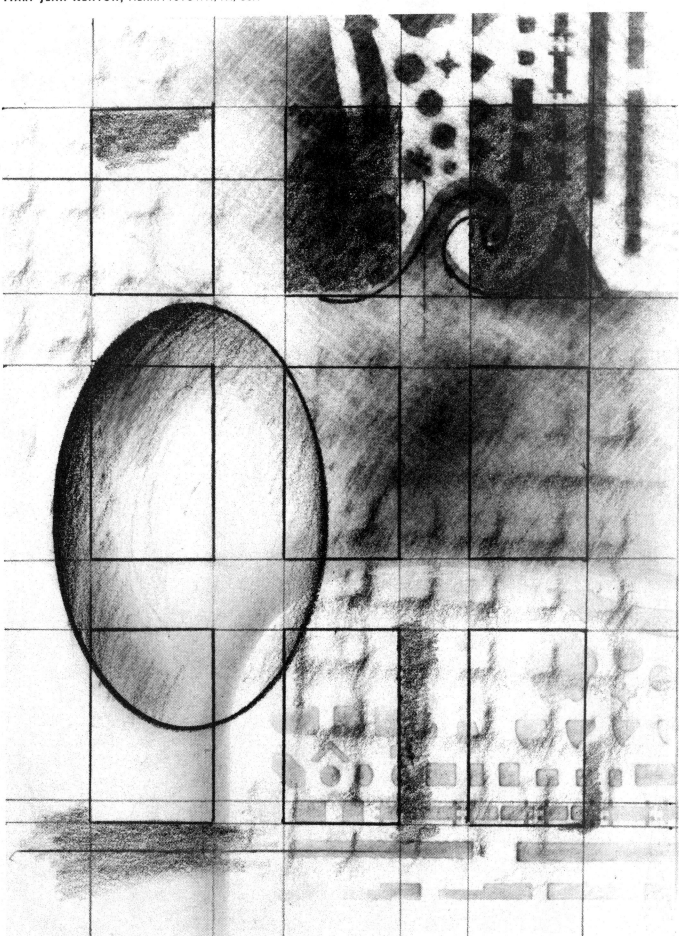

YOSHIKO SHIMADA, TOKYO JAPAN

Comfort Women

Comfort Women
Some Asian women were forced into sex slavery by the Japanese military. What were Japanese women saying and doing at that time?

The Japanese military collected women in their teens and twenties to serve as military sex slaves ("comfort women") For this purpose, "military comfort stations" (*ianjo*) were established in areas which the Japanese military had invaded (China, Hong Kong, the Philippines, Indonesia, Thailand, Burma), in Japanese colonies (Korea, Okinawa, Manchukuo) and in military bases in Japan.

The Japanese women who worked there were prostitutes from public brothels, who had been sold into prostitution due to poverty. They might have been unwilling, but at least they knew they were there to serve soldiers sexually. Other Asian women, on the other hand, were forced to be sex slaves. In Korea and Taiwan, some were kidnapped or "hunted" by military and police forces. Others were lured, by military-connected merchants, with the prospect of well-paid jobs in factories. Many women from Okinawa were also tricked in this way.

The Japanese army took these women to front lines in military warships. In *ianjo*, the women were kept under strict surveillance and their daily life was completely controlled by the military. Except for a few who succeeded in escaping, they were imprisoned until the end of the war. Many are said to have been killed when defeat in the war became evident, so as to cover up the military's deeds. Some were forced to work as nurses in short-handed military hospitals as well.

Yoshiko Shimada, TOKYO JAPAN

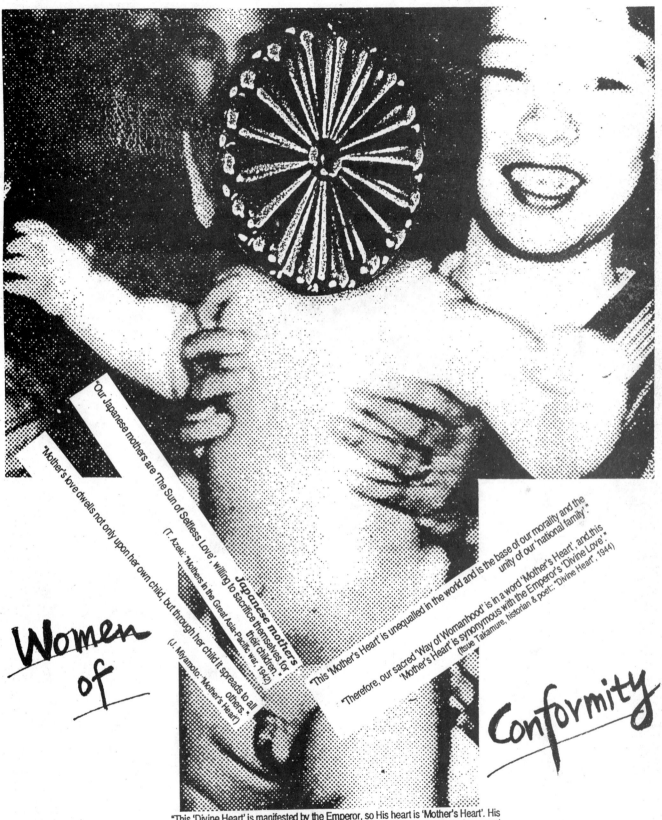

"Our Japanese mothers are 'The Sun of Selfless Love', willing to sacrifice themselves for their children."
(T. Azeki: "Mothers in the Great Asia-Pacific war, 1942)

"Mother's love dwells not only upon her own child, but through her child it spreads to all others."
(J. Miyamoto: "Mother's Heart")

Japanese mothers

Women of

This 'Mother's Heart' is unequalled in the world and is the base of our morality and the unity of our 'national family'."

"Therefore, our sacred 'Way of Womanhood' is in a word 'Mother's Heart', and this 'Mother's Heart' is synonymous with the Emperor's 'Divine Love'."
(Itsue Takamure, historian & poet:: "Divine Heart", 1944)

Conformity

"This 'Divine Heart' is manifested by the Emperor, so His heart is 'Mother's Heart'. His aim in *hakko ichui* is to spread His heart, which is 'Mother's Heart' not only to Japan and Asia but to the world."

"Japanese mothers must keep this notion of 'His heart' in their own hearts, and raise their children not as their own but as 'the Emperor's treasures', and be willing to return them to Him whenever it is necessary."

Y. Shimada

LYNNE YAMAMOTO, NEW YORK, NY, USA

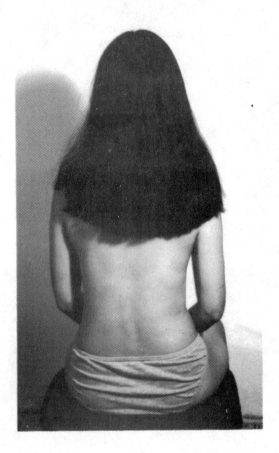

Sold Out.

KHARA NEMITZ, BROOKLYN, NY, USA

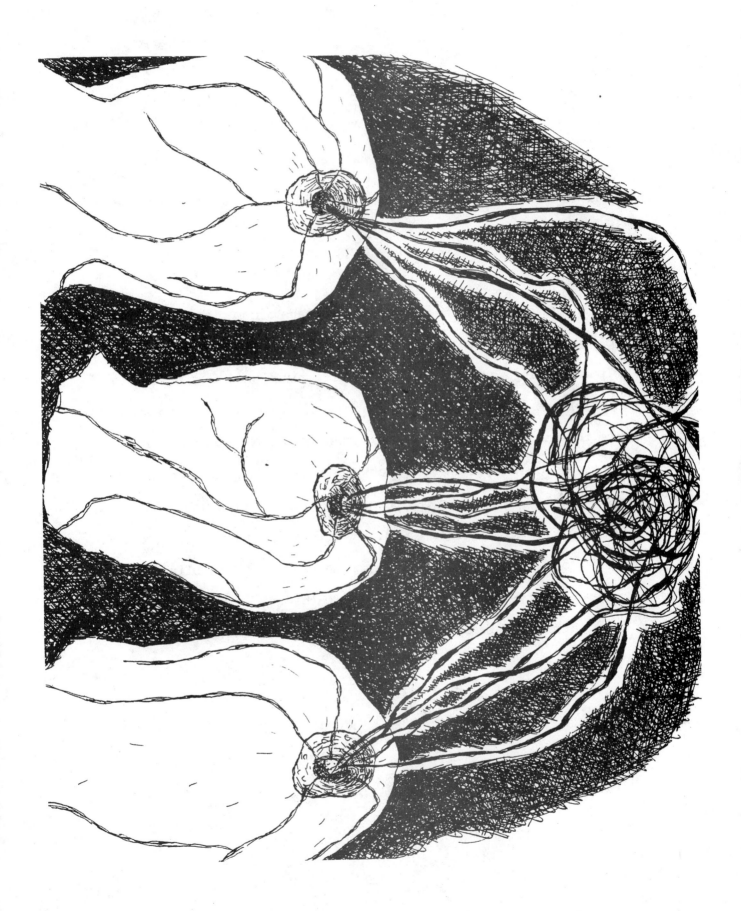

CHRISTINA SILLARI, NEW HAVEN, CT, USA

Christina M. Sillari   40 Westwood Road   New Haven   CT   06515   (203) 389-9610

Consciousness

fumbling in darkness with soft strength tears are replaced with sweat

cool wood bleeding its roots inside my belly the moon lingers like a

dolphin waiting for the wave that never arrives when i am scared to

death of the power in my bones are crawling with thorns of consciousness

from the dna restructuring you will restructure me beginning with a

kiss as we break down the illusion that covers the purple roses and

black blood i receive a sound through my spine remembering broken

eyeballs with gentle tones i would love to eat you now secrets are

always looking at the river flows to the sky but we are blind so we

pretend it flows to the sea where inside the middle of the earth

lives a very old beautiful woman i would love to meet

JUDITH WEINPERSON, NEW YORK, NY, USA

RENT-A-FRIEND
TRANS-GENERATIONAL

212-465-3347

coffee	dancing	opinions
lunch	tours	laughs
dinner	walks	movies
phone	talks	events
shopping	problem solving	

!! GIFT CERTIFICATES AVAILABLE !!

VIOLETTA ALVAREZ MONTILLA, MOGAN, SPAIN

Seguro que quieres irte? - No es que quiera irme, es que creo que tu quieres que me marche. Podriamos intentar ser amables con los otros. Nunca te he entendido, creo que deberias disculparte con ellos. Sera mejor intentar que todo vuelva a ser como antes.

La jodida experiencia en la que tu creias, no ha funcionado en absoluto. Lo siento, esto no va a ser facil. Sera mejor que te sientes,sera solo un momento. - Estoy bien...de verdad.

Odiaba lo que hacias con tu vida, pero siempre te he querido. Discute conmigo, puedo encajarlo.

Viene se duerme y se va, el asunto se complica. Me impresiona como has organi-zado tu vida de forma que nadie pueda tocarte. Es mas facil ser amable con gente que se queda poco tiempo. Hay personas a las que hablo con frecuencia y no me entienden. Tu eres una mujer brillante, no tendras problemas en ningun sitio, tu unico problema ahora es que no estas sola.

A veces me doy cuenta que no hablo porque no puedo hablar de ti, supongo que debo estar obsesionada. Anoche sone con sus padres, trabajaban en una pelicula de vaqueros.

Llego ese dia tarde, habia cogido un autobus se habia bajado al final del trayecto, entonces tomo un taxi y regreso a casa. Penso que quiza podria estar muerta, metida en un ataud y asomando algodon entre los dientes, el mientras tanto con esa pasividad que le venia de repente en situaciones dramaticas se limitaria a decir cosas como..." que terrible, que terrible" o " no puedo creerlo, no puedo creerlo ".

- Quieres cafe ? -. Si por favor, con azucar.

Con el siempre que ella queria podia hacer el amor, dejaba el cepillo al lado de la cama se desataba el cinturon de la bata y arrodillandose sobre el, dejaba sus pechos en forma de v que tocaran sus ojos, su boca, su barbilla. Hacia que su coño bajase y aun cerrado lo balanceaba de arriba a bajo contra el pene todavia blando, el cogia entonces sus brazos anillandolos con fuerza como si fueran dos columnas. Le conozco desde hace 14 anos y continua hablando de lo mismo, de lo del huevo y la gallina.

DEVON DIKEOU, NEW YORK, NY, USA

Artist's Coupon — Expiration date 12/31/95

Save 20% or $299

on any size art piece by
DEVON DIKEOU

with the purchase of

Time Capsule: A Concise Encyclopedia by Women Artists, Performers, and Writers

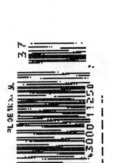

This coupon good only on the purchase of of an art product of Devon Dikeou at the Supastore Middlesbrough. Any other use constitutes fraud. **COUPON NON TRANSFERABLE. LIMIT - ONE PER PURCHASE, ONE PER CUSTOMER**

To the Gallerist: Devon Dikeou will honor this discount against her split of the purchase price of a piece of art. Valid only if redeemed at galleries authorized by the artist to represent her work.

Artist's Coupon — Expiration date 12/31/95

Save 20% or $299

on any size art piece by
DEVON DIKEOU

with the purchase of

Time Capsule: A Concise Encyclopedia by Women Artists, Performers, and Writers

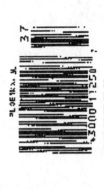

This coupon good only on the purchase of of an art product of Devon Dikeou at the Supastore Middlesbrough. Any other use constitutes frau.. **COUPON NON TRANSFERABLE. LIMIT - ONE PER PURCHASE , ONE PER CUSTOMER**

To the Gallerist: Devon Dikeou will honor this discount against her split of the purchase price of a piece of art. Valid only if redeemed at galleries authorized by the artist to represent her work.

Artist's Coupon — Expiration date 12/31/95

Save 20% or $299

on any size art piece by
DEVON DIKEOU

with the purchase of

Time Capsule: A Concise Encyclopedia by Women Artists, Performers, and Writers

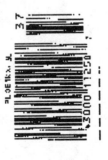

This coupon good only on the purchase of of an art product of Devon Dikeou at the Supastore Middlesbrough. Any other use constitutes fraud. **COUPON NON TRANSFERABLE. LIMIT - ONE PER PURCHASE, ONE PER CUSTOMER**

To the Gallerist: Devon Dikeou will honor this discount against her split of the purchase price of a piece of art. Valid only if redeemed at galleries authorized by the artist to represent her work.

Artist's Coupon — Expiration date 12/31/95

Save 20% or $299

on any size art piece by
DEVON DIKEOU

with the purchase of

Time Capsule: A Concise Encyclopedia by Women Artists, Performers, and Writers

This coupon good only on the purchase of of an art product of Devon Dikeou at the Supastore Middlesbrough. Any other use constitutes fraud. **COUPON NON TRANSFERABLE. LIMIT - ONE PER PURCHASE, ONE PER CUSTOMER**

To the Gallerist: Devon Dikeou will honor this discount against her split of the purchase price of a piece of art. Valid only if redeemed at galleries authorized by the artist to represent her work.

HOLLY MORSE, BROOKLYN, NY, USA

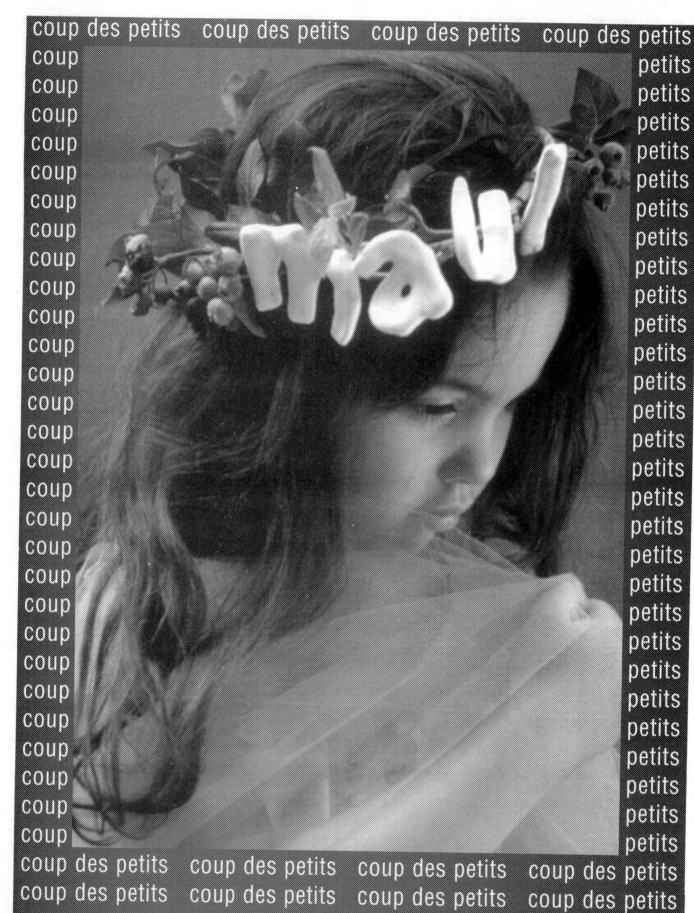

HOLLY MORSE, BROOKLYN, NY, USA

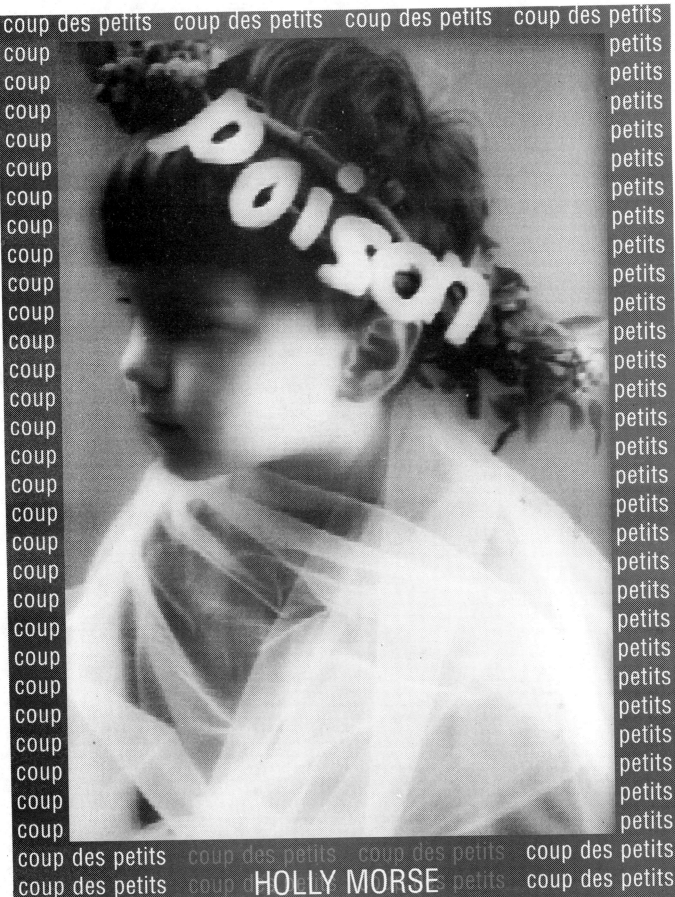

coup des petits   coup des petits   coup des petits   coup des petits

HOLLY MORSE

ANN DeVere, BROOKLYN, NY, USA

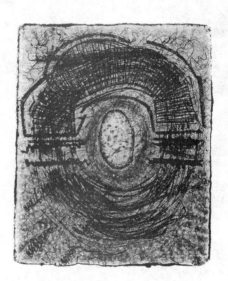

IMAGE #5

ANN DEVERE, BROOKLYN, NY, USA

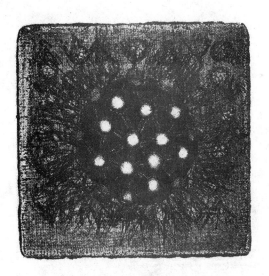

IMAGE #9

NEFERTITI C GOODMAN, MONTCLAIR, NJ, USA

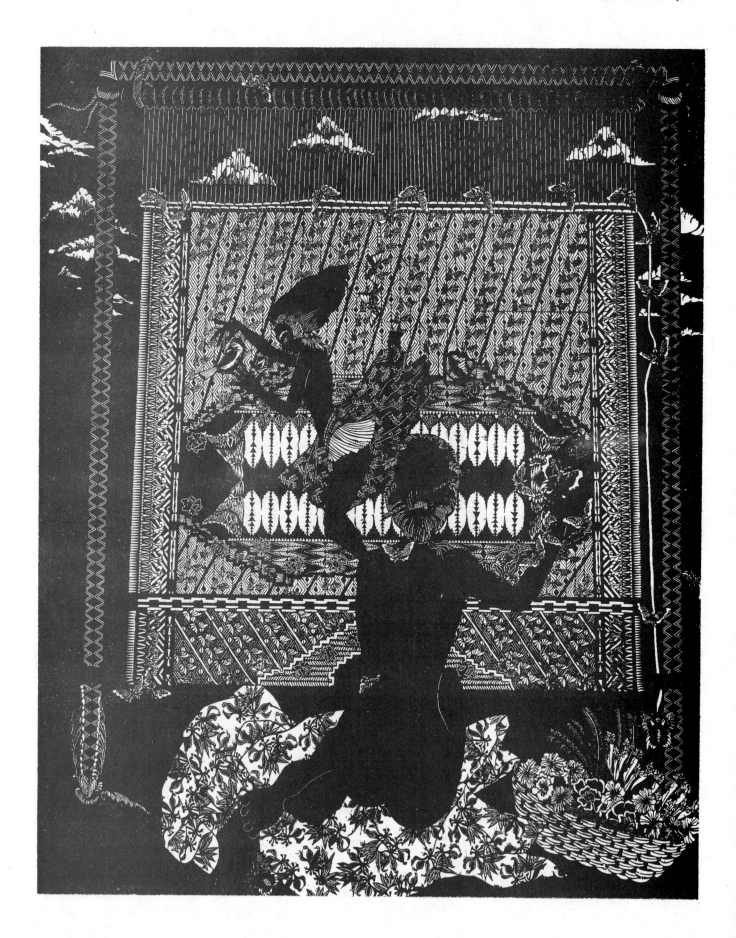

JOAN JONAS, NEW YORK, NY, USA

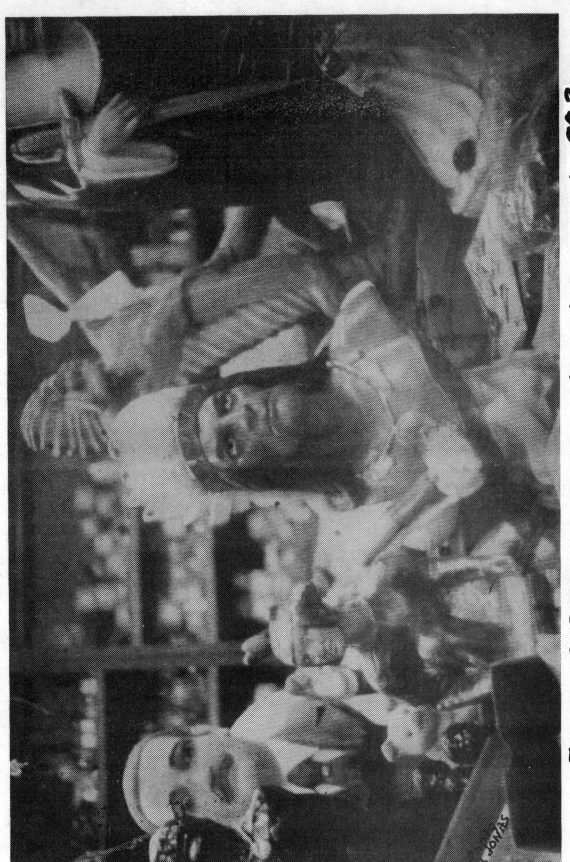

CROSSROAD DANCE   THE CENTER OF THE CITY

ESSEX STREET MARKET, NEW YORK CITY, 1993

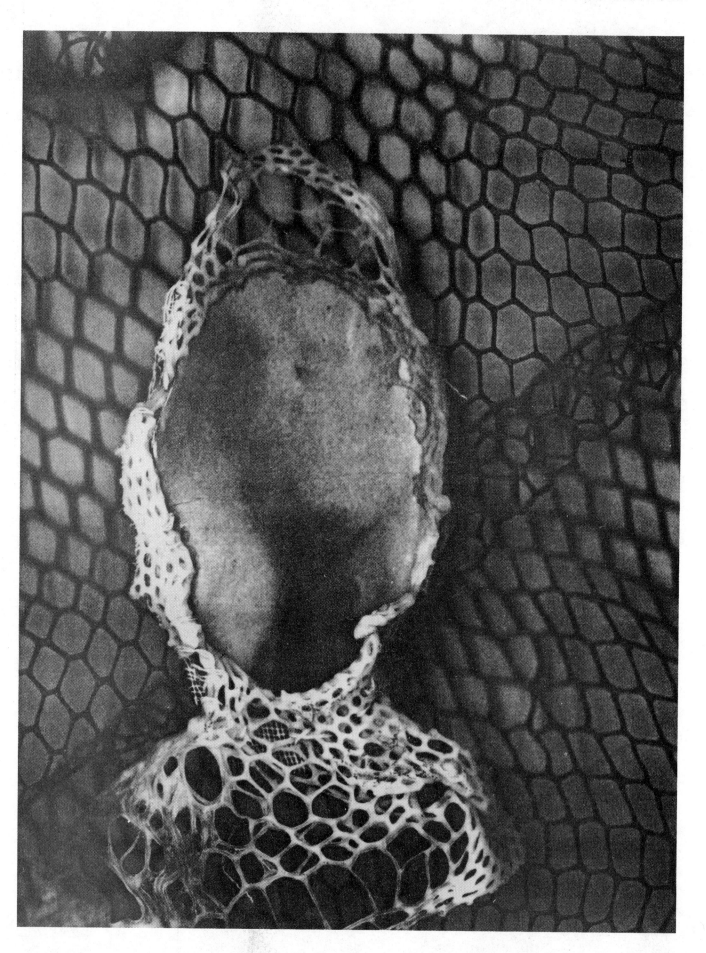

JACQUELINE LIMA, BROOKLYN, NY, USA

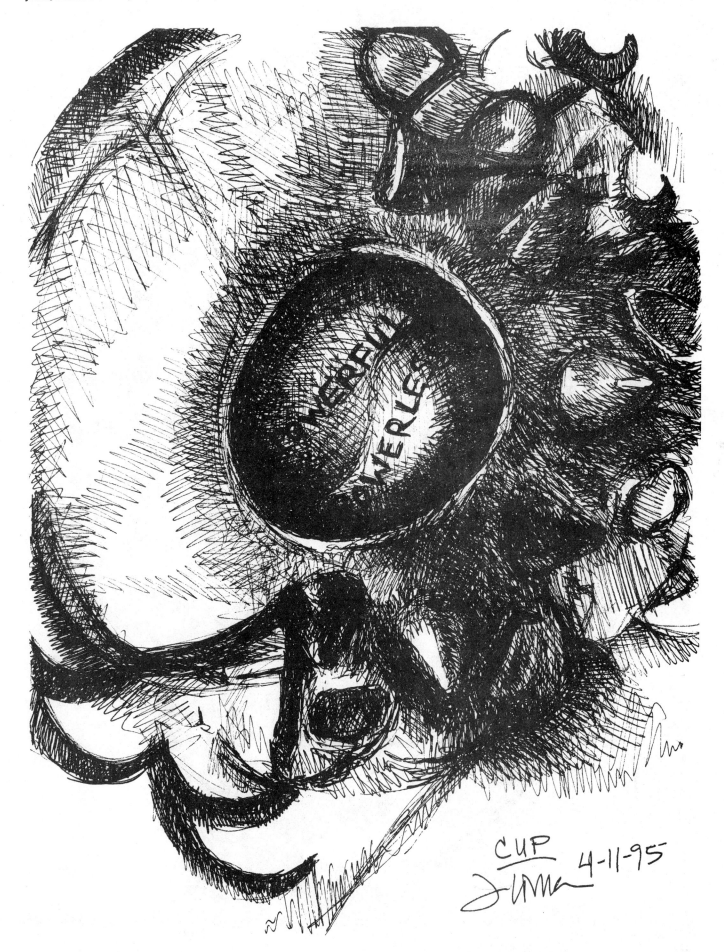

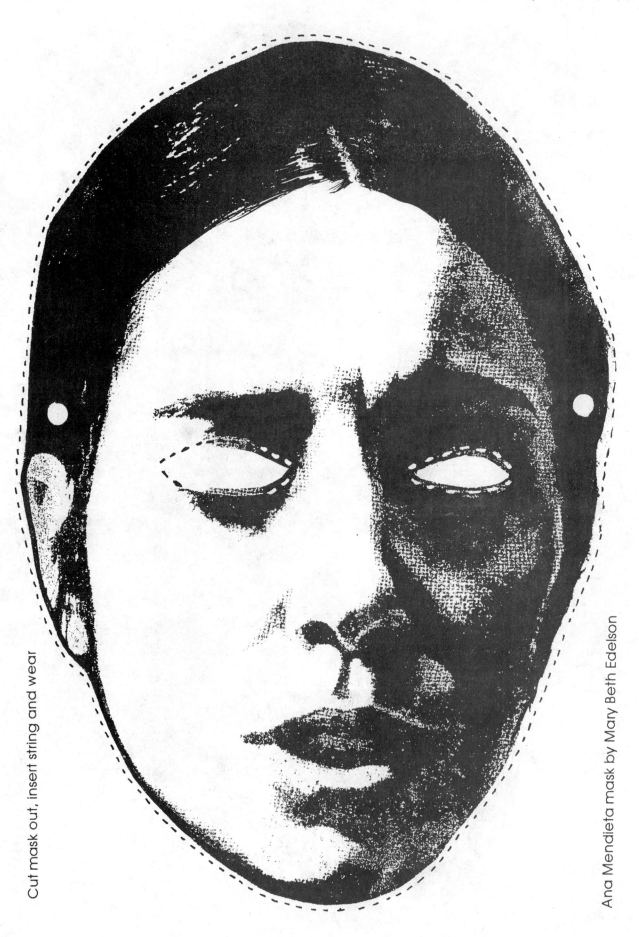

Cut mask out, insert string and wear

Ana Mendieta mask by Mary Beth Edelson

MARY BETH EDELSON, NEW YORK, NY, USA

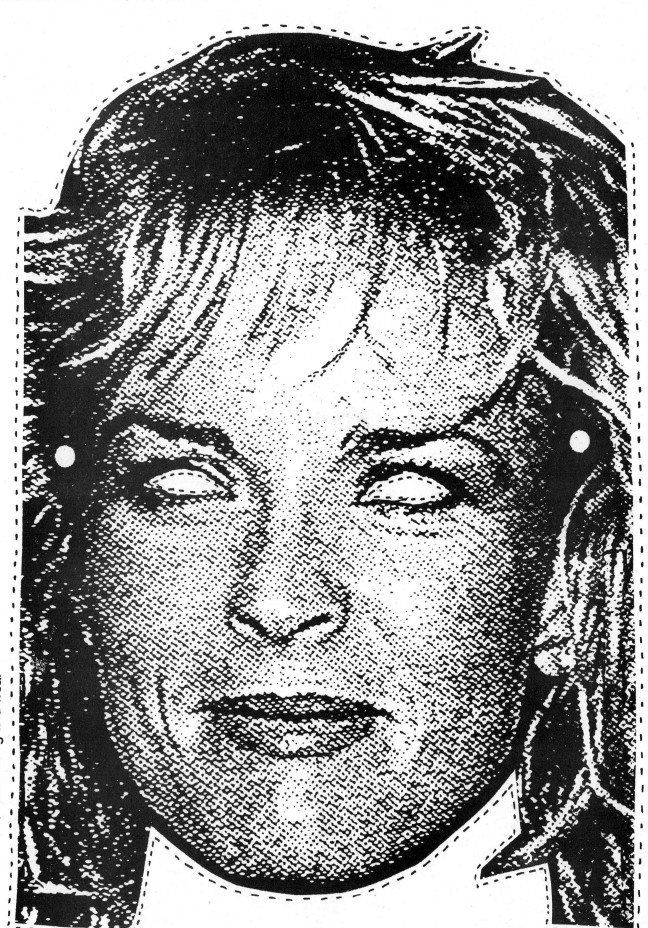

Cut mask out, insert string and wear

Nicole Brown Simpson mask by Mary Beth Edelson

TYYNE CLAUDIA POLLMANN, BERLIN, GERMANY

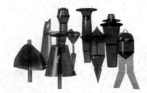

"Die Junggesellen von ihrer Braut nackt entblößt, sogar."

Tyyne Claudia Pollmann, BERLIN, GERMANY

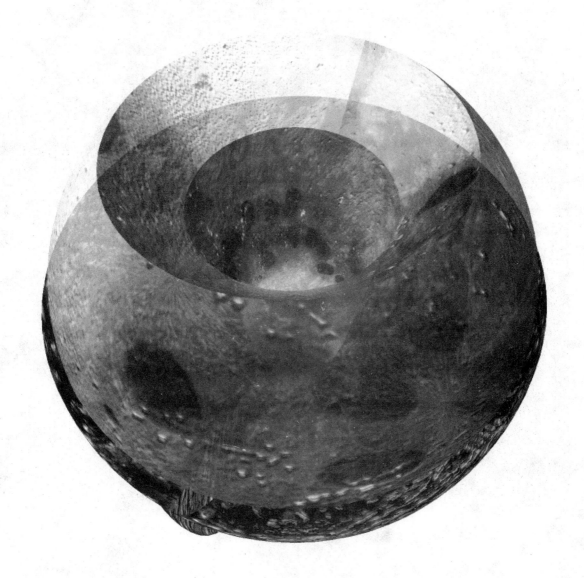

AHNE 3

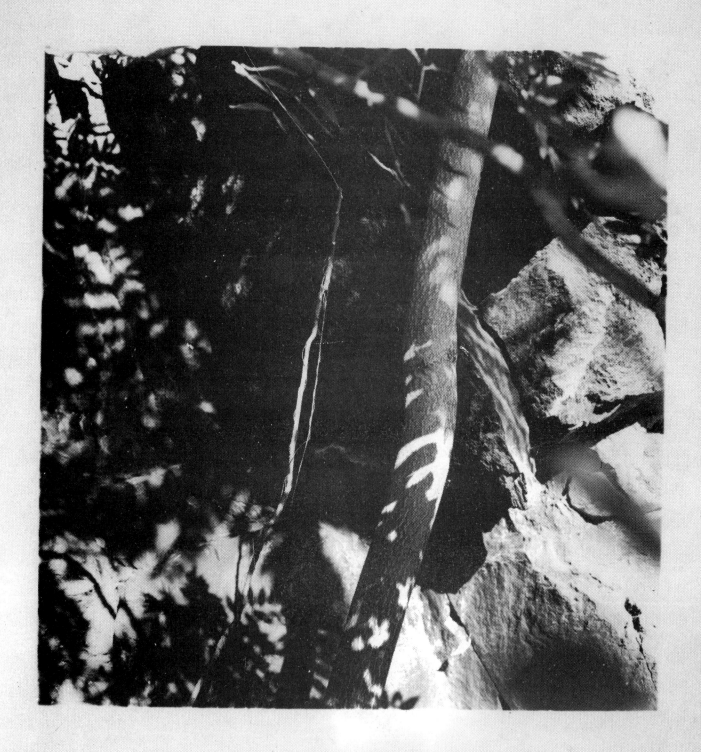

MARIE DURQUET, BALTIMORE, MD, USA

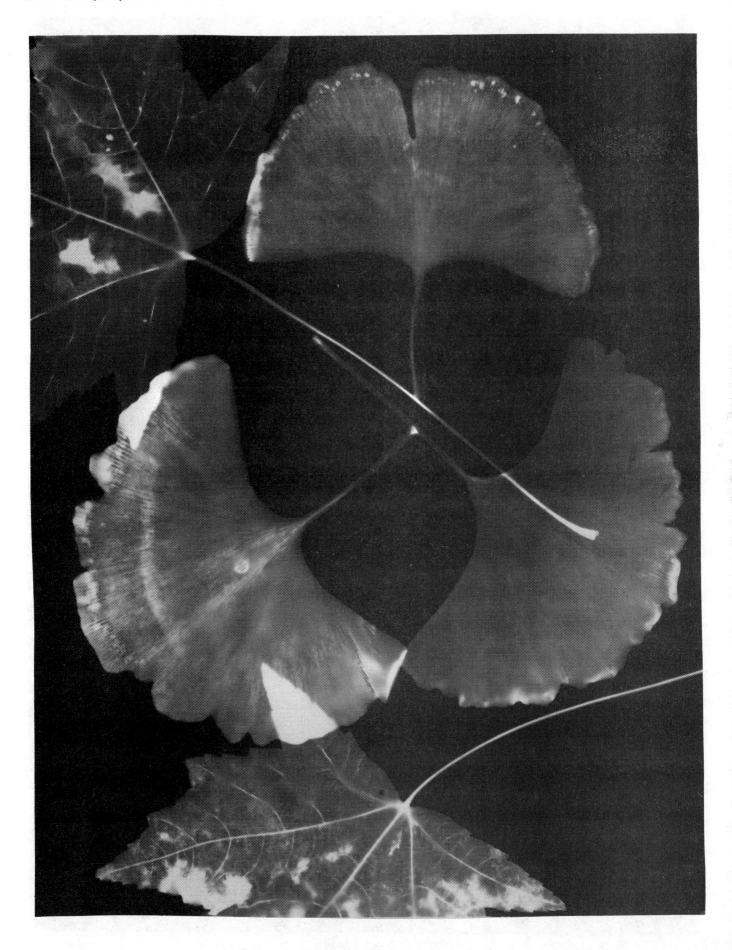

FREYA HANSELL, NEW YORK, NY, USA

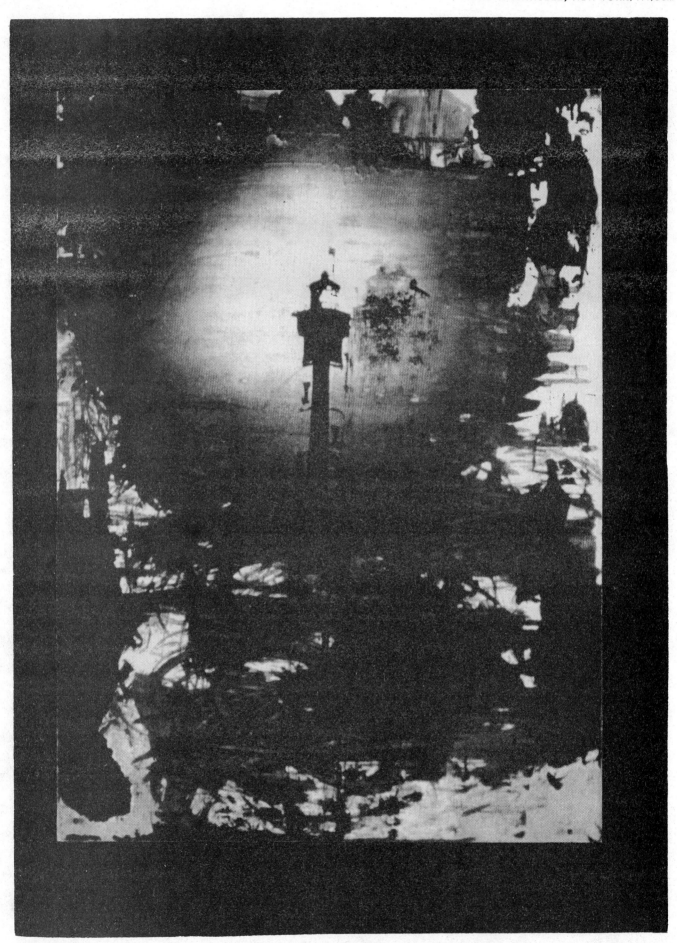

FREYA HANSELL, NEW YORK, NY, USA

LITTLE PARTICLES

INTERRUPT MY VISION

ALL THE TIME.

ROBIN TEWES, NEW YORK, NY, USA

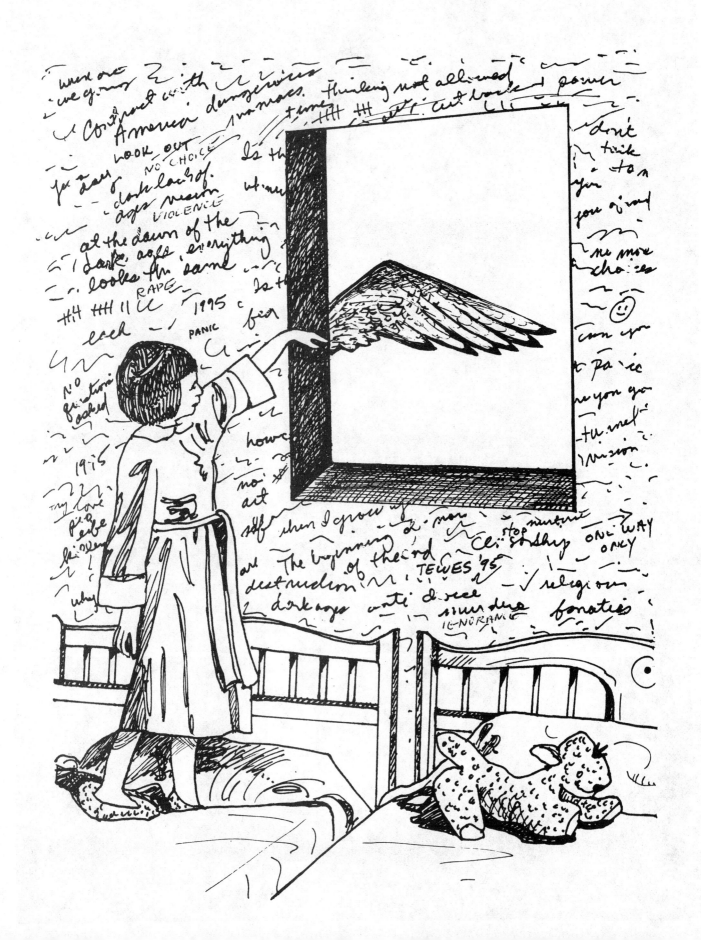

Tatiana Garmendia, SEATTLE, WA, USA

Now What I Ask

As the cycle's fist clocks the apex
of day and night, all you taught
me revisits this hour. Such
cruxes evade the fastened gaze.
Just sum the creased
brow and provoking chin
that recognize your charges.

I am not surprised.
Take them back, doing
what your want inclines.

Now what I ask for
is another gulp of dark faith.
Hot brew.
Without sugar or milk.

JILL O'BRYAN, NEW YORK, NY, USA

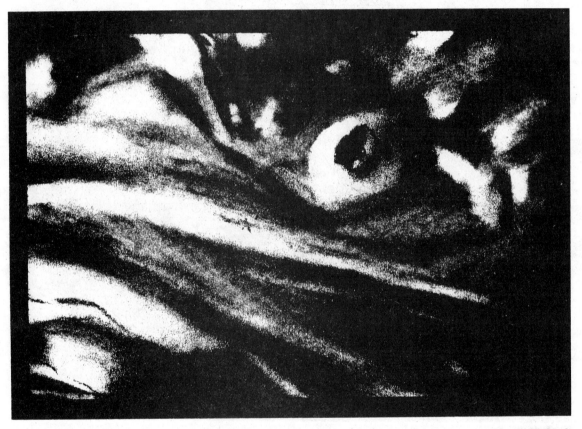

De-Stilled Life

Jill O'Bryan

JILL O'BRYAN, NEW YORK, NY, USA

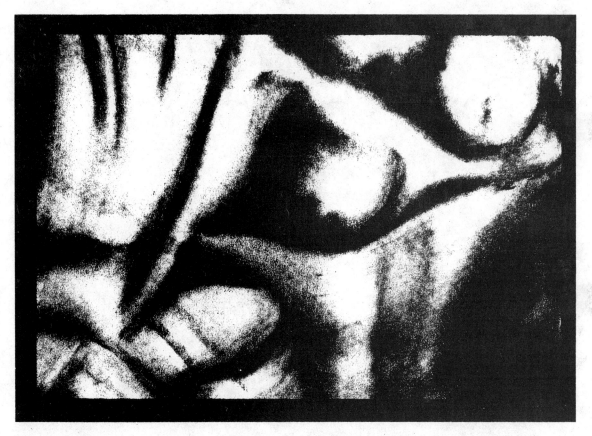

Re-Stilled Life

212.995.8113

Dear Mother,
    That's great that you will be over on the 17th. Be sure to come in the morning so you can go with us to Radio City Music Show. I will give you Diane's room in the back. I have slipcovered the chair and made a new spread, so it is really attractive.

December 8, 1971

CATHY HAVEMEYER, NEW YORK, NY, USA

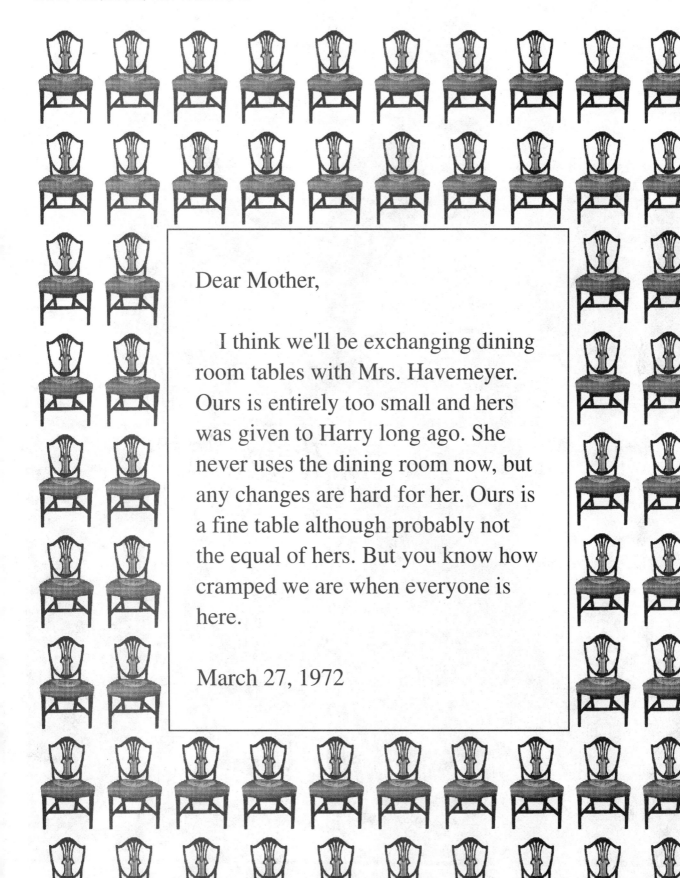

Dear Mother,

I think we'll be exchanging dining room tables with Mrs. Havemeyer. Ours is entirely too small and hers was given to Harry long ago. She never uses the dining room now, but any changes are hard for her. Ours is a fine table although probably not the equal of hers. But you know how cramped we are when everyone is here.

March 27, 1972

KATE LAMBERT, NEW YORK, NY, USA

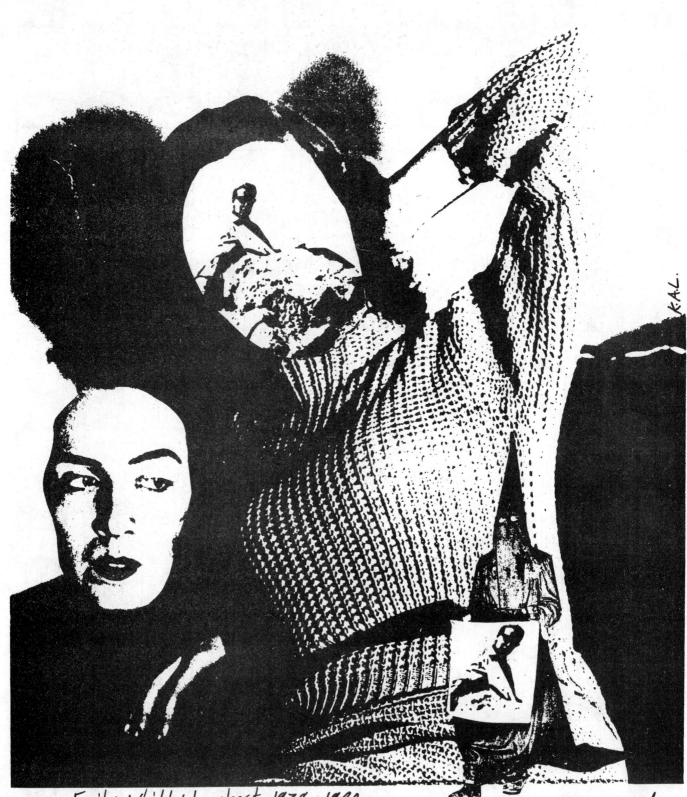

Emily Whitty Lambert 1928-1980

I love you mom, even though you offed
yourself.
— XX oo Rag-a-Muffin

MILENA DOPITOVÁ, PRAGUE, CZECH REPUBLIC

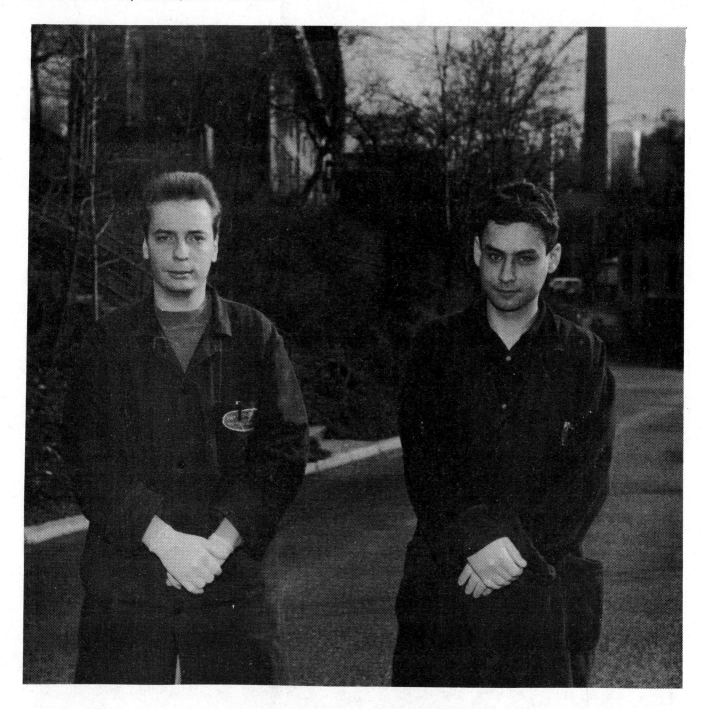

IS THIS THE WAY
YOU ARE LOOKING FOR?

BONNIE RYCHLAK, NEW YORK, NY, USA

Dear Maria,

Finally getting around to typing you a letter.

I went into St. John't Hospital and had that light run down my throat to my stomach. This is the fifth time I've had it done. I don't like having to go through it but I have done before. I don't like having to go through it but I have no choice. Well I ddin't have a cancer thou caused the spec. said I did have a great deal of acid which eventually causes more bleeding.

They could tell something was wrong with me. So they tested everything they said definitely could I make the trip & alone because I'd gotten so excited they don't want that to happen to me again.

All I can say you'll have to forgive me. My thought and love are with you and Peter.

I was just doing fine emotionally a week or so ago & all of a sudden it hit me & I panicked about it all. Couldn't think straight anymore. It was wrong on my end because I just hated disappointing you.

I even clled the train station. It would be quite nice. Straight through from New York to Chicago & then change of train to San Francisco. Also the meals were seven hundred but I did enjoy the scenery on my trip to Oregon but did hate sleeping on the train. It was so difficult to sleep really on that after the ordeal I had al-ready going through. Actually would take one night to Chicago then two nights to get to San Francisco. When we were traveling we did meet a number of people, you meet travelling all over the country, Some from Germany & etc. also.

Weather here lousy. Very over-cast until noon time when the sun comes out but we do live near the beach & can expect that.

Kelly called a couple nites ago & we had quite a long talk on the phone. I was glad she understands how I feel & etc. Actually I shouldn't give a dam what my family thinks. Either they love me for what I am or don't need to bother with me. I'm getting to dam old now for all that stuff. I have never had to ask any of you for a penny & I hope it will stay that way. I would die first before I would ask any of you for help. You are eager to help your father but you all seem to feel differently about me. I think I've done well so far. Have gone through a great deal of heartache & problems I thought I could never face due to your Father's illness. Like my ladyfriend, Jeannie says, Margaret your to hard on yourself. I think oe of the most horrible things I ever experienced was having that bone marrow taken from my hip as the specialist never sedated me.

I guess you've been reading & watching on T.V. about the election in California pertaining to Prop 187. It's really getting bad with the Mexicans. They are even considering bringing in the Nat. Guard out here. Hope it doesn't end up like those rois in L.A. Anything can happen but I can't worry about that, even though you live out there. They say it will pass & I hope so as Calif is going broke taking care of those that are not citizens.

I should have saved the clipping in the paper which you'd love. It was in with pictures. Remember where we used to live before we moved here. Nyland. Acme well the Mexicans just have taken over the pk. The mobile we lived in there were eleven people living in that mobile. The one next to ours another Mexicn family lived. The man was doing mechanic work in his drive-way. Make money re-pairing cars. Stupid guy was working under the hood using gasoline & it caught fire & burned up. Also the mobile burnt to the ground. They were on welfare & had no ins. plus owed a great deal of money on the mobile. Ken told me he heard they were going bk. to Mexico. Also the one we owned also caught on fire as the whole side was burned. Boy I am sure glad we moved out of that place when we did. Your Dad was ill then & let me handle the selling of that one & buying of the one we live in now. I'm happy here & live very comfortably which I am grateful for.

Coming near the end of the paper so will sign off for now. Please excue my mistakes I've made, but you'll still understand it all I hope.

Love, Mom

BONNIE RYCHLAK, NEW YORK, NY, USA

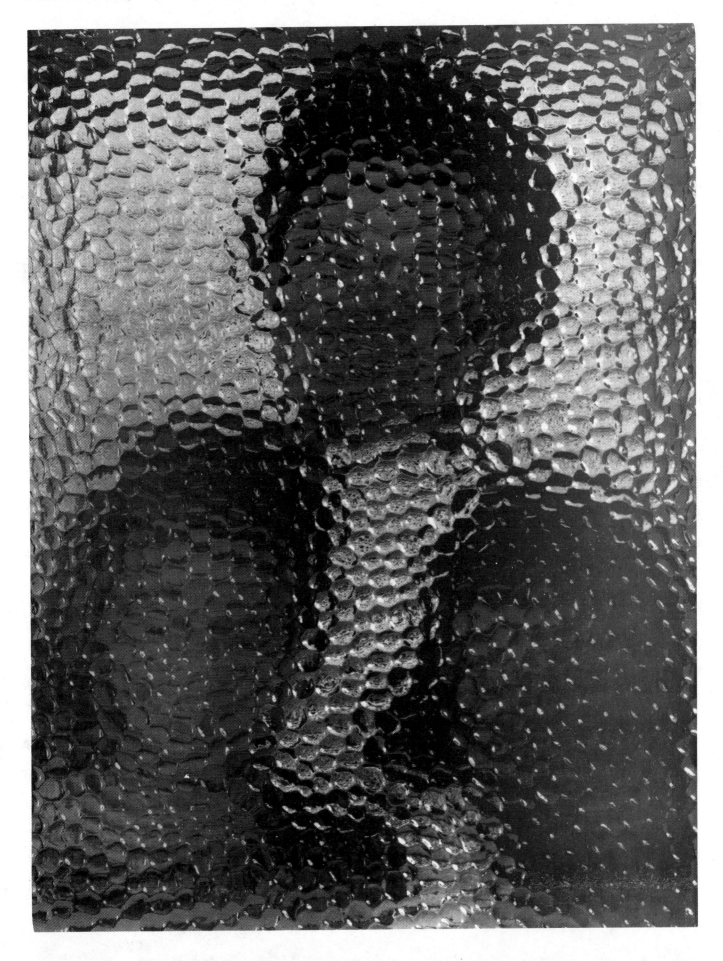

Szófia Harmati, BUDAPEST, HUNGARY

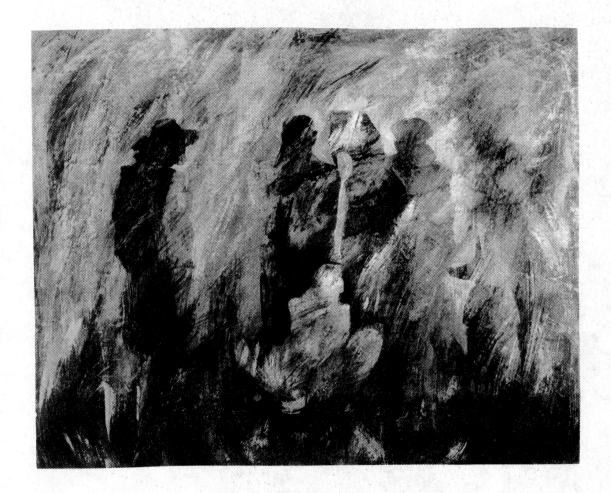

GRACIELA-GACHI HASPER, BUENOS AIRES, ARGENTINA

DIRECTION

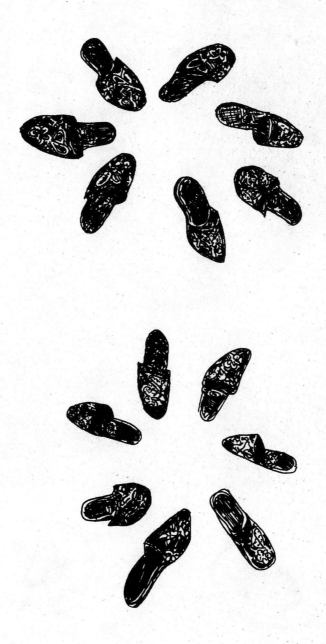

GACHI HASPER.

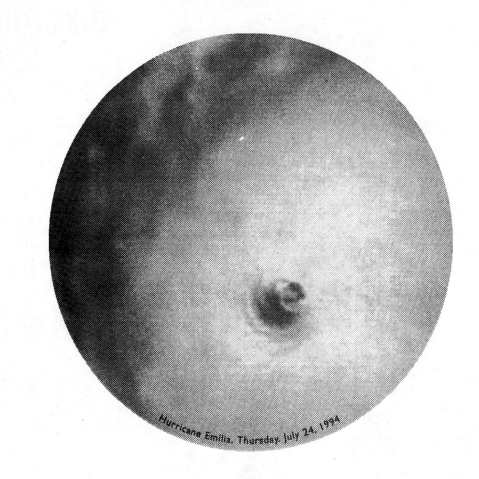

Hurricane Emilia, Thursday, July 24, 1994

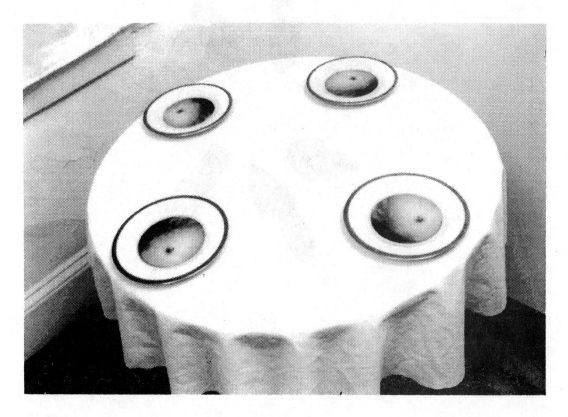

DEBORA WEINSTEIN, PARIS, FRANCE

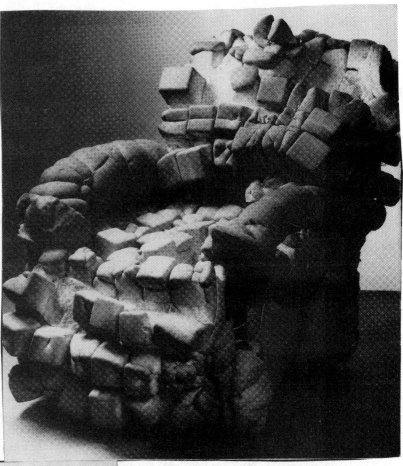

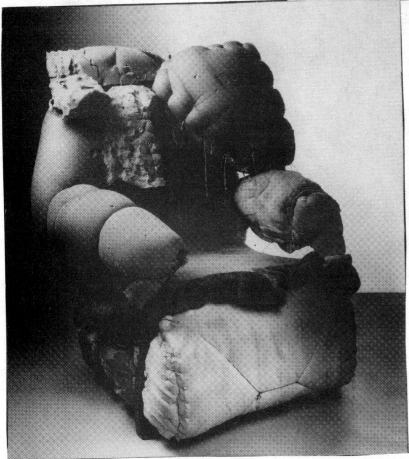

→

DEBORA WEINSTEIN, PARIS, FRANCE

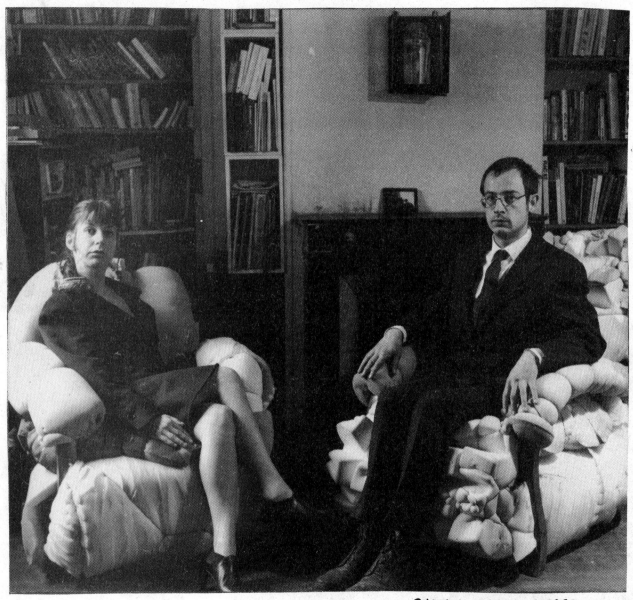

PHOTO: FRAÇOIS GIRARD

DENISE SHAW, NEW YORK, NY, USA

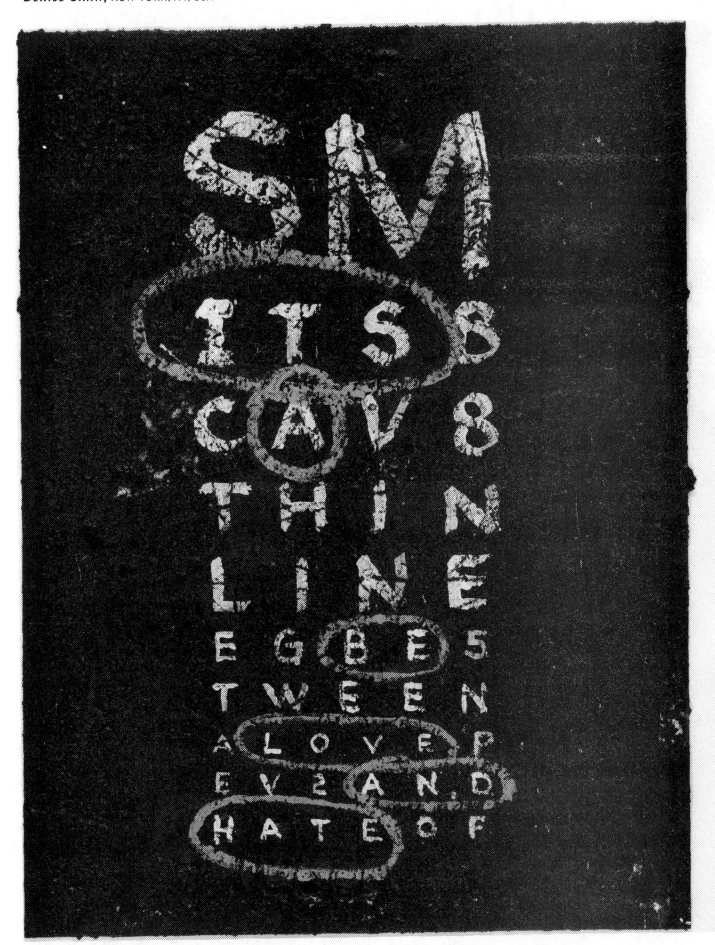

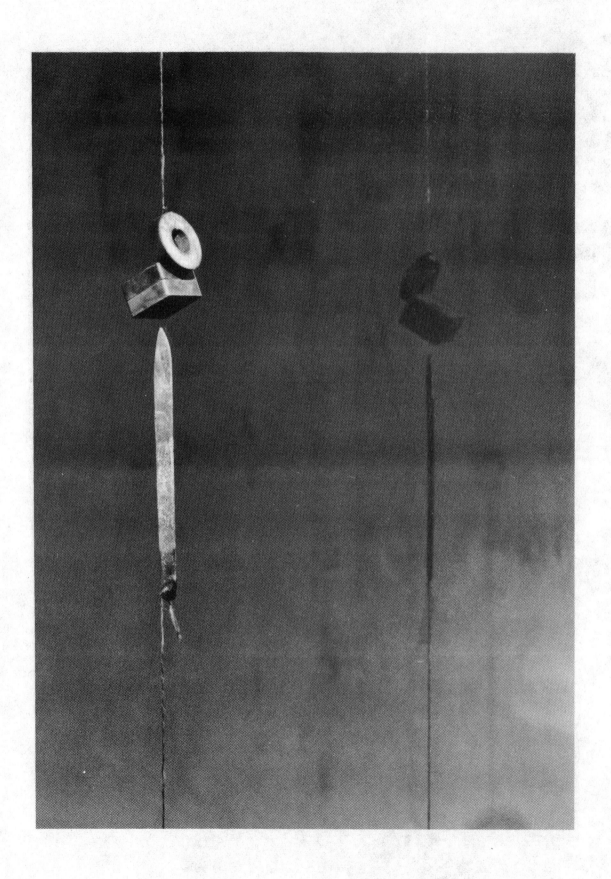

MARGITA TITLOVÁ YLOVSKY, PRAGUE, CZECH REPUBLIC

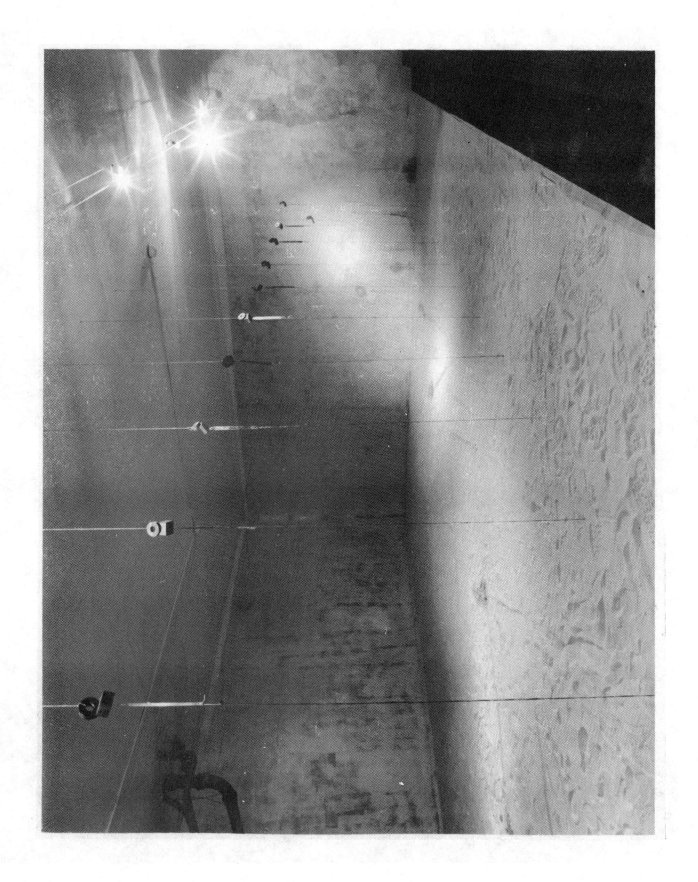

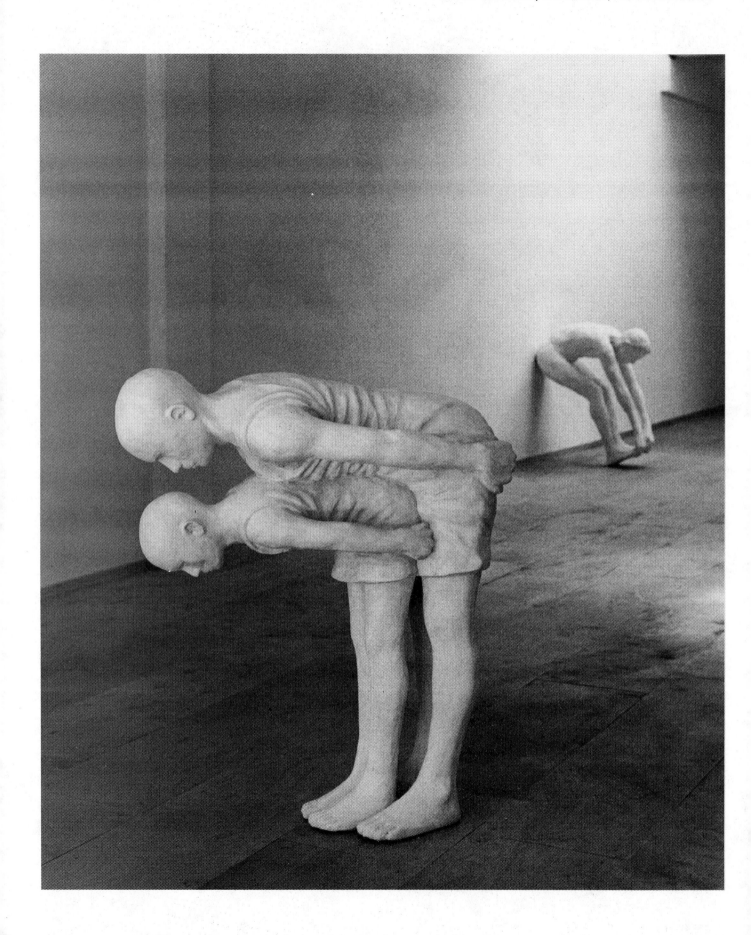

PETRA MORENZI, AMSTERDAM, THE NETHERLANDS

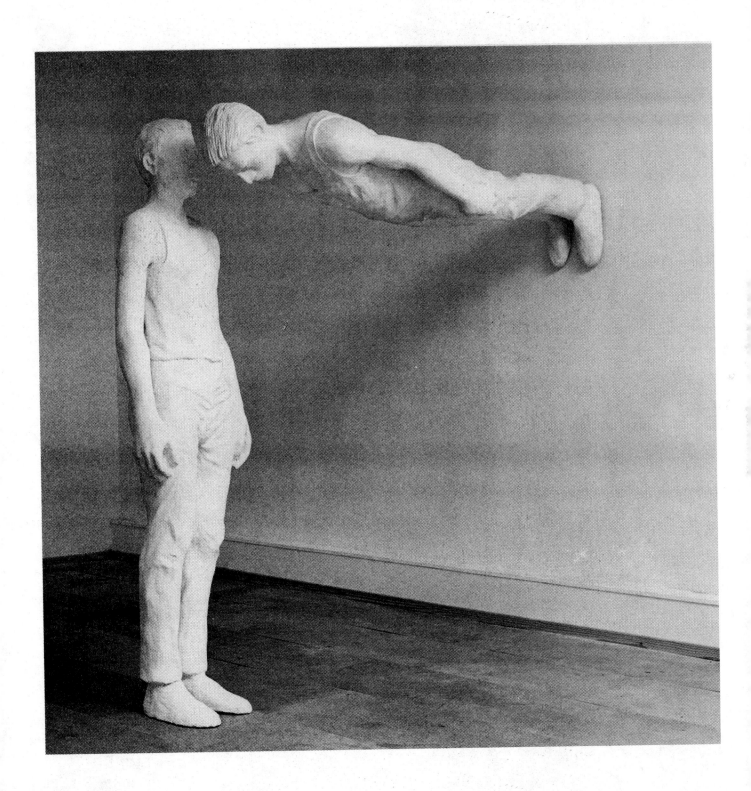

CORNELIA RUEHLICKE, NEW YORK, NY, USA

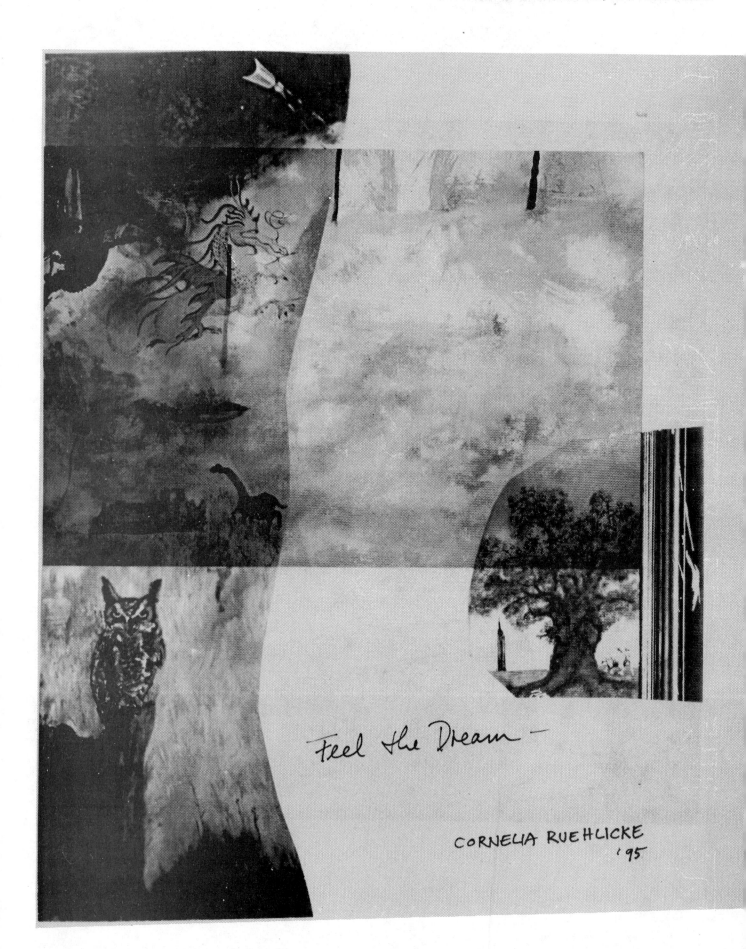

Feel the Dream —

CORNELIA RUEHLICKE
'95

CORNELIA RUEHLICKE, NEW YORK, NY, USA

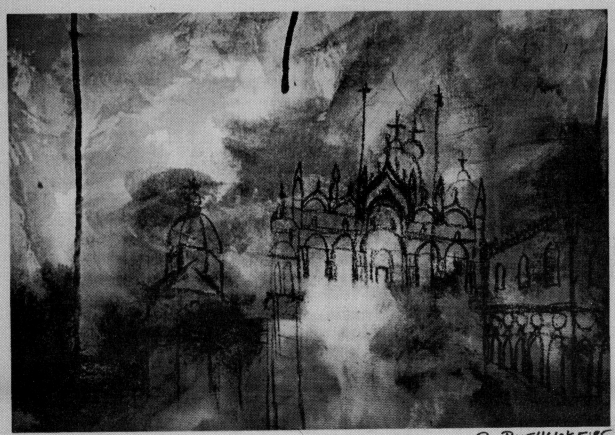

C. RUEHLICKE '95

you can't steal love —

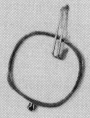

JUDY THOMAS, BROOKLYN, NY, USA

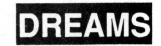

Dream Journal 12-29-94

"The Hide Out"

I was in a large apartment, and we were barricading the place because these guys were after us. The living room was wrapped in windows. I crawled on my belly and carefully pulled the blinds closed to about three inches from the window sill. Everything was dark in the apartment. Microwave foodstuffs were in a box in the kitchen. There was chocolate brownie mix. My friend said "You can eat a lot of sugar under pressure."

I am crawling on the floor, checking around the living room and I look out of the window. A police car is there and some punks are being arrested. It is almost sunset. A lot of people are watching the commotion and I realize this could be a distraction by the bad guys to get into the building. I am alone, the others have left. I decide to find my companions and go to the elevator door. It opens. Three bad guys are standing there - just like in the movies.

They are just as surprised to see me as I am to see them; they have their guns and are just about to shoot me when I say, " This isn't how it is supposed to happen, the door wasn't even locked - you are early. I am here all by myself and I'm worthless (they are really after my friends). So you have to leave while I lock up, and then you have to find a way to get in."

I was so surprised when they agreed, and so I went to find my friends who they were after. I pushed the button for the 20th floor (the top), but I realized that plan wouldn't work and we would all die. I was going to push all the buttons, but that wouldn't work either. I had nothing with me, but I knew I had to just 'get out.' Somehow I grabbed an extra jacket, it had a Chinese pattern, and I found fifteen bucks.

I was in the elevator going down, then the door opened and I could see the street. Some Chinese people were getting on and I asked, "Is this the way out?" "Yes," a woman said, "This is Chinatown." I had never gone out that way before.

I was in a large square, like the City Hall area, surrounded by buildings. I just started walking.. "I'll get lost in Chinatown," I thought. It was dark now. I arrived at a narrow alleyway. It looked like a dead end, and I asked the woman standing there if it was safe to go down there. "OK?" I asked, and she said, "Maybe not OK, maybe Marshals up ahead." There were only two guys sweeping up the street. Maybe they were sentries or something, I had heard such stories. I realized I should not be talking to anybody.

I walked down the alley and at the end, on the right, there was a tall open room the size of a gym crowded with people. It was raining in the room like something out of Blade Runner. The water was coming from the sprinkler system, the room had a greenish glow. I turned to the left, and another warehouse-like rainy room was there, just like the other side. There were doors at the back of this room, which I figured must lead to the passageway. I had to pass through this room first, though. The sprinklers were wrapped in foil to 'contain' the water so it didn't go all over the room. I was at the door, opened it, and walked through a series of dimly lit passageways, up and down stairs, through basements and sub-basements, then through another door that led up some stairs to another door.

JUDY THOMAS, BROOKLYN, NY, USA

I opened this door to find a brownish, 70's style room. Wood cabinets lined one wall, and large windows streamed dusty light across the dull carpet. About ten people were hanging out, on a sofa and at a table. No one expected me, but no one was surprised to see me, either. Bits of conversation. There was a left-over, acrid stale smell, but it was not unpleasant. Longhair hippie types. Tobacco on the table. Outside there were trees, and abundant green foliage growing out of abandoned buildings that once were elegant - brick red with columns and ironwork. The dense blue sky contrasted with the dark dampness below.

I ask a woman if I could buy a cigarette, roll my own. I give her a dollar and tussle over the papers, she wants a cigarette too. In the corner a guy is going on about "being high for a week, man." I am at the table. Then I am laying in a lounge-like cot and say " I just need to rest for a few days." I take a sip of hot coffee and think how wonderful it tastes and I go to sleep and dream that I am narrating the story of this dream. When I wake a messenger, a young boy, comes to tell me that they are asking about me. They are on their way. I get ready to leave. There is a tree branch just outside the window. I look down - I think I can make it. I thank the young boy and say goodbye. I awaken in my bed, the morning sun warm on my face.

© Judy Thomas

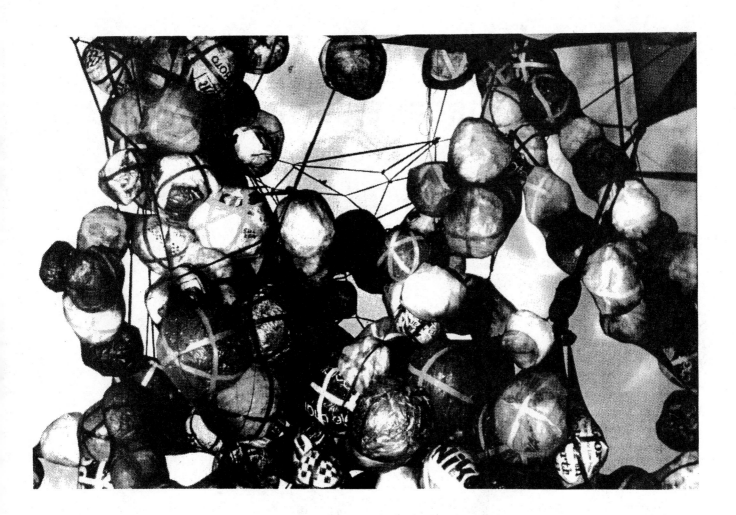

Judy Thomas is a sculptor living and working in Brooklyn. New York.

JENNIFER ELSNER, BROOKLYN, NY, USA

lie face down

JENNIFER ELSNER, BROOKLYN, NY, USA

The Indians were chasing me and all the people I am with, almost everyone there had been hit by an arrow, the Indians would not stop chasing us until we were all dead, so I pretend to have been hit and I lie **lie face down** down in the dirt, I held my breath when they came around to inspect the bodies, I could feel them around me kicking the other dead people and shooting the ones they thought may still be alive, I can hear them stabbing the dead with their daggers just because and I remember that sound of sword through flesh.

I cannot see them but I know they are there, the Mafia was approaching the kitchen and about to blow us all away. Bullets were flying and I pretending to be dead. I feel a Mafia guy standing above me, I say to myself don't breathedon't move. A knife starts at the base of my spine, I try not to move but I arch my back exposing my insides. I remember knowing I was going to die, he was going to take my kidneys and I would not be able to survive that kind of an infection.

Jennifer Elsner. The above is an interpretation of an earlier performance, DREAM CARDS, where the differences between experiencing, telling and reading dreams is acknowledged in different mediums.

JERIANN HILDERLEY, NEW YORK, NY, USA

"Taking Charge of our Dreams,"
From the novel, <u>Movement,</u> by Jeriann Hilderley

.... I wonder, can you dream another's dream? Can someone slap you awake with their deepest longings, their cruelest defeats? I still feel a sting from this dream I had where my work, not Lucina's was demolished by blows.

In the dream, I was in a park -- it could have been Riverside Park -- and I was stomping in deep snow. Why not make something out of this stuff, I thought.   When my crude shape wouldn't stand, I packed it against the ground, like a relief. I wasn't sure what   I was making until I backed away and saw it was a person, in fact a woman because it, she, had large breasts that looked like big eyes. I guess, it's no coincidence that my own breasts are quite large.

I decided to take a walk and think about what I had just made. The thought of going about the park, making more of these mounds, amused me. I knew for certain I was in a park because there was a children's playground and some benches nearby. But something called me back to the one I had made. I was a short distance from my Icy Woman, considering if I should now give her legs, when I saw three kids, running toward her. With their woolen caps on, I couldn't tell if they were boys or girls. And suddenly, they were kicking at my figure with such vehemence I felt the blows in my own body. I wanted to cry out but I was frozen in my rage. I woke up with an oppression in my chest.

JERIANN HILDERLEY, NEW YORK, NY, USA

When I told Lucina my dream, she quickly brought me back to reality. "The spring sun would have melted the piece anyway," she concluded, I thought smugly.

"Why do you say, 'spring sun,' when this is December?" I asked.

She reflected then spoke. "I don't know exactly. It seems like a Spring Equinox dream to me. You've either got Demeter on the ground about to descend to look for her daughter, Persephone, or vice-versa. You remember the myth, don't you, Ruth? How Persephone, like vegetation, is devastated in the fall and is revived in spring. Maybe you have Persephone coming up for air to find her mother and escape from that rapist, Pluto. Anyway you look at it, there's reality in your dream," she said. "Just as there is reality in that Greek myth of mother and daughter being separated by a domineering, possesive husband."

"It's time to change reality," I said.

"And our dreams," she said.

It had struck me that she was taking liberties with my dream, but then, I wasn't sure if it were my dream, or hers. I would have preferred some happy dream about finding treasure or rainbows. Then she reminded me of her continual ordeals with dream sticks and stones. How she is supposed to do something with them, and her quest is to find out what.

I've definitely decided Lucina is in my life as a challenge, whether she likes that word or not. She is like a real sabré. Just to consider writing about a creative spirit such as hers tickles my soul....
"Taking Charge of our Dreams,"
From the novel, <u>Movement</u>, by Jeriann Hilderley

JUDITH FLEISHMAN, NEW YORK, NY, USA

Drie Schone Panoramen
or
A Professional Virgin's Suicide

3 subterranean windows
3 views of (the life)
3 human humans

Kunfurstendam, Berlin
passing tick
going tock

posing always posing
and as I understand it
now... and then

the main stop
for sheiky Mickey
and

hungrily perusing
the evening's
tender

wo(men) pass it
and vice versa too;
jokes end as we know them

a red satin march
listens:
white roses

Come

take the tram,
metro
or taxi

walk by
watch
the bloom still fresh on her stem.

Judith Dimitria Fleishman
Berlin 1995

Judith Fleishman, NEW YORK, NY, USA

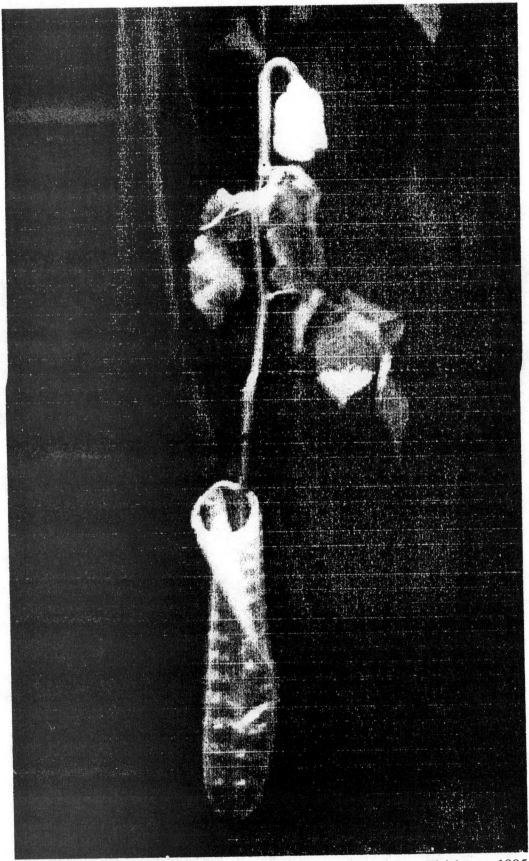

"A Professional Virgin's Suicide"   Fleishman 1995

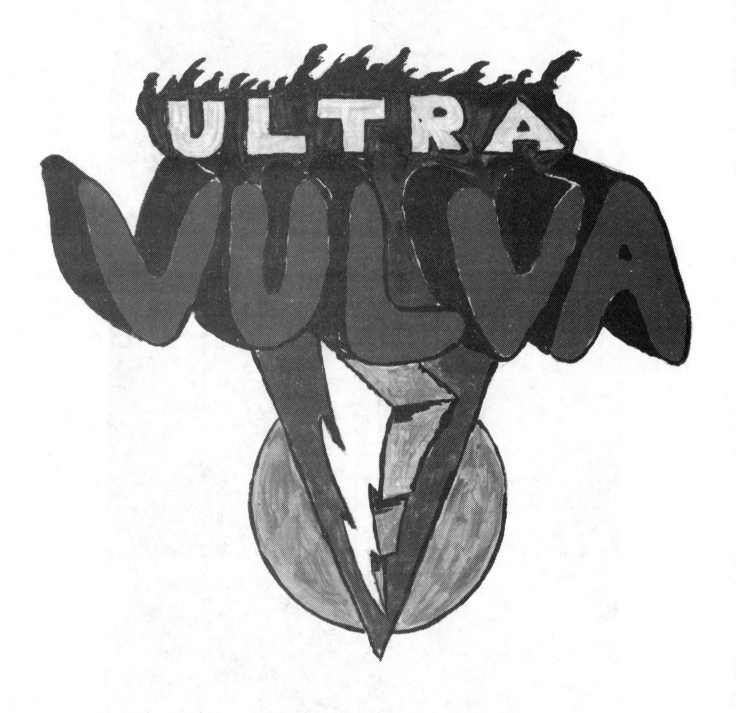

JANET PASSEHL, NEW BRITAIN, CT, USA

A house of many rooms, inside and out

the body is a room in the house,

a piece of clothing, a room.

The camera is a room

All rooms contain the spirits

of time

and desire.

Listen carefully to the walls of your house

they will speak to you

the way the trees

speak to you in the woods,

ask you,

can you leave this house?

Janet Passehl '92-5

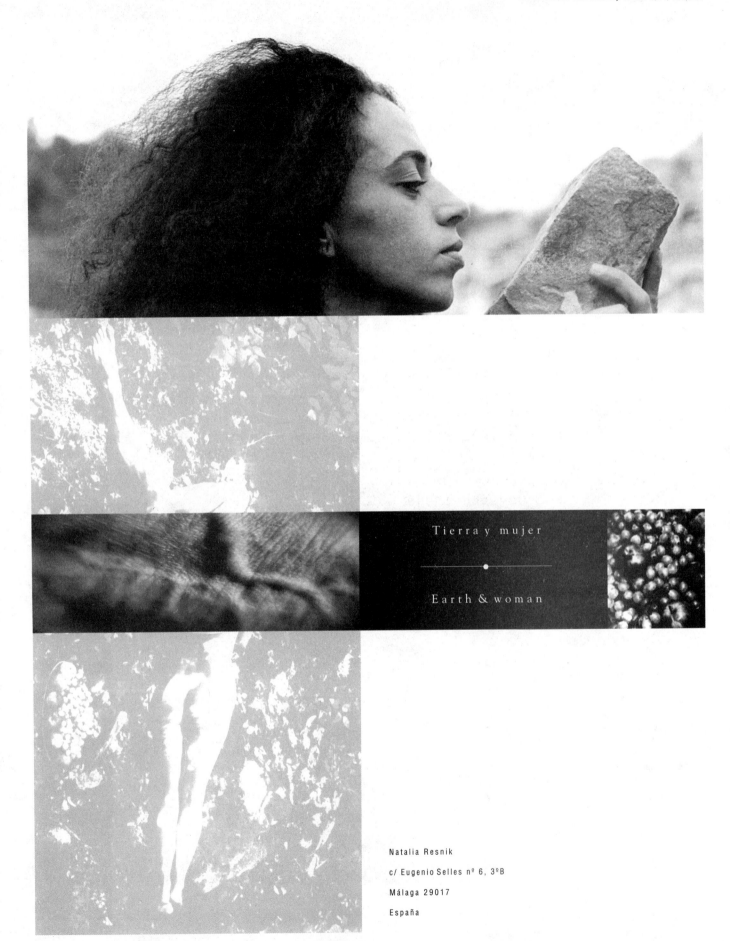

Tierra y mujer

Earth & woman

Natalia Resnik

c/ Eugenio Selles nº 6, 3ºB

Málaga 29017

España

ROSEMARY KOTHE, AMHERST, NY, USA

Pretty Pretender

Purple loosestrife
Pretty pretender
Invader from Eurasia
Mauve marauder of wetlands
Mesmerizing man, while destroying a mainstay of wildlife, the native
marshland species.
Where have you gone, variegated refuge for birds, insects and frogs?
Purple, the royal intruder has taken over our symbiotic democracy,
Crowding out the golden dandelion,
Brown cattail, white Queen Anne's lace and amber tiger lily.
The purple plague persists:

When will it end?

SANDY GELLIS, NEW YORK, NY, USA

HYDROGEN   HELIUM   LITHIUM   BERYLLIUM   CARBON   NITROGEN   OXYGEN

BORON

FLUORINE   NEON   MAGNESIUM   ALUMINUM   SILICON   SULPHUR

SODIUM   PHOSPHORUS

SCANDIUM

CHLORINE   ARGON   POTASSIUM   CALCIUM   TITANIUM   VANADIUM

GERMANIUM

IRON

CHROMIUM   MANGANESE   COBALT   NICKEL   COPPER   ZINC   GALLIUM

ARSENIC   SELENIUM   BROMINE   RUBIDIUM   STRONTIUM

KRYPTON

YTTRIUM

RHODIUM

ZIRCONIUM   MOLYBDENUM   TECHNETIUM   CADMIUM   INDIUM   TIN

NIOBIUM

SANDY GELLIS, NEW YORK, NY, USA

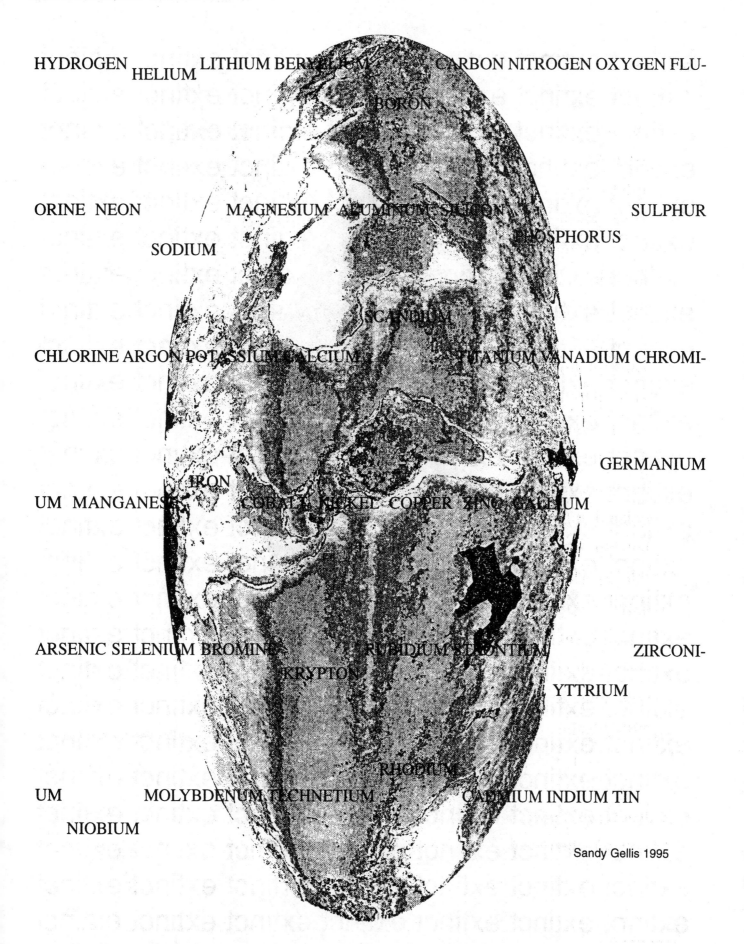

HYDROGEN HELIUM LITHIUM BERYLLIUM CARBON NITROGEN OXYGEN FLU-

BORON

ORINE NEON MAGNESIUM ALUMINUM SILICON SULPHUR

SODIUM PHOSPHORUS

SCANDIUM

CHLORINE ARGON POTASSIUM CALCIUM TITANIUM VANADIUM CHROMI-

GERMANIUM

UM MANGANESE IRON COBALT NICKEL COPPER ZINC GALLIUM

ARSENIC SELENIUM BROMINE RUBIDIUM STRONTIUM ZIRCONI-

KRYPTON YTTRIUM

RHODIUM

UM MOLYBDENUM TECHNETIUM CADMIUM INDIUM TIN

NIOBIUM

Sandy Gellis 1995

MICHELLE STUART, NEW YORK, NY, USA

extinct extinct extinct extinct extinct extinct extinct
extinct extinct extinct extinct extinct extinct extinct
extinct extinct extinct extinct extinct extinct extinct
extinct extinct extinct extinct extinct extinct extinct
extinct extinct extinct extinct extinct extinct extinct
extinct extinct extinct extinct extinct extinct extinct
extinct extinct extinct extinct extinct extinct extinct
extinct extinct extinct extinct extinct extinct extinct
extinct extinct extinct extinct extinct extinct extinct
extinct extinct extinct extinct extinct extinct extinct
extinct extinct extinct extinct extinct extinct extinct
extinct extinct extinct extinct extinct extinct extinct
extinct extinct extinct extinct extinct extinct extinct
extinct extinct extinct extinct extinct extinct extinct
extinct extinct extinct extinct extinct extinct extinct
extinct extinct extinct extinct extinct extinct extinct
extinct extinct extinct extinct extinct extinct extinct
extinct extinct extinct extinct extinct extinct extinct
extinct extinct extinct extinct extinct extinct extinct
extinct extinct extinct extinct extinct extinct extinct
extinct extinct extinct extinct extinct extinct extinct
extinct extinct extinct extinct extinct extinct extinct
extinct extinct extinct extinct extinct extinct extinct

MICHELLE STUART, NEW YORK, NY, USA

extinct extinct extinct extinct extinct extinct extinct
extinct extinct extinct extinct extinct extinct extinct
extinct extinct extinct extinct extinct extinct extinct
extinct extinct extinct extinct extinct extinct extinct
extinct extinct extinct extinct extinct extinct extinct
extinct extinct extinct extinct extinct extinct extinct
extinct extinct extinct extinct extinct extinct extinct
extinct extinct extinct extinct extinct extinct extinct
extinct extinct extinct extinct extinct extinct extinct
extinct extinct extinct extinct extinct extinct extinct
extinct extinct extinct extinct extinct extinct extinct
extinct extinct extinct extinct extinct extinct extinct
extinct extinct extinct extinct extinct extinct extinct
extinct extinct extinct extinct extinct extinct extinct
extinct extinct extinct extinct extinct extinct extinct
extinct extinct extinct extinct extinct extinct extinct
extinct extinct extinct extinct extinct extinct extinct
extinct extinct extinct extinct extinct extinct extinct
extinct extinct extinct extinct extinct extinct extinct
extinct extinct extinct extinct extinct extinct extinct
extinct extinct extinct extinct extinct extinct extinct
extinct extinct extinct extinct extinct extinct extinct

michelle stuart

LOIS NESBITT, NEW YORK, NY, USA

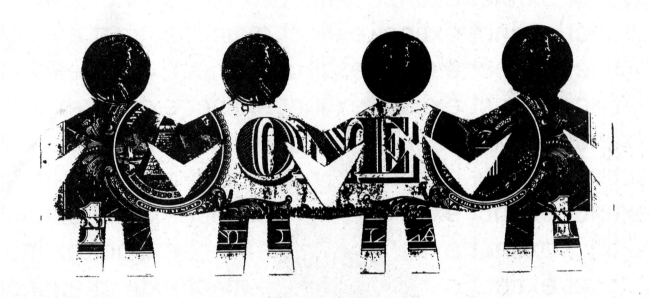

ECONOMICS 101

It's just too big. The millennium. The globe. My brain just can't wrap itself around that broad circumference or sprawl across all those digits. Confronted with huge numbers, I feel like Pooh Bear, a little dazed and confused. Unable to take in the long sweeps of time and space, I don't feel equipped, as the editors requested, to contribute something reflective of our "historical moment."

But I do know that my brain, limited as it is, is always busy thinking about something--usually the same things, which it circles round and round, over and over again. And, recently, those local thoughts have seemed to apply to the big picture.

The ideas aren't new. And they aren't "mine." They come, in part, from the writings of Patanjali, an Indian sage writing some 5000 years ago (another inconceivable number). They have to do with economy. Not necessarily a financial economy, not strictly about money (unless you think of money as a kind of "green energy" that's just out there circulating among all the other kinds of energy). They have to do, specifically, with three principles: ahimsa (non-violence), asteya (non-stealing), and aparigraha (non-greed).

I got to these principles the hard way, through a two-decade-long battle with my own body. As I learn to love and not to destroy my body, to respect its "economy," one day at a time, I'm learning what it means to care. And as I begin to care about one thing, I start to care about other things and other people.

LOIS NESBITT, NEW YORK, NY, USA

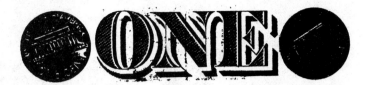

Patanjali believed that karma is a boomerang. If you practice non-violence, people will treat you well. If you don't steal from others, things will come to you. If you don't act on greed, you will always have what you need. I've felt this in action. Several years ago I began an art project called <u>Dispossession</u>, in which I systematically began giving away everything I own. I found that I will never reach my goal (to rid myself of all material goods), because more and more things keep coming into my hands. No matter how much I give away, intake exceeds output.

But it's not about ownership. We're all renters, in the cosmic sense--renters of the things we claim to possess, of the land we live on, of the space we occupy and the air we breathe, even of our physical bodies, these shells that carry our spirits through this life. Nothing, nothing is ours to destroy, to waste, to squander. We can use what we truly need, but it's better to make ourselves useful.

All of this is at odds with how the world works--or seems, through jaded eyes, to work. It means not accumulating or holding onto or coveting anything--materials or money or fame. It's also at odds with a lot of things I thought <u>I</u> wanted. But whenever I start thinking of the self, of myself, as body, as object, I start to feel very small and very alone. I start to feel that I'm competing with an unmanageable number of other object-bodies, all different from me, all separate from me. I start to fear that there won't be enough--stuff, attention, love--for me, and I start to clamor and to hoard. I start taking instead of giving.

I think, from my limited knowledge of history, that this is how nations work too, oscillating between giving and unifying (peace treaties, the United Nations, Earth Day) and me-first grabbing that divides and destroys (colonialism, purges, world wars).

Economics 101, as we enter the first century of the new millennium and the second century of shrinking resources and contracting distances, goes as follows: We're all in this together. What you do to the net, you do to yourself. And what you do to yourself, you do to the net.

Lois Nesbitt
New York, 1995

McCrady Axon, MADISON, CT, USA

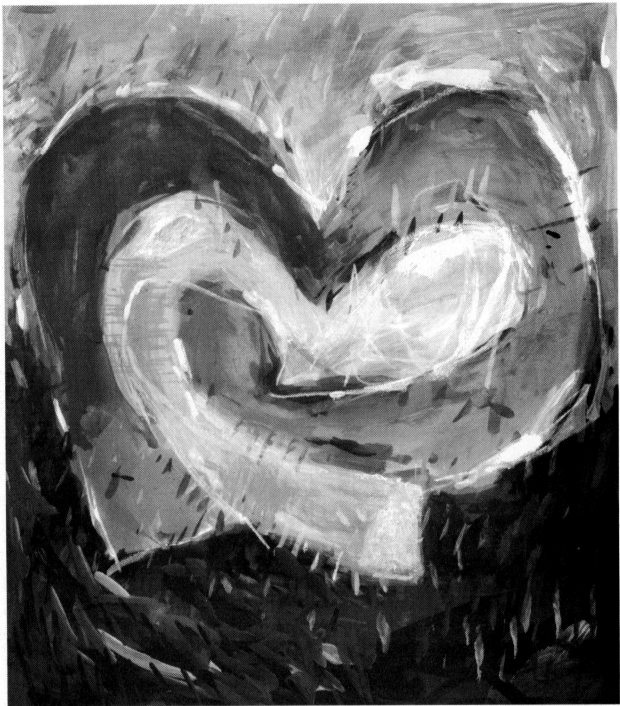

S111, Relentless Seed

In the 90's we are scientizing for an evolved divine. Now is the chaotic and precious and fleeting
moment when, on rehearsed instinct, we embrace the flickering unexpected.
As when you look out to sea, focus on the infinite. In this decade,
I use red as a neutral. These paintings are five foot red monochromes
in a series on The Sublime begun in 1988.

S130, Inferno

MᴄCʀᴀᴅʏ Axᴏɴ, MADISON, CT, USA

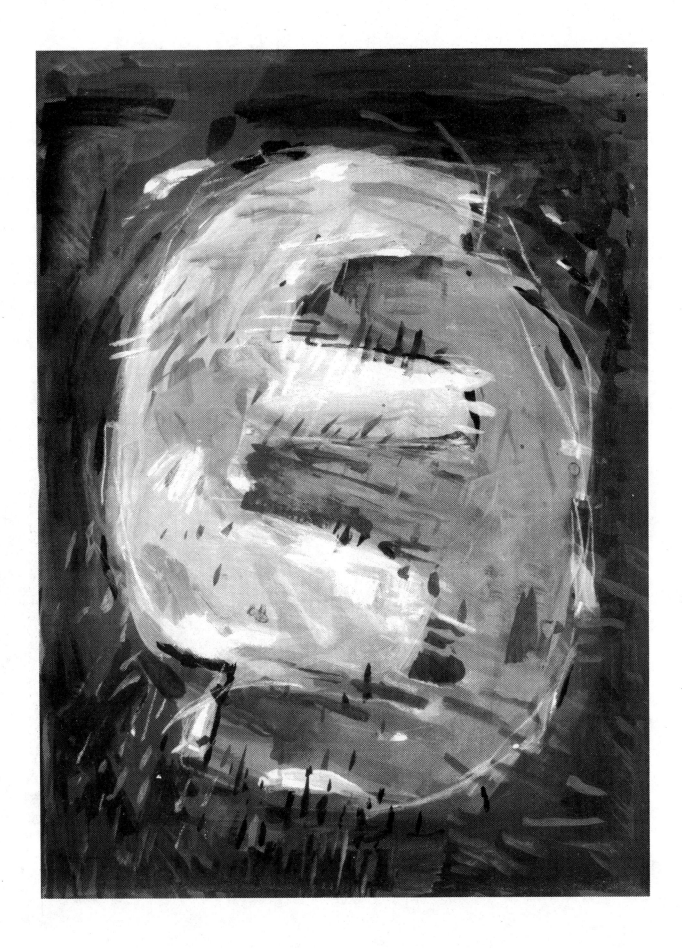

KATHLEEN WEBSTER, NEW YORK, NY, USA

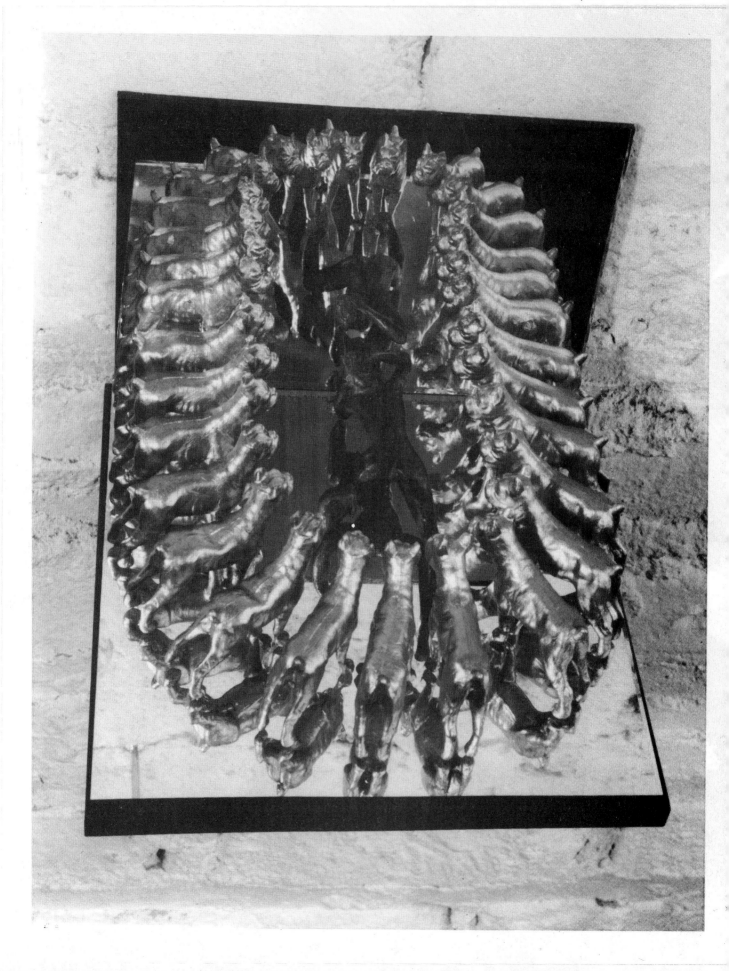

KATRIN VON MALTZAHN, BERLIN, GERMANY

22 C   Talk about "typical"
women's and men's occupa-
tions.

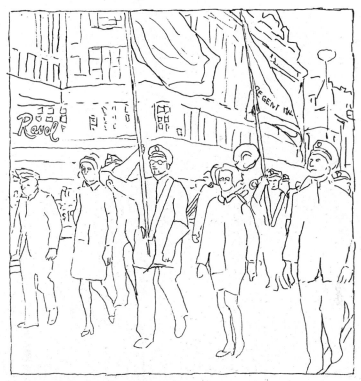

*No sex discrimination from the start - in the Salvation
Army men and women have always had equal rights*

22C-22D   91

KATRIN VON MALTZAHN, BERLIN, GERMANY

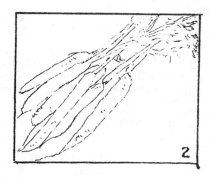

*carrots   ['kærəts]   a vegetable → 2

ANN MENEBROKER, SACRAMENTO, CA, USA

a bird enters the undulating dream of life

the bird of reality and sorrow
lands on the rim of a dream.
a whale plays flute
in an ocean of oil and debris.
nickle-head buffalo
sit in the string section
fiddling to a tune, in search
of the land where they once
roamed for weeks.
There are drums beating,
from the desert and high mountain vistas,
where lizzards bang their tails
on tight-pulled skins.
life is a holy ceremony, a glad
and sacred noise.
we who have forgotten
are reminded about truth
in the exploration of our dreams.
there is no need for this bird
to be here. we need to be awakened.
we need to open our eyes
in the stirring of the first light
at the beginning of time, coming up
through the surface
with songs so full of love
it almost hurts to sing them.
a small sigh escapes
from the dreamer. it startles
the bird away. now we must
wake up by ourselves.

Annie Menebroker
2738 4th Avenue(alley)
Sacramento, CA 95818 USA

RUTH LIBERMANN, BROOKLYN, NY, USA

The True Account
of
Fritzy Agny, *written by herself,*
together with
The Behaviour and non-Confession,
taken by the person who attended her while
in prison, and to the place of execution.

What a way to die. I had not anticipated this.

The woman whose fate gives rise to this narrative was born about the year 1759, in a village near Norwich.

Soon after her arrival in the city, she found herself in a very painful and disagreeable situation; for she had no friends capable of supporting or even assisting her.

My own country was so miserable a place, that it would not afford me provision to subsist on, wood to hang me on, nor earth to bury me in.

As our readers have a claim upon us for matters of entertainment as well as instruction, we insert the following for the sake of whimsical singularity of the prosecutor's evidence, which was delivered in the following terms:

As for the event: I would have liked to undertake to writing an account on how these eyes stared at my death, how I saw them see me dying, so distant was I. Now I deem that my death belongs to me no more. It is for the same reason, that is, because they did not grant me the dignity to die alone, that they spied on my death. It must be confessed that I have been perpetually occupied with this sentiment. In speaking my thoughts upon the subject of their watching me dying and disowning me thus of my death, my capability of discernment and judgment is slowly being restored. (Doubtless those wretches have some consolation, but I have none, save for the liberty to write). But certainly there must be some mistake in this matter. This argument I see holds good against writing the possibility that my dying image was cast back on me; that the moments I watched them see me, my death reflected on their faces as though it was my own death mask that I beheld.

I shall not dislodge myself further with such futile ruminations; futile, for it is too late to comprehend that I had already been looked into the wall and had become a part of the collection, a chapter. I would cherish the idea of asking any one of the others here if they, too, tried to remember the instant which crystallized perhaps all they had hitherto known, all that was knowable and that could be known no longer. Or else, the thoughts of that instant may have been of great banality. Be that as it may, I should wish to commend to them that before, so much as during, the event they should put in writing what is being thought, for if they do not remember they will forever be doomed to reassemble. How vain my intents: The others I do not see—mine remains a very lonely and solitary existence; my sanity has become my greatest curse in this abode of horrors. My heart is corroded by grief and agitated by fear. Left to myself, unhappy in my disposition, nevertheless, the oblivion I bring upon myself by retreating from the gruesome awareness of this stale and putrid collection, aids me in centering my mind on that which is my chief concern.

She continued writing till about twelve at night, when she went to bed and requested silence, that she might repose in quiet—waked at three next morning, wrote a few lines and then lay down again and slept till seven, when she got up, washed herself, and breakfasted at eight o'clock.

My imagination is compelled to relinquish the prospect of receiving intelligence from a source other than my own memory about the thought I must have had during my most fatal moment. My mind is so entirely filled with the object of remembering this thought that I cannot entertain any other. Nor can I indulge in the one I seek, for the very one is unknown to me. Yet I must endeavour to track my consciousness back to the event. In so doing I shall reach the moment of my death. But, alas, at that very instant it tends to leap to the one but last before my death, always leaving the trace of a gap, the gap that I must regain. Allow me to try one more time. I recall having at length decided to pass my concluding moments with the pursuit of contemplating what it would be like to see the outside one more time, if only for a glance. Yet I endeavored to reason myself out of this. (Nor was it until the decline of life that I had actually taken fancy to the idea of dying as a free person.) How dangerous it is to foster the will to die free. When facing desire of that kind in such an imperfect state of existence, one cannot but yield to the unmitigated forces of frenzy. I would not have regained tranquillity, had I not abandoned the thought that could have been brought within the utmost verge of possibility: to die free. After rejecting the decision to occupy my final thought with the notion to die free, I had set out to find a different, a more significant thought, one that was less subsumed by my recent deplorable state or my current affairs, rather it had to be a thought that was sustained by my inner being. But what I decided this thought to be, I do not know.

Lucky is she who cherishes some secret she cannot disclose. My secret I do not even know. Perhaps it is not entirely fitting to be speaking of a secret, for is not a secret precisely that which is known to the owner of the secret? My chief concern is to know of an event that threatens to be forever concealed from my knowledge, a secret that , in all likelihood, no one is in the possession of. Yet I must not, therefore, conclude that it cannot be regained by me, although this is certainly a conceivable outcome the mention of which ought not here be omitted. Had I been so provident as to put in writing—which I could have done were it not for my inordinate propensity for indecision—I might have now had a most satisfactory account of the decision that I had made, if such had been made. It is with great reluctance that I admit here, and suffer the consequences of, my neglect. Alas! It has been my ruin in this world. However, I have, as yet, no grounds to accept that I shall not arrive at coming upon the substance of my decision.

And she constantly confirmed that from that time she was always in a hurry and confusion of spirits, and could have no rest day or night, seldom shut her eyes to sleep, or if she did she was disturbed with starts and fears. She was continually running up and down stairs, and could never sit down long to business, her spirits being continually agitated and flurried, but by what means she could give no account: she said, she had been several times tempted to lay violent hands on herself, at other times on her own children, of which she acquainted her husband, who only said she was whimsical or maggoty; but never took any pains to find out the cause of this disorder in her senses. After the warrant for execution came down she seemed much better but could give no farther or better account than as the following.

2

I see not what good a minister can do me, for the matter lies upon myself. I am at this time reduced to the necessity of asking relief, having nothing to carry one on in my intended prosecution of adventures.

I fear, though: Could indeed my memory have been destroyed? Then where or what will it be now? It may be reconstituted in some matter. For the force by which my memory must have been destroyed, almost too insupportable to bear up with, thoroughly shattered it against this wall. I had not anticipated such a vast force, so instant, so irretrievably faster than the speed of my perception. But the memory of it is perpetual. What am I saying—memory? It is precisely that which is outside the realm of perception that is so memorable; it is not what I perceived that my memory is occupied with; not any more: It is the irretrievable moment, the moment I shattered, irretrievable to memory, so it seems, to conscious memory. In consequence of this predicament, I should resign myself to be eternally occupied with searching for what cannot be found. In that, however, I would not succeed according to my wishes. For, would I resign, I would have to continue to remember, which is indeed my very wish: to bring to memory the object of my thought during my most fatal moment; in this wish I cannot succeed, lest what I propounded earlier is false.

While she was in prison she was seized with the gaol distemper, which occasioned some idle reports; for the people not knowing the nature of her disorder, imagined she had taken poison. But that was false; for she never attempted any such thing; and except in the article of levity, when she related her adventures, her behaviour in general was sober, pious and resigned:

There was no possibility to make my escape, every one turning my enemy now at the last extremity; when if Love of Man had influenced them, they should have befriended me.

I cannot, nay, must not abandon the active forces springing from my urge to excavate a fact that, however hidden to my perception, is nevertheless a fact and therefore must exist. If there was but a trace, I may succeed to know what, prior to my death, I had decided to think in the course of my dissolution. Behind the wall, I had thought it all through several times since I was sentenced. I had imagined it all and all turned out to be very much according to my imagination: the place I would occupy on the wall; the waiting; the impending decision on what exactly it is that I should want to think last; what precisely that should be, and the order in which it ought to be thought; the apprehension of the moment's brevity; hence the torment if there be enough time to think all that I would still want to think; and finally the doubt if what I decided was really essential and true to my life, to its unfolding, perception, and thinking. And that is almost exactly the way it was—it all went according to my imagination—except the moment that cut me off. This sudden, however temporary, arrest of my memory I had not anticipated: I had not understood that I would indeed cease to perceive to be thus to remember that I ceased.

Though very agreeable to the nature of her case, this was penned in [a] manner not likely to come from the hands of a poor ignorant woman; but let us read more:

He went first and then I with a candle and lanthorn in my hand, a carbine upon my shoulder, my hair wet and about my ears, and in a linen night-gown and slippers. I exercised the most powerful restraint that could be thought of. The eye has an expression of anguish unspeakable, and a languor in its movement, an inclination

3

to shut out all objects. Neither the thought of the place, nor the apprehensions of death in the least terrify me.

Yet being inextricably fixed in the moment after it happened, I can but remember the moment before the moment it happened. I can do nothing but remember nor can I abstain from attempting to uncover, or rather: to remember just what it was that I had in the end decided would be my last thoughts. Or had I not arrived at a decision? I have been pondering this question. I cannot recall if I had ever resolved with myself to come to a decision on what my final thought ought to be. It was an important decision and one that could not easily be cast aside as nonsense. It was almost all that I was thinking since I was sentenced, all that my mind was occupied with; nothing else was important to me, not my past life, nor the future that I did not have, not even the sentence itself.

It is very probable this journal might be a contrivance, to confront the evidence against her if ever she should be sentenced to death.

Prior to being sentenced, the silence and confinement I lived in had become more and more odious, and I had thought a lot about the impending sentence. But it was not long before that sentence was actually passed on me; it was but a matter of days. Here they do not waste time on formalities concerning something that is already decided prior to any process of determining what exactly the decision ought to be. Some decisions are well made in advance. It is then as though the decision preexisted the case for its application. However, whilst such decision regarding my continued or discontinued existence may have been known to the judges, I was as yet ignorant about it, until it was announced to me. The theme of death and of a public death as might have awaited me then, was undeniably on my mind. I had even indulged myself in various analyses on the subject of executions and had come upon some conclusions, the most significant of which still seems to me that the one executed must be like a transient item similar to a patient briefly occupying the physician's chair to at once make place for the next patient.

It is but reasonable to think that this fleeting visit is of great consequence to the "patient's" life which, in our case, is thus ended. For the patient then the visit is not at all so fleeting, but is likely to be a more enduring one. Indeed there is one thing to be considered: Me is here, though me, that is my story. It has been lingering here since it all happened, from the moment of my dissolution. And it is that moment which so ardently begs of me to be completed; for complete it is not until I gain knowledge of what it was that was thought by me in the very instant of my death. Alas! I cannot recall. I fear no one will have the ability to retrieve knowledge of it for me. In order to aid my capacity to remember what exactly it was that my thoughts were about, I have been considering to retrace the very decision that must have preceded the actualization of that which I had decided. To that decision alone, I mused, I might have access because the decision must have happened while I was still able to perceive and thus remember. My potential for conscious memory of the decision that I must have formed with regard to what it is that I ought to think last, is unlike the potential to remember what of that decision was put into action, that is, my last thought, for this must have occurred during the most fatal, most traumatizing event I have ever lived to experience. What I do remember and must be sure of, is the fact that I was, prior to my death, perpetually considering possible topics for my final thoughts. I know this to be true for I am in possession of my writings.

I enter upon this part of my story with great hesitation for fear of appearing pedantic. Yet it is only in order to proof that the aforementioned consideration regarding the uncovering of a decision about my final thoughts is founded upon evidence, which I deem so conclusive, that I cannot but believe that I must have finalized my decision.

Based on the assurance of this probability I might learn to be contented, but I was

4

RUTH LIBERMANN, BROOKLYN, NY, USA

not formed to be satisfied. I must admit to a spark of a doubt present that challenges the very existence of such a decision ever having been made by me. Supported with unshaken resolution I am determined to further explore the matter.

Certainly I was born with some determinations, and instinct and survival frequently induced me to rapid decision making; yet concerning the decision on my final thought I was entirely unprepared, for the circumstance of knowing the hour of death was never by me anticipated, nor was it anticipated that I should worry myself with the substance of my thinking during that last hour, and finally the last moment, of my life, nor further more that, after it happened, I should still concern myself with those thoughts which—even worse: I cannot recall. It is no longer within my power to return. Hereupon I must concede that my current tendency to search for various excuses for not remembering—one such excuse of course being that it all happened much too fast—prevents me, unfortunately, from achieving precisely that which I am so eager to discern and am so perpetually occupied by: The very decision on what my thoughts ought to be during the brief moments I know to be my last. For if I refrained from finding excuses for the lack of memory—the lack I so ardently perceive—then, and only then, would I possibly have a chance, slight though it may be, to remember. From the moment I conceived this idea, my reason was not only restored, but I took a mighty disgust in having been so defensive about the fact of my memory's deficiency. Furthermore I had almost exhausted my spiritual strength by dwelling at length on the possibility of how different my current knowledge would have been, had the matter been taken into consideration before the event had happened.

Upon realizing that this lack of preparation I must but accept, my passions were raised to a great height, for I entered upon one further possible solution. Before I elaborate, let me, however, say that this further solution, if a solution indeed it were, could also be a cause of great anxiety for me. The conclusion I have just alluded to, I have pondered it recently, could be that, assuming I have never in fact made any such decision as aforementioned, that I may make it now, retrospectively as it were. I would have delighted in the prospect of this.

All the time that she remained in this gloomy prison, her mind seemed to be tortured with the most agonizing pains, on account of the horrid crimes of which she had been guilty; and she expressed a sense of her torments in the following striking words, which she spoke to a Clergyman who attended her: He only can judge who is acquainted with the secrets of all hearts and who, as he is not to be deceived, so his penetration is utterly unknown to us, who are confined to appearances and the exterior marks of things.

But could I live with the uncertainty that perhaps my retroactive decision supersedes, or undermines the possibility of coming upon, the original one, if after all there was one. The latter I shall possibly never be able to be entirely sure of. However, the inversion of this problem lies in precisely the same uncertainty: If there never was a decision—a possibility which after all cannot entirely be ruled out, as discussed earlier—then, what I am so fervently trying to remember would be something that never in fact happened. This leads me yet further into the depth of the matter: My recent concerns have been with the nature of the decision that I have assumedly made regarding the contents of my last thoughts; now, I cannot be certain of having implemented that decision, if indeed there was one.

Accordingly, if there was none, I may nevertheless have had some final thoughts. In consequence of this affirmation I should now restrict myself to the bare facts of the

5

substance of my last thoughts, thus limiting my search to only two items: Item A being the question as to what precisely I have thought at the very instant that I expired. Item B must then consist in the question of what to do should I never reconstitute Item A—after all not a wholly impossible eventuality. That is, should the content of my last musing never become known to me, then what am I to do? And now: When shall I decide that this is the case? In answer to the first question, I may decide to at last make a decision on that very content, as though that final thought still needed to be thought. In answer to the second question, I must plainly say, that I do not know at what moment I should determine that I have strained my memory and patience and can justifiably conclude that any further attempts will yield no result. It appears to me now, from what has been stated, that my first step should be a decision as to what further considerations I should have before I may safely conclude that knowledge of my actual last thought shall never be regained by me. Respecting all that has thus far been stated, that moment may have arrived and I should ready myself to decide what I should want to think, knowing that no other thought will ever be thought by me again. Whoever reads this may rely upon the truth of the account which I have here given.

If you find a story, or but one sentence in all her scribbling, that is even tolerable, depend upon it, she stole it.

But certainly there must be some mistake in this matter. There is no possibility to make my escape, every thought turning my enemy at the last extremity. I would have liked to undertake to write down the process of determining the substance of my concluding thought, for such record would now be for me a most perfect aid in gaining further knowledge regarding that thought. It must, however, be confessed that I have been perpetually occupied with the sentiment, that the actual thought I had had may not have been the actualization of a preceding decision concerning such thought, but may indeed have been a novel, spontaneous thought, springing from the immediacy and brevity of the situation. This argument I see holds good against writing the possibility of a decision. For such decision does not carry within it the assurance of having been implemented. In speaking my thoughts upon this subject, allow me to try one more time to retrieve what little I do remember.

I recall having at length decided to entertain the fantastic idea of dying free. Yet I endeavored to reason myself out of this. I would not have regained tranquillity had I not abandoned the thought that could have been brought within the utmost verge of possibility: to die free. After rejecting the decision to occupy my final thought with the above notion, I had set out to find a different, a more significant thought, one that was less linked to my recent deplorable state, rather it had to be a thought that was sustained by my inner being, not by my current affairs. My mind was so entirely filled with the object of determining that thought that I was unable entertain any other. Nor could I have indulged in the desired thought, for the very one was as yet unknown to me.

My chief concern now is to know of an event that threatens to be forever concealed from my knowledge, a secret that is likely to be in no one's possession. Yet I must not, therefore, conclude that it cannot be acquired by me, although this is certainly a conceivable outcome the mention of which ought not here be omitted. Had I been so provident as to put in writing—which I could have done were it not for my inordinate propensity for indecision—I might have now had a most satisfactory account of the decision that I had made, if such had been made. It is with great reluctance that I admit here, and suffer the consequences of, my neglect. Alas! It has been my ruin in this world.

It is precisely what is outside the realm of perception that is so memorable; it is not

6

that which I perceived that my memory is now occupied with; not any more: It is the lost moment, the moment I shattered, so irretrievable to memory, memory, it seems, to conscious memory. In consequence of this cognition, I should resign myself to abandoning the search for what cannot possibly be found. In that, however, I would not succeed according to my wishes. For, would I resign, I would have to continue to remember, which is indeed my very wish: to bring to memory the object of my thought during my most fatal moment; in this wish I cannot succeed, lest what I propounded earlier is false. But certainly there must be some mistake in this matter.

I had thought it all through several times since I was sentenced. I had imagined it all, and all turned out to be very much according to my imagination: the place I would occupy on the wall; the waiting; the impending decision on what exactly it is that I should want to think last; what precisely that should be, and the order in which it ought to be thought; the apprehension of the moment's brevity; hence the torment if there be enough time to think all that I would still want to think; and finally the doubt if the thought I decided upon was really essential and true to my life, to its unfolding, to my former perception and thinking. And that is almost exactly the way it was—it all went according to my imagination—except the moment that cut me off. This sudden, however temporary, arrest of my memory I had not anticipated: I had not understood that I would indeed cease to perceive to be and thus to remember that I ceased. I had not anticipated such a vast force, so instant, so irrevocable, so shamelessly faster than the speed of my perception.

Finding the day of dissolution at hand, her crime being of too high a nature to admit her longer continuance on earth, she appeared to be in great confusion, from the unsettled state of her mind concerning her imminent death.

There was no possibility to make my escape, every thought turning my enemy at the last extremity. Yet, being inextricably fixed in the moment after it happened, I can but remember the moment before the moment it happened. I can do nothing but remember nor can I abstain from attempting to uncover, or rather: to invent just what it was that I had in the end decided would be my last thought. Or had I never arrived at a decision? I have been pondering this question. I cannot recall if I had ever resolved with myself to come to a decision on what my final thought ought to be. It was a momentous decision and one that could not easily be cast aside as nonsense. It was almost all that I was thinking since I was sentenced, all that my mind was absorbed by; nothing else was of importance to me then, not my former life, nor the future that I did not have, not even the sentence itself.

In order to aid my capacity to remember what it exactly was that my ultimate thought reflected, I have been considering to retrace the very decision that must have preceded the possible actualization of that which I had decided. To that decision, I mused, I might have access, because the decision must have happened at a time when I was still able to perceive and thus remember. My potential for conscious recollection of the decision that I must have formed with regard to what it is that I ought to think last, is greater than the potential to recall what of that decision was put into action, that is, my last thought, for this must have occurred during the most fatal, most traumatizing event I have ever lived to experience. What I do remember and must be sure of, is the fact that I was, preceding my death, perpetually considering possible topics for my final thoughts. I know this to be true for I am in possession of my writings. Yet this is only in order to proof that the aforementioned consideration regarding the uncovering of a decision about my final thoughts is founded upon evidence, which I deem so conclusive, that I cannot but believe that I must have finalized my decision. I must admit to a spark of a doubt present, which challenges the very existence of such a

7

decision ever having been made by me. Supported with unshaken resolution I am determined to further explore the matter.

I was entirely unprepared, for the circumstance of knowing the hour of death was never by me anticipated, nor was it anticipated that I should worry myself with the substance of my thinking during that last hour and finally during the last moment of my life, nor further more that, after it happened, I should still concern myself with those thoughts which—even worse: I still cannot recall. It is no longer within my power to return. There is no possibility to make my escape, every thought having turned my enemy at the last extremity. It all had happened much too fast. The insurmountable loss of memory prevents me, unfortunately, from achieving precisely that which I am so eager to discern and am so perpetually occupied by: The very decision on what my thought ought to be during the brief moment I knew to be my last. Assuming that I have never in fact made any such decision as aforementioned, I could conclude, as a possible solution, that I may make it now, retrospectively as it were. I would have delighted in the prospect of this. But perhaps my impending, retroactive decision will supersede, or undermine the possibility of coming upon, the original one, if after all there was one, an eventuality that can and should never by me be wholly excluded or overlooked; though I shall possibly not be able to be entirely sure of the mere existence of such an ultimate thought, let alone its content. This returns me to the search for the decision, for it is likely that in the weight of the uncertainties regarding the mere existence of a last thought, the preceding decision might just be what is of greater significance. Perhaps the actualization of the thought is, because it may be for ever unrecoverable, therefore irrelevant. However, this inversion of the problem entails precisely the same uncertainty: If there never was a decision—a possibility which cannot after all entirely be ruled out, as discussed earlier—then, what I am so fervently trying to remember would be something that never in fact happened. This takes me yet further into the depth of the matter. My recent concerns have been with the nature of the decision that I have assumedly made regarding the contents of my last thought; but, because I cannot be certain of having implemented that decision, if indeed there was one, why then would my knowledge of that decision be of any relevance to me now? Accordingly, if there never was a decision—it is possible to conceive of my final moment approaching faster than my arriving at a final decision—if there never was one, I may nevertheless have had some final thoughts. In consequence of this affirmation, what am I to do, should the content of my last musing never become known to me?

And now: When shall I decide that this is the case? In answer to the first question, I may decide to at last make a decision on that very content, as though that final thought still needed to be thought. In answer to the second question, I must plainly say, that I do not know at what moment I should determine to have strained my memory and patience to the utmost extent that I could justifiably conclude that any further attempts at receiving intelligence of the thought I assume to have had, will yield no result. It appears to me still now, from what I have stated thus far, that my first step ought to be to arrive at a decision as to what further considerations I should have, before I may safely conclude that knowledge of my actual last thought shall never be obtained by me, either because the impact of my dissolution was so disgraceful that it expelled from me all potential for the continence of memory, or that because I did not succeed to think at all during a moment that may well have been so exactingly abridged that it offered no duration at all. Respecting all that has thus far been stated, the moment of resignation, as I still prefer to call it, may have arrived and I ought to ready myself to decide what I should want to think, knowing that no other thought will ever by me be thought again. That is, the very decision on what my thought ought to have been during the brief moment I know to have been my last, seems to be impending. Every thought turning my enemy at this last extremity, there is no possibility to make my escape.

8

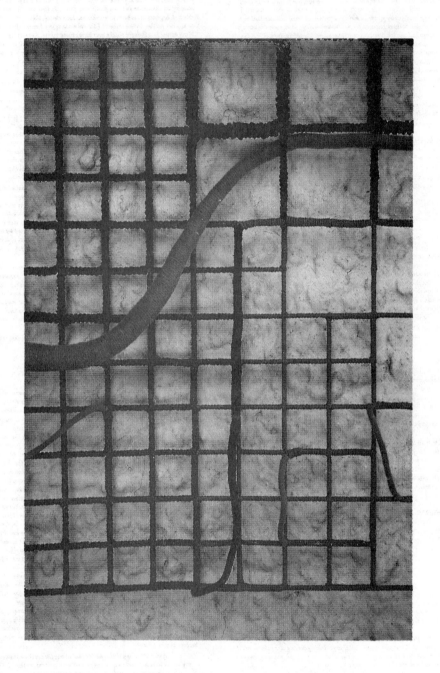

ISABELA PALAU, MALAGÁ, SPAIN

T E   X   T   I   L

C   O   L   I   D   A   L

F L E X I B I L I D A   R

M   E   T   L   A   D

G E O M   E   T   R I   L

F R   A   C   T   A   A

M O V I M I E N T   O

L   U   Z

D I   A   L   O   G   O

S   O   M   B   R   A

A   E   R   E   R   A

L   I   G   E   R   R

N A T U R A L E Z A

F   L   O   T   A   A

F   O   R   M   Z   R

D I N A M I Z A   R

A   Z   A   S

I   S   L   A   N

M   A   E   R   I   A

P R O Y E C C I O R

O R G A N I   C   S

E T A   R   C   A

T E C N R   C   A

A I C I N R   E

E S   P   A   C   I   O

LEIGH BEHNKE, NEW YORK, NY, USA

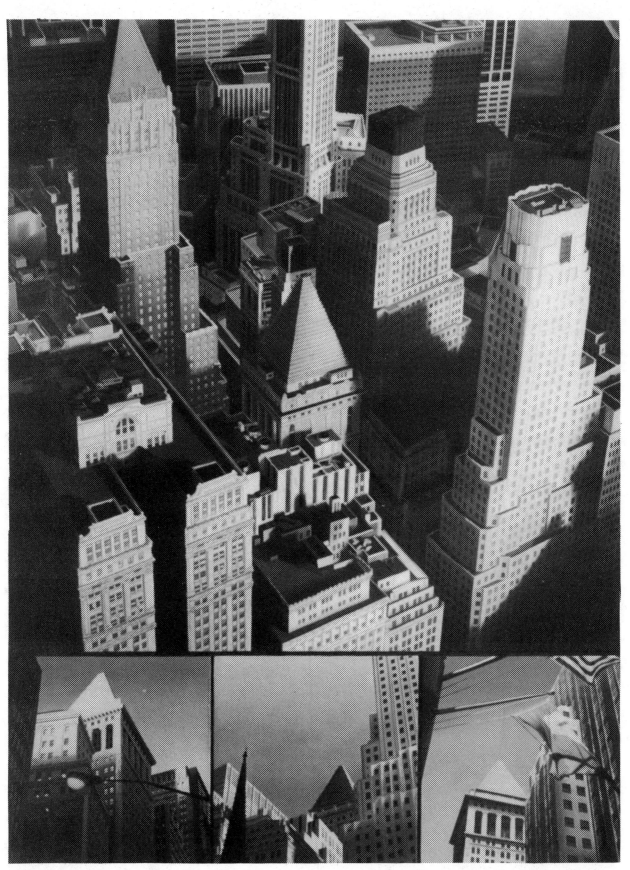

Wallace's Heresy   Leigh Behnke

LEIGH BEHNKE, NEW YORK, NY, USA

Alfred Russel Wallace (1823-1913) and Charles Darwin (1809-1882) came independently to the notions of evolution now associated with Darwin.

They met in 1862, four years after their individual works had been simultaneously published, and ex--changed ideas for their remaining lives.

In 1871 Wallace wrote to Darwin that he was unconvinced by the appli-cation of natural selection as app-lied to humans. His "special heresy" was that human mental and spiritual development was non-Darwinian in origin and the harbinger of some other, higher process.

<u>Wallace's Heresy</u> poses one of the central unanswered questions in the development of all species.

<u>Wallace's Heresy</u>, 1995,Leigh Behnke

DENISE MARIKA, BROOKLINE, MA, USA

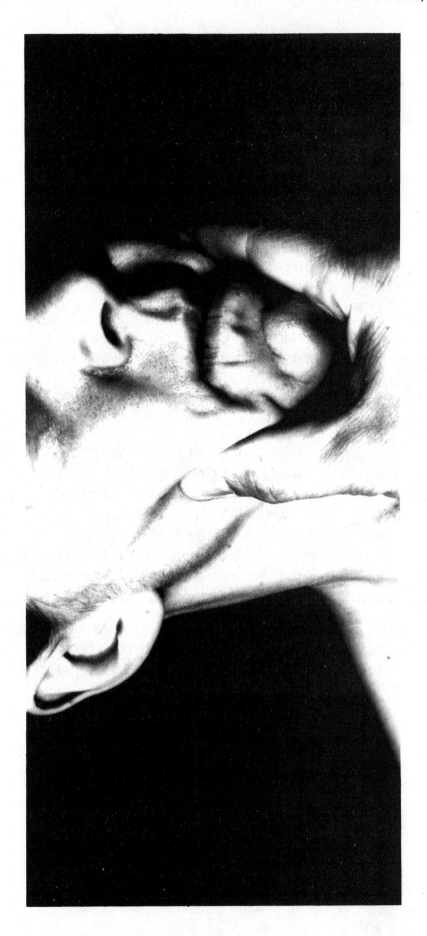

DENISE MARIKA, BROOKLINE, MA, USA

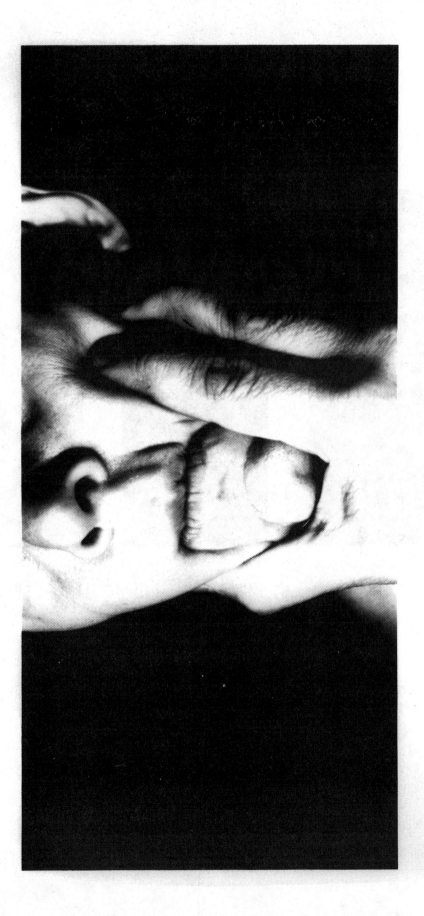

DENISE MARIKA "FACE TO FACE" 1991
Photo series / video sculpture

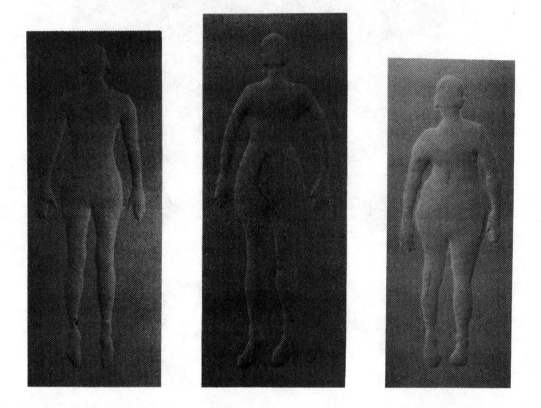

Self Portrait with Mother and Grandmother

ALEXANDRA MCGOVERN, NEW YORK, NY, USA

Alexandra McGovern
135 hudson Street #5R
New York, NY 10013

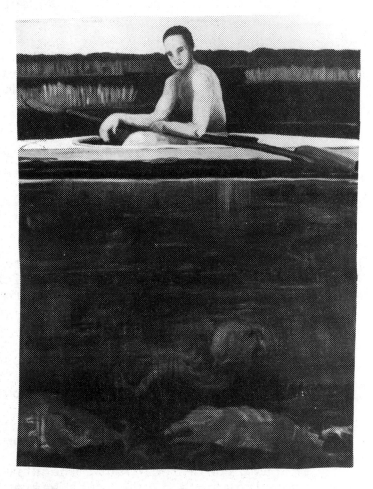

<u>The Marshes,</u> 1994
30"X24", oil on canvas

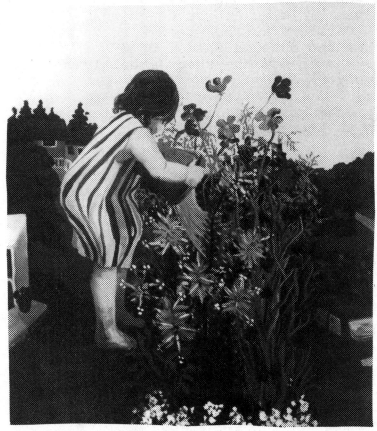

<u>Miracle Grow,</u> 1994
44"X40", oil on canvas

Three questions from Claude Rutault to **Rosemarie Castoro**
in the form of a Fax interview for publication in
Le *Journal de Expositions*:

*Q: In all your working time, what is the work that you think
has the most strength and actualization?*

A: As I am every age I have ever been, I am responsible for
all the work I have ever made. I take out of each work a seed
that I cultivate.

For example, To make the transitory permanent, I fused
graphite, (transitory), onto thickened gesso broom strokes
painted on a solid masonite board, which I cut out with a hand
held saber saw. The spontaneous broom stroke was executed in a
gesture of imperative necessity. The rest was carpentry
(permanent), and as my own best assistant, executed. I had used
graphite pencil (seed) on canvasses in the past. To make the
transitory nature of drawing to become as solid and permanent
as painting and sculpture, the boundaries of the three
disciplines were transgressed.

These strokes became the seed for relational groupings in how I
was perceiving people, and how I was looking into myself:
choreographic sociology. The stroke became linear, the
groupings more dense. Wire was added to the same material, a
need to communicate when I was Visiting Artist teaching
sculpture for two months in California. The steel wire inside
two pieces of masonite became the outside shadow of my
"underconsciousness" series and is now the sheet steel I am
welding to dimension the line.

*Q: Is there a work, a body of works or a direction which is
today distant or aloof from your preoccupations?*

A: Painting. Still, I love to see painting. There is a romance
about painting. I consider myself a sculptor but I probably
think like a painter, with three dimensional responsibilities.
My paintings from 1964-1969 are rolled up except for a few
small gems. They are investigations into the nature of
rhythmical discipline, of wall building with paint, of decision
making, of thinking and doing. One of the decisions was to
eliminate all but one color, so that structure would become
prominent without the distraction of color. Through monochrome
painting, I was able to isolate a predominant shape, the "Y". I

followed the "Y"'s extension to the edges of the canvas, which led to a grid structure. In eliminating the initial "Y", and the grid, I concentrated on one angle and its manner of dynamics on the canvas, brushing in thinned paint and reinforcing the one angle with colored pencils.

The decision to eliminate all but one angle placed me in a gray space and time and led me to investigate my activities with a stop watch which led me to take inventory of my world surroundings. I "cracked" open my space with metal tape that led to wall building with free-standing panels painted with giant broom strokes.

Q: *Is there a work you have never been able to make? Why? What would you need to make it today?*

If there is a "never", there is always a "way". Artists think of the most unlikely scenarios and find a way. I dreamt of a tall ladder that came out of the chimney of a house. The ladder was as tall as a small airplane could fly. I understand the economics of vision. I never made that work, but I started with the action of the ladder as it bent over beaches, under bridges, around small towns. I made that ladder perform in concert with like-minded other ladders. The ladder fragmented and became a graphic symbol for a tree trunk. I started using trees rescued from the back of a pickup truck while I was Visiting Artist for sculpture in Boulder, Colorado. The "Flasher" at first was a tree trunk. Groups of 8' tall black painted metal "Flashers" were made for the three levels of the theater at ArtPark, Lewiston, New York. They have since been choreographed and were temporarily installed for two outdoor street areas in New York City.

There is a work I would make: Three 12' tall concrete "Flashers" in choreographic proximity to one another.

I started with three 4' tall concrete works built in my studio (now outdoors in New Jersey at Hal Bromm's residence), one 9' tall Paris Flasher at the old American Canter on Boulevard Raspail, and one 12' tall Ethereal Concrete Flasher at Socrates Sculpture Park, Long Island City. It is now on 43rd Street between 9 & 10 Avenues in New York City.

What do I need? A construction crew, money, materials, and a site.

Rosemarie Castoro
February 10, 1995

CARLA KIRKWOOD, NORTHHAMPTON, MA, USA

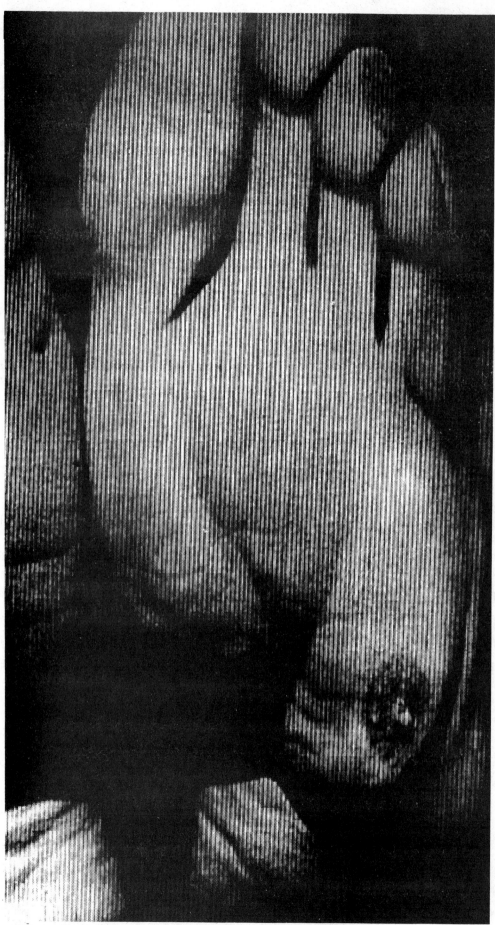

She is running, running very fast. It is the first time she has been on her feet since the surgery, since the operation to remove the bone left by the accident. It hurts to be so upright, every muscle tensed, moving so decisively, cutting the wind in half with every step. She is laughing. She doesn't stop to think where she is running. She doesn't hear her mother's voice very clearly anymore.

She wants something new, she doesn't yet know what.

CARLA KIRKWOOD, NORTHHAMPTON, MA, USA

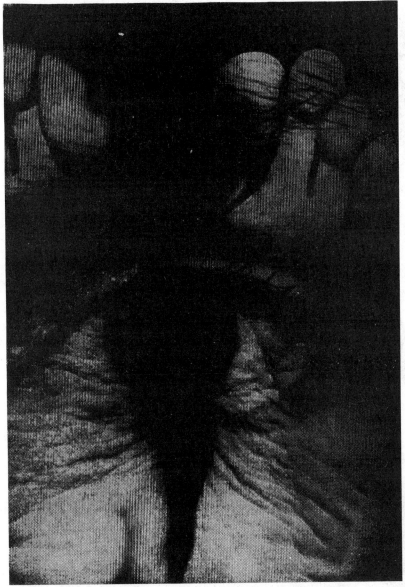

running, her mind making more noise than the sound of her bare feet hitting the pavement. She is trying to position herself in the race. Taking a path that is laid out by friends. She turns her head to the road. She runs naked through the streets, she finds the ocean. She runs for days. The sound of singing emanates from her torso. Her feet move over rock and sand. She finds her house. She falls asleep on the rug. She dreams of water, glass, steel and fire.

She is glad to be on her feet again, glad to feel the power of her own body, separated from the wound. In the place where the surgery was done she had a lot of time to think, to pull things back together, throwing out the useless things and grabbing ahold of things she felt had all but disappeared.

She thinks about her life as she is

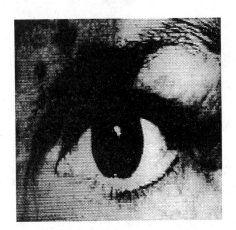

Images and text
Carla Kirkwood

Photographer - S. Chapman • Computer layout - S. Rush & C. Kirkwood

KATIA SANTIBAÑEZ, NEW YORK, NY, USA

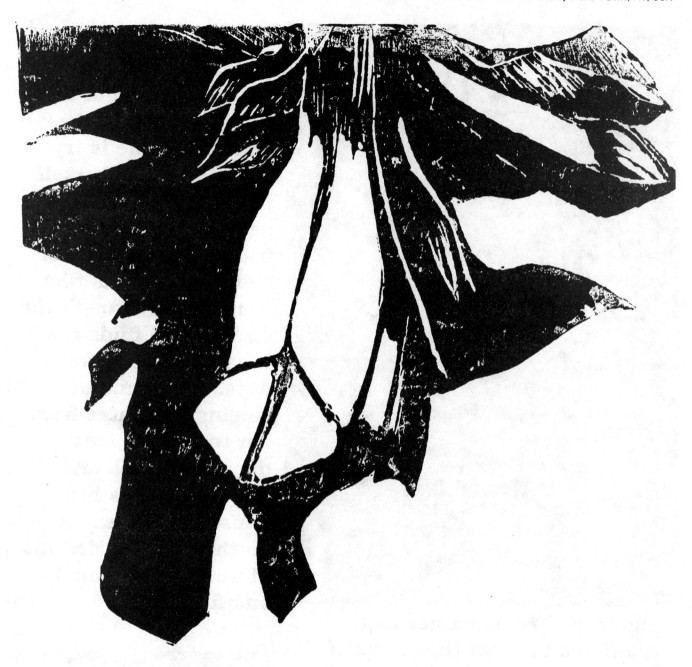

JOAN BANKEMPER, NEW YORK, NY, USA

Fertility- Abortion
"The Medicinal Garden
For a Woman's Choice"

Joan Bankemper
1995

In this garden I am growing Red Clover, Motherwort and Black
Cohosh. Red Clover is used as a tea to increase fertility.
Motherwort and Black Cohosh are used to bring on menstruations-
to cause an abortion.

This is a garden made for a woman.
It is not a garden about morals, it is a garden about choice.

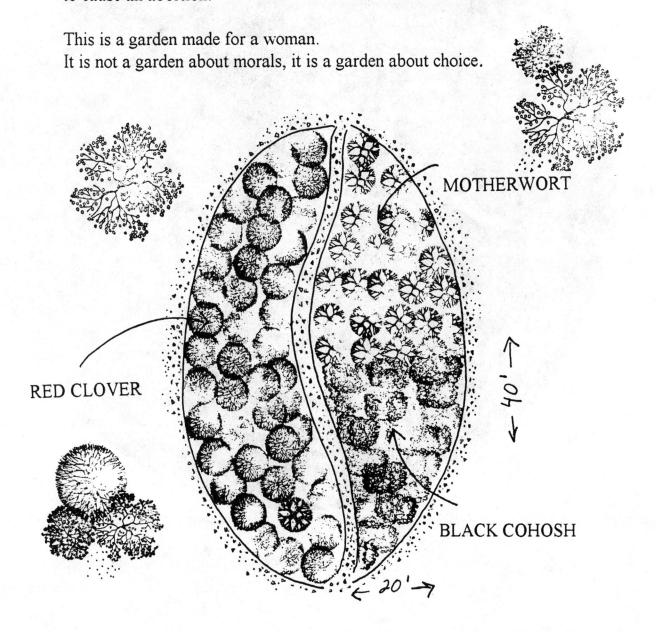

MOTHERWORT

RED CLOVER

BLACK COHOSH

← 40' →

← 20' →

CRISTINA BIAGGI, PALISADES, NY, USA

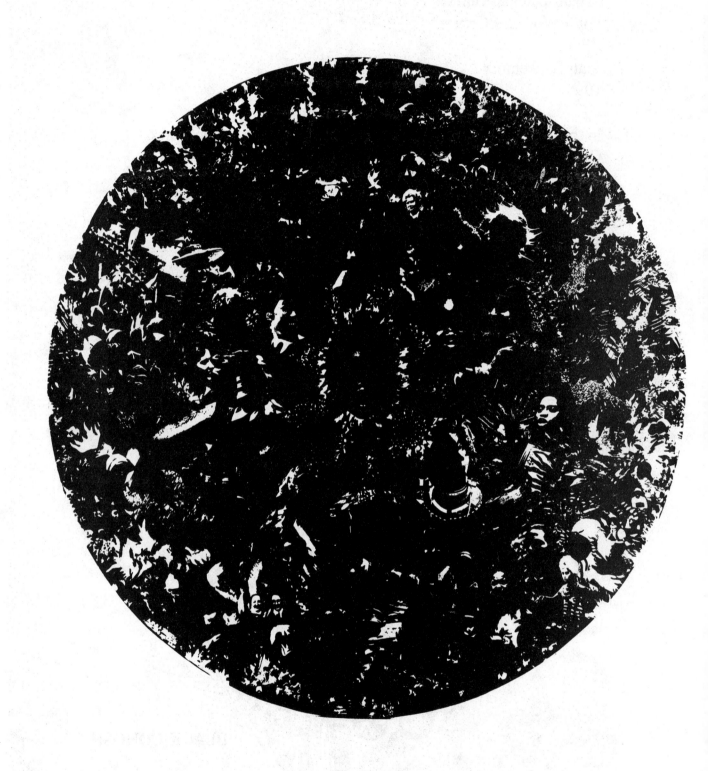

ANNE RUSSINOF, BROOKLYN, NY, USA

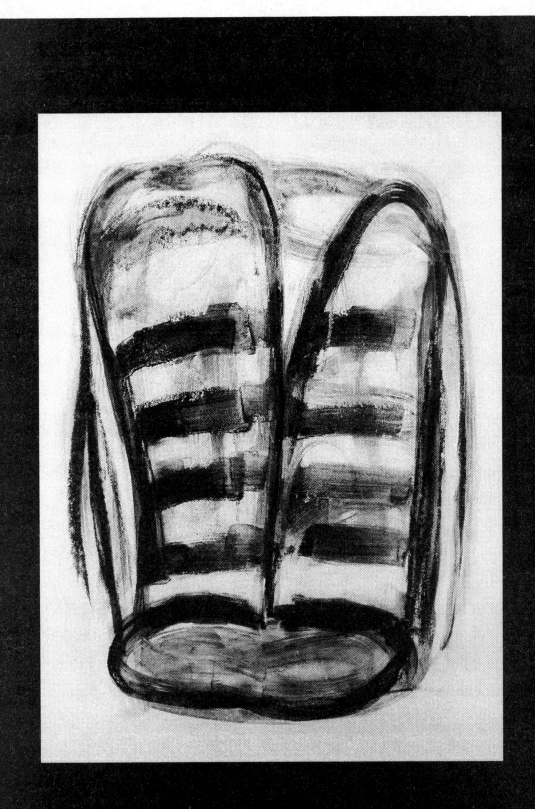

"Vest" charcoal and gesso 1994
© *Anne Russinof   1208 8th Avenue Brooklyn, NY 11215 (718)768-8992*

ANNE RUSSINOF, BROOKLYN, NY, USA

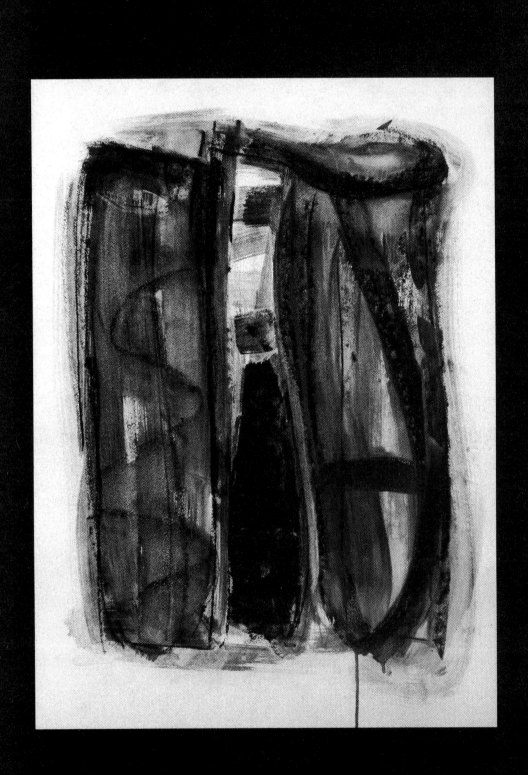

"Breather" charcoal and gesso 1994
© *Anne Russinof   1208 8th Avenue Brooklyn, NY 11215 (718)768-8992*

Victoria Uchalova, ST PETERSBURG, RUSSIA

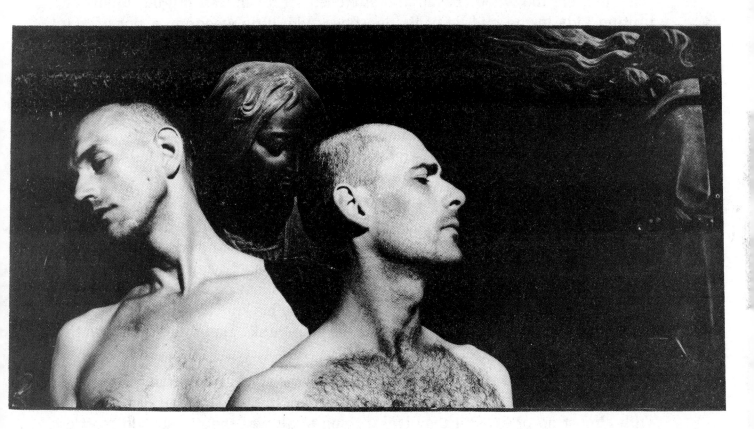

JOYCEANN MASTERS, NEW YORK, NY, USA

FILTERING
by
Joyceann Masters

Iused to go into the woods with boys. They wore their hair over their eyes, flicking it back with a swift upward nod of the chin. They wore sneakers with magic marker initials bleeding through the canvas. They were pale boys in black jeans, with slick smiles and bad teeth-- almost teenagers. I'd ride my purple boy's stingray bicycle down to the back of the elementary school where the woods began and stretched on for miles bridging towns and uniting kids in the middle of its denseness like little weeds in a pot of giant lillies. We all seemed so ordinary in that extraordinary place where animals crawled on their bellies and berries grew and light filtered over fiddleback ferns as gently as mist on your face. The ground crackled with life-- dry leaves, moss-covered rocks moving under our feet. We were spiders riding light.

We hid our bicycles in brush and ambled deeper into the place where day never looked quite the same. You could find anything in the woods, parts of peoples lives dumped there, melting with the afternoon.

I didn't want girlfriends. I just wanted to be the girl who was part of this caravan that walked around in a place as close to underworld-ly as we could get. I went to the woods to use L.J.'s pocketknife, flick it open and see it slice through a stem, see the milky blood trickle onto my hands. I went to feel my heart rumbling, wondering what we'd find during our silent parade. I went there to sit on logs and smell L.J.'s punks burning down to his knuckles, burning holes in yellow strips of newspaper. I wanted to see the punks glowing like insects that turned orange in the breeze.

We found lots of things, the arm of an ax, the springs of a chair, the bottom of a man's pajamas, oil cans, a rusted trap, jars of buttons, bites of fur, beer cans with almost no print. But the biggest thing of all was the pin-striped mattress we came across under a tangle of thick grape vines.

I watched L.J. and P. Haw eyeing it. They poked it with sticks, kicked it, spoke to it-- asked it how it was. They sliced away the grape vines. The sun hit the back of their dark heads and shone white and round. I watched their bodies, the way they kicked in short, fast jabs, the way L.J.'s back showed through a rip in his plaid shirt. I watched sweat run from his temples and pool up with dirt near his ear and trickle down, staining the side of his cheek. I saw P. Haw laughing, poking the mattress as though it had ribs, his small face beaming, shadows darkening his eyes and striping his chest. I kept moving closer to L.J., silently trying to get just close enough to touch him but never actually doing it.

JOYCEANN MASTERS, NEW YORK, NY, USA

We all piled onto the mattress and jumped as hard as we could. We pounded it, bouncing and laughing, wondering whose it had been. There were no urine stains. I felt my body tiring but kept up, jumping, falling and picking myself back up, staying out from under L.J.'s feet. On the count of three we all held hands, sprung up and fell onto the mattress laughing. The afternoon began to die and we sat watching it slide through the trees, fall to their trunks and lay there burning golden with the blue evening above it.

We got our bikes and headed away. For a moment L.J. met my stare. We rode off in the different directions to our homes. We rode without arms, slumped over the high handlebars, our heads slouching into our shoulders. I watched L.J. head off with something more than a smile on his face.

I could feel my head sweating. I could feel myself sweating all over. And I could smell it. I felt it trickling down my chest and then I felt it gathering in the pocket where my arm was bent. I took a finger and drew the sweat up toward my armpit. I felt the little breeze I was making, drying the line of moisture as I drew. And all I could think of was the way the sweat had streaked L.J.'s face, the way I didn't mind his small grey teeth, or the thin ribbed back I'd seen through the rip in his shirt. I rode along as the sun finally gave into the earth, leaving only the faintest red glow over fields. And as I rode I felt something moist between my legs, something that sneaked out as I pedaled faster, something that wasn't sweat at all but had to do with the feeling of sweat and the image of it on L.J.'s face.

No one had said anything but the next day L.J. was waiting by the woods. I rode up, let my legs straddle over the bar. I looked around for sight of P. Haw but I knew he wouldn't be there.

We hid our bikes and went deep into the woods and with each step I felt myself growing less and less aware of what I was passing. I let the feeling in my heart take over for my eyes, skip over the light, the still air, the leaves moving beneath us, the spots of sun on our feet.

Our mattress was still there. Our muddy footprints had dried and we brushed them into dust. Without saying a word we sat, and without glancing around us we started to kiss. I kept my eyes open and watched his closed ones, thinking how fast they seemed to be moving, wondering if I was suppose to close mine. As we leaned back onto the mattress I saw a blur of green leaves. I closed my eyes as L.J.'s hands traveled my body. And as each part of me became known to him, I felt the mystery of the place slipping away, losing itself under the shadows of trees.

THE END

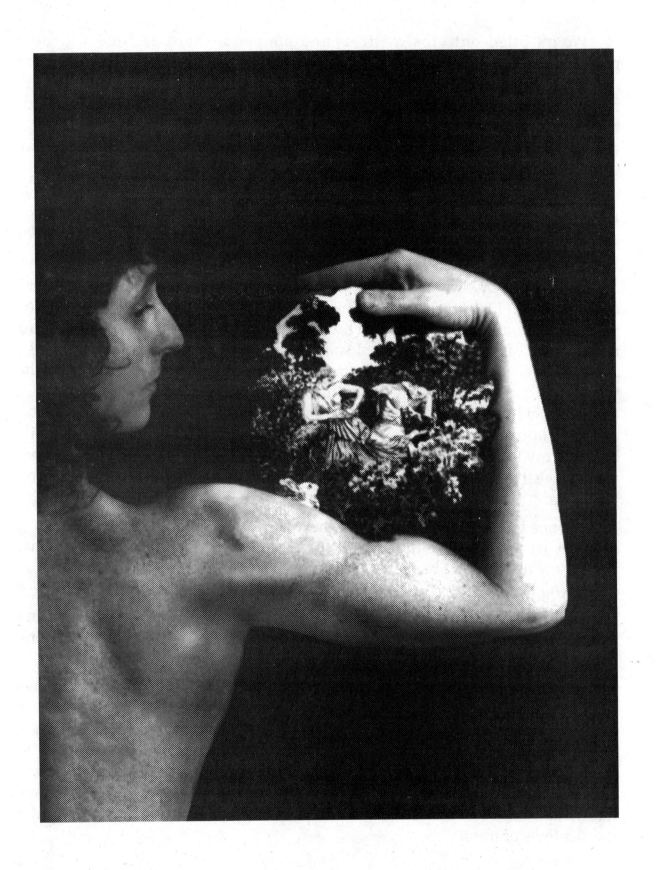

Betty Tompkins,
Limb from Limb, 1993.

BETTY TOMPKINS, NEW YORK, NY, USA

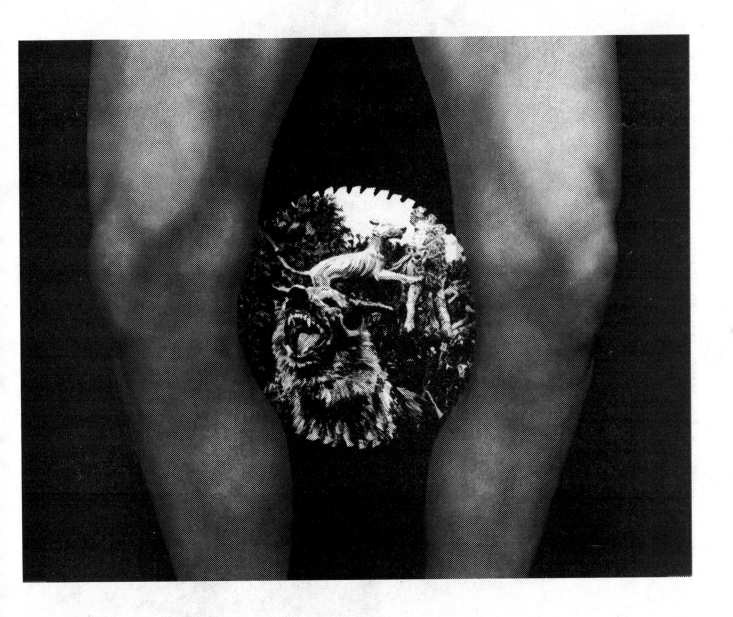

Betty Tompkins, *Bitch*, 1994.

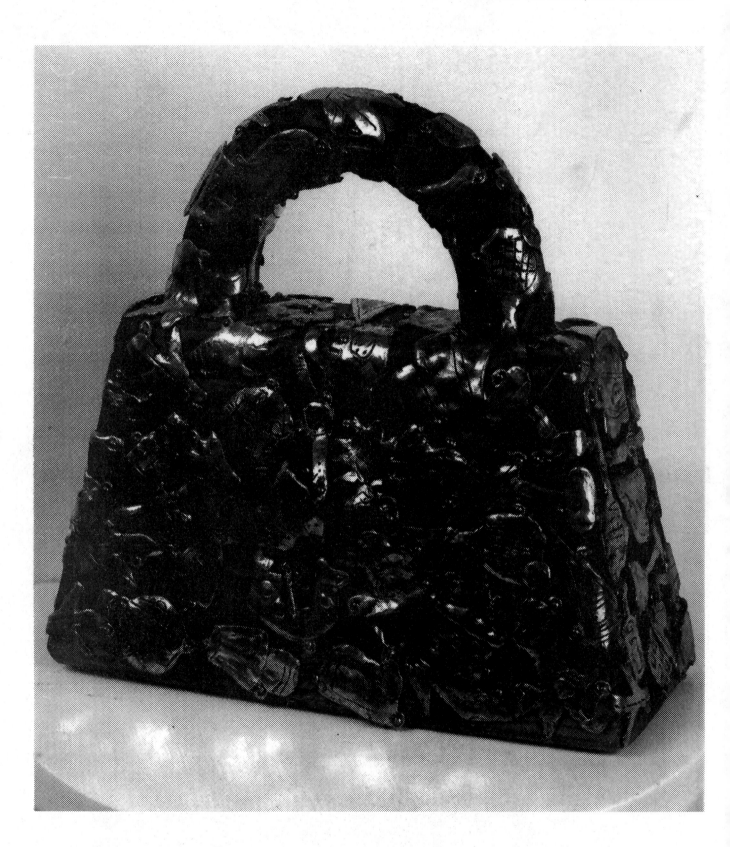

Claudia DeMonte,
Female Fetish: Handbag,
1993, wood, pewter, 9" X 9" X 3½".

ELISABETH KLEY, NEW YORK, NY, USA

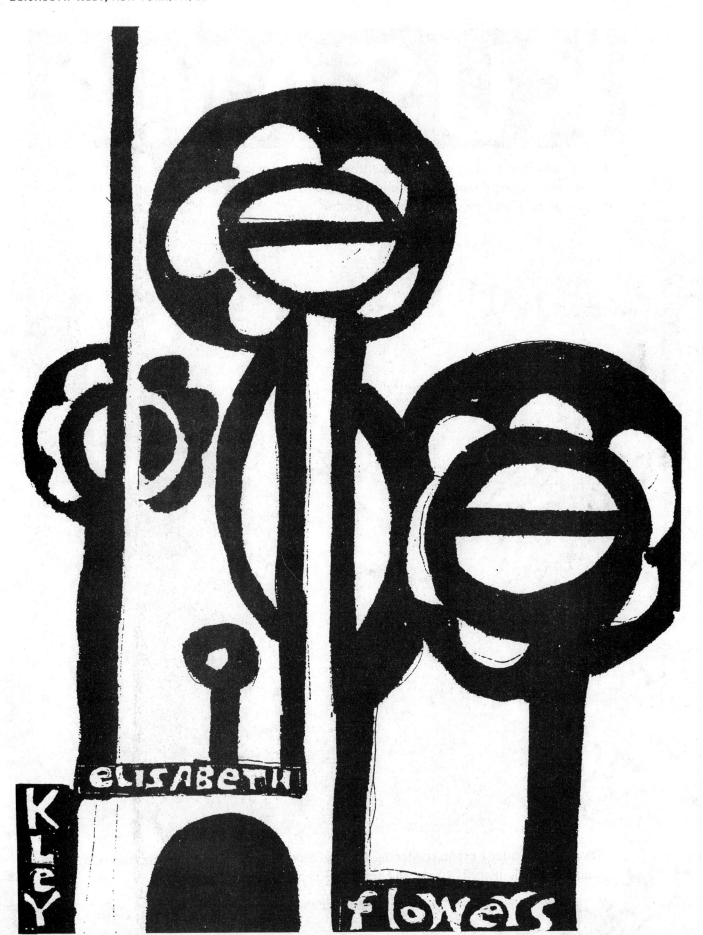

KUSAMA

I have described the origin of the repetitive vision so basic to my imagery as coming from hallucinations I experienced as a child, and intermittently ever since. My art-making is both the symptom of and the cure for my Obsession.

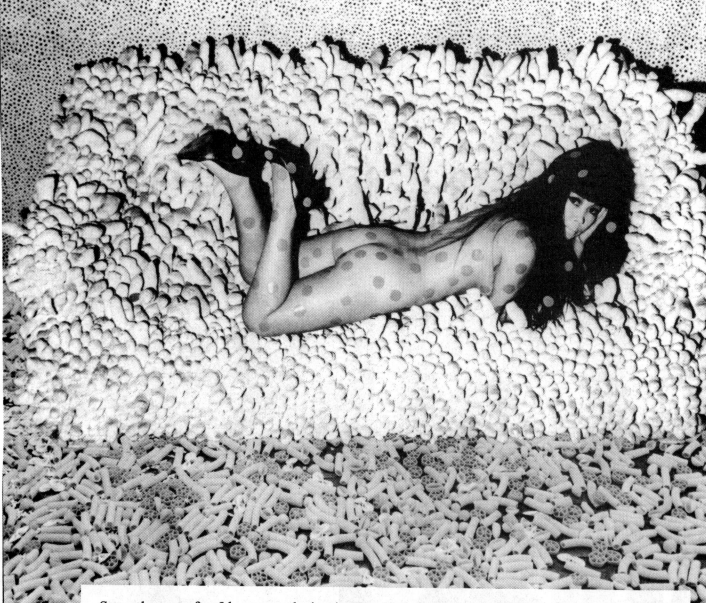

Several years after I began producing in New York, I developed infinite meshes of a net into sculptures with images of food and sex. This is a Sex Food Obsession.

YAYOI KUSAMA, TOKYO, JAPAN

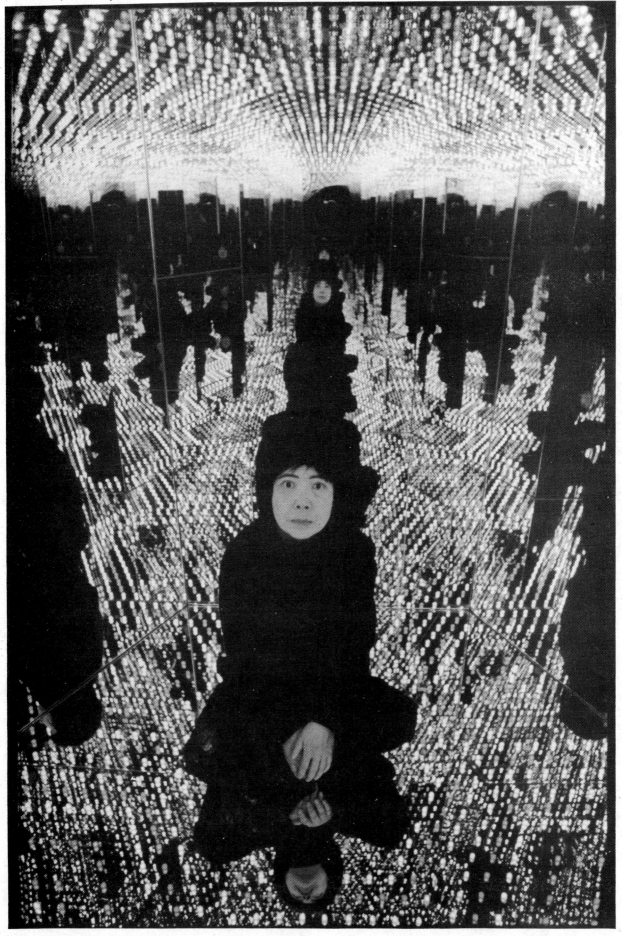

SUSAN EDWARDS, BOULDER, CO, USA

DREAM ELIXIR   O Peregrina, Go to The Lady With The Pomegranate   Tomb of Mother's Blood   Where the many-seeded apple gives birth through the pillared womb of Solomon   O Exile, Drink Astarte's sour and sweet juice   Pierce the veil   Fecundate thunder   Sound Amnesty for the New World   O Pilgrim, Your hair a slice of Pomegranate   the rind tough   the tears garnet   No one said it would be easy   S.H.E.

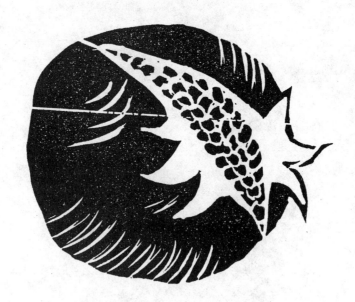

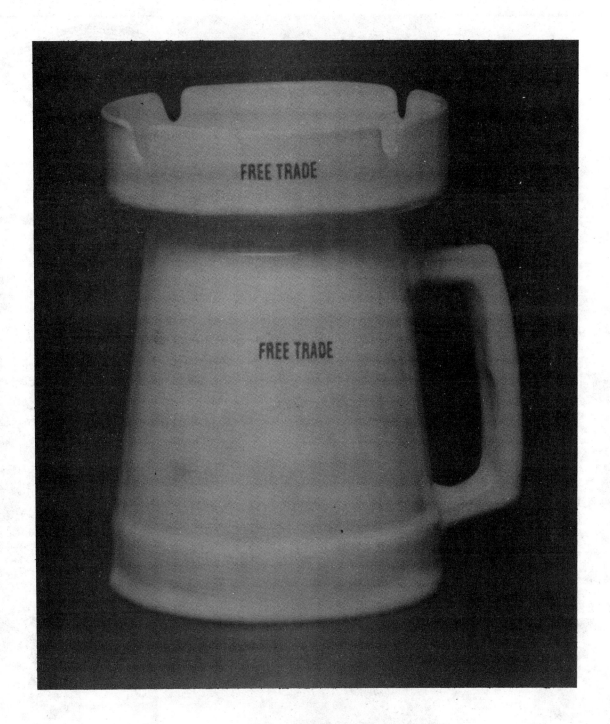

FREE TRADE
Mug with Ashtray

Jackie Chang   Brooklyn, New York

Completed through the generosity of the John Micheal Kohler Arts Center, Art/Industry Program, Sheboygan, Wisconson.

LIZ YOUNG, LOS ANGELES, CA, USA

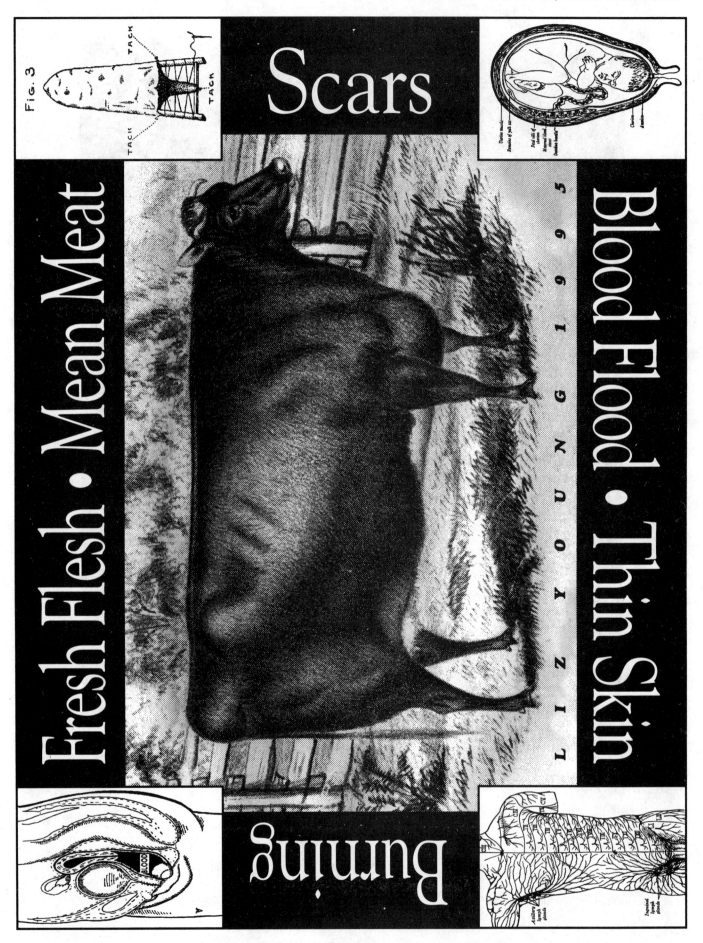

Scars

Blood Flood • Thin Skin

LIZ YOUNG 1995

Fresh Flesh • Mean Meat

Burning

FIG. 3

LAURA STEIN, NEW YORK, NY, USA

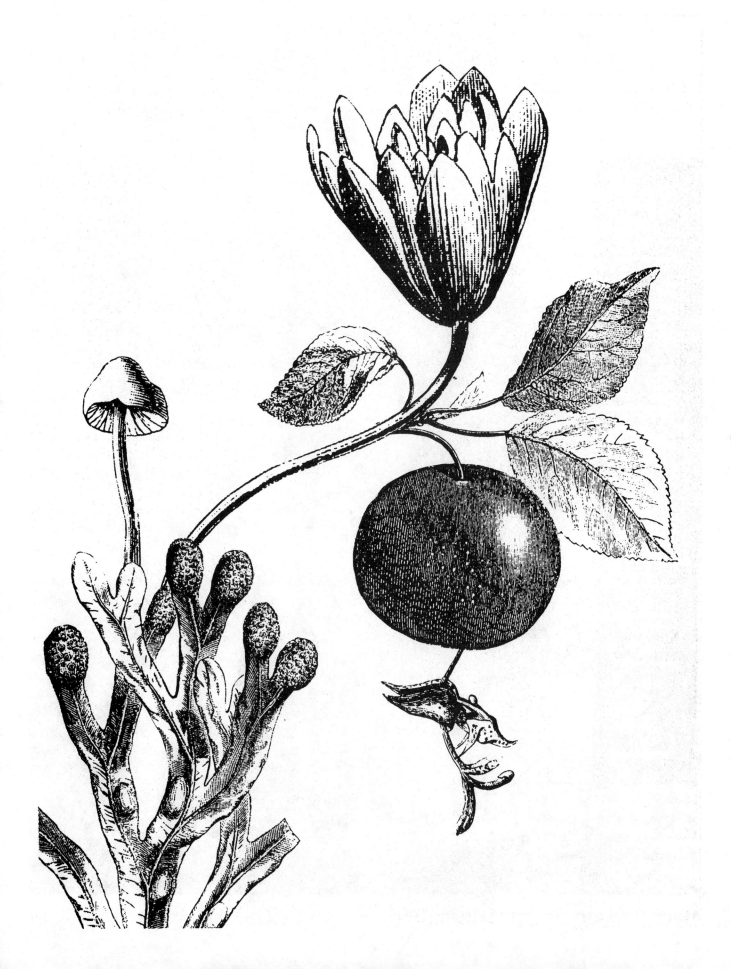

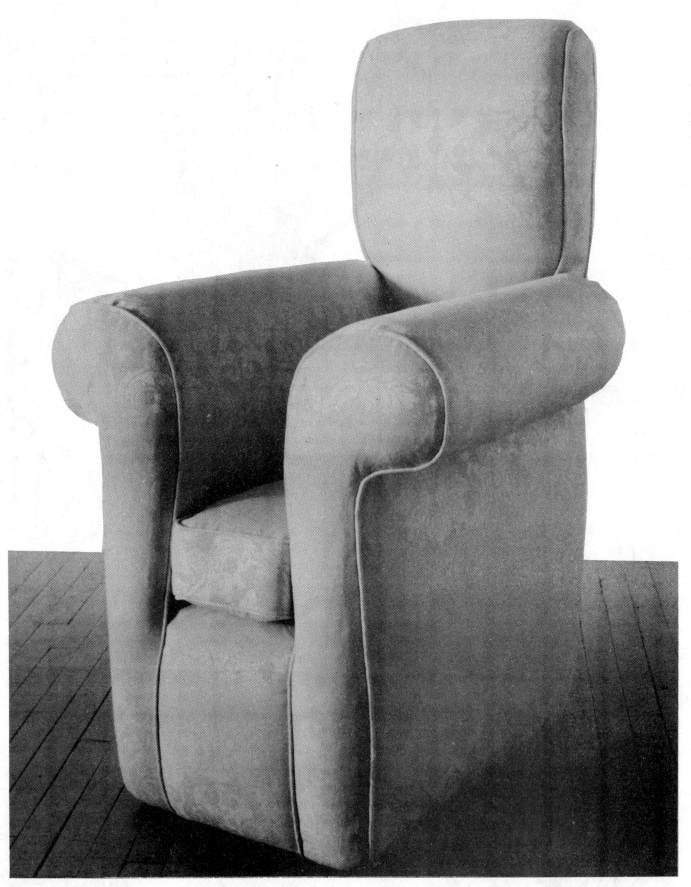

Mary Carlson, *Brocade Chair*, 1995, 45 x 28 x 32", wood, batting and fabric

MAJA GSPAN VICIC, LIVARSKA, SLOVANIA

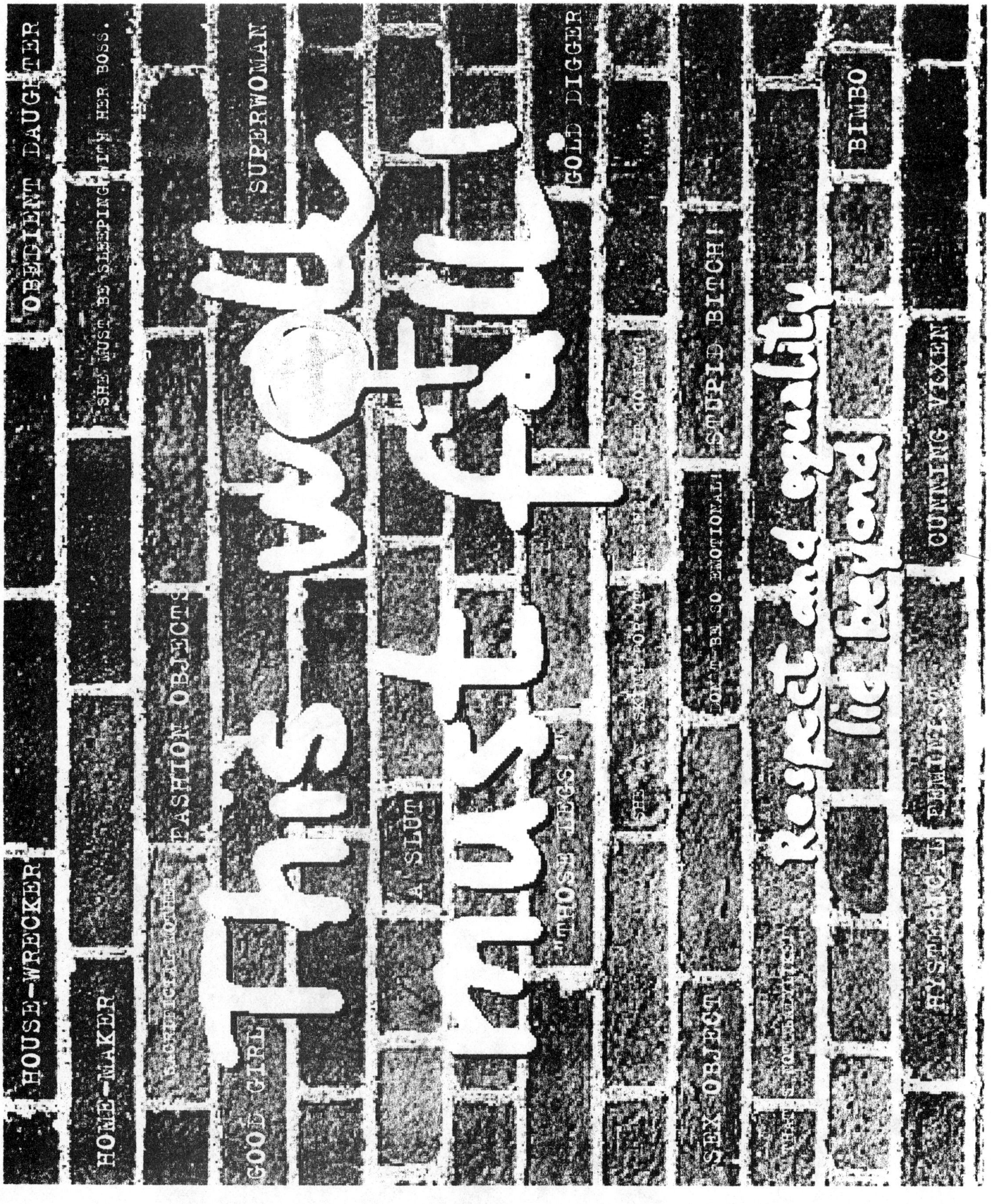

This will just must still just

This will just

This must still

OBEDIENT DAUGHTER

SHE MUST BE SLEEPING WITH HER BOSS.

SUPERWOMAN

GOLD DIGGER

BIMBO

STUPID BITCH!

DON'T BE SO EMOTIONAL!

CUNNING VIXEN

HOUSE-WRECKER

HOME-MAKER

FASHION OBJECTS

GOOD GIRL

A SLUT

THOSE LEGS!

SEX OBJECT

HYSTERICAL

Respect and equality lie beyond

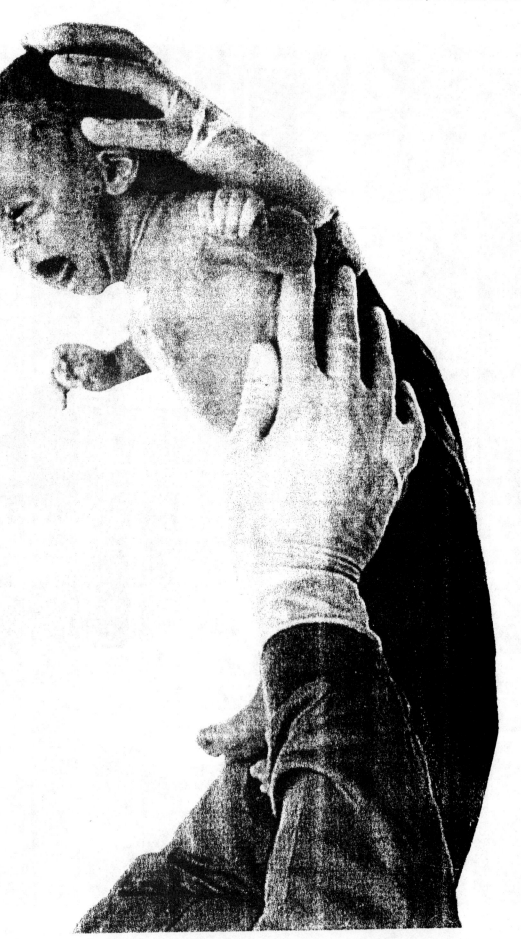

"IT'S A GIRL!

SHE'LL DO THE IRONING FOR YOU."

GERDA PEER, VIENNA, AUSTRIA

"Domino"

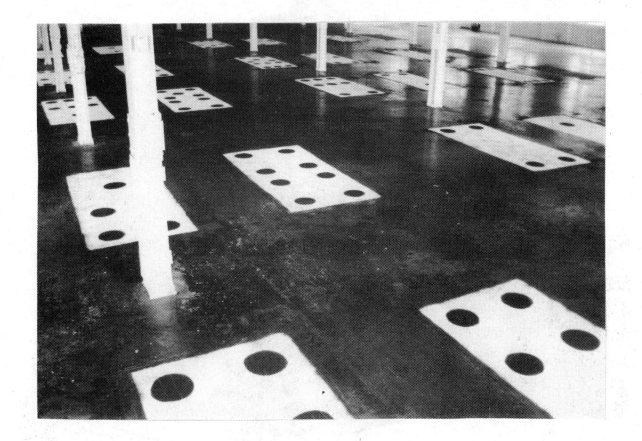

Gerda Peer
Gassergasse 2-8/3
A-1050 Vienna

RUTH HARDINGER, NEW YORK, NY, USA

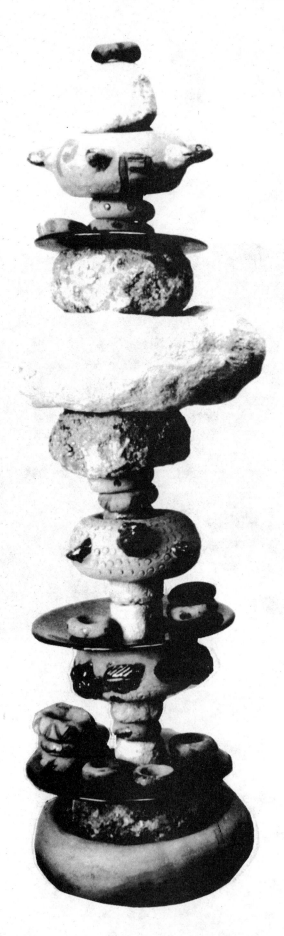

DIANNA COHEN, PACIFIC PALISADES, CA, USA

Oh the waste

We all live like there is no tomorrow. Yet, we wake up each new day with no thought to the future. No recognition that each "new" day is the future. That it all starts today. No guilt, no feeling of responsibility. We must be insane. to think that we can create, pollute, & throw things away... Somewhere else. And that all of this refuse will somehow simply dissappear - vanish into the air. Imagine life over a 10 or 20 year period - expand your overview of time... current recycling efforts seem futile. They must be reconceived. Think in terms of a continuum - a cycle.

In my perfect world there would be no "garbage" and no "waste."

RHODA MUCHOKI, NAIROBI, KENYA

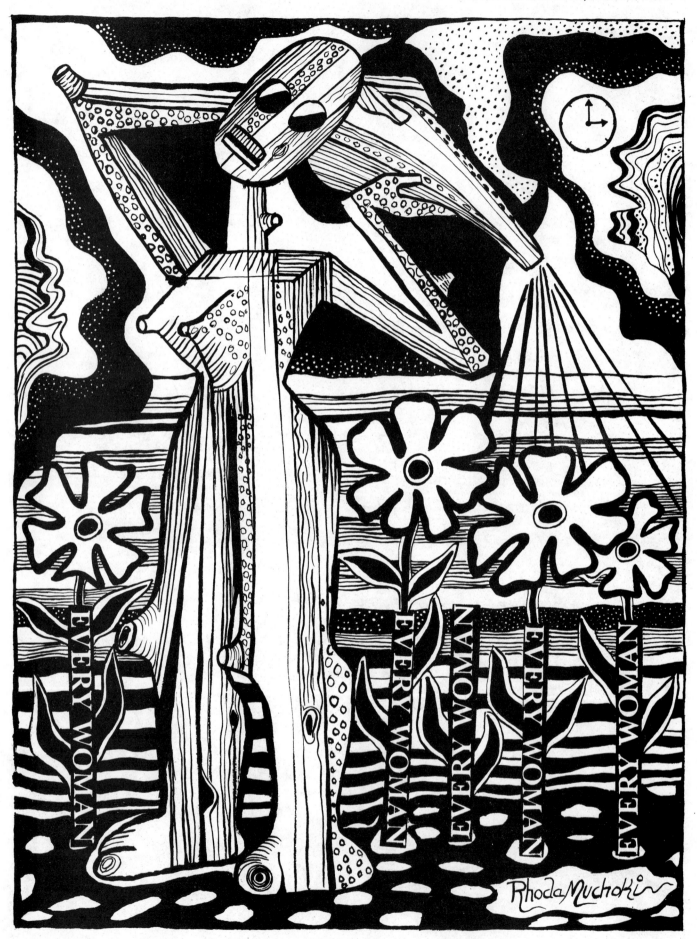

RACHAEL ROMERO, NEW YORK, NY, USA

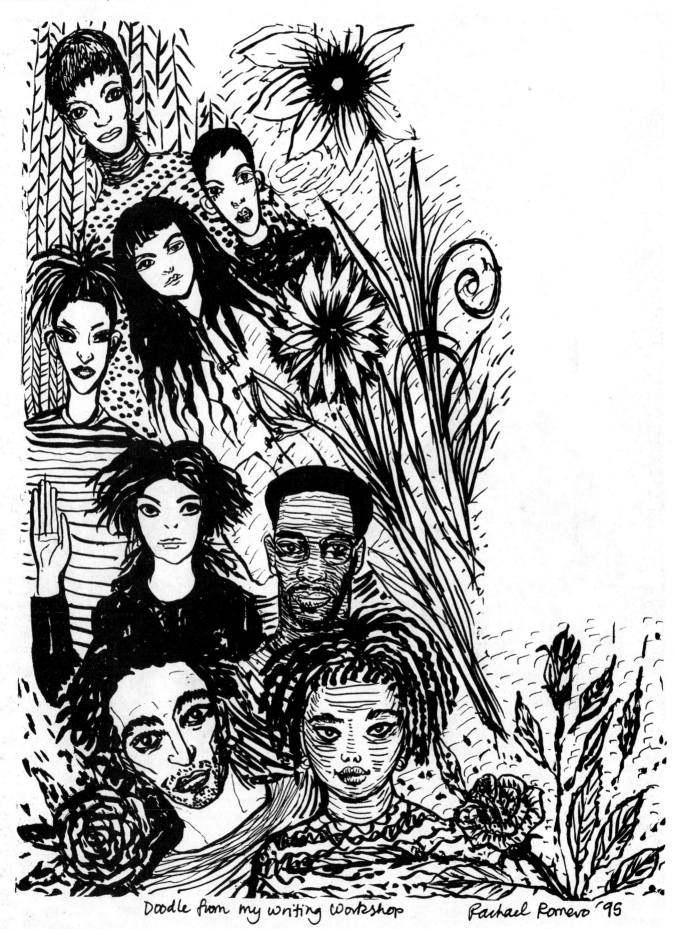

Doodle from my writing Workshop   Rachael Romero '95

DIANA AISENBERG, BUENOS AIRES, ARGENTINA

genesis

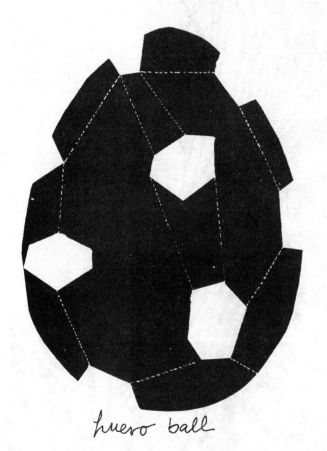

huevo ball

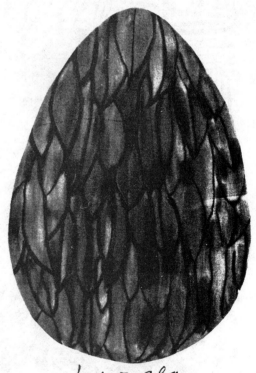

huevo ala

DA95

DIANA AISENBERG, BUENOS AIRES, ARGENTINA

GENESIS

TO KILL   THE GOOSE THATH LAYS THE GOLDEN EGGS.

THE SUFLOWER_EGG/ THE PARAGUAYAN-EGG/ THE WING-EGG/THE GAUCHO-
EGG/THE ARGENTINIAN CAB-EGG/ THE WATTERMELON-EGG/ THE CAW-
EGG/THE SOCCER BALL_EGG/ THE TENNIS-EGG / THE ART -EGG/THE
SOCCERBALL-EGG/ THE BROKEN- EGG/ THE HARDBOILED-EGG/ THE
DESGUSTING -EGG/ THE DADDY &MAMY -EGG/ THE PRETTY-EGG/
THE COCK IN LOVE-EGG?THE CRIOLLOCOUPLE-EGG.

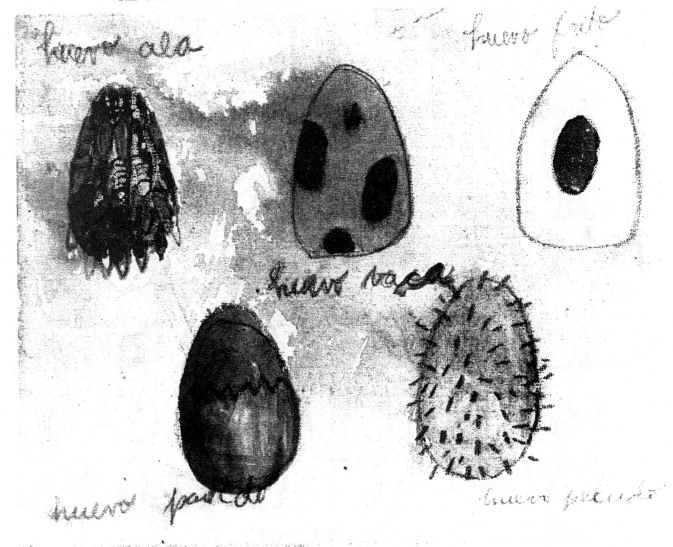

DA 95

SUZANNE ANKER, EAST HAMPTON, NY, USA

GGtTCGTaGcTAA
TCGaTCGTACTAATC
GaCLONALAGCTAA
TCSELEctIONATC
AcTaAtCgAgTAG
CTACTAATCGAG
TAGCTACtaaTCGA
ReproductIVeRIgh
TsGCTACTAATCGA
TAGCTACTAATCGA
GCTACtaaTCGAGt

SUZANNE ANKER, EAST HAMPTON, NY, USA

SUSAN HOELTZEL, NEW YORK, NY, USA

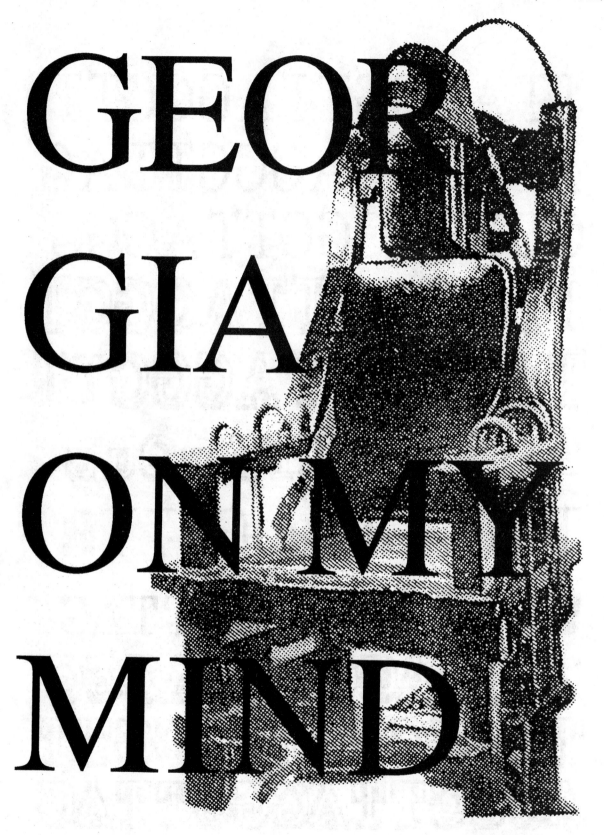

GEOR GIA ON MY MIND

Susan Hoeltzel

NANCY ESAJIAN, SACRAMENTO, CA, USA

1995 * APRIL

The times are ripe for artists. Artists in a myriad of mediums continue to struggle at having a respected voice. The voices are sensitive, thoughtful, colorful and always seem to desire acknowledgment. The emotions expressed are full range, while the personalities repeatedly exhibit strength of character and courage.

The times are ripe for voices. Artists say what is hard to say. They sing songs about what many of us feel. They play instruments in ways that describe places where no words go. Artists perform theatrical vignettes which enliven behaviors which may shock, thrill and or even reassure audiences. Artists portray real and fictional characters that we wish we'd met, that we shudder at the thought of encountering and others that we're satisfied to observe.

The times are ripe for hope. Artists continue to chronicle time. They mark history with paintings, tiles, weavings, photographs, drawings, etchings, prints, rugs, sculptures, fountains, monuments, fabrics, costumes, characters on stage and in film, words, poems, carvings, tombstones, advertisements, earthworks, computer generated images, animated movies and cartoons, sound recordings of voices, nature, instruments and every combination. Artists depict the sacred, the daily and the rare moments of life.

When will artists be honored in ways that reflect these contributions? No way to tell and no way to assume it is not happening on parts of the earth.

My hope and continued effort in the arts is reflective of my earliest teachings at sunday school. Treat others, as you would hope they treat you.

Nancy Lee Esajian, Visual Artist & Public Art Consultant, 1049 38th Street, Suite C, Sacramento, California, 95816-5512, United States.

ANN PHELAN, ELLICOT CITY, MD, USA

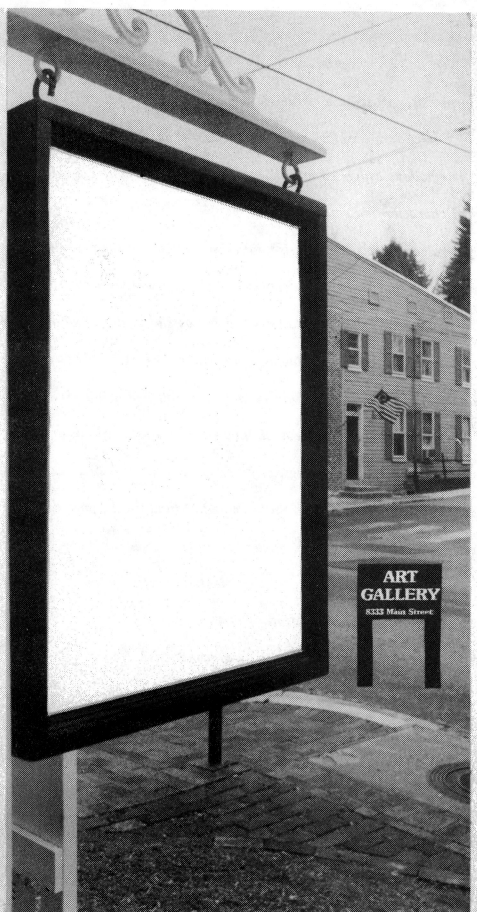

GLOBAL-LOCAL

This space is available
for images or words

ROTATING SIGN EXHIBITION
Ann Phelan
8333 Main Street
Ellicott City
Maryland, 21043
(410)750-7349
Contributers will be
in library and receive
copies of all work
at year's end

Image currently on sign
The Veil of Veronica
April, 1995

With hope,
Saint Veronica
won't be carrying
the same burden
into the next century

ANN PHELAN, ELLICOT CITY, MD, USA

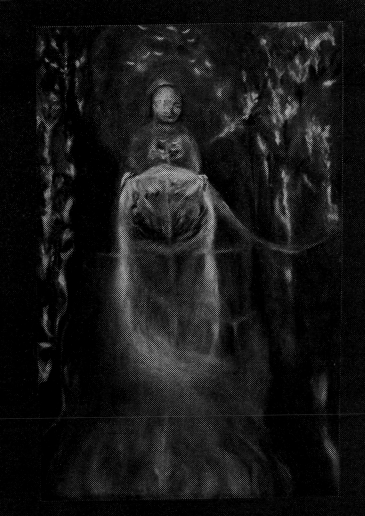

VIRGINIA AREY, ELLICOT CITY, MD, USA

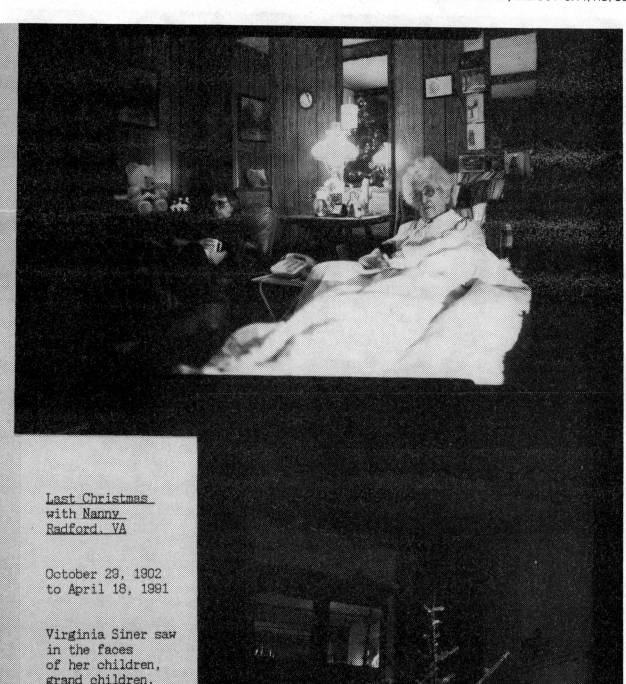

Last Christmas
with Nanny
Radford, VA

October 29, 1902
to April 18, 1991

Virginia Siner saw
in the faces
of her children,
grand children,
great-grand children,
the future,
the next century

Virginia grew up
in Southern poverty
uneducated
she saw her family
attend high school
and college

Virginia Arey
410-461-8284

KIRSTEN BECKERMAN, BALTIMORE, MD, USA

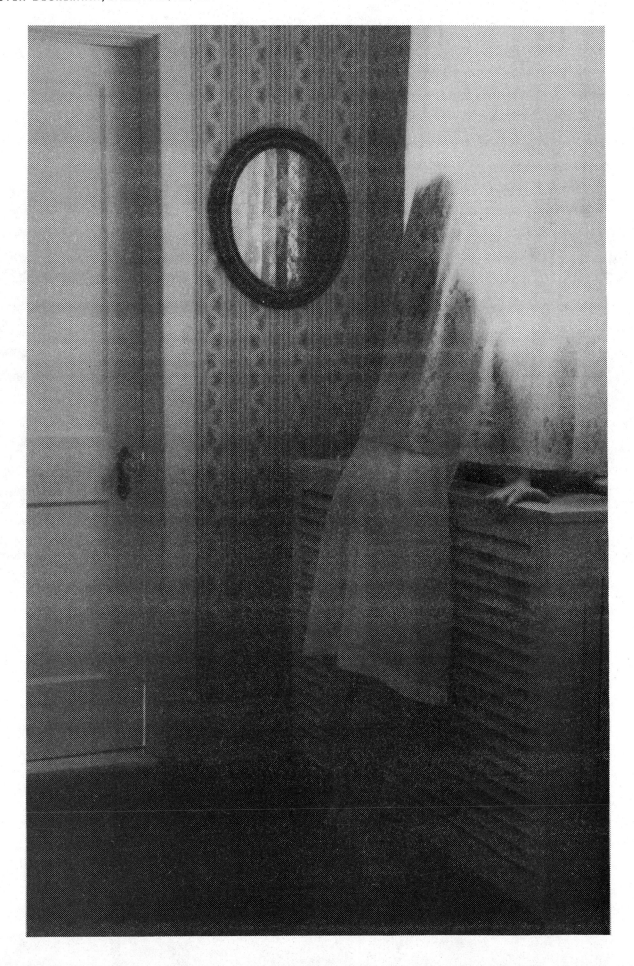

STEPHANIE PEEK, SAN FRANCISCO, CA, USA

G L O B A L - L O C A L

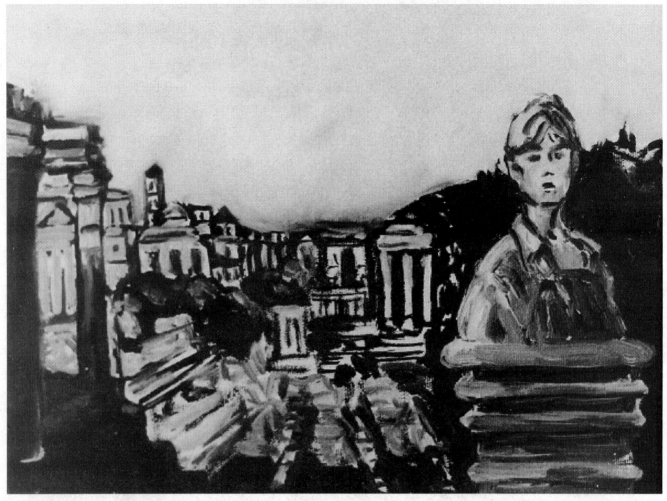

When in Rome

S T E P H A N I E   P E E K

Tel 415.387.3750

**3 5   S E V E N T E E N T H   A V E N U E
S A N   F R A N C I S C O   C A   9 4 1 2 1**

Fax 415.387.5373

ANN KOSHEL VAN BUREN, NEW YORK, NY, USA

Home Life

The kitchen is long and narrow
as a Chinese finger-trap.

Passive at either end
the couple must ease in and out
the way evening melts with day.

Young man
back to the fire
the shadows play before him

like a hand of cards
he cannot grasp
among the china.

All this is passed down
as darkness is passed down upon them
deepening the shadows that soften their bed.

It is better to just relax
accept and give.

                    Ann Koshel van Buren

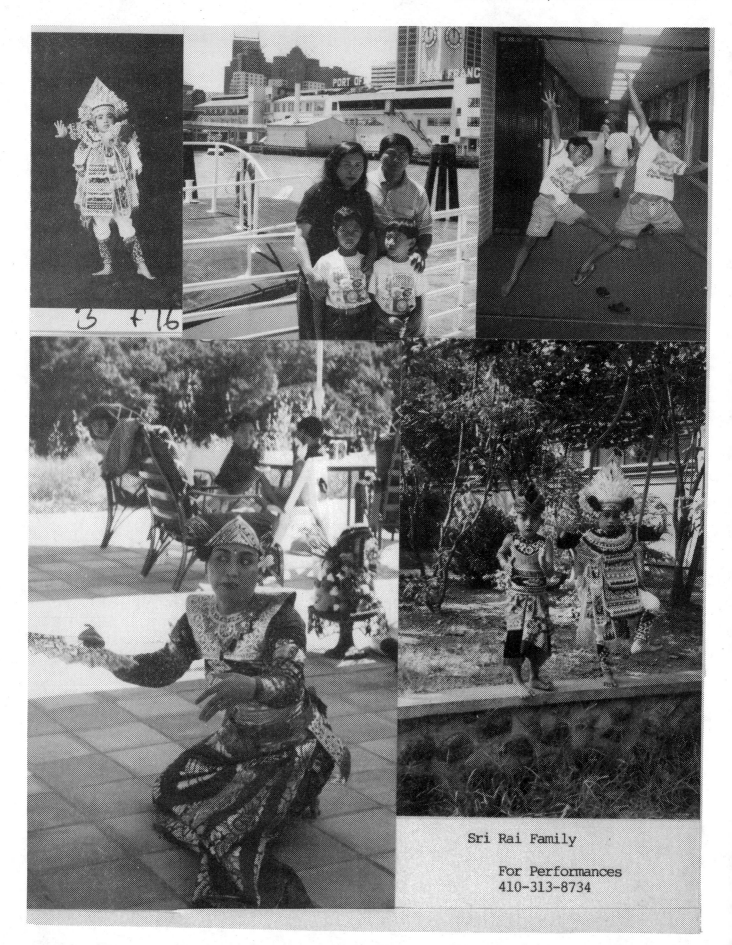

Sri Rai Family

For Performances
410-313-8734

Danica Lorincz, BALTIMORE, MD, USA

12/18/94

There was a pang – a rush
like love on an empty stomach,
A flow of warmth in the chest
of melting tears, of raw connection
unbound by I and Thou
but simply Us –
An Us, no doubt with inner distinctions
and richly allowing
despite its infancy;
Don't go yet, sweet treasure
of all that matters within me –
thoughts, inclinations, allowance, uplifting
and the exalting recognition
mirrored between us.
This I wish to cherish in your presence
as long as life allows it,
to merge light deeply into the horizon
from the early dark of an almost
winter morning, moist and warm like
spring's beckoning, uncommonly promising,
bestowed with deep roots already formed, –
a gift with no precarious pedestal –
Sweet Chimes on a Sunday.

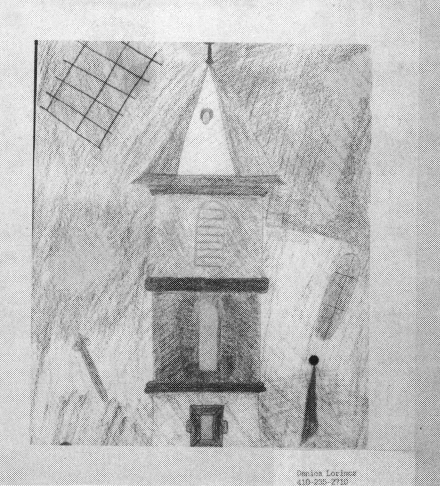

Danica Lorincz
410-235-2710

MA PYONE HTUN, COLUMBIA, MD, USA

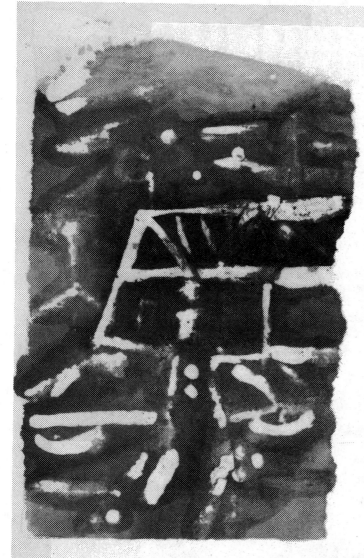

ဒီဇင်ဘာ ၁၇ရက်နေ့
၁၉၉၁ ခု

ဒေါ်အောင်ဆန်းစုကြည်သည်အဘကြွားသော
ခြေကိုလိုက်နာသည့်သမီးဖြစ်ပါသည်။
ကျွန်မ မြိုးထွန်း ကချီးရဲ့ပါသည်၊
ကျွန်မသည်မိဘ၏ခြေကြားသောခြေကို
လိုက်မနာခဲ့ပါ၊ ဒါကြောင့်ကျွန်မနိုင်
ငံခြားမှာ နေ ရ ပါသည်။

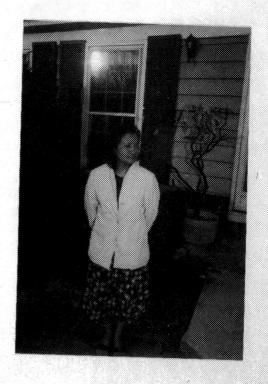

Aung San Suu Kyi
is the daughter who
follows in the footsteps
of her father.

I, Ma Pyone Htun,
admire her.
I did not follow my
parent's footsteps,
so I am here in a
foreign country.

Ma Pyone Htun
Columbia, MD
301-596-5820

Jubillee Early, INVERNESS, CA, USA

Rebirth of Women in the 21st Century

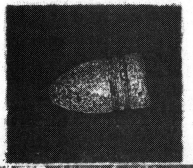

Confederate
bullet

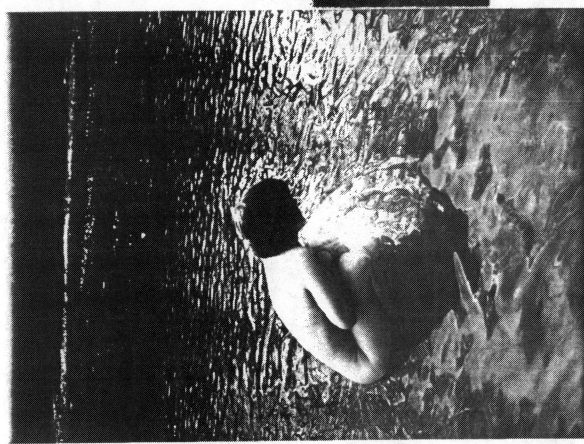

Jubillee Early in the Gunpowder River, MD

Sal Arey & Jubillee Early
c/o Slattery
General Delivery
Inverness, CA 94937
415-669-1432

Rebirth of Women in the 21st Century

MANY THINGS

ONE OF THINGS

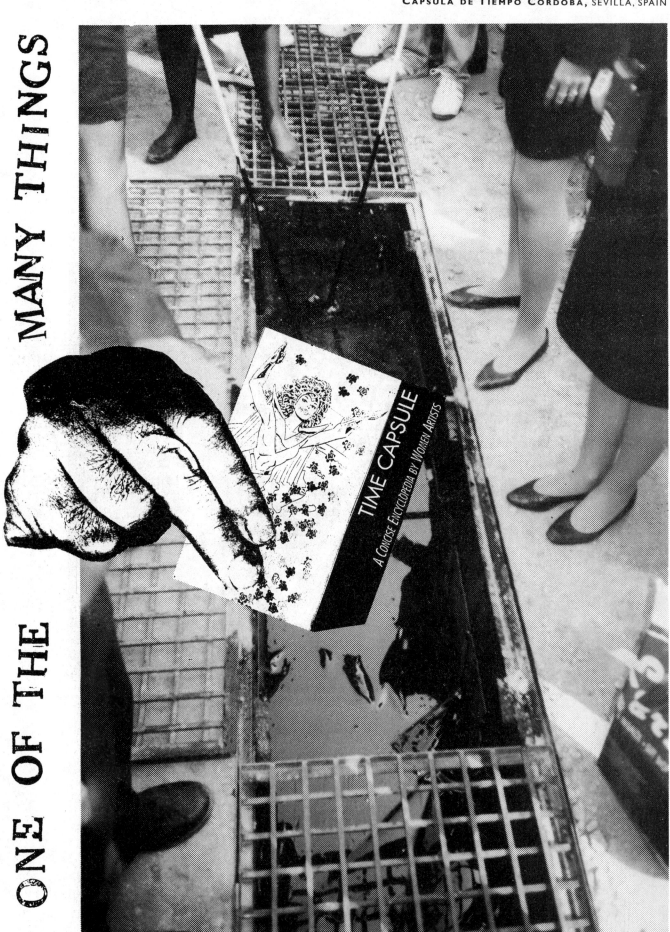

TIME CAPSULE

A CONCISE ENCYCLOPEDIA BY WOMEN ARTISTS

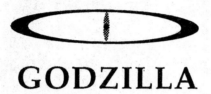

GODZILLA

**Asian Pacific American
Art Network**

Godzilla is a New York-based collective group of Asian Pacific American artists, curators and writers, founded in 1990. Our aims are to function as a support group interested in social change through art, bringing together art and advocacy; to increase visibility and opportunities for Asian Pacific Americans otherwise isolated with limited resources. We want to contribute to changing the limited ways Asian Pacific Americans participate in and are represented in our society. We undertake a range of public activities aimed at information exchange and self-empowering group projects.

**P.O. Box 1116, Cooper Station
New York, NY 10276
Phone 212.228.6000 ext. 400**

MARY MAGSAMEN, BROOKLYN, NY, USA

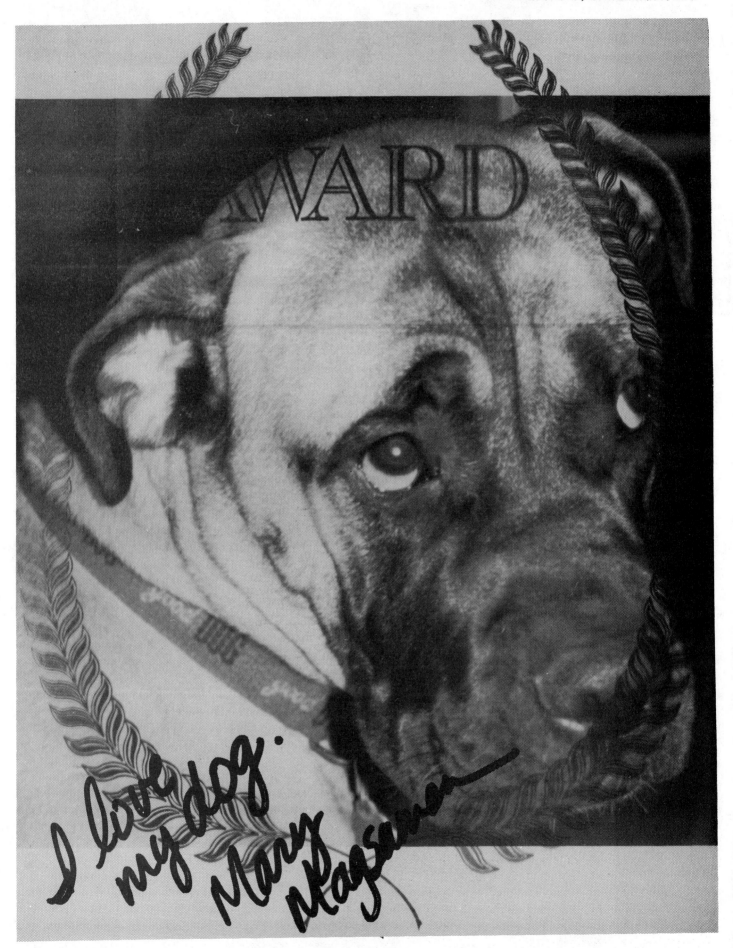

I love my dog. Mary Magsamen

ARLENE RAVEN, NEW YORK, NY, USA

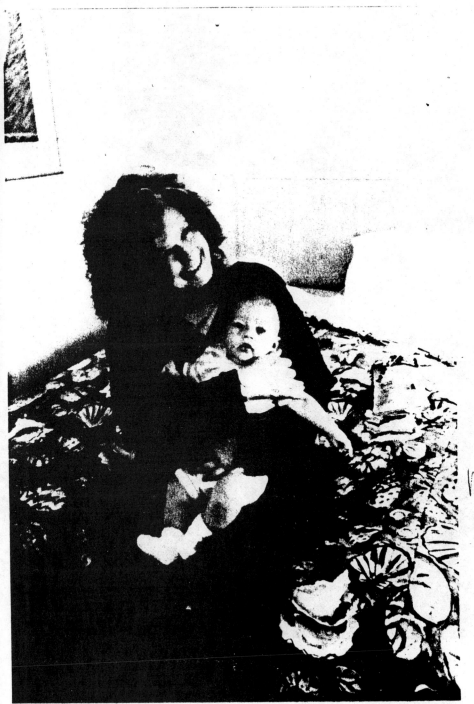

Arlene Raven
and granddaughter
Mariana Best

PAULA GABRIEL, MADISON, CT, USA

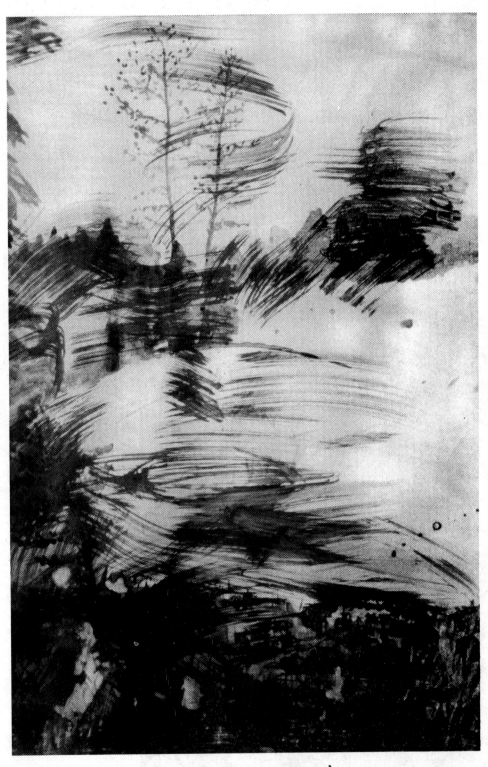

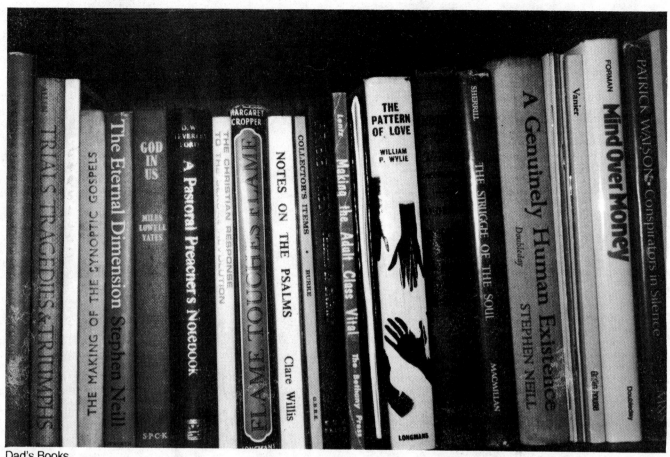

Dad's Books

EDWARD DAVID BUSBY
August 14, 1928 - November 21, 1994

You were always busy. You were always caring. You were always sensitive.
You were always hopeful. You loved and you were loved.

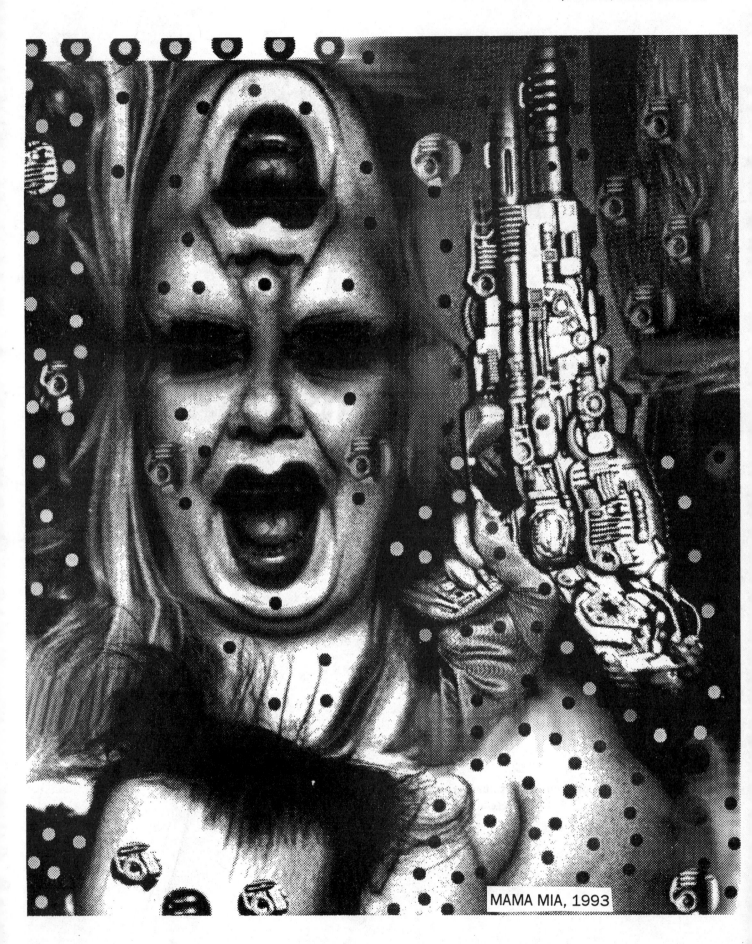

MAMA MIA, 1993

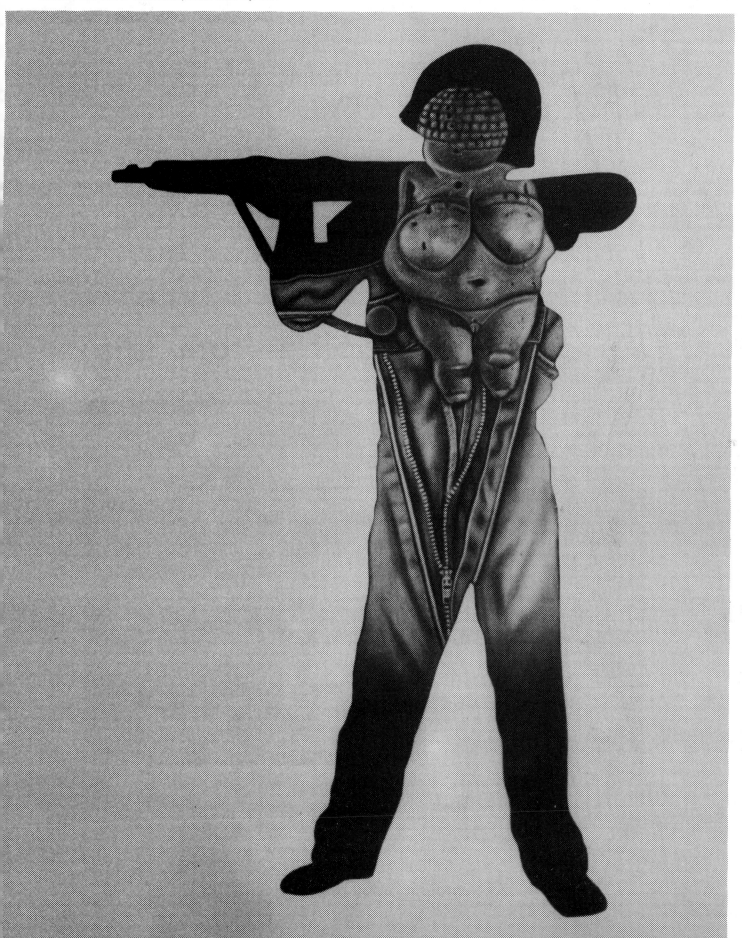

Those who cry:

"Save the world

are going from this

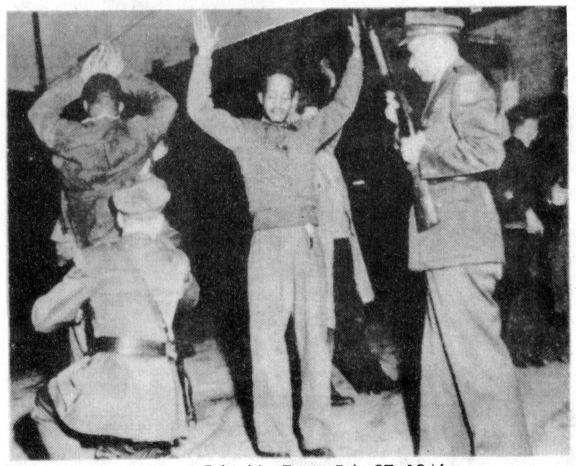

Columbia, Tenn., Feb. 27, 1946.
75 Negroes arrested by lynch mad cops.

from Communism"

to this

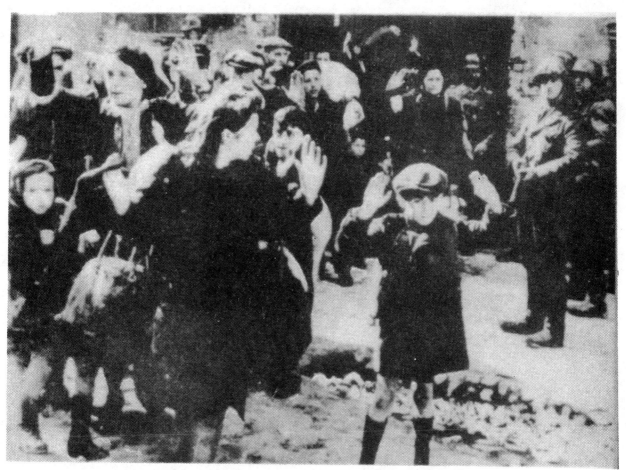

Warsaw, 1943. Nazi stormtroopers
round up Polish women and children for execution.

SUSAN TURCOT, BERLIN, GERMANY

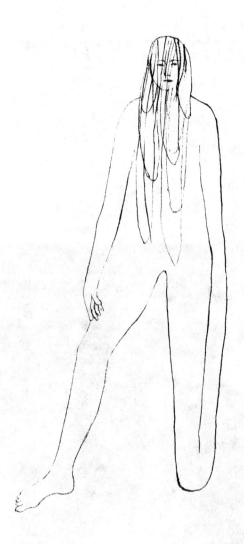

Susan Turcot, BERLIN, GERMANY

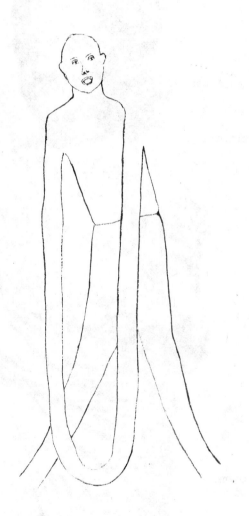

KIMBERLY CONNERTON, BROOKLYN, NY, USA

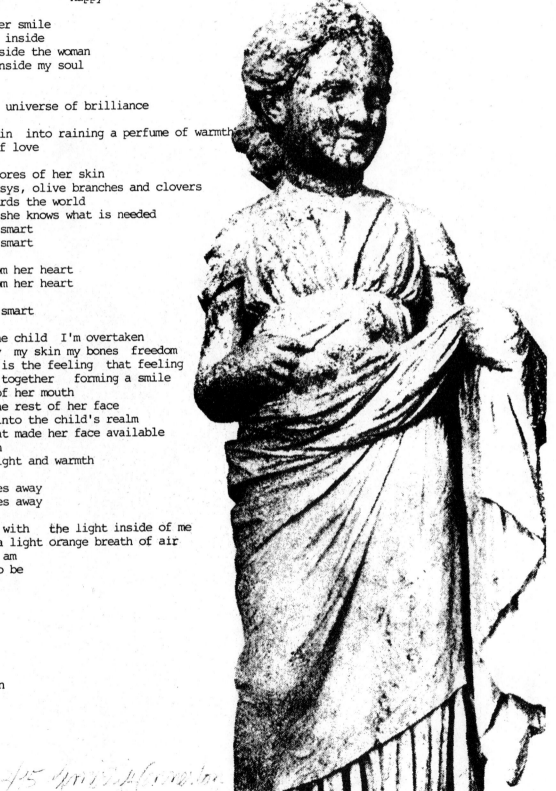

happy

she   I see her smile
she smiles   inside
the girl   inside the woman
the child   inside my soul
smiles

her face is a universe of brilliance
her smile
lights my brain into raining a perfume of warmth
in the form of love

through the pores of her skin
she rains daisys, olive branches and clovers
outward towards the world
intuitively she knows what is needed
she is so smart
she is so smart

she lives from her heart
she lives from her heart

she is so smart

her smile the child I'm overtaken
all goes away my skin my bones freedom
what is left is the feeling that feeling
lips pressed together   forming a smile
the corners of her mouth
along with the rest of her face
elevate me into the child's realm
my hands what made her face available
through touch
feel only light and warmth

her image goes away
her image goes away

I am flooded with   the light inside of me
today it is a light orange breath of air
thats what I am
she ceases to be
I am only me
I am a child

Kim Connerton
02/14/95

JOANNE ROSS, NEW YORK, NY, USA

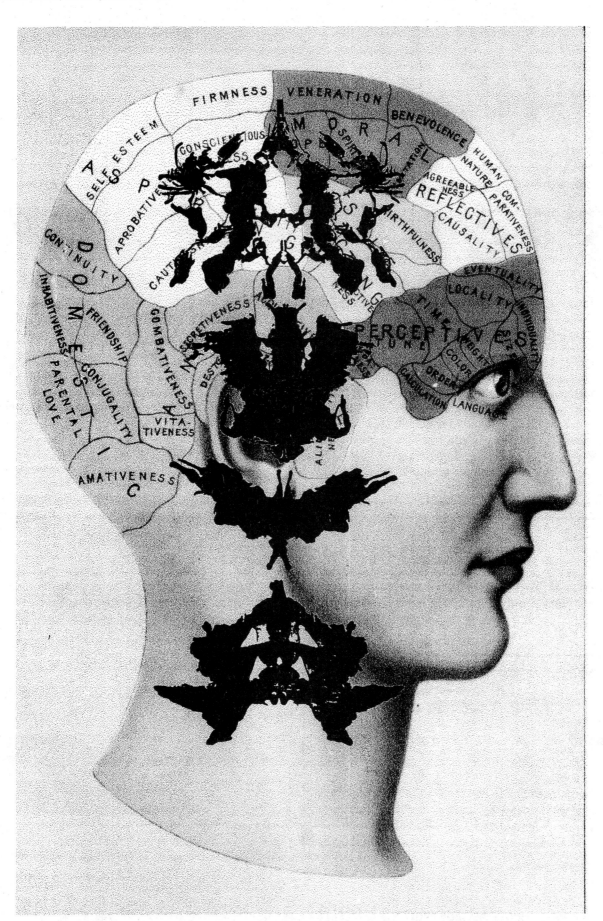

THE Token Times

CLASSIFIED

HELP WANTED, ART WORLD

OUTSTANDING CAREER OPPORTUNITY: CURATORIAL ASST TO ASST-CURATOR AT MAJOR MUSEUM. ENTRY LEVEL POSITION.
Ph.D from Top School, publications & 10 years experience required.
Must know Word Processing, answer own phone, conduct own research.
Possibility of curating shows at branch museum, providing you can raise the money. EOE; Women and minorities encouraged to apply.

WELL-DRESSED ART HISTORY MAJOR?
Blue chip NYC art gallery, wanting to change male, pale image; seeks multicultural receptionist with drop-dead appear. & clothes to match; ivy league education & attitude a must; NO ETHNIC ACCENTS. Minimum wage, no health insurance. Fringe benefits include: attending fancy parties and meeting the right people.

$$$$$$$$$SMILES$$$$$$$$$$$$

DEVELOPMENT ASSISTANT: person of color needed to intimidate foundations, corporations, and collectors into giving large amounts of money. Successful candidate must relish being only minority staff member. High visibility in public, silence at staff meetings required. Photogenic a plus.

EARN A GREAT P/T INCOME !!!!

MAJOR MUSEUM seeks 1 artist of color EVERY year for next five years (or as long as multicult. lasts) for solo shows. Prefer artist already discovered by major galleries, collectors and other museums. Must restrict artistic output to ethnic issues: FORMALIST NEED NOT APPLY.

GRAND OPENING! ARTIST CALL!
Female African-American, Latina, Asian or Lesbian artists wanted for large summer group show in out of the way location.
No honorarium, no sales.
Must deliver own work.

CATHERINE ALLPORT, BERKELEY, CA, USA

Remember Our Herstory
Remember Our Heroines

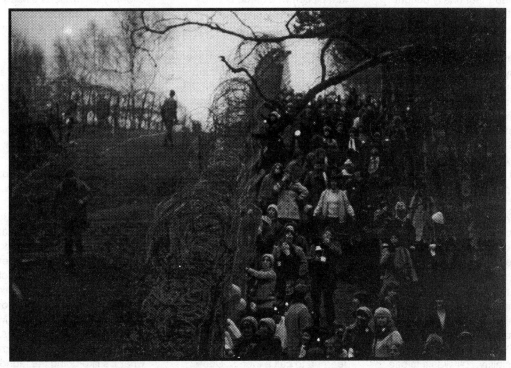

Greenham Common, England. December 11, 1983. 30,000 wimmin circled the nine mile perimeter of the nuclear base at Greenham Common. First there was silence. Then a wail arose. Then came the beating of pots and pans. Then the wimmin shook the fence until it came down.
Remember our power. Circle for survival.

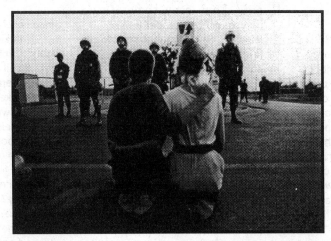

Women's Encampment for a Future of Peace and Justice, Seneca Falls, New York. July, 1983. These two wimmin came from Greenham Common and were the first wimmin arrested at the Seneca Army Depot, a transshipment site for Cruise and Pershing missiles. Over 10,000 women participated in actions at Seneca during the summer of 1983.

Catherine Allport • Photographer/Activist • 2828 1/2 Cherry St.• Berkeley, CA 94705 • USA

HIS/HERS

I dreamed that I finally bought myself the antique clock I had passed by daily on my commute to and from work. I brought it home and in immediate dream-time, my two-year-old broke it. I don't remember if I took the time to cry or not but I did take the car to the train station, rode to New York, left a message on the machine so that Peter could find the car in the parking lot and jumped a cab to the airport. I woke up in Italy.

Actually, I woke up. In my dream I had escaped to Italy where I had lived for four years before art school, marriage, career and child. I woke up definitely in New York but with the recognition of that timeless fantasy - to leave everything: child, husband, work - and do something for myself. To be relieved of the endless responsibility. Or was it to see how far someone might go to look for me? Would I even be missed? I knew the answer for my son. He's clearly in some stage of the Oedipus cycle and feels fairly confident that he took over his father's position when Peter wasn't looking.

And so I woke up to hear my son happily amusing himself with my purse and his diaper bag - opening and closing, taking things out and putting things in. Then I heard a crash and I put together "pot-luck dinner with friends the night before, too tired to put things away when I came home, dish left in the diaper bag" in the swift moment it took my ceramic bowl to shatter on the living room floor. I fell on my knees shouting "oh no, oh no, oh no" and no one came to my rescue. I sat there unwilling to open the plastic bag and witness the shards. It was my fault - I had

designated the art piece as utilitarian. Now it was gone - the last piece I had made before I stopped making art. Gone. Where was everyone? And then the tears came.

I had to go through everything alone. When we discovered this winter that my son's sitter was abusive, my husband plowed through his work while I took a short leave to heal Alexander and find new childcare for him. Whereas Peter used to shop, cook and clean, now he left the house before we were awake and came home after we were in bed in the evening. I had a miscarriage about nine months ago and the next day Peter and Alexander came down with the flu. I did three loads of laundry, cleaning up the vomit. The lost child went unmourned. If I had any conflicts about my teaching or the absence of any artistic production, I had learned to call a friend. Does Peter feel the same about his conflicts? Does he talk to anyone about them? He doesn't talk to me.

And then I felt a patting on my arm. "Sorry, sorry, sorry.....Otay, otay, otay." Alexander was leaning from his chair to dry my tears. "Tears," he said. "Tears," I said. Peter remained in bed. "Broken," he said. "Broken," I said.

How does a couple reconcile enormous love and respect with vast neglect? You are there for your child and your child is somehow very grown-up and pulls through for you but you are not there for each other. You are parents but you are no longer lovers. The support that earned income provides in no way replaces the support that a soul mate provides. "I thought you had

married 'the new man,'" a friend of mine recently remarked dismayed over my frustrations since Peter had never 'gendered' responsibility and had always shared freely. Yet income demands obliterate any recognition of a personal life and of a soul - there is just no more energy.

In lieu of conversation I have sleep...and fantasy.

The bowl was not enough to get me on an airplane. But now anyone would know where to find me if I did take off. How much do I need to rattle my marriage and how much do I need to think of myself? Meals prepared get eaten not appreciated. Should I start that PhD.? Did anyone notice that I was home every evening on time to relieve the baby sitter? Maybe I should take that yoga class, I would feel better. Do you know what it's like doing the laundry in the summer with your child continuously running out the laundromat door? What do you think, should I go for job security, career advancement or self-fulfillment (whatever that is)?

Since childhood, I imagined myself making a film when I am eighty. I'm halfway to that age now. If I sit out a few more years to see where wife, motherhood and job take me will I recognize an individual who is not reflecting someone else? Will I disappear into the good life of family, home and peace of mind and never make that film? Or is there a way to take Peter and Alexander with me to Italy? Is going their way, going mine? Can inspiration be found in the mundane and silenced spaces? Can energy grow out of fatigue?

Kathleen MacQueen, May 1995

KATHLEEN MACQUEEN, NEW YORK, NY, USA

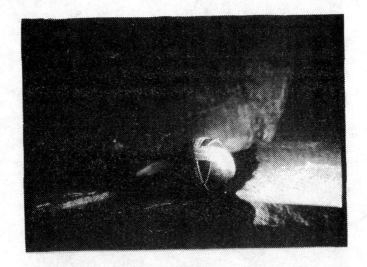

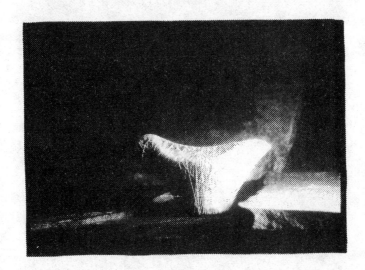

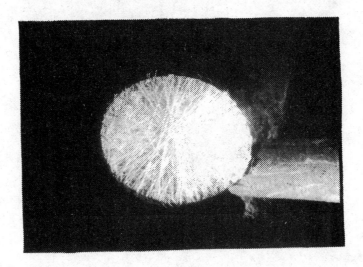

JENNIFER PEPPER, BROOKLYN, NY, USA

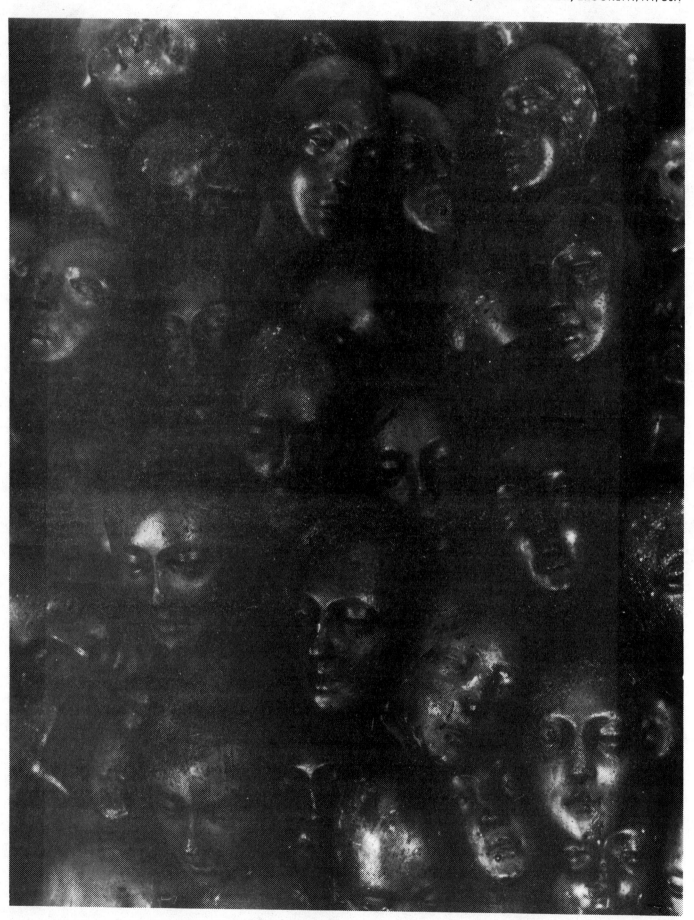

ANA TISCORNIA, NEW YORK, NY, USA

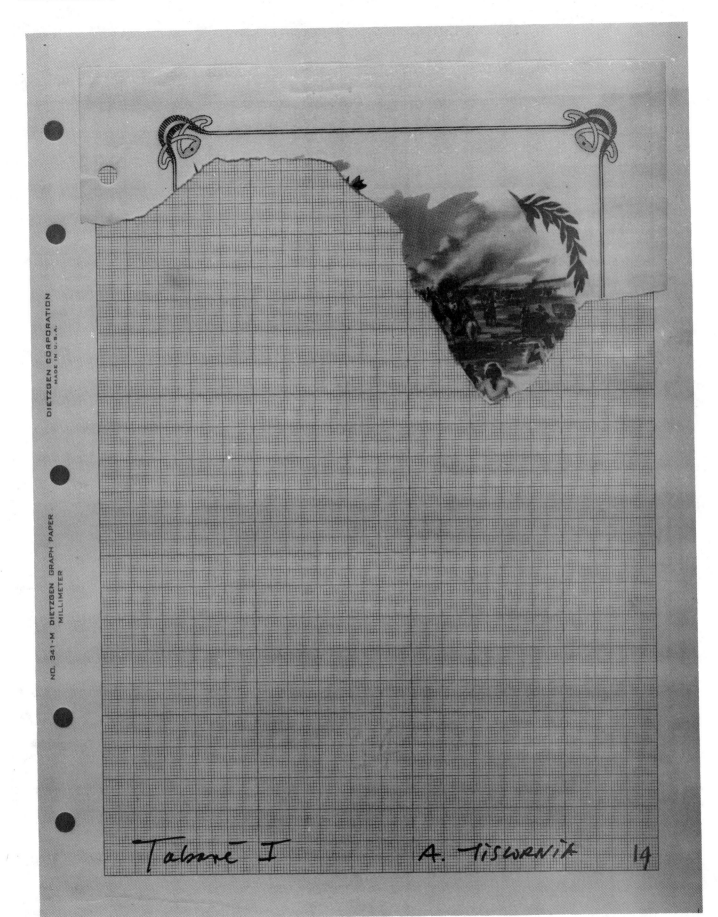

Tabaré I   A. Tiscornia   14

DEBORAH MUIRHEAD, STORRS, CT, USA

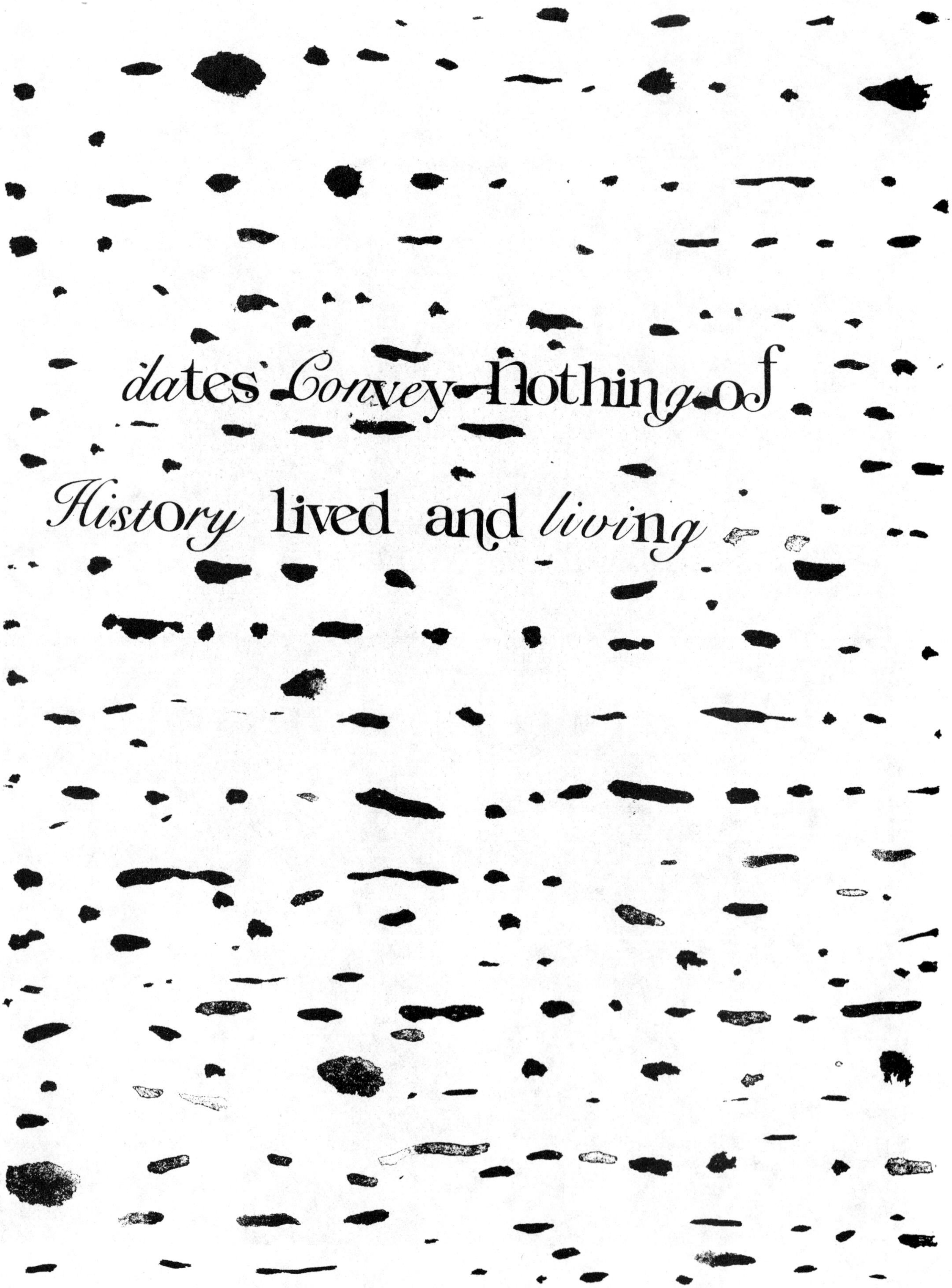

dates Convey nothing of

History lived and living

DEBORAH MUIRHEAD, STORRS, CT, USA

Advertising Negro Martha & child

Daniel Kassie Amos & Sally *also*

Fugitives 1829

LIZ LARNER, MALIBU, CA, USA

<u>hlaefdize</u>

A definition is hard until it is deluged in the pliancy of other meaning. As a young girl I never liked the words woman or female due mainly to the attachment of the prefixes wo and fe, to words that otherwise named the sex that I am not (human was similarly displeasing.). Girl, was OK because it had nothing to do with boy and had one more letter but soon I sensed the powerlessness *Girl* had to carry. Being under age - under somebody else's control "little girl". Around this same time(raw, bright 12) I took a shine to the word *Lady* as a description for myself and others of my sex. *Lady* like *Girl* has no man or men or male at the end of it.. It seemed to me a word that stood on it's own associatively, and imbued a sense of power that some may argue has to do with social or economic position. My definition, did not connect with class issues as much as a sense that a Lady could take care of herself and do so with great style - her own.

Ladize,

It has been pointed out that language (especially written) is, very possibly, a male construct. This is disappointing but not entirely intractable. I recently looked up the words *Lady*, *Woman*, *Female* and *Girl* in the Oxford English Dictionary. This small research was not inspiring. In fact the OED's definitions and summaries of usage of these words reads like a history of oppression salted with slander. The word *Woman* was originally wife and then wifeman. Very disappointing. *Lady* originally meant bread, loaf that is kneaded or dough(this etymology baffles the dictionaire as it seems to have nothing in common with the later corresponding masculine designation -lord.) In contrast to *Woman*, *Lady*, has a more complex and not entirely typical definition in the OED, The inexplicable link to nourishment complexities the definition. Bread- not merely a raw

Liz Larner, MALIBU, CA, USA

material but a proportioned combine of elements, various ingredients making loaves that sustain. In this sense, a means to concoct a unique blend.

Hardness must first be transformed to a state of pliancy before it can turn into anything else -even hard again.
Hardness aspires towards intractability. Hardness can be some thing to hide behind . It can also be gotten around.. Experiments may be done against control's hard background but experiments themselves are always in flux (something that hard, never is, once it is.). Pliancy allows recapitulation. It is hard to call something pliant an object as it is always ready to transform.

STEFANIE NAGORKA, MONTCLAIR, NJ, USA

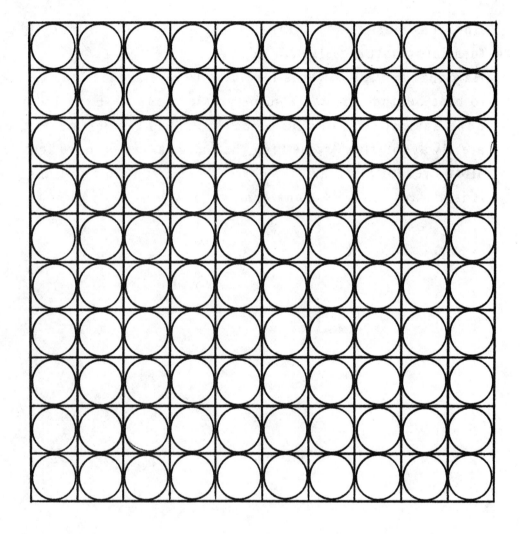

STEFANIE NAGORKA, MONTCLAIR, NJ, USA

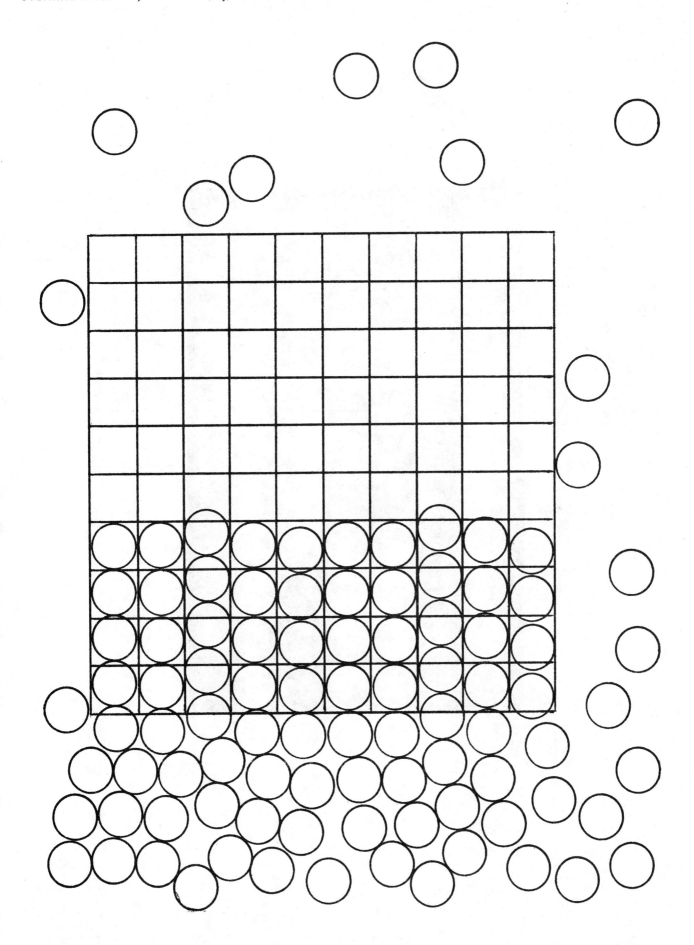

ROBERLEY ANN BELL, BUFFALO, NY, USA

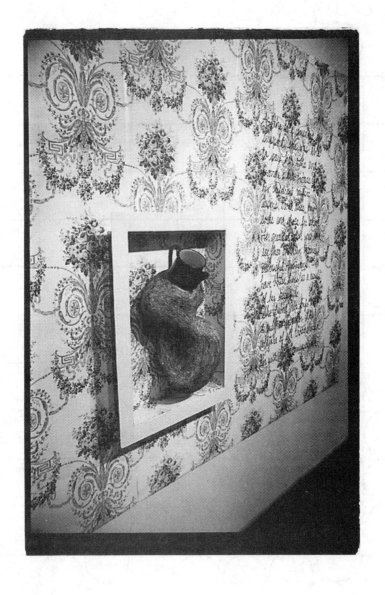

RONDA MUSIC, NEW YORK, NY, USA

Washing My Mother's Hair
-for Karen-

I hold your head in support under the tepid water
and softly lather as your breaths come more deeply,
and your eyes close to relax into my care.

I notice the small lines accentuating the beauty of your age,
and the shininess of your skin next to the fresh youth of my own.

This stay in the hospital is temporary,
but your fight to kill this disease has left you weak,
and as I rinse out the soap,
your hair envelopes my hand like a silken liquid.
I know this all will come again,
Not from disease, but the age that is inevitable.

Last night I held my brother, who cried into the evening for his mommy. He
tested me like a substitute teacher, and I couldn't
make the sandwich right, or set the table like mommy does.

He tired me so quickly.

And now as I pull the covers around you,
and force you to swallow the green liquid and pills,
I admire your strength and sacrifice.

This caring, for you and the family, that makes me feel so old,
is as minor as the simple dissonance of a lullaby.

You are things I want to be: strength, earth, woman, kindness, .
passion, sister

Mother

LAURA CLOUD, EAST LANSING, MI, USA

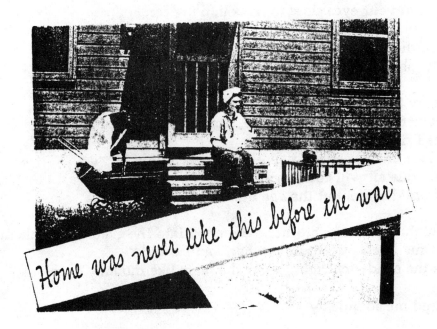

LAURA CLOUD, EAST LANSING, MI, USA

vords on the news each night for months, even be-
. Soldiers and pilots squinted into the sun and
nsciously, as if they were somehow sorry that they
thing better to say. "I just want to do the job and
at should they have said? The promise of home is
in victory, more tangible than peace.

be, in the broadest sense, the reason wars are
to war to protect our homeland, or to preserve
e at home or to
s' homes when
m seem like big
s to us. But home
than a cause; it
ation. "I can pic-
in front of me,"
er in Vietnam,
ie and our chil-
much the things
anted can mean.
of cut grass, the
over the lake
the trees and
Small things—
ings—gain the
s during a war;
strangely sanc-
ice and by risk.
u fighting for?"
asked the Ma-
lcanal. "A piece
pie." "Scotch
mes." "Books."
vies," they said.

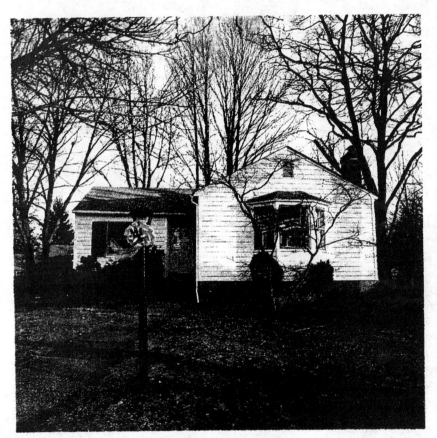

Persian Gulf War 1991

ness. Home isn't a church. It is where we argue,
on mantels, measure our wants and try to finc
meaning of home is changed by war, and not jus
fight it. For those who stay behind, home become
to keep intact. So Christmas trees are left sta
write that everything's just the same, which of c
possibility. Homes cannot be static; life goes on
to, and the hole left by an absence will start to clos

The fear of c
change—the fe
one will fit in, oi
of the saddest
But it doesn't le
sy of reunion, oi
fantasy has.
home!" the Con
were told at Ge
member, home
those hills!" Ho
sweet word, and
image we have o
for a war to end.
ware ad showed
a ravishing red
HOME FOR KI
"It's Christmas
giving, it's the
you're laughing,
there are stars
it's the day yot
home." Dated?
tunistic? You be
age is fixed in

t grown any closer since then, which is stranger
t the same moment that we're watching high-tech
lance in midair, soldiers are standing on line at a
ir the Kuwaiti border, waiting to use a telephone
l stateside. Technology brings so much of the war
that we sulk when we can't see live footage. But
h more of the home in war than there was a hun-
. Soldiers in the Gulf still carry home in their
a picture, a letter, a pebble, a coin.
rmal times is not a talisman but a setting: It is the
r lives, with varying degrees of success and happi-

Wars start on maps, with armies, but they end i
Children all over the world draw houses the s
dows are eyes, doors are mouths. Tracy Kidder v
England homes were designed with reference to pa
right down to the chimney, "the breast in which
which resembled the hearth, which contained th
stood for the soul." It's a beautiful way to think at
home isn't always that beautiful and, at its best
Home should be thought of without metaphor, ye
regret. War makes us see homes as symbols. The
home again, as it is, without really needing to see i

JANE GLUCKSMAN, BOZEMAN, MT, USA

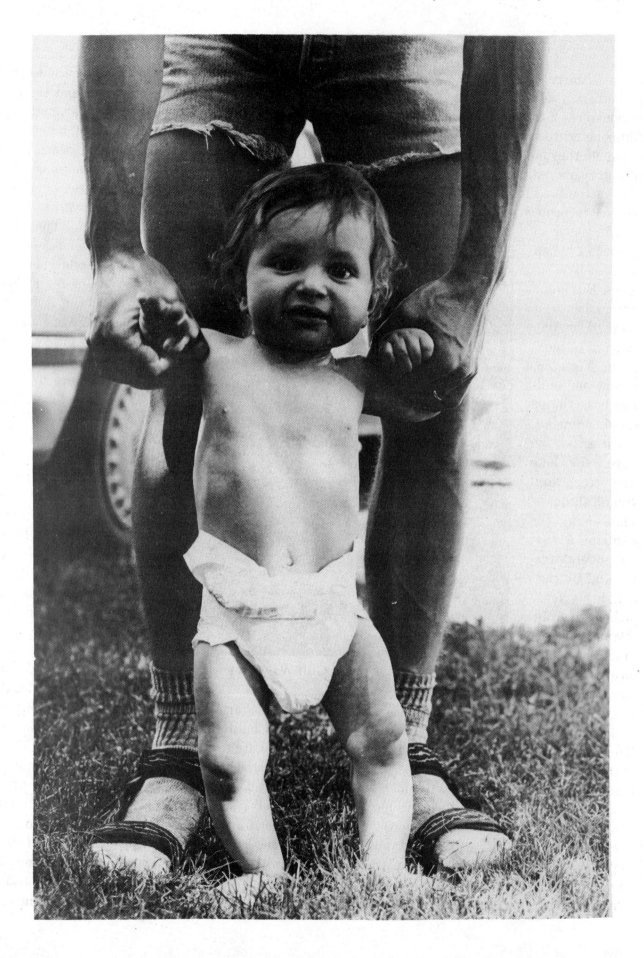

JANE GLUCKSMAN, BOZEMAN, MT, USA

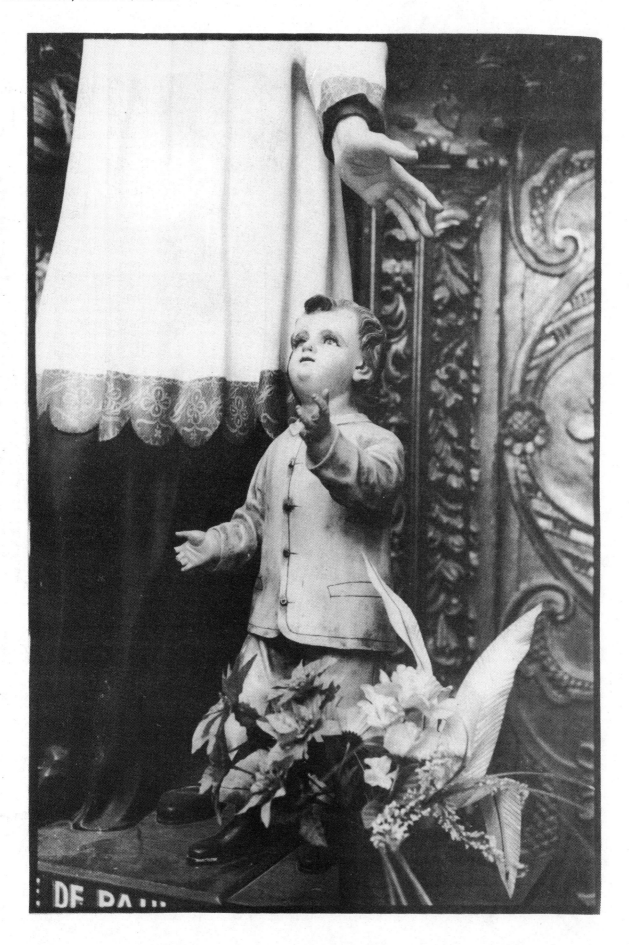

CAROL FICKSMAN, NEW YORK, NY, USA

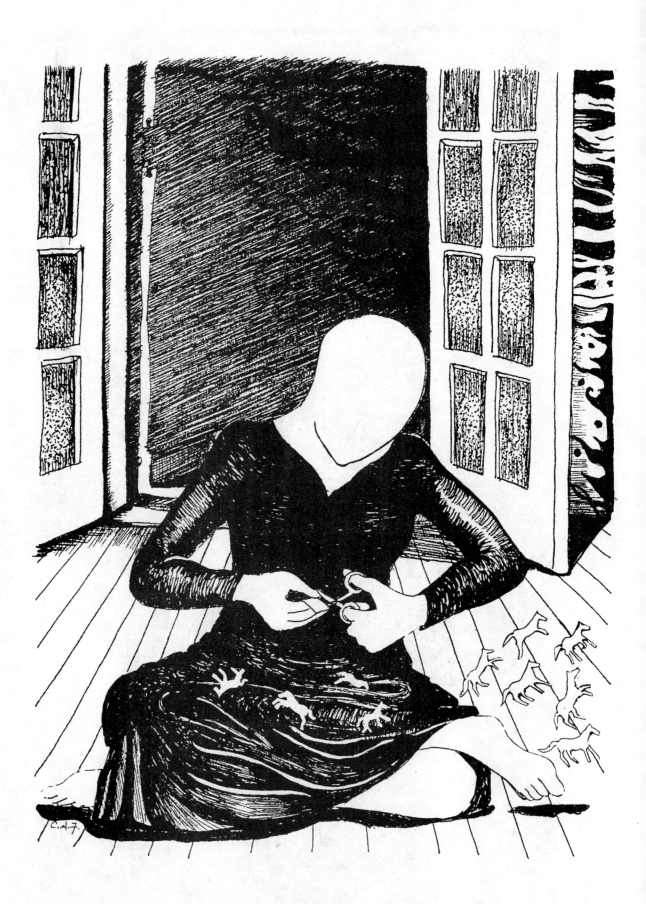

CAROL FICKSMAN, NEW YORK, NY, USA

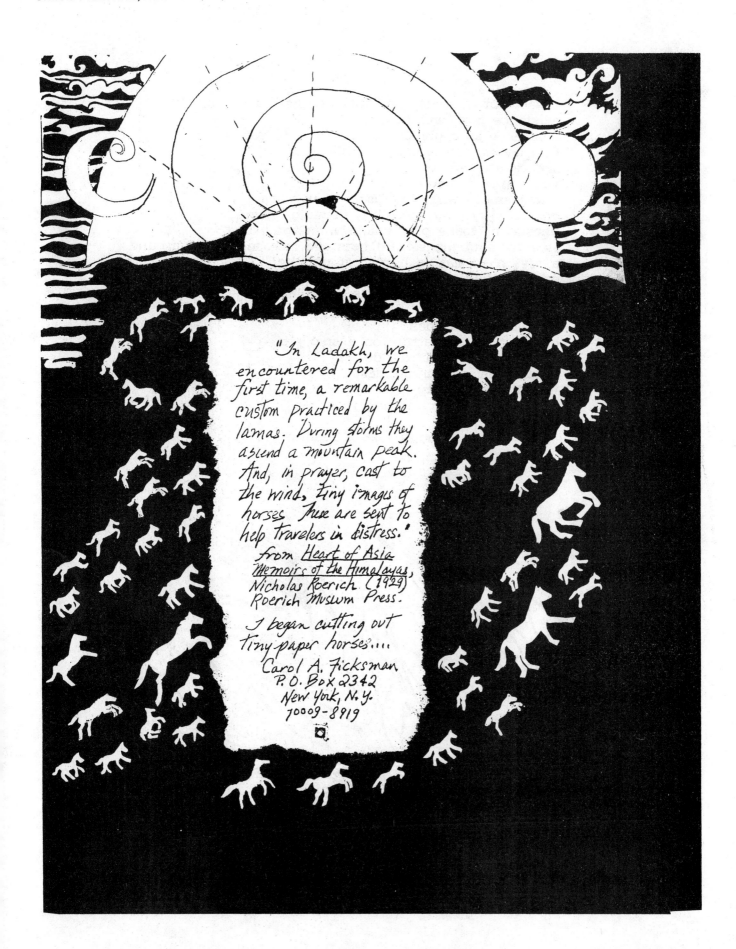

"In Ladakh, we encountered for the first time, a remarkable custom practiced by the lamas. During storms they ascend a mountain peak. And, in prayer, cast to the wind, tiny images of horses. These are sent to help travelers in distress."

from *Heart of Asia Memoirs of the Himalayas*, Nicholas Roerich (1929) Roerich Museum Press.

I began cutting out tiny paper horses....

Carol A. Ficksman
P.O. Box 2342
New York, N.Y.
10009-8919

JUDITH REN-LAY NEW YORK, NY, USA

I walk out of a role and into another dimension
existence is a crutch
I observe as a ghost, cause tables to rattle
find my way invisibly and take food
a dark stuffed bat
you broke through
I was human with you, more than warm
gezellig, gezellig, gezellig, gezellig, gezellig
ghosts in cloaks play shadows on the walls
as birds and planes and bats are released to fly around
a cry, a scream, a horror of unbelief
death - livin', breathin'
the little worm inside trails droppings
infesting the rest
screams and tirades
of the skeleton rattlin' on a shaky tree
a healthy distrust to ride
a dark vision, runnin' fast
immediate intensity
genitals and heart strung together

with a through line of feeling...........

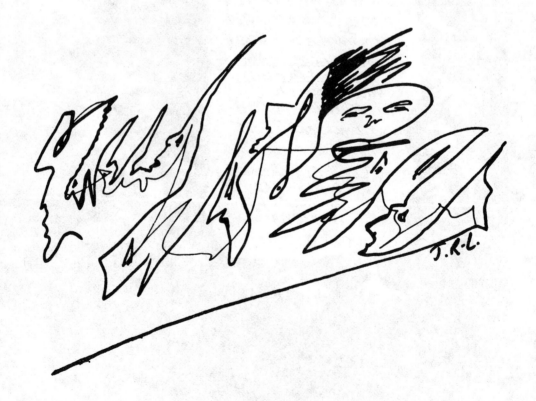

JUDITH REN-LAY NEW YORK, NY, USA

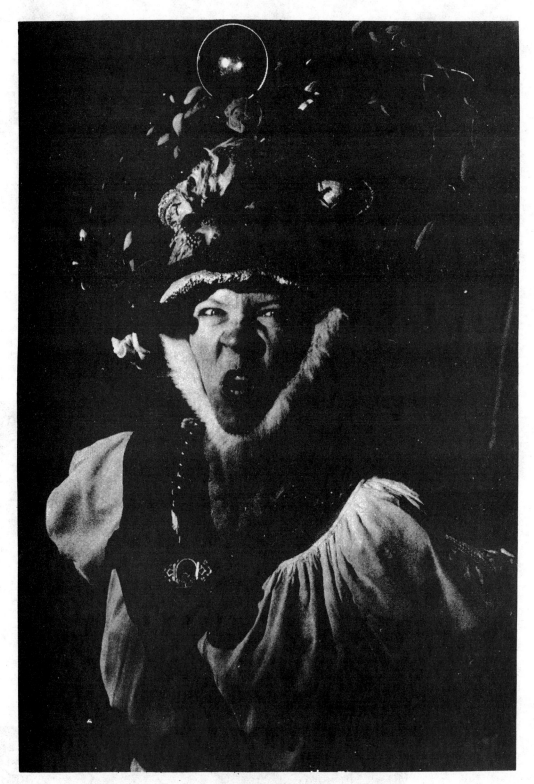

Performance of UNDERCURRENT EVENTS by Judith Ren-Lay
at Performance Space 122/ New York City/ 1992
Performance photograph by Dona Ann McAdams
Drawing & text by Judith Ren-Lay

amaLIA
perjovschi
berthelot street 12
bucharest
1/70749 romania
e-mail
perjo@r22.sfos.ro

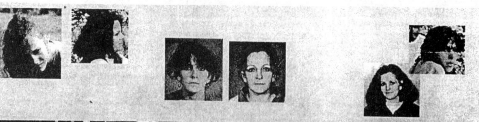

I don't want
to go
to sleep

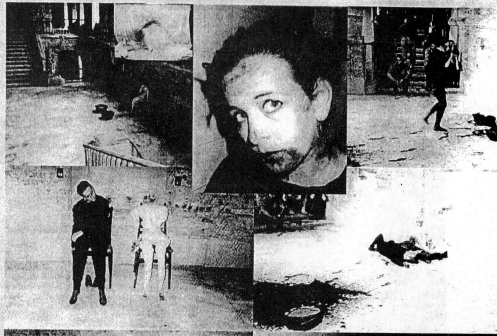

I am
fighting
for my right
to be
different

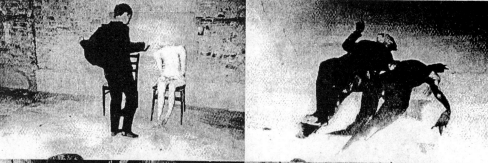

what is
for me
it's scattered
everywhere

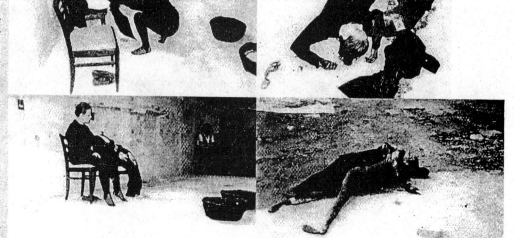

identity

AMALIA PERJOVSCHI, BUCHAREST, ROMANIA

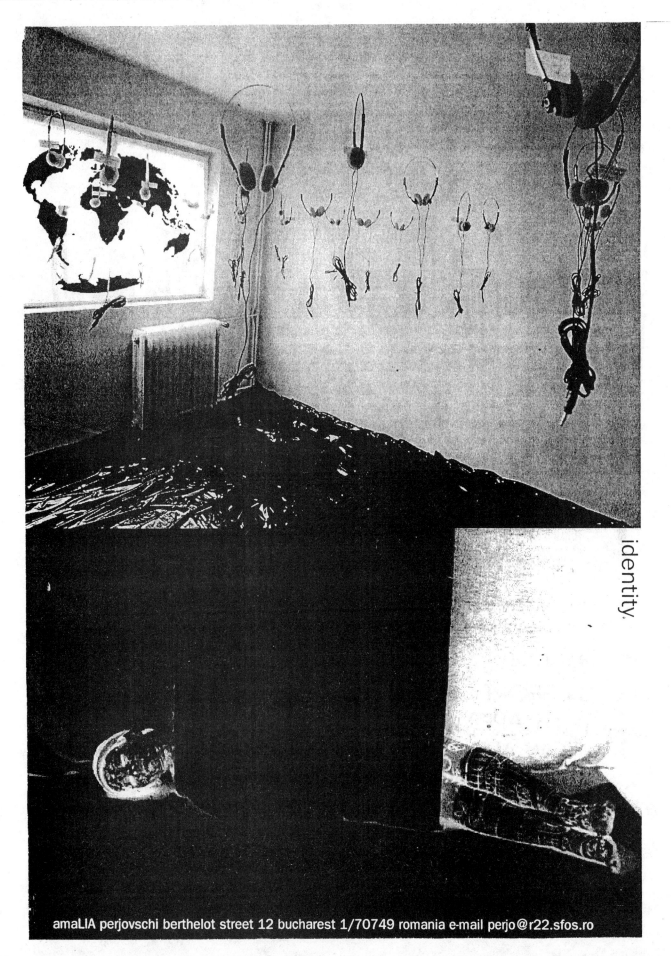

identity

amaLIA perjovschi berthelot street 12 bucharest 1/70749 romania e-mail perjo@r22.sfos.ro

CASSANDRA LANGER, JACKSON HEIGHTS, NY, USA

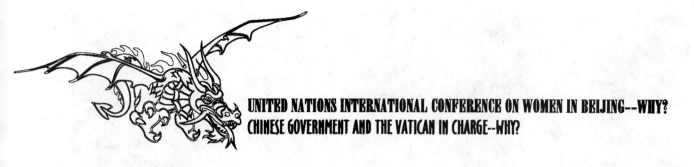

UNITED NATIONS INTERNATIONAL CONFERENCE ON WOMEN IN BEIJING--WHY?
CHINESE GOVERNMENT AND THE VATICAN IN CHARGE--WHY?

Where Are The Tibetan Women?

- DENIED
- BARRED
- MURDERED
- TORTURED
- CATHOLICS FOR FREE CHOICE - TAIWANESE - LESBIANS DENIED CREDENTIALS TO ATTEND MEETING

WOMEN'S ISSUES DENIED BY PATRIARCHY!

1. WHY ARE WOMEN SPENDING THEIR MONEY TO SUPPORT TYRANNY?
2. WHY ARE YOU HERE?
3. HOW ARE YOU COLLUDING IN YOUR OWN OPPRESSION AND THAT OF OTHER WOMEN?

Everything here will out live us
Except Shame

Cassandra Langer
Art Historian/Critic

TRUDI VAN DER ELSEN, AMSTERDAM, THE NETHERLANDS

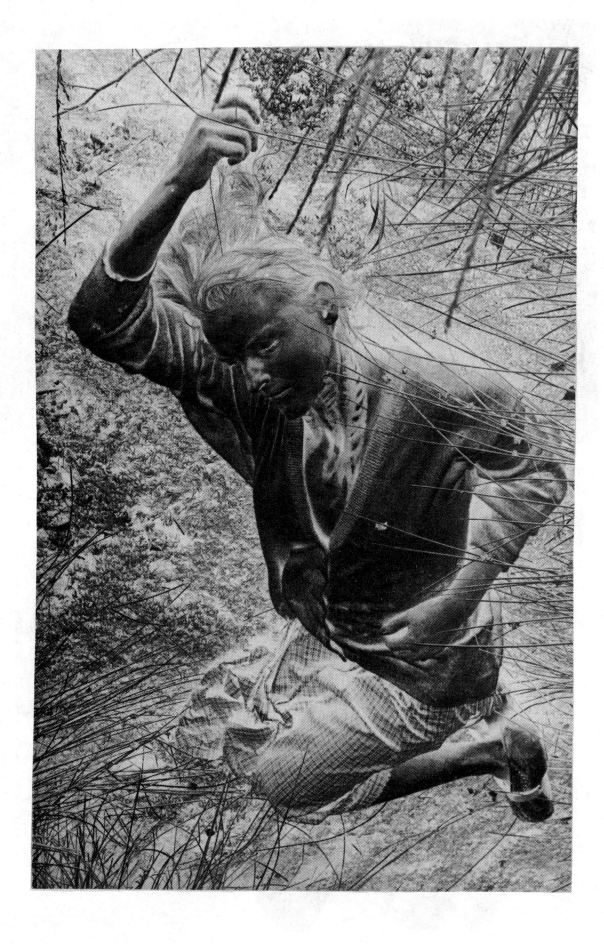

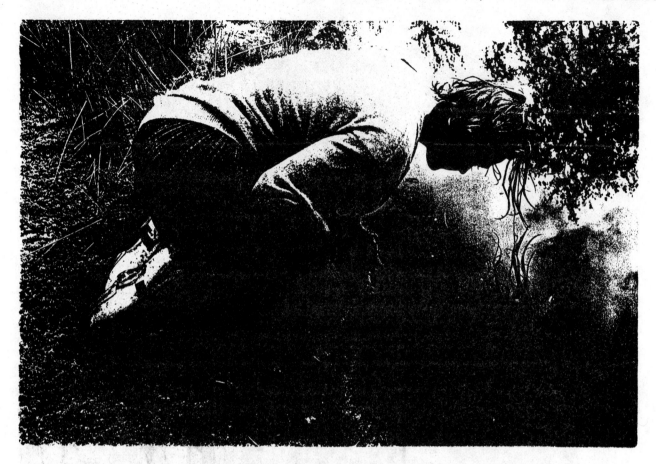

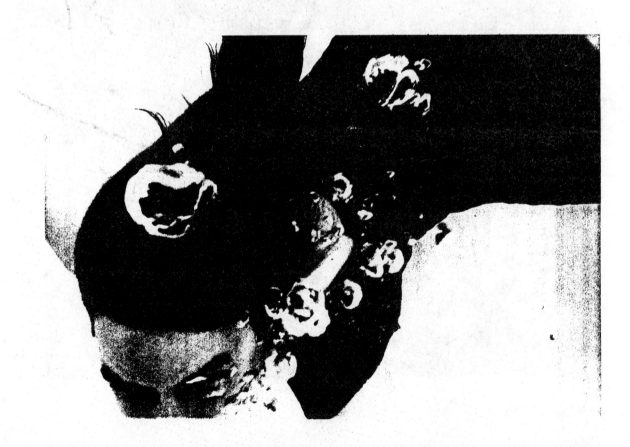

LAURA LONDON, LOS ANGELES, CA, USA

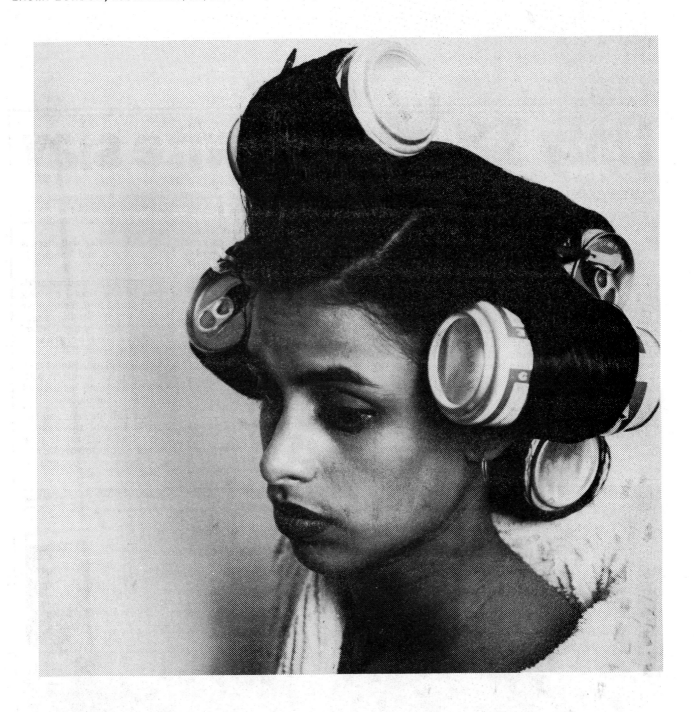

"Untitled"/Extremes, Black & White Photomural, 24"x24", 1992

"Untitled"/Extremes grew out of a body of work entitled the Cosmetic
Ritual Series. These images are concerned with the extremes people
go to create beauty and the contradictions inherent within
these practices.

O 26

Only 18 mos. in wife slay

THE ASSOCIATED PRESS

TOWSON, Md. — A man who shot his wife to death after finding her in bed with another man was sentenced to 18 months in prison by a sympathetic judge who said he felt he was forced to impose a sentence.

Circuit Judge Robert Cahill's comments drew immediate fire from women's activists yesterday, who charged that the sentencing amounted to giving spouses a license to kill.

"This case explodes the myth that there is justice for domestic violence victims in Maryland," said Carol Alexander of the House of Ruth shelter for battered women. "He's sanctioned and approved an execution."

Cahill said he was reluctant to give any jail time to 36-year-old Kenneth Peacock, who killed his wife hours after finding her in bed with another man. He could have received 25 years in prison.

"I seriously wonder how many men married five, four years would have the strength to walk away without inflicting some corporal punishment," Cahill said Monday. "I am forced to impose a sentence ... only because I think I must do it to make the system honest."

Sandra Peacock, 31, was shot in the head with a hunting rifle Feb. 9 after her husband came home unexpectedly during a snowstorm. Finding her in bed, he went downstairs, had a few drinks,

got into an argument with her and killed her. Her lover was not hurt.

The judge's comments dominated Baltimore-area radio talk shows yesterday and generated sharp criticism from women's groups and advocates for battered spouses.

"This is 1994, and we have a judge who excuses a man who gets so jealous that he murders his wife," said Judith Wolfer, a lawyer active in domestic violence issues.

"If this judge's message gets out that it's okay, that's not a society I want to live in," she said.

The judge did not immediately return calls for comment.

Susan Carol Elgin, a member of the Maryland Bar Asso-

ciation's committee on gender equality, said she wasn't aware of any past complaints against Cahill.

The committee will discuss his sentence and comments today, she said.

Prosecutors also drew criticism for letting Peacock plead guilty to manslaughter and for recommending a sentence of three to eight years. Peacock was originally charged with murder.

Prosecutor Ann Brobst said the deal was discussed with the victim's family beforehand and that no one objected.

"Given all the facts and circumstances of the case, I don't think a first-degree murder conviction would have been an easy one to achieve," she said.

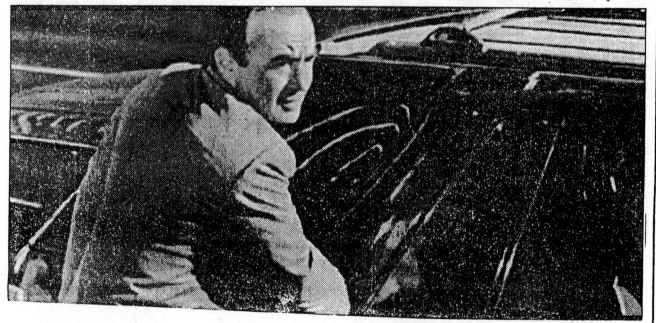

ELIZABETH HENDLER, DALLAS, TX, USA

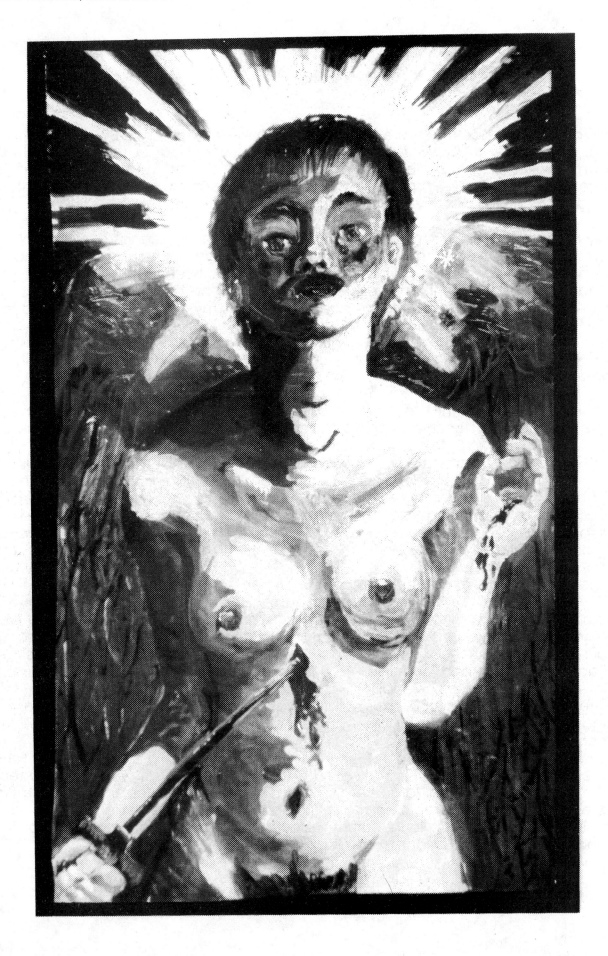

INCLEN

It is no coincidence that there was an earthquake in October, 1989, and that these paintings follow that event. These are not paintings about earthquakes. Yet the earthquake led to a building inspection by the city bureaucracy and the consequences of that inspection resulted in an eviction from a perfectly fantastic studio which was also my home.

My home is essential to my definition of self, as are family, friends and work. In my art I generally use primary colors, bright and cheery. After the quake and the inspection I felt uneasy. My vulnerability became overwhelmingly clear to me and I began to have inklings of deeper fissures in the bright and cheery colors I work with. I started the works on paper to express my anger, frustration and fear. Just before Christmas of 1989 my father had a massive stroke that seemed to leave him on the brink of a vegetative state. The potential of blackness had never been so clear, dramatic or fraught with substance. Clearly larger paintings were called for.

These paintings are not to be seen as somehow representative of these events. The earthquake jeopardized my studio, my home and my work. There is continuity. The structural and color field elements of my earlier paintings are in these pictures. I have extracted and emphasized some of the details of this past work. I am pleased with the strength of the rich, brushy blacks contrasted with hints of color. I am pleased how they seem to absorb, to suck up, all the light to the exclusion of everything else. I like these paintings because they are fluid and expressive. Because they are linked to a natural disaster, I like the factured, but strong color fields that lie beneath the event.

I have been able to come to this darkness in my work in a time frame that is linked to the earthquake. The earthquake caused aftershocks in my existence which have focused that dispair and pain that runs through all of our lives. For me these black paintings will always be there to remind me of the unlit chasm that surrounds our rational, lit, colorful world. I am not ready to give myself over to that blackness. I acknowledge it and I want to use it to triumph over its awesomeness. I am not interested in sharing the real or imagined personal tragedies of my life. I am interested in sharing successful paintings as reflective of the process of life. Yet they are just paintings and they are either successful or not in how well they convey the picture.

These paintings are surprising to me. I have a large body of work that precedes the quake. It is by and large very different in concept, color and structure from these works. The quake jarred me in substantial ways. I believe that the body of paintings that will follow in the future will contain elements of these black paintings and will be far richer because of this experience.

Jeanne Jo L'Heureux   P. O. Box 597, Venice, California 90294

INCLENS 283

Inclens
Jeanne Jo L'Heureux

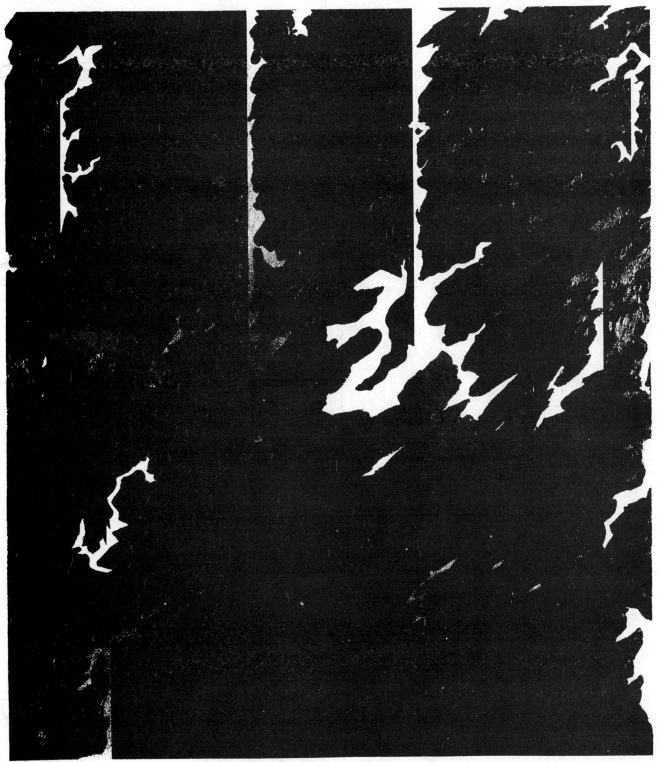

Inclen #9, 1990   54" x 48", oil paint on gessoed canvas

Jeanne Jo L'Heureux   P. O. Box 597, Venice, California 90294

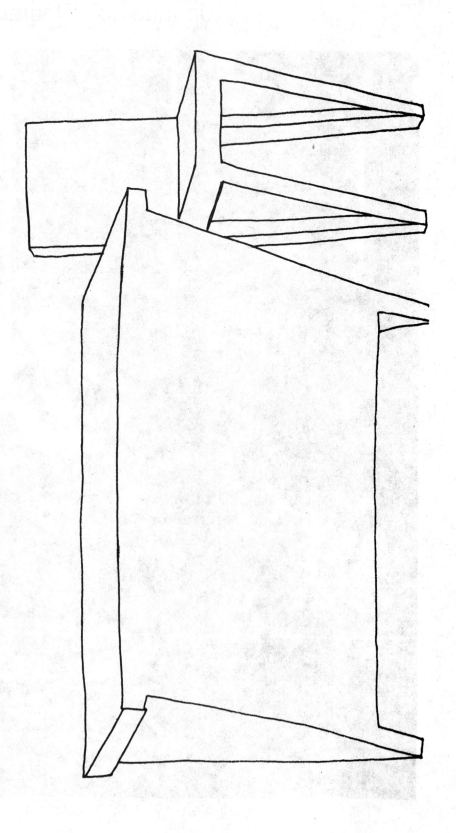

MARTA CHILINDRON, NEW YORK, NY, USA

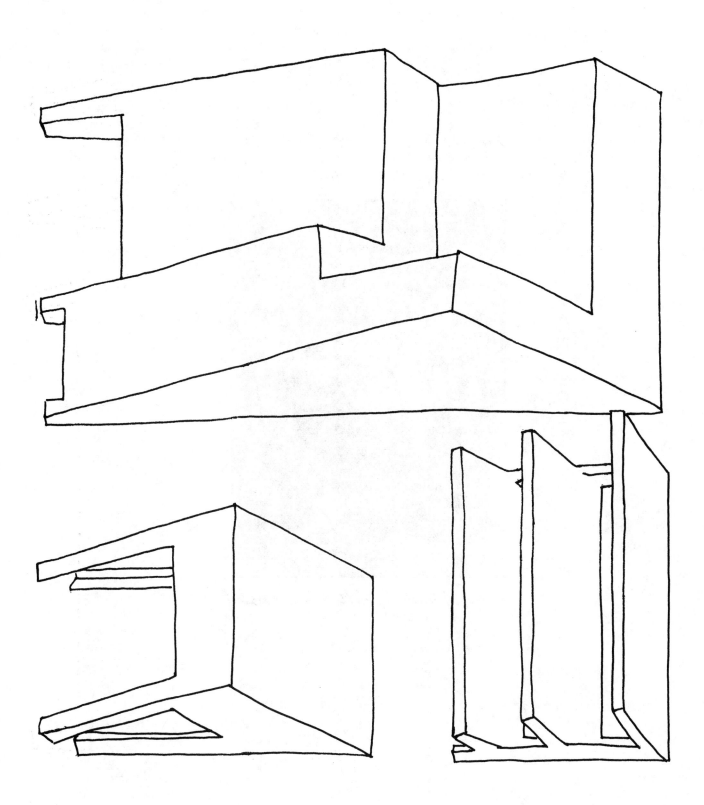

ANN MESSNER, NEW YORK, NY, USA

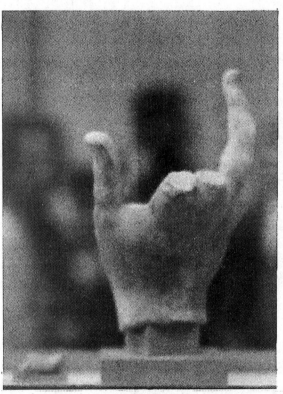

winged victory with broken hand

ANN MESSNER, NEW YORK, NY, USA

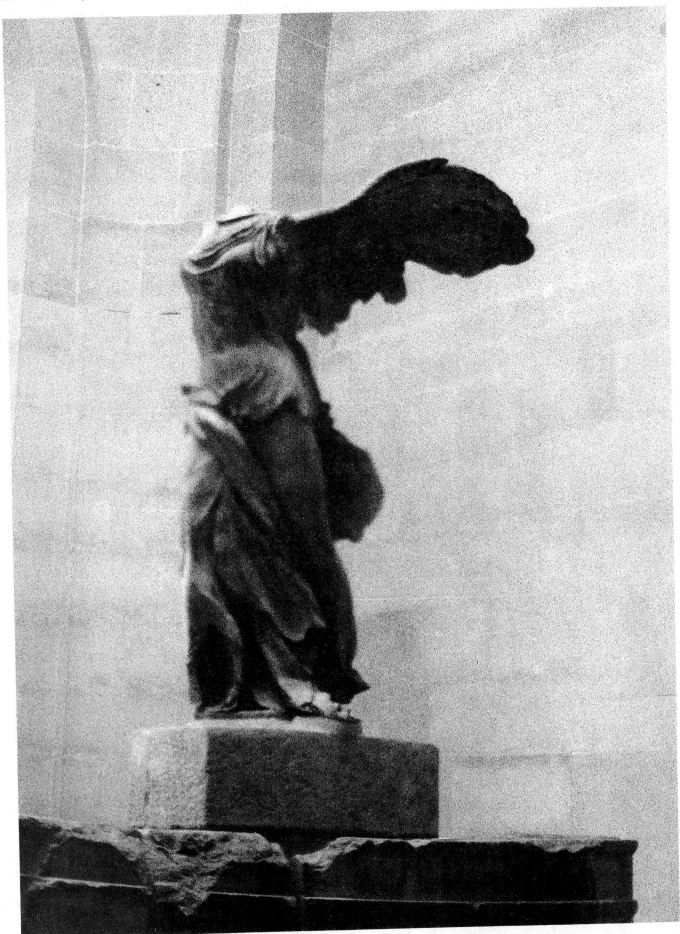

SKOWMON HASTANAN, NEW YORK, NY, USA

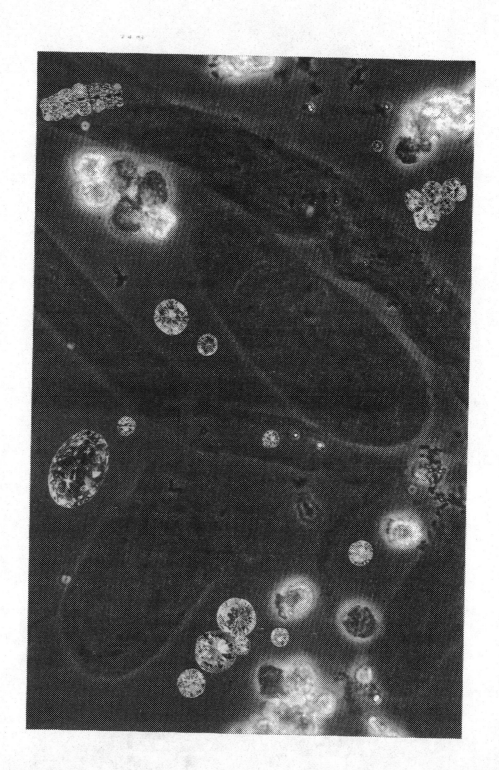

SUZAN ETKIN, NEW YORK, NY, USA

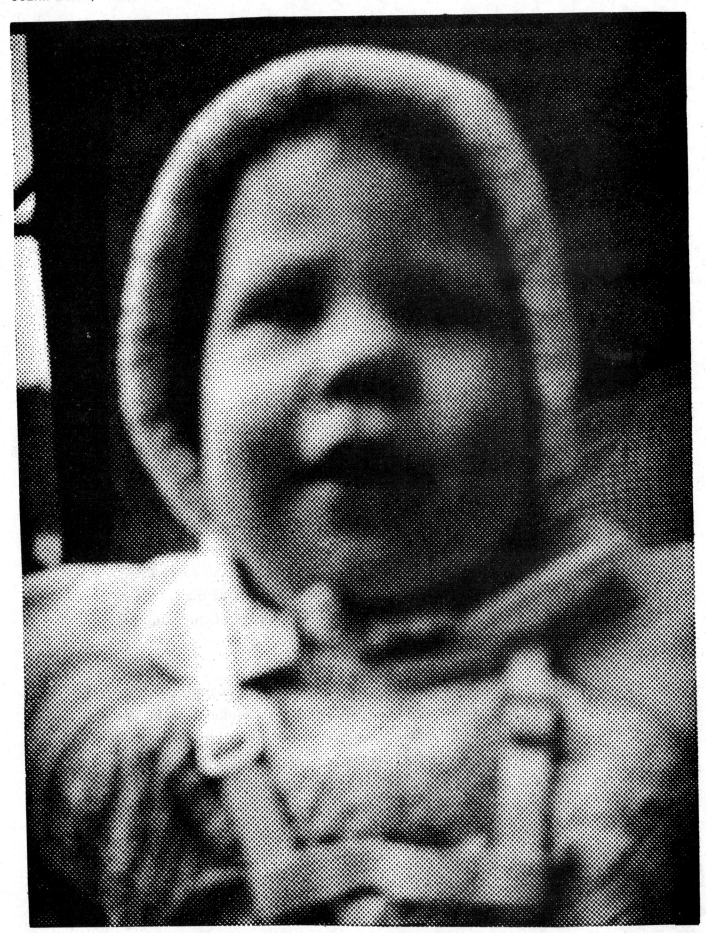

The exhibition project *Inside the Visible* is unfolding as an open-ended process, prompted by the observation of multiple convergences in aesthetic practices both in time (over different periods of the 20th century) and in space (in different countries of the world). From experience, one knows that a museum is a house securing order through its own rules. However, the display of this exhibition should generate amazement, in the manner of a *Wunderkammer*. The *Wunderkammer* is a private collection of objects assembled according to personal perception, desire and reminiscences, but not according to an 'objective' system of classification as in the case of a contemporary museum. The *Wunderkammer*, a personalised collage of realtiy, is both reflective of the mainstream, authoritarian systems of communication and also of puzzlement. It is within this space of amazement shared by the art work, the maker and the beholder - which could be called "participatory relation" - that the exhibition is conceived.

The curatorial process may be likened to an excavation of material traces and fragmentary histories which are recombined into new statigraphies or configurations to produce new meanings and insights of reality. If a structure has to be conceived for the exhibition it is that of several possible recurrent cycles, rather than a linear survey with its investment in artistic originality and genealogies. Moreover, as work crosses different temporal and spatial zones, finding new audiences each with their own symbolic world views, so it undergoes shifts in meaning and significance. Thus it is towards the specificity of the encounter between work and viewer and the continual reinvention of the aesthetic experience that the concept of the exhibition is directed.

As a manifestation of culture, art is both a reflection of changing sociopolitical and economic circumstances and the expression of singular thought, yet it is not reducible to either. Despite the recurrence of similar life crises throughout the 20th century, such as the periodic rise of state repression, nationalism and xenophobia, different times demand different resolutions. Nonetheless, at such times of crisis, there seems to be a need to deconstruct existing representational codes, to search for "new beginnings", in order to imagine the world anew. With this in mind, we must also consider that, at any time, there exist different perceptions of the same reality, or material

CATHERINE DE ZEGHER, KORTRIJK, BELGIUM

expressions of coexisting and often conflicting realities, which have too often been dismissed, or rendered invisible, by the priviledged terms of hegemonic elites whose very existence is nevertheless predicated on this eclipse of difference. One of the aimes of the exhibition is to break down such polarities, to ask if it is possible to think 'difference' without naming it and subsuming it under reductive and totalising systems of thought. It is possible to de-racialise and de-genderise difference and think it in positive, non-reifying terms ; to seek work in which 'sameness' and 'difference' are in a perpetual state of mutual negotiation where the one neither swallows nor ejects the other (*Matrix and Metramorphosis* by Bracha Lichtenberg Ettinger).

The works selected are those which risk 'incoherence' through their acceptance that the act of marking the blank surface, so to speak, may constitue a refiguring or coming-into-language from a space of uncertainty. The meanings and expressions privileged in drawing and those intuitions of reality would be explored in the exhibition as "new beginnings". This act is not to be interpreted as the sign of a transcendent subject, but as a continuous process of redefing existence, open to remappings and negotiations with alterity, seeking the limits of the self and the knowable ...

An analogy may be made between this attitude to 'drawing' and Derrida's play of the supplement or trace - that which both adds to and substitutes for an imaginary "origin" : a perpetual movement of reinscription which resists hierarchies and fixed positions. In this sense, the notions of "interdependency" and "co-emergence" are basic to the selection of works and the developement of the exhibition. The exhibition will attempt to echo the potential of the selected works, seeking to reveal content through its formal process rather than impose a form on a predetermined content. The image that comes to mind is a web insofar as it is a network of traces formed not from any a priori image but through the working process itself.

Catherine de Zegher
September 1994

The exhibition, *Inside the Visible*, will be open to the public at ICA Boston from January to April 1996.

RUTH TURNER, SAN FRANCISCO, CA, USA

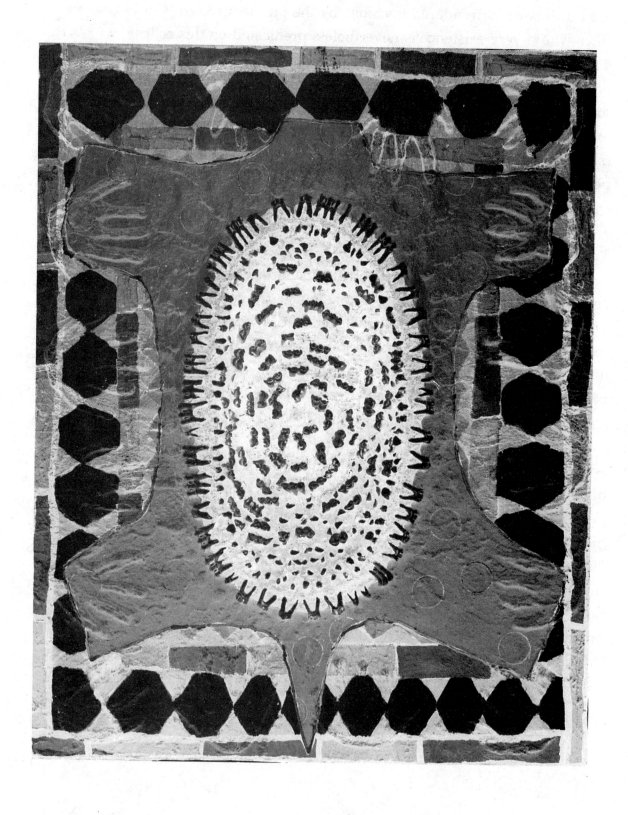

BARBARA MILMAN, DAVIS, CA, USA

TOO MANY WOMEN ARE INVISIBLE

WOMEN WHO LACK POWER ARE INVISIBLE

WOMEN WHO HAVE POWER ARE VISIBLE

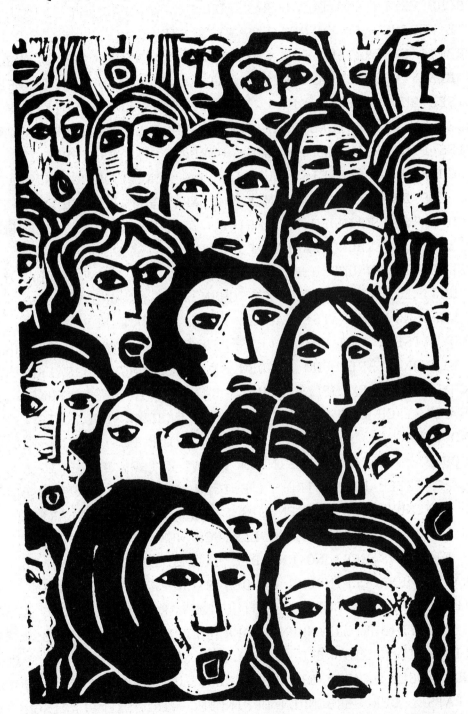

WOMEN ACTING TOGETHER MAKE THEMSELVES VISIBLE

HEIDI SILL, PARIS, FRANCE

RÄTSEL UND WERBUNG GINGEN ALLEIN IN DAS EWIG EXEMPLARISCHE EIS HINEIN:

EXEMPLARISCH FANDEN WERBUNG UND RÄTSEL EIN EWIGES EIS: ERFINDUNG

EIN EWIGES EIS: DIE ERFINDUNG FAND WERBUNG UND RÄTSEL

EXEMPLARISCHE ERFINDUNG DURCH RÄTSELHAFTE WERBUNG IM EWIGEN EIS

RÄTSELHAFTE WERBUNG IM EWIGEN EIS WIRD EXEMPLARISCH ERFUNDEN

FINDEN WERBUNG UND RÄTSEL DIE ERFINDUNG IM EWIGEN EIS EXEMPLARISCH

IM EWIGEN EIS FINDEN EXEMPLARISCH RÄTSEL UND WERBUNG DIE ERFINDUNG

FANDEN RÄTSEL UND WERBUNG EIN EWIGES EIS ZUM ERFINDEN EXEMPLARISCH

ZUM ERFINDEN IM EWIGEN EXEMPLARISCHEN FANDEN SICH WERBUNG UND RÄTSEL

RÄTSELHAFTES FINDEN IM EWIGEN EIS: WERBUNG UND ERFINDUNG

EXEMPLARISCH EIN EWIGES EIS: ZUR FINDUNG VON WERBUNG UND RÄTSEL

EIN EWIGES EIS DER ERFINDUNG IM EXEMPLARISCHEN RÄTSEL DER WERBUNG

WERBUNG UND RÄTSEL ERINDEN EIN EWIGES EIS UND FANDEN ES EXEMPLARISCH

RÄTSEL ERFINDEN, WERBUNG FANDEN ES EXEMPLARISCH IM EWIGEN EIS

WENN RÄTSEL ERFINDEN UND WERBUNG ERFANDEN: EWIGES EXEMPLARISCHES EIS

DIE ERFINDUNG: EIN EWIGES EIS ZWISCHEN WERBUNG UND RÄTSEL

EWIGLICHE WERBUNG DES RÄTSELHAFTEN EISES WIRD EXEMPLARISCH ERFUNDEN

WERBUNG UND RÄTSEL: EIN EWIGES EIS DER EXEMPLARISCHEN ERFINDUNG

IM EWIGEN EIS DER ERFINDUNG FINDEN SICH WERBUNG UND RÄTSEL

FINDET SICH WERBUNG EXEMPLARISCH IM EWIGEN EIS DES ERFUNDENEN RÄTSELS

FANDEN EXEMPLARISCH DIE ERFINDUNG DURCH WERBUNG UND RÄTSEL

RÄTSEL FAND WERBUNG: DAS EXEMPLARISCHE EWIGE EIS: KEINE ERFINDUNG

EXEMPLARISCH FAND WERBUNG ERFINDUNG: ZUM RÄTSEL DES EWIGEN EISES

WERBUNG DES RÄTSELHAFTEN WIRD IM EWIGEN EIS EXEMPLARISCH ERFUNDEN

RÄTSEL UND ERFINDUNG IM EWIGEN EIS FANDEN SICH EXEMPLARISCH

EWIGLICHES FINDEN ERFINDET EXEMPLARISCH WERBUNG UND RÄTSEL

EIN EWIGES EIS: DAS WERBUNG UND DIE RÄTSEL ERFINDEN EXEMPLARISCH

WERBUNG, RÄTSEL UND ERFINDUNG FINDEN SICH EXEMPLARISCH IM EWIGEN EIS

RÄTSELHAFTES FINDEN IM EWIGEN EIS: EXEMPLARISCHE WERBUNG ALS ERFINDUNG

ERFUNDENES RÄTSEL DER ERFINDUNG ODER WERBUNG IM EIS EXEMPLARISCH

ERFINDUNG IM EWIGEN EIS WERD EXEMPLARISCH ZU WERBUNG UND RÄTSEL

WERBUNG UND RÄTSEL FANDEN EINE ERFINDUNG IM EWIGEN EIS EXEMPLARISCH

DAS EWIGE RÄTSEL DER WERBENDEN ERFINDUNG WIRD EXEMPLARISCH EIS

RÄTSEL FAND WERBUNG ERFINDEN EXEMPLARISCH: EIN EWIGES EIS

WERBENDES RÄTSEL ALS EXEMPLARISCHE ERFINDUNG IM EWIGEN EIS

DIE ERFINDUNG DES EISES FANDEN RÄTSEL UND WERBUNG EWIG EXEMPLARISCH

FANDEN RÄTSEL UND WERBUNG DIE EXEMPLARISCHE ERFINDUNG EWIGLICH

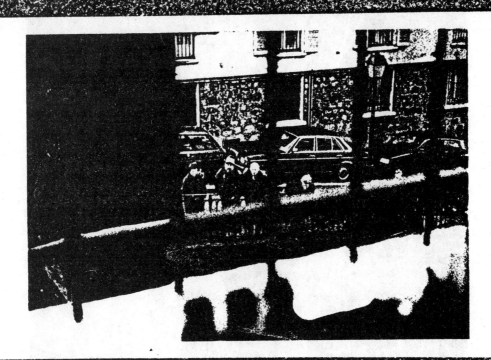

HEIDI SILL

PERSPECTIVE

VERNISSAGE LE SAMEDI 18 MARS 1995   DE 16 A 20 HEURES
EXPOSITION DU 21 MARS AU 20 AVRIL 1995

ESPACE E1 CUSINE
24, rue Norvins   75018 Paris   Tel. 42 51 06 61

CATHARINA COSIN, NEW YORK, NY USA

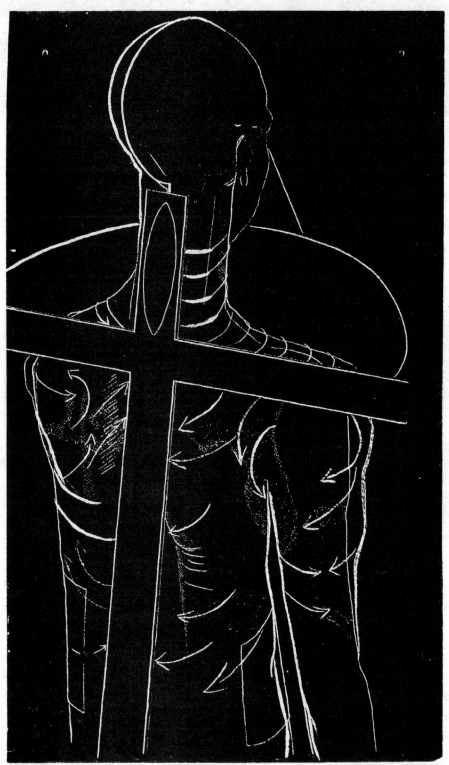

*W*hat makes my blood **boil:**

THE SILENCED WOMAN

C. Cosin '95

CATHARINA COSIN, NEW YORK, NY USA

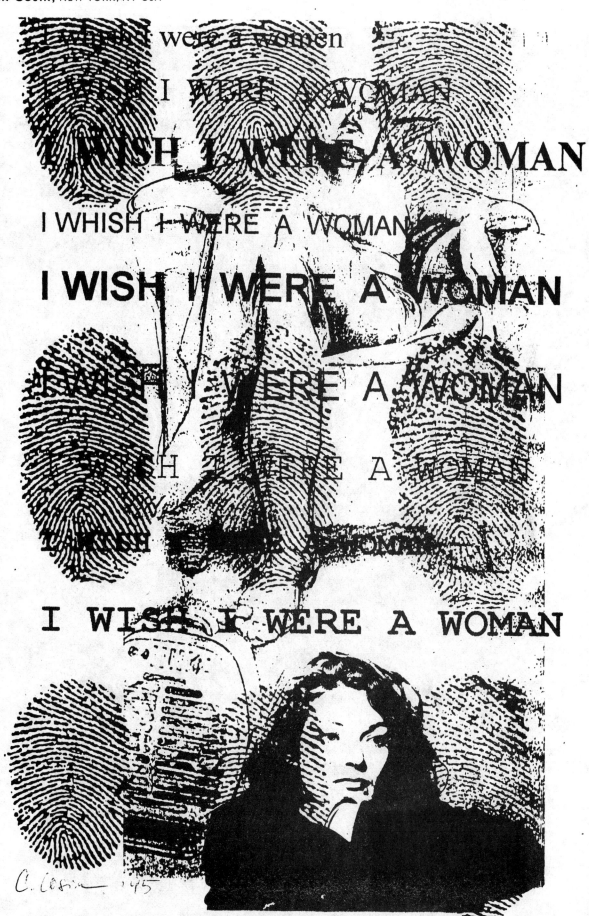

LESLIE KIPPEN, JERSEY CITY, NJ, USA

I TAPED THE TIP OF MY NOSE TO MY FOREHEAD

TIGHTLY PULLING ON MY UPPER LIP AND NOSTRILS

TO CHANGE THE SHAPE OF MY NOSE

IT WAS THE INFLUENCE OF MY ORTHODONTIST

IF HE COULD RECONSTRUCT MY OVERBITE WITH WIRES

I COULD EASILY DO THE SAME WITH MY NOSE

BEING A VISIONARY AT 10 YEARS OLD I HAD A PRECONCEIVED NOTION OF WHAT

A SWEET SIXTEEN RITUAL FOR A JEWISH GIRL FROM QUEENS WOULD REQUIRE

ASSIMILATION

A NOSE JOB

DR. DIAMOND WAS A FAVORITE IN THE NEIGHBORHOOD

A PARTY, A NOSE JOB, OR JEWELRY

I OPTED FOR THE MATERIAL

I DECIDED I'LL CONTINUE TO TAPE -

I'LL TAKE CARE OF THE NOSE.

YOU CAN CHANGE THE SHAPE OF YOUR BODY

INCREASE YOUR ATTENTION SPAN

HEIGHTEN LEVELS OF AWARENESS

EXPAND YOUR CONSCIOUSNESS

CONTROL YOUR DESTINY

BUT YOU CAN'T CHANGE THE SHAPE OF YOUR NOSE

- LESLIE KIPPEN

LESLIE KIPPEN, JERSEY CITY, NJ, USA

I HAD A HAIR COMPLEX

AND IT WOULDN'T GO AWAY

AS SOON AS I THOUGHT

I HAD IT UNDER CONTROL

THOSE HAIR FOLLICLES EMERGED

ON PARTS OF MY BODY THAT CAUSED

GENDER CONFUSION

AND

JEWISH GUILT

IF ONLY I WERE A GENTILE

- LESLIE KIPPEN

HILDA DANIEL, BROOKLYN, NY, USA

LORRIN THOMAS, BROOKLYN, NY, USA

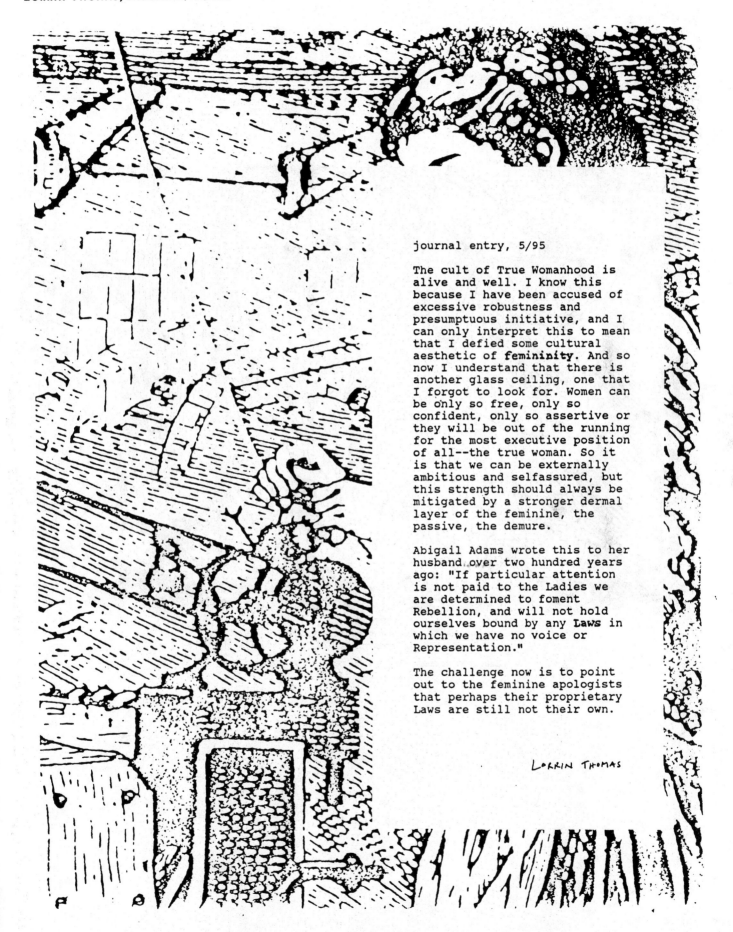

journal entry, 5/95

The cult of True Womanhood is alive and well. I know this because I have been accused of excessive robustness and presumptuous initiative, and I can only interpret this to mean that I defied some cultural aesthetic of **femininity**. And so now I understand that there is another glass ceiling, one that I forgot to look for. Women can be only so free, only so confident, only so assertive or they will be out of the running for the most executive position of all--the true woman. So it is that we can be externally ambitious and selfassured, but this strength should always be mitigated by a stronger dermal layer of the feminine, the passive, the demure.

Abigail Adams wrote this to her husband over two hundred years ago: "If particular attention is not paid to the Ladies we are determined to foment Rebellion, and will not hold ourselves bound by any **Laws** in which we have no voice or Representation."

The challenge now is to point out to the feminine apologists that perhaps their proprietary Laws are still not their own.

LORRIN THOMAS

LOUISE KRAMER, NEW YORK, NY, USA

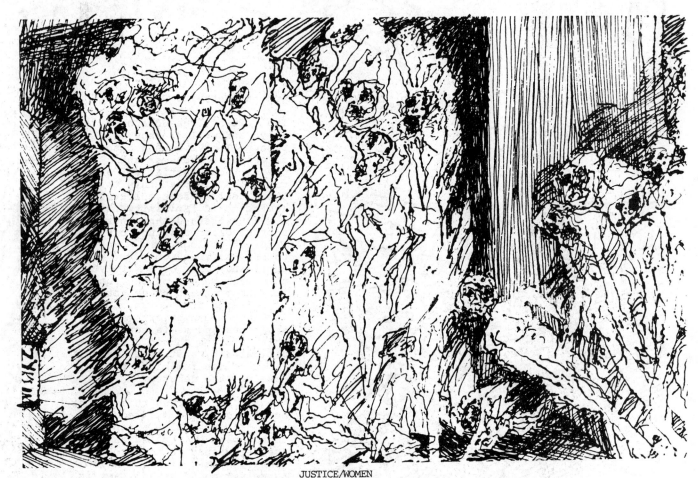

JUSTICE/WOMEN
LOUISE KRAMER,sculptor-graphic artist 212 344-2137
A.I.R. GALLERY, 40 Wooster St,NYC, NY 10013 212 966-0799

Cauldron series: Auschwitz pen/ink drawing

LOUISE KRAMER, NEW YORK, NY, USA

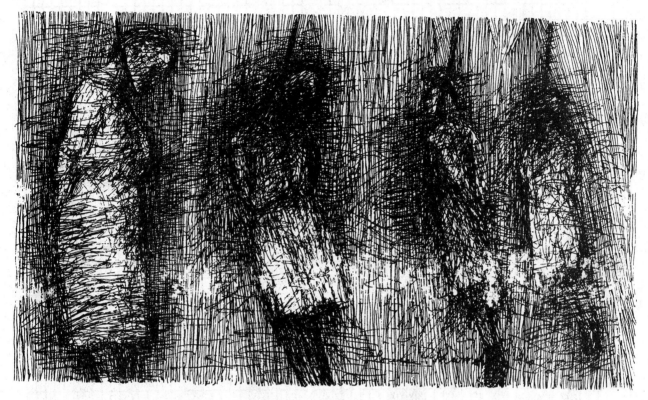

JUSTICE/WOMEN
LOUISE KRAMER,sculptor-graphic artist 212 344-2137
A.I.R. GALLERY, 40 Wooster St,NYC, NY 10013 212 966-0799

Cauldron series: Auschwitz pen/ink drawing

MEIRA MARRERO DIAZ, HAVANA, CUBA

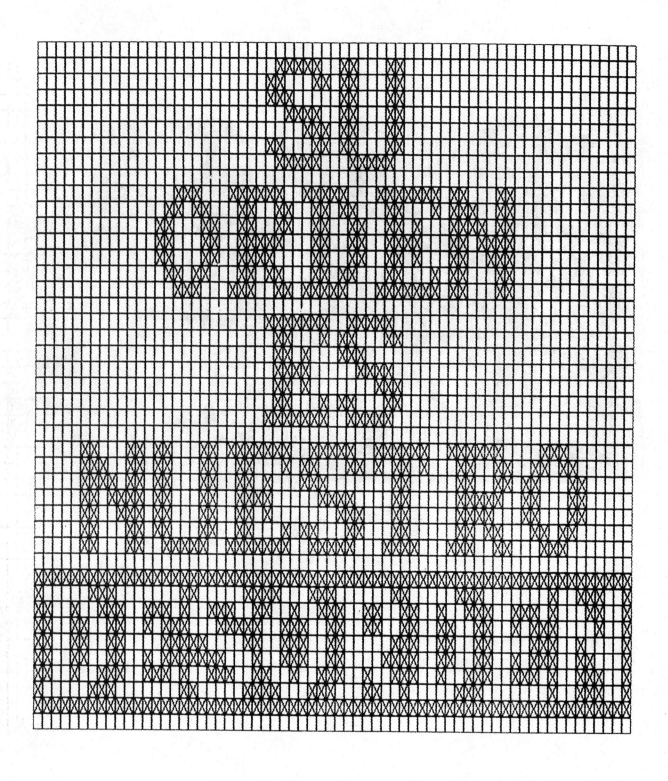

MEIRA MARRERO DIAZ, HAVANA, CUBA

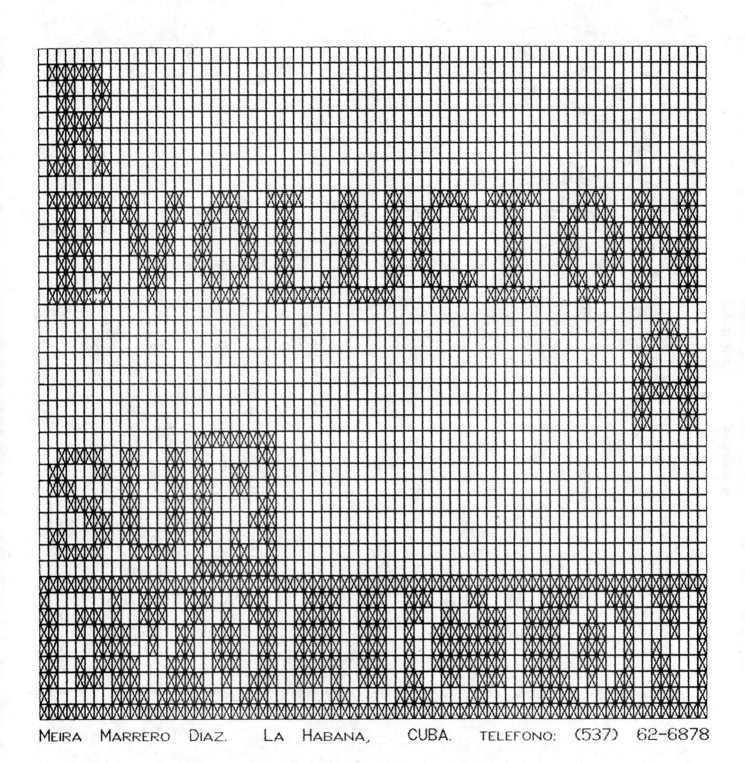

MEIRA MARRERO DIAZ. LA HABANA, CUBA. TELEFONO: (537) 62-6878

VIKKY ALEXANDER, VANCOUVER, BC, CANADA

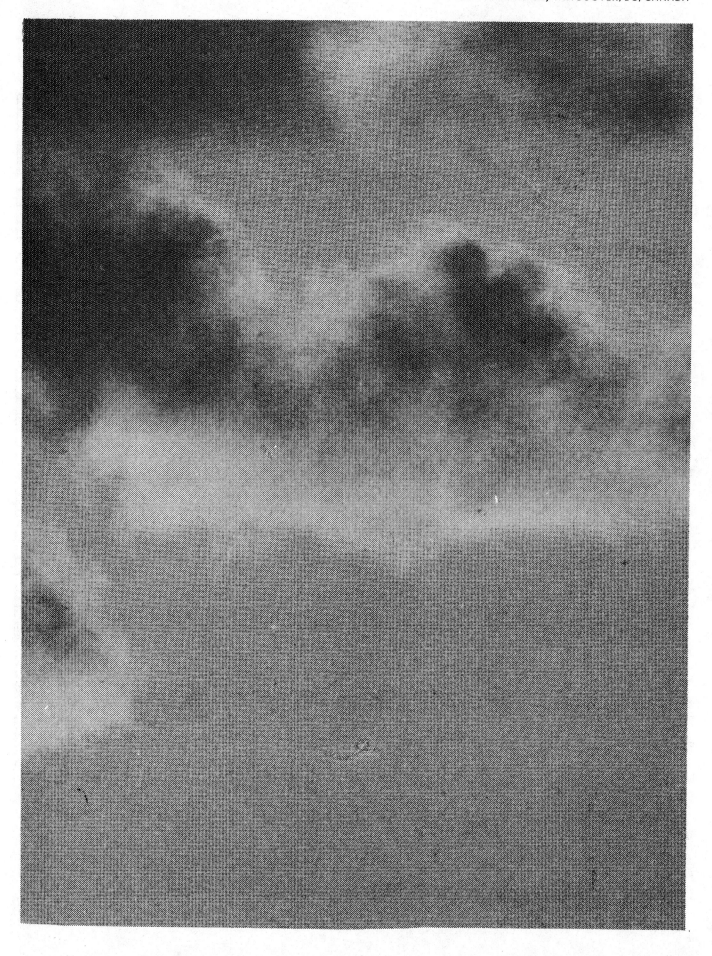

VIKKY ALEXANDER, VANCOUVER, BC, CANADA

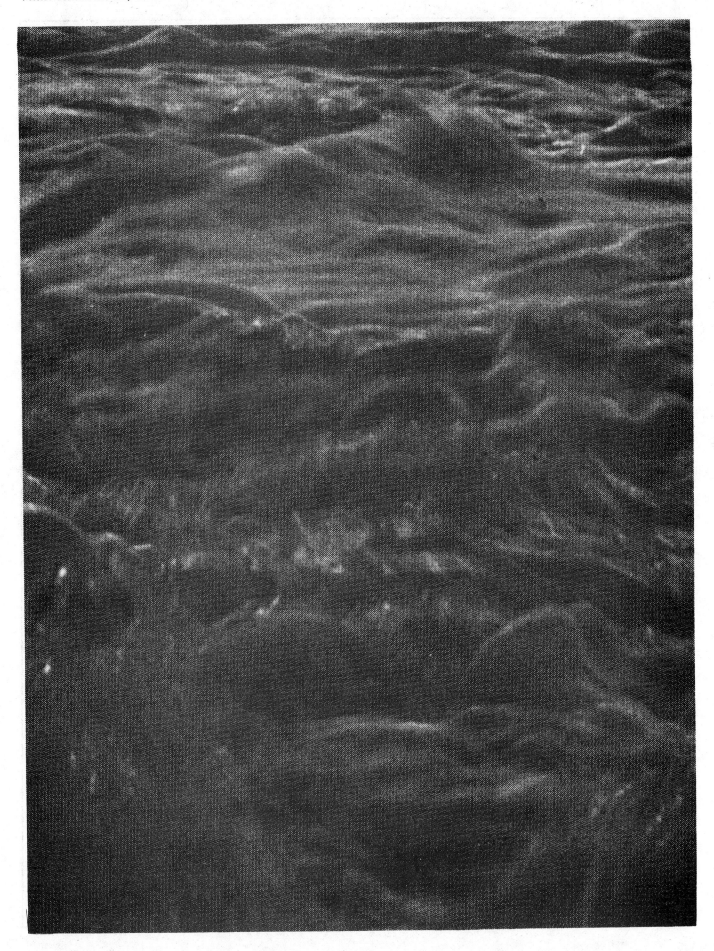

VIKKY ALEXANDER, VANCOUVER, BC, CANADA

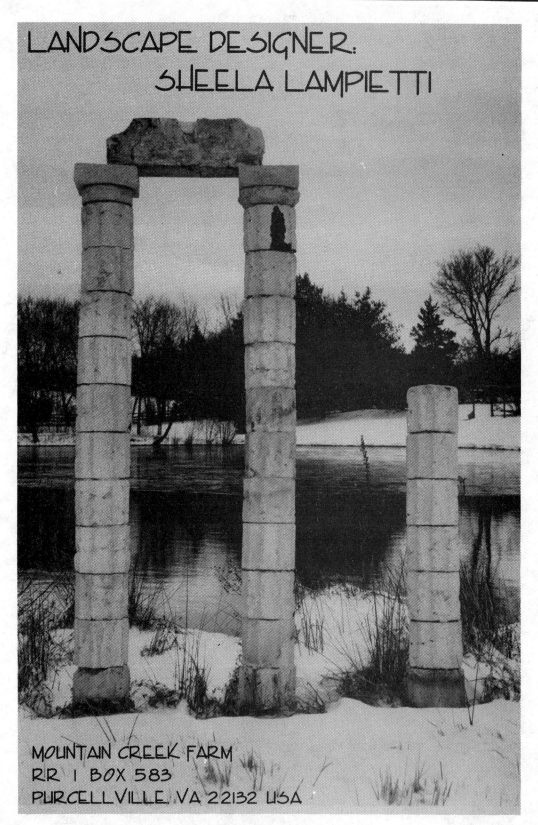

LANDSCAPE DESIGNER:
SHEELA LAMPIETTI

MOUNTAIN CREEK FARM
RR 1 BOX 583
PURCELLVILLE, VA 22132 USA

703 668-6101 PH.
703 668-6952 FAX
LANDSCAPING = ART + ARCHITECTURE

STEPHANIE STRICKLAND, SCARSDALE, NY, USA

ON FIRST LOOKING INTO DIRINGER'S *THE ALPHABET: A KEY TO THE HISTORY OF MANKIND*

I wanted...a *Guneaform*--a woman's form--of writing
and thought, perhaps, Cuneiform it, so tactile that script, palpable
wedges pressed in wet clay: writing "at once," as a fresco

is painted.   But in this book, in the pictographs
that underlie Cuneiform, there is only one sign for woman,
pudendum.   Slavegirl and male servant, also

given by genital description.
Man is head, with mouth in it, plus beard.
I thought apart from Diringer's claim, *origin* of alphabets,

this script is just one instance.   Hieroglyphic
determinatives for man and woman in Egypt look more
matched, both stickfigure-like, both kneeling on one shin--   Except

the woman has longer hair, no arms, no *difference* between
first- and second-person-singular.   How quietly here ancient grammar states
what our marital law, or canon teaching on abortion, legislates:

"I am--not only yours--but you."
I began to wonder whether, somewhere in the world, different
thinking existed.   Flipping through the book,

I was struck by Chinese trigrams, their elegant
abstraction: just three lines
above each other meant, the footnote said, sky and dry and prime

and creative: grandfather-life.   Slashed, into six
little lines, the sign meant secondarily
and destruction, and foreboding, and grandmother, and earth.

Later Chinese for man, an upright stroke, hook rising to the left.
For woman, a buckling crook, large bundle at the shoulder.
Woman, next to woman, meaning quarrel--

and man, next to word, meaning *true.*
I did find toward the end one group of people, the Yao
or Miao, or Miao-tzu tribe, called

by the Chinese "wild Southern barbarians."
Fifty thousand in Viet Nam and Laos before our war.
The Yao had, I found nowhere else, four

different signs of *equal* complication:
mother, father, person, heart
--but as I said, wiped out.

Stephanie Strickland

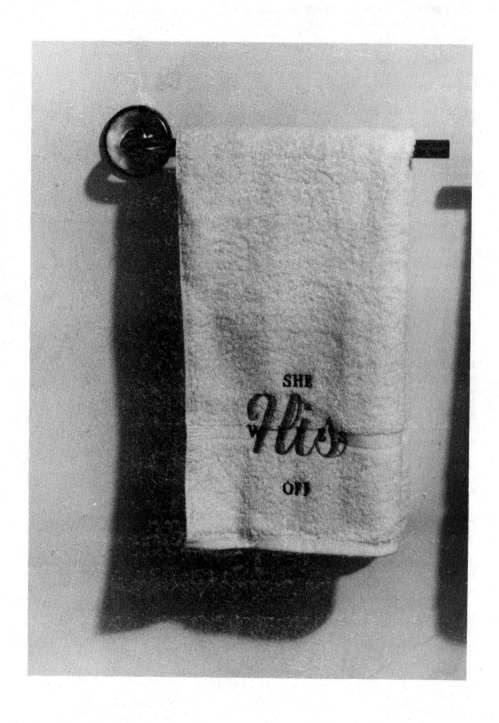

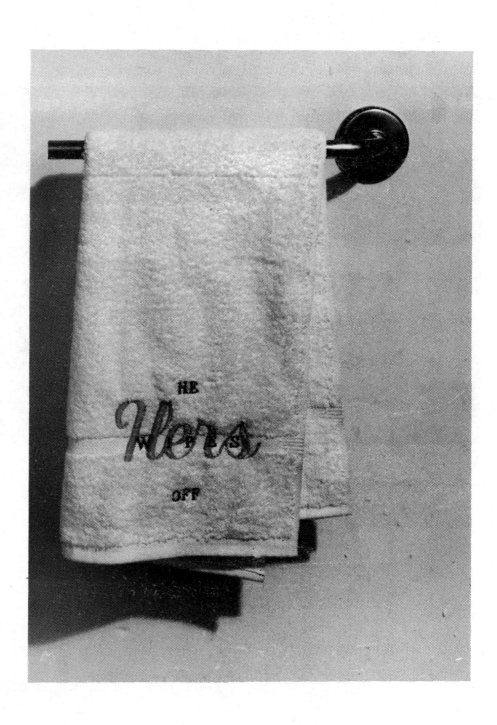

GABRIELLE WAMBAUGH, PARIS, FRANCE

Using video and photography, I Juxtapose images of the near and the far, as compared to breathing (inhale and exhale), at times regular and in cadence at other times arrhythmic and disordered.

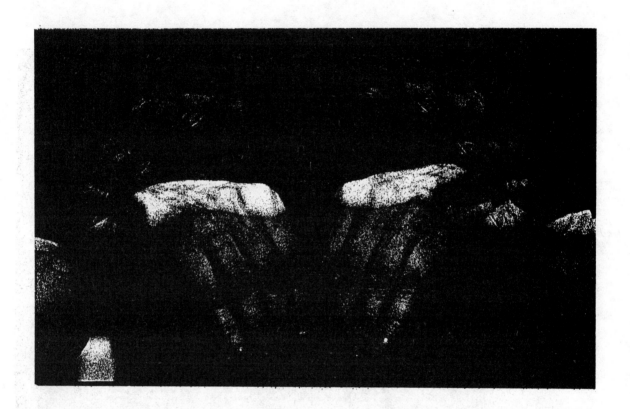

DROP

JANICE MOVSON, NEW YORK, NY, USA

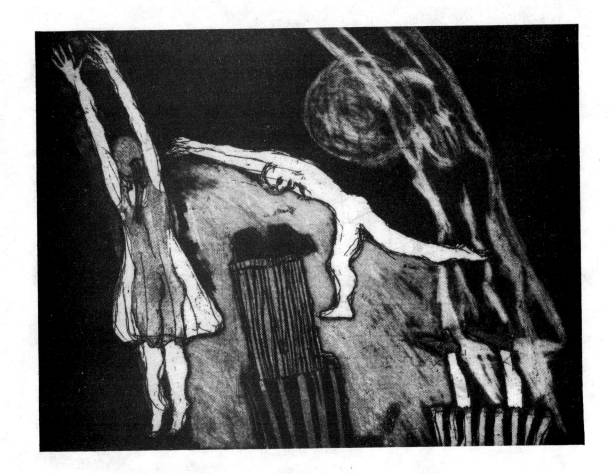

EUGENIA POP, CLUJ, ROMANIA

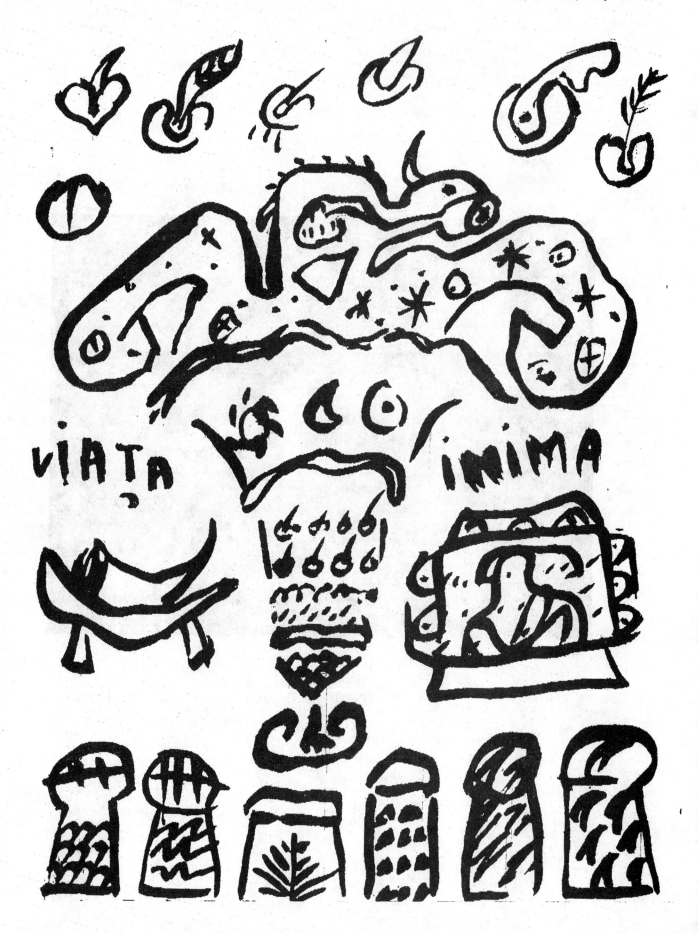

AUDREY STONE, BROOKLYN, NY, USA

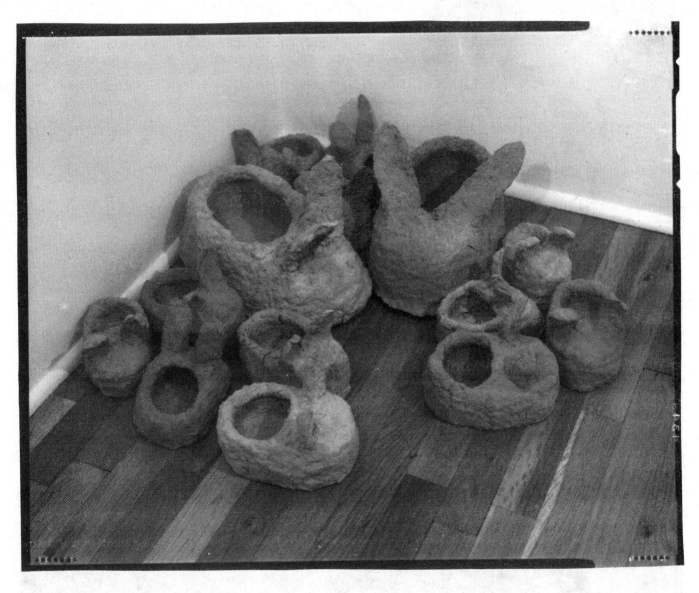

"LIKE BUNNIES"   **1993**   **AUDREY STONE**
paper pulp and acrylic
dimentions vary, approx. 30x36x8.5"

LISA DALE MILLER, LOS GATOS, CA, USA

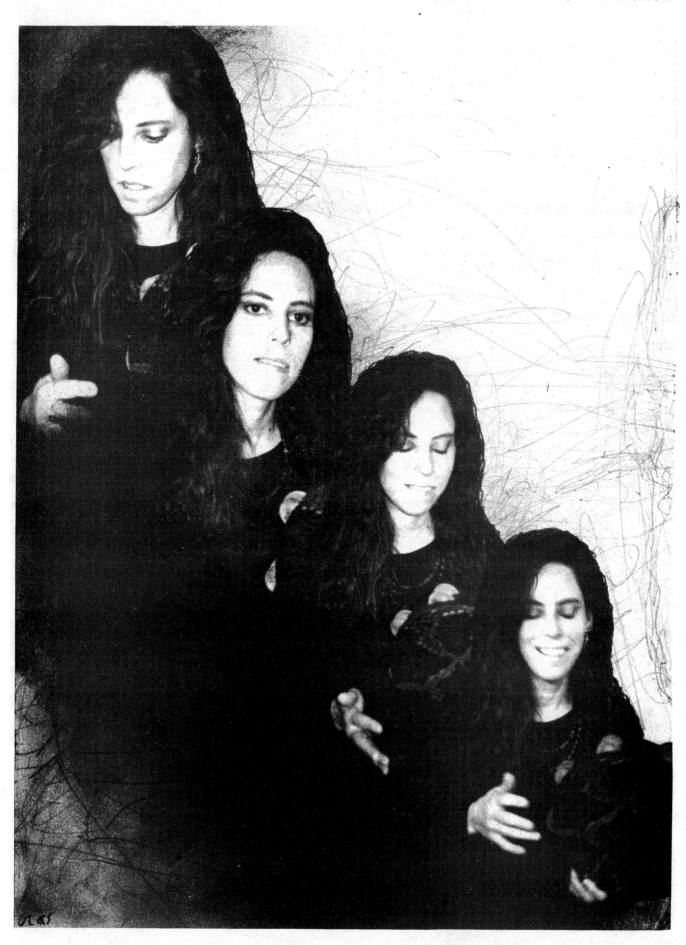

LISA DALE MILLER, LOS GATOS, CA, USA

Listen and Heal

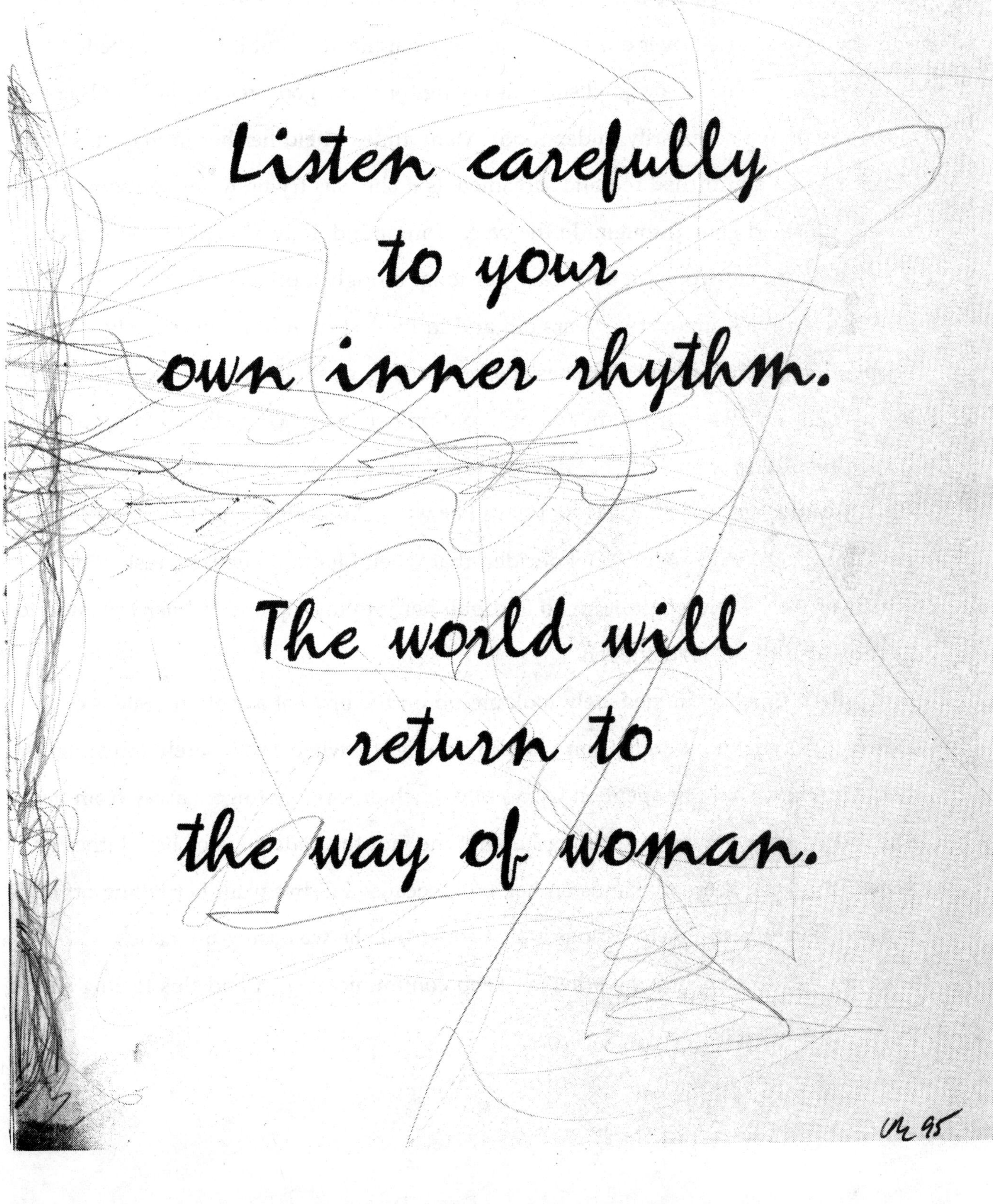

*Listen carefully
to your
own inner rhythm.*

*The world will
return to
the way of woman.*

LM 95

GINNY PYE, PHILADELPHIA, PA, USA

Ever since Eva was a newborn, John and I have made an effort to listen to her when she seemed to need to cry. Of course, we'd always check first to make sure her diaper wasn't wet, or we'd try to see if she felt too hot or too cold or to tell if she was hungry. We worried over our baby as all new parents do. But if nothing needed to be fixed right away, we decided she was crying for some good reason, although not not a reason we necessarily understood. Many times I held her her in my arms and she struggled and turned red and screamed as if she was trying to tell me something just awful she'd gone through. In the back of my mind, I always wondered if she was telling me how painful and scary her long, though routine, birth had been.

Now Eva's almost two years old and in the last month my previously cooperative and delightful child has she been acting pissy and mad most of the time. We've had days when she didn't want to put on her winter coat, didn't want to be picked up, didn't want to be put down, didn't want to go in her car seat and then didn't want to get out of it. When I gave her what she wanted she'd just find the next thing to be mad about. So, I decided that when I had the time, I'd just stop whatever we were attempting to do and pull her into my lap and tell her I wanted to hear all about how mad she felt.

Each time she immediately took me up on the offer of attention. She'd cry and say, "Too tight, too tight, don't hold me so tight," when I was barely touching her. Her fury would be spent on trying to wrench or slap my fingers away from her. She didn't want anything touching her, not me, not the bedcovers or her clothes or shoes. But I did keep my hands on her, both because I didn't want her falling off my lap and also, in a strangely curious way, I could tell she was using my hands touching her to somehow help herself keep communicating. I had this feeling she

GINNY PYE, PHILADELPHIA, PA, USA

was trying to tell me something.

One day, in the midst of one of her tantrums, she stopped crying and looked at me as she sat on my lap and said, "Mommy tummy hurt?" I smiled, thinking how lovely my daughter was to be concerned about my discomfort while she was feeling so badly herself. "No, honey," I said, "I'm alright, you're not hurting Mommy's tummy. You can stay on my lap." Eva then looked more closely at me and I could tell she was thinking hard. "No," she said finally, "me in Mommy tummy hurt."

I felt a flush of excitement and pride and maybe even horror. "Really honey, you hurt?" "Yes, Mommy," she said, "Mommy tummy too tight." My heart was racing the way it had when we'd watched as she took her first step. "Where did it hurt?" I asked. I think I half hoped we'd have a lengthy discussion about her birth. She'd tell me her version, then I'd tell her mine.

But Eva didn't look at all interested any more. Her big cry left her relaxed and ready to play. "Eva body hurt all over," she said almost happily, then she hopped off my lap and trotted over to her toys.

I lamely trailed after her. "When you were born?"

"Yup, Mommy," she said. Then far more urgently, "Hey, Mommy, where are Ernie and Bert, Mommy?"

I don't know why I was so stunned by Eva's telling me about her birth. It hadn't happened that long before and now she had language: now, of course, she'd both remember and want to tell. Still, it seems to me like a special gift of communication she was offering back after all those times John and I had listened and wondered what it was she was saying. Now, perhaps, we know.

HOPE SANDROW, NEW YORK, NY, USA

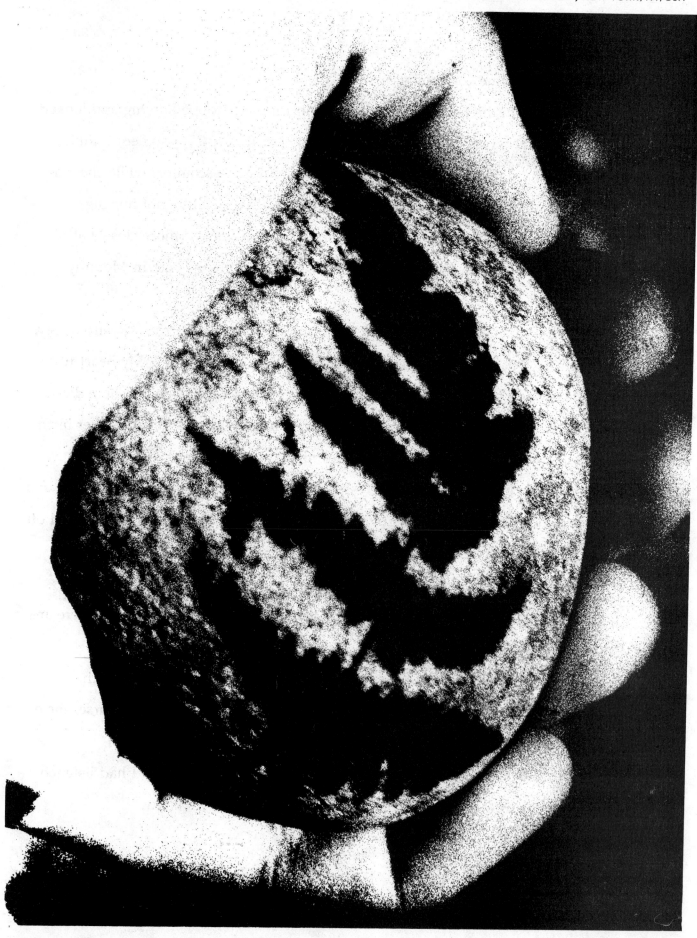

MIMI YOUNG, BROOKLYN, NY, USA

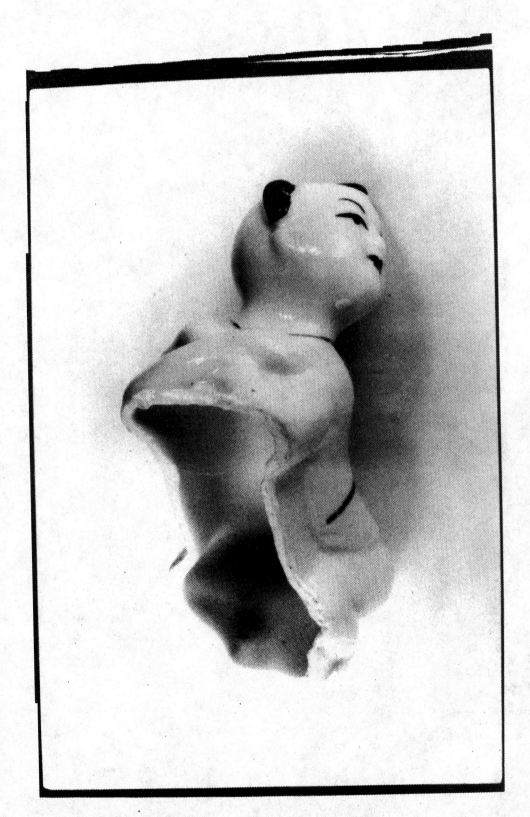

Mimi Young
Untitled (flip-side)
1995

ELAINE CHOW, NEW YORK, NY, USA

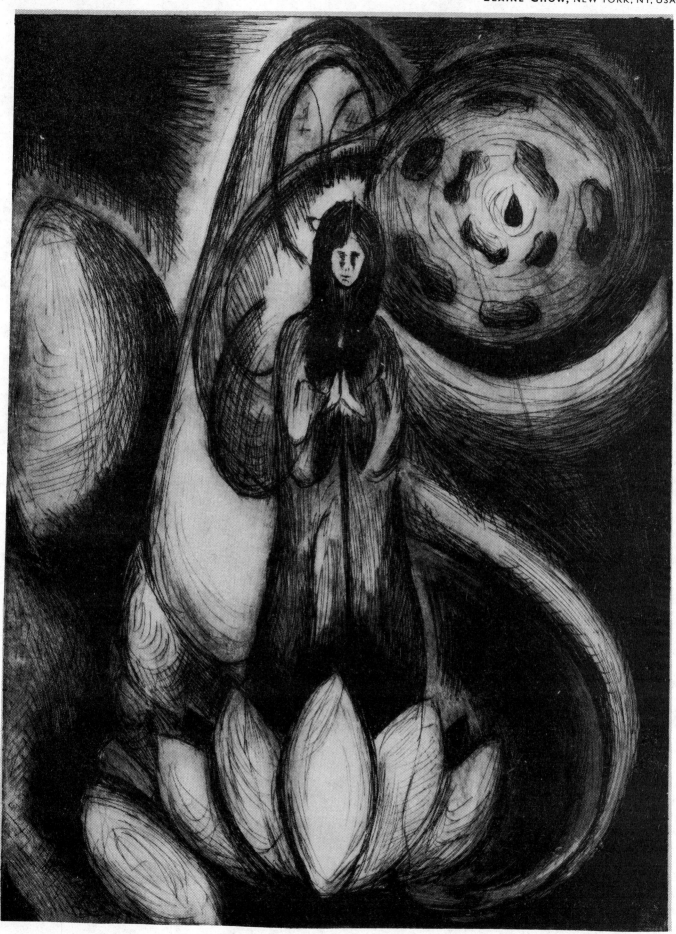

ELAINE CHOW, NEW YORK, NY, USA

i dreamt of my birth one night i was born
out of the ancient roots
buried deep
out of the living that pushed out from
below to up high i dreamt of
out of the lotus flower
the lin
i dreamt of her the goddess
on the throne of the
lotus flower
the lin
eyes open as brightly
and she said
Yi-Lin
you are me i am you
we are the maiden the mother the death crone
we are of the lotus flower
the lin
this is what i dream true the
archaic charge of the goddess that i must
remember
and keep the roots alive
to forget would be the death of her
existence
and the storms will ravage and not subside
until a lotus flower blooms.

Elaine Y. Chow

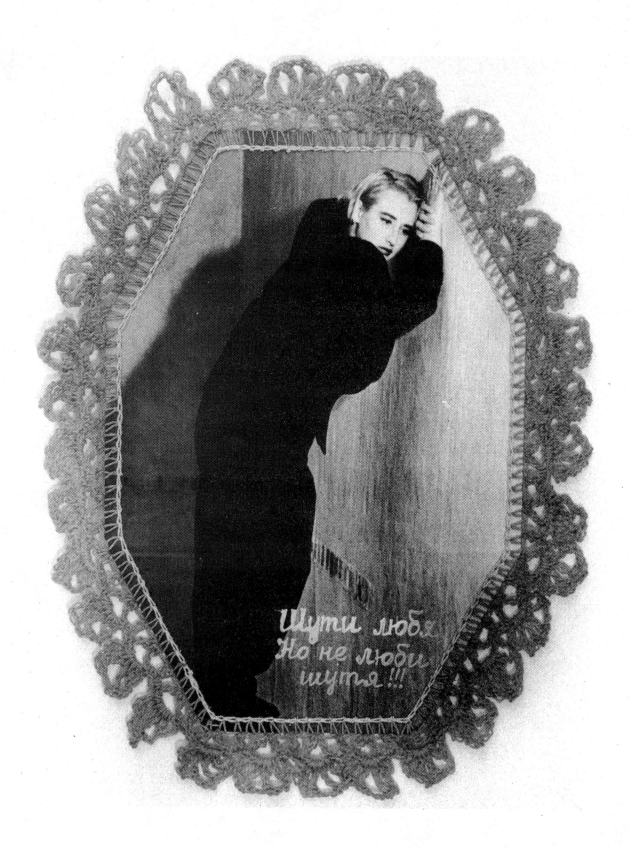

VITA BUJVID, ST PETERSBURG, RUSSIA

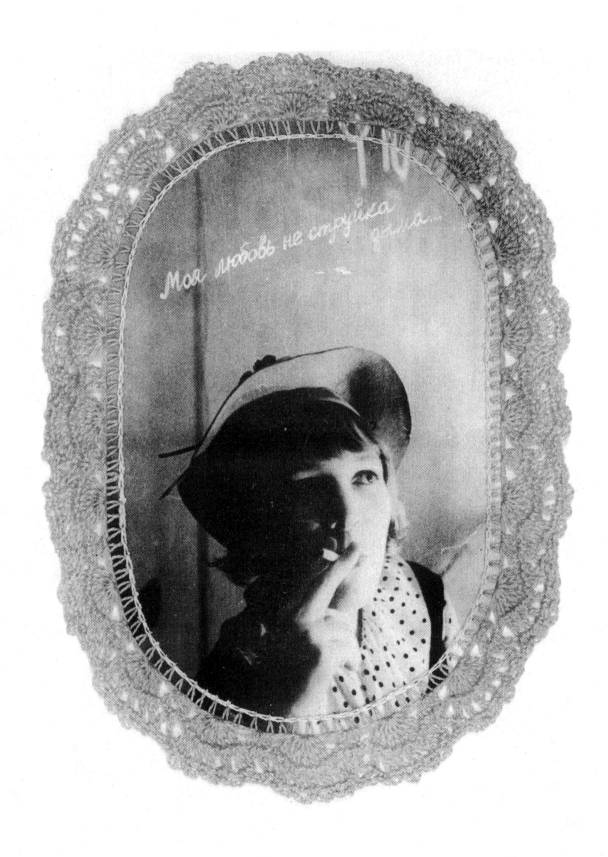

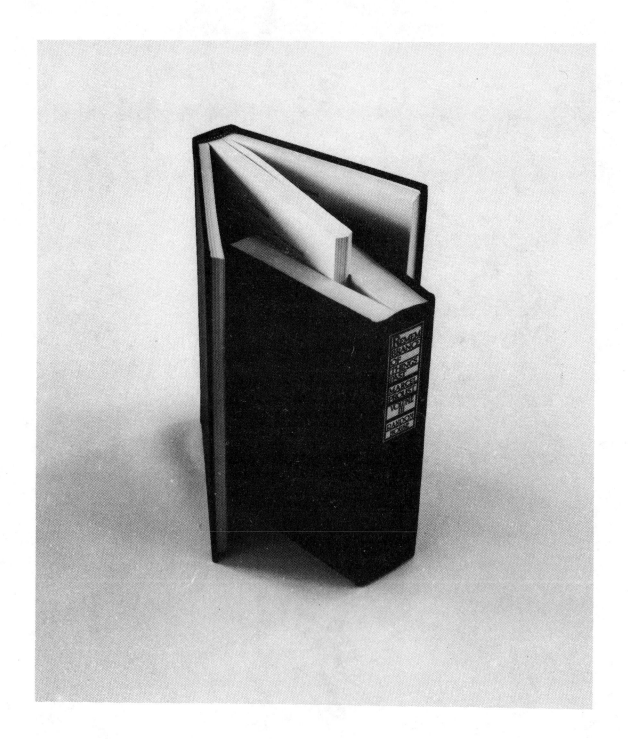

NANCY MEBANE SHAKIR, MONTCLAIR, NJ, USA

BIG LOVE

I like big love
No holds barred,
Laughing from the gut,
Sunday, hunk of cake
Kind of love

I like big love
Complete immersion,
Baptismal,
Cold lemonade on a hot day
Kind of love

I love big love

JANIS WILKINS, NEW YORK, NY, USA

JANIS WILKINS, NEW YORK, NY, USA

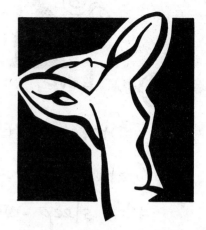

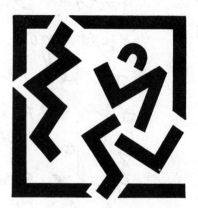

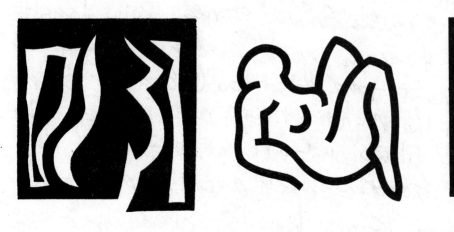

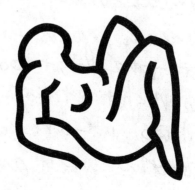

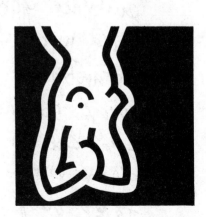

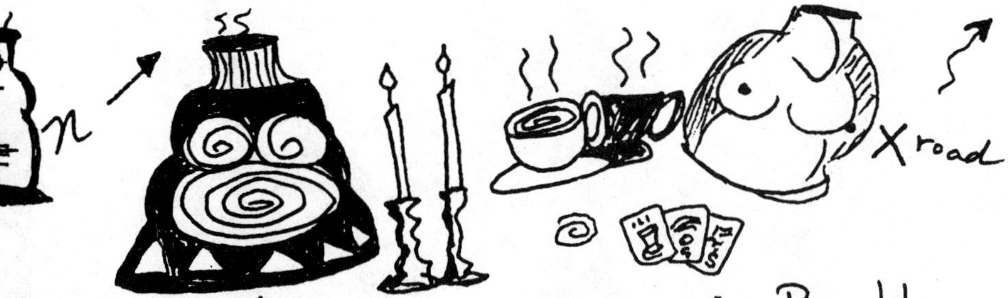

Dear Love,

Stars sparkle on the night streets in Brooklyn. Galaxies, salsa, rap & hot streets calling to the sleep walkers. Look at me you sleeping fools! Stay awake & eat mangos & know that you are not alone! Stars sparkle on the night streets of Brooklyn & all the taxis are free tonight. Gorgeous elegant drivers smile & sing your favorite song. Tall women in African robes light incense in your wake. Children embrace you with raging smiles filled with life juice & really funny stories. Belly laughs, strawberries & cream, good strong coffee & the urge to paint the tattood waiter. Stars sparkle on the night streets of Brooklyn - the clear wind blows, we are sure footed & take deep breaths with ancient potential. The corner store has stocked up on my brand. The old women on the corner know my name.

I'll write when I can—

Your Love

MEREDITH McNEAL, BROOKLYN, NY, USA

Dear Love,

The night has slipped into morning. The shadow of lilies
hovering on the wall and the ceiling like a jungle,
huge and daunting.
Our bodies filled with potential.
Poison snakes set loose by careless trespassers.
Beautiful vines that choke and strangle when left untended.
Shiny red leaves - lethal when ingested
Fierce tigers that silently   stalk
                                                wait
                                                stalk
                                                attack from behind

And the most beautiful and precious
of all flowers
sweet, strong
                        perfume
unable to blossom without
swiftly drumming wings
wildly racing heart
shaped to fit just so
                        evolution insured perfection

On this safari we must be each others guide.
Fear the dangers
                        they are quite real.
Learn to protect and nurture the treasures
                        their beauty is unequaled
There is magic here, accept the peril
and we will walk with the gods.

                Your Love

Meridith McNeal 333 Washington Avenue Brooklyn, NY 11205 USA 718-857-0255

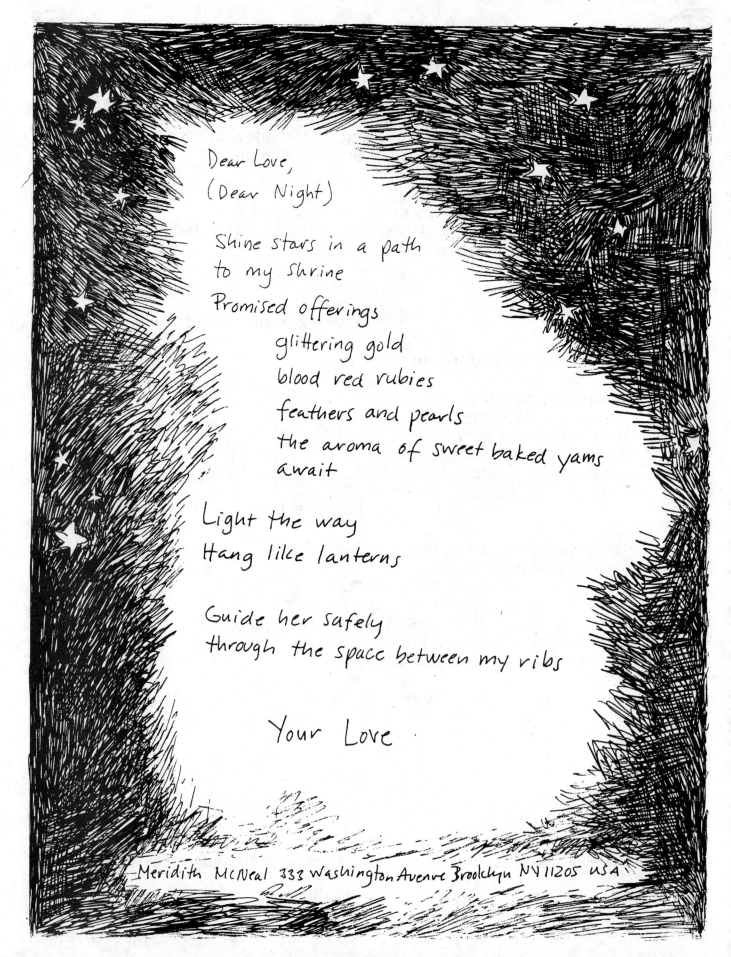

Dear Love,
(Dear Night)

Shine stars in a path
to my shrine
Promised offerings
    glittering gold
    blood red rubies
    feathers and pearls
    the aroma of sweet baked yams
    await

Light the way
Hang like lanterns

Guide her safely
through the space between my ribs

    Your Love

Meridith McNeal 333 Washington Avenue Brooklyn NY 11205 USA

LYNN A TONDRICK, BROOKLYN, NY, USA

The Luck To Be

The Luck To Be Rich	The Luck To Be Earning Enough	The Luck To Be Sensitive	The Luck To Be Thick Skinned
The Luck To Be Gay	The Luck To Be Straight	The Luck To Be Female	The Luck To Be Male
The Luck To Be Believed	The Luck To Be Convincing	The Luck To Be Available	The Luck To Be Uninvolved
The Luck To Be Fruitful	The Luck To Be Beautiful	The Luck To Be Home	The Luck To Be Far Away
The Luck To Be Jaded	The Luck To Be Childlike	The Luck To Be Famous	The Luck To Be Unnoticed
The Luck To Be Experienced	The Luck To Be Innocent	The Luck To Be Nubile	The Luck To Be Sophisticated
The Luck To Be Towering	The Luck To Be Impish	The Luck To Be Wild	The Luck To Be In Control
The Luck To Be A Favorite	The Luck To Be A Black Sheep	The Luck To Be Royalty	The Luck To Be Equal
The Luck To Be Found	The Luck To Be Hidden	The Luck To Be Round Eyed	The Luck To Be Almond Eyed
The Luck To Be Held	The Luck To Be Released	The Luck To Be White	The Luck To Be Black
The Luck To Be Proud	The Luck To Be Humble	The Luck To Be The Only One	The Luck To Be On The Team

KAREN HARMELIN, PHILADELPHIA, PA, USA

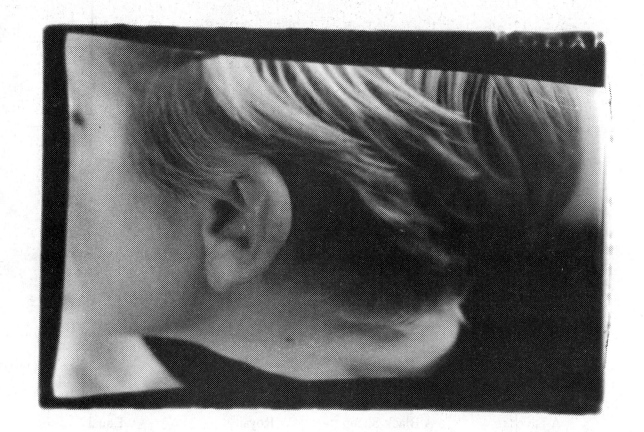

KAREN HARMELIN, PHILADELPHIA, PA, USA

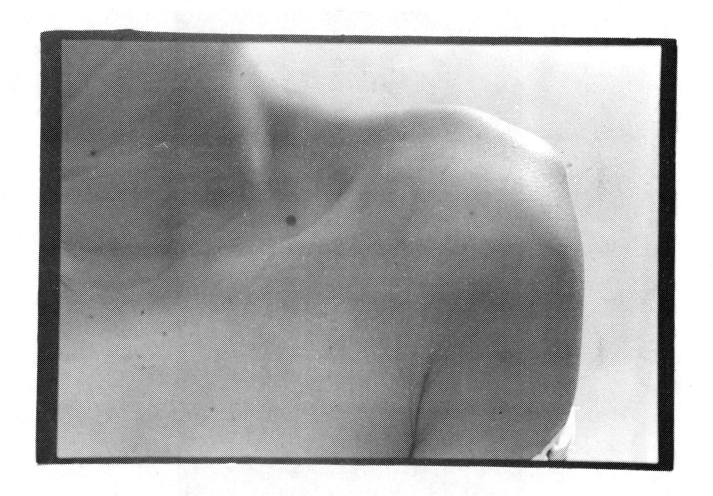

BARBARA WESTERMANN, NEW YORK, NY, USA

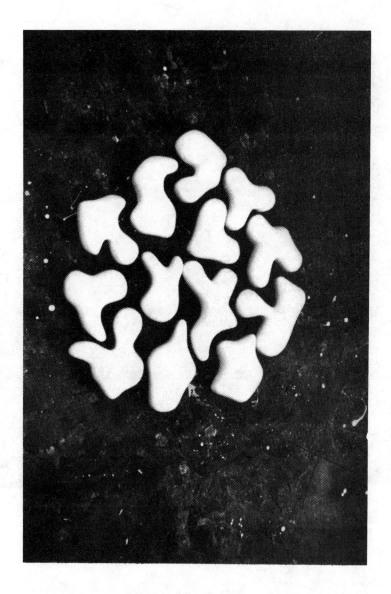

SPIRITUS MUNDI-GUDRUN ENSSLIN-FONTAINEBLEAU
BARBARA WESTERMANN, (plaster and enamel, 7x3'), 1995

BARBARA WESTERMANN, NEW YORK, NY, USA

Materiality and Social Sculpture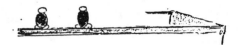

2772 7 SESSIONS FRI. 6-9   SPRING 1995
BARBARA WESTERMANN

This course explores the concept of social sculpture, and its relationship to particular materials. The term originates with Joseph Beuys, whose work we will examine along with other artists from his time and after, including Daniel Spoerri, Rosemarie Trockel, David Hammonds, Jenny Holzer, Janine Antoni, Paula Hayes, and Rirkrit Tiravanija, with a weekly, one-hour slide lecture/discussion and a two-hour sculpture studio, as we work with non-traditional materials (cooking, knitting, gardening, readymades, found objects, talk, etc). I'll outline Beuys' sources, influences, oeuvre and ecopolitics from a gender-specific and material point of view. Beginning with his inference that " everyone is an artist, " we'll will consider the radical implications of sculpture as it is discovered in social processes, as we explore the social sculptures of others as they impact our own material creations.

Required Readings
Allen, William, " Notes on Poetry & Art, " *Pequod,* 1987
Bachelard, Gaston, from *Water & Dreams,* Pegasus, 1978
Cembalest, Robin, " The Ecological Art Explosion, " *Art News,* Sep. 1991
Gookin, Kirby " The Morality of Materials, " unpubl., 1995
Moffit, John, *Occultism in Avante-Garde Art: the Case of J.oseph Beuys,* UMI Press, 1989
Spector, Buzz, " A Profusion of Substance, " *Artforum,* Oct., 1989
Tachelhaus, Heiner, *Joseph Beuys,* Abbeville Press, 1989

Materials-- To be outlined in class.

Other Requirements--
Three assignments: food collage, independent project, & " dinner plate. "

Shows and panels to attend: " Chocolate " at the Swiss Institute, Felix-Gonzalez Torres at the Guggenheim; as much as the Joseph Beuys seminar as you can (see brochure).

COURSE OUTLINE
March 31 Introduction: Joseph Beuys, 7000 Oaks and Materials. Food collage. Prepare an additional work for discussion next week. Read Spector and Bachelard.

April 7   Daniel Spoerri's social museums of eating. Read Allen and Gookin.
                8:00-9:30: Beuys and Spirituality--we'll go over as a group.

April 14   The Morality of Materials--Independent project. Prepare dinner plates. Design
                a moral object lesson. Read Tachelhaus and Moffit.

April 21   Beuys and Anthroposophy/Spirit and Matter. Read Cembalest.

April 28   Contemporary Artists: Rosemarie Trockel, Jenny Holzer, and David
                Hammonds.

May 5   Contemporary Artists: Paula Hayes, Janine Antoni, and Rirkrit Tiravanija.

May 12   Garden Party with R. Tiravanija--Meet at 151 Ave. A/Apt. 9 (9 & 10th)/982-9880.

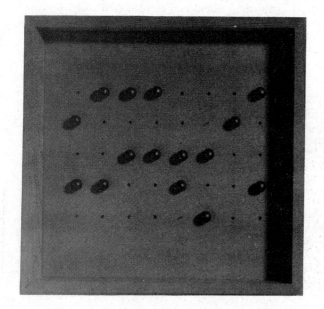 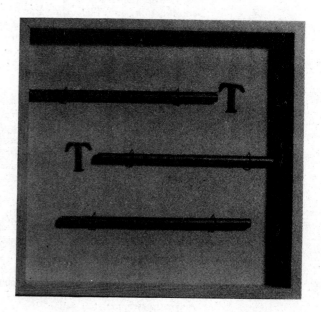

Serie "LA LÍNEA DEL TIEMPO". 1994
Collage/cajas. 35 x 37 x 5 cm.

Linda Tonetti, PITTSBURGH, PA, USA

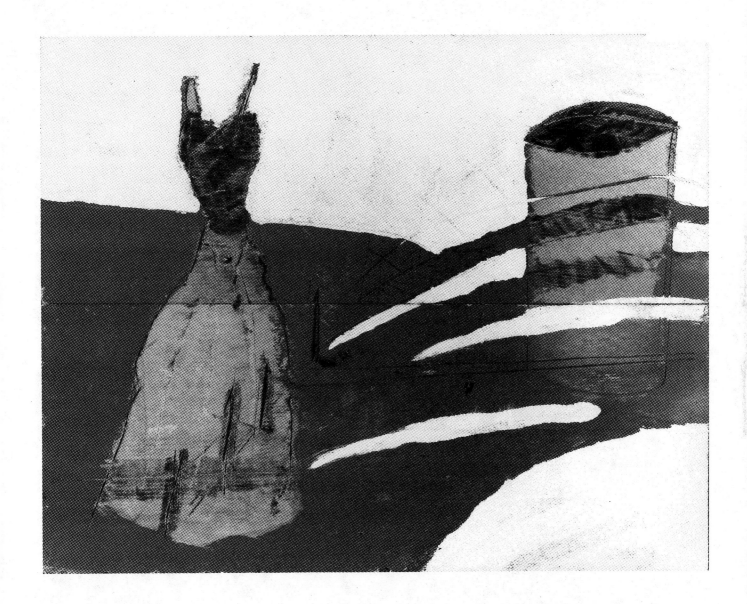

GLADYS TRIANA, NEW YORK, NY, USA

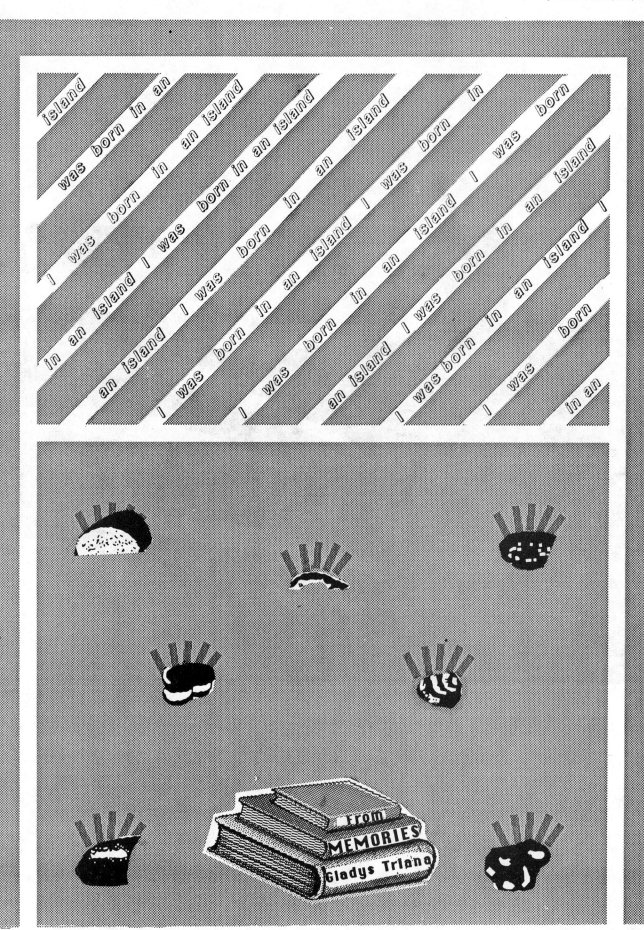

GLADYS TRIANA, NEW YORK, NY, USA

MEMORIES

My artistc expression, founded in "memories", represents a search for roots- a link with that, which has true meaning and escapes in the nebulousness of time.
These images revealed an intimate protest, an aggressive revolt against my own ability to communicate.
I began to elaborate a new visual language, capable of representing and encompassing my chaotic and fragmented experience.
The agglomerated fragments in my memory are replicas of the emotional conditions which express the alignment of man in this society.

Gladys Triana
401 First Ave 14E
New York 10010

SARAH BARNUM, NEW YORK, NY, USA

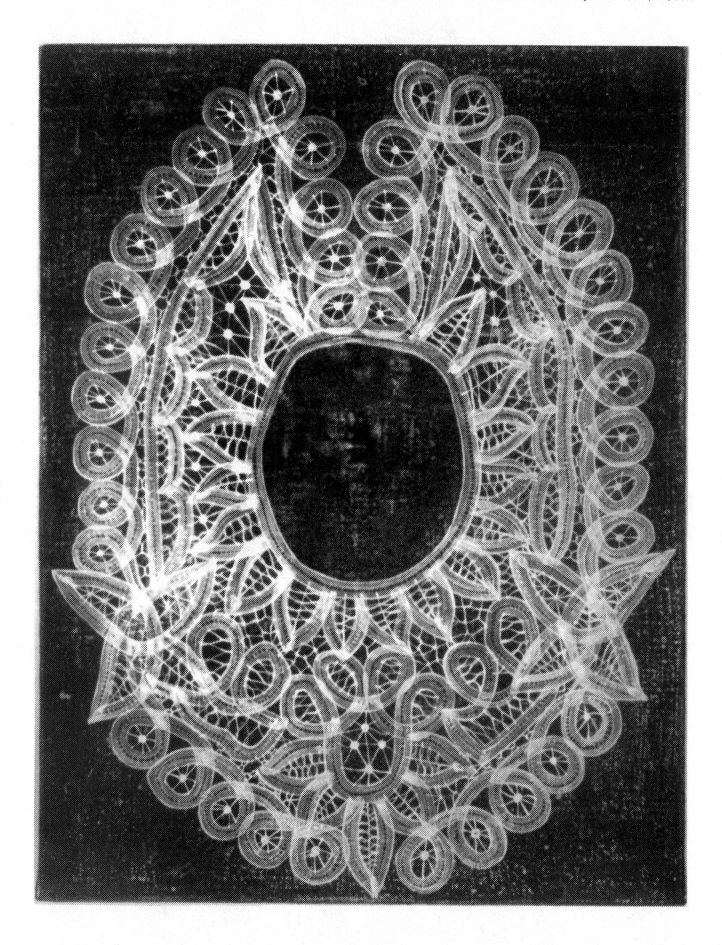

SARAH BARNUM, NEW YORK, NY, USA

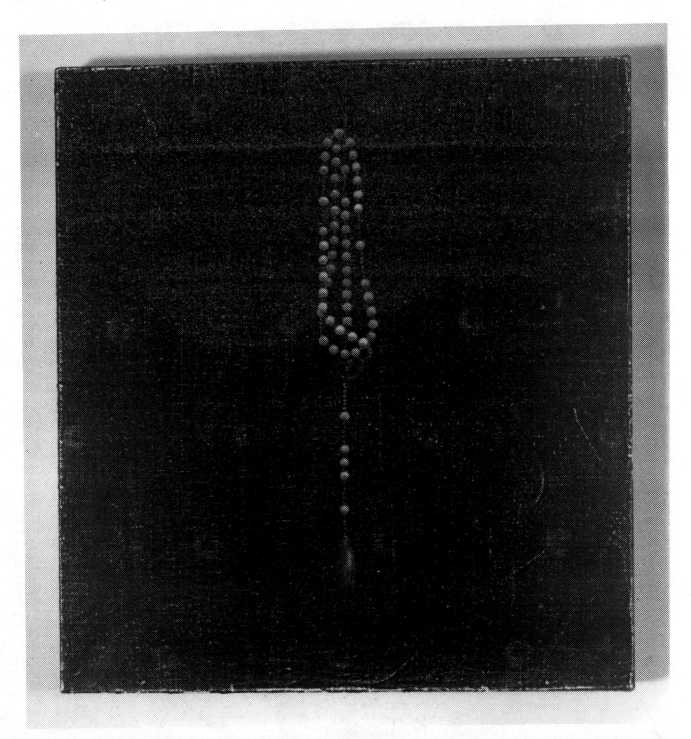

ANN-SARGENT WOOSTER, NEW YORK, NY, USA

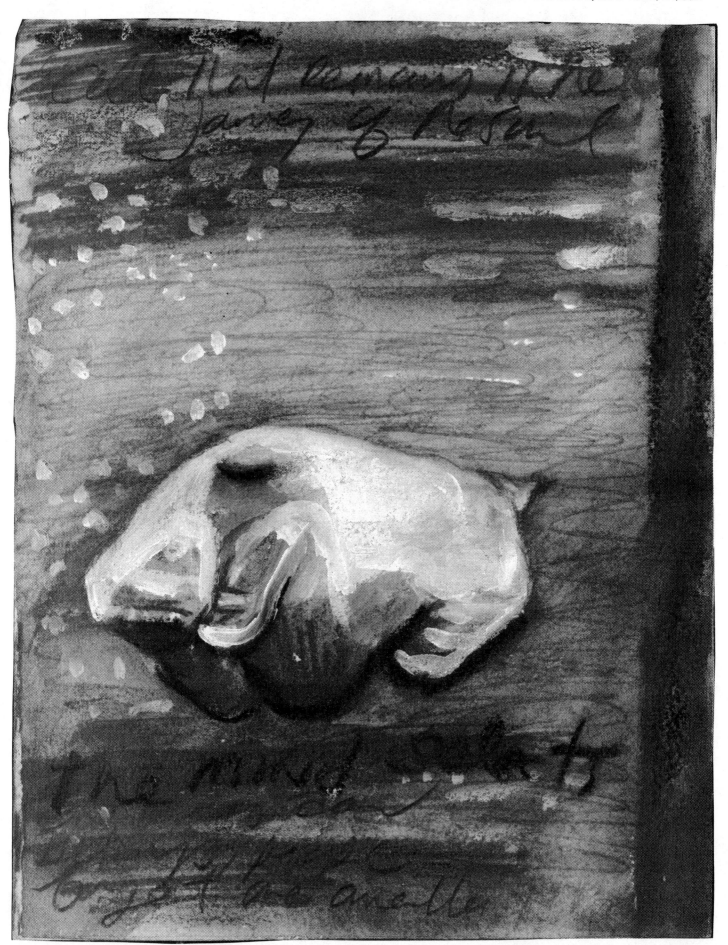

ANN-SARGENT WOOSTER, NEW YORK, NY, USA

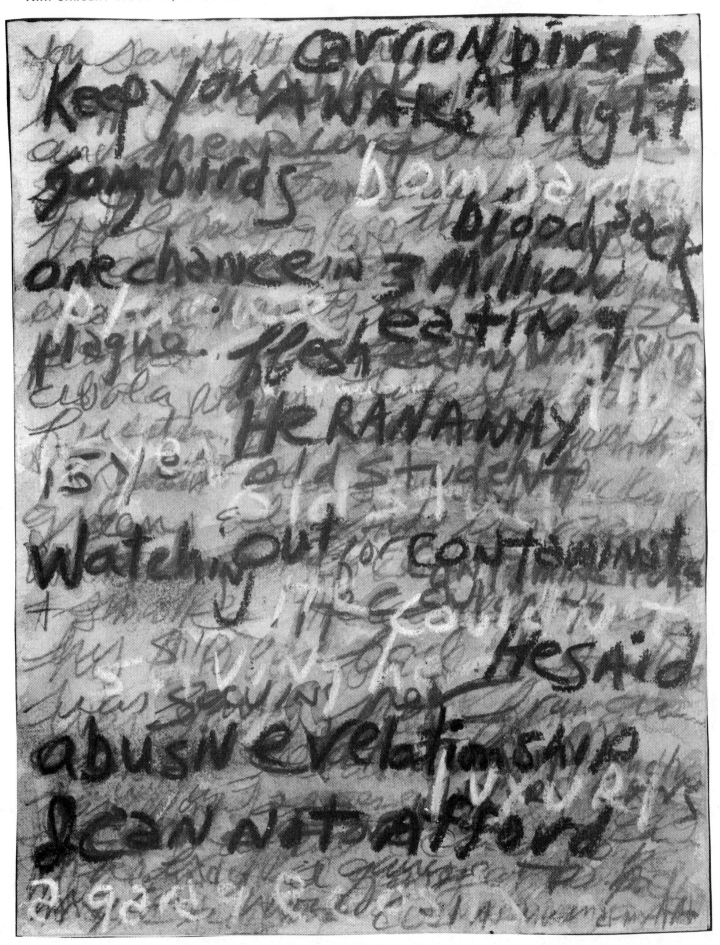

MARIA ANTONIA HIDALGO, MILAN, ITALY

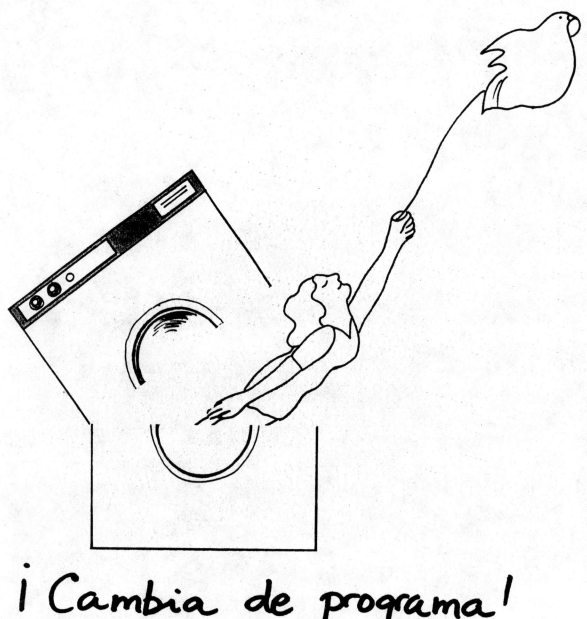

¡ Cambia de programa !

MARIA ANTONIA HIDALGO ◊ VIA FAVRETTO 8 ◊ 20146 MI
LAN ◊ ITALY ◊ TEL. 02 - 427322 ◊ NO TENGO FAX

PILAR IBAÑEZ, GRANADA, SPAIN

hola!

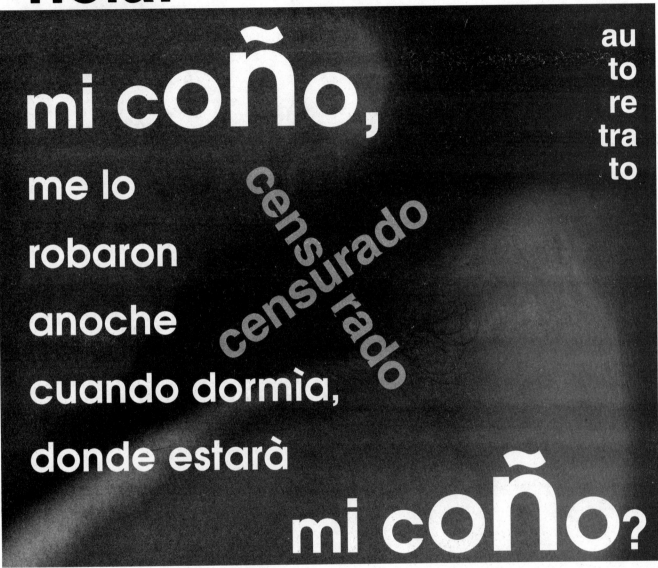

mi coño,

au
to
re
tra
to

me lo

robaron

anoche

censurado
censurado

cuando dormìa,

donde estarà

mi coño?

mi
direcciòn
es
calle
santa
catalina
18293
obeilar
granada
mi
teléfono
958
454271

pilar ibaÑez, españa

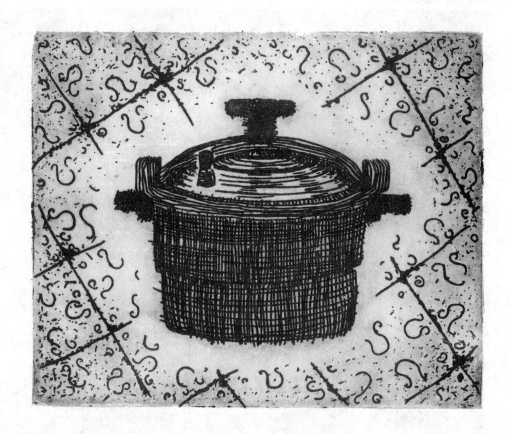

Mujer en la oficina
A U T O R A
Gala Placidia Zarzo Rodriguez
Nacida el 17 de abril de 1966 en Granada España
Direcciòn: Puente Verde 1, pta. 4, 2°H
teléfono 958 - 816085, Granada 18008, España

MARIA ANTONIA HIDALGO, MILAN, ITALY

MICRO COSMOS

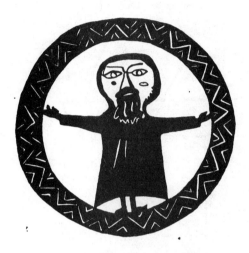

EL hombre, microcosmo
dentro de un circulo
(España Romana)

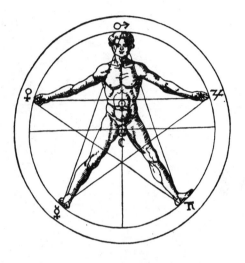

EL hombre, microcosmo
en la imagen del
pentagrama (siglo XVI)

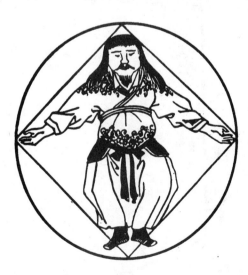

EL hombre, microcosmo
dentro de un cuadrado
(China, siglo XI)

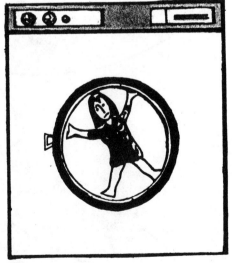

Una mujer.
Microcosmo de muchas
mujeres en el siglo XX

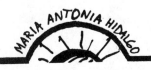

CAROL SZYMANSKI, BROOKLYN, NY, USA

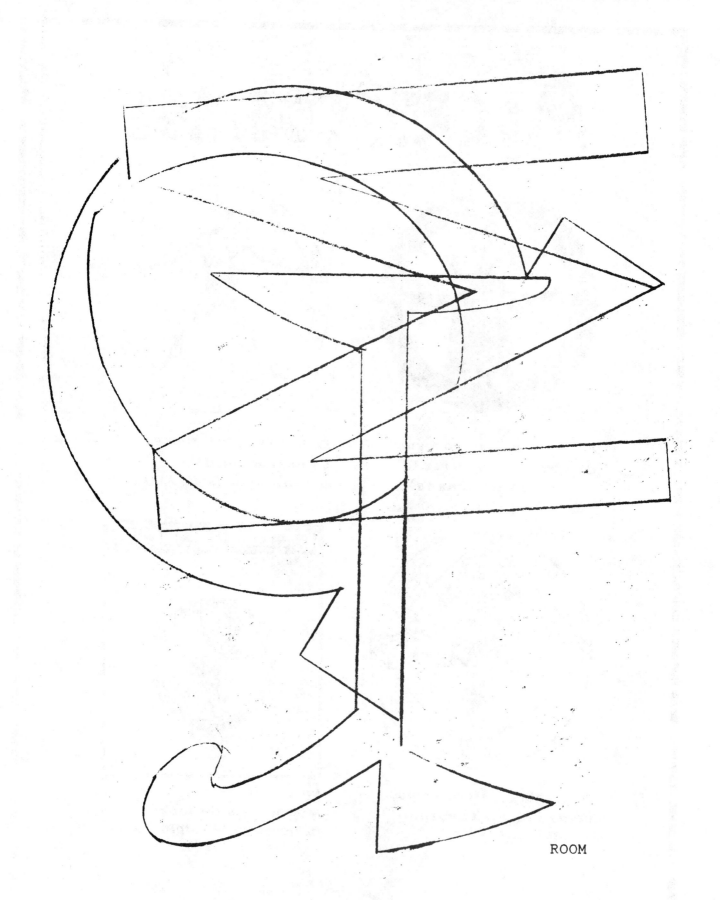

ROOM

CAROL SZYMANSKI, BROOKLYN, NY, USA

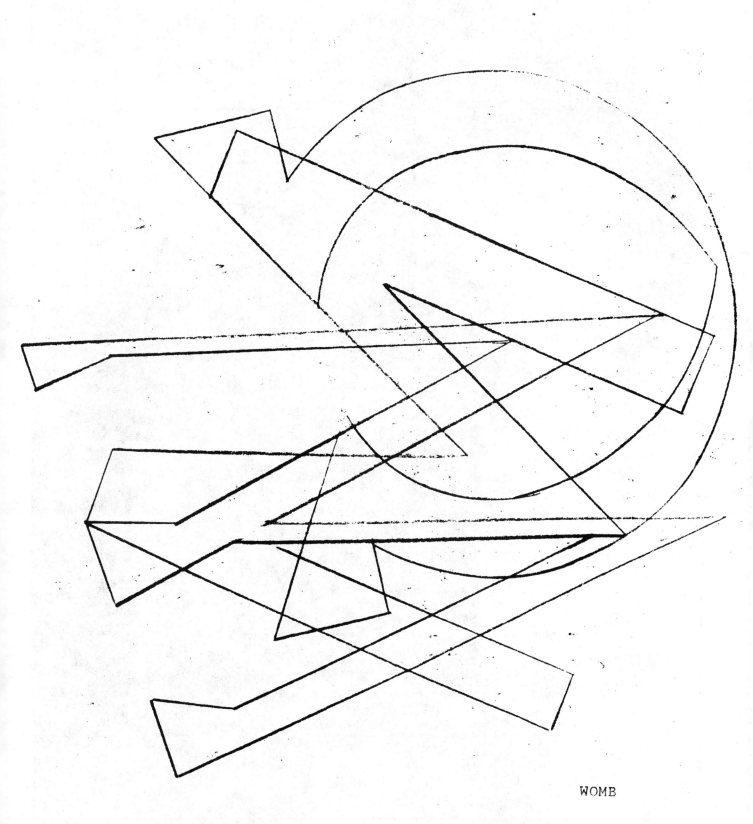

WOMB

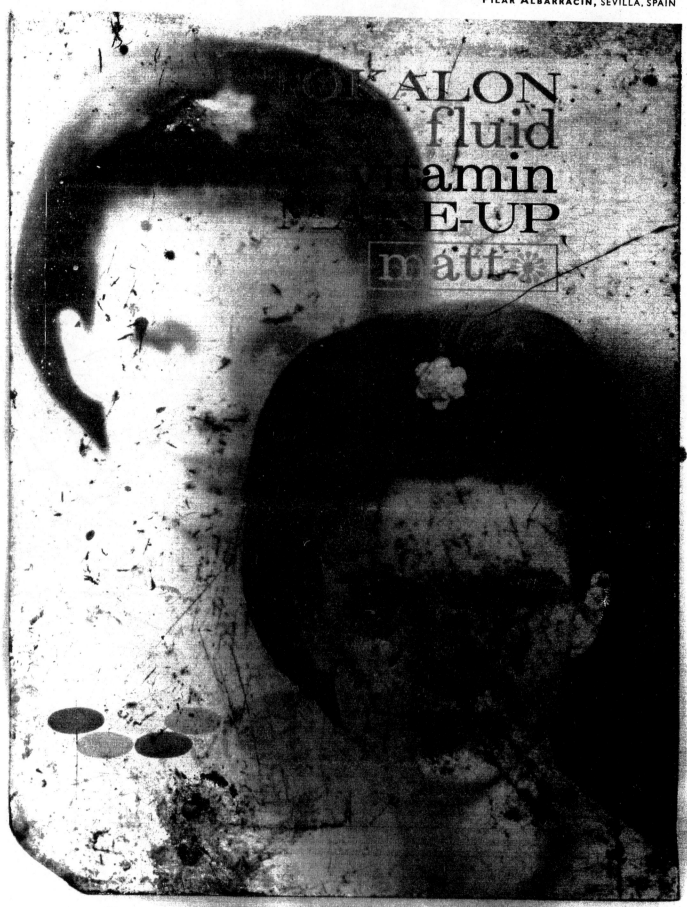

PILAR ALBARRACÍN, SEVILLA, SPAIN

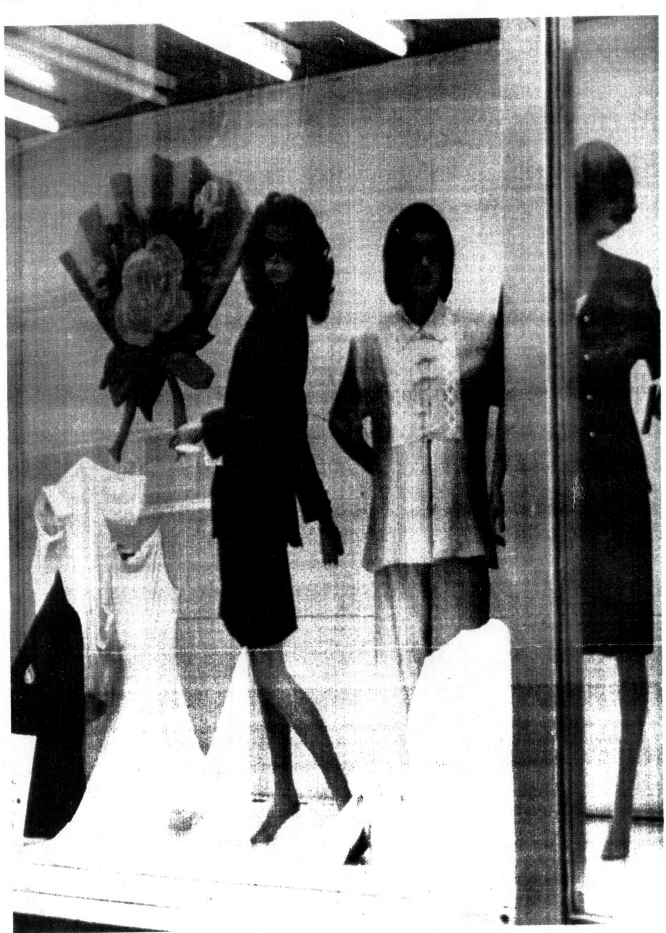

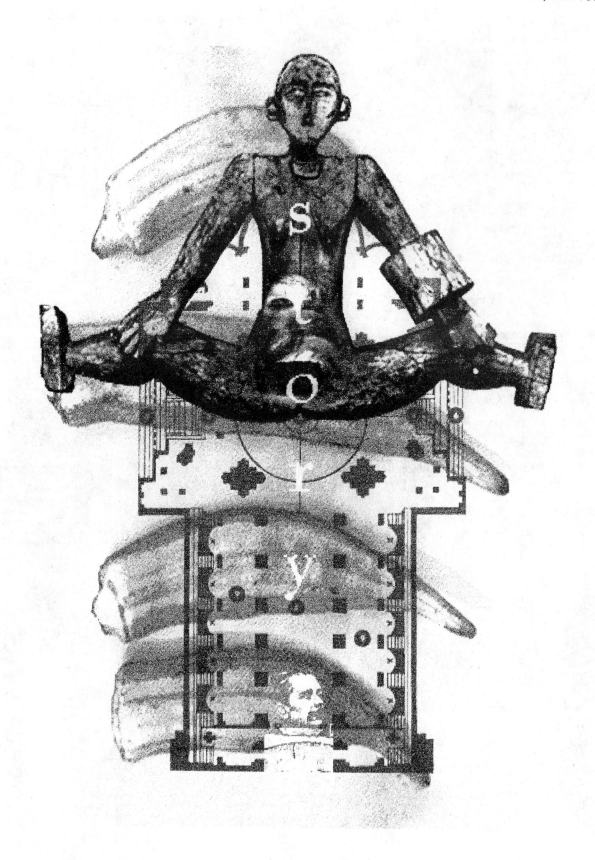

Tennessee Rice Dixon

TENNESSEE RICE DIXON, NEW YORK, NY, USA

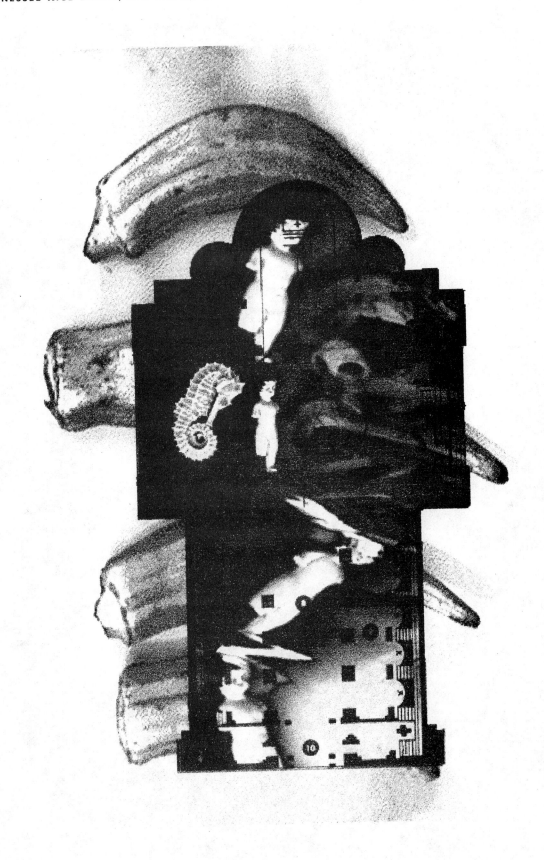

Tennessee Rice Dixon

"mom in mirror making up" m. minter 1970 - 95

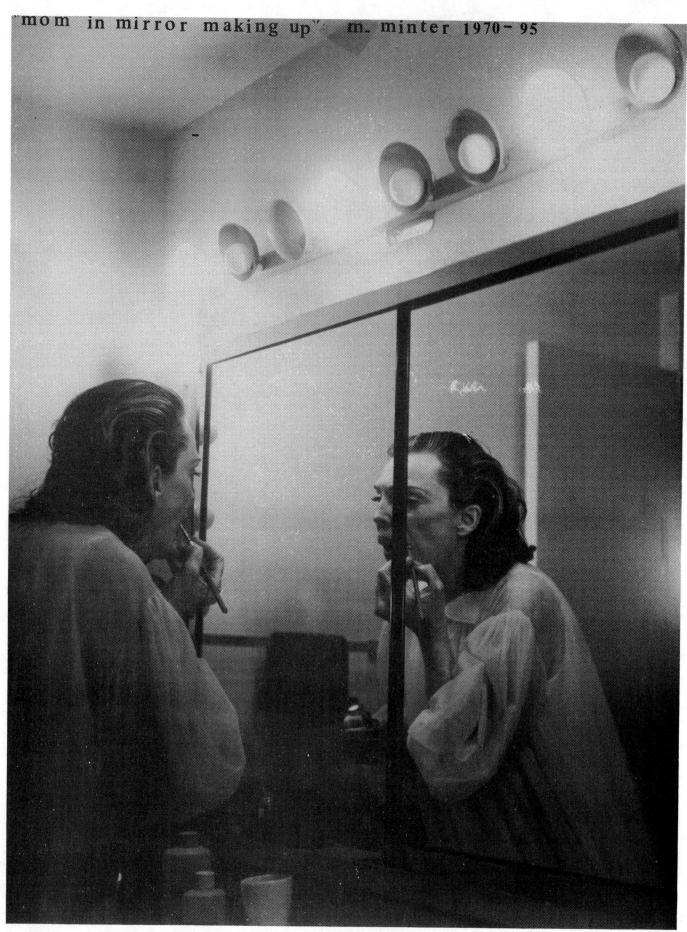

"mom in mirror making up" m. minter 1970 - 95

MARILYN MINTER, NEW YORK, NY, USA

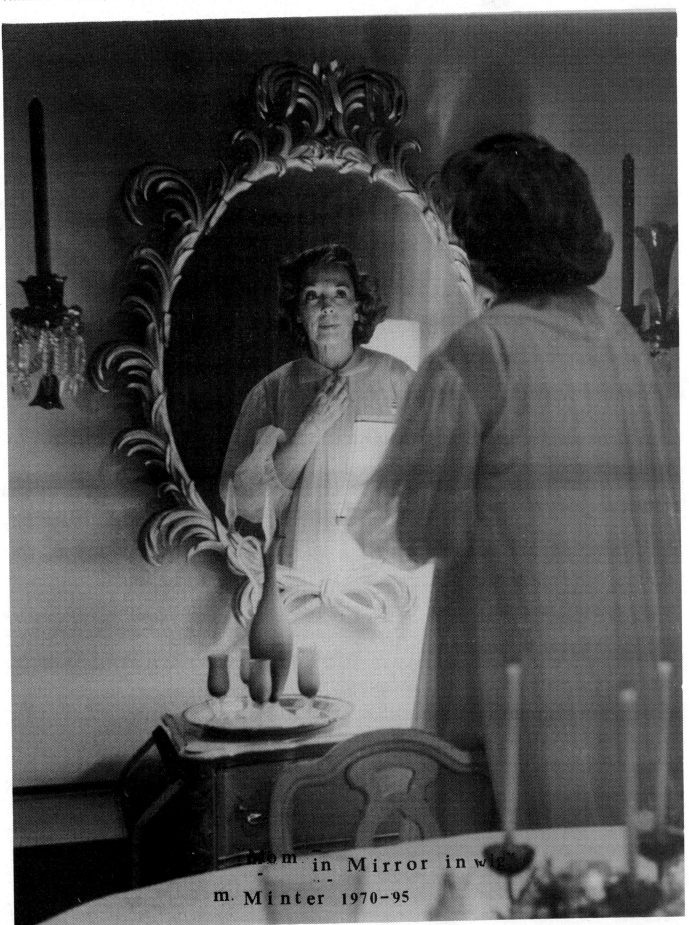

Mom in Mirror in wig
m. Minter 1970-95

SUSAN SILAS, BROOKLYN, NY, USA

I WANT TO BUILD A MONUMENT TO MYSELF. I WANT TO BUILD A MONUMENT TO MYSELF. I WAN
ILD A MONUMENT TO MYSELF. WANT TO BUILD A MONUMENT TO MYSELF. I WANT TO BUILD A
NUMENT TO MYSELF. I WANT TO BUILD A MONUMENT TO MYSELF. I WANT TO BUILD A MONUME
TO MYSELF. WANT TO BUILD A MONUMENT TO MYSELF. I WANT TO BUILD A MONUMENT TO M
ELF. I WANT TO BUILD A MONUMENT TO MYSELF. WANT TO BUILD A MONUMENT TO MYSELF.
O BUILD A MONUMENT TO MYSELF. I WANT TO BUILD A MONUMENT TO MYSELF. I WANT TO BU
IONUMENT TO MYSELF. I WANT TO BUILD A MONUMENT TO MYSELF I WANT TO BUILD A MONUM
TO MYSELF. I WANT TO BUILD A MONUMENT TO MYSELF. I WANT TO BUILD A MONUMENT TO MY
WANT TO BUILD A MONUMENT TO MYSELF. I WANT TO BUILD A MONUMENT TO MYSELF. I WAN
BUILD A MONUMENT TO MYSELF. I WANT TO BUILD A MONUMENT TO MYSELF. I WANT TO BUIL
MONUMENT TO MYSELF. I WANT TO BUILD A MONUMENT TO MYSELF I WANT TO BUILD A MONU
T TO MYSELF. I WANT TO BUILD A MONUMENT TO MYSELF I WANT TO BUILD A MONUMENT TO M
LF. I WANT TO BUILD A MONUMENT TO MYSELF. I WANT TO BUILD A MONUMENT TO MYSELF. I W
O BUILD A MONUMENT TO MYSELF I WANT TO BUILD A MONUMENT TO MYSELF I WANT TO BUILI
A MONUMENT TO MYSELF. I WANT TO BUILD A MONUMENT TO MYSELF I WANT TO BUILD A MON
MENT TO MYSELF. I WANT TO BUILD A MONUMENT TO MYSELF. I WANT TO BUILD A MONUMENT
TO MYSELF. I WANT TO BUILD A MONUMENT TO MYSELF. I WANT TO BUILD A MONUMENT TO M
YSELF. I WANT TO BUILD A MONUMENT TO MYSELF. I WANT TO BUILD A MONUMENT TO MYSELI
TO BUILD A MONUMENT TO MYSELF. I WANT TO BUILD A MONUMENT TO MYSELF. I WANT TO B
MONUMENT TO MYSELF. I WANT TO BUILD A MONUMENT TO MYSELF. I WANT TO BUILD A MON
IENT TO MYSELF. I WANT TO BUILD A MONUMENT TO MYSELF. I WANT TO BUILD A MONUMENT
O MYSELF. I WANT TO BUILD A MONUMENT TO MYSELF. I WANT TO BUILD A MONUMENT TO MYS
WANT TO BUILD A MONUMENT TO MYSELF. I WANT TO BUILD A MONUMENT TO MYSELF. WANT
UILD A MONUMENT TO MYSELF. I WANT TO BUILD A MONUMENT TO MYSELF. I WANT TO BUILD
MENT TO MYSELF. I WANT TO BUILD A MONUMENT TO MYSELF. I WANT TO BUILD A MONUMEN
TO MYSELF. I WANT TO BUILD A MONUMENT TO MYSELF. I WANT TO BUILD A MONUMENT TO M
YSELF. I WANT TO BUILD A MONUMENT TO MYSELF. I WANT TO BUILD A MONUMENT TO MYSELF.
TO BUILD A MONUMENT TO MYSELF. I WANT TO BUILD A MONUMENT TO MYSELF. I WANT TO B
MONUMENT TO MYSELF. I WANT TO BUILD A MONUMENT TO MYSELF. I WANT TO BUILD A MON
UMENT TO MYSELF. I WANT TO BUILD A MONUMENT TO MYSELF. I WANT TO BUILD A MONUMEN
O MYSELF. I WANT TO BUILD A MONUMENT TO MYSEL. I WANT TO BUILD A MONUMENT TO MYS
WANT TO BUILD A MONUMENT TO MYSELF I WANT TO BUILD A MONUMENT TO MYSELF I WANT
BUILD A MONUMENT TO MYSELF. I WANT TO BUILD A MONUMENT TO MYSELF. I WANT TO BU
BUILD A MONUMENT TO MYSELF. I WANT TO BUILD A MONUMENT TO MYSELF. I WANT TO BU
NUMENT TO MYSELF. I WANT TO BUILD A MONUMENT TO MYSELF. I WANT TO BUILD A MONUM

SUSAN SILAS, BROOKLYN, NY, USA

IT TO BUILD A MONUMENT TO MYSELF. I WANT TO BUILD A MONUMENT TO MYSELF. I WANT TO B
MONUMENT TO MYSELF. . WANT TO BUILD A MONUMENT TO MYSELF. I WANT TO BUILD A MON
NT TO MYSELF. I WANT TO BUILD A MONUMENT TO MYSELF. I WANT TO BUILD A MONUMENT
YSELF. I WANT TO BUILD A MONUMENT TO MYSELF. I WANT TO BUILD A MONUMENT TO MYSEL
WANT TO BUILD A MONUMENT TO MYSELF. I WANT TO BUILD A MONUMENT TO MYSELF. I WAN
ILD A MONUMENT TO MYSELF I WANT TO BUILD A MONUMENT TO MYSELF. I WANT TO BUILD A
ENT TO MYSELF. I WANT TO BUILD A MONUMENT TO MYSELF. I WANT TO BUILD A MONUMENT 1
YSELF. I WANT TO BUILD A MONUMENT TO MYSELF. I WANT TO BUILD A MONUMENT TO MYSELF.
T TO BUILD A MONUMENT TO MYSELF. I WANT TO BUILD A MONUMENT TO MYSELF. I WANT TO
D A MONUMENT TO MYSELF. I WANT TO BUILD A MONUMENT TO MYSELF. I WANT TO BUILD A N
MENT TO MYSELF. I WANT TO BUILD A MONUMENT TO MYSELF. I WANT TO BUILD A MONUMEN
YSELF. I WANT TO BUILD A MONUMENT TO MYSELF. I WANT TO BUILD A MONUMENT TO MYSELI
ANT TO BUILD A MONUMENT TO MYSELF. I WANT TO BUILD A MONUMENT TO MYSELF I WANT T
D A MONUMENT TO MYSELF. I WANT TO BUILD A MONUMENT TO MYSELF. I WANT TO BUILD A M
NUMENT TO MYSELF. I WANT TO BUILD A MONUMENT TO MYSELF. I WANT TO BUILD A MONUME
TO MYSELF. I WANT TO BUILD A MONUMENT TO MYSELF. I WANT TO BUILD A MONUMENT TO M
YSELF. I WANT TO BUILD A MONUMENT TO MYSELF. I WANT TO BUILD A MONUMENT TO MYSEL
T WANT TO BUILD A MONUMENT TO MYSELF. I WANT TO BUILD A MONUMENT TO MYSELF. I WAN
UILD A MONUMENT TO MYSELF. I WANT TO BUILD A MONUMENT TO MYSELF. I WANT TO BUILD
UMENT TO MYSELF. I WANT TO BUILD A MONUMENT TO MYSELF. I WANT TO BUILD A MONUMEI
TO MYSELF. I WANT TO BUILD A MONUMENT TO MYSELF. I WANT TO BUILD A MONUMENT TO MY
ELF. I WANT TO BUILD A MONUMENT TO MYSELF. I WANT TO BUILD A MONUMENT TO MYSELF.
TO BUILD A MONUMENT TO MYSELF. I WANT TO BUILD A MONUMENT TO MYSELF. I WANT TO B
A MONUMENT TO MYSELF. I WANT TO BUILD A MONUMENT TO MYSELF. I WANT TO BUILD A MO
T TO MYSELF. I WANT TO BUILD A MONUMENT TO MYSELF. I WANT TO BUILD A MONUMENT TO
YSELF. I WANT TO BUILD A MONUMENT TO MYSELF. I WANT TO BUILD A MONUMENT TO MYSE
I WANT TO BUILD A MONUMENT TO MYSELF. I WANT TO BUILD A MONUMENT TO MYSELF. I WA
UILD A MONUMENT TO MYSELF. I WANT TO BUILD A MONUMENT TO MYSELF I WANT TO BUILD
UMENT TO MYSELF. I WANT TO BUILD A MONUMENT TO MYSELF. I WANT TO BUILD A MONUME
IT TO MYSELF. I WANT TO BUILD A MONUMENT TO MYSELF. I WANT TO BUILD A MONUMENT TO
ELF. I WANT TO BUILD A MONUMENT TO MYSELF. I WANT TO BUILD A MONUMENT TO MYSELF.
TO BUILD A MONUMENT TO MYSELF. I WANT TO BUILD A MONUMENT TO MYSELF. I WANT TO B
ILD A MONUMENT TO MYSELF. I WANT TO BUILD A MONUMENT TO MYSELF. I WANT TO BUILD A
ILD A MONUMENT TO MYSELF. I WANT TO BUILD A MONUMENT TO MYSELF. I WANT TO BUILD
ENT TO MYSELF. I WANT TO BUILD A MONUMENT TO MYSELF. I WANT TO BUILD A MONUMENT 1

Katrin Asbury, CHICAGO, ILL, USA

Eiffel Tower

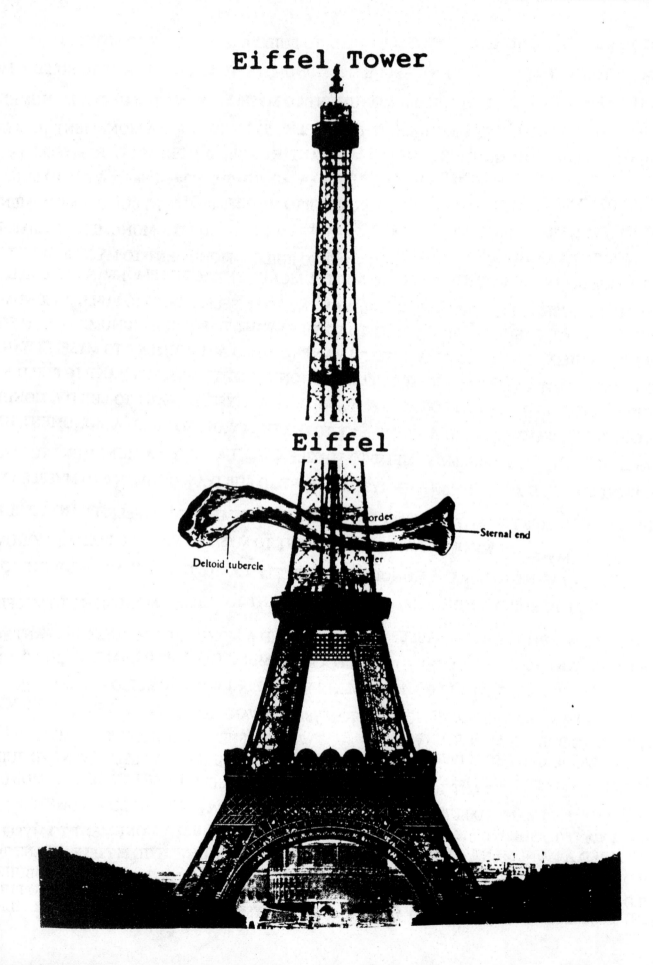

Eiffel

Deltoid tubercle

Sternal end

MIRIAM BEERMAN, BAYSIDE, NY, USA

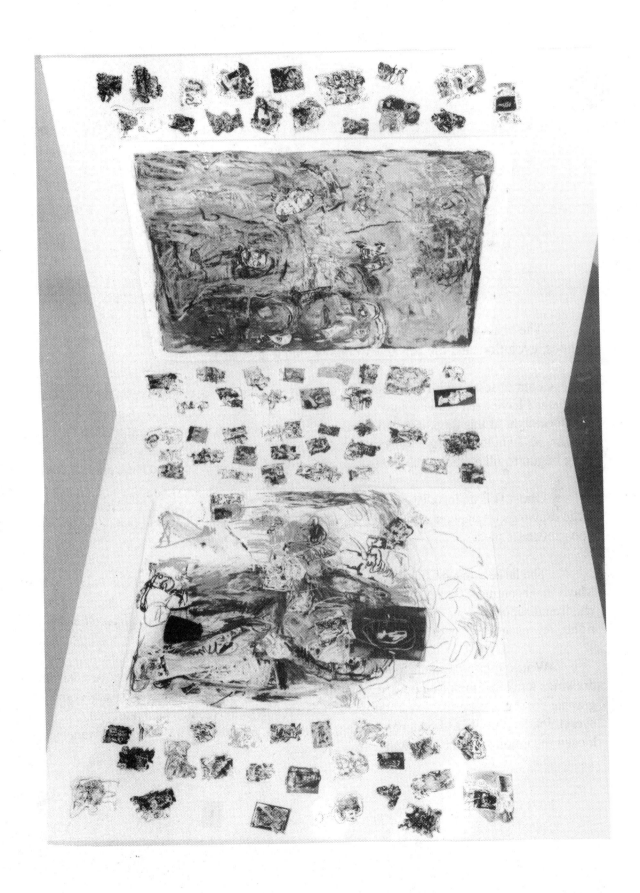

MIRIAM BEERMAN, BAYSIDE, NY, USA

Artist Statement

The history of my work is my response to the history of everything: art, nature, politics, evolution, and the human psyche (including my own).

I am obsessed with drawing. For me, it is an intensely personal experience. In the past year I have been drawing into printed and non-printed books; and have completed seven or eight at this time. From hundreds of these small sheets (mostly automatic drawings), I am led to larger works. Some drawings made up of large and small parts have begun to fill a whole wall; often reaching around and continuing on the adjacent wall.

Ghost II is an installation work measuring 108" x 185". It consists of two very large drawings on paper surrounded by almost one hundred smaller stream of consciousness pieces.

The large work on the left was made to memorialize the Mothers of the Plaza De Mayo in Argentina. These were the mothers of missing sons and daughters. These children disappeared during a time of great political oppression. The Ghost figure on the right...represents the children.

Working into printed and non-printed books, I work small; covering the text with drawings and superimposing new text and drawings upon the old. As such, they become graphic commentary or bizarre notations and like the large works are the history of everything: art, politics, the human psyche, nature and evolution. These memory traces loosen the emotions in strange and unexpected ways.

BEVERLY DECKER & JANET DUNGAN, SUMMERLAND, CA, USA

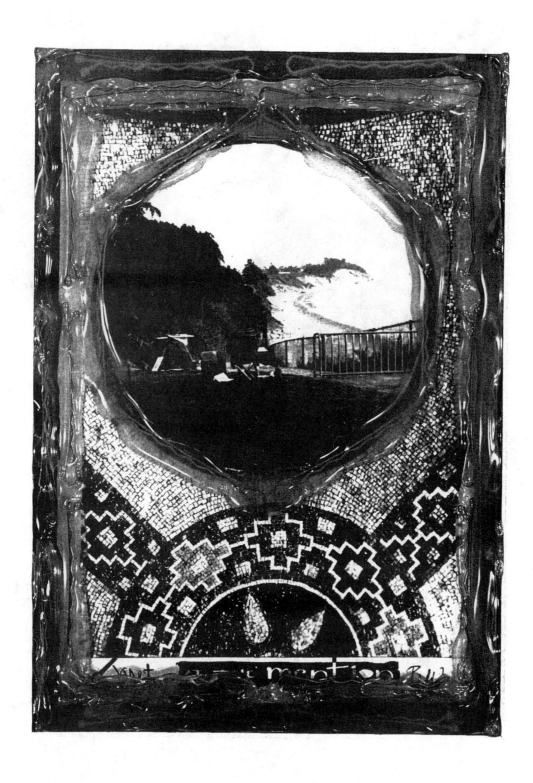

NINA LEVINTHAL, PARIS, FRANCE

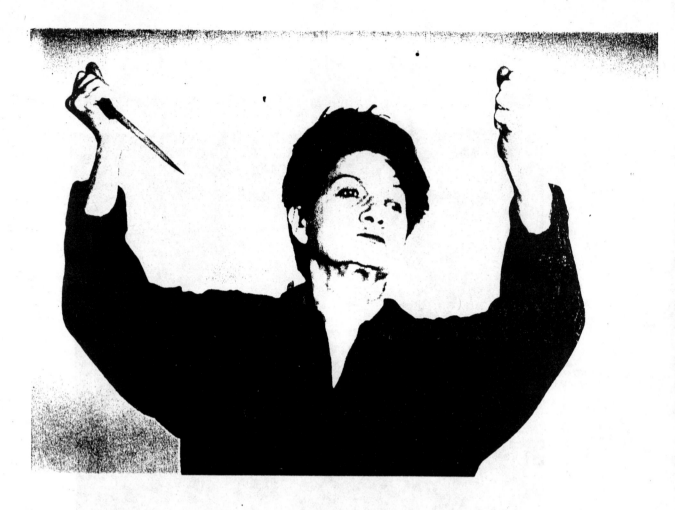

What kind of person is happy? In a word,
a strong person. And who is unhappy? A
weak person. A strong person can enjoy
everything in life, and whatever obstacles
arise only make that person even stronger.

Joy of Living, p.73
Daisaku Ikeda

NINA LEVINTHAL, PARIS, FRANCE

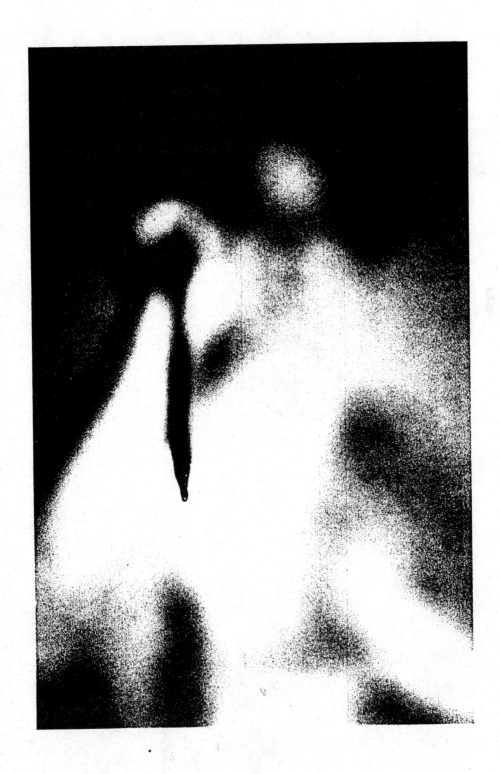

ANILA BENJAMIN, BROOKLYN, NY, USA

Motherhood :ö:

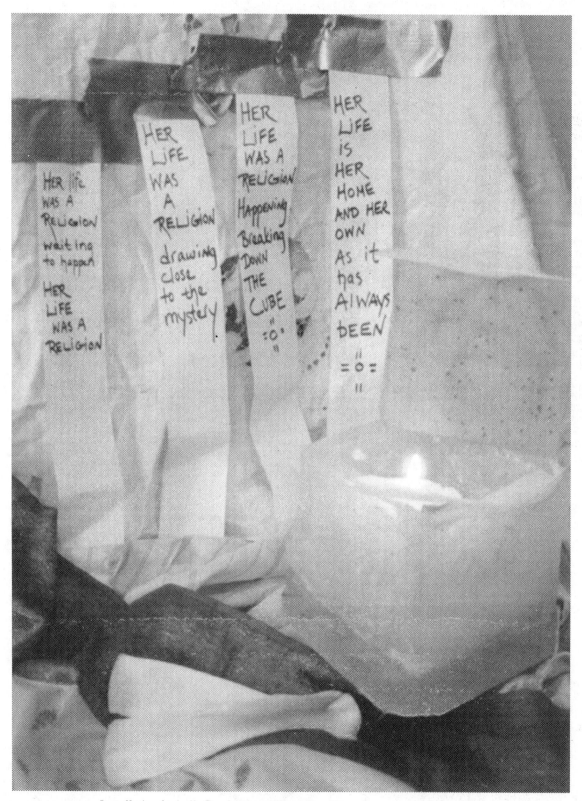

Installation by Anila Benjamin   *Cast glass, linen, bone, tape, ink, paper.*

AVITAL GREENBERG, NEW YORK, NY, USA

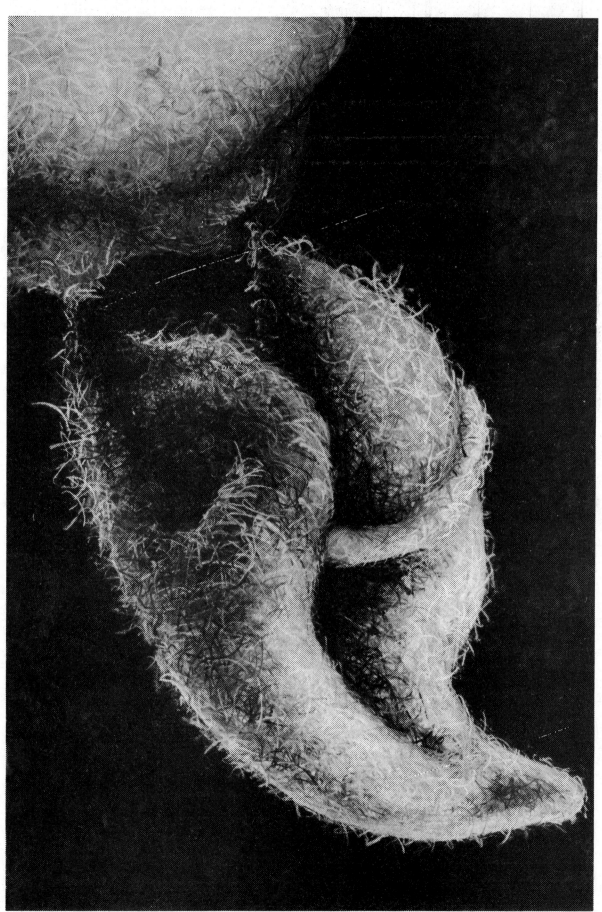

AVITAL
GREENBERG

CONGRUOUS

PASTEL
on paper
mounted
on canvas.
30"/44"

Mrs. Emanuel Silverman
33 Alexander Avenue
Upper Montclair, NJ

Thursday, Feb. 20, 1958

My dearest Marcia,

Daddy has just left for the office, and I'm still in my
bathrobe with you on my mind. Warren is still sleeping. He is
on vacation this week.

Daddy as you know has had a cold and so he has been
getting home early. In fact the last few days he has left
between 2 and 3 P.M. - not like him at all. While his cold is
better he has complained of feeling depressed. In fact, he
didn't feel like going in at all on Tuesday. Business is bad
and no money coming in. There are too many problems to face
etc. etc. I can't tell you how I worry sometimes. Well this
morning the comment was "my cold is coming out now. I suppose
that was really why I felt so depressed." It probably was. I
have come to realize that physical well being plays a great part
in mental attitude.

At any rate- your letter came yesterday and I only read it
when I came back from Newark before supper time. I was so upset
I could have cried. Don't misunderstand now - you don't know
how heartwarming it is for us to have you pour your heart out -
or write frankly like you do. It is how you feel that bothers
me so much. I thought about it all night, and reread the letter
before. It sounded so different in the morning light. Last
night I could only see that you were terribly unhappy. Today I
see a mature sensible girl who is emerging into a fine young
woman with a growing sense of values and the time to stand off
and look to see where she is heading. Any wonder why you are
lonely? There are not many - a good deal older - who can do
that - or realize the need to. It is such sensitive people as
you who give meaning to life and add to growth. You as usual
are just so much ahead of your physical self that it takes much
more adjustment. Your surroundings are so necessary though.
One needs the padding - if you know what I mean. Much can be
gained from understanding and getting along and loving those not
so keenly aware. Tolerance comes with knowledge and
understanding but then I'm only repeating what you have already
said. You show so much growth- you amaze me.

As for love - that great big word is everything. Give it
and get it is life's meaning. To have it is every person's
strive.

Daddy after reading your letter said "I can remember when
I felt just that way." I look back and can too. Let me
reassure you. Your time will come and you will find such
happiness but you must cultivate patience to achieve it. For
surely there are others who feel as you do. You have met some
in older people. In the meantime continue to add to your self
worth - so that as you look within you can say to yourself - I'm

MARCIA TUCKER, NEW YORK, NY, USA

good, kind (as you always were) trustful, honest, etc. etc.
Truly we think you are wonderful already.

You wrote as you felt. I wrote as I felt - that makes us
even. If you are lonely - do know that even if you think we
don't understand - 4 arms are open to you always. We love you
very dearly. As for Warren (you may not believe this) he
idolizes you.

I'm sorry your valentine came on Saturday. I sent it off
on Tuesday - time enough I thought. Please let me know what
food you can use - besides nosh - and I'll send a package.

May I add my 2 cents please - don't take up with sailors
or chance acquaintances. It isn't nice - please.

In the meantime - write as often as you can. We are
always ready to listen and want to help. If there is anything
you need - say so. I will try to find a black bag for you when
I next go shopping.

Here's hoping your next letter will be a happy one. They
say hard work is good medicine-- anyhow

                    All our love,
                    Mother

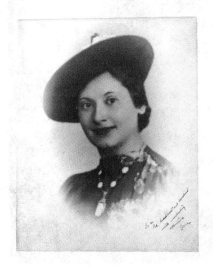

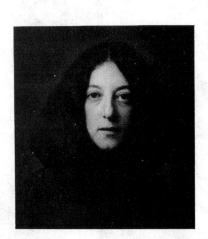

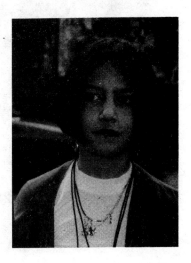

| Dorothy (Dora) Wald Silverman | Marcia Ruby Silverman | Ruby Dora McNeil |
| b. 1911, d. 1960 | (Tucker; McNeil), b. 1940 | b. 1984 |

ANN ROSEN, BROOKLYN, NY, USA

MOTHERS HEROES

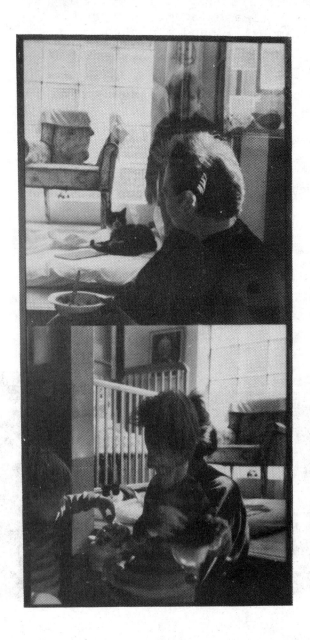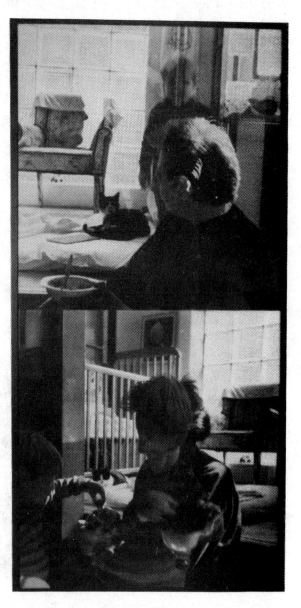

ANN ROSEN

LANNY FRANCES DE VUONO, SPOKANE, WA, USA

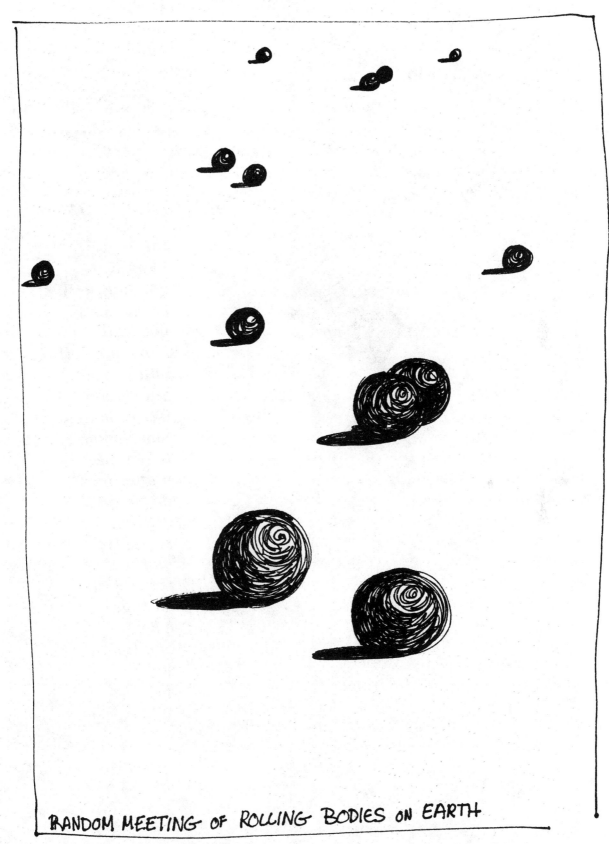

RANDOM MEETING OF ROLLING BODIES ON EARTH

LDEVUONO -95

Coco Gordon, NEW YORK, NY, USA

,,.,<,`,.,   in   ,.;;.,,   ;',' '.`` ,.,,.;',   ,.,;.`'',    ;'.`^
,,.,<,`,.,          ,..;;.,,`   ;,'.'.` ,.,,.;',   no   ,.;.''' time
';.'`^    ,,.,<,`,.,   as   ,.;;.,`   ';.'.'`` ,.,,.;',   ,.;.''
';.'`^    ,,.,<,`,.,   ,.;;.,,   ';.'.'`` ,.,,.;',   ,.;.''
';.'`^    ,,.,<,`,.,   was   ,.;;.,,   ;',' '.`` ,.,,.;',   ,.;.''is

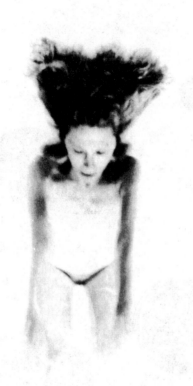

this
I know
you will
know
you will
know you will
now
now know
(strike match)
SkyWoman,,.,., ;'>
take time
blow time
do time
get time
to use time
on time
for all time
let time
a hell
of a time
go

COCO GORDON, NEW YORK, NY, USA

Becoming SuperSkyWoman

I keep empowering myself as an aging woman to make visible deep cultural inquiries, to make an impact on the thought/behavioral ethic and integrated mind/body/spirit of our modern construct. My process is informed by the trance speakings & teachings of Quileute elder David Forlines during the 80's in La Push, WA.

Coco Gordon

TO BE SO FORGET

*as I sing from
Haudenosaunee Skywoman creation story
retold by Paula Gunn Allen in
Grandmothers of The Light*

under *t*ree *O*f light ```` *b*lossom she opens her l*e*gs

it````falls   *S*he blue world dives through

galaxy f*O*rget home forget origins *f*alling fall f*OR*get

````begin coming forget end *g*oing

awareness B*e*aver waterfowl turtle slow her endless fall

````her fall rests in their arms drift a coherence
a form within order of all that is she sleeps dreams
they call a waterfowl earthcall timeless place
beaver searches formless sea for spin slow motion ```clutches shapely in
potential nurturing in possibility loving in being substance becomes
her earth he blows pattern about her
like fur down beads of rain early light crystal highnotes

swims endlessly away ````*t*urtle's circleswimming slows

````they sing into stars night spiral void tree of light she births breathes
on dries waits tamps in dark on turtle's back
pole thickens branches form ````song change ````balls of light
when tree blossoms skywoman sleeps beneath it wakes
````daughter emerges many cycles ````lies in spot her mother
aeons before and sleeps ````luminous shadow merge
````with coming of grandsons Sapling Bud
````````time to ready earth
ride turtle through darkness to a new plane

ELENA CARRODEGUAS ROJO, HAVANA, CUBA

Crucificción        Resurrección

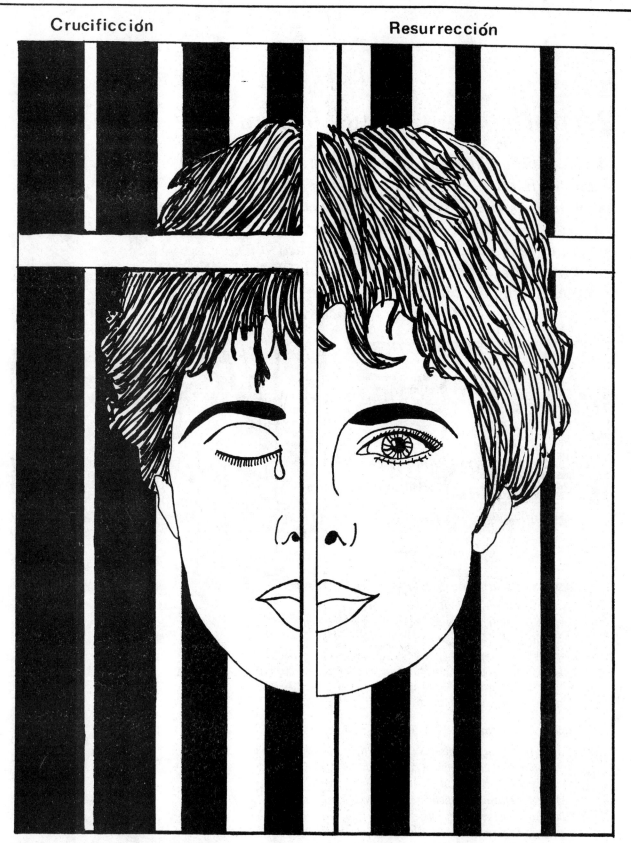

Elena Carrodeguas Rojo

Marquez Glez. 668, e/ Maloja y Estrella. Habana 3. Cuba. CP. 10300

ELENA CARRODEGUAS ROJO, HAVANA, CUBA

Crucificción                    Resurrección

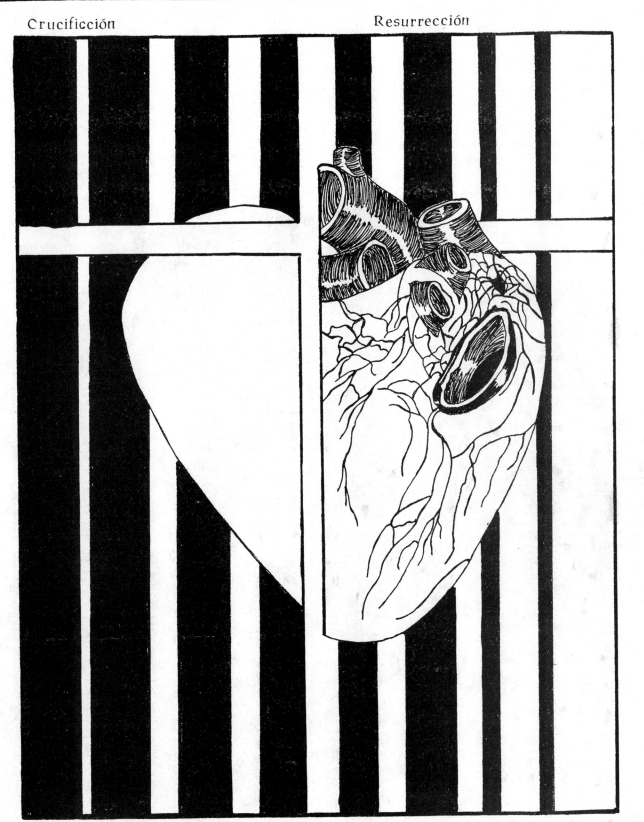

Elena Carrodeguas Rojo

Marquez Glez. 668 e/Maloja y Estrella. Habana 3. Cuba. CP. 10300.

MARIA JOSE BELBEL, SEVILLA, SPAIN

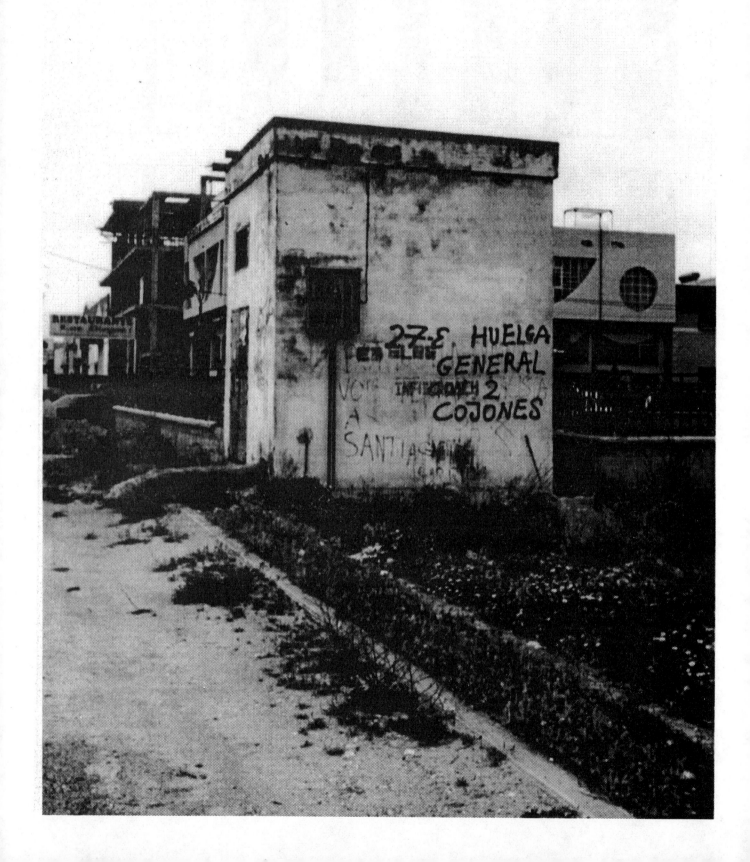

**MARIA JOSE BELBEL**, SEVILLA, SPAIN

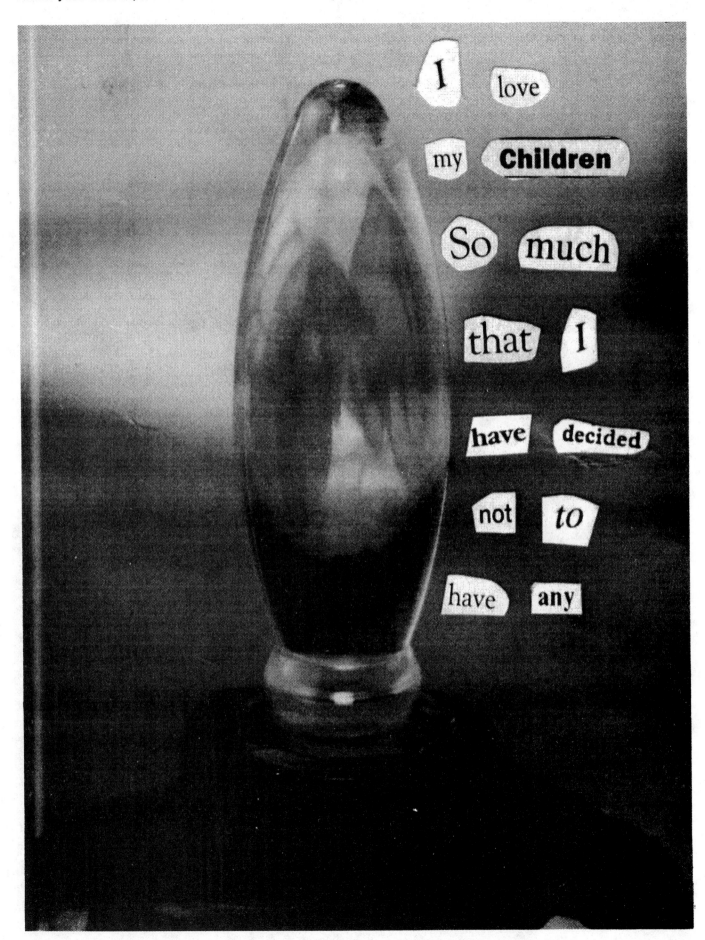

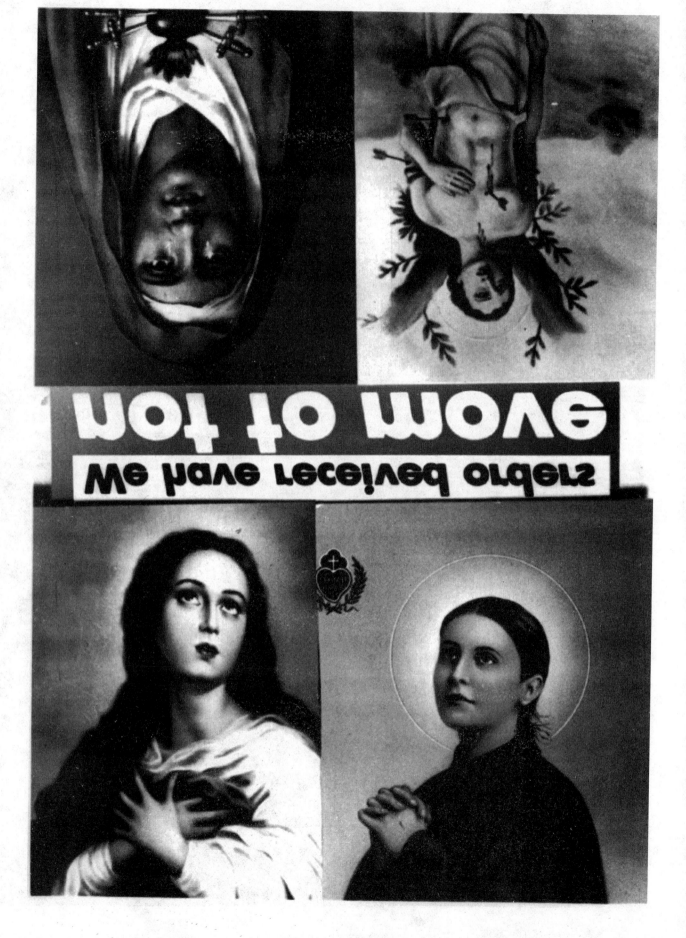

MARGARITA VILLAREJO, MALAGÁ, SPAIN

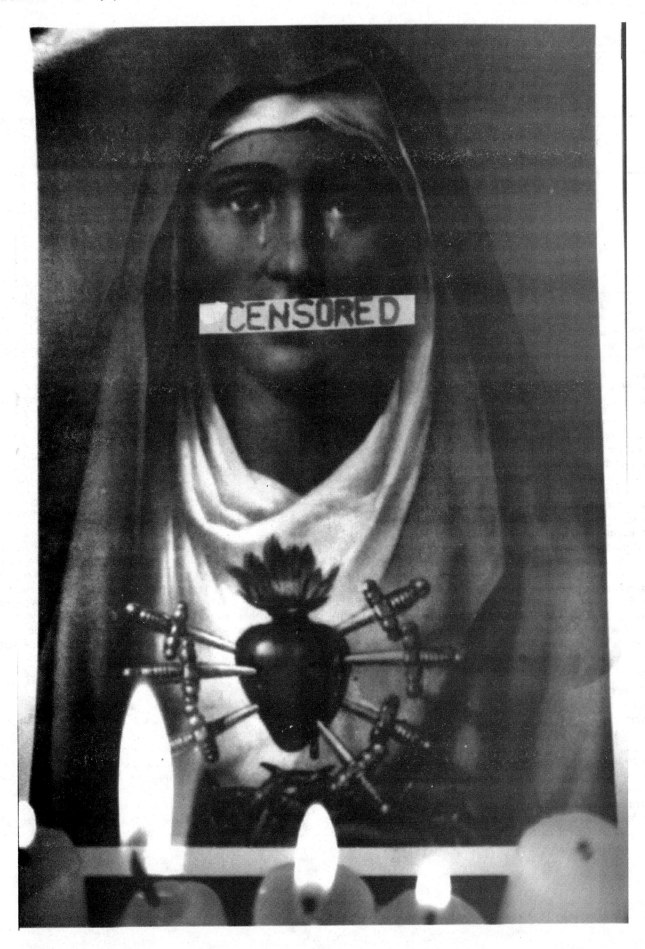

# NEWSLETTER

## WOMEN'S CAUCUS FOR ART
## New York City Chapter

**WCA** Fall 1994

P. O. Box 2646 New York, NY 10009  718 727-8125

## Interview: Elyse Taylor, Artist and Activist

When asking Elyse Taylor about the different aspects of her career, the theme of "linking surfaces" appeared over and over again. This theme is important to an artist with her strong commitment to her local community, a long history in the WCA, and an ongoing exploration of personal growth in her art.

The most recent manifestation of the concept of making connections and forging links is a project Elyse Taylor is currently working on for the Mr. Natural Snapple Distribution Plant in Red Hook, Brooklyn, under the auspices of CityArts, Inc. She was chosen to organize and produce a mural for the plant with approximately twenty teenagers from the local area. Many years of teaching experience have taught her how to set up workshops, teach technical skills, and inspire students to create work about their lives, dreams, fears and problems. Her unpretentious and natural manner are key factors here. She hopes that the project will help each teenager learn simultaneously about who they are as they collaborate with each other to give something back to their community. Three workshops a week, field trips, and a Creative Time and Dance Theatre Workshop are planned so that the young participants will have a wide range of experiences and inspiration.

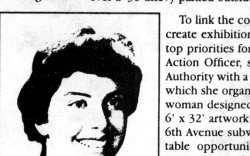

*Elyse Taylor, Brookline H.S. Yearbook '59*

Elyse's commitment to community is not restricted to Brooklyn. She has been an active member of WCA/NYC, working with different presidents. Presently, she is treasurer of the organization, a position she has held for over two years. In her own words, "activism is an ongoing process needing constant maintenance and requiring that one always have a plan of attack." She has collected "watchdog" statistics on the number of women artists shown at major NYC art museums, made flyers of these horrifying statistics, and organized their distribution in front of the Metropolitan Museum of Art as visitors poured in on Saturdays. She also participated in demonstrations at the Whitney, the Guggenheim and MOMA, For the latter, she designed the banner, "MOMA Has Antique Ideas About Women Artists" and draped it over a '36 Chevy parked outside the museum.

To link the community of women artists and to create exhibition opportunities for them are also top priorities for Elyse. As WCA/NYC Affirmative Action Officer, she approached the NYC Transit Authority with a project called "On The Move," for which she organized thirty-two WCA artists. Each woman designed a panel that became part of the 6' x 32' artwork exhibited at the 42nd Street and 6th Avenue subway station. It was a "totally equitable opportunity, with each artist having the same space and all names included."

As an artist, Elyse has worked many years exhibiting in commercial galleries as well as in museums and colleges. She has been as consistent in showing her work in group and individual shows as she has been in her steady activism. However, her latest work seems to be a more personal exploration–a literal "linking" together of her own life for her own awareness–"Growing." An ongoing multi-paneled and quilt-like autobiography, it is made up of 16" squares. Now numbering over one hundred, twenty-five of them were exhibited in Paris last year.

Incorporating various found and traditional materials, these panels are personal statements, sometimes painful, sometimes funny, sometimes "just life." They document her passage, but most importantly, "relate to everyone's growth experience." Elyse says that she's found that many people identify with different pieces of "Growing" and some panels seem to elicit very powerful responses. As "Growing" panels continue to be produced, the forging of links goes from the community to the studio, from her world to ours, as her art and activism connect us to each other. For Elyse, this is an ongoing collaboration. *Maria Epes, Artist*

ELYSE TAYLOR, BROOKLYN, NY, USA

MURAL

MURAL TITLE: A DREAM GROWS IN BROOKLYN
LOCATION: Pier 12 - 212 Wolcott St., Red Hook, Brooklyn, NY.

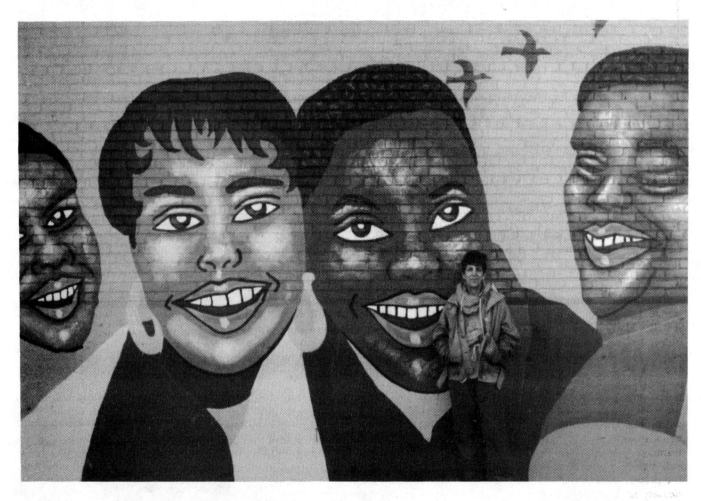

DETAIL OF THE MURAL WITH ELYSE TAYLOR - ARTIST

A DREAM GROWS IN BROOKLYN is a 32x93 ft exterior mural painted
on the side wall of Snapple's distribution plant facing the New
York Harbor. This community project was created with the help and
imput of local teenagers. The first step was a series of workshops
in which I taught technical skills and inspired the volunteers to
create work relevant to themselves and their environment. Next I
created a maquette and transferred it to the brick building. All
the faces and figures in the mural are likenesses of the actual
teens who worked on the project.

ELYSE TAYLOR  407 DOUGLASS ST., BROOKLYN, NEW YORK 11217
TEL NO. 718 622-8840

**MILLIE CHEN**, TORONTO, ON, CANADA

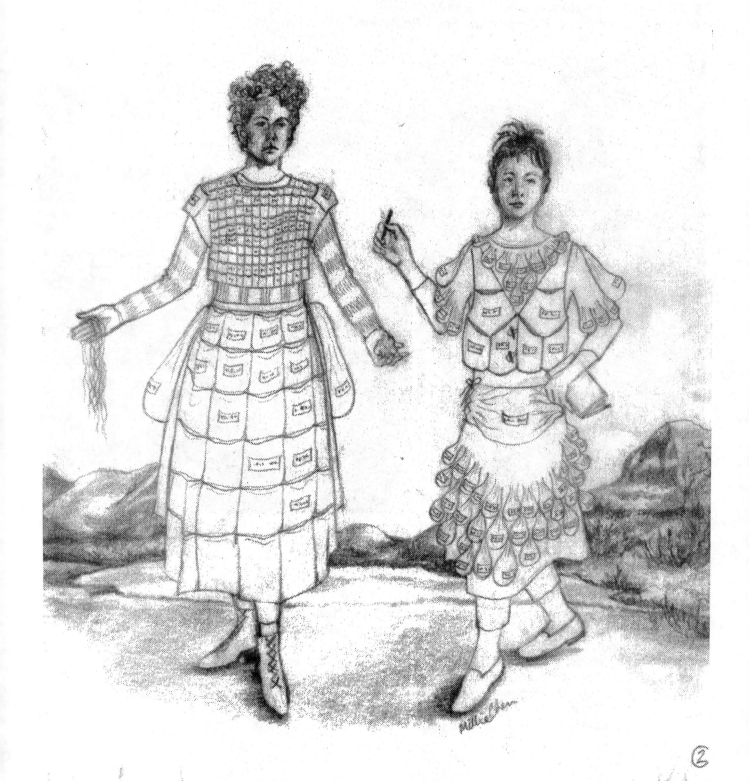

Yurtopia: costumes

EVELYN VON MICHALOFSKI, TORONTO, ON, CANADA

# Yurtopia:
## portable museums

becoming
moving
permeable
sweating
mutable
displays

disrupting the habitual ways that information is collected

VICKY CLARK, PITTSBURGH, PA, USA

# speakeasy

*Each month, the New Art Examiner invites an art-world personality to write a "Speakeasy" essay on a topic of his or her choice. The ideas and opinions expressed in the "Speakeasy" are those of the writer alone, and not subject to editorial interference.*

*Vicky A. Clark is a curator at the Carnegie Museum of Art in Pittsburgh, Pennsylvania, where she has worked for 13 years. She is currently working on an exhibition titled "International Encounters: The Carnegie International and Contemporary Art 1896-1996," about the Carnegie's 100-year history. She also teaches twentieth-century and contemporary art at the University of Pittsburgh, and has written articles on contemporary art and women's issues for a variety of publications and periodicals.*

Those who know me well realize that I am rarely left speechless. Last spring, however, while teaching Postmodernism at the University of Pittsburgh, I found myself momentarily stunned. I had assigned Hélène Cixous's "The Laugh of the Medusa," Laura Mulvey's "Visual Pleasure and Narrative Cinema," and Craig Owens's "The Discourse of Others: Feminists and Postmodernism" for a lecture on the feminist critique. A female student in her twenties questioned the validity or necessity of such ideas in today's world. In further conversation several women revealed that they felt the feminist battle had been won: there was equality in the art world and women were showing their work in galleries and museums. In response, I recounted statistics from the Guerrilla Girls and my own research about representation in galleries, art magazines, exhibitions, arts festivals, and academic departments. The statistics told a continuing story of exclusion that could not be denied.

But statistics and even feminist and Postmodern critiques rarely penetrate that charming and charmed circle of the art-museum world. People frequently talk about male curators who are not open to work by women yet insist their decisions are based on quality—as if quality can somehow be removed from issues of gender, age, and race. Few people talk about the small number of female curators, especially in major museums. Having operated in the museum world for 13 years now, I have become increasingly frustrated at the lack of support for women in the inner circle while I have watched many talented women leave institutions for more rewarding avenues.[1] I am angry about the hard reality that things are not likely to change in my lifetime as art museums remain instruments for maintaining the status quo, especially with current funding problems and virulent attacks from the conservative Right.

Why can't, and more accurately, why *won't* art museums change? Art critic Christopher Knight wrote a persuasive article for the *Los Angeles Times* on March 27, 1994, entitled (in large, bold letters): "These Are the Only Three Women Running Major Art Museums in the United States. Can You Believe It?" Small pictures of Mary Gardner Neill, newly appointed director of the Seattle Art Museum; Anne d'Harnoncourt of the Philadelphia Museum of Art; and Kathy Halbreich of the Walker Art Center in Minneapolis illustrated his point. Knight, a writer not known for championing women in the arts, cited the usual dreary statistics (75% of the members of American Association of Museum Directors (AAMD) are men, etc.), but then proceeded to define museums as nonprofit corporations where "women are held back by a corporate Establishment that is simply not yet comfortable with their presence."

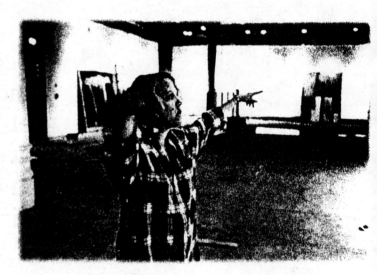

Photo by William Wade; courtesy of Carnegie Museum of Art

Museums, like corporations, are innately conservative, concerned with validating culture and the status quo; they have created the same glass ceiling that exists in the corporate worlds (as recently as 1993, there was only one female CEO of a Fortune 500 company). The crossover, of course, comes with the board of trustees, whose members are generally suc-

VICKY CLARK, PITTSBURGH, PA, USA

cessful businessmen, who, even if they are unaware of their intentions, are interested in perpetuating their own comfortable world and thus contribute to the existing tension between the public and private aspects of a museum.

Knight's linking of a corporate mentality with the art museum relies on widespread theories about patriarchal dominance, the vertical hierarchy of that ideology (museum departments, for example, are rigidly circumscribed despite recent blurring of boundaries that traditionally have separated the different media), and the different ways in which men and women think and act. (Deborah Tannen's popular theories about differing conversational techniques, now taken into the business world, have caused great debate.) Women are not welcomed in many worlds, but this is especially so in art museums, where the investment in the status quo is enormous. Three female directors does not a revolution make, and they hardly counteract the number of talented women who have left the museum world entirely because of its inhospitality and limitations.[2] Museums have effectively silenced the voices of women, especially in contemporary art, where gender issues play such an important role. Museums, based on the principle of exclusivity for their entire history, are slow to move to a new world of inclusivity.

Knight introduced another slant on the problem by drawing upon Ann Douglas's 1977 book, *The Feminization of American Culture*. Douglas credits the Industrial Revolution with bringing about an abrupt shift in gender roles as men left the home to work and women acquired leisure time. Art began to be perceived as feminine, and therefore of secondary importance. In order to counteract this feminization—Knight cites the popular stereotype of a wife dragging her reluctant husband to the opera or the ballet—arts organizations have turned to men as directors to maintain patriarchal control.

One wonders what will change the power structure. Feminist activist groups in the '70s picketed the Museum of Modern Art and the Whitney Museum of American Art, perhaps effecting a small increase in the number of women artists shown there. Last year, however, Women's Action Coalition (WAC) members protested at the opening of the SoHo Guggenheim, showing that little has changed. Women have joined museum staffs, but they are rarely hired for power positions. When, in exceptional cases, women do ascend to major curatorial posi-

tions, many find the atmosphere untenable. The struggle for power develops, as usual, along traditional oppositional lines. Instead of finding room for a variety of voices within the institution, museums generally support safe, non-controversial art and curators.

Institutions are naturally conservative entities. When challenged, they tend to retreat to safe ground. I remember my graduate research into the fourteenth century, when the winds of change challenged the authority of the nobility, who reacted by becoming even more courtly, almost becoming caricatures of themselves, as they attempted to hold on to their power. In many ways, the current situation in art museums is remarkably similar. Under attack from many sources, museums are retreating just when they desperately need to change.

Change *is* happening elsewhere, and eventually it will infiltrate the art world and its institutions. People working on artificial intelligence, for example, have had to regroup after their efforts to recreate a vertical structure—a patriarchal model—failed. New efforts here, as well as in robotics and virtual reality, are focusing on a more horizontal system of thinking and working, a system stressing interdependence and multiple options rather than the single authority of the vertical organization.[3] The sciences, those disciplines so valued in our empiricism-happy culture, have even begun to emphasize connections rather than the breaking down of systems to their smallest bits. As new methods of thinking emerge, perhaps there is hope for new visions, even in old-fashioned art museums.

Whenever I feel the most defeated by the lack of support for women in art museums, I seem to find a small ray of hope. Just this week, someone sent me a list of ways to facilitate change in museums offered by Harold Skramstad at the Museum Management Institute:

1. Change starts at the top—and the bottom.
2. Learn to listen. Listen to everybody.
3. Find ways to measure what you do.
4. Support risk and failure.
5. Recognize limits—but stretch!
6. Look outside your organization for best practices.
7. You can't deal with diversity outside your organization if you don't have diversity inside it.
8. Challenge every assumption.
9. Develop new metaphors for your organization.
10. Keep searching for the common ground between your mission and your audience's needs.

Sounds like a feminist agenda to me!

**NOTES**

1   I work, after all, at The Carnegie Museum of Art and have witnessed four "Carnegie Internationals" where the presence of women has been almost non-existent. Currently studying the history of this exhibition, I have confirmed that this bias has existed for its entire 100-year history.

2   One should note that museum directors in general are becoming an endangered species as few can meet the high expectations of boards who want and need a charismatic miracle worker skilled in finance, management, public relations, and yes, even art history.

3   I am indebted to Simon Penny, an artist who teaches at Carnegie Mellon University, for these insights which I gained when he lectured about his work this fall at Carlow College.

**BERTA SICHEL**, NEW YORK, NY, USA

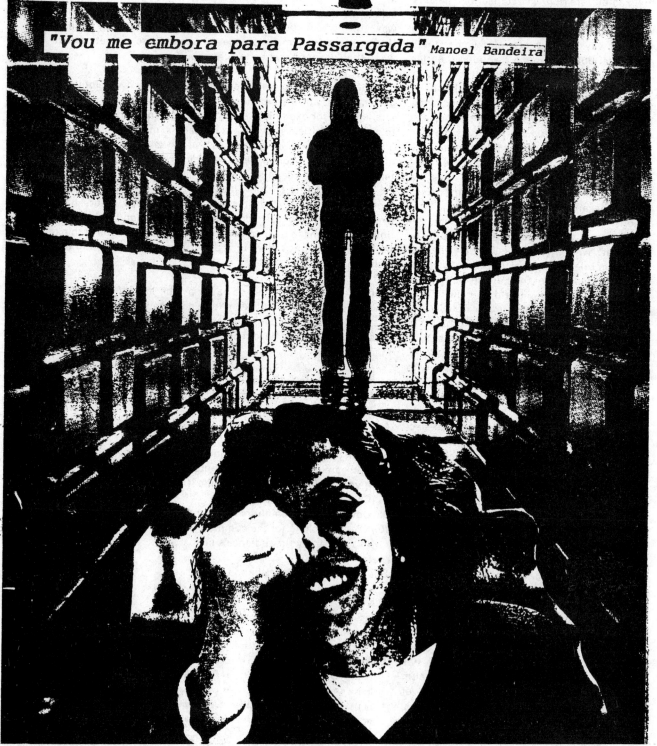

JUDITH GOLDMAN, NEW YORK, NY, USA

My Alibi

He never decided to kill her, not consciously. He
hadn't planned it. In fact, it had come about quite
naturally, and once he made the connections, the pieces
had just fallen into place. In retrospect, it had been
easy. There was never a choice, and to this day, he has
not once doubted the rightness of his action. His only
regret is that no one knew he did it. He had wanted
someone to know. In an age when every one had time in the
limelight, he would have liked a little credit. The sad
part is there were never even suspects. No one considered
her death suspicious. It was not murder by a long shot --
but one of those tragic, mysterious cases like an
infant's crib death or the people one reads about who go
to sleep one night in the prime of life and never get up
again. The obituary attributed death to an allergic
reaction. To shellfish or peanuts -- someone said. They
wanted to do an autopsy, but her husband objected. He
could not bear the idea of them cutting her up.

Food poisoning, as a cause of death, satisfied him.
After all, she was an indiscriminate eater. For a chic,
much-photographed lady, she totally lacked self-control.
The first time we met, she turned to my wife and said
"I'm sure you don't lunch." I didn't know what she was
talking about, but my wife said she was a bitch. We
didn't know then that she couldn't keep the weight off or
about the exotic binges. She would consume a bucket of
chicken wings or plate of corn fritters at a sitting. Her
taste in food was down and dirty. Afterward, she'd starve
and take her older daughter, the fat one, to the spa
where they'd drink hot water with lemon juice. Sometimes
she went on a regime of pills. There was talk she died
from an overdose of amphetamines. That was a real
possibility. And there was a small group of friends who
suspected suicide. They were the people who knew her
well. I was counting on them. They were my alibi.

MAXINE KAHN, NEW YORK, NY, USA

My mother was a lion. She fiercely guarded her domain and woe to anyone who tried to break in, or who was the least bit cutting or disrespectful about her family. She saw cuts even when they were not intended and banished poor unsuspecting friends and relations from her lair. We all tried to point out to her that we'd be left all on our own if she persisted but she gaily went on her own way certain of her course.

She never preached at us but by her example I learned a ferocity or tenacity of spirit of survival with humpur. Her laugh was deep and the tears would pour out of her eyes when she was taken by a fit of laughter. It was infectious when it began and everyone around would have no choice but to join in. The children particularly loved when this happened and would talk to one another about it.

The children's children fell into the category of those who could do no wrong.It didn't matter what they were up to she knew that she had the cleverest, most wounderful grandchildren in existence. She bragged about them unmercifully to anyone who lent an ear. And she kept careful track of their days by incessant phoning, letter writing, card sending and the usual preparation of family dinners on Holidays. If God Forbid one of them couldn't return from boarding school or College for Passover or Hanukah she showed her displeasure then forgot about it in preparation for those who would be coming.

All the children's friends were included in our holiday dinners as were our friends when we were growing up. This kind of existence engendered a loyalty and fierce pride of family which I don't see much anymore. My mother was always sitting with my Dad in the hospital rooms when the children were born or were hurt or she would simply take one or another if there were too much going on at home. If one of them achieved honors or some special award she dined out on it long after.

Even after I was married I knew I always had a place to come home to. She gave me that place and now it is inside of me and I pray that I can do as much for my children and their children.

MAXINE KAHN, NEW YORK, NY, USA

My father has spent the last fifty odd years worrying about his
kids, his fgrandchildren and now his great grandchildren. I think
if you asked him he would have described himself as a happy man.
His work was something that fulfilled him and he was proud of his
accomplishments and the friends he made in business over the year

He literally described himself as having no regrets.  And those who
were among his friends seemed to enjoy his company as much as I did
^Not that I saw a great deal of him as I raised my family. He had
a habit of not being obtrusive in one's life, but if ever he was
needed he was there.  sIt was not that I always agreed with him,
and it was not that he led a particulary examined life, it was just
that he didn't judge others harshly and liked to be of use, if
possible.

It always took him a while to come up with a decision but he did
think about what concerned him and those he cared about.  when I
needed a lawyer he came with me to interview them. When I was in
Hospital he came to sit with me. It was not what he said but the
fact that he was there that was important. When he played golf with
my sister and me he taught the game as if we were potential olympic
golfers and if we didn't line up properly or used the wrong club he
would make us try again and again until the shot was well made.

It never ocurred to him that we might not care as much about the
game as he did but just liked being out there with him
When Annie had decisions to talk over his ear was available and he
was never to busy to take any of the kids to lunch or dinner if
they had the time. He loved us all without talking much and even
enjoyed the tales about the kids when they weren't around

As for my mom I remember him telling me as a child that he loved
her more in her little finger than he would ever love anyone else
in this lifetime.   'm not even sure now about what he was saying
but I think that he could not live without her. They are a good
example to the next generation of a devoted couple.

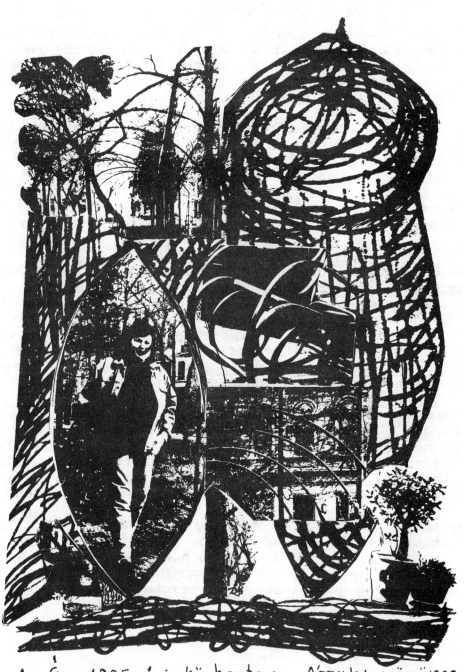

Az Ém 1995-évi közkertem - Áprilisi gyümölcs?
NEM, PONT MÁJUSI - VÁRADI - NAPOS KERT.

SONYA GROPMAN, JACKSON, NY, USA

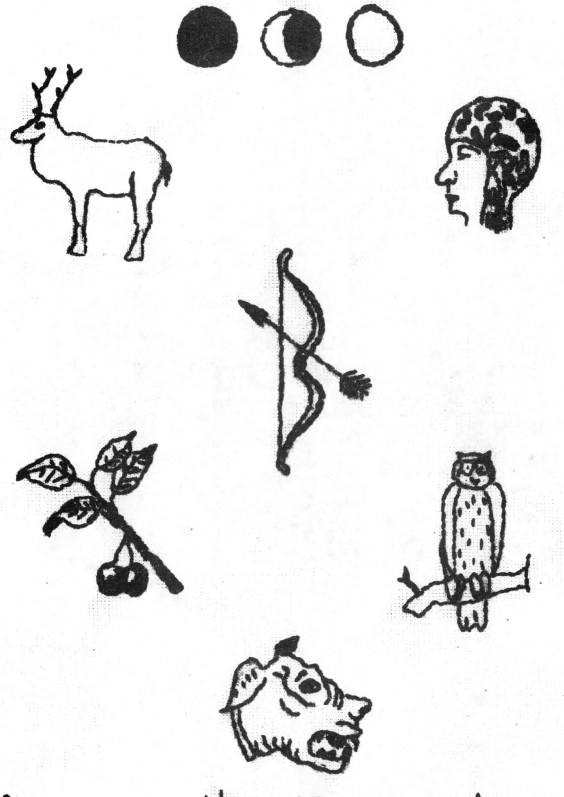

Diana          Hecate          Athena

**SUSANNE GREVEN**, KÖLN, GERMANY

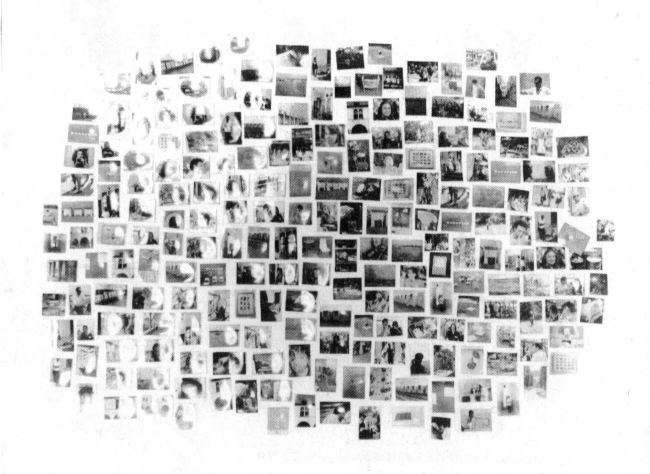

SUSANNE GREVEN, KÖLN, GERMANY

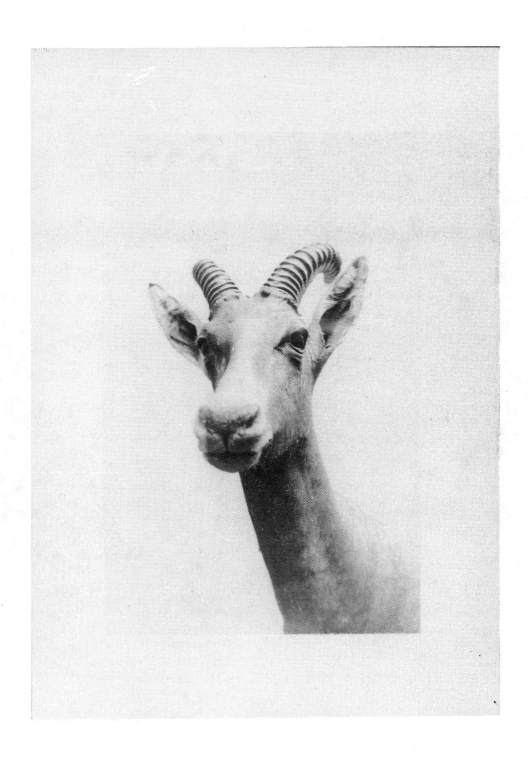

**CARMEN BISTE**, KOLN, GERMANY

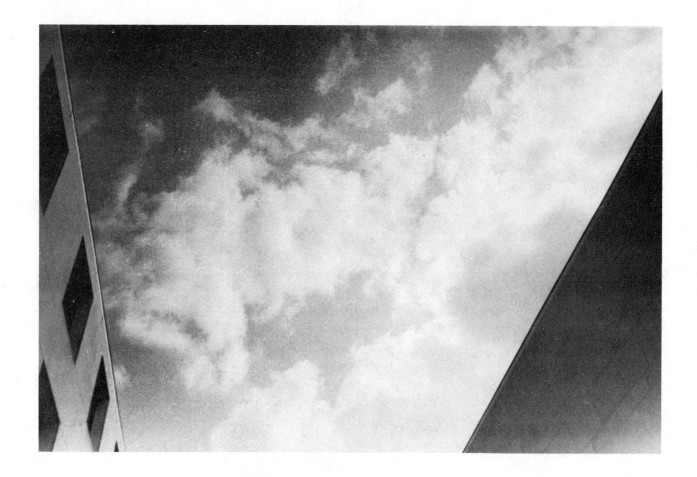

CARMEN BISTE, KOLN, GERMANY

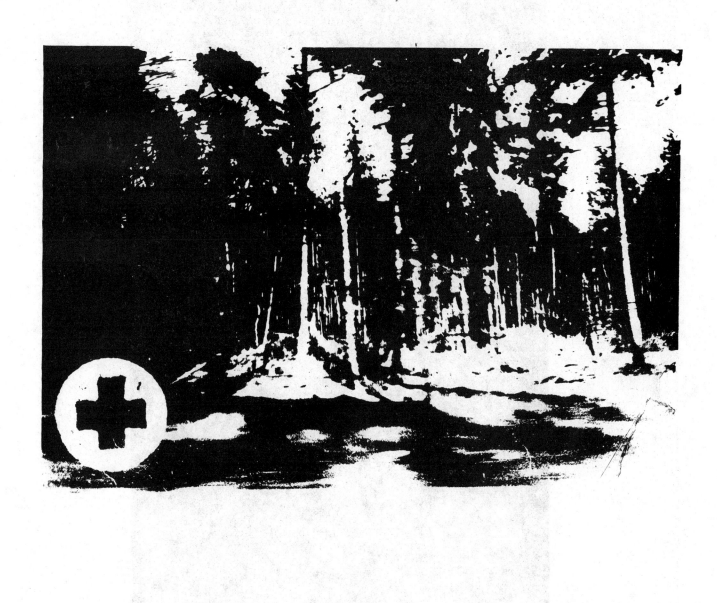

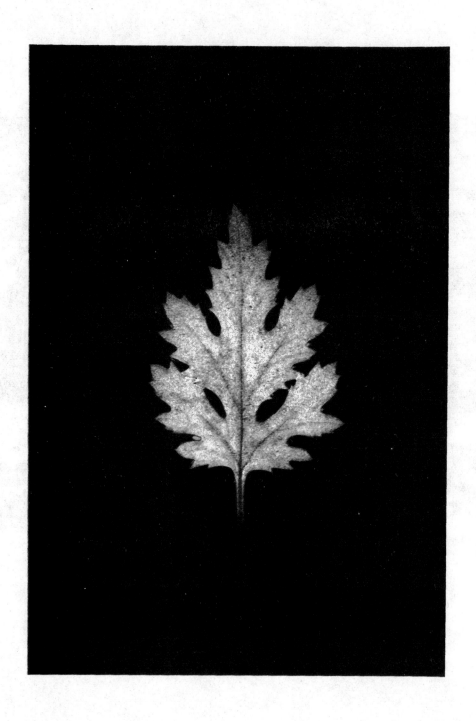

LUTZ BACHER, BERKELEY, CA, USA

nature

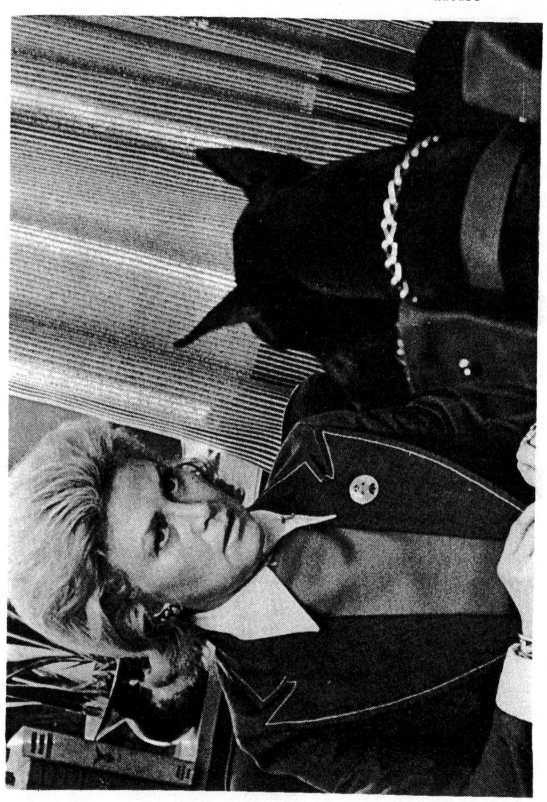

lutz bacher

now I know you and your dog like nature

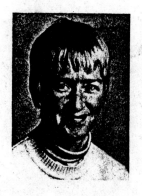

Nature Art


Inken N. Woldsen
Paulstr. 16
D 25421 Pinneberg
Germany


<u>Vita</u>
1948          born in Northern Germany
1966 - 70     studied art teaching in Kiel

since 1978    free lance artist
since 1987    working with natural pigments like earth,
              rust, mould, peat etc.
since 1988    member of the German Artists Association




<u>One-woman-shows</u>
1986     Glückstadt      Brockdorff-Palace
1987     Pinneberg       Gallery under the roof
1987     Hannover        Gallery for arts and crafts
1989     Pinneberg       Gallery under the roof
1990     Hamburg         House of arts
1993     Kiel            Gallera in Akkerboom Farmhause
1994     Oldenburg       Producers Gallery Karg e.V.




<u>Symposiums</u>

1990   "Holzsignale", wood sculptures, Pinneberg
1991   "Lagewechsel", installations, performances, Hamburg
       Internat. Nature Art Symposium, Kong Ju, South Korea
1992   Internat. Nature Art Symposium, Ammersbek, Germany
       Internat. GAIA-Symposium, Gelsenkirchen, Germany
1993   Internat. Nature Art Symposium, Tsukui, Japan
       Art  Architecture III, Kyoto, Japan
1994   Internat. Nature Art Symposium, Samkawa, Japan

INKEN N. WOLDSEN
BOOKS     1993

Installation in Bad Segeberg, Germany

48 books wrapped with cotton and wire layed for four months
in the soil of a park. The long process of changing showed
a synthesis between human culture and natural elements.

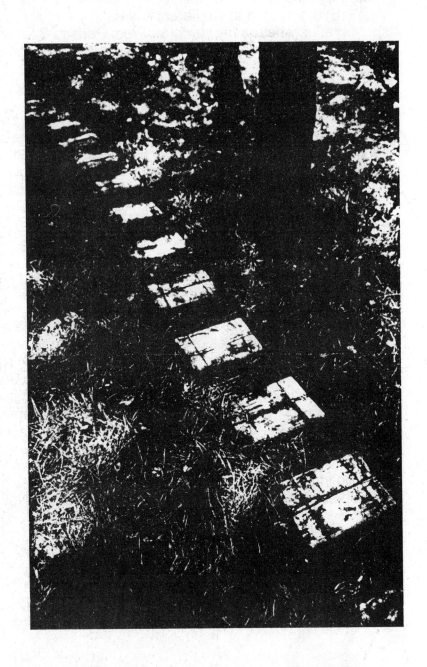

## ARTISTS' STATEMENT

### JILL WATERMAN - NEW YEAR'S EVE SERIES

New Year's Eve is the holiday of anticipation. As a young artist in a foreign land, I became curious about the significance of a celebration I had previously taken for granted. As a woman photographer considering the history of the documentary medium, I thought it a challenge to assign myself an on-going photographic project. In December 1983 I resolved to capture the rituals of New Year's Eve, traveling to a different city each year to photograph events occurring spontaneously before my camera. From Paris to Shanghai the sites of my project currently span a dozen locations, numerous social climates and a telling cultural array.

Among the places and festivities captured on film :
Parisian society gathered along the Champs Elysees; London bobbies in a shaving cream fight; the apple high atop Times Square in New York; Canadian punk rockers at a club in Montreal; waitresses at a San Juan Casino Resort; Boston's genuine "First Night" events; outfitted party-goers in Georgetown, D.C.; San Francisco's Exotic Erotic Ball; festivities at a Karioke Bar in Burlington, VT; a Masked Ball Discotheque in Tucson, AZ; a curbside all-niter for Rose Parade fans in Pasadena, CA and students playing dragon tag on the Bund in Shanghai, China.

The end of the millennium is now offering another perspective from which to view this project. In the past 12 years my focus has evolved to incorporate organized festivities such as "First Night" events, as well as cultures where celebrations take on varied meanings and traditions. Over time I have found increasing attention given to activities providing fun for different ages and lifestyles. Recently, I have begun to gather information about the traditions and history of New Years' past, with a plan to propose this project in book form. I will continue photographing New Year's Eve celebrations through the turn of the century, alternating between U.S. and foreign cities every other year. A portfolio of images from this series have already been exhibited in sites around New York City, and proposals are currently being offered to galleries and cultural centers both near and far. In spite of the diversity of locations covered in this project, the portfolio images are united through a narrative of candid gestures received from the subjects and by their shared expectations for the New Year.

JILL WATERMAN, NEW YORK, NY, USA

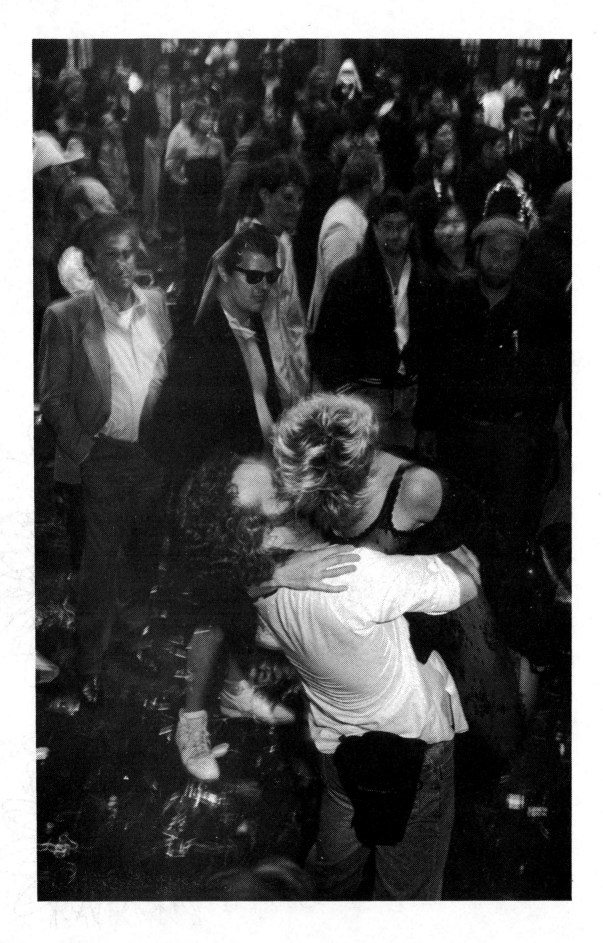

**AMY DREZNER**, SANTA MONICA, CA, USA

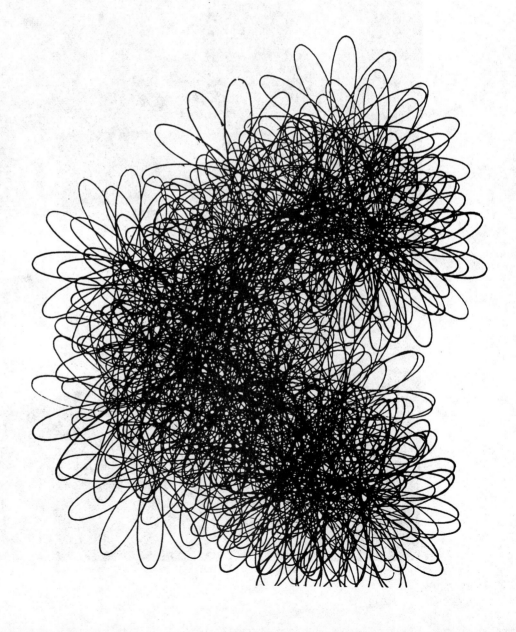

MICHELLE WEINBERG DE PEREYRA, PROVINCETOWN, MA, USA

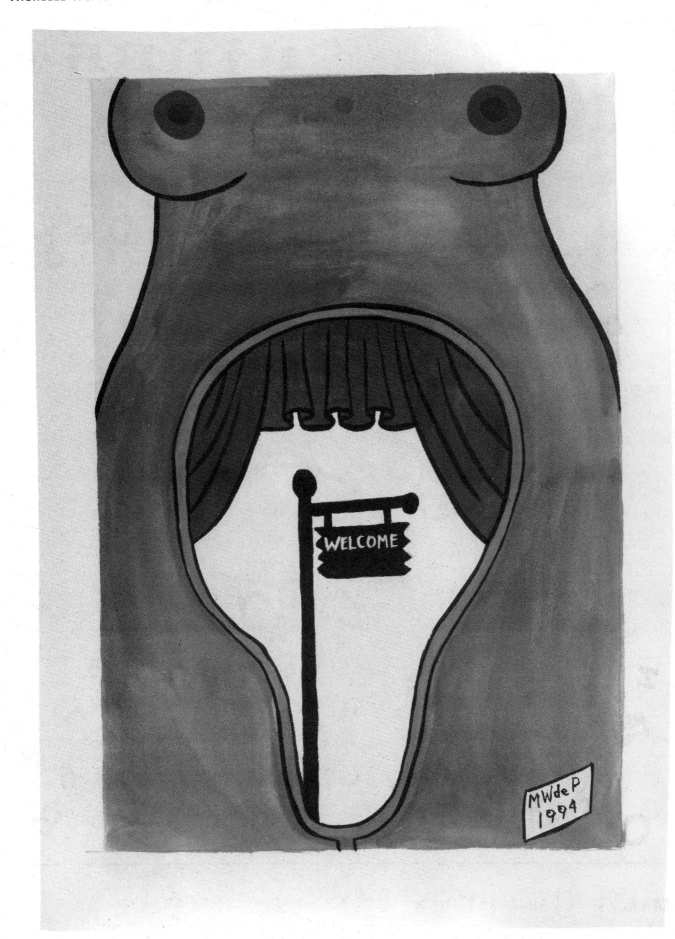

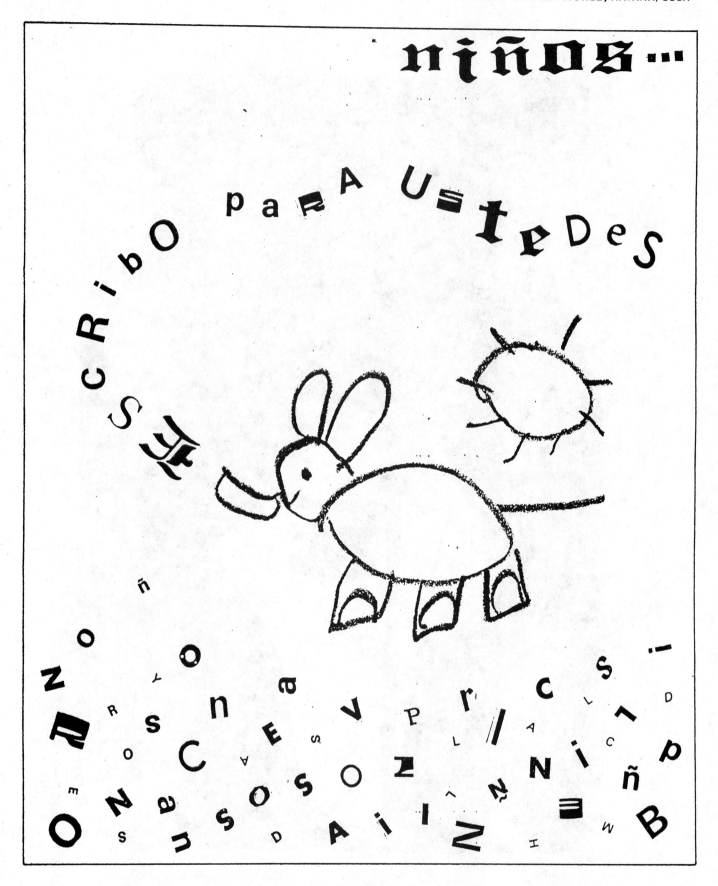

MARLEN garcia nuñez      Ciudad de La Habana, Cuba      (53,7) 62 6878

MARLEN GARCIA NUÑEZ, HAVANA, CUBA

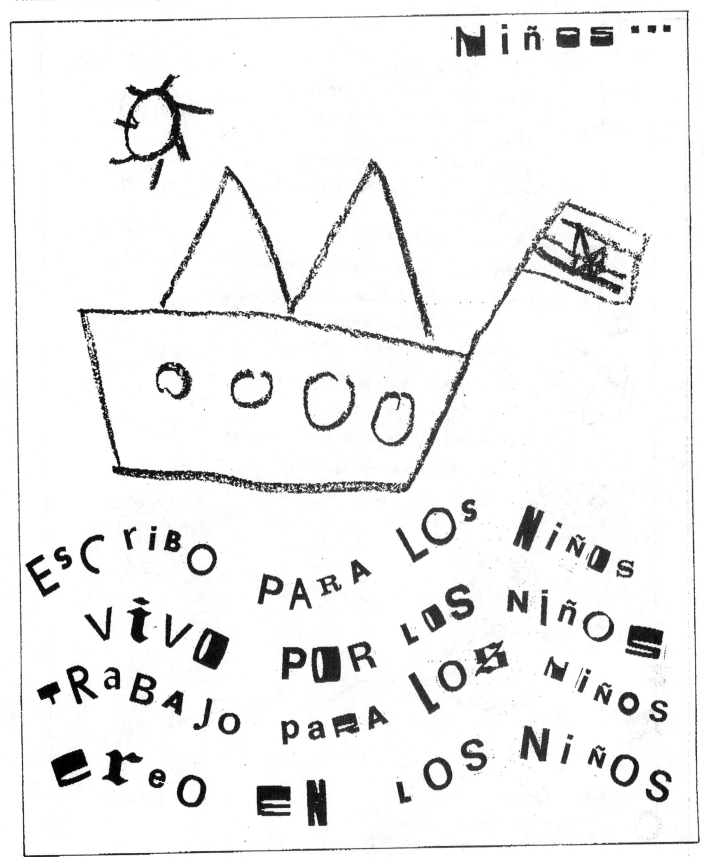

MARLENE GARCIA NUÑEZ    CIUDAD DE LA HABANA, CUBA. (537) 626878

IRINA LEYVA, HAVANA, CUBA

POESIA

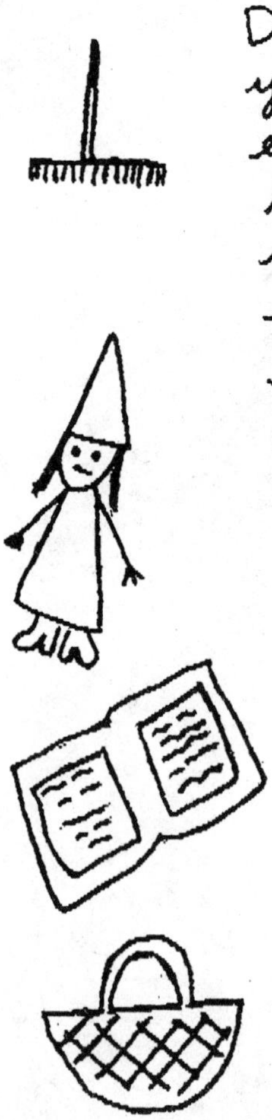

Doy la espalda
y cruzo por el silencio
en mi escoba de papel,
trato de barrer
hasta el último rincón
en el que pueda encontrar
un pelo tuyo.
A veces aparece alguien
con tu nombre en el rostro,
sonriendo le sacudo las orejas
y caes lentamente
hasta hacerte pedazos.
Después recojo cada uno
y los pego al azar.
Siempre vuelve a funcionar
y apareces otra vez
como papalote al viento

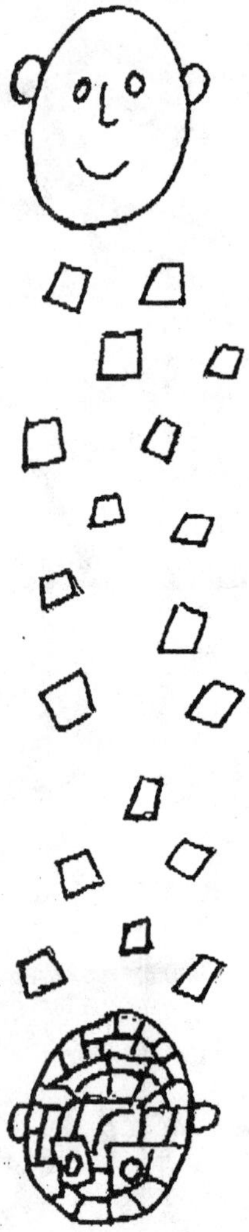

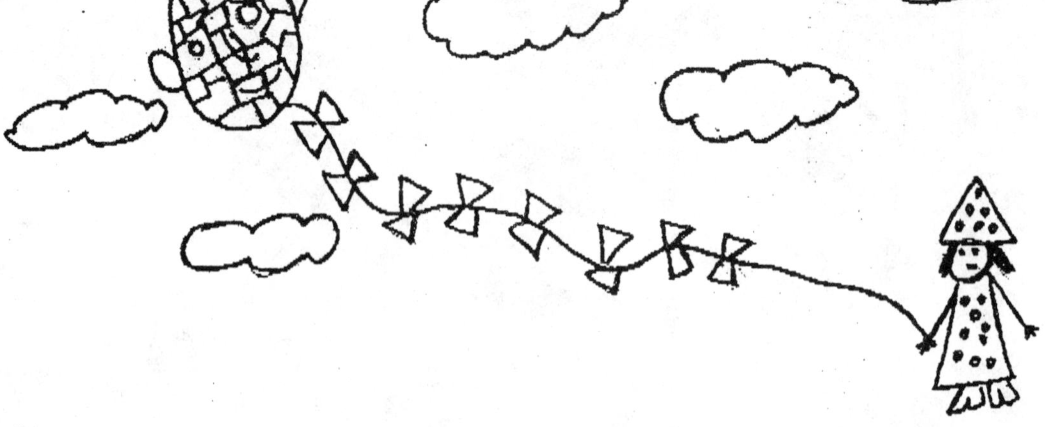

IRINA LEYVA
8 EAST KINGS HOUSE CIRCLE
KINGSTON 6. JAMAICA W.I.
9783188 (phone)
9228540 (phone)
9228544 (Fax)

Irina

IRINA LEYVA, HAVANA, CUBA

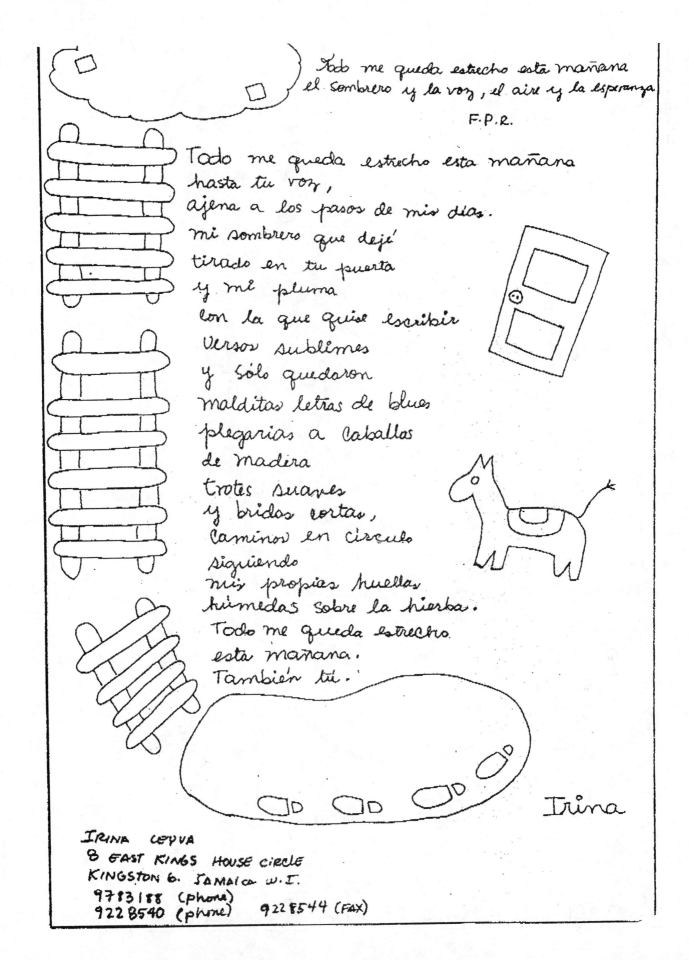

Todo me queda estrecho esta mañana
el sombrero y la voz, el aire y la esperanza.

F.P.R.

Todo me queda estrecho esta mañana
hasta tu voz,
ajena a los pasos de mis días.
mi sombrero que dejé
tirado en tu puerta
y mi pluma
con la que quise escribir
versos sublimes
y sólo quedaron
malditas letras de blues
plegarias a caballos
de madera
trotes suaves
y bridas cortas,
caminos en círculo
siguiendo
mis propias huellas
húmedas sobre la hierba.
Todo me queda estrecho.
esta mañana.
También tú.

Irina

IRINA LEYVA
8 EAST KINGS HOUSE CIRCLE
KINGSTON 6. JAMAICA W.I.
9783188 (phone)
9228540 (phone)    9228544 (FAX)

Niños

Siempre para los niños

por la complicidad de los sueños.

Porque la llave que abre el

Por la frescura, la ingenuidad, y

es una sonrisa

un beso

Universo Infantil

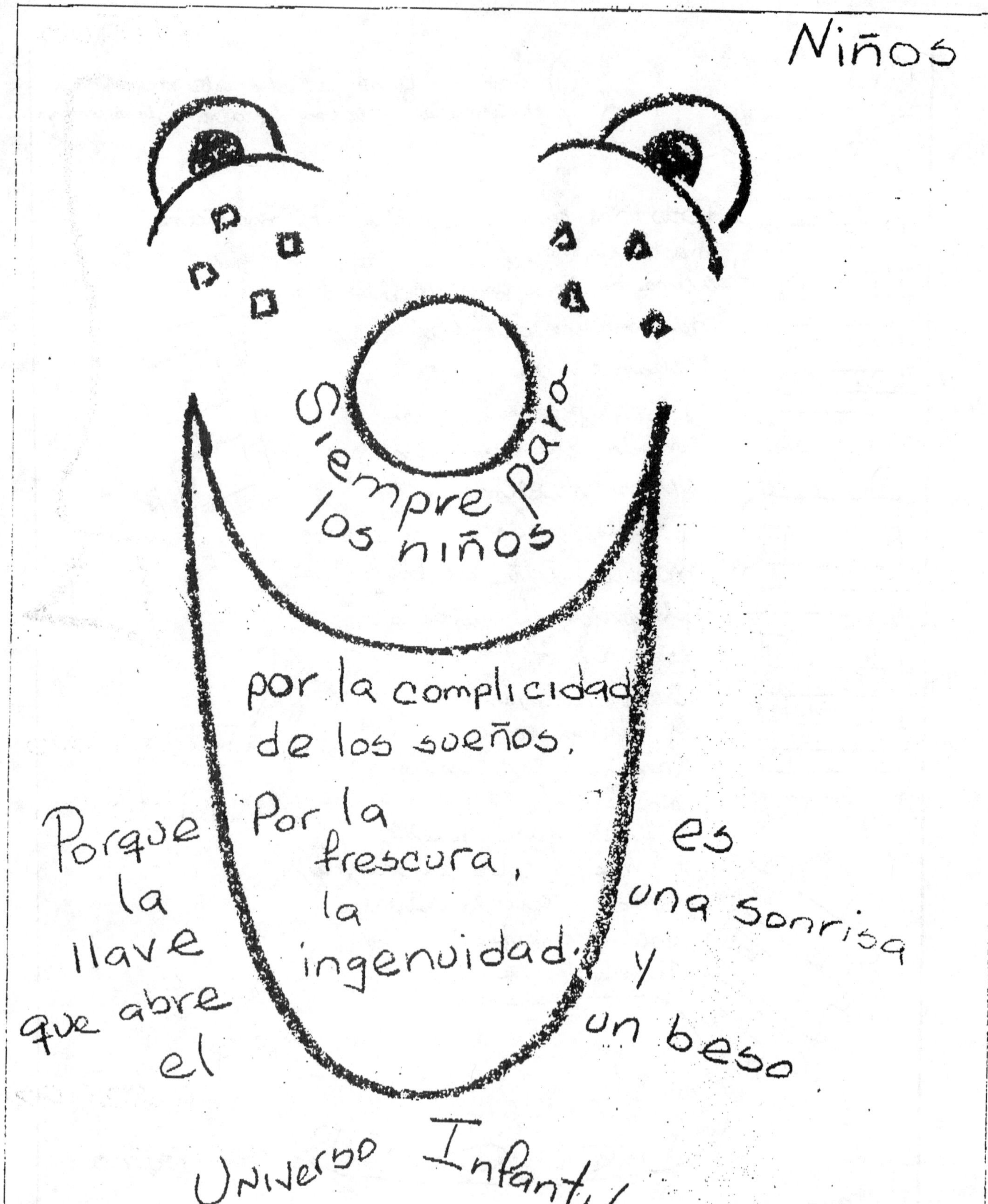

MAITE LUIS RUIZ, HAVANA, CUBA

Niños

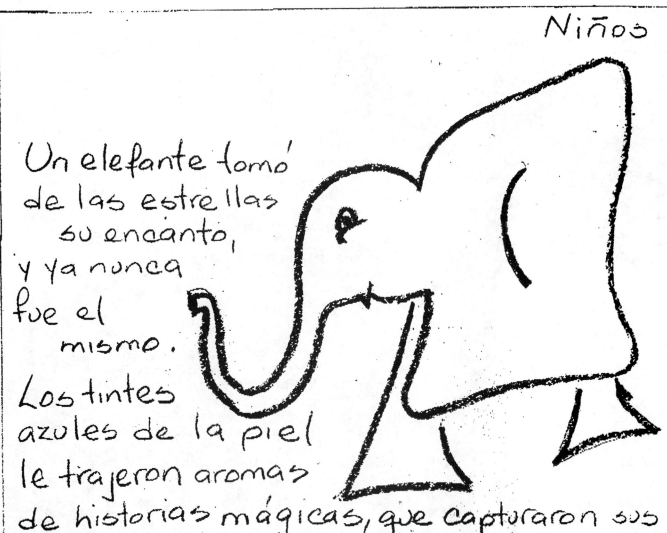

Un elefante tomó
de las estrellas
su encanto,
y ya nunca
fue el
mismo.
Los tintes
azules de la piel
le trajeron aromas
de historias mágicas, que capturaron sus
orejas de los secretos del viento.
Comenzó su tarea de
inventar los sueños,
cada noche, entre las bromas de
las ciudades tristes.
Y encontró la puerta de los misterios
en un pliegue del tiempo.
Una vez, en
un cuento...

Maite Luis Ruiz. Ciudad Habana. Cuba (537) 90-8077

Pamela Jacobs, NEW YORK, NY, USA

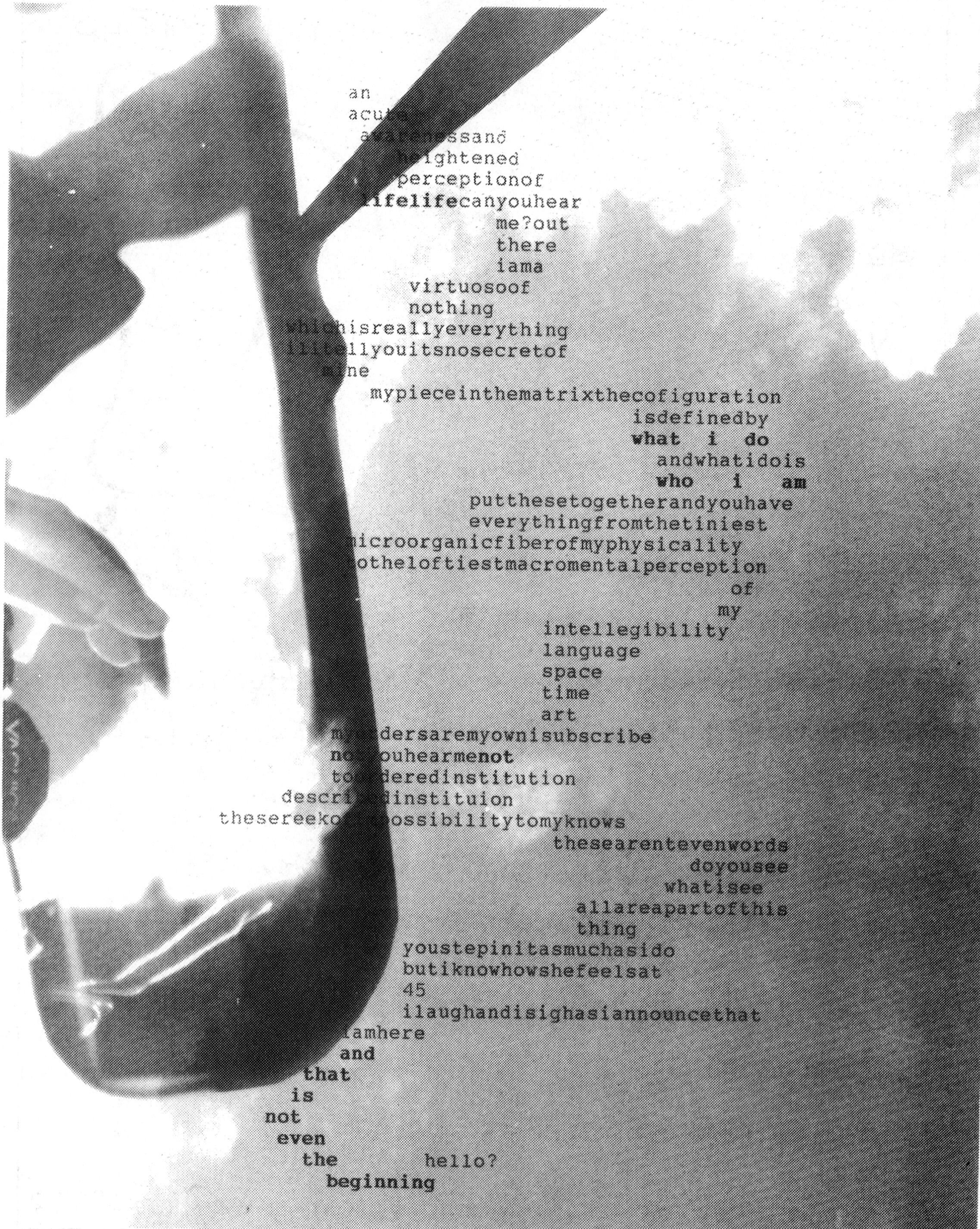

an
acute
awarenessand
heightened
perceptionof
**lifelife**canyouhear
me?out
there
iama
virtuosoof
nothing
whichisreallyeverything
illtellyouitsnosecretof
mine
mypieceinthematrixthecofiguration
isdefinedby
**what  i  do**
andwhatidois
**who  i  am**
putthesetogetherandyouhave
everythingfromthetiniest
microorganicfiberofmyphysicality
totheloftiestmacromentalperception
of
my
intellegibility
language
space
time
art
myordersaremyownisubscribe
**no**youhearme**not**
toorderedinstitution
describedinstituion
thesereekofpossibilitytomyknows
thesearentevenwords
doyousee
whatisee
allareapartofthis
thing
youstepinitasmuchasido
butiknowhowshefeelsat
45
ilaughandisighasiannouncethat
**iamhere**
**and**
**that**
**is**
**not**
**even**
**the**      hello?
**beginning**

**PAMELA JACOBS,** NEW YORK, NY, USA

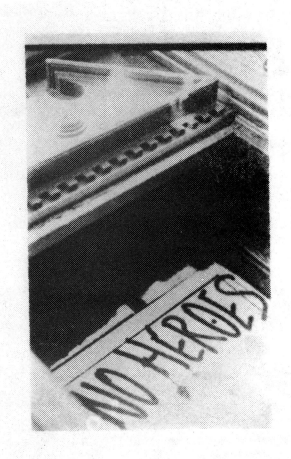

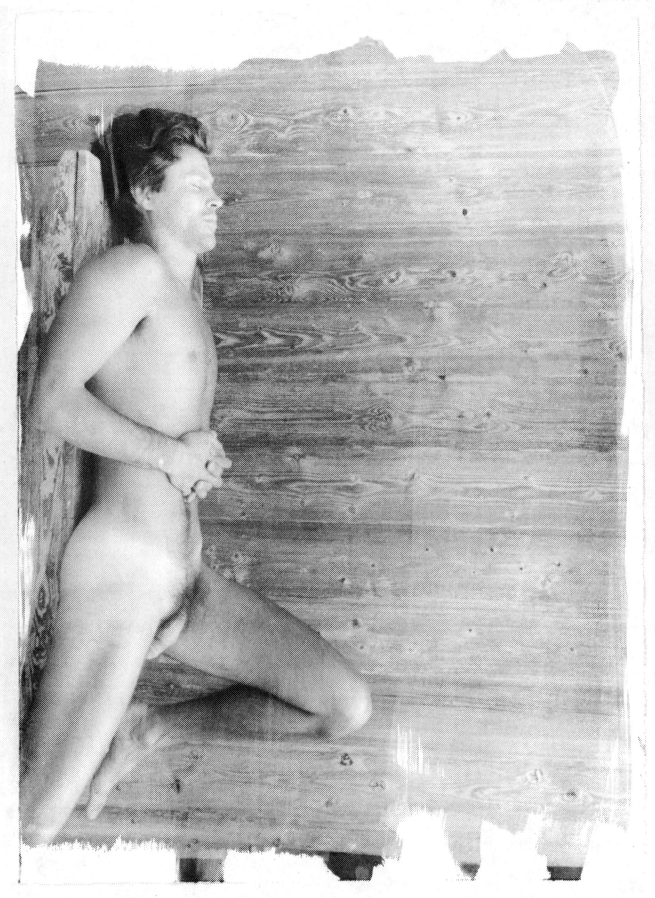

ELLEN T BIRRELL, LOS ANGELES, CA, USA

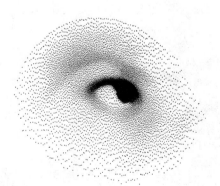

ELLEN T BIRRELL, LOS ANGELES, CA, USA

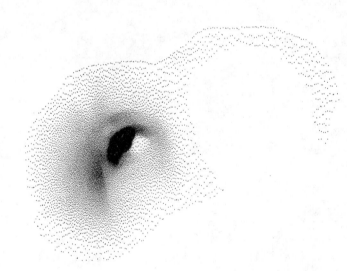

KAY ROSEN, GARY, IN, USA

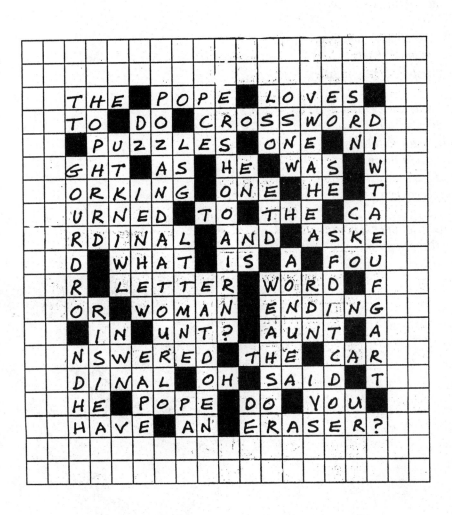

ROSALIND SCHNEIDER, IRVINGTON, NY, USA

*The Millennium Approaches*

---

*I look to the rocks*
*for answers*
*for time marked by humans*
*is consumed as quickly*
*as the mountain's shadow*

*Surfaces layered with memory*
*textured and reflective ·*
*speak the language of possibilities*

*These vistas, once claimed*
*will sustain me...*
*with quick notation*
*I carry them*
*to nurture the unfolding dream*
*that has become my vision*

*These marks of my existence*
*will speak for me*

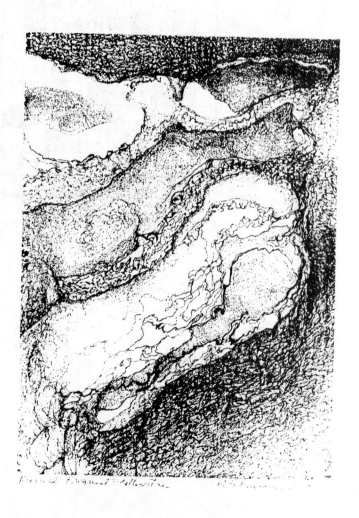

SOFIE TOBBACK, BOECHOUT, BELGIUM

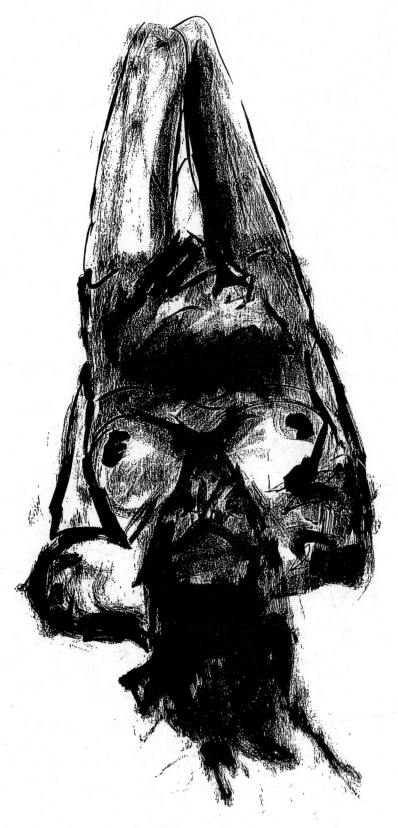

**MEREDITH B DANLUCK**, NEW YORK, NY, USA

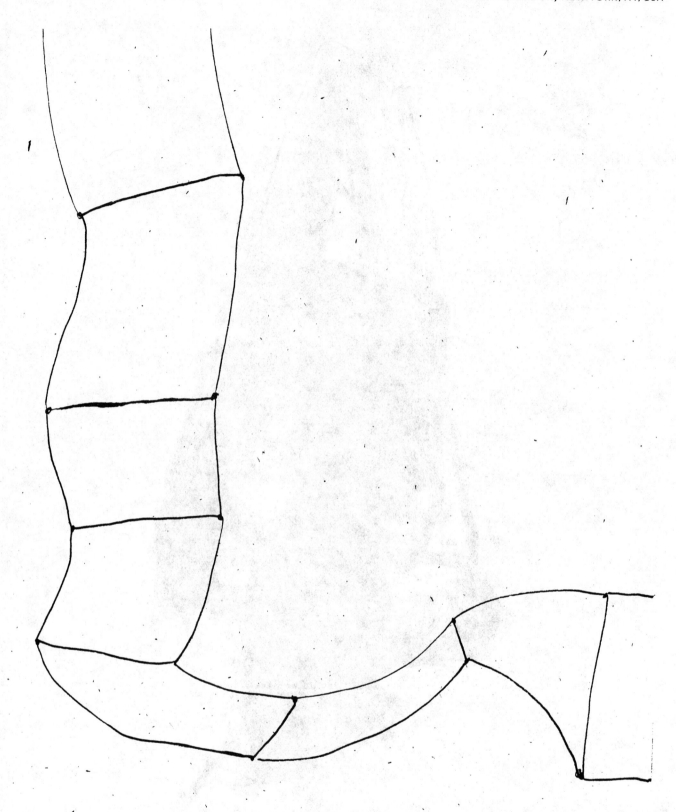

**MEREDITH B DANLUCK,** NEW YORK, NY, USA

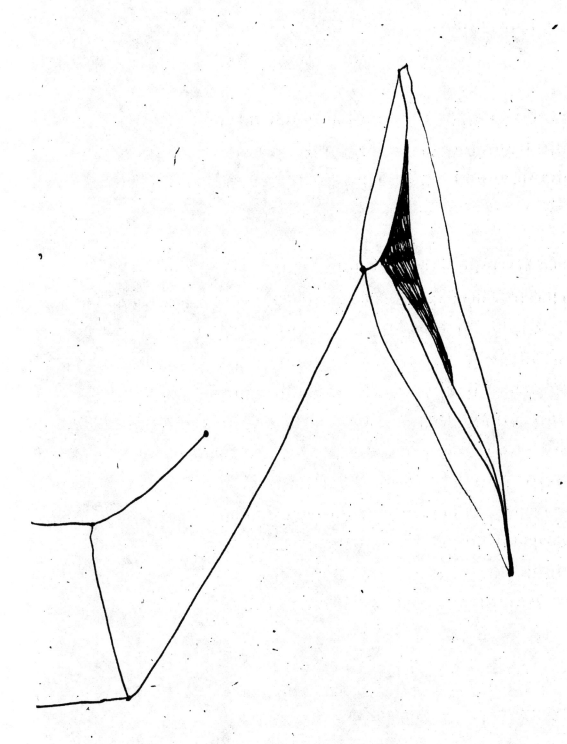

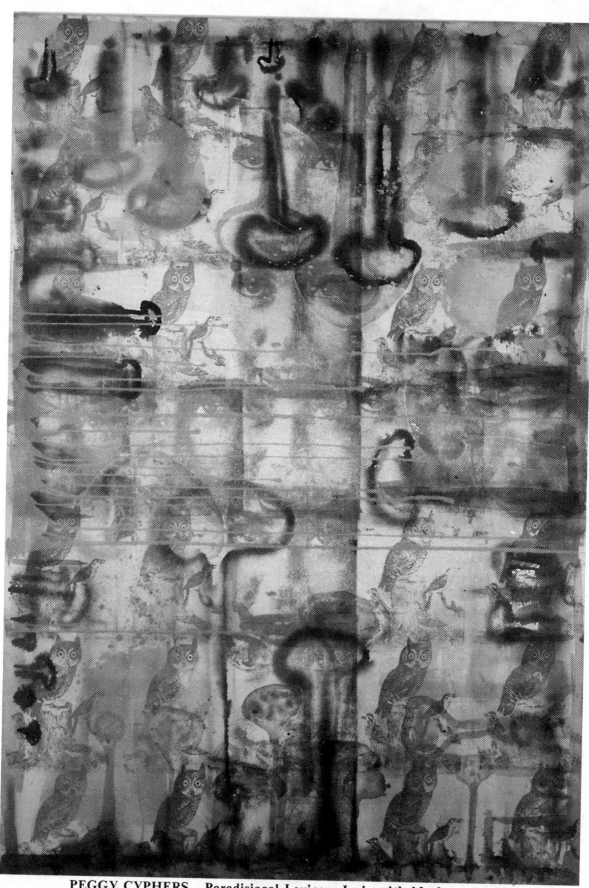

**PEGGY CYPHERS**  Paradisiacal Lexicon, Lady with Mushrooms, 1995
acrylic & sand on silkscreened canvas  69" x 48"

PEGGY CYPHERS, BROOKLYN, NY, USA

**Peggy Cyphers (American b.1954) Notes of a Painter**

**My activity is game-playing. These games allow me infinite hours outside adult consciousness to "SLAY THE DRAGON."**

*The Childhood Fantasy: The Owl that inhabits the mansions of my mind likewise inhabits my hybrid 2-Dimensional Objects. I have known an owl personally, his message was clear. BE Still. Watch the lizard sun himself on the bleached wooden steps. A slippery sheen of psychedelic hue weighs upon his flesh and bones like a wizards cloak. Up on the edge of the hill mushrooms grow. The mushrooms, the "suns of god," sprout like erect penises - integrating with field and forest. Their psychedelia is a wild realm, "fertilizer for human conciousness." (Why not, they grow prolifically in the dung of livestock!)*

*Meanwhile the Owl, hunter of the night, closes in, scanning the cavernous void of before and after historical time. (Harrowing stillness there.) You can hear the Owls heavy wings. Along clay cliffs of infinite greyness the sand moves in and out, ushered by a procession of aquatica. Licking the wounds of your innards the seaweed rolls with the waves. Butterflies enter, decorated in colors that mock the glory of sun and moon. Where sand meets cliff, the dandelion weed grows. Her job is to push oldness (stuckness) out so that the journey (digestion of life) is ever-new. The QUEEN is talking very LOUD through the plant world - we ingest her botanical kingdom to be fortified with wisdom. It is the "taste of wilderness."*

**I crave the material of my ancestors. The grandmothers taught us to listen to the birds - to be still enough to listen. They taught us how to *let* things grow. Darwin listened to the activity of life as he navigated the globe. This journey gave him mystical revelations with Gaea. Darwin's personal life journey never negates his worship of this Deity. The message, simply, of these objects (paintings) is love of nature. (Think of St. Theresa writhing in orgasmic ecstacy as she communes with her Logos.)**

**I play on a cross game-board now. The historical illusion is Early Christian - a limited thought system whose message is simple: love.**

**Giotto's crucifix jumps with pictorial authority. These painting games are merely maps which reroute my transcendental thought-narrative into pictorial energy.**

VIVIAN McDUFFIE, MONTCLAIR, NJ, USA

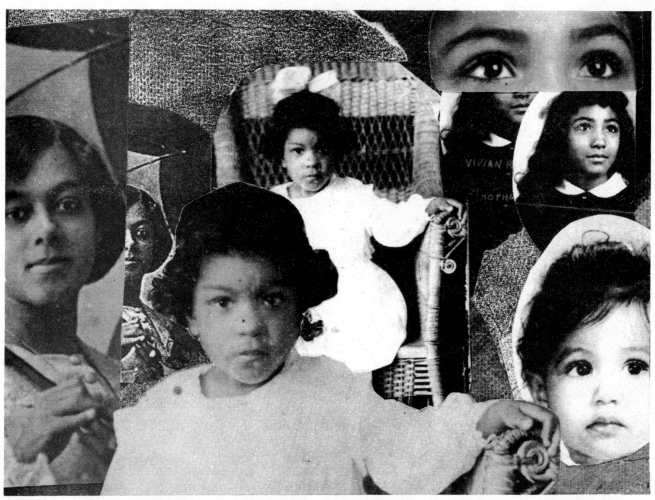

Vivian Ramming Dorman Bain    Agnes Christine Dorman Reynolds    Vivian Rochelle Reynolds McDuffie
Mother:   Christine Ramming *Baby its you*                    Dorian Christine McDuffie

TITLE:  The Fruit of Our Mother's Womb Is The Hope Of The World
ARTIST:  Vivian McDuffie.                    1995   Mixed Media

This page is dedicated to my parents, Agnes Dorman Reynolds and
Albert Alexander Reynolds

The Fanny Lou Hamer Chapter of the Rainbow Coalition of Montclair
The Montclair Pearl Lagoon Sister City Project
The Montclair Women's History Month Project
WAM, Women Artists of Montclair

"THINK GLOBALLY . ACT LOCALLY."

VIVIAN McDUFFIE, MONTCLAIR, NJ, USA

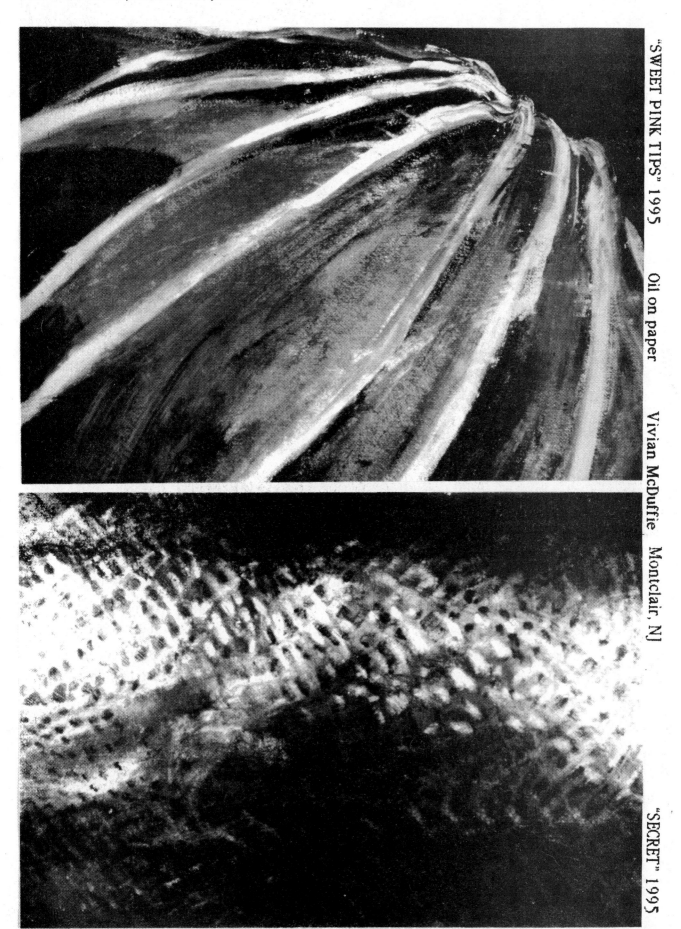

"SWEET PINK TIPS" 1995     Oil on paper     Vivian McDuffie     Montclair, NJ

"SECRET" 1995

STEPHANIE SHEPHERD, MONTREAL, QUEBEC, CANADA

### Notes on Flying Saucer Phenomena and the Behavioral Scientist
Stephanie Shepherd

### Item 1:  The Photographic Evidence

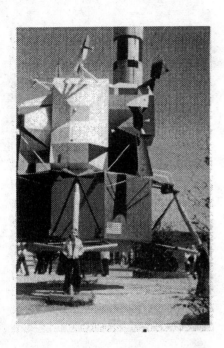
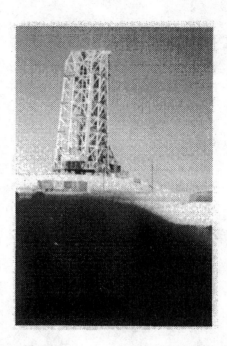

In 1975, when I was thirteen years old, my family took a winter vacation down in Florida. Other than seeing the hitherto unknown Goodyear blimp fly noisily past our hotel window at close range, the most memorable experience was the visit we made to Cape Kennedy Space Centre, or Cape Canaveral as my father insisted, and still insists, on calling it.  When we had finished taking a guided tour of the astronaut training rooms, launch pads, and space craft replicas, my parents bought me a model of the Apollo lunar landing module which I took back to Toronto and constructed in my bedroom.  My squat landing module had four articulated legs that concluded in concave saucer shaped feet designed for settling onto the moon's dusty surface.  I used tin foil to cover its base, in imitation of the metallic covering found on the real module.  My favourite part of the model was the simulated moon surface that was provided with the kit.  The little lunar facsimile was made of molded gray plastic and replicated the exterior of the moon down to its craters and undulating surface.  As a preventative measure, four indentations were pressed onto its surface for the space module's feet to securely sit and thus forestall any accident arising from the model slipping off this barren synthetic face.  Thus displayed, the model no longer was earth bound like its parent back at NASA, but instead sitting on a tract of the moon's surface, still up in outer space.

STEPHANIE SHEPHERD, MONTREAL, QUEBEC, CANADA

## Item 2: Rubbery, Rudimentary and/or Miniaturized

During the beginning of the seventies I was in my early teens and attending junior high school. In those years, on Saturday night or Sunday afternoon my entertainment of choice was watching sc-fi films and monster movies on television. These films were made in the fifties and early sixties and possessed what I deemed to be the requisite qualities of unbelievability and fakeness. Stories had to be implausible while special effects strictly adhered to standards most simply referred to as: rubbery, rudimentary and/or miniaturized. I never watched vampire or werewolf movies; the paranormal scared me too much and made sleep impossible. Once having mistakenly watched a too credible story about a murderous mutated creeping vine, I spent a tormented night wide awake fearing that the birch tree in the backyard was going to break into our house and strangle my sister Pam who slept by a window.

## Item 3: Abstract

Lying back in the grass on the side of the mountain, I let the sun soak into me through a filter of birch tree and clouds. I lay completely still but for an occasional hand movement to brush away stray ants that tried to make their way across my arms. Periodically I'd open my eyes just wide enough to confirm my position. It's a funny thing about stillness, that it makes me think I've gone somewhere. At one of these moments of lazy verification I saw a shape up in the sky. The object was motionless, positioned twenty meters above me. Not directly above, but a bit to my right side. It seemed flat on the bottom yet curved on top like an over turned dinner plate. Its size was that of a small house, like a post war bungalow. I could faintly hear a soft hum emanating from it. Maybe it was actually spinning, I couldn't tell. It looked to be composed of some sort of whitish metal, not the cold glow of steel or aluminium, but more like silver with its dull warm haze. I could imagine it in miniature, putting it in my mouth like a silver spoon or like butter and feeling its softness on my tongue.

KIM P MAENAK, TORONTO, ON, CANADA

**KIM MAENAK**

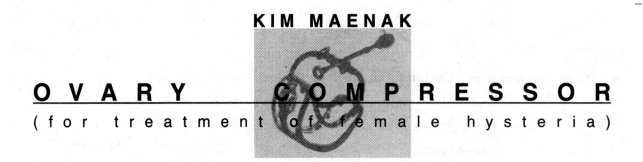

# O V A R Y   C O M P R E S S O R
(f o r   t r e a t m e n t   o f   f e m a l e   h y s t e r i a)

### H y s t e r i a

Uterus, woman's disease, feminine disorder, hysterical suffocation, disturbance of femininity. The ovary compressor was a device used to stop an hysterical attack by compressing the woman's ovarie's in the nineteenth – and twentieth centuries, age of the womb. Every woman carries with her the seeds of hysteria, deemed unfit to breed, too rebellious to be tolerated. Hysteria, hysteric, and hystercal may become anachronisms. It should be possible for a man's attack to put pressure on the man's testicles. The womb is like an animal within an animal, all women are hysterical. Today hysteria has become a great interest to feminist intellectuals, literary critics and artists. Hysteria major, hysteria minor, hystero-epilepsy.

### S y m p t o m s

Troublesomeness, eating like a ploughman, masturbation, attempted suicide, erotic tendency, or persecution mania, simple cussedness, and painful menstruation.

### C u r e

Became tractable, orderly, industrious, and cleanly.

OVARY COMPRESSORS ©1994
Pigment on Panel 60" x 96" Diptych
image credit: Progrés Médical, 1878

KIM P MAENAK, TORONTO, ON, CANADA

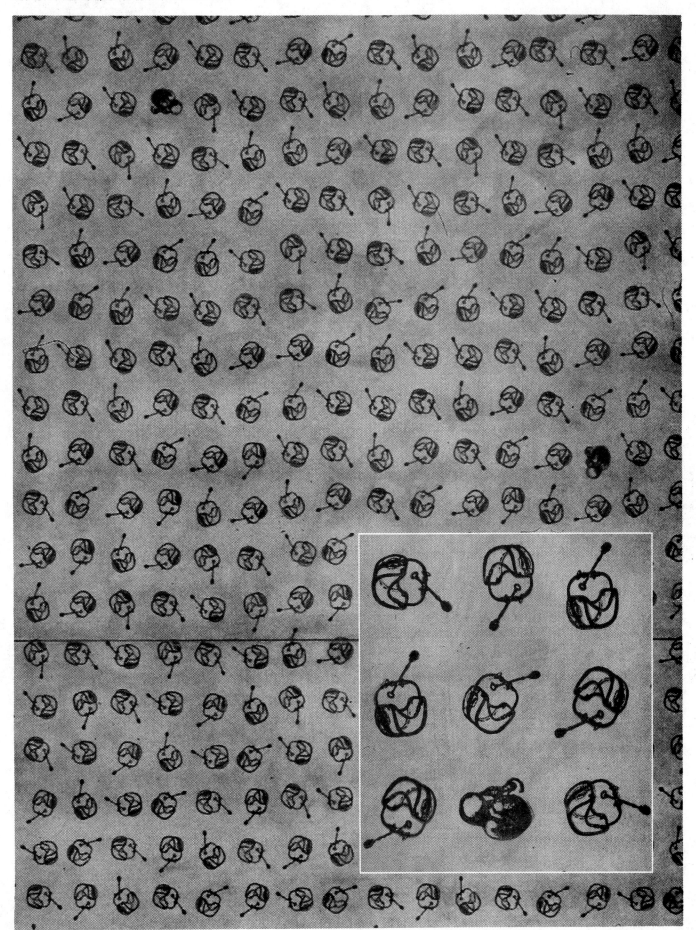

## EMPLOYMENT 1970-1995

**Sales Clerk**, Sears Department Store, Rockville, MD
**Dishwasher**, Saga Food Corporation, Middletown, CT
**Food Server**, Alpha Delta Phi, Wesleyan University, Middletown, CT
**Typist**, English Department, Wesleyan University, Middletown, CT
**Clerk Typist**, GS-1, Department of Health, Education, and Welfare, Rockville, MD
**Clerk Typist**, GS-3, United States Department of State, Office of Soviet Union Affairs, Washington, D.C.
**Security Guard**, Visual Art Studio Building, Wesleyan University, Middletown, CT
**Statistical Typist**, Arthur Andersen & Company, Boston, MA
**Legal Secretary**, Pillsbury, Madison & Sutro, San Francisco, CA
**Temporary Secretary**, Compu-Temps Temporary Services, San Francisco, CA
**Part-Time Legal Secretary**, Gregory S. Stout, Esq., San Francisco, CA
**Part-Time Legal Secretary**, Pillsbury, Madison & Sutro, San Francisco, CA
**Temporary Word Processor**, Pro-Temps, Inc., New York, NY
**Floating Legal Secretary**, Stroock & Stroock & Lavan, New York, NY
**Floating Legal Secretary**, Pillsbury, Madison & Sutro, San Francisco, CA
**Part-Time Legal Secretary**, Alan J. Pomerantz, P.C., New York, NY
**Temporary Word Processor**, Temporaries Network, San Francisco, CA
**Temporary Word Processor**, Continental Word Processing, New York, NY
**Part-Time Word Processor/Weekends**, Cravath, Swaine & Moore, New York, NY
**Assistant Supervisor**, Word Processing Department/Weekends, Cravath, Swaine & Moore, New York, NY
**Assistant Director**, Socrates Sculpture Park, Long Island City, NY
**Instructor, Lithography I**, Rutgers--The State University, New Brunswick, NJ
**Part-Time Word Processor**, Ween & Associates, New York, NY
**Administrative Director**, Socrates Sculpture Park, Long Island City, NY
**Project Director**--Long Island City Art Map Project, Queens Council on the Arts, Jamaica, NY
**Acting Executive Director**, Lower East Side Printshop, New York, NY
**Screenplay Typist**, Screenwriter Warren Leigh, New York, NY
**Project Director**--MetroTech Center Public Art Program, Public Art Fund Inc., New York, NY
**Project Director**--Sculpture Center at Roosevelt Island, Sculpture Center, New York, NY
**Project Director**--Flushing Art Map Project, Queens Council on the Arts, Flushing, NY
**Development Director**, Thread Waxing Space, New York, NY
**Project Consultant**, Brooklyn Academy of Music, Brooklyn, NY
**Project Director**--*Artists in Action*: BAM's Visual Arts Initiative, Brooklyn Academy of Music, Brooklyn, NY

**JEAN FOOS,** NEW YORK, NY, USA

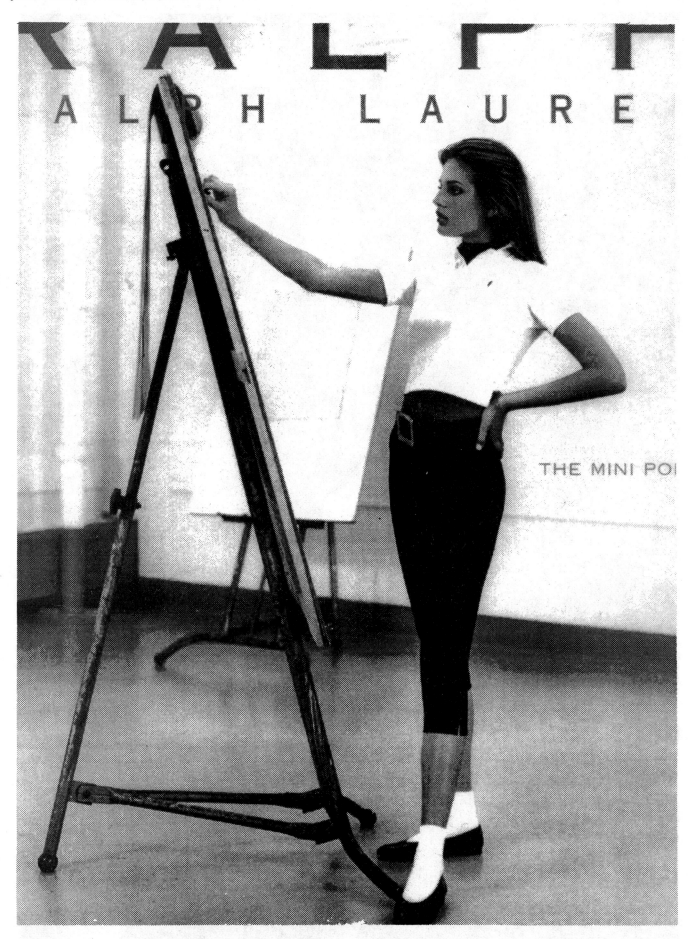

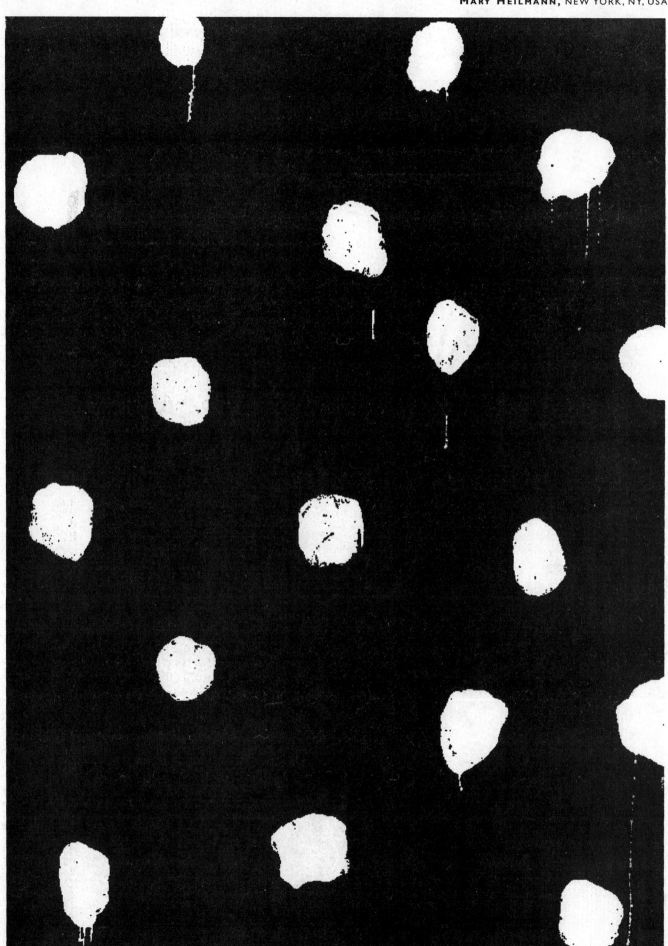

RIKKI ASHER, REGO PARK, NY, USA

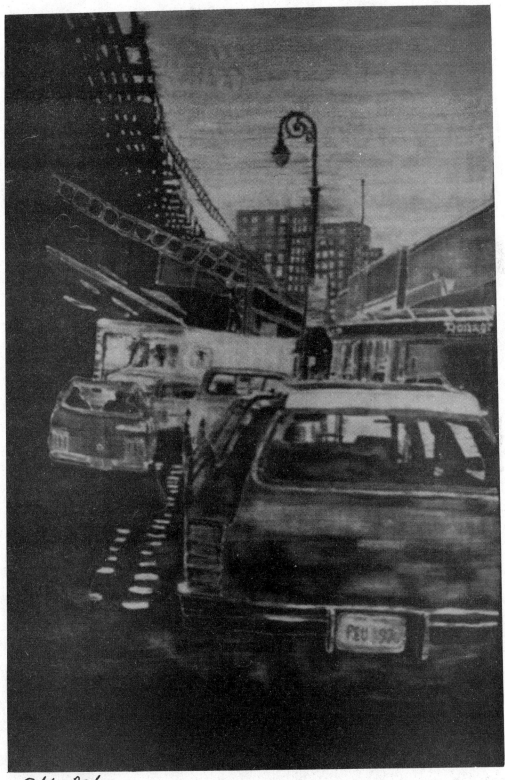

*Rikki Asher*
85-26 65th Road
Rego Park, New York
11374

GABRIELA DAUERER, NURNBURG, GERMANY

**B § 18**

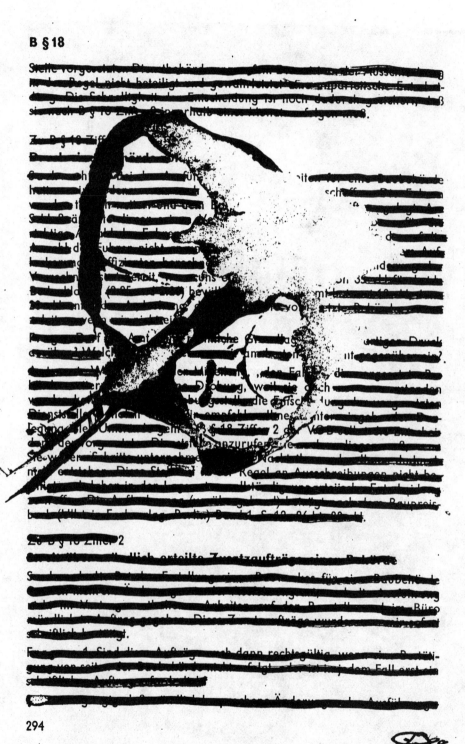

294

LISA DiLILLO, NEW YORK, NY, USA

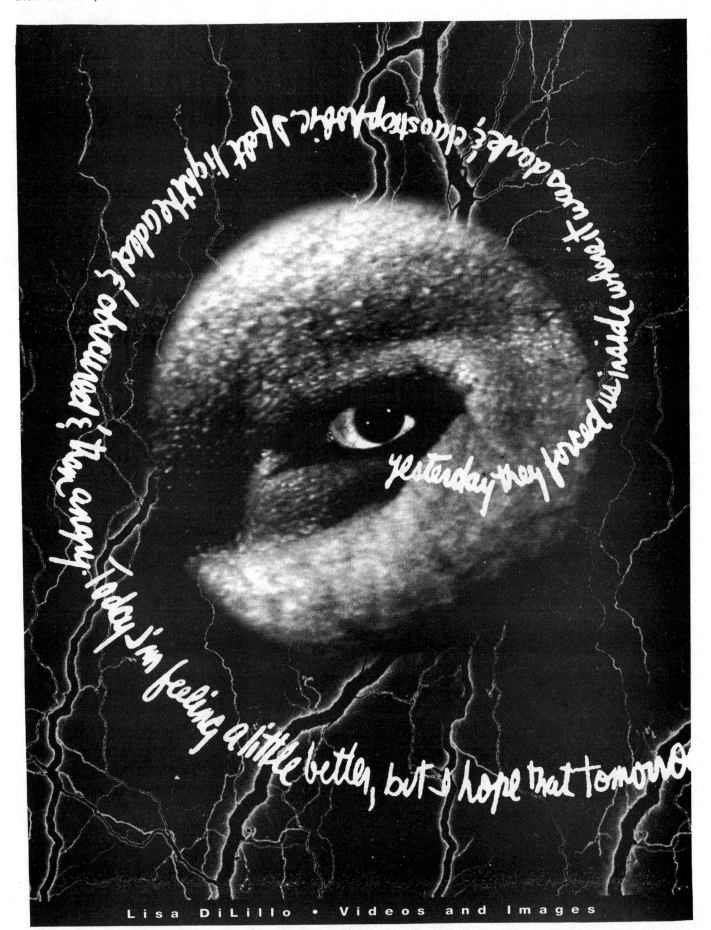

Lisa DiLillo • Videos and Images

TEI KOBAYASHI, TOKYO, JAPAN

patriarchal pathos of being

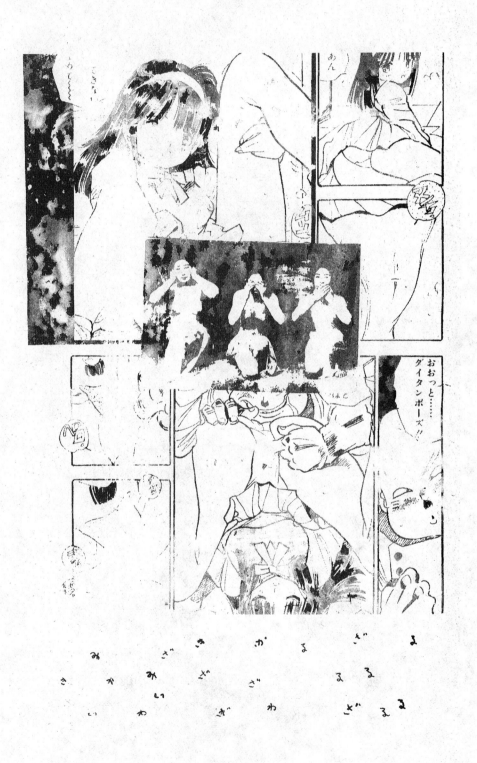

TEI KOBAYASHI, TOKYO, JAPAN

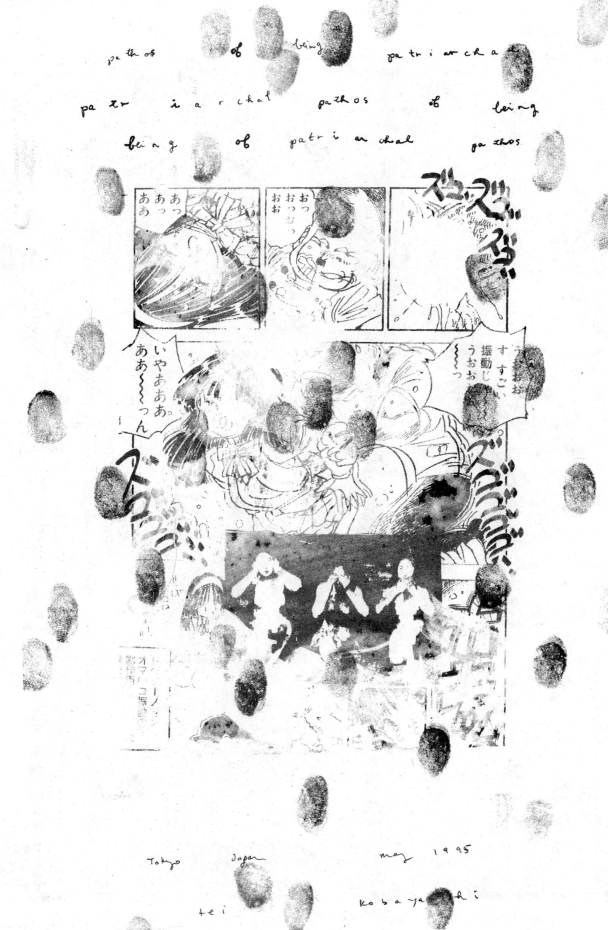

NEFERTITI C GOODMAN, MONTCLAIR, NJ, USA

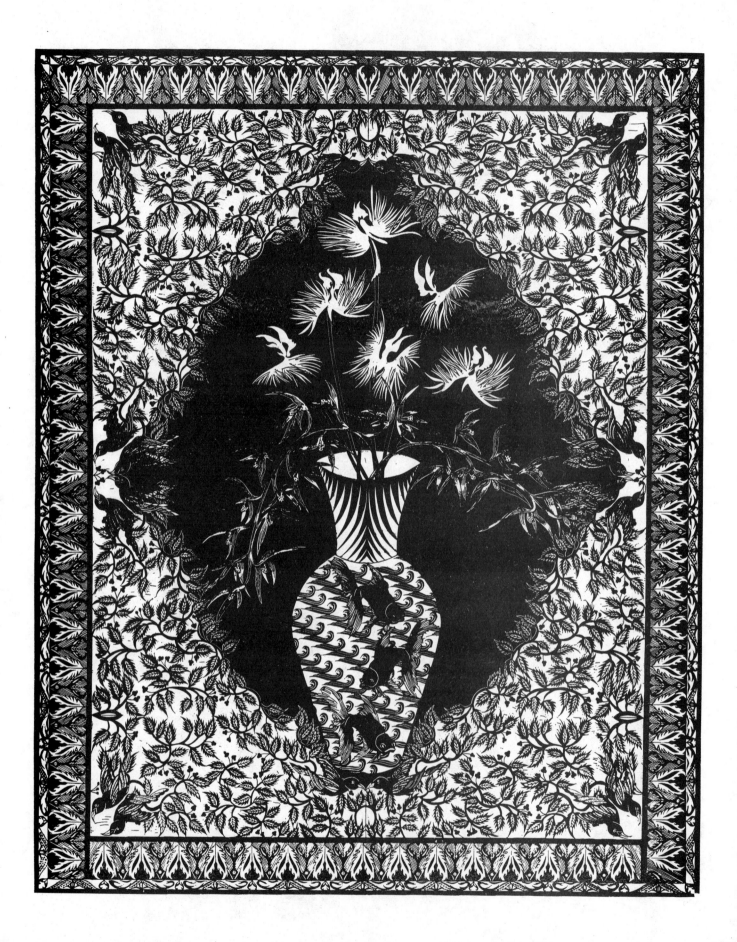

TRACY ANN ESSOGLOU, NEW YORK, NY, USA

*Aggression*
*Neglect*
*Territorialization*
*Impunity*
*Complacency*
*Wastefulness*
*Willful Ignorance*

*Emphasizing, volition, decision making and opportunity, SINs of the New Millenium assume global interdependence and affirm the significnce of our constant status as active and decisive beings: each sin infers terms of accountability that girder the interdependency of living forms.*

*SINs of the New Millenium delineates those conditions which threaten personal safety and identifies those behaviors which result in the transgression of fundamental human rights. It is the mission of Los Pecados not to sentence or chastise, but to advocate critical reflection, willful participation, and thoughtful anticipation, as being well within our grasp.*

*SINs of the New Millenium posit that between habit and gesture is an opportunity -- perhaps the only original moment -- to do and be decisively observant and circumspect, socially and geopolitically clairvoyant.*

*SINs of the New Millenium acknowledges not religious or political authority, but rather the intimacy of our own authority as individual social participants: inciting the development of a more profoundly intra-planetary consciousness; commissioning us to make change.*

*Los Pecados Nuevos: Sins of the New Millenium*
*Tracy Ann Essoglou*
*NYC -- 1995*

SARAH SCHWARTZ, NEW YORK, NY, USA

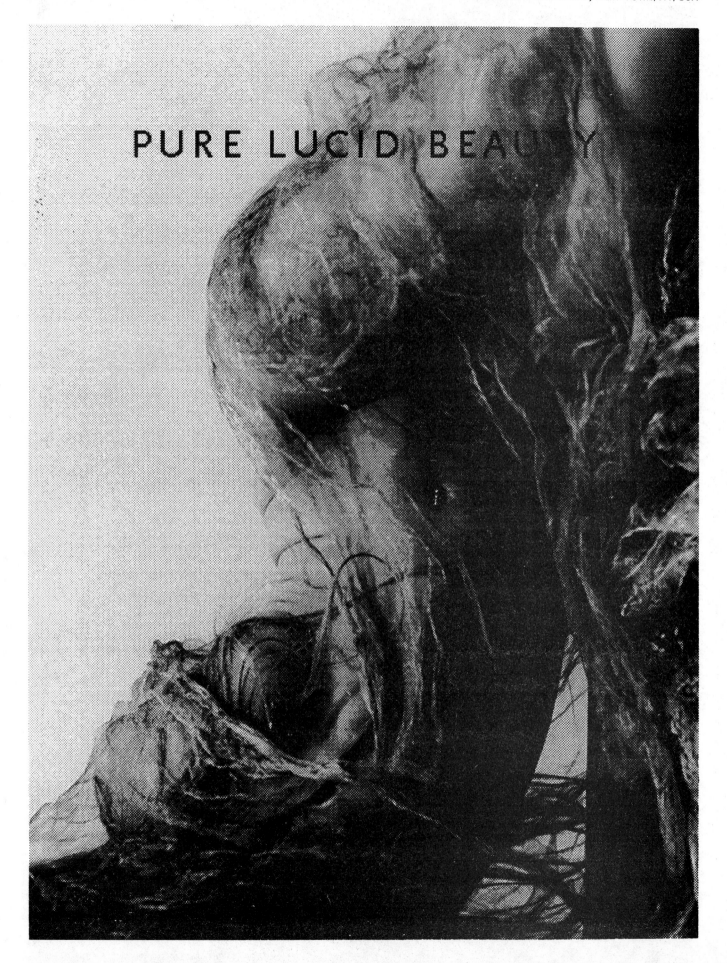

PURE LUCID BEAUTY

**SARAH SCHWARTZ**, NEW YORK, NY, USA

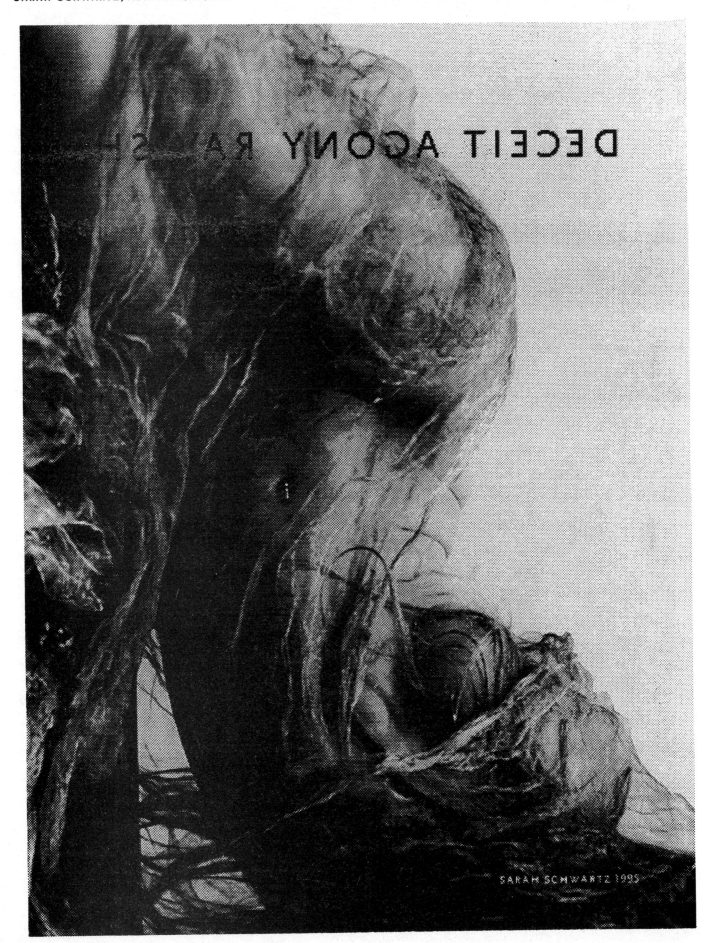

Elizabeth Lamourt, FOREST HILLS, NY, USA

Elizabeth Lamourt, FOREST HILLS, NY, USA

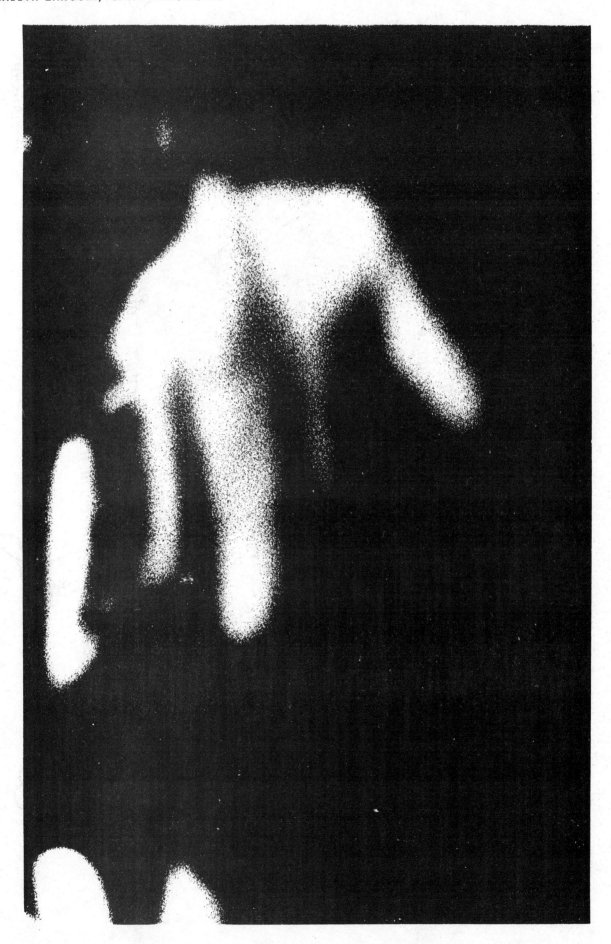

CLAUDIA NAGY, NEW YORK, NY, USA

Claudia Nagy
230 Mulberry Street, A
New York, NY 10012-5714
USA (212) 941-7535

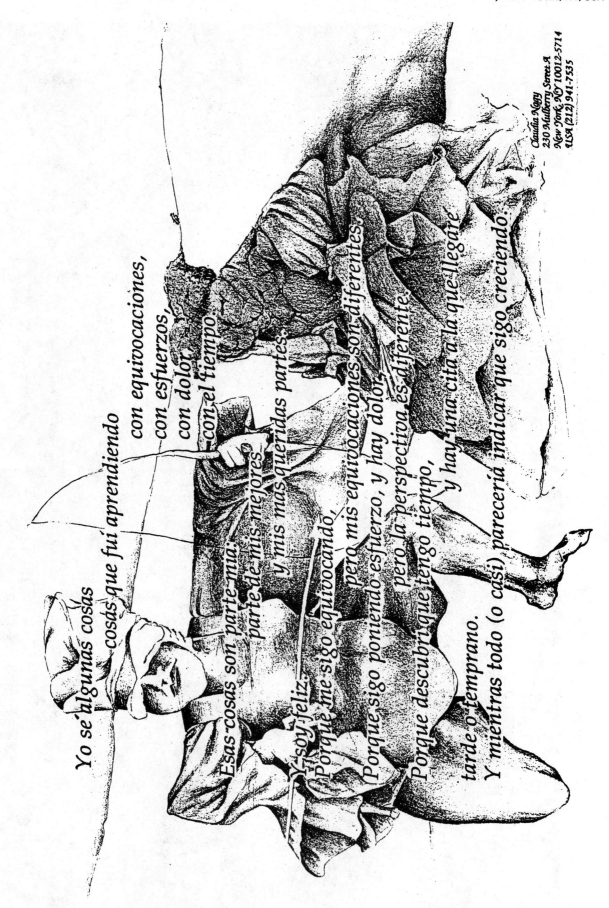

Yo sé algunas cosas
cosas que fui aprendiendo
con equivocaciones,
con esfuerzos,
con dolor,
con el tiempo.

Esas cosas son parte mía:
parte de mis mejores
y mis más queridas partes.

Y soy feliz.
Porque me sigo equivocando,
pero mis equivocaciones son diferentes.
Porque sigo poniendo esfuerzo, y hay dolor,
pero la perspectiva es diferente;
Porque descubro que tengo tiempo,
y hay una cita a la que llegar
tarde o temprano.
Y mientras todo (o casi) parecería indicar que sigo creciendo.

**CLAIRE FLANDERS**, WASHINGTON, DC, USA

# LE TEMPS PERDU

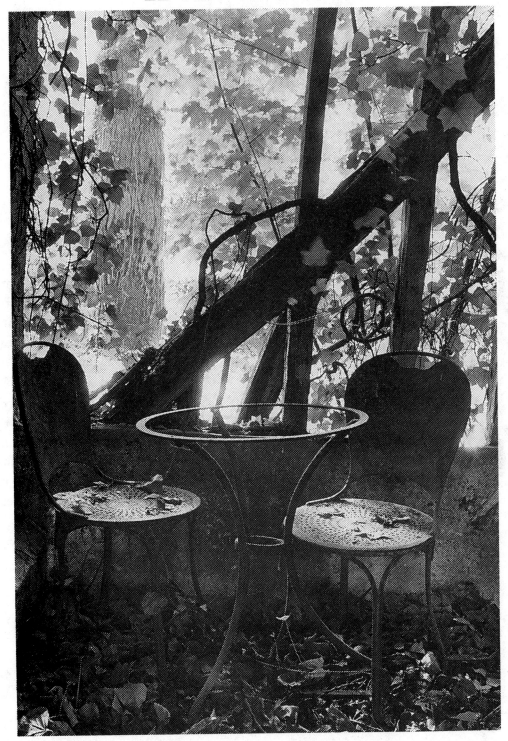

# LE TEMPS RETROUVÉ

## CLAIRE FLANDERS
PHOTOGRAPHY
WASHINGTON, DC
202-244-5137

**DONA ANN MCADAMS,** NEW YORK, NY, USA

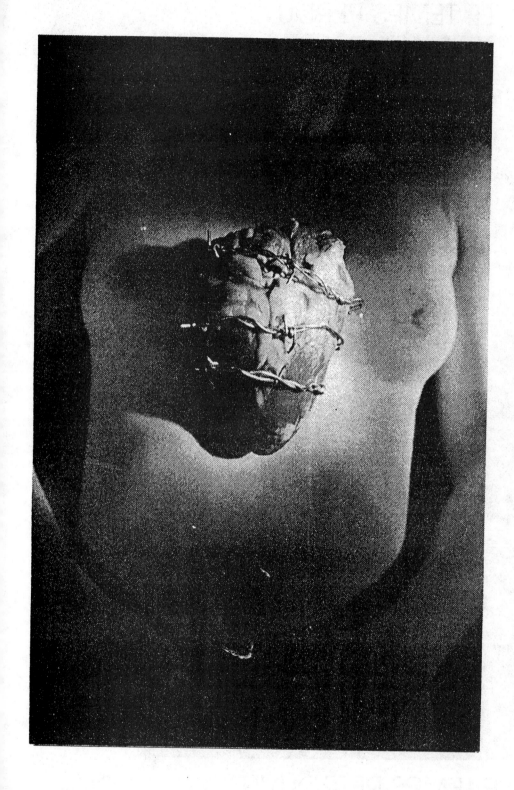

As the plague removes an entire generation of artists, we lose a cycle of growth and inspiration. Too many men and women are dying too young. And when a life of work is cut short, the artist falls into obscurity, or becomes a hero before their proper time. Neither is a replacement for the life and work that would have been. To see their lives unfinished leaves my heart exposed.

—*Dona McAdams*

**FERN SHAFFER,** CHICAGO, IL, USA

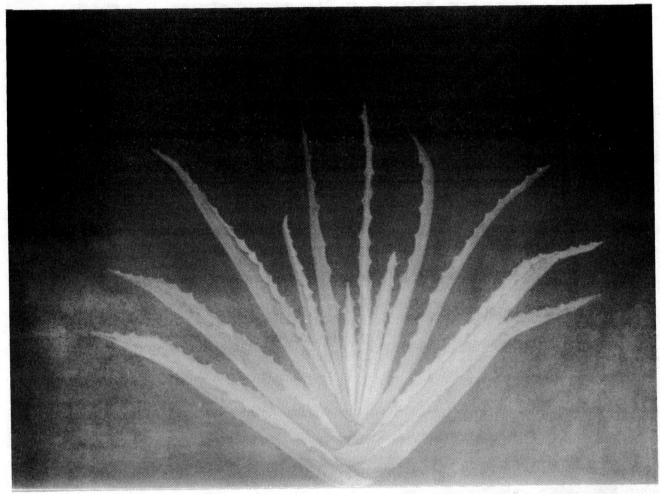

"Aloe"    acrylic  5'x7'  1995

ALOE BARBABADEBSUS-ALOE VERA

AN IMPORTANT HERB FOR OVER 3,000 YEARS. THE PLANT ORIGINATED IN THE CAPE VERDE ISLANDS OR THEREABOUTS, AND BY EARLY HISTORICAL TIMES IT HAS APPEARED IN EGYPT, ARABIA AND INDIA.

ALOE: USED FOR EXTERNAL APPLICATION TO HEAL WOUNDS, BRUISES AND IRRITATIONS AND TAKEN INTERNALLY AS A TONIC, PURGATIVE, AND JAUNDICE REMEDY. CAN BE USED FOR RADIATION BURNS.

FERN SHAFFER, CHICAGO, IL U.S.A. 312-226-7220

Rosa Lopez Camacho, MALAGA, SPAIN

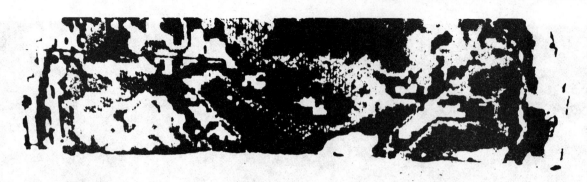

```
MEDULAR
UNIVERSAL
JUGO
ELECTRIZAR
REIVINDICAR
ENGENDRAR
SEDICION
ALMA
LABRAR
PROMISORIO
OBRA
DESEAR
```

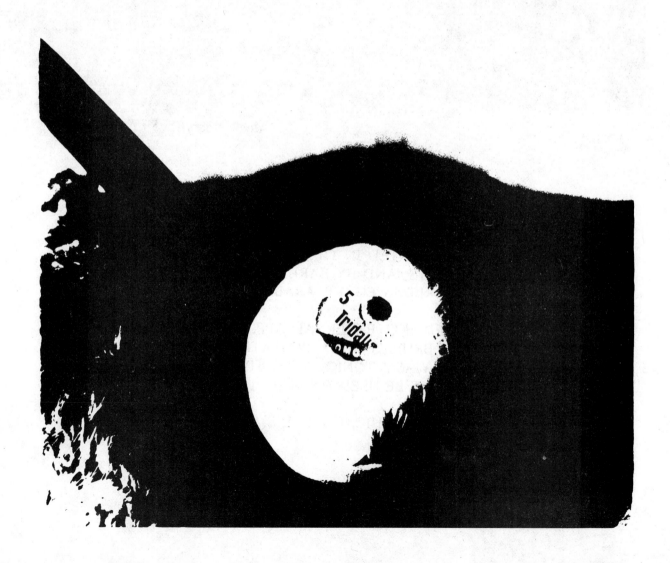

Rosa Lopez Camacho, MALAGA, SPAIN

ESTADO   ESTAFAR ESTOFADO           ESTOMAGO   ESTRATEGIA
ESTRAGO ETOLOGIA ETNIA  EXILIO ECO ECONOMIA  EGOISMO  EMPLEO
ENDROGARSE  ENGAÑAR ENSEÑANZA  ENTREPIERNA           ABORTAR
  ACELERADOR  ACTIVISMO AGUA  ASTRO  ASTROLOGIA ATROFIAR  ATROCIDAD
AUGURAR AURA  AURORA      ABRACADABRA ABORIGEN  ABOLIR  AUTOCTONO
ANSIAS LIBERTAD LUCHA LICITAR  LUPA LUNA LUNAR LESBIANO LIBERAR
VINDICATIVO  VIOLACION VIOLENCIA VIRGINAL  VISADO  VISCERAL VITAL
        VISUALIZAR  VITAMINICO VIVERES   VOTAR VOYEUR VUDU  VULVA
MARGINAL  MARGINADO MARICA  DENUNCIA  DEPORTAR DESCOLONIZACION
 DESEO MITIGAR DESIGUALDAD  DESNUTRIDO DICTADOR  MACHO
COLOR  COMUNICAR CONCIENCIAR  CONDON CORREO CONTRACEPTIVO CORRUPTO
 COSMOS  RACIAL RACIOCINIO RADIO REIVINDICAR  RAZA          CUBA-
LIBRE  SANGRE  SANIDAD  SATELITE HUELLA SECUELA SECUENCIA DEVASTADOR
 SED SEDICION SEGREGACIONISMO SENSIBILIZAR  SENSORIAL SENSUAL SINDICAL
  SINDICALISMO SOLIDARIDAD SERRALLO  NOESIS NEGRO NECESITAR NEXO
NECESIDAD  NUDO NUTRIDO NEGOCIO    OBRERO  OLLA OLOR OBSERVAR
 OPINION  OREAR  ORGASMO ORIENTAL  OXIGENO OZONOSFERA  POLITICA
        POLITICO  PREDESTINAR  PREDOMINAR POLLA  PREEMINENCIA
PREFERIR  PREMIO         PRENSA  PRIMICIA  PRIMITIVO PROGRESO
 PROGRESISTA PROPINA  PROSTIBULO        PROHIBIR  PROSPERIDAD
 PRONUNCIAR  PROPAGANDA  PROPALAR PROVECHO PROVIDENCIA  PROYECCION
 PROYECTO  PUBIS PUBLICAR  PULSO PUTATIVO  PUCHERO PUTO POBREZA
PODER POAR  PODAR  PUDIENDO  PODIDO JODER JODIENDO JODIDO
 FISCO  FIRMAMENTO           OUTPUT.

# POEMS
## Omographic Translations

"The only things I like to take seriously are games ..."

Therefore, why not consider poetry as a game, why not create new, crazy rules that last the duration of this intellectual game and end with new, crazy artistic productions?

A new concept of "the artist" is born: poets as mice that would like to escape from the labyrinth they build themselves!

Thus, I try to "escape" from this rule:

"A unique sequence of letters is submitted to two different splitting processes. The results - even if by punctuation adjustment - are two different texts, in two different languages, with different, related* meanings".

This rule is called "Omographic Translation", and the game is played in Italian and English.

**Elena Addomine**
Via Vassallo 31
20125 Milano (Italy)
+39 (2) 6880084
or
428w 23 Street Apt. 4D
New York, NY 10011 (U.S.)
+1 (212) 366-4745

---

\* The relationship could be: similar contexts (i.e.: love and betraying, art and music), opposite concepts (i.e.: day and night), and so on.

ELENA ADDOMINE, MILAN, ITALY

# POEMS
## Omographic Translations

Lo vedi,
paga in amore,
tremo rapita.
Ma fine porterò fatale ...

*Love dip,*
*again a more tremor:*
*a pit, a ...*
*'m a fine porter of a tale ...*

Musicisti:
meno talenti ma geni
che offron tal passione a rare amanti e sacri dei.
Inganni, celate com'eran, note ...

*Music is time, not a lent image:*
*niche of frontal passion,*
*ear area.*
*Man ties acrid ey'ing an' nice;*
*latecomer, an' note.*

MARIE PAVLICEK WEHRLI, SILVER SPRING, MD, USA

Spring Poem for Albina, My Grandmother


As rain falls upon the stones of Bower Hill
and water flows in rivulets
along the edges of the street,
I climb to the click of a wood-toed cane
and the swinging red flare of Albina's babushka.

Today the hedges bloom tall at my side,
the weeping willow at the corner of Grandview and Ridge
is a blur of drifting buds,
in Mrs. Bonacci's yard a yellow coat of paint
freshens the shed's wood frame door
and by the fence near the blue Madonna
the fig trees sway
freed of their burlap wraps.

In April all the streets of my town
are washed clean, grit gathers
aside the curb at the bottom of the hill,
in the laps of old women
riding home on the Braddock bus
are sleeves of flower seeds, a pail,
some paint, a white bristled brush.

I'm climbing a sidewalk cracked and heaving
behind the barreled hips of a woman
whose face is flush
with the fever of spring.
She moves with the bulk of a listing cart,
her chest spills round and wide,
filled with the scent of marigolds and bread.
The valley between her breasts cradles tissue and change,
inside the elastic bands of her stockings
ride the folded dollars.

For all the wide hipped mothers from Europe
whose last stop on the tracks leaving New York
was the foot of these hills,
these narrow frame houses,
through whose thighs passed
the clenched bud hands and the slippery backs
of newborn children, for you,
who often outlived them,
I'll carry your bags of soup bones, parsley, and lemons,
I'll follow you slowly up this rain drenched hill,
if you pause at your gate
near the opening viburnum,
I'll wait behind you,
in April when the small white blossoms fleck with pollen,
I'll scrub your walls clean
though you no longer can see them.

MARIE PAVLICEK WEHRLI, SILVER SPRING, MD, USA

Song for the Trains and the Small Lost Towns


I'm singing to the trains in my head tonight,
they light out beyond the rim of Matta's hill,
follow the Monongohela along its blighted
shores, the tunnels and watchtowers, stacks of the steel
mills shine like hard metal buttons behind my eyes.
I'll write a symphony of hissing tracks and
clanging water, by the rivers in my skull no town ever dies,
each crossing is clear and every thing bears the mark of a hand.
Who would I tell where I go as I lie here alone?
The window opens out over a flowering hedge, it's spring,
along the rails winter's dried brush cracks and drifts, stones
spray as the engines speed left and right, who'd know why I sing
of twisting curves and matchbox towns?  It's all gone
now but for here, in this room, where I'll sing until dawn.

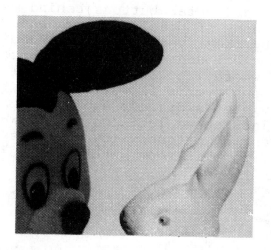

the dialogue

Liliana Porter.

**LILIANA PORTER**, NEW YORK, NY, USA

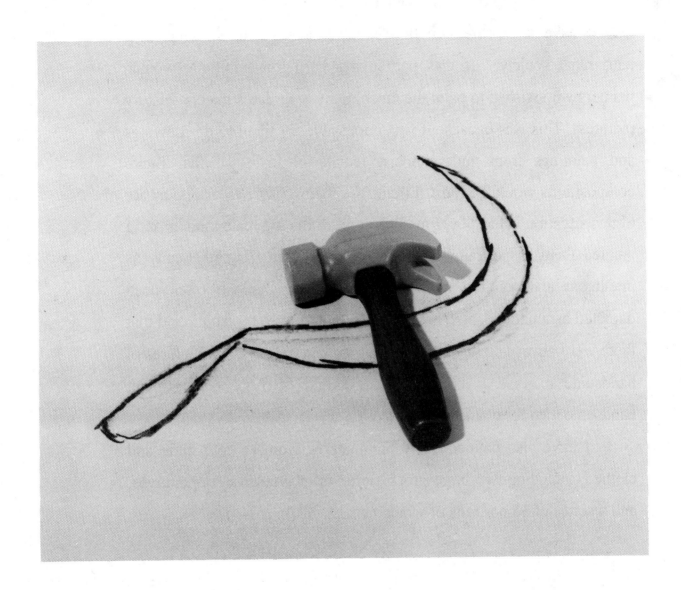

Drawing with plastic hammer      .

Liliana Porter.

SYLVIA SLEIGH, NEW YORK, NY, USA

It has always been difficult for women to do creative work or indeed have any profession that endows prestige in our chauvinist patriarchal society.  It was particularly hard for ambitious women painters who wished to paint the most highly regarded subjects--history pictures.  This was because it was impossible for them to do drawings and paintings from nude models, female or male, so that figure compositions would be most difficult for them.  Once I became aware of this situation in the '60s, I made a point of finding male models and I painted them as portraits, not as sex objects, but sympathetically as intelligent and admired people, not as women had so often been depicted as unindividuated houris.  I had noted from my childhood that there were always pictures of beautiful women but very few pictures of handsome men so I thought that it would be truly fair to paint handsome men for women.

I have also painted many paintings of women, both nude and clothed, including two large group portraits of women's cooperatives, and a series of 18 portraits of women artists (all 36 x 24").

Sylvia Sleigh
© 1995

**SYLVIA SLEIGH,** NEW YORK, NY, USA

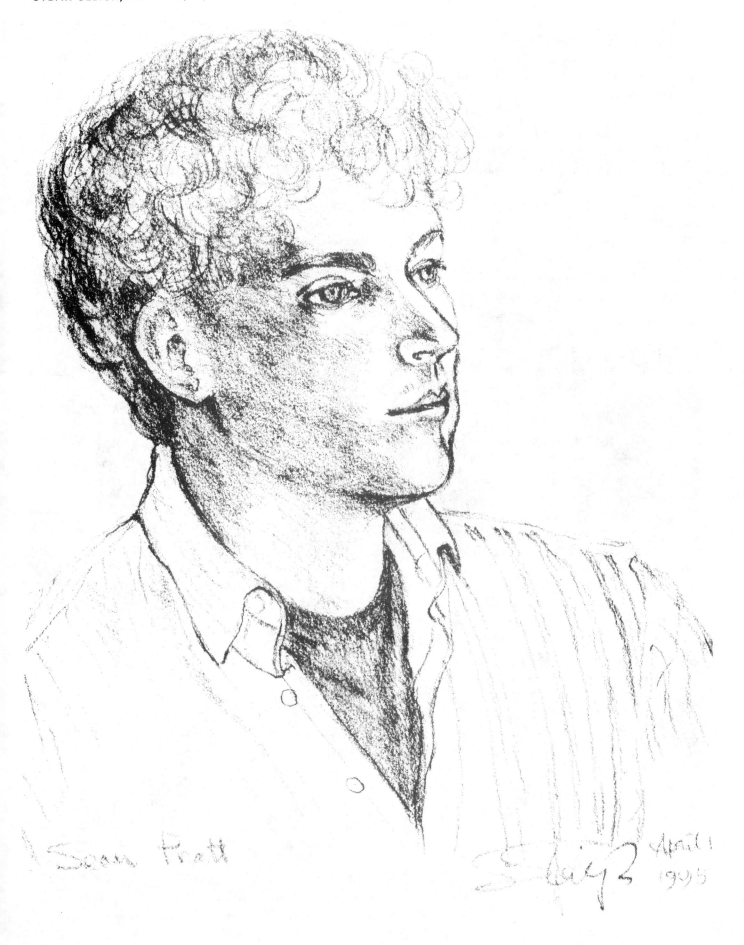

Sean Pratt                                    Sleigh April 1
                                                     1995

At once, the little mermaid's tail disappeared, and she was human once again. Prince Eric awoke to see his beloved Ariel standing beside him on the shore. He kissed her and soon they were married. Prince Eric and Ariel sailed off together, and they lived happily ever after.

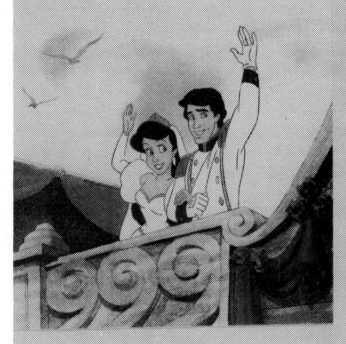

Keron Joseph

Ariel wanted to go some Where. And Eric said do not go. Eric said where are you going to And a job. She found one fast. She was a librarian. Ariel made 98$ a day. When people couldn't find a book She sang to them. When she Worked out she played tennis. They had twins. Aries will ask her father to make them in to merkids for 1½ months.

story by Keron Joseph, 2nd grade, 1995

PUBLIC SCHOOL 29, BROOKLYN, N.Y.
ARTIST/INSTRUCTOR: BARBARA VERROCHI

CREATIVE WRITING PROJECT:

**"**"The Little Mermaid" ends with the wedding of Prince Eric and Ariel. Using Ariel's character traits as a mermaid, write a story about her life after marriage."

**STEPHANIE PEEK,** SAN FRANCISCO, CA, USA

SELF PORTRAIT AS SUBJECT

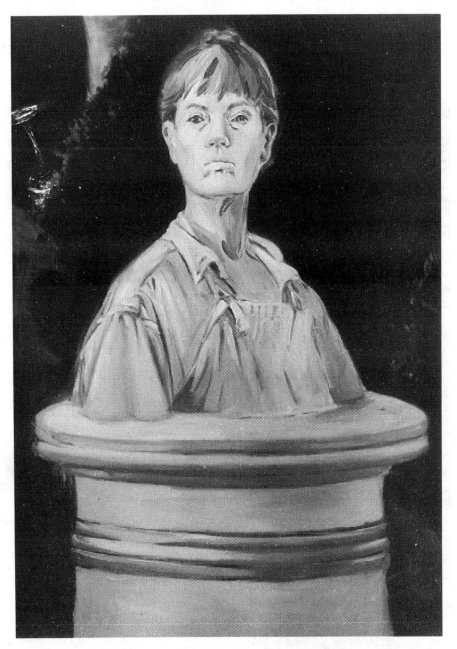

STEPHANIE PEEK

*Tel 415.387.3750*

35 SEVENTEENTH AVENUE

SAN FRANCISCO CA 94121

*Fax 415.387.5373*

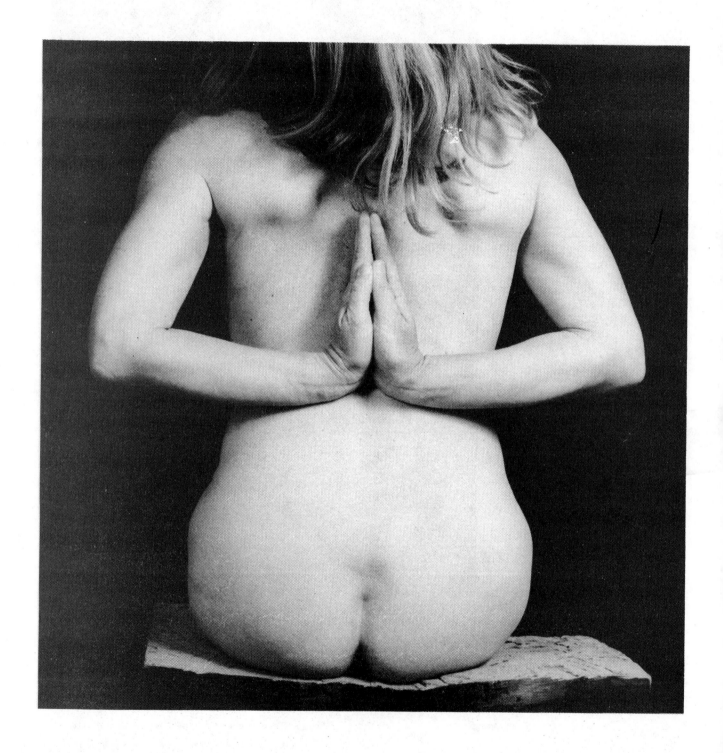

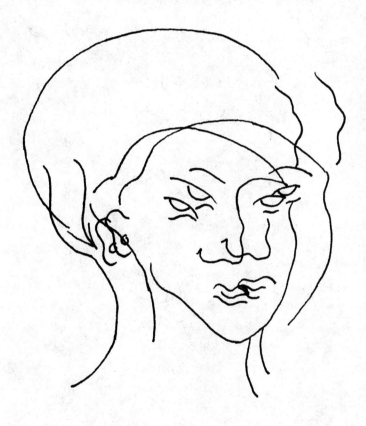

**RACHEL SCHUDER**, NEW YORK, NY, USA

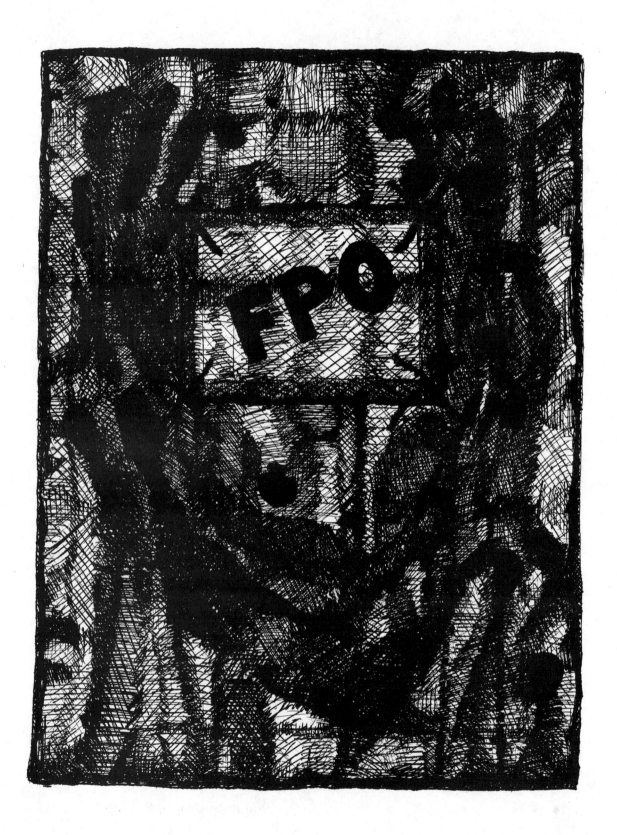

KATIA CANTON, SAO PAOLO, BRAZIL

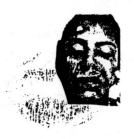

# FAIRY TALE WOMEN

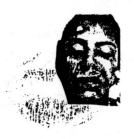

KATIA CANTON

KATIA CANTON, SAO PAOLO, BRAZIL

Amanhã,
    TUDO ÁZUL.
Hoje, o sangue
    escorre com lágrimas.

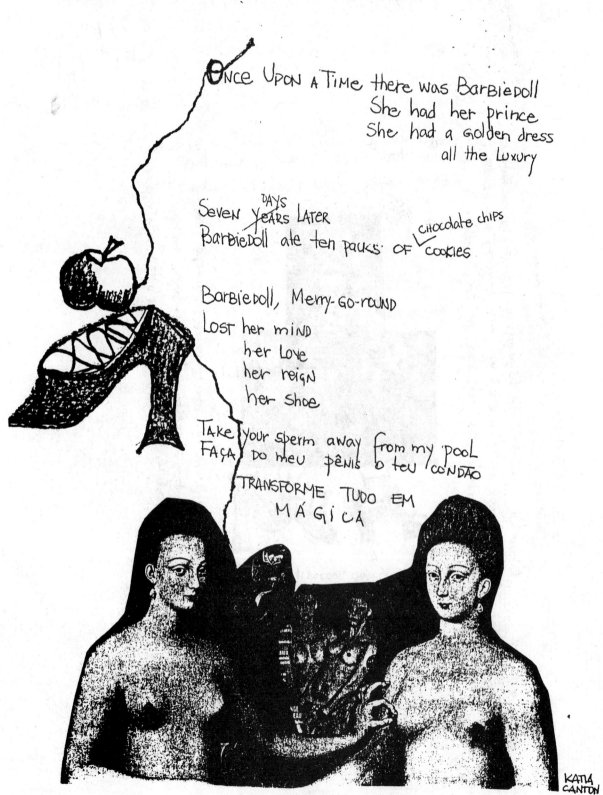

Once Upon a Time there was BarbieDoll
    She had her prince
    She had a golden dress
        all the Luxury

Seven ~~YEARS~~ DAYS LATER
BarbieDoll ate ten packs of chocolate chips cookies

BarbieDoll, Merry-GO-round
Lost her mind
    her love
    her reign
    her shoe

Take your sperm away from my pool
FAÇA DO MEU PÊNIS O TEU CONDÃO
    TRANSFORME TUDO EM
        MÁGICA

KATIA CANTON

**ESTHER REGUEIRA MAURIZ**, NEW YORK, NY, USA

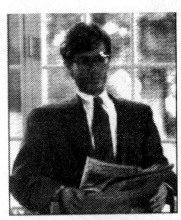

*Safe-T-Man keeps intruders away.*

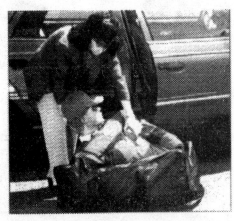

*Folds compactly into carrying tote for discreet portability.*

### Safe-T-Man: Your personal bodyguard.

Designed as a visual deterrent, Safe-T-Man is a life size simulated male that appears to be 180 lbs. and 6' tall, to give others the impression that you have the protection of a male guardian with you while at home alone or driving in your car. This unique security product looks incredibly real, with movable latex head and hands, and air-brushed facial highlights.
Made of soft fabric polyfiber, he weighs less than 10 lbs. Dress him according to your own personal style (clothing not included); the optional button-on legs complete a total visual effect, if desired. Safe-T-Man can be stored and easily transported in the optional tote bag.

*#4851931  Light Skin/Blonde Hair Man  $99.95*
*#4851907  Light Skin/Gray Hair Man  $99.95*
*#4852178  Dark Skin/Dark Hair Man  $99.95*
*#4852194  Button-on Legs (Specify Light or Dark)  $19.95*
*#4840017  Optional Zippered Carrying Tote  $34.95*

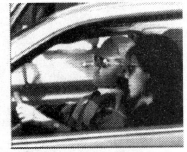

*Give the appearance of having a driving companion.*

**ORDERING IS EASY,** *SEE ORDER FORM*

KATHRYN WALTER, TORONTO, ON, CANADA

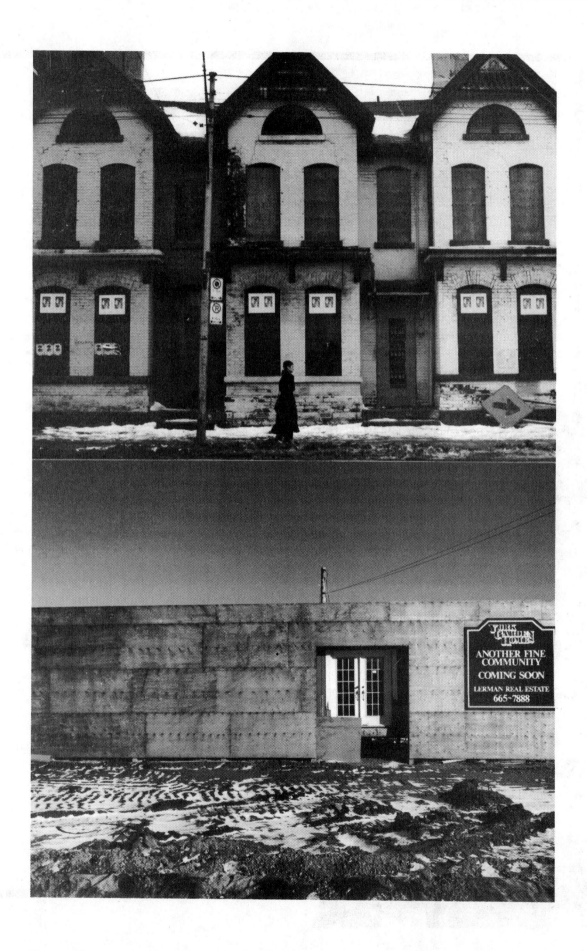

SALLY ETTA SHEINFELD, NEW YORK, NY, USA

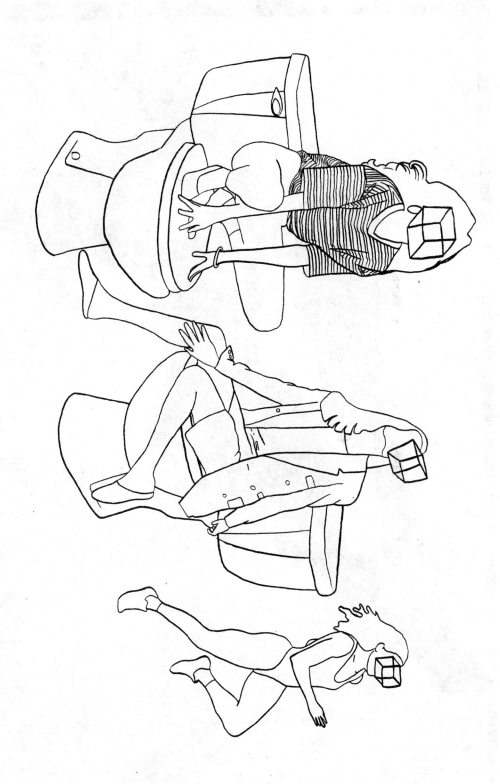

MARIETTE LINDERS, AMSTERDAM, THE NETHERLANDS

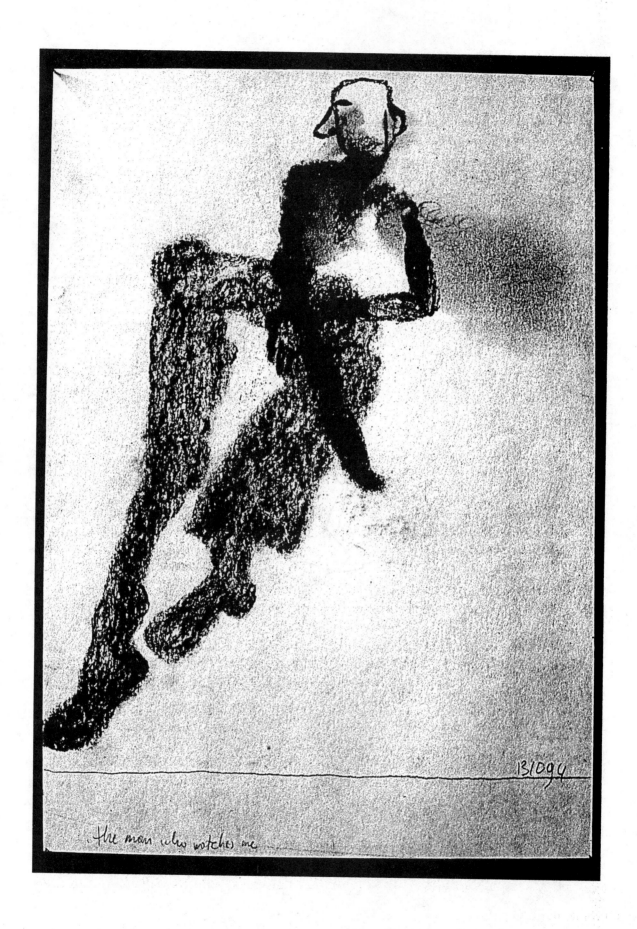

131094

the man who watches me

MARIETTE LINDERS, AMSTERDAM, THE NETHERLANDS

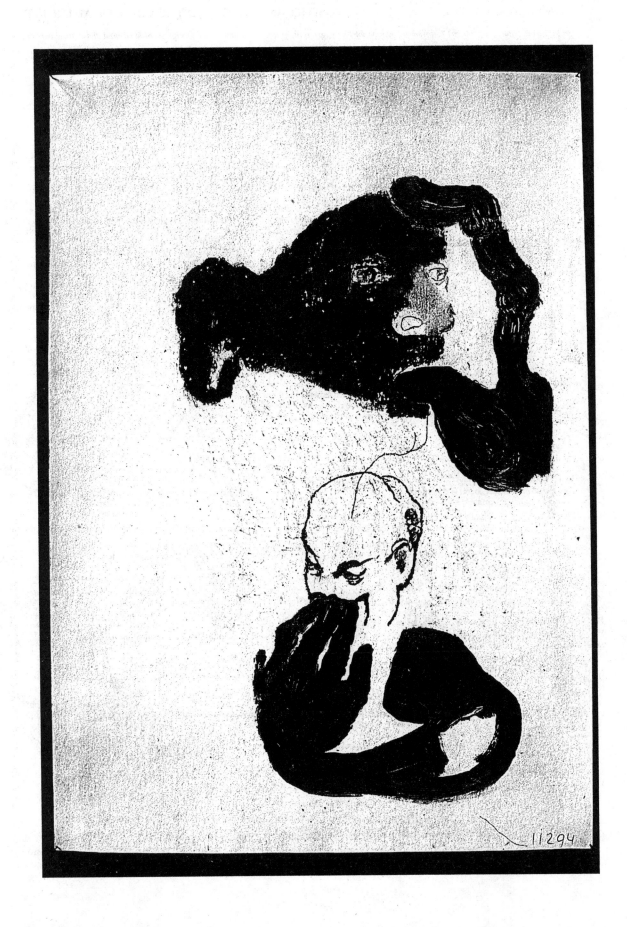

**ANNA NOVAKOV, PhD**, BERKELEY, CA, USA

ANNA NOVAKOV, Ph.D.          **POSITIONING: TEXT AND THE VOICE OF AUTHORITY**

*grid (grid) n. [short for gridiron] 1. a framework of parallel bars; gridiron, grating. 2. a network of evenly spaced horizontal and vertical bars or lines, esp. one for locating points when placed over a map, chart, building plan, etc.* [1]

Language gives voice to ideas through a grammatical and cultural pattern system that is based on a sense of metaphorical and philosophical symmetry, apparently in harmonious balance with the desires of its speakers. Language, as a transmitter of dominant social and cultural information, is structured on a grid-like network based on location within that greater authoritarian structure. Utterances become imbedded not only with personal nuance but with signifiers that wed the speaker with their time and culture. The voice of the individual is manifest as an unsevered umbilical cord which is nurtured by the voice of the father who has usurped the position of the primordial mother tongue. As in the case of most patriarchal frameworks, the child becomes the progeny of the father, who births his children through his brow, as Athena from Zeus, they emerge fully grown and permanently inscribed with the linguistic patterning of domination and subordination.

New York City is also structured on a vast, orderly grid pattern. The streets merge onto square corners creating a kind of topographical conduit resembling an elaborate computer chip. Visual and textual information flows from one geometric urban arena to the next, assuming the semblance of a kind of linguistic metaphor. Radiating patterns spread from the central square. Texts are perpetually inscribed and reinscribed into the body of the city as people are continuously assaulted with a myriad of ocular stimuli from billboards to neon signs to posters for upcoming concerts at local clubs.

As you come above ground from the 42nd Street Subway station you may notice that the stairs are stained and littered with debris from the local fast-food establishments. At noon on a week day, people are rushing, seldom looking up or even left or right. One senses the cool of the air as it mingles with the stale stench from the subterranean subway labyrinth. It is around and all through Times Square. It no longer resembles what could have been its forefather, the Italian piazza. In the 16th century, Michelangelo's grand Campidoglio in Rome, a magnificent town square, symbolized the center of ancient Rome, the top of the Capitoline Hill. The design of this piazza is simultaneously Imperial as well as intimate, public and private, making the casual visitor feel as though they were enveloped in a grand open-air room.

In New York's Times Square, the centuries-old meeting place has been superseded by the modern Mecca without a center. People hurry, avoid each other with agility and continue on their way. There are no outdoor cafes, no majestic fountains and yet the import of Times Square to New York City is on some levels equivalent to the significance of the Eiffel Tower in Paris. Roland Barthes comments about the steel structure are equally relevant when thinking about the Square.

"... [it] is there incorporated into daily life until you can no longer grant it any special attribute, determined merely to persist, like a rock or the river, it is as literature, a phenomenon of nature whose meaning can be questioned to infinity but whose existence is incontestable." [2]

Through both reproductions and personal experiences, the sites of New York and Paris have become more than man-made constructions they have become cultural and linguistic signifiers, symbols of an entire metropolitan area and even a whole way of life. The Times Square Spectacolor lightboard continuously displays advertisements for the world's most famous products. The brightly colored light bulbs flicker at rapid pace as you watch your body progress through dozens of messages. While walking you are assaulted by newspaper sellers distributing flyers and you feel the constant pushing and shoving of the endless sea of humans time and again.

Standing on a public plaza you hear the blend of deafening sounds of car horns, ambulance sirens, radios, and at the moment when the lightboard stops momentarily flashes:

INFORMATION WITHHELD INFORMATION WITHHELD INFORMATION WITHHELD
The clarity of Juan Downey's public project, sandwiched between advertising slogans and news briefs, jumps out against the gray sky. In a 1992 interview with the writer he recalled that, "'Information withheld' is the title of a video tape that I did in 1983. It is not about censorship specifically, but it is also about semiotics. The tape referred more to the difference between everyday signs and fine art. In everyday signs, information is given quickly and clearly, but in art, information is delivered very slowly, in layers that are peeled off gradually.... Conceptually it operated in the mind of the viewer." [3]

The size of the lightboard mildly displays the Messages to the Public. Texts appear out of scale with the clutter of the newsstand below.

The visual brilliance of the words and short fragments bring to mind Ludwig Wittgenstein's references to "pictures of facts." [4] The Spectacolor lightboard and the newsstand below it are in many ways in the same business, spelling information -- to the 1.4 millions people that move through Times Square daily.

Texts in public art and advertising images are often founded on the physical presence of language in a space. As in the case of concrete poetry, the word rises out of a semiotic vacuum, like a sound and a sign devoid of background, like 'fury and mystery'." [5] Works such as this, these elements are concerned more with the function of the linguistic metaphor than the visual metaphor. resulting in a kind of authoritarian structure. In this society, structured through a compilation of language, the primordial mother tongue, and its authoritative nature. In textual works such as this, in the case of certain ideas of the posters, the text functions as a linguistic frame which is assembled out of reconstructed cultural values, displaying the ideas and creating visual as well as linguistic punctuation marks within the urban visual field. As Lisa Phillips wrote, posters such as these are:

In mural functioning as intervening within the flow of editorial and advertising matter, while reflecting on the codification of language and image systems. This proliferation out into the world, of changing and of frame and context, enabled artists to broaden their audience as they mediated between the world of fantasy and culture and the commercial realm of the mass media. [6] Juan Downey used his stark poster in the vertical windows of 60 plus shelters throughout Harlem in 1992. Employing simple devices the black and white photograph showed a vacant lot with a supermarket cart and a dilapidated old couch, and was inserted into the scene. Underneath the black-and-white photograph is printed the following text:

on a scalding hot/ summer day in Harlem/ wedged in a vacant lot/ a field ...

[1] *Webster's World Dictionary*. Second College Edition. New York: Prentice Hall Press, 1986.

[2] Roland Barthes. The Eiffel Tower and Other Mythologies. New York: Hill and Wang, 1979, p.

[3] Juan Downey. Interview with the Writer. New York, January 1992.

[4] Ludwig Wittgenstein. Tractatus Logico-Philosophicus. New York: Harcourt, Brace and Company, 1922, p. 2.1.

[5] Roland Barthes "Writing Degree Zero" from A Barthes Reader. New York: Hill and Wang, 1982, p. 57.

[6] Lisa Phillips and Marvin Heiferman. Image World: Art and Media Culture. New York: Whitney Museum of American Art, 1989, p. 64.

ANNA NOVAKOV, PhD, BERKELEY, CA, USA

/mo' watermelon/ mo' watermelon/ mo' watermelon

The vivid references to poverty and racial stereotypes resonate within this poetic phrasing which is constructed and bracketed by the inscribed bus shelter and its surrounding environment. The shelter, a unit of urban containment, is monumental and stoic as passersby glance at it, read it and continue walking. While waiting for a bus, the text/image is kept in a nebulous holding pattern, as people read and re-read the poem waiting for the bus to transport them to another place. As Marcel Duchamp wrote, "All in all, the creative act is not performed by the artist alone: The spectator brings the work in contact with the external world by deciphering and interpreting its inner qualifications."[7] [...] the shelter's advertising space for public art messages that target the neighborhood that they are imbedded in. The project is [...] address to the people waiting at the bus stop, driving by in cars, or walking along the side [...] of interv[...] everyday lives. An attempt to impart a momentary pause, or opportunity for ref[...] setting[...]

In [...] positioning refers to "segmenting a market by creating a product to [...] the [...]
[...] appeal to meet the needs of a specialized group. . ."[8] [...]
employed [...] of the public audience, or readership, into human phrase patterns which [...]
collective despon[...] of the dominant language. As in the case of Allen [...]
the system. It is also [...] of infusing private ideas and private space into [...]
the city is the backdrop for both art and advertising which attempts to transform [...] which must be mediated, or partially, assimilated, in order to be subverted.[...]

Paid advertisement placards within the subway cars or subway stations have become [...] as Jacques Derrida writes, "open to all possible investments of sense"[9] and in so doing are often indistinguishable from [...] The visual texts in works such as Les Levine's We Are Not Afraid, subway car poster, can be seen as overtly [...] the [...] of writing"[10] by [...] work of art which has displaced itself from the high art world to the commercial world of mass communication [...] visual texts [...] metaphysical to an everyday use."[11] In speaking artists like Levine [...] Materials [...] and others, have fabricated a [...] or new mutation in the history of writing [...] or text, equalized the previous [...] hierarchical [...]

Starting in the 1980s John Fekner stenciled words onto discarded cars and building, buses and garbage dumps. The words "LOST HOPE" or "ABANDONED" merged with these [...] of despair to form text images which [...] urban conditions as well as providing a verbal link between the physical manifestations of poverty and their [...] counterparts. In doing so, he facilitates the inclusion of such topics into the cultural discourse as well as enabling the repositioning. [...] concept within the dominant dialogue. "Fekner's stencils functioned as epitaphs on unintended monuments, marking the end of an industrial era dependent on petrochemical plenty. . . [his] words are also working by labeling. [...] of past destruction, he transforms them into omens of troubles to come."[13] Fekner's projects are reminiscent of Les Levine, who in 1968 littered Forty Second Street with Kleenex tissues stamped with the phrase "dirty words." The same year, Levine made his Process of Elimination in a vacant lot on Houston Street. This project involved the installation of 300 sheets of polyexpandable foam. Each day, a portion of the foam was removed. The piece thus, involved subtracting rather than adding things to the environment.

Through something of a deconstructive descent, "the written word, the advertising slogan, and the [...] of the Times Square street [...] could be on the same interpretive level as the flashing signs on the Messages to the Public spectacolor board. Both [...] Wittgenstein and Derrida have made references to pictures of facts, and the "paint[ed] language" [...] by [...] they suggest that [...] visual manifestation of [...] to illuminate the different art-like quality of words. The Messages to the public [...] and [...] is information Withheld, is a convergence of art and language, and more notably [...] by [...] own [...] work as well as the public art placards done by [...] advertise group GRAN FURY. [...] within their [...] between the expected and the unexpected. GRAN FURY [...] constantly attempt [...] situating their work in the "public realm [...] diverse, non-homogenous audience [...] creating dominant media techniques, we [...] to make the social and political subtexts . . . visible and to incite the viewer to take the next step."[15]

The semiotic shift between the art world and the real world as well as the shift from the public to the private art is complete. The geometric grid pattern is assimilated and subsequently subverted. The utterance of the other is inserted into the [...] completing the subversion of the single, dominant voice into a [...] individualized, multifarious voices.

Anna Novakov, Ph.D. is Assistant Professor of Art History, Theory and Criticism at the San Francisco Art Institute. She holds a doctorate from New York University in the area of twentieth century art, with a specialization in contemporary public art. She also holds degrees in Art History and Literature from the University of California and the Universite de Paris. She is a regular contributor to Artpress, New Moment, Public Art Review, Sculpture, and other national and international publications. She has contributed essays to museum and gallery exhibition catalogs and has written extensively about issues of gender, public art, and contemporary installation art. She is currently writing a book "Public Penetration: The Convergence of Advertising and Public Art."

[7] Marcel Duchamp, quoted in Jeanne Siegel, "Uncanny Repetition: Sherrie Levine's Multiple Originals," Arts, Summer 1991, p. 35.

[8] Otto Kleppner. Advertising Procedure. Englewood Cliffs: Prentice-Hall, 1986, p. 640.

[9] Jacques Derrida. Of Grammatology. Baltimore: Johns Hopkins University Press, 1976, p. 200.

[10] Ibid., p. 55.

[11] Ibid., p. 55.

[12] Ibid., p. 55.

[13] Louis E. Nesbitt, "John Fekner, Exit Art" Artforum, May 1992, p. 120.

[14] Op, cit., Derrida. Of Grammatology, p. 45.

[15] Gran Fury. "This is to Incite You" in Mark O'Brien and Craig Little, eds. Reimaging America: The Arts of Social Change. Philadelphia: New Society Publishers, 1990, p. 264.

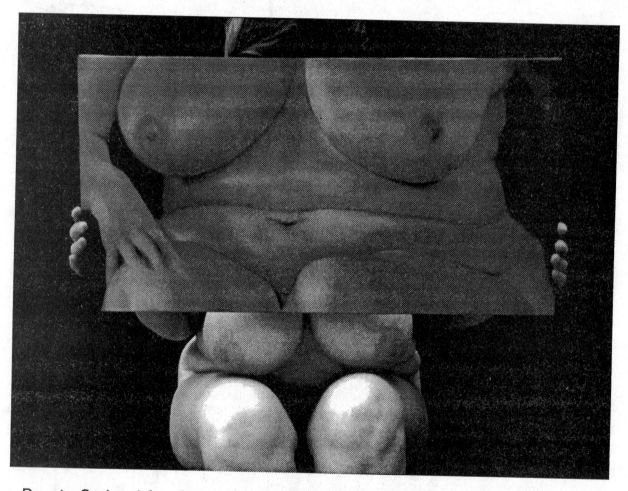

Dorota Sadovská : „Quarterfool" 1994 [oil painting on canvas, cibachrome]

KEIRA ALEXANDRA, BROOKLYN, NY, USA

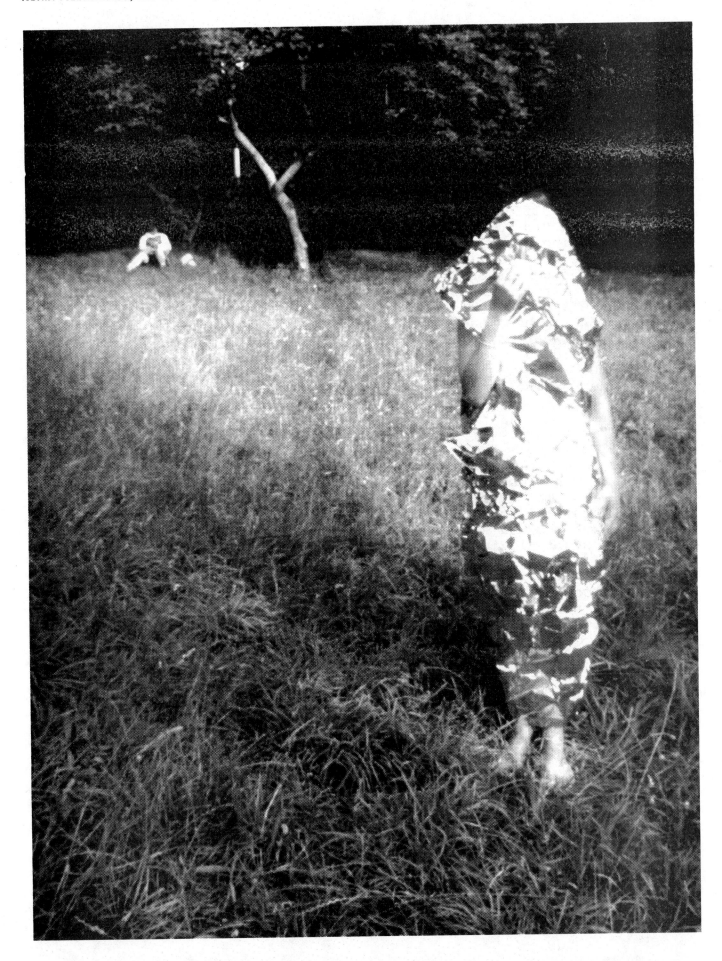

HETTIE JONES, NEW YORK, NY, USA

# Sisters, Right?

*Hettie Jones*

"Sisters, right?" says the woman who owns the grocery, when my middle daughter and I step up to her counter.

At the same time she says "sisters, right," she gives a little squeeze to my hand and a gesture just short of a wink to show us she's well aware that this is a mother-daughter duo.

My middle daughter and I burst out laughing. She--like her sisters--is a grown woman, a black woman in her thirties. I am white, in my sixtieth year. In the past week, we have encountered two different women who could not see our relationship.

"How did you guess?" my daughter asks the grocery woman, who is laughing with us.

"Because you look exactly alike!" she shouts gaily.

My daughter and I have been together this week for a rite of passage: from minor we have progressed to major surgery. Both of us have survived the knife.

What, then, had the grocery woman seen that the others hadn't? What has appeared to augment our resemblance--pain?

And does this shared pain create the same face, differently skinned?

And who else sees it?


In the recovery room I had asked on my daughter's behalf for pain medicine. "Not yet," said the nurse of the snapping eyes.

A few moments later I asked again. "Sorry," I said, "but you know how mothers are."

"You're her mother?"

Courtesy falling like rain.

But who had she seen before? Who was that woman hung over the bedrail, loving someone?


Soon, another nurse--a young one, mean to the bone--has my daughter out of bed and in the bathroom with the water running full force.

I offer instead to whisper in her ear, the way I used to when she was little.

"What are mothers for?" I joke to the nurse, who overreacts with more noise than the splashing water, about how I couldn't possibly be, I'm too young, but we know what she's covering.

"Loud," says my middle daughter, back in bed, thumbing the painkiller button.


Later, I muse about these two women.

Flowers on the bed table, heart balloons in the air, my daughter, propped up and frowning dismissively, says, "Oh, they probably just thought we were dykes."

HETTIE JONES, NEW YORK, NY, USA

At her house, in the beautiful spread of her life, I tell her I'm going to write this story.  That I'll begin with the grocery woman, because she had good eyes.

My middle daughter jumps on this.  She says, "There you go, Ma."

## 2.

And off _she_ goes, to work again.  The two of us sit side by side in the small city airport.

There's always something at the airport.  This time it's a young black man, with a young white woman seeing him off.  They're not lovers, that much is clear, perhaps new acquaintances.  They sit facing us in the narrow lobby.  The plane is delayed, and we four--he, she, my middle daughter and I--have nothing to do but scope each other.

Suddenly, between us intrudes a noisy, excited group, led by a sexy overcontrolling mother in a black catsuit, missing her two top front teeth.

Into my ear my middle daughter whispers, "Somebody couldn't take it and popped her."

I laugh out loud.

"Ma, it's rude to laugh at people in airports," she says, laughing, and when I look up, still laughing, I catch the eye of the young black man.  He's now standing, his face a mask of controlled amusement.  He almost smiles.  Perhaps, as he passes me, the one who catches his smile is my middle daughter.

Or perhaps not.  Gently, gallant in the bumrush, he spreads a protective hand on the back of the woman he's with.

I know my daughter doesn't miss this.

I think about black and white women in competition.  For what hard reasons?  What's to be addressed?  What will happen if we don't?  If my middle daughter--my sister, right?--is black, and I am white, we have to keep thinking.

We lean against each other and talk.  She says, "Three minutes more, you'll have to pay to park another hour."

She's old enough to dismiss me; still I dawdle, kiss her goodbye twice.  On the way out I'm thinking in Spanish, _m'ija_, _mi hija_, such a pretty way to say it.

The parking lot gate is manned by a boy, whose sweet smile recalls to me my middle daughter's high school boyfriend.  I know his mother loves him.  I wish I were looking at a million of him, because of that number how many will survive?  And he doesn't charge me for another hour, although according to the clock in my car I am nearly _five_ minutes late leaving.

In my gratitude I fumble a dime, which gets lost on the seat.

"Well," he says with a pleasant laugh, "at least you know where it's _at_."

Which, I suppose, is both the problem and the start of any solution.

MIRRIAM LIPPMAN, BROOKLYN, NY, USA

# Recycling

IT HAS ALWAYS INTRIGUED ME THAT LIFE WORKS IN CYCLES. PERHAPS SINCE I'M SO SENSITIVE TO THIS PROCESS IN MY OWN LIFE. EVERY TIME A MAJOR CHAPTER ENDS, IT'S LIKE A DEATH — ALWAYS FOLLOWED — — EVENTUALLY — BY A REBIRTH.

I LOVE BREATHING NEW LIFE INTO THE MATERIALS I FIND (OR SEEM TO FIND ME). IT MAKES ME HAPPY TO RENDER VALID AN OBJECT DEEMED "DEAD" OR "USELESS" — — A WASTE PRODUCT — BY GIVING IT A NEW CONTEXT. TO NOT WASTE IT — TO TRANSFORM IT, GIVING IT NEW LIFE, IS TO SEIZE AN OPPORTUNITY TO SALVAGE OUR PLANET'S RESOURCES.

**MIRRIAM LIPPMAN,** BROOKLYN, NY, USA

# Recycling

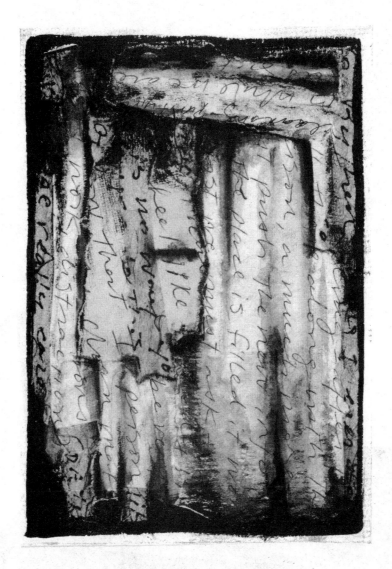

*Mirriam Lippman*

MIEKE SCHOBBE, AMSTERDAM, THE NETHERLANDS

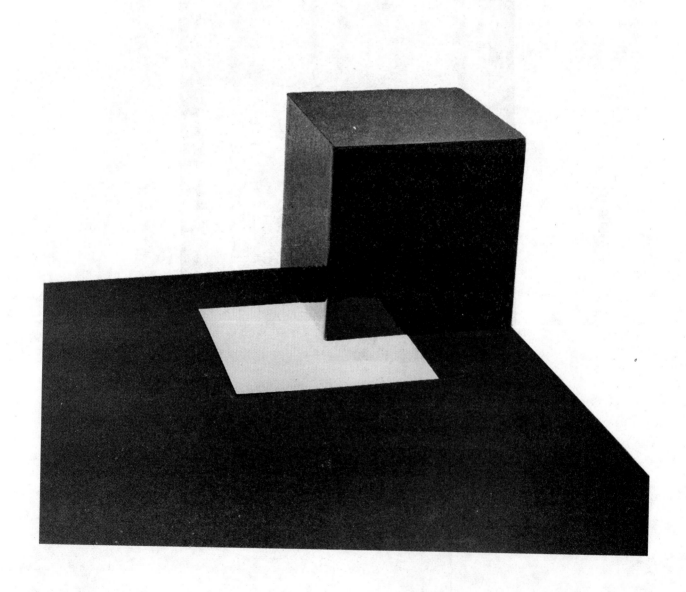

**MIEKE SCHOBBE**, AMSTERDAM, THE NETHERLANDS

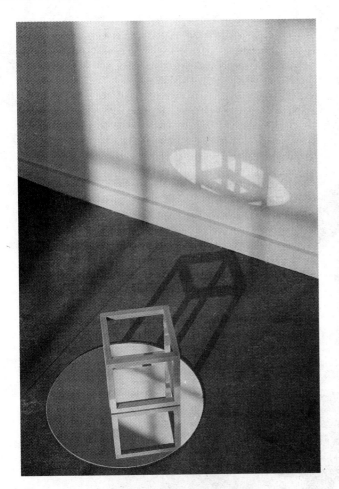
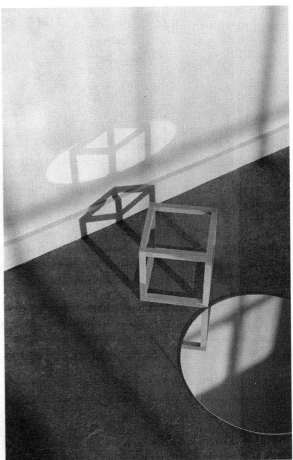
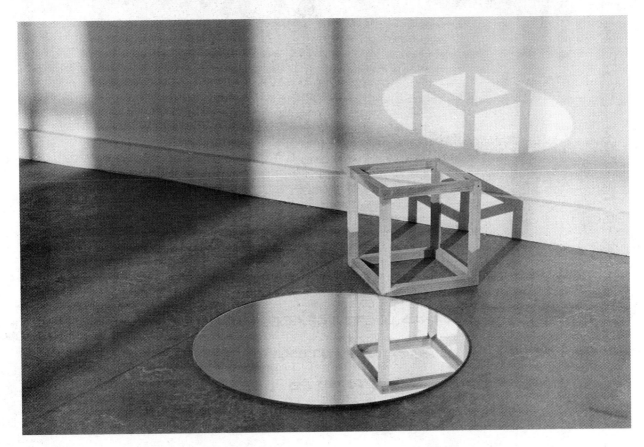

**FRAN BEALLOR**, NEW YORK, NY, USA

FRAN BEALLOR   MIDDLE EAST PIECE   OIL ON CANVAS   40" x 36"

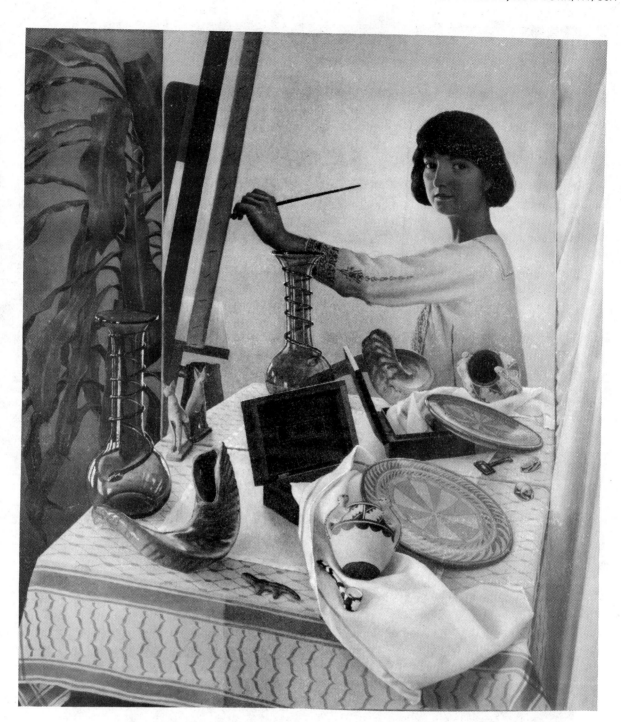

# REFLECTIONS OF PEACE

ARAB & ISRAELI OBJECTS PEACEFULLY COEXIST ON CANVAS,
WITH A LITTLE AMERICAN INTERVENTION.

(PAINTED DURING THE GULF WAR)

Nuria Carrasco, SEVILLA, SPAIN

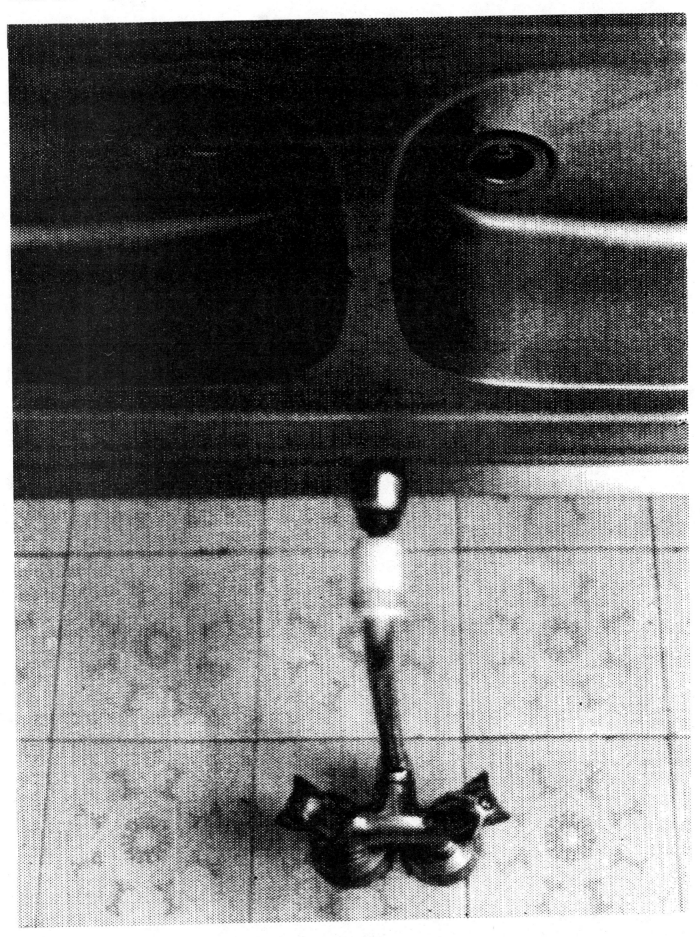

Nuria Carrasco, SEVILLA, SPAIN

RACHEL MOSES, JERUSALEM, ISRAEL

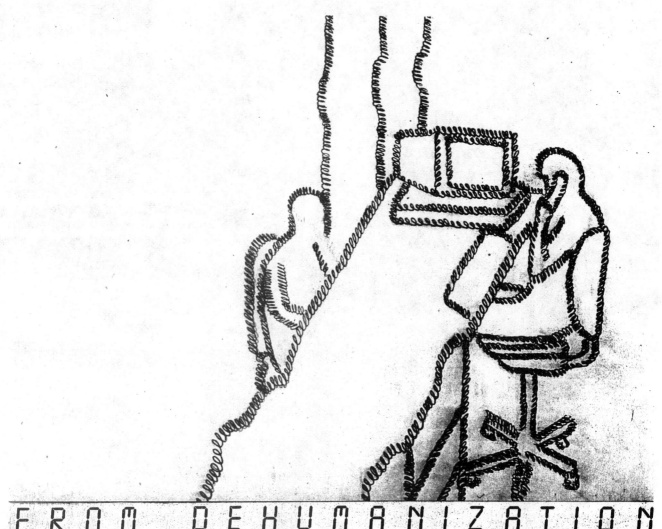

FROM DEHUMANIZATION

RACHEL MOSES, JERUSALEM, ISRAEL

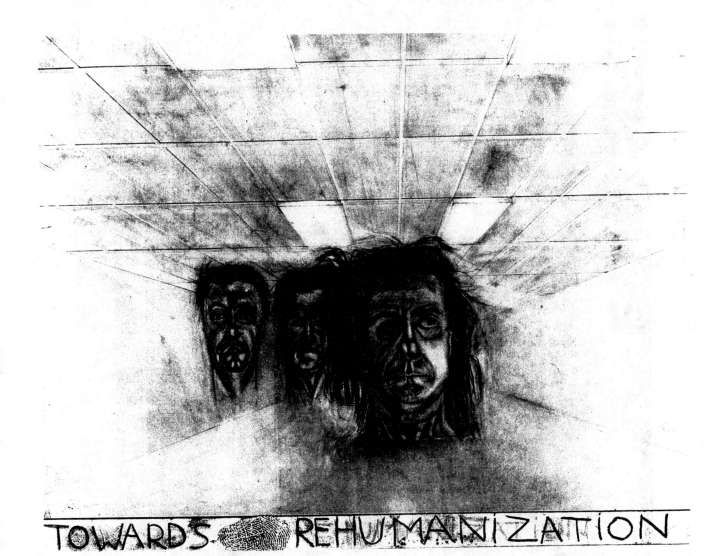

TOWARDS REHUMANIZATION

**SARITA AHOOJA**, MONTREAL, CANADA

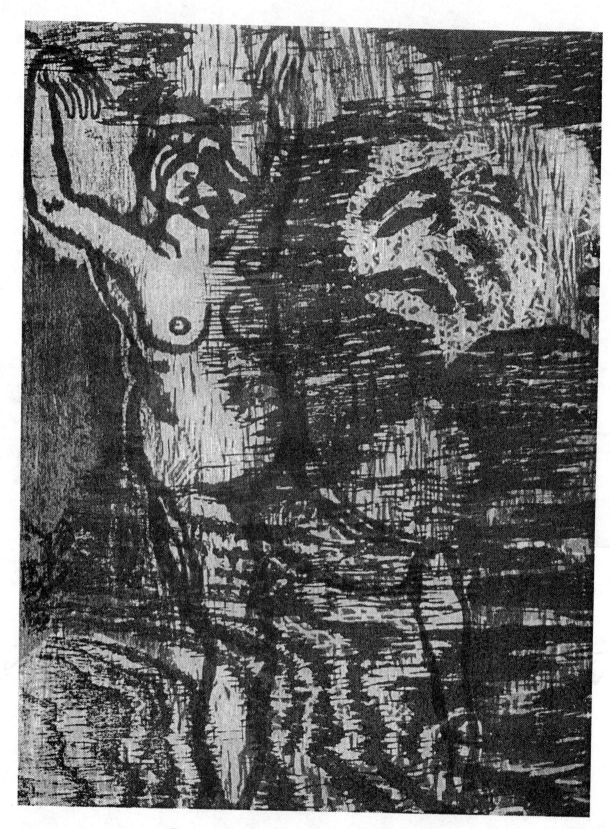

Resistance Can Be Repetition...Find A Place

ANGELA LUBIC, BERLIN, GERMANY

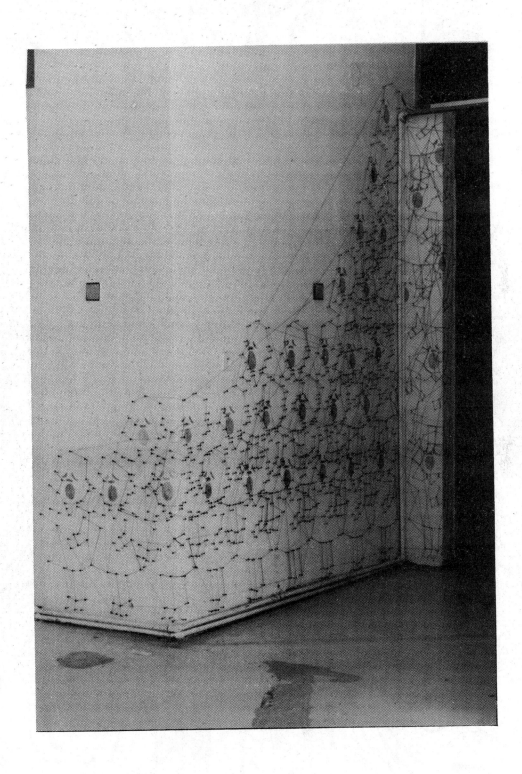

EILEEN DOSTER, NEW YORK, NY

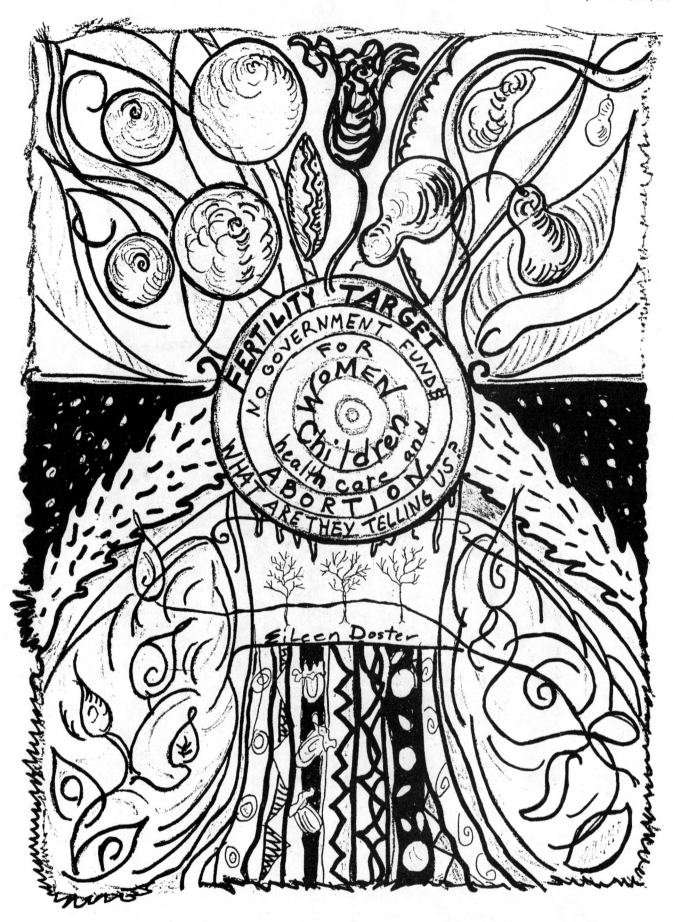

EILEEN DOSTER, NEW YORK, NY

EiLeen Doster
637 East 6th Street #10
New York, N.Y.  10009
Telephone   # (212) 982-2379

Artist's Statement

Anything can happen in the paintings of EiLeen Doster. In the dishscape paintings the teapots appear to be spying on the wineglasses and the sunflowers are listening in.  These oil paintings range in size from the side of a tin can lid to 10 by 18 feet and practically every size in between.  They are dramas, with crockery levitating, floating and flying AND taking on human emotions and characteristics if one is really looking. These paintings have a surrealist edge and have definitely been affected by such disjointed influences as Matisse, Morandi, stage set design, cell animation, American quilts and folk art. The Celtic background of the artist is apparent in the highly, intimate landscapes which have been described as borderline minimalist paintings.   The palette is both charged and quiet, rich and warm, subtle and aggressive. These qualities contribute to a small but select section of work which consists of portraits of saints and graveyards from around the world.  The poet and critic Michael Sobsey wrote in 1986 "She paints great skies".

E. Doster
Spring 1995

LILLIAN BALL, NEW YORK, NY, USA

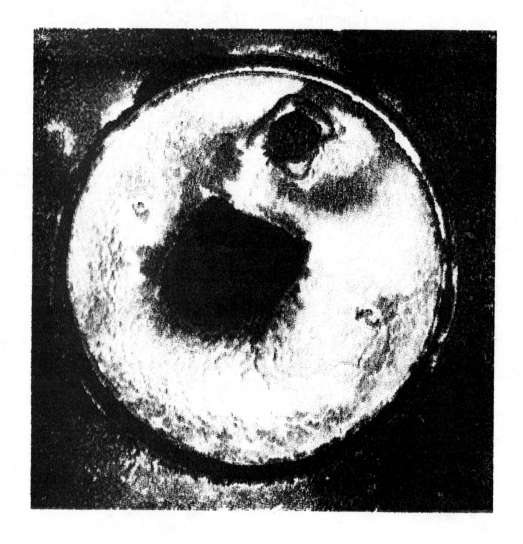

LILLIAN BALL, NEW YORK, NY, USA

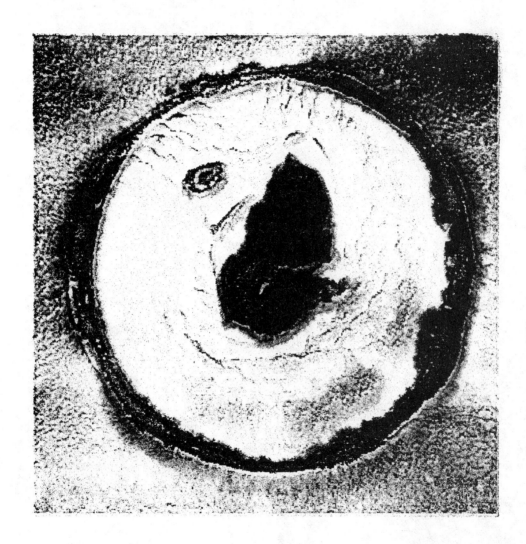

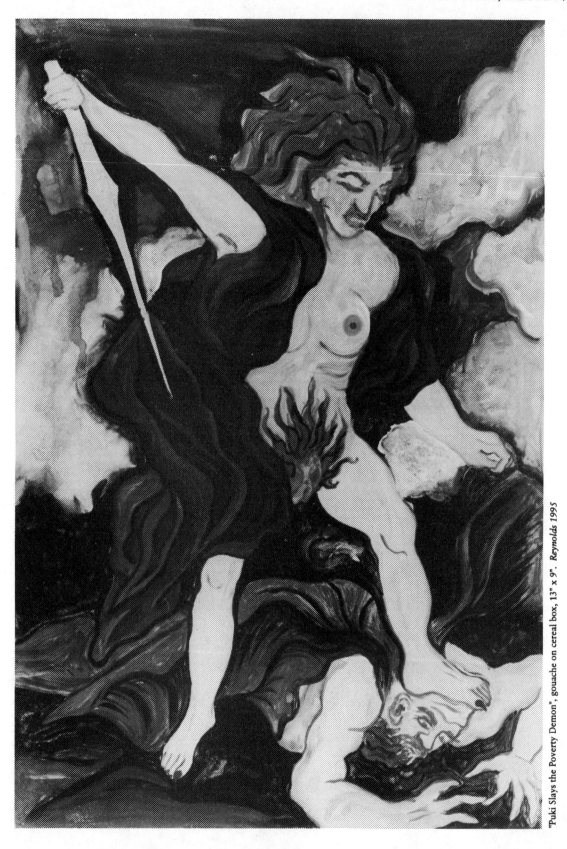

"Puki Slays the Poverty Demon", gouache on cereal box, 13" x 9". *Reynolds 1995*

**Revenge**     I started the series of Puki Monsters in 1991, in response to *Documenta IX*'s underrepresentation of women. The first Puki (meaning vagina in Filipino),  was born under the monument of Hercules in Kassel.  The local women had deposited tampons between the supporting rocks of the statue to protest the glorification of phallocentrific power. Puki monsters avenge the heroic with the comic.

SIDNI LAMB, WESTBANK, BC, CANADA

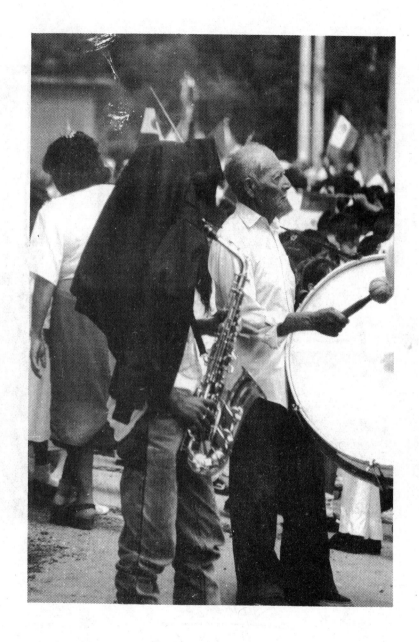

**FAY CHIN,** NEW YORK, NY, USA

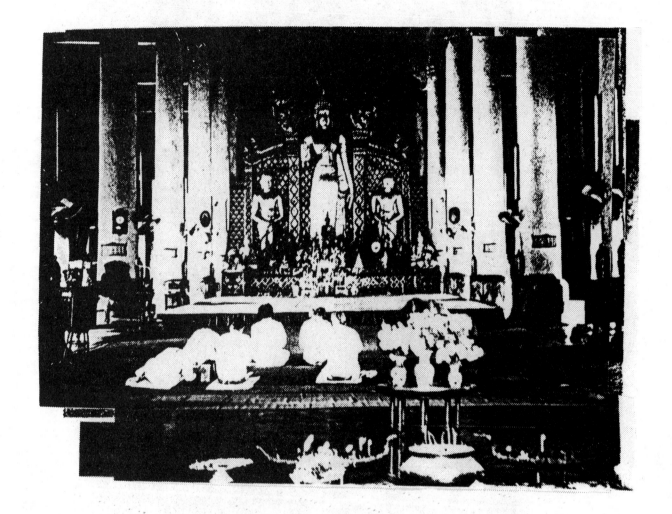

**FAY CHIN,** NEW YORK, NY, USA

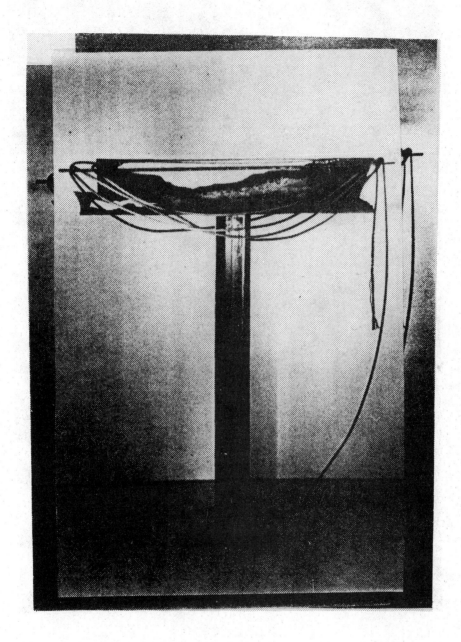

**JO YARRINGTON,** FAIRFIELD, CT, USA

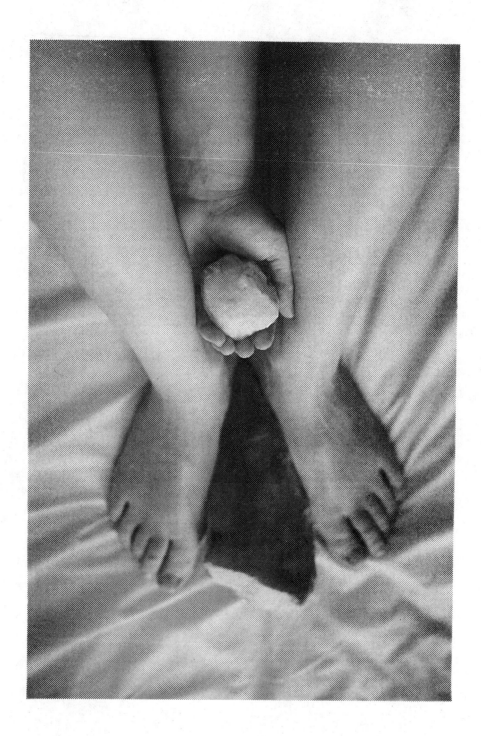

The work I'm doing now is evolving out of process, a desire for language, the building of an alphabet. Piece by piece, objects and materials are collected and woven into a record of sensation. I am slowly finding my way through touch, in to cultures, in to histories, in to the belly of the earth. Gliding my hand over rock and grass, through water and air, I search for a resting place, for a shape, a texture, a color, a light that resonates, that returns my caress. I stop only when the touch is yes (yes).

**BABETTE SEMMER,** LONDON, ENGLAND

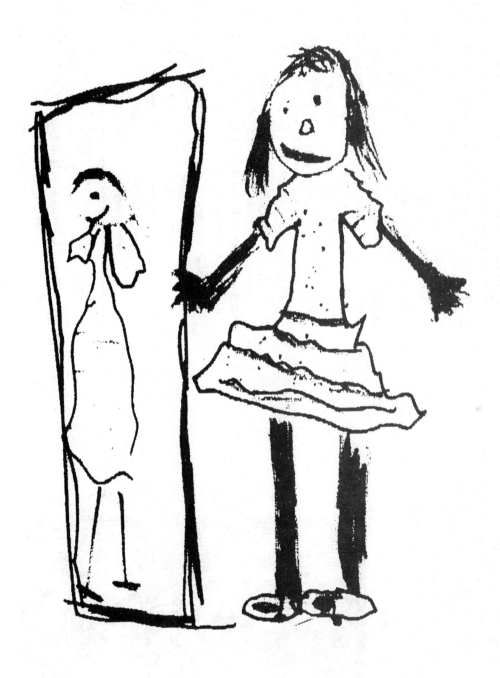

KATHLEEN L OETTINGER, ROCKVILLE, MD, USA

# I'm part of the Sandwich Generation now

*Oettinger: K.L., Kat, Kathy, Kathleen, Mom, Sis*

## Love is a decision Retirement - HOW?

Yes, world, you need another artist! I'm an artist, wife, mother, daughter, in-law, sister, friend. I want to focus on my art full time now. I **need** time in the studio. Some of my life choices were based on the premise that when our three daughters grew up and my husband retired I would have freedom to explore the productivity of Cronehood. I've done it all - been superwoman. I'm a Crone now but the flexibility I craved, the gratification I delayed, are threatened. I'm sandwiched between the needs of two generations. My mother-in-law has the resources to reside in an assisted living community but I'm still, in some ways, her primary caregiver. My parents are beginning to have needs that concern me. Our children aren't settled - one is married, the youngest will be graduating college soon - but they have chosen to work in creative fields which don't have guaranteed career tracks, stability, home bases... When I hear Congress talk about the responsibility families have to take care of their own, I translate that to "women have to care for everyone." Mostly it works out that way. How can women be supported so we can do these jobs with love and still have lives of our own? Men retire to second careers, Can we?

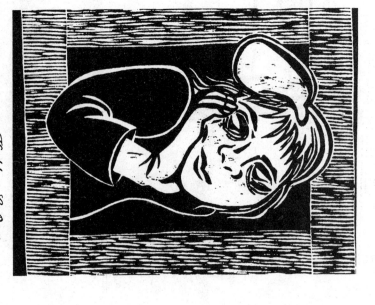

*Kalevala Woodcut Series by Kathleen L. Oettinger*

Lack of arts funding and the current mercenary situation in the art world take me away from my studio and into the marketplace. My preferred job would be as art faculty at a college or university but those positions go to younger people. Don't get me wrong, I am happy with the choices and results of the first half of my life. I have achieved "success" in art and life. But I want to pursue art **full time**. My family agrees and helps - but will all the support systems be taken away?

ANA VEGA, ROSELLE PARK, NJ, USA

improprieties of the mind

You would
Wouldn't you
If I let you

catch the light in my eyes
beckon me still
soft whispers
your touch like lighting
yet as tender as dew on a morning petal
the caress of a warm breast
yours
mine

You would
Wouldn't you
If I let you

tongue frolicks
using my body as its playground
searching
finding
searching once again
quenching its thirst on the moisture of my lips
mouths ajar
we exchange sustenance
come
come close
closer closer
you want me to invite you in
don't you
quench your thirst
feed on my reserves
I have been waiting for you
don't suffocate
inhale me
be a part of me

You would
Wouldn't you
If I let you

drops
drops
torrential floods
of sweat of sweet nectar
your fragrance would overpower mine
5 more minutes
5 more minutes
5 more minutes you plead
minutes that turn into hours
into an eternity
hold me for such a long time
that the heat of your body would brand me

You would
Wouldn't you
If I let you

make me yours

You would
Wouldn't you

moment by moment
with an innocent air
leave your mark on me
your hunger is insatiable
my body is not enough for you
ah
but my mind is fertile ground

You would
Wouldn't you
If I let you

suck my brain
leave me as autumn leaves
so dry that a spark would ignite
take me to places far away
no concept of space or time
almost to the point of loosing
consciousness
it's so unbearably hot
i can not breathe
i no longer have thoughts
just sensations
i am no longer in control
my consciousness is yours

You would
Wouldn't you
If I let you

**Diyan Achjadi**, NEW YORK, NY, USA

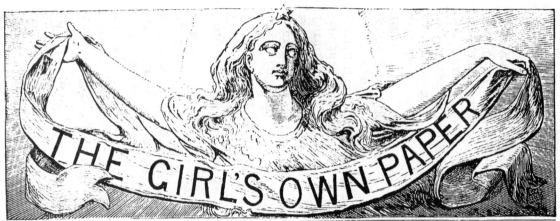

VOL. XIV.—No. 672.]  NOVEMBER 12, 1892.  [PRICE ONE PENNY.

## LITTLE MISS MUFFET.

By ROSA NOUCHETTE CAREY, Author of "Nellie's Memories," "Our Bessie," "Averil," etc.

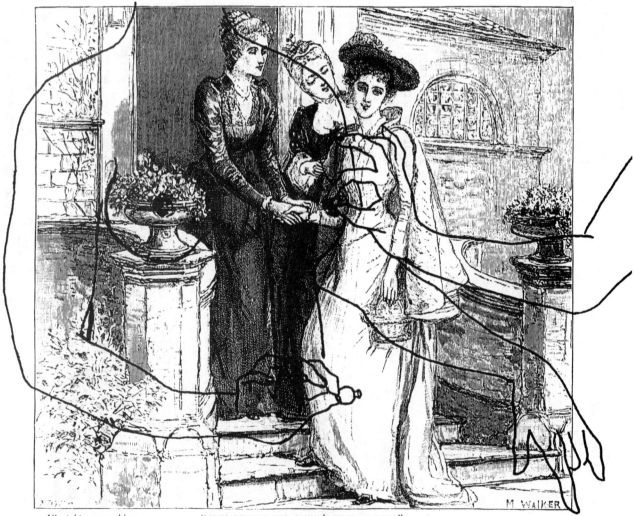

"STILL KEEPING HER COUSIN'S HAND IN HERS."

M. WALKER

DIYAN ACHJADI, NEW YORK, NY, USA

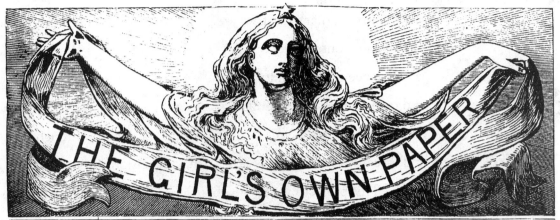

VOL. XIV.—No. 713.]          AUGUST 26, 1893.          [PRICE ONE PENNY.

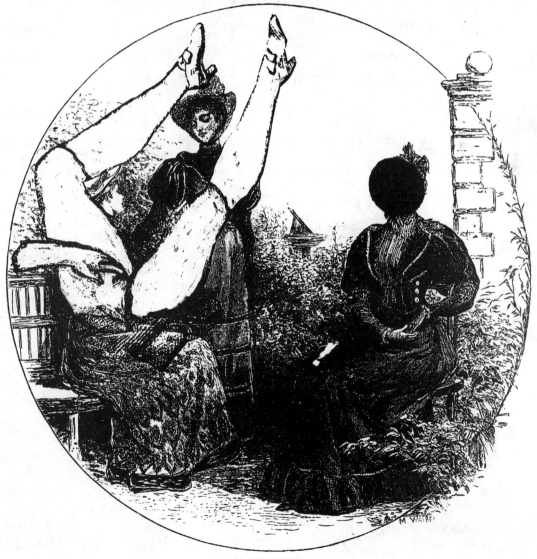

IN THE GARDEN.

(See *Frocks and Gowns for the Month.*)

## THE SCARLET LETTER PROJECT

Born guilty — that's what we are. According to the men who would like to gain control over our lives, women are guilty — guilty because we have been raped, guilty because we have been sexually abused, and guilty because we found ourselves with an unwanted pregnancy and got an abortion. We are guilty at birth and guilty through life, and, because of our guilt, unable to make decisions for ourselves.

This project has several goals in mind: to break through the silence of the guilt and shame forced on us at the moments of our most severe pain, to allow us to openly deal with the events that have touched us deeply but we have been unable to express and to understand that we are not alone but part of a brigade of millions and millions just like us, who hide in our silence.

Now, we can wear a small pin, a scarlet letter A to show our solidarity with the reproductive rights of women around the world a symbol of our experience and to show one another we don't have to be afraid.

The Scarlet Letter represents common experience. It is a symbol of solidarity in the face of attacks from anti-choice groups and the right. It allows a recognition of one woman for another. It can be a secret sign for those who know and an object of curiosity for those who don't. It will overwhelm us with our numbers.

These pins will be sold, the ultimate goal being to support the continuing fight for abortion rights around the world. The Scarlet Letter Project will give its proceeds to groups that aid in disseminating information about reproductive rights and are committed to making and keeping abortion an option until the time when that option is no longer needed.

*Terry Berkowitz, The Scarlet Letter Project, 1995*

**TERRY BERKOWITZ**, NEW YORK, NY, USA

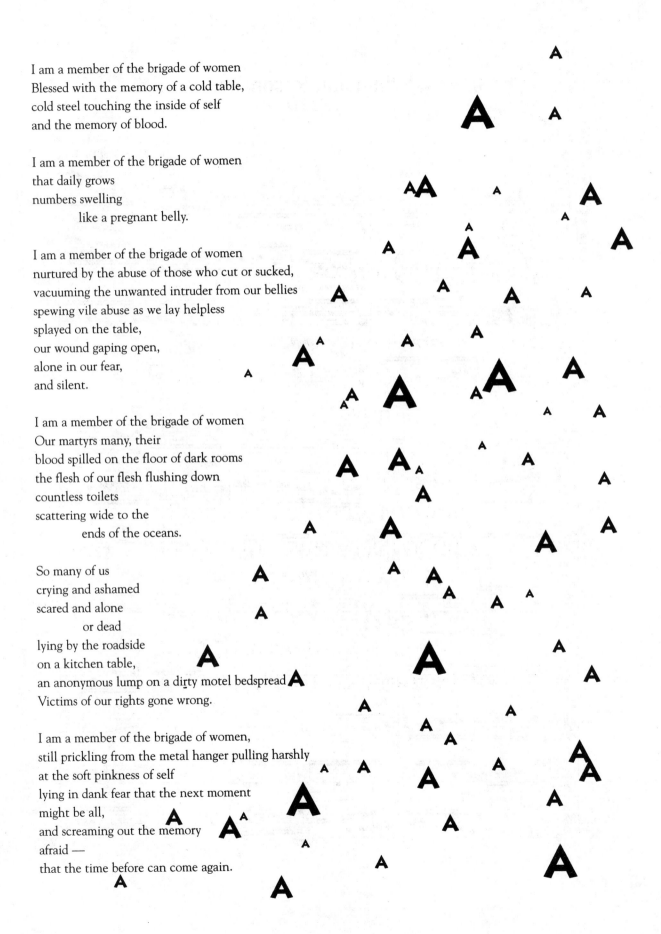

I am a member of the brigade of women
Blessed with the memory of a cold table,
cold steel touching the inside of self
and the memory of blood.

I am a member of the brigade of women
that daily grows
numbers swelling
       like a pregnant belly.

I am a member of the brigade of women
nurtured by the abuse of those who cut or sucked,
vacuuming the unwanted intruder from our bellies
spewing vile abuse as we lay helpless
splayed on the table,
our wound gaping open,
alone in our fear,
and silent.

I am a member of the brigade of women
Our martyrs many, their
blood spilled on the floor of dark rooms
the flesh of our flesh flushing down
countless toilets
scattering wide to the
       ends of the oceans.

So many of us
crying and ashamed
scared and alone
       or dead
lying by the roadside
on a kitchen table,
an anonymous lump on a dirty motel bedspread
Victims of our rights gone wrong.

I am a member of the brigade of women,
still prickling from the metal hanger pulling harshly
at the soft pinkness of self
lying in dank fear that the next moment
might be all,
and screaming out the memory
afraid —
that the time before can come again.

**MARGARET DEWYS,** ANNANDALE ON HUDSON, NY, USA

# Schumann Resonance
## 7.83 Hz.

Margaret De Wys

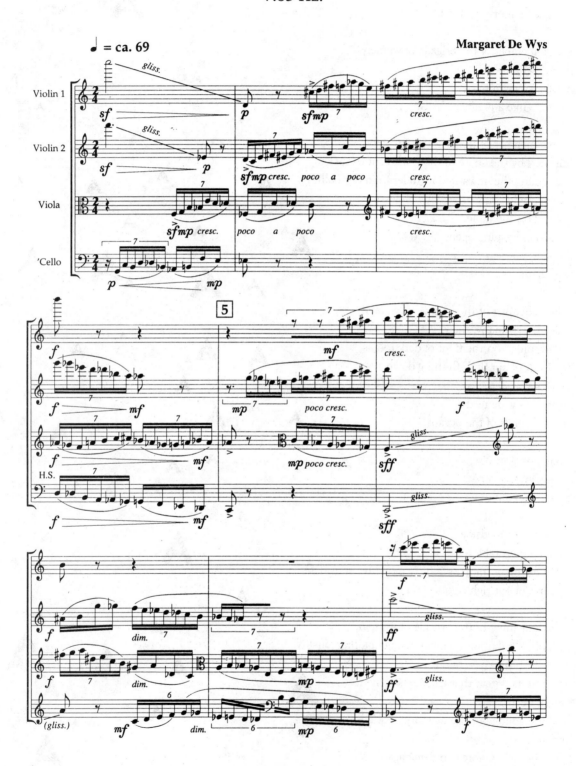

MARGARET DEWYS, ANNANDALE ON HUDSON, NY, USA

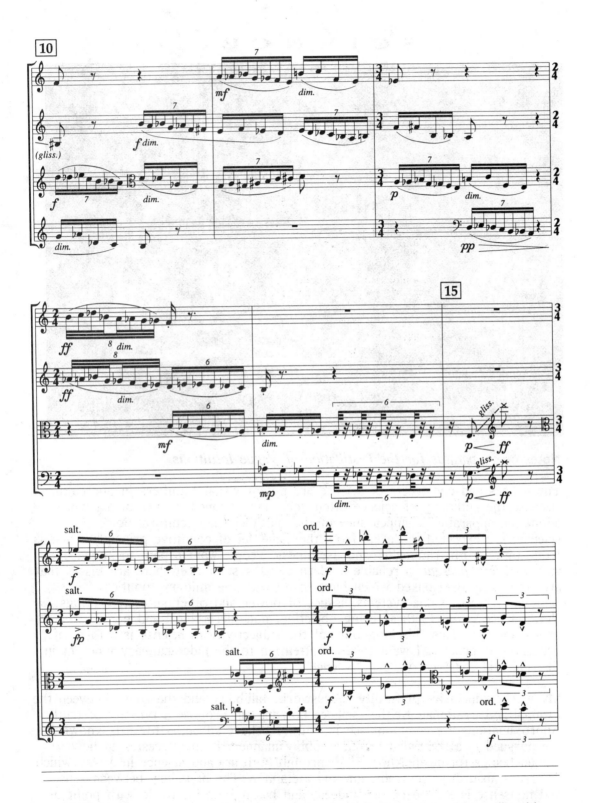

Can there be any way to express that wave form in the dream without disturbing the illusion . . . or is the design exactly that, to disturb the dream?          *Robert Monroe*

EVE ANDRÉE LARAMÉE, BROOKLYN, NY, USA

# S C I E N C E

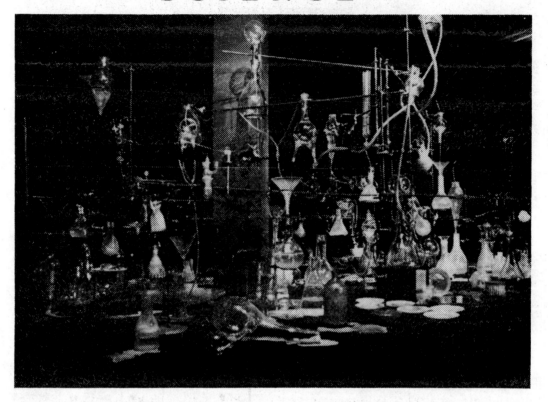

### Notes on *Apparatus for the Distillation of Vague Intuitions*

The images and constructs of science are potent visual signifiers in our culture. Because the authority of science often goes unquestioned, works of art which adopt the apparatus or appearance of the "authoritarian" cultural voice of science, are expected to derive from the same set of cognitive principles, that is from logic, truth, rationality and usefulness. People want a path to knowledge and science *represents* a reliable modern belief system. Yet there are biases that are frequently overlooked which have to do with the military, politics, economics, social value systems, issues of power and other subjective things. Yet, science is put forth as being objective, non-hierarchical and non-propagandistic. This "blacking-out" of the subjectivity in science is a form of occlusion or opacity. I want to draw attention to the indeterminacy inherent in that cultural construct we call "Science".

My work is inclusive of futility, guesswork, fallibility and the zones between the rational and irrational. Neither science nor art can propose a tyranny of truth. Approximations are commonplace in both. I believe all paths towards knowledge are pursued in a somewhat errant, wobbly manner. I am interested in how human beings formulate knowledge through both art and science in a way which embraces absurdity, contradiction and metaphor. The boundary between sense and nonsense is a slippery one indeed, and has quite a bit to do with point of view. I like to wander in such ambiguous zones.

## Eve Andrée Laramée

**MARU HOEBER**, SACRAMENTO, CA, USA

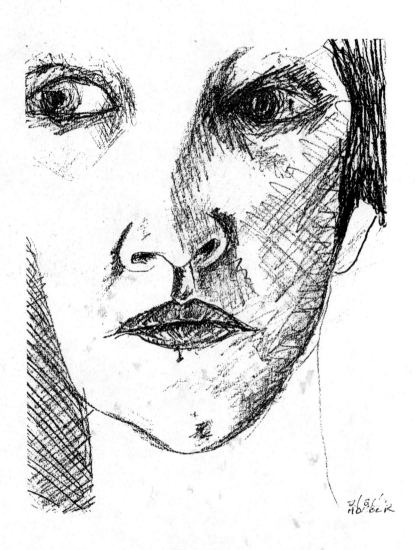

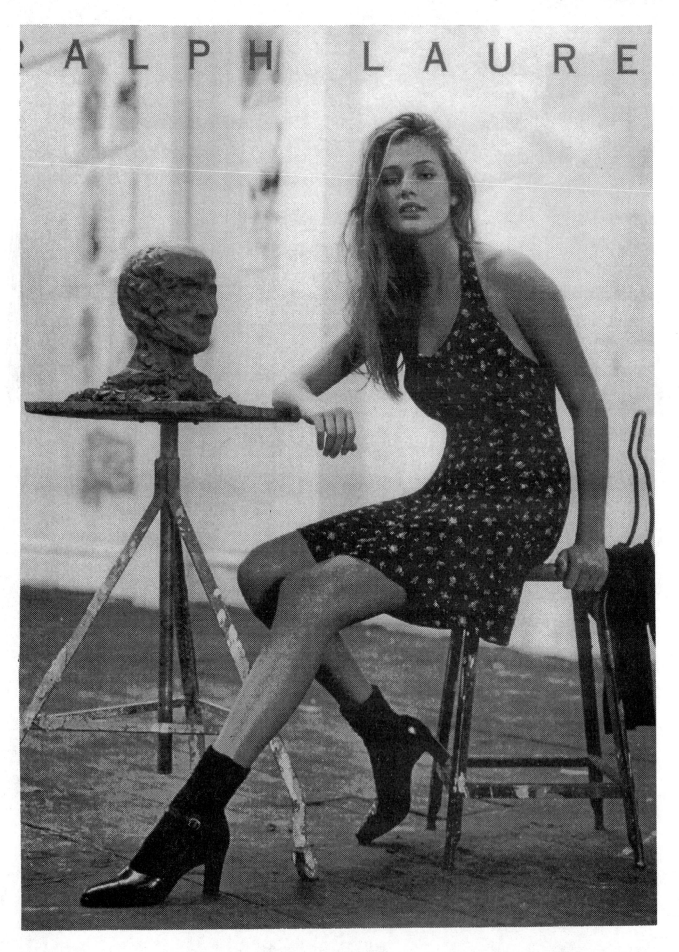

**APRIL GORNIK,** NEW YORK, NY, USA

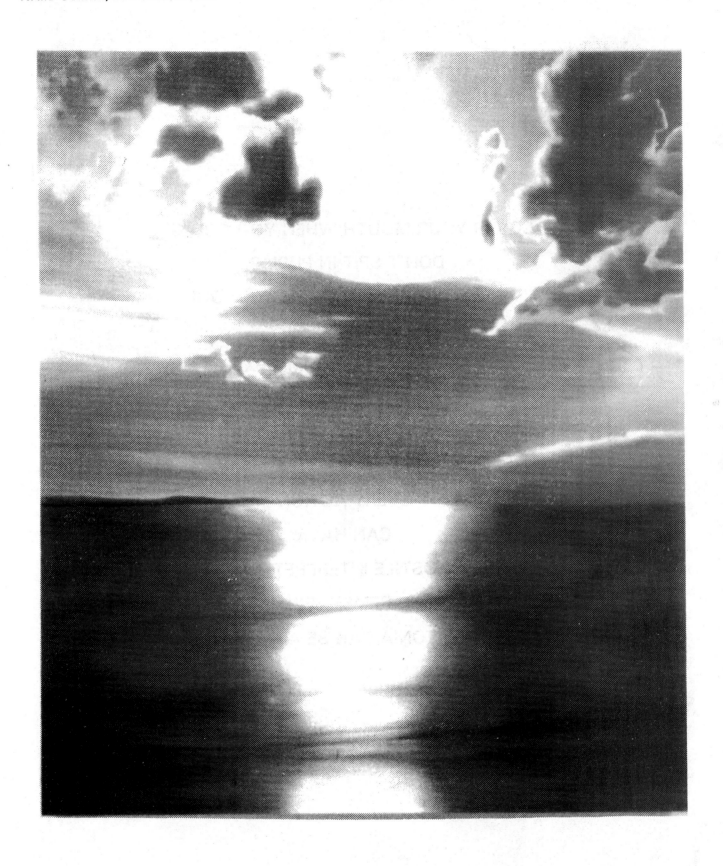

"Sea Light"  1995  Oil on Linen  70" x 60"  April Gornik
Art crosses time and space.  Art creates time and space.

**SHIRLEY IRONS**, NEW YORK, NY, USA

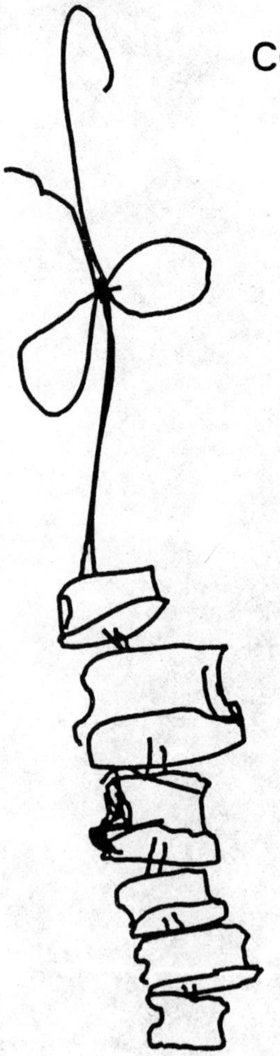

COVER YOUR MOUTH WHEN YOU COUGH.

DON'T SPIT IN PUBLIC.

SAY "PLEASE" AND "THANK YOU"

WITH FREQUENCY.

DO NOT SPEAK OF COMPLEX IDEAS,

SLIP EASILY INTO THE VERNACULAR,

BE INOFFENSIVE IN YOUR DISRUPTIONS.


EVERY ACTION

CAN HAVE

A HOSTILE INTERPRETATON.

REMEMBER,

CATATONIA CAN BE AN ASSET.

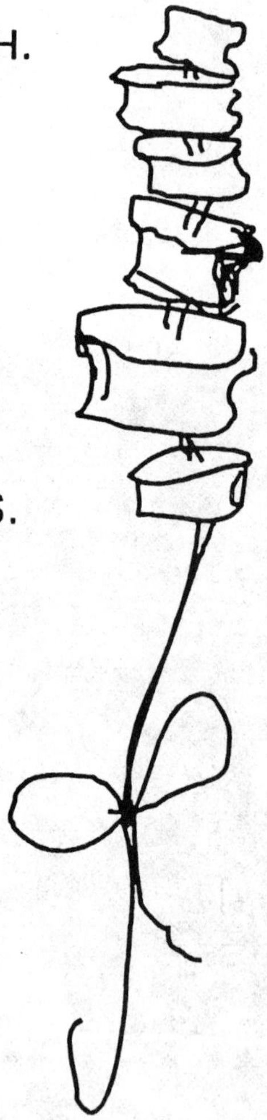

SHIRLEY IRONS, NEW YORK, NY, USA

When Marguerite was bored she cut (usually with symmetry) 3" pieces off her hair.  When Marguerite was anxious she shaved neat corkscrews of skin off her hands and feet.  When Marguerite was in love she got thin.  When Marguerite was angry, she aimed for control.  The rest of the time she tried to oblige.

Her doctor told her that she was experiencing a failure of primordial psychological activity, distorted and masked by human cognitive and affective superstructures, a hereditary predisposition to paranoia, mythomania, a persistence of omnipotent feelings from childhood and a low sense of self esteem.  "Aha," Marguerite said, "Arbeit macht frei."  And she became a painter.

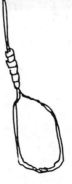

# MARNIE CARDOZO
## pinhole camera self-nudes

c/o Bernard Toale Gallery
11 Newbury Street, Boston, MA, USA 02116
1-(617)-262-0211

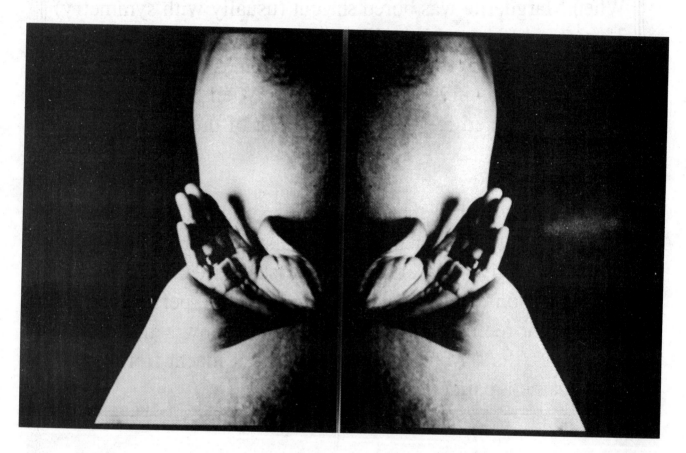

courtesy of Bernard Toale Gallery, Boston, MA USA

diptych self-nude #5

MARNIE CARDOZO, BROOKLINE, MA, USA

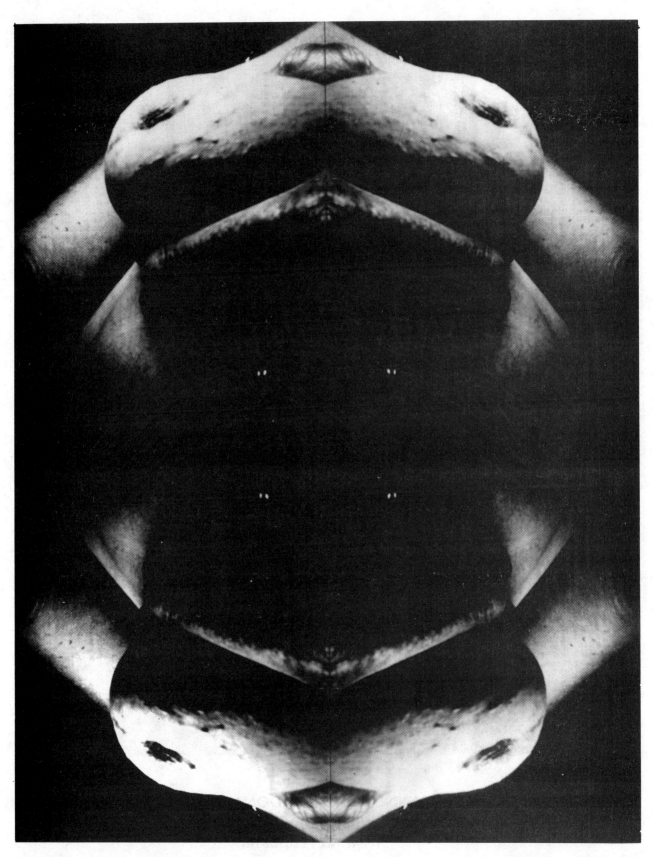

courtesy of Bernard Toale Gallery, Boston, MA USA

kaleidoscope self-nude #4

ANNE ARDEN McDONALD, BROOKLYN, NY, USA

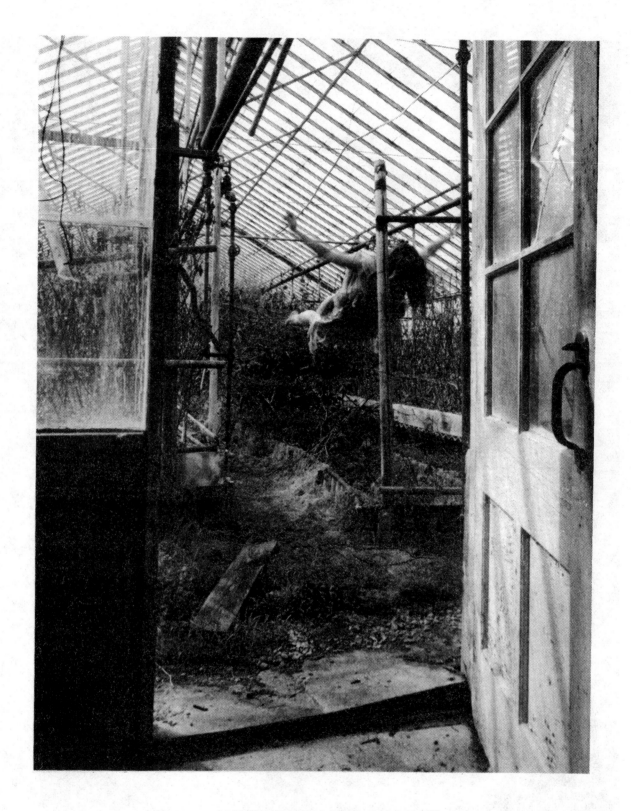

**ANNE ARDEN McDONALD**

Tel. & Fax 718.852.8816

ANNE ARDEN MCDONALD, BROOKLYN, NY, USA

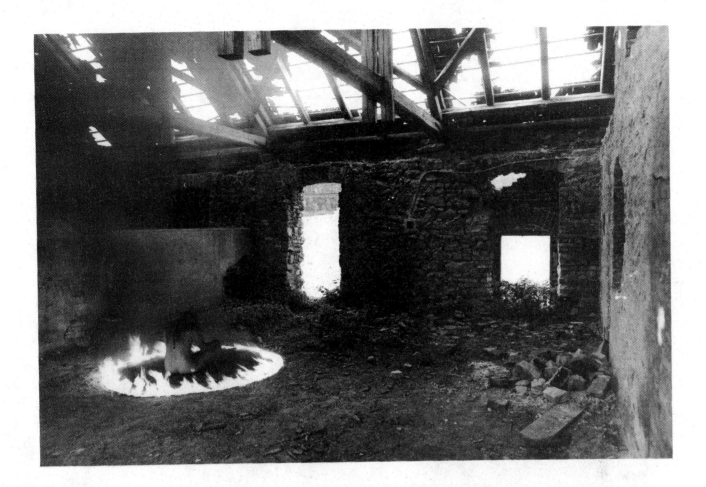

I daydream to escape the everyday world of details and paperwork--or I go completely crazy. I have many fantasies that I can not achieve in life as I have known it--including being able to breathe under water and to fly--and am frustrated by the limitations of an earthbound body. In some of my photographs, I have watched myself achieving these goals. More recently, my work has centered around struggles we face every day: tensions and balances, keeping hope alive against the obstacles, and living in a vulnerable way without being crushed.

**JEANNE CRISCOLA**, NORTH HAVEN, CT, USA

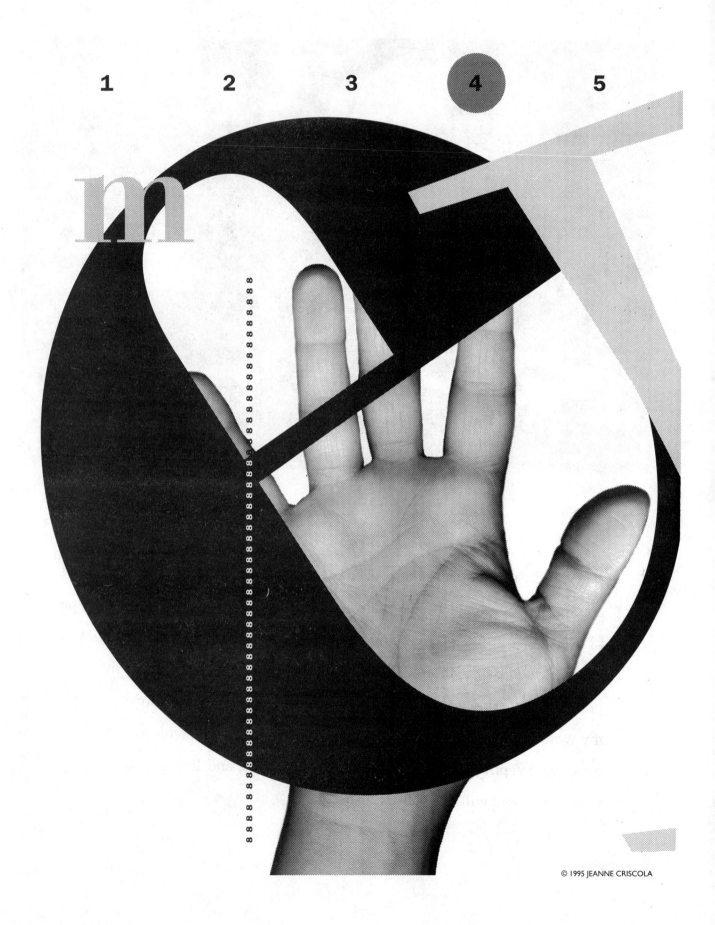

JEANNE CRISCOLA, NORTH HAVEN, CT, USA

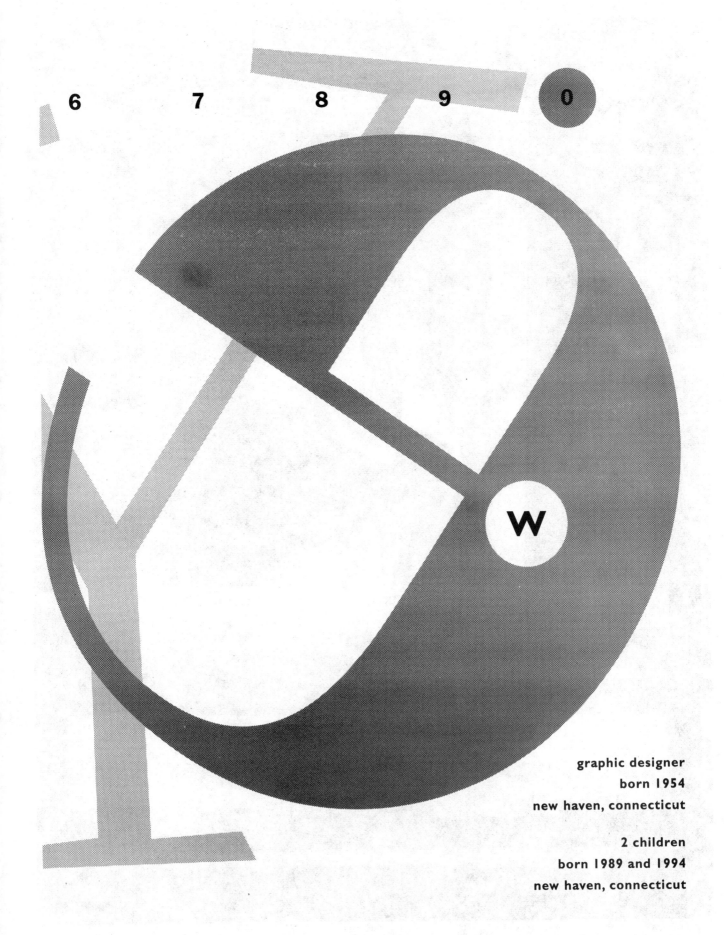

6 7 8 9 0

w

graphic designer
born 1954
new haven, connecticut

2 children
born 1989 and 1994
new haven, connecticut

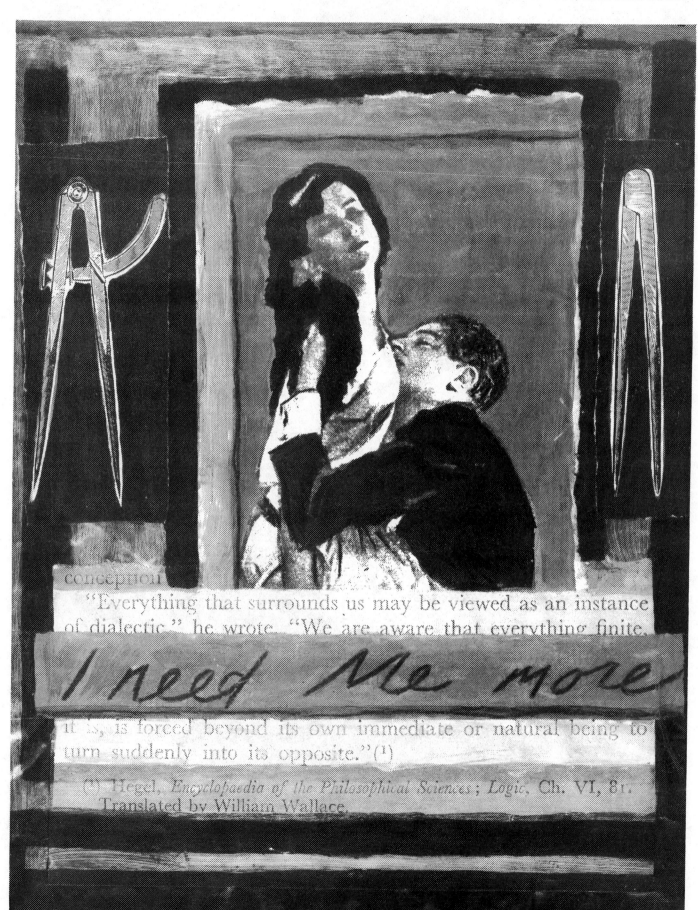

conception

"Everything that surrounds us may be viewed as an instance of dialectic," he wrote. "We are aware that everything finite,

*I need Me more*

it is, is forced beyond its own immediate or natural being to turn suddenly into its opposite."(1)

(1) Hegel, *Encyclopaedia of the Philosophical Sciences; Logic*, Ch. VI, 81. Translated by William Wallace.

MJ CONNORS, BROOKLYN, NY, USA

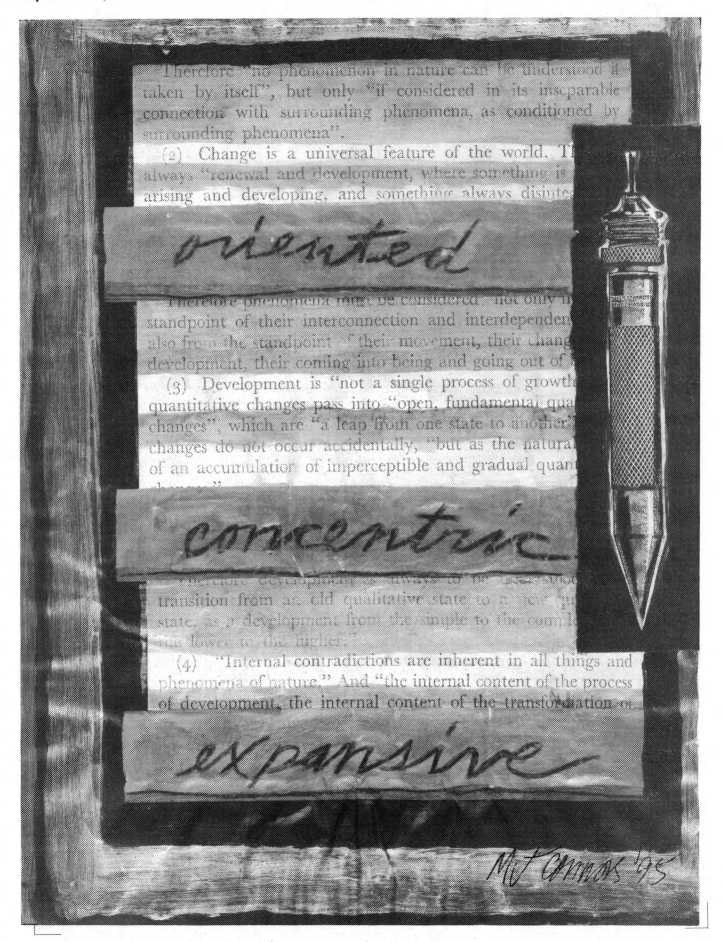

**KATALIN KOTVICS**, NEW YORK, NY, USA

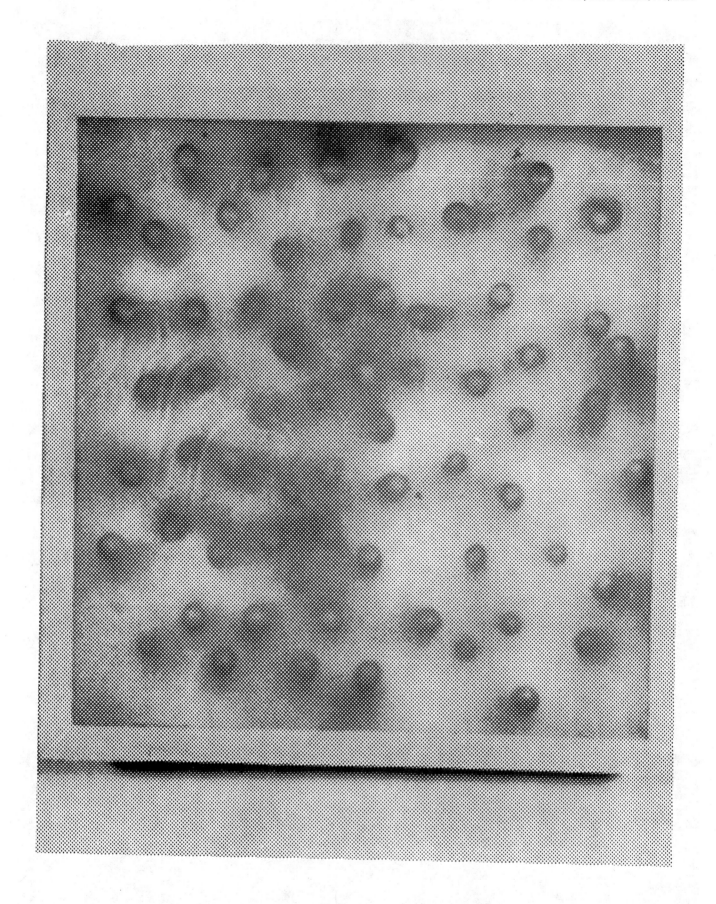

**PATRICIA SULLIVAN,** NEW YORK, NY, USA

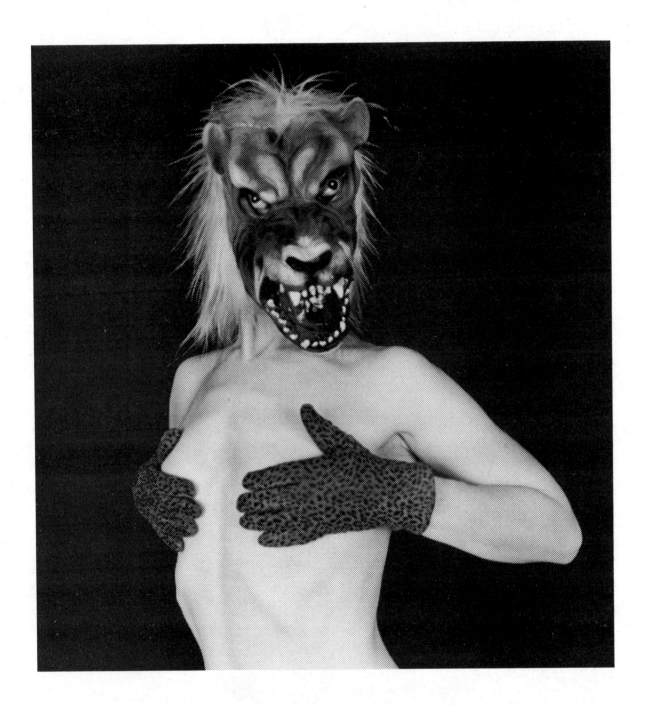

*Ode to Nature*

*P. Sullivan '95*

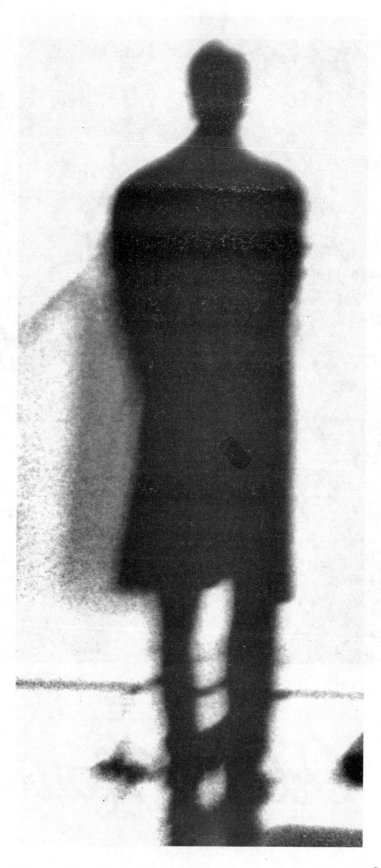

*"The man of the airport"* - Photograph black and white. Ana Fernández. ESPAÑA

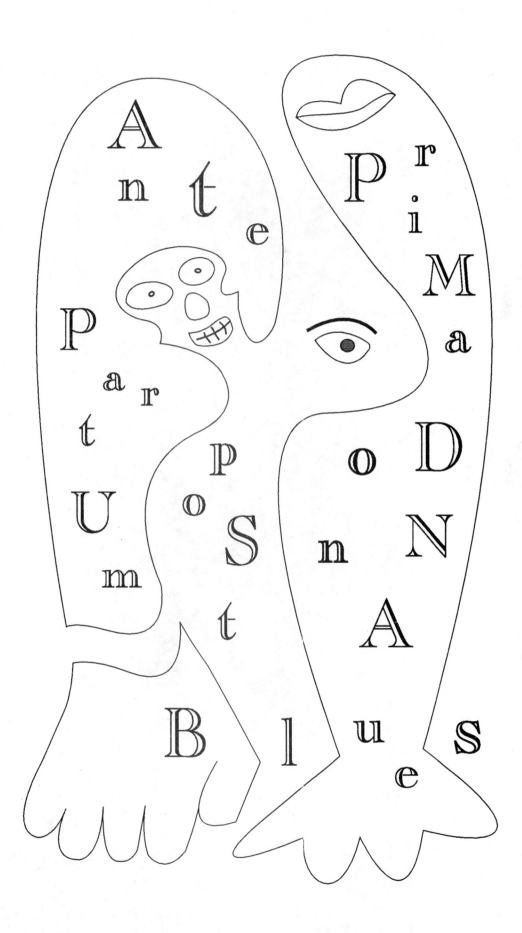

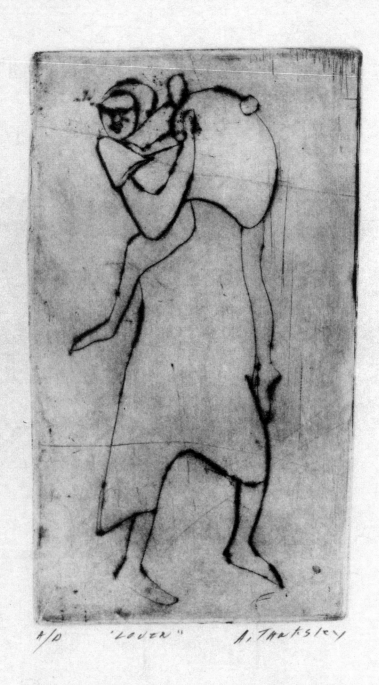

A/D      "LOVER"      A. Tanksley

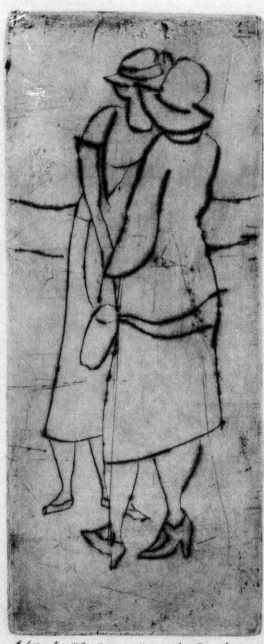

**TRACY ZUNGOLA**, NEW YORK, NY, USA

# Tit Steaks

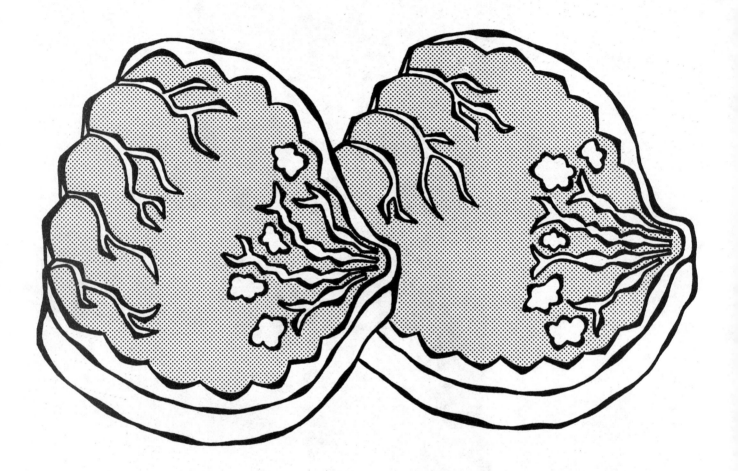

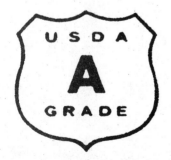

USDA
**A**
GRADE

**LEAN & MEATY**
**$2.29** lb.

©1994 TRACY ZUNGOLA

MICHELLE HANDELMAN, SAN FRANCISCO, CA, USA

# SEXBITCHGODDESS

```
O V E I NO U O   R D A   A R L O
L O N T GR N R E O U   M O E L
O L O E E N T R A R G   N TA D
U N     SA     O S     H E     I Z
T       TD     R Y     T Y     D T
I       O      T E     C
O              R
N
```

C. 1995  MICHELLE HANDELMAN

**VICTORIA VESNA**, SANTA BARBARA, CA, USA

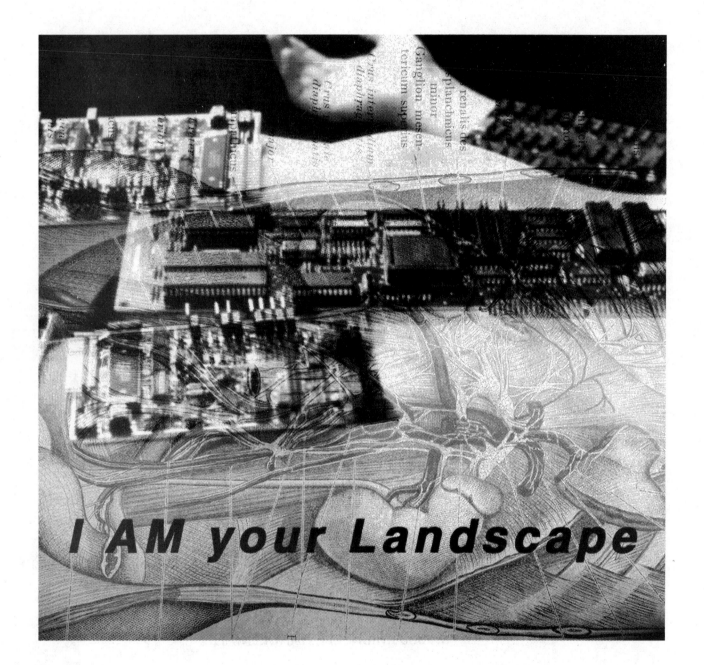

ERIKA ROTHENBERG, LOS ANGELES, CA, USA

Once a year, everyone in our

neighborhood has sex

with everyone else.

Then we return to our spouses.

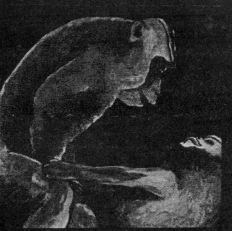

CALLICEBUS MONKEY

She crawls inside my body

and we have sex lots of times

and then she crawls out.

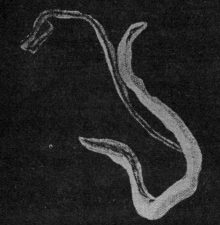

FLUKE

I like to kiss males

and they like to kiss each other,

but I'd never kiss

another female.

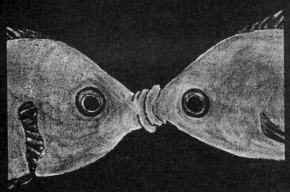

GOURAMI

MI CUERPO NO

SE MUEVE

SE RAMIFICA

FORMA PARTE

DE TODO.

QUIZAS.. MI

SUEÑO

NO SEA

EL TUYO

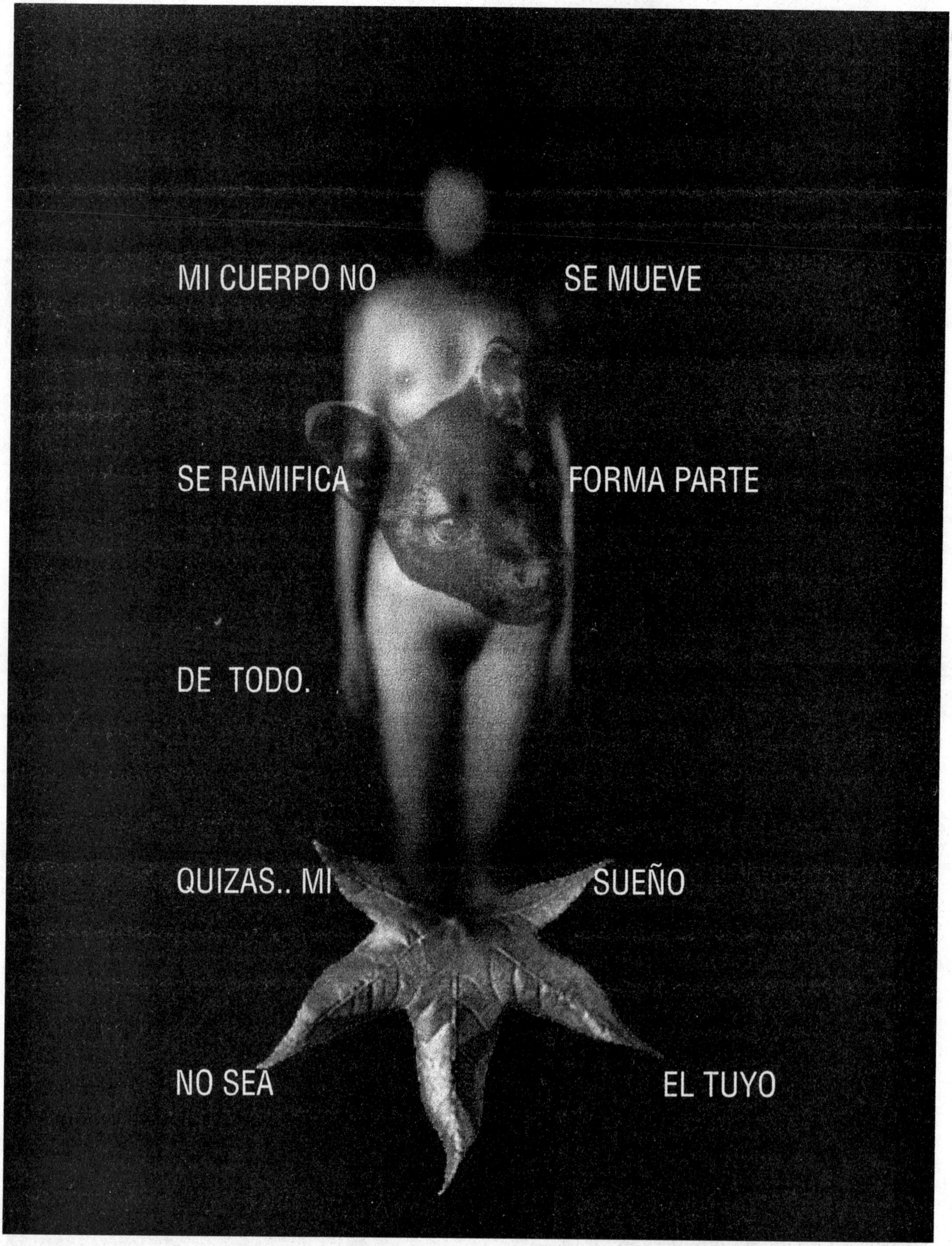

Sofía Fernández Sigler, GRANADA, SPAIN

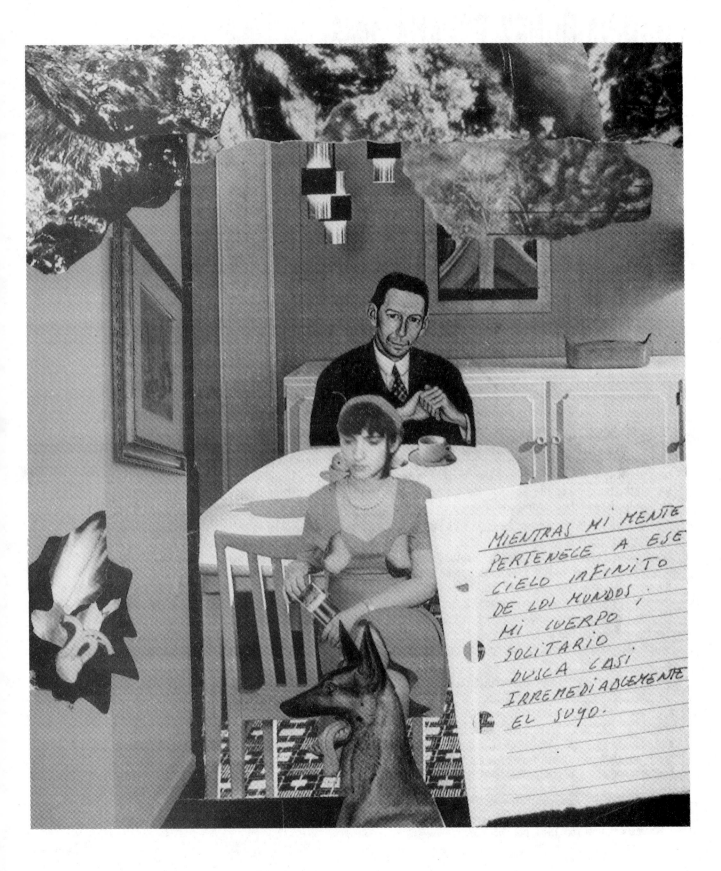

# MARINA NUÑEZ. ESPAÑA, 1966

According to the myth, it was Atenea, jealous of the beauty and romances of Medusa, who changed her hair into snakes and ordered that her glance would petrify any man who dared to look at her. However, the Medusa's story is not one of rivalry between women, but rather one of masculine obsessions.

The other possible narration (myth?) is rather amusing: men, scared to death because of the possibility of the absence or the loss of the penis —their poor mother hasn't any, so their own one is in danger— react trying to forget this traumatic menace. Female's body frightens men by her lack, by her otherness. To reconstruct the imaginary and lost phallic mother who guaranteed their own security, they create fetishes: substitutes of the maternal penis in which the little boy believed and wishes going on believing to avoid castration fear.

It's in these bewildered moments when that esquizofrenic alternation between men's dependence and repulsion from women appears. "Generated at this intersection of knowledges and still sliding meaning are twin images of what will later be linguistically fixed as woman (as difference). One is the compensatory fantasy of the pre-œdipal mother, still all-powerful, phallic; the other is the fantasy of woman not only as damaged, but as damage itself, castrated and the symbol of castration"[1] (*femme fatale*).

The Medusa's head is paradoxical: on one hand it's full up with those false, compensatory penises: the vipers/fetishes, which should mitigate the horror of the absence and remind the wholeness of the mother of childhood; but on the other hand, this overloading repletion, far from releasing, cancels the desired effect out, because, as Freud said, a multiplication of penis symbols means castration. Soothing fetishes hook around her, but so many, that they achieve the opposite target.

There is no doubt about the misogynist origin of the Medusa: it's a sign of patriarcal dread towards any difference, stereotype and reduction of femininity to the other (but a domesticated other) of reason. However, her existence, like that of so many other femme fatale, seems to spread into an uncontrolled and personal life of her own. It goes beyond the foreseen intentions, it ruins the narration which it was intended to contain it, in the end it reveals the fissures in the own narrative system: the insecurity in the source of the myth, the incapability to exorcise the threat, the revenge of a powerfull image that women glance stealthily to read their own translations.

Because the Medusa doesn't resign with enjoying the horror she provokes as the other, if this otherness continues being defined as pure reverse of masculine discourse (that is, as the same). Mystified as the monstruous feminine by an ideology captured in castration dogma, which is not her problem, she realizes it's time to live her own life, to escape from the rule of the Presence and Absence of the Phallus. "Wouldn't the worst be, isn't the worst, in truth, that women aren't castrated, that they have only to stop listening to the Sirens (for the Sirens were men) for history to change its meaning? You only have to look at the Medusa straight on to see her. And she's not deadly. She's beautiful and she's laughing. (...) If woman has always functioned 'whitin' the discourse of man, a signifier that has always referred back to the opposite signifier which annihilates its specific energy and diminishes or stifles its very different sounds, it is time for her to dislocate this..."[2]

When the Medusa understands that the signification system that defines her with the sign of the lack is not hers —she hasn't made it, she has not any place in it to signify anything distinct from not-masculine—, her revolt bursts. Perseus forces her to stare her image, and that is precisely what he should have prevented. Perhaps she was momentarily weakened, but finally, her understanding of herself is going to make her laugh. First because of so many Perseuses, trying to kill a sign created by them but that seems to debilitate their manliness. Afterwards, because she is going to have better things to do, and she is going to look another place, probably funnier.

---

[1] Griselda Pollock: "Vission and Difference", Routledge, London, 1989, p. 139.

[2] Hélène Cixous, "The Laugh of the Medusa", in E. Marks and I. de Courtivron (eds.): "New French Feminisms", Harvester Wheatsheaf, New York 1981, pp. 255, 257.

MARINA NUÑEZ, MADRID, SPAIN

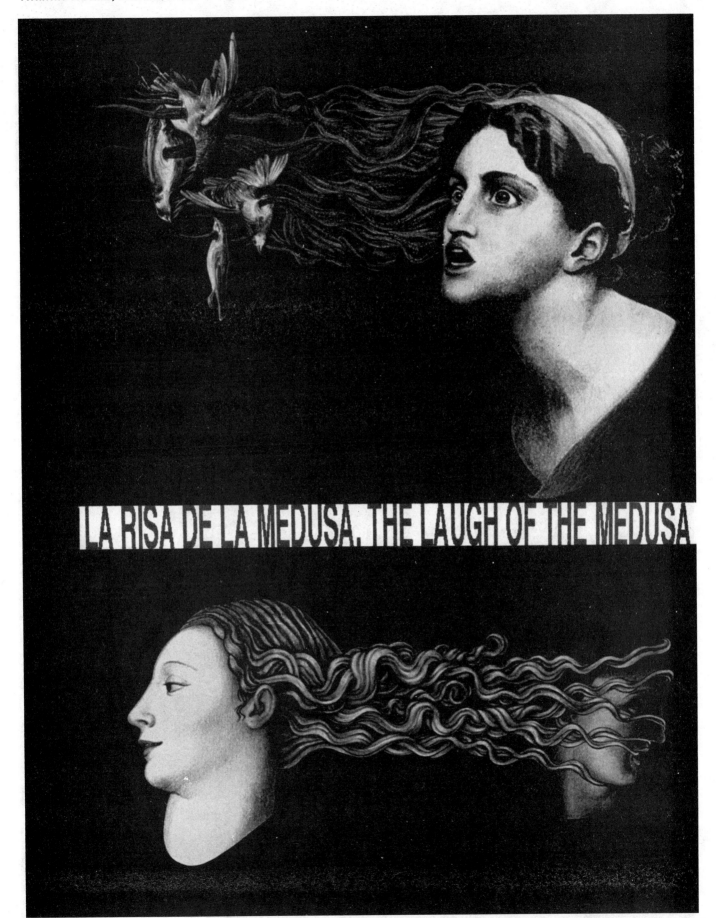

LA RISA DE LA MEDUSA. THE LAUGH OF THE MEDUSA

MARINA NUÑEZ, MADRID, SPAIN

BELÉN SÁNCHEZ ALBARRÁN, MADRID, SPAIN

"Available: a liberated girl in exchange for a monumental glass of Beefeater."

"When you told me that you were a swimming instructor, i thought we would swim a few laps and then you would take me out for a soft drink."

"She needs to feel loved. Giving her peace of mind is one way of letting her know."

"Her ugly sisters were determined to fit into the small glass slipper one way or another, in order to marry the prince, but their feet were enormous and ugly."

"Lateral protection system, automatic seatbelts, powerful back lights, ABS and airbag. The actress wears a silk dress by Moschino Couture, shoes by R. Clergerie, bracelet by Majorica and earrings by Del Pino."

"I grant you sweetness." "And i beauty." Thus spoke the fairies at Aurora´s birth.

"Mr. McKinney..." "Call me John, sweetheart." "I...need to find my husband." "If i were to tell you what i need! for the moment let´s start with a bit of ice and... some long John."

"Smoother and younger skin in 30 days."

**ELLEN LOUISE SMITH,** NEW YORK, NY, USA

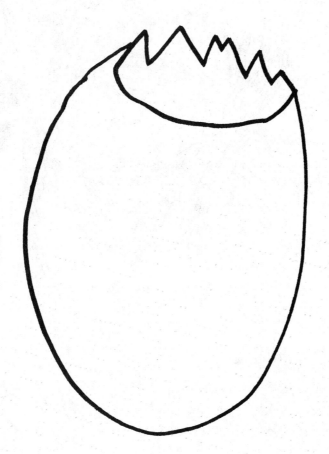

ELS

**MAY STEVENS**, NEW YORK, NY, USA

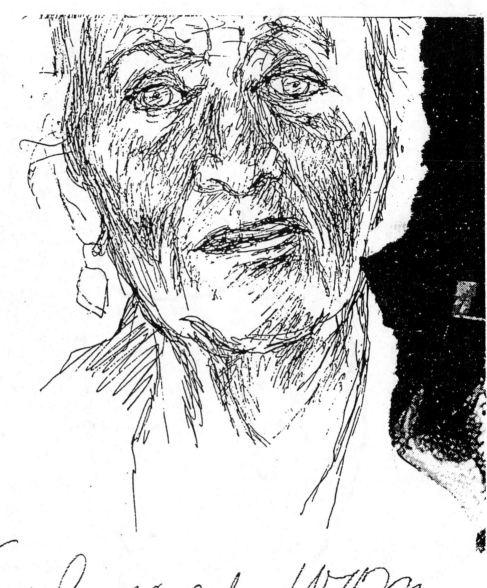

**MAY STEVENS**, NEW YORK, NY, USA

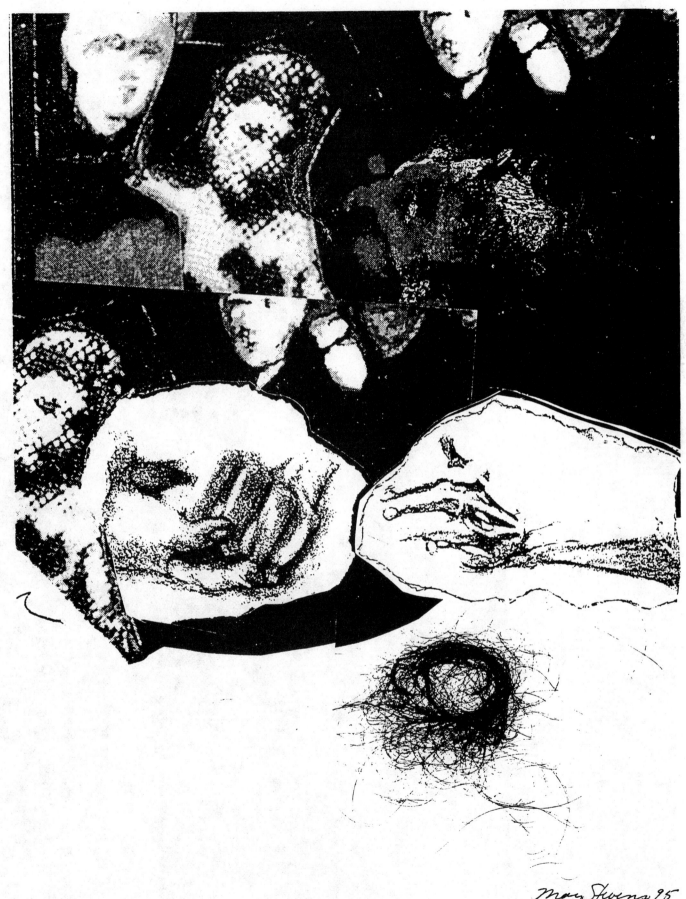

May Stevens 95

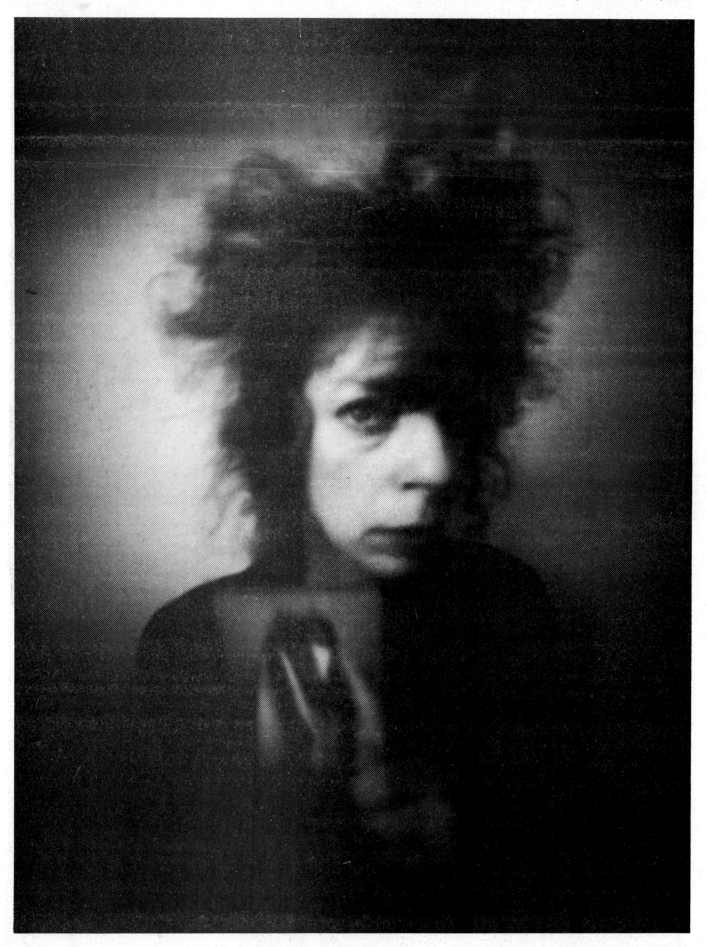

**BARBARA ESS,** NEW YORK, NY, USA

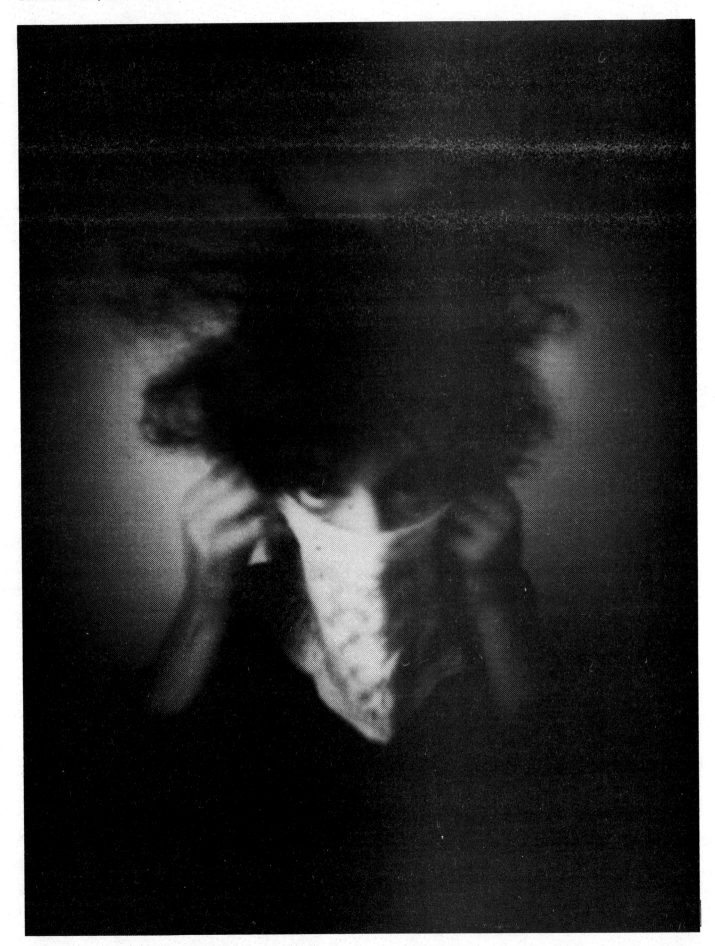

**MALIKA RA,** BASKING RIDGE, NJ, USA

M A L I K A   R A

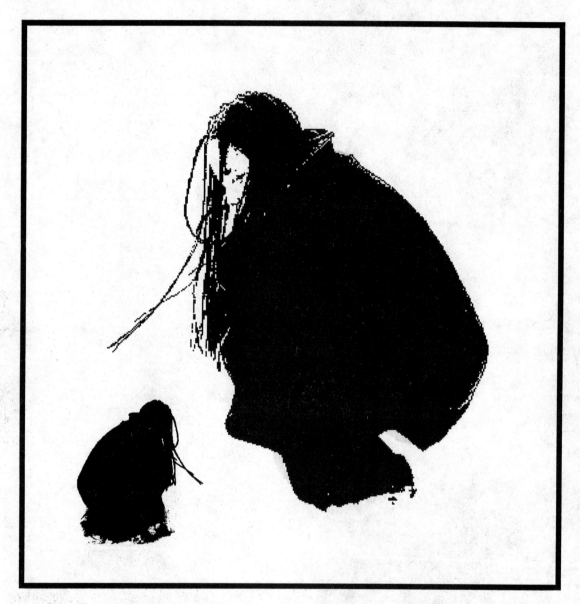

SISTERS IN THE SNOW

UNTIL THYSELF BELOVED

LET THE SUN TORCH THE SKY.

MALIKA RA, BASKING RIDGE, NJ, USA

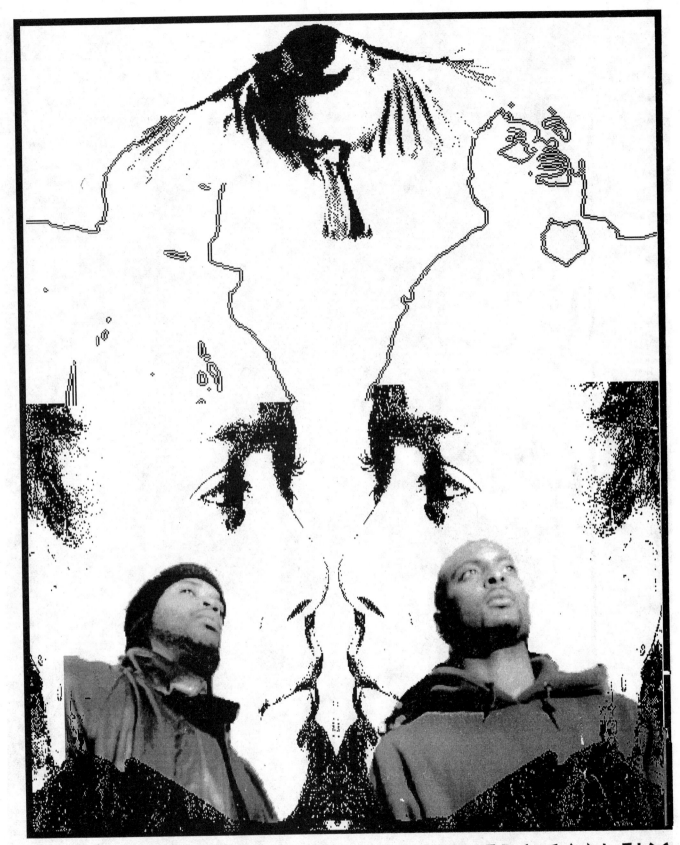

THE SISTERS AND THE BROTHERS CAN FLY

 PHOTOGRAPHICS BY MALIKA RA
908 •766•9177

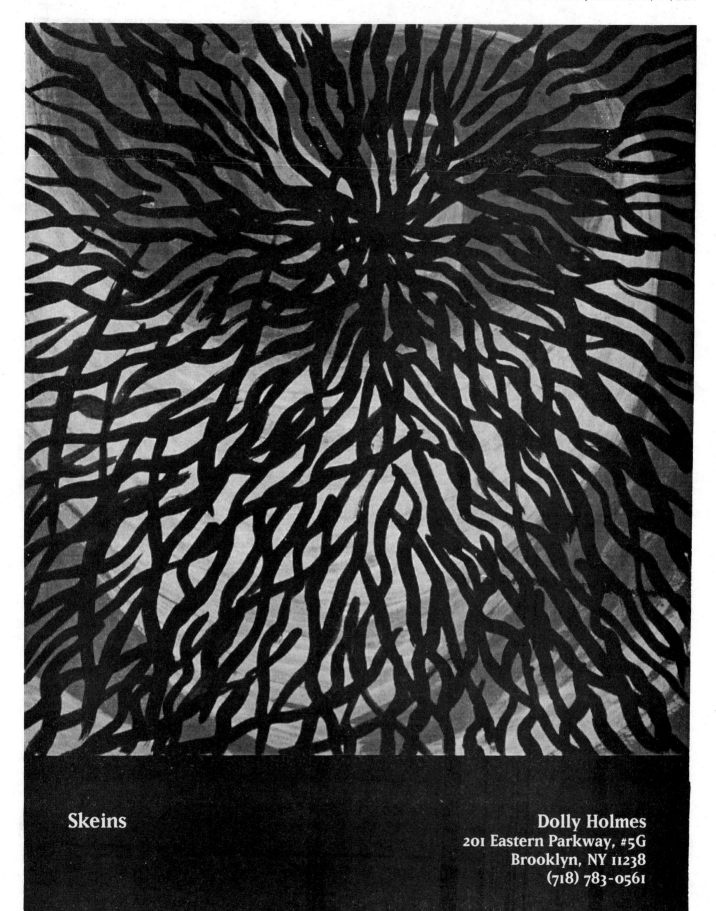

**Skeins**

**Dolly Holmes**
201 Eastern Parkway, #5G
Brooklyn, NY 11238
(718) 783-0561

DOLLY HOLMES, BROOKLYN, NY, USA

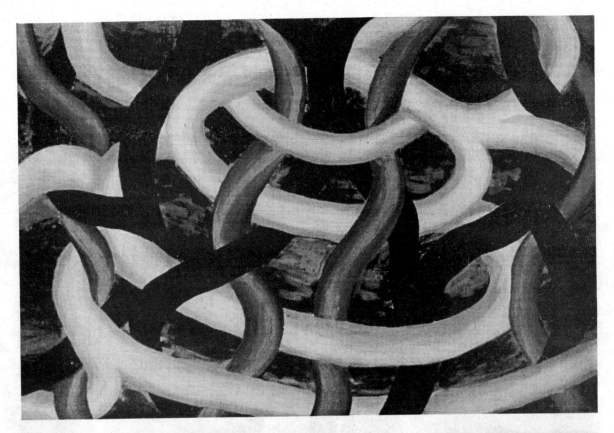

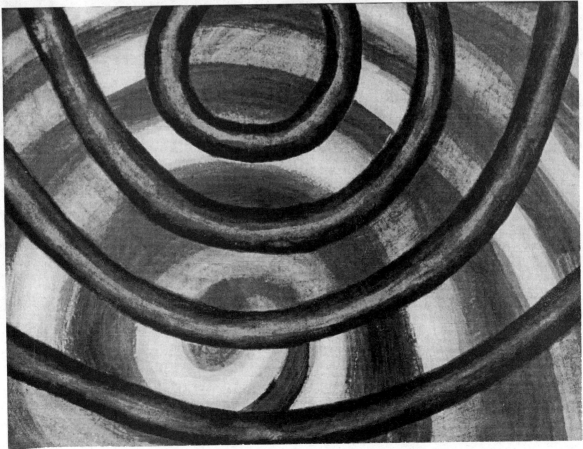

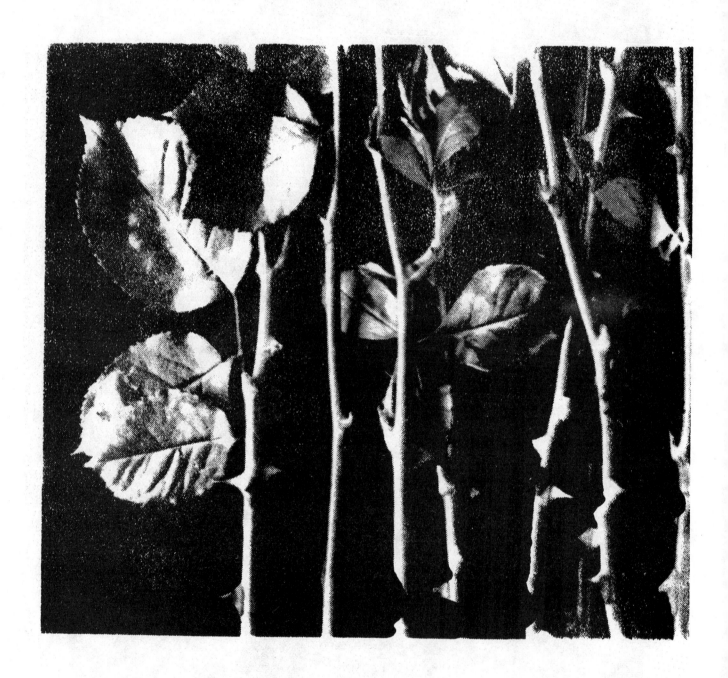

MARY WEATHERFORD, NEW YORK, NY, USA

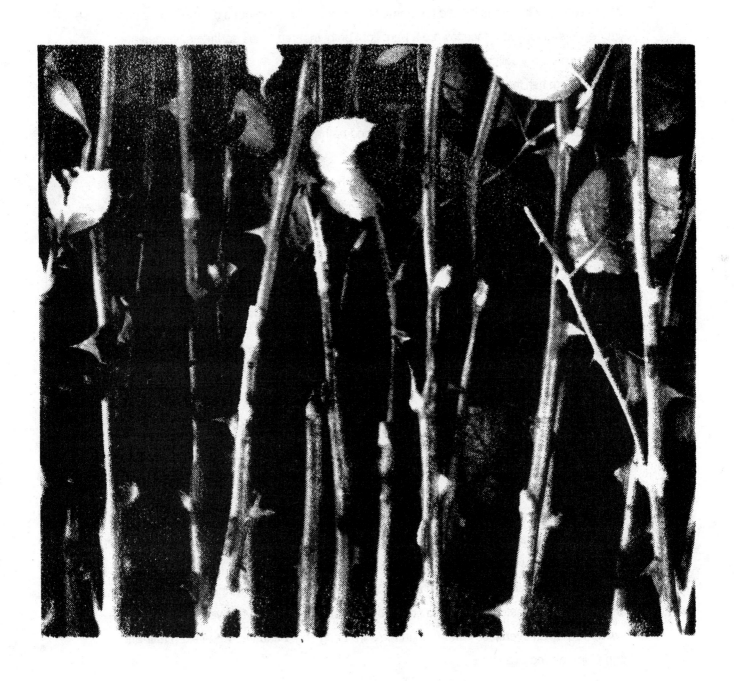

ANDREA CODRINGTON, NEW YORK, NY, USA

## Small Things Float

by Andrea Codrington

Would you think it strange if I said I remember swimming in my mother's belly 30 years ago? Close your eyes and turn your face toward a bare light bulb: that red-black darkness, veined and throbbing, was my daily view.

More fish than female, I passed the sticky fluid through my gills, wiggled my tail. My mother might have looked at my father. She might have said, "I felt it, Jerry. I felt it." Or maybe she bent silently over the brutal porcelain rim in a cramped bathroom.

Happy, I was.

Is it any wonder that months later, under the cold metallic light of some hospital delivery room, I refused to come out for a good two days? That once out, all blood and curd, I cried myself to sleep in a nurse's arms? My mother—slim-hipped, ill-fated—died soon thereafter.

Shed a tear and open your mouth: it tasted just like that.

As a child I lived on a canal that led to the ocean, learned to crawl on my grandfather's tar-treated pine dock. One day, knowing that small things float, he tossed me into the water with a careful arcing gesture of his arm. I was three, and felt no fear—just a faint sting on my bottom as my body entered the water and bobbed like a Halloween apple.

Alone, I watched barnacles open their flinty armor and taste the brine with vermillion tongues. But at low tide they hung in mid-air off the dock's wooden pylons, pimpled and lifeless until the warm wash of evening came.

It wasn't until I was seven that I recalled my own warm, moist tenancy. I had been sick with a sore throat when my grandmother, looking down my gorge with a black rubber flashlight, announced that I was to gargle. Sitting on her kitchen counter, laving my swollen tonsils with warm salt water, I suddenly remembered bumping against those soft, sanguine walls—surrounded, as I had been, with the hushed train-chug rhythm of my mother's pulse.

I had seen pictures of her in a small box hidden in my grandmother's underwear drawer, amidst frayed polyester panties and stiff-cupped brassieres. She, a few years older than me, swallowed by an oversized inner tube in the surf. Laughing, beautiful, with flaxen hair and pumpkin-colored eyes.

I visited my father on occasion, boarded buses that drove me away from my life of blue into the glaring Western sun. I came to know that dusty parking lot where he would meet me with a car full of bug-eyed children and his wife sitting stiffly in the front seat.

ANDREA CODRINGTON, NEW YORK, NY, USA

She would look at me in the rear-view window, appraise her husband's past in my squinting face.

What did she see? I would like to have known, for I knew nothing of it. Did time stop for him after my mother died, after her parents took me from him? My father—a green beetle trapped mid-crawl in resin—lived in the perpetual present.

He laughed a lot, my father did, tried to get me to laugh along with him and his stupid progeny, who sat in front of a wood-grain TV with slack mouths. But a drooping mustache made him look sad even as he threw his head into the air with a hearty, helpless yelp.

His house smelled like the chlorine, thick and stinging, that issued from his swimming pool in the backyard. His children, not knowing the first thing about water and its properties, disturbed the turquoise surface with their flailing white arms and legs, their noisy, strident games. I sat on the grass and watched their Kool Aid—stained mouths call and respond.

Brutes, they were.

Like dogs, they smelled my difference but mistook it for fear. Certain I couldn't swim, they chased me across that cramped back yard with wet, snapping towels, tied me up and threw me in. I sank slowly to the bottom like a leaf to the ground and stayed there motionless, feeling the water softly fill my ears. I heard them run screaming into the house. My father jumped in the pool, jeans plastered to his ham-hock legs, and winched me up and out to the summer-scorched grass. I opened my eyes one minute later—the time was right—and looked up at his mustache, hanging like two inverted horns into my face.

How long can *you* hold your breath?

It's evening and I wake up. Submerged in a fading dream, I hear myself crying and know enough to be quiet. Around me, three stepsisters sleep like baby tigers.

I move outside and down the stairs. My father's gray, straggly schnauzer eyes me, cocks an ear.

Outside it is hot and black—that landlocked atmosphere that makes summer skies over Kansas turn the color of bile. I slide into the pool and the water makes my skin glow moon-rock white.

I swim along the bottom of the pool with my eyes open, my snub nose lightly scraping the painted cement. My lungs grow tight and I cry. I cry and my tears are clear as any seaside day. They fill my mouth—welcome salt.

Lie quietly in a bathtub: don't you know that with every breath you are floating and sinking?

**KERSTIN KARTSCHER**, HAMBURG, GERMANY

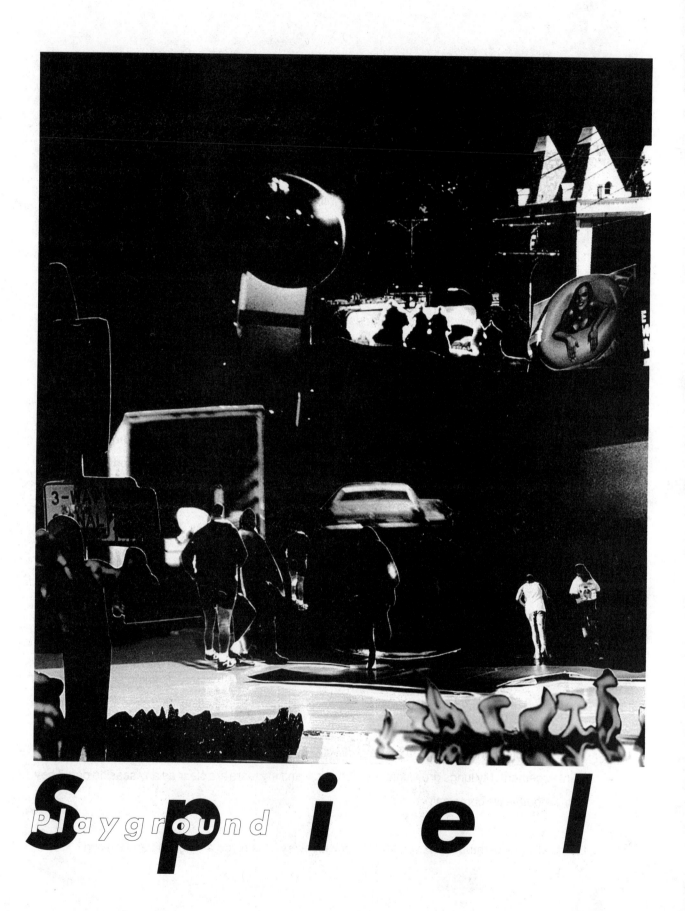

KERSTIN KARTSCHER, HAMBURG, GERMANY

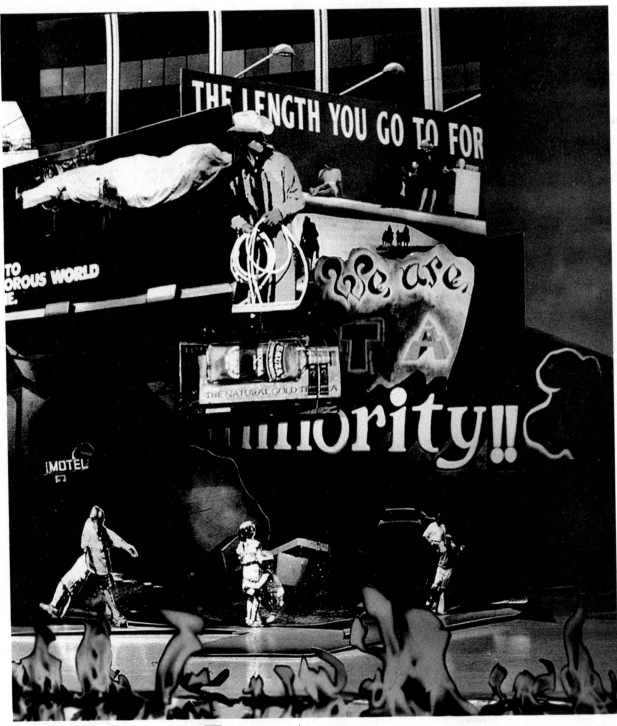

platz

**VERA KRIVOSHEIN**, ASTORIA, NY, USA

WATER SHALL DISSOLVE THE DARKNESS OF INK AND THE LETTERS INSCRIBED SHALL VANISH BUT THE UNWRITTEN WORD THAT THE HEART KNOWETH THIS ALONE SHALL NO MAN DESTROY

Calligraphy by Vera Krivoshein

**ADRIANA MUÑOZ,** S MIGUEL DE ALLENDE, MEXICO

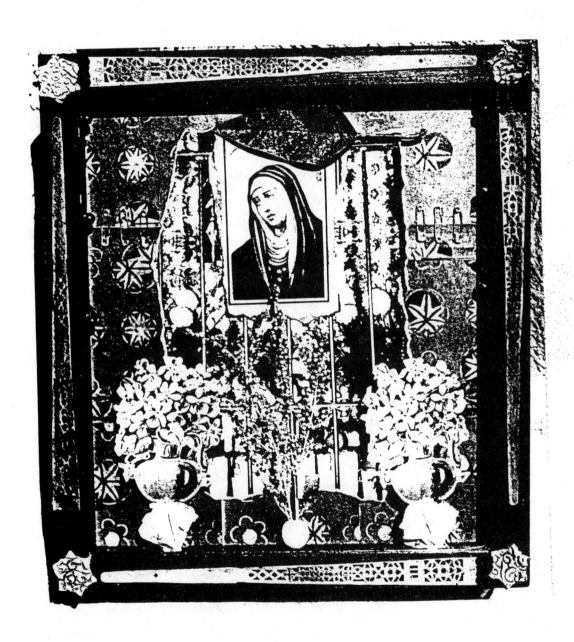

LOUISE LANDES-LEVI, BARRYTOWN, NY, USA

TENTATIVE/

Alienation, 'HUNG', the

Power of suggestion/ suggested, to the

Chinese, FREE TIBET, there has been enough genocide

on

GAIA, 'The Hotel Gaia', Bagnore,

the lower E. side of the

world, of the D.C.

world,

The lamas meant no harm, the monks were not animals, the women were

not, yet, ghosts,

When the rabbi asked if I

followed Jewish law I said I obey the 10

commandments, & silenced him. A. was not a Buddha, I

was not Mira-B., but this was not a reason to cre-

mate us, before our time,

Kham was a nice place. Tibet

did not want to be a nuclear depository.

Avilokiteshwara hurt no one. Tara shed a tear for us. I

shed a tear for you, "Il mio papa non voleva morire di fame"/ My

hunger for you alone was appeased. Farlo per il tuo

papa. & when realized how wld. it look, wiping

away the temple dust, suddenly, a goddess

playing a violin,

We wouldn't let 'Venezia' sink.

Natascha Kassner, BERLIN, GERMANY

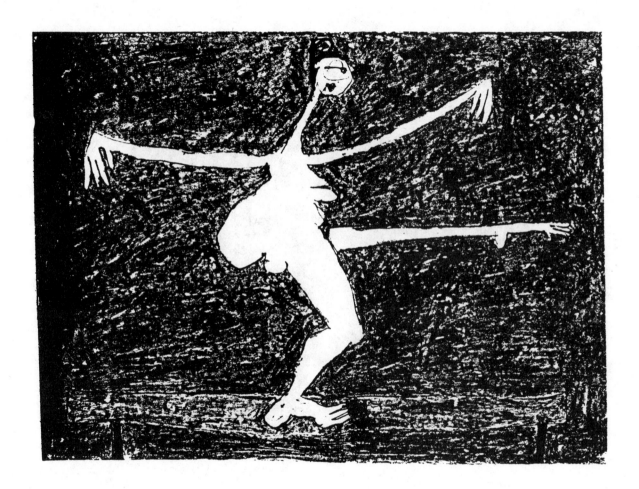

MÁRTA JACOBOVITS, ORADEA, ROMANIA

—Coordinates to find out a starting-
-point in the sky.  ⸺⸺⸺

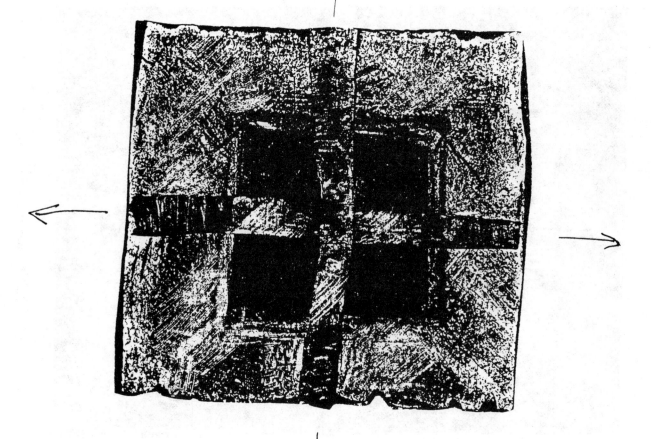

JAKOBOVITS MÁRTA —3700 ORADEA.
                    Str. Brasovului. Nr. 39.
                    ROMÁNIA.

„Coordinates to stretch reality" -paperwork

**MARIE LEGROS,** PARIS, FRANCE

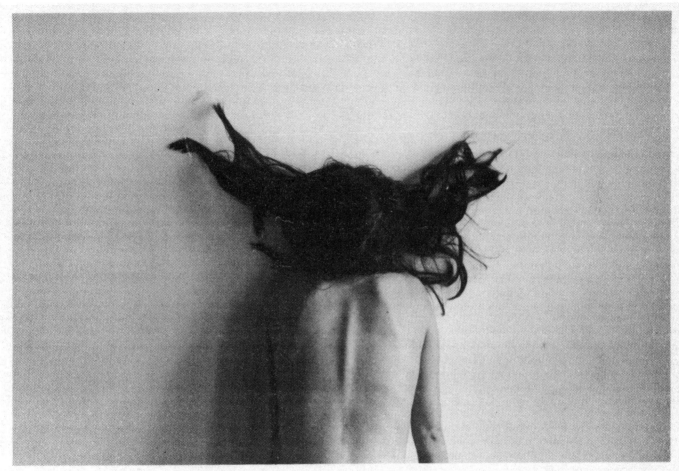

"STUCK" © MARIE LEGROS 1992.

A space between the desire to say and the act of pronouncing.
The impossibility to control our lives with words.
Our experience of the outside world is fragmented.
It is more an imperceptible rupture  than a meaningfull cut.
 - I use stutter in my artistic work like painters  were using pointillisme.
 -This parodic moment is a farcial view which could be a meditating force,
that acts upon gestures and emotions,coating them with the gloss of absurdity.

SARAH BLAKE, NEW YORK, NY, USA

The Dumb Language of Things


Moored to his shirts in my mother's closet,
my father can't sail away,
though fifteen years gone
and her new husband's suits side by side.

All the dead things my mother belongs to.
Demure, her debutante dresses sleep
beneath her children's beds, smudged kisses
from the fifties folded, boxed, and safe.
Snowboots in the attic, linen
from her "first successful party" packed
behind the sofa with the clippings,
read once and then marked:
send to Sarah, or Whitney, or Elinor.

And her mother before her
who never repainted the house
after her husband died, so
long strips of color
from the late-nineteenforties
swung free above the rounded staircase
and our feet clattering up
shook loose the old paper
snowing down in feathery scraps.
Beneath the stairs
her parents' love letters
lay cozy in their boxes, labelled
Correspondence: 1890, 1880, 1910.

As if to say:
women must carry the dead
set up houses with the past in tow.
This way we can save our own lives.

This leaves
no room
in the house
for the living.

But how can I throw their bundles away?
I understand the impulse to things.

SARAH BLAKE, NEW YORK, NY, USA

There was a woman
we thought crazy in college,
who tore at the wooden window-seat
with her fingers and a dining-hall spoon
to get at the hollow beneath the bench
and find what she thought
she had buried there.
Now I think,
who can call her mad?
She just came early
to the search for the things
that will call her by her name.

I patch pieces of memory to stuff
from a life, lived and now broken:
wedding ring, handwriting, letters
from a man I called husband.
Perhaps these can tell...

Who will bury me?

No dead to hold me here,
no house I might speak to
saying, *Listen, listen,*
*I am dying*

*and what was I?*

Hair ribbon. Hair-ribbon. Ring.

Sarah Blake

ANN KOSHEL VAN BUREN, NEW YORK, NY, USA

# *Suicide Threat Ends Peacefully At Penn Station*

A woman who said she was distraught over the breakup of her marriage held the police at bay for more than three hours last night with a pistol pointed at her temple in a concourse at Pennsylvania Station, the police said.

The incident caused a good deal of confusion in the station, but only

only one train, the Lake Shore Limited, bound for Albany and Chicago, was delayed, by 20 minutes.

ANN KOSHEL VAN BUREN, NEW YORK, NY, USA

## Composite Figure

You expected a half a million dollars from his estate
but he left it to your stepmother instead.

Your wife left you with your three kids
but then she came back.

After working at the same job for 15 years
they fired you, drunk.

The kids wouldn't speak to you because you
didn't stop drinking.

Your son became addicted to drugs.
Your daughter became addicted to drugs.
Your other son became addicted to drugs.

There was a small earthquake.
The hole in the ozone got bigger.

Your commute was too long.
You got stuck in traffic.
Your train was delayed.
Your daughter was sick.
Your son was demanding.
Your wife wouldn't sleep with you.

You could have gone to a Carribean Island
but you didn't.
You lived in Westchester instead.
You commuted everyday.
You lost hair.

The job you moved back to do was cut
in the latest incision of budgeting
and it seemed that simultaneously
a doctor removed your wife's womb.

Your daughter loved you but
you were woking too hard to say you really knew her.
Your son hated you and said so.
The youngest said nothing and
you were grateful for that.

Your wife died
not of the suicide she always threatened
but of something else.

This has become
a family tradition.

                                        Ann Koshel van Buren

**JANE DICKSON**, NEW YORK, NY, USA

SUDDEN INSPIRATIONS

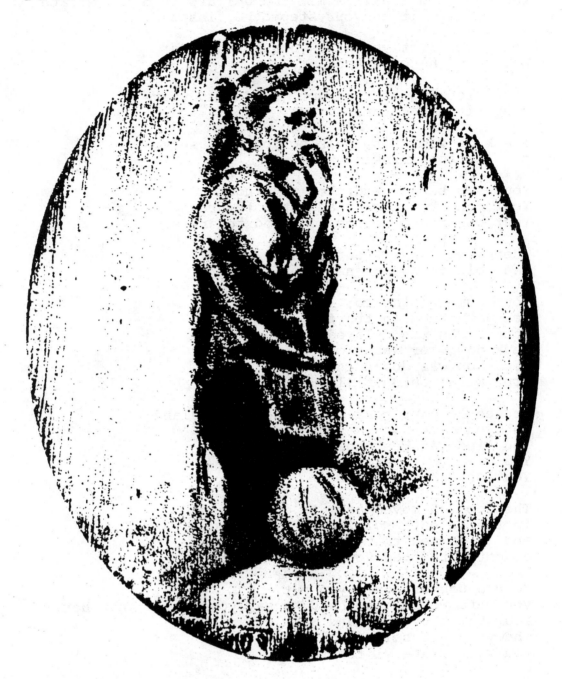

I know everything is perfect but still.

I worry.

**LINDA YABLONSKY,** NEW YORK, NY, USA

Jane Dickson, Image

Linda Yablonsky, Text

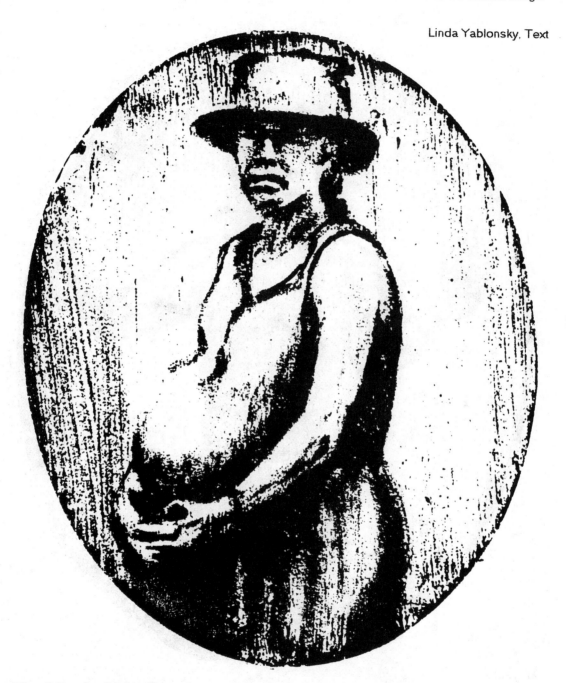

## The Sting by Sister Tsouris

"What's it all about?" said the baby to the bee. "Life is sex and laughter," the bee replied, "and beside these, sorrow takes its place and waits to be served."

**LINDA YABLONSKY,** NEW YORK, NY, USA

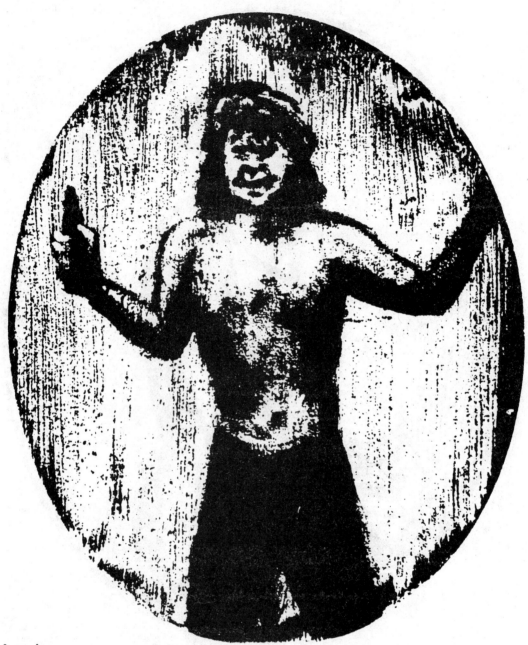

## Angel

His mother called him "My Angel" when he was a boy and let him do whatever he wanted. Later he had a girlfriend. Her name actually was Angel. He called her "Mommy." At first she liked it and let him do anything he wanted. Then she changed her mind. She left him. He didn't understand. He suffered and ran amok, drinking and picking fights and gambling, and always losing his shirt. Now people called him a loser and the minute he heard the name, he lost everything. He lost his house. He lost his job. He lost his mind. He hated this. He knew something was wrong, but he didn't know what. He felt perfectly justified in everything he did and could find no one to tell him different. *A man with nothing to lose still has something to say,* he thought. When last seen he was directing traffic at the crossroads of the world.

**JANE DICKSON** NEW YORK, NY, USA

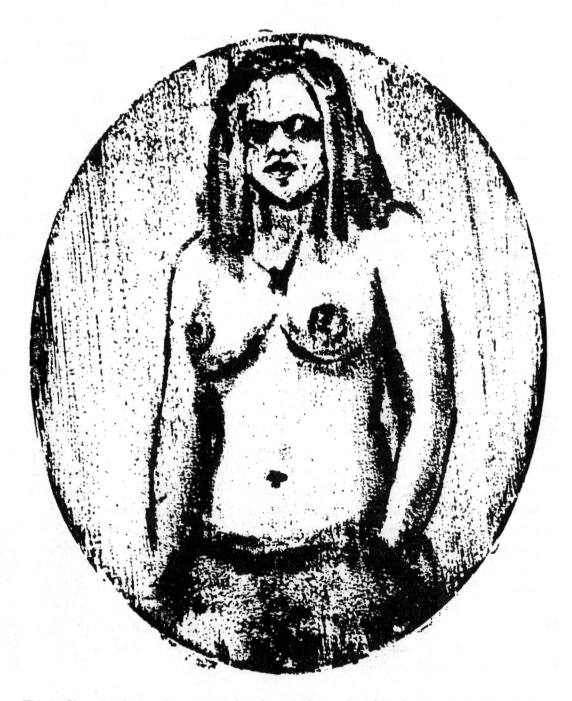

This is Sister Lookame, the patron saint of narcissism, a late 20th Century virgin. "Look a' me, look a' me!" she shouts from every rooftop and street corner. "Look a' me!" They say if you look you'll be struck by lightning. I was feeling bored one day and I looked. She didn't notice and nothing happened but that night I slept on top of the world. I wasn't pretty and I wasn't smart but brother, was I proud! What a bitch I was. So what? Should madmen rule alone?

LAURA SOROKOFF, NEW YORK, NY, USA

### Today...

I'm in a good mood. That's why I can think so articulately. I wish I could always think this way. I wonder if I've ever been schizophrenic. It's this sort of lack of contact with people. When I was younger (I don't quite remember if it was middle or high school), I used to curl up in the corner of my canopy bed with a book. I used to read under the covers so that if anyone came in they thought I was sleeping and I wouldn't have to confront them. But Dad used to come in and shut off the light because he thought I'd left it on. Somewhere along the way he figured out that I always slept with a book, not a teddy bear. He would tell me I was hurting my eyes by reading in the dark, but I didn't care. Dad usually wanted me to read history books instead of what I'd pick, so while I knew he liked that I read, I thought he found my reading inconsequential compared to what I should have been reading. I remember he found me reading this book *The Virgin Suicides* in high school and called it crap. That book won some award in the New York Times, so I left the section out for him to see on the kitchen table. I used to do subtle things like that because I didn't know how to bring things up again once they'd past. I thought he'd think I was smart; maybe I wanted to be a more modern thinker than him. I know that all those little hints I'd leave to prove that I was an intellectual (I always thought intellectuals would be subtle with their gifts) were probably never noticed.

### One day later...

 Turbulence in my body. Turmoil between something sweet and something inevitably fatal. When? I can hardly wait any longer, but I must allow it to do it on it's own. I can't control it anymore. Energy is abundant, but positive energy so scarce, smiles so rebellious, laughing so sarcastic. Being is not being anymore. Existence is killing me. Worthwhileness is a hypocrisy. I am so sane right now that even the most sane and rational people wouldn't understand my sanity. I feel relaxed and I know that things will happen on their own. I haven't felt this good in so long. I feel orgasmic, and gosh, I haven't felt orgasmic in months. Anyone would think I'm nuts because my sanity is beyond their sanity. My being is in a separate place, but it is so sophisticated and sitting here I feel smart. I don't feel like talking to anyone or watching the hockey game or doing my homework or eating or smoking or anything. I am alive! I am so alive that I am ready to nonexist. I do sort of nonexist, because the girl that was living inside me crawled out (I hope she's ok). My plain beauty, my easy smile, my soft brown hair, my giggle, giggle, giggle, my subtle nature...they have all crawled out and what is left is so true. I have more integrity than I have ever had. I am here being and I am liking it. I am ugly to someone who is peeking, I'm sure, but leave me alone and hide the mirrors because I am so beautiful! Don't let anyone see me, because the peaches and cream have spoiled rotten so I dropped them in the dumpster.

JUDE TALLICHET, BROOKLYN, NY

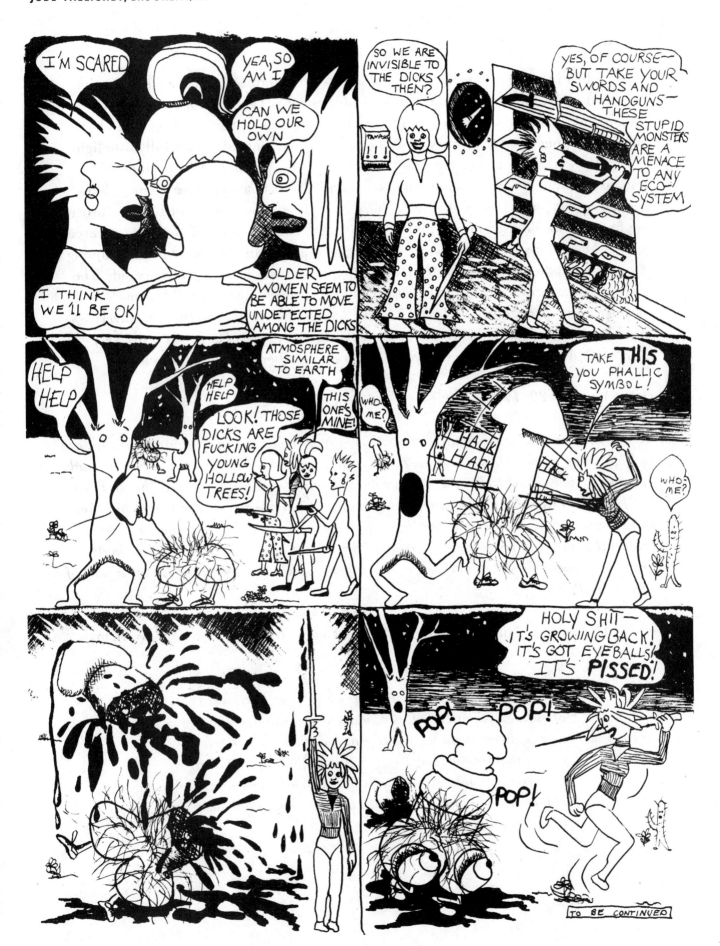

When I am behind the camera or with my photographs, I am in a state of calm. This is an irony, for my art would hardly be described as calm. It makes a sound - blatant and timeless. The calm creates a darkness which I recognize, observe, and embrace, hoping that the journey of shadows will bring me and my art fully into light.

My work is of its own mortality. It describes the life and decomposition of humans, inanimate objects, environments, and itself. Primarily, I create "narratives" - singular or combined images that tell a story. Yet there is no story to be found. Instead, one finds worlds desiring to tell; they want the viewer to ask, but still they do not reveal.

Most of my work intertwines with dreams. For example, I have been dreaming of rooms and other spaces, usually made of dirt, since I was at least ten years old. The influence these dreams have had has led me to create three-dimensional "rooms". I consider these spaces inner worlds. They are worlds the eye and psyche can travel through yet with mysterious areas that are a struggle to reach. These pieces are very intimate and change illusion as the viewer changes his/her position of viewing.

### DREAM: July 29, 1989

*Once again, I was about to enter those inner rooms of Rhea's apartment that are so frightening to me. Only this time, Rhea's apartment was also my own. Rhea is dead now but some nurse was wheeling her around. I guess I should have said "hi" to Rhea but I was very anxious about entering the rooms. I have been in them before but they still remain vague. It's like a maze - very big and musty with lots of cobwebs. The rooms, though I can never remember them, are a part of me that is overwhelmingly familiar. I guess I am getting closer to these rooms if Rhea's apartment is now a part of mine as well.*

The words of Minor White create an ideal summary for in essence they are my words as well:

> *The moment of illumination of a monster in ourselves is oftentimes experienced as a moment of beauty. Out of intense excitement we photograph such moments. As if that action were not strange enough, another person, finding that such photographs mirror his inner conflict, is for a moment released from that tension! The power of the demon turns to light.*

M ARY R F ULLWOOD, LOS OSOS, CA, USA

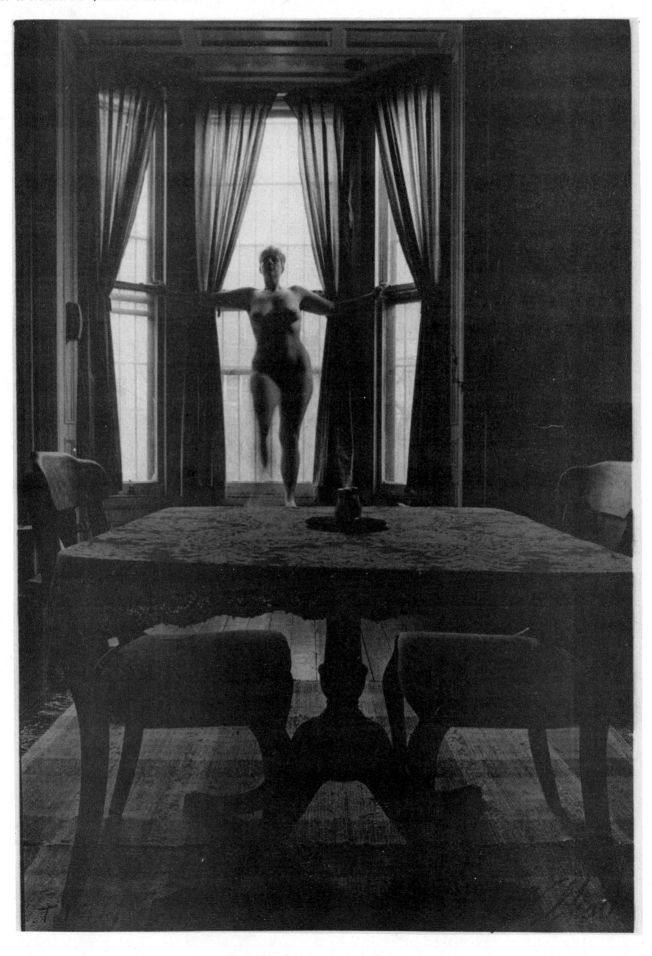

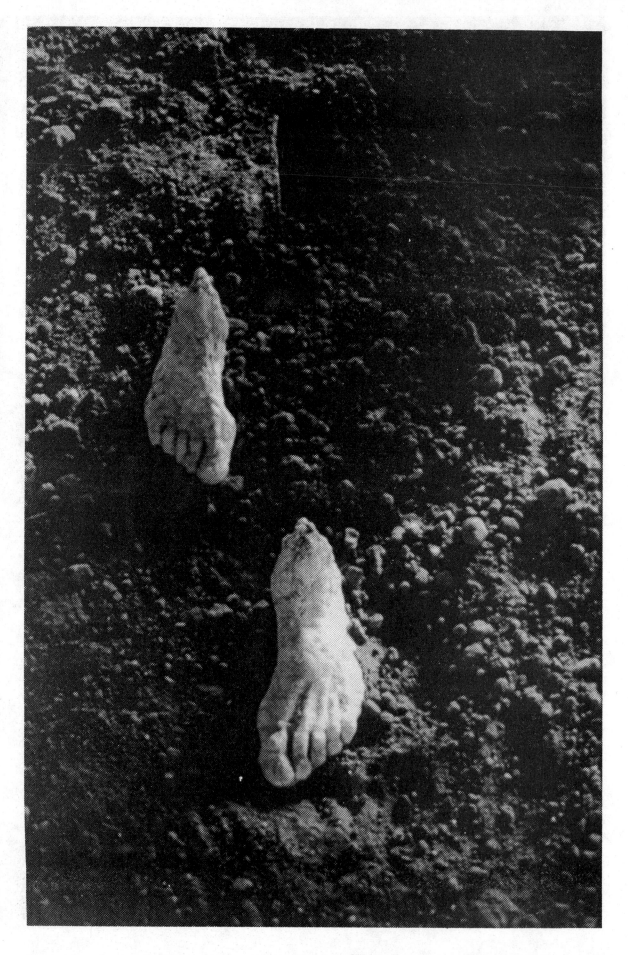

JACKIE BROOKNER, NEW YORK, NY, USA

# The New York Times

TUESDAY, MARCH 14, 1995

# Deadly Nuclear Waste Piles Up With No Clear Solution at Hand

## By WILLIAM J. BROAD

INCREASINGLY, the world is awash in plutonium, the deadly gold of the nuclear era, the man-made element that is produced in all nuclear reactors and prized for making atom bombs. And increasingly, no one knows what to do with it, as big nuclear arsenals become passé and as alternative plans for the perilously radioactive stuff lose their luster.

The simplest option is to bury it. But that is now under fire as scientists debate, and Federal agencies study, whether a proposed underground dump in Nevada might eventually blow up in a nuclear explosion fed by waste plutonium. For years the dump has been seen as a crucial solution to the plutonium problem, and its rejection would be an enormous blow to nuclear planning.

And globally, plans to burn plutonium in commercial nuclear reactors are floundering for political and economic reasons.

Scientists are proposing many new methods and machines meant to rid the world of surplus plutonium, including new reactors, annihilators and special ways to discard it. But costliness and political inertia have kept these schemes largely in limbo. Meanwhile, the glut of plutonium is growing, stirring fears that sooner or later some will fall into the hands of nuclear terrorists.

"Plutonium is the bottom-line danger because it's always atom-bomb material, even when it's declared for peaceful purpose

# Evolution Of Humans May at Last Be Faltering

**N**ATURAL evolutionary forces are losing much of their power to shape the human species, scientists say, and the realization is raising tantalizing questions about where humanity will go from here.

Is human evolution ending, ushering in a long maturity in which Homo sapiens persists pretty much unchanged? Or will humankind, armed with the tools of molecular biology, seize control of its own evolution?

# Modern Life Suppresses An Ancient Body Rhythm

As it turns out, human biological clocks do change but only in about half of all people — the half who are women. In men, however, the songs of the seasons apparently hit a deaf ear. The contemporary industrialized world, which blazes with artificial illumination, has suppressed men's ability to react to changes in day length.

In production of the hormone melatonin, women were found to respond to the song of seasons but men were tone deaf.

INGRID JEJINA, AMSTERDAM, THE NETHERLANDS

SUPERHEROES        DON'T

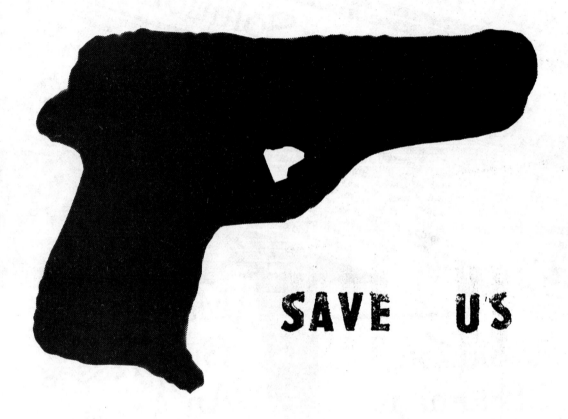

SAVE    US

ANY   MORE

Ingrid Jejina, AMSTERDAM, THE NETHERLANDS

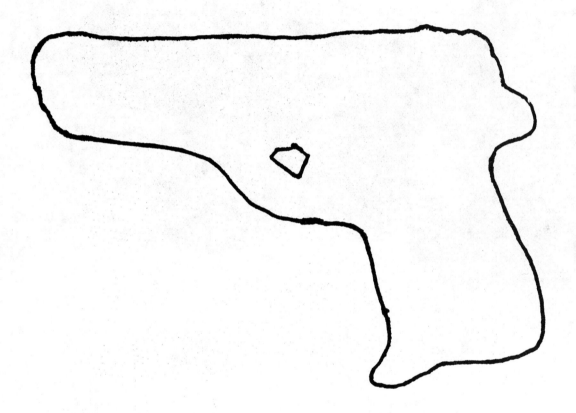

CAN WE ALLOW OURSELVES TO GIVE A PRECISE ANSWER TO THE
FACT  SUR - VIVA - L ? CONSIDERING THE DICTIONARY THERE
IS MORE THAN ONE MEANING - WE WILL GET A DOZEN OF DIFFERENT
ANSWERS DEPENDING ON   WHERE   WE ARE IN THIS WORLD.

JUDITE DOS SANTOS, NEW YORK, NY, USA

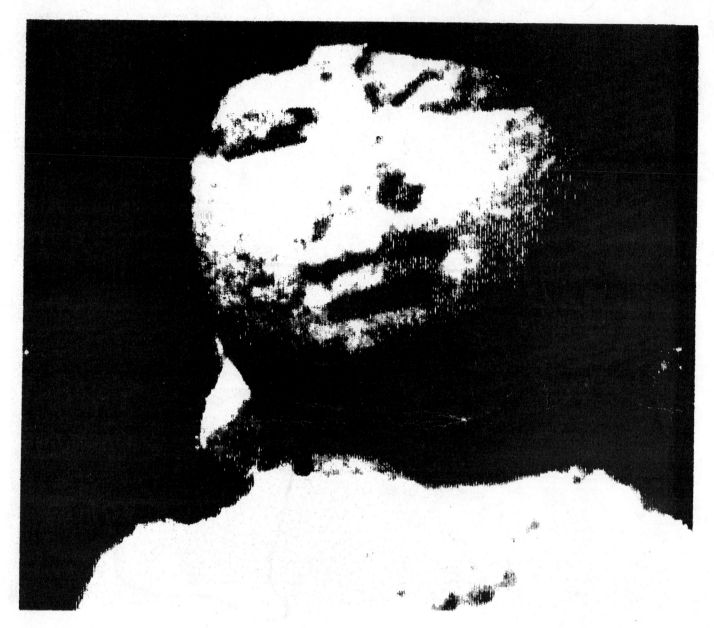

*TASTING
DREAMS*

*SMELLING
EARTH*

*HEARING
SILENCE*

*SEEING*

*HOLDING TOGETHER*

*NIGHT LIGHT*

**JUDITE DOS SANTOS**, NEW YORK, NY, USA

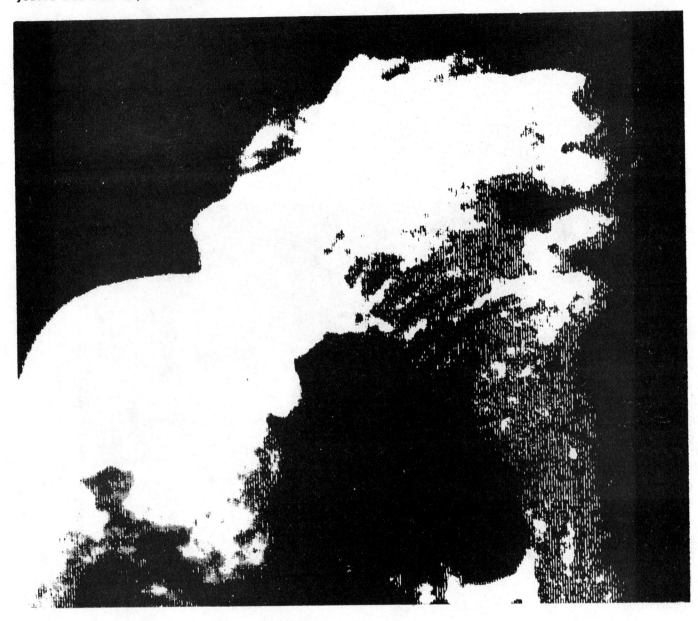

*BEING*          *INTEGRAL*          *SENSING*

*FULLY*          *BODY*          *TOUCHING*
*ALIVE*          *MIND*          *SKIN*

USA KAFTORI, SANTA BARBARA, CA, USA

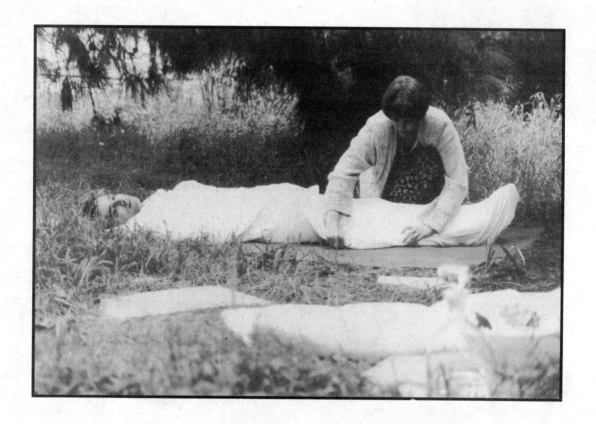

Title of contribution: ***"Swaddling"*** **from the** *Nurture and Surrender Series,* *detail of performative interaction.*

*Themes of memory, identity, human vulnerability, and nurturing form the central narrative that flows through my art work. I am interested in approaching art making as a process that renews meaning or allows meaning already present, to emerge. Developing an understanding of the relationships of artist to society and art to transformative experience has become a compelling aspect of my artistic practice. During the past few years these issues, combined with a longing for a kind of conversation that underscores the importance of reconnecting art to the activity of making meaning in everyday life, inspired me to experiment with forms of interactive sculpture, emphasizing wholeness, shared experience, and collaboration.*

ALISA DWORSKY, RANDOLF, VT, USA

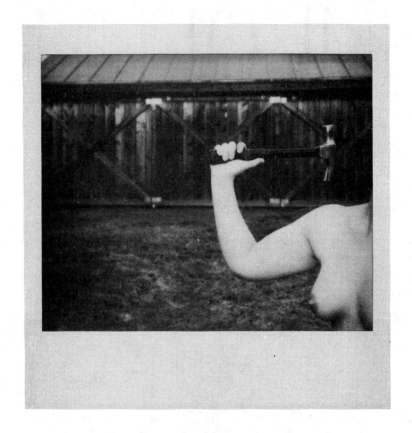

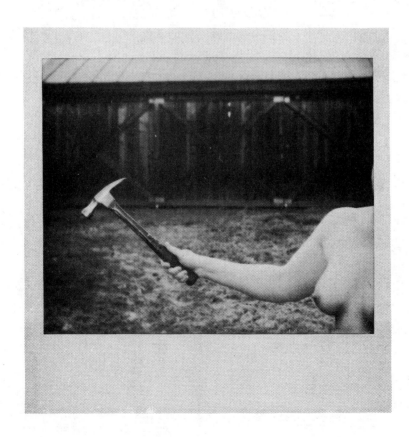

VALÉRIA MERÉNYI, BUDAPEST, HUNGARY

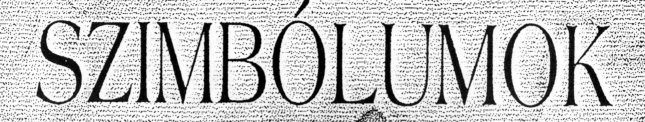

# SZIMBÓLUMOK

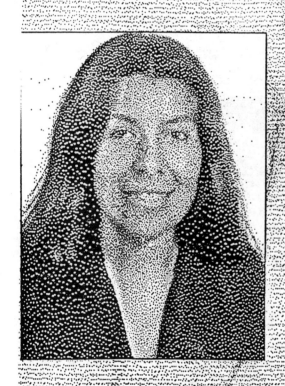

Merényi Valéria
festő- és grafikusművész
kiállítása megtekinthető
1995 május 10.-től
a Jókai Klubban.
(XII. Hollós u. 5.)

**ILEANA B LEAVENS, PhD,** SEATTLE, WA, USA

"Teaching art history as a fine art."

Ileana B. Leavens

Teaching art history as a fine art means to consider art history as a source for visual images. As art history and the fine arts are intimately connected, (the very existence of the former depends on the latter), there are well known examples of art works that formally derive from art historical precedents. My intent however is not to continue with further examples of this tradition but to visually express the broader concepts and themes of art history. As art and its history are but reflections of attitudes and ideas of each and every society at a particular time, there are art historical themes of universal character. I wish to address these.

Within the academic world, the separation of art and its history is as artificial as the dichotomy between the arts and the sciences; they have been products of ways of thinking that places knowledge inside nicely labeled, discrete containers, all wrapped up for instant consumption. These have nothing to do with reality, where everything is intricately related to create a whole which goes beyond national boundaries or frontiers.

How can teachinng art history as a fine art be part of this holistic view of reality?

Unlike words which originate from a diversity of languages, there are images of universal significace, such as motherhood, for example. Others that at one time were the prerogative of a particular society have become widely known through global communications, and have become part and parcel of art historical studies.

I propose that as the study of art has given rise to art historical ideas and themes, these in turn can be reinterpreted visually.

How many times have we heard the phrase of a picture being worth a thousand words?

Some ten years ago I introduced what has been called an art project as a requirement for the successful completion of my art history courses. The project consists of interpreting through visual images any art historical topic or theme that has been of particular interest. Students are encouraged to create according to their individual needs and abilities; there are no restrictions and their success is measured in terms of imagination and clarity and not technique. Using images that are understood by all, students have been able to visually represent both abstract and specific concepts in their paintings, sculptures and collages. For the most part they have been very successful in making their themes clear.

Considering the globalization of images, could it be possible that through a process similar to the one just described, visual representations and not the written or spoken word be the universal language of the future?

LESLEY DILL, NEW YORK, NY, USA

**LESLEY DILL**, NEW YORK, NY, USA

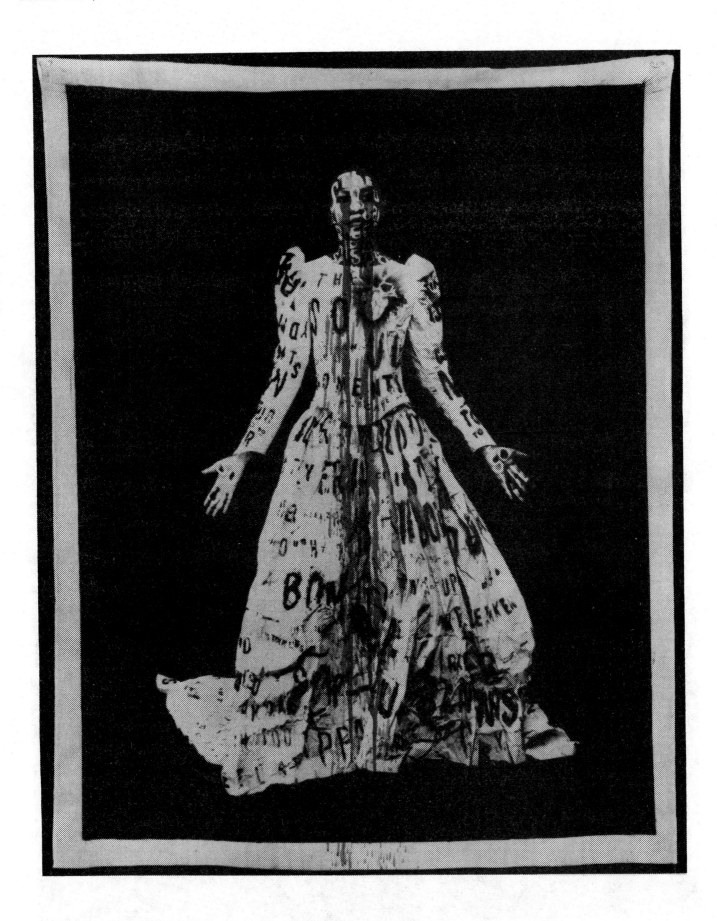

**ANA FERRER**, NEW YORK, NY, USA

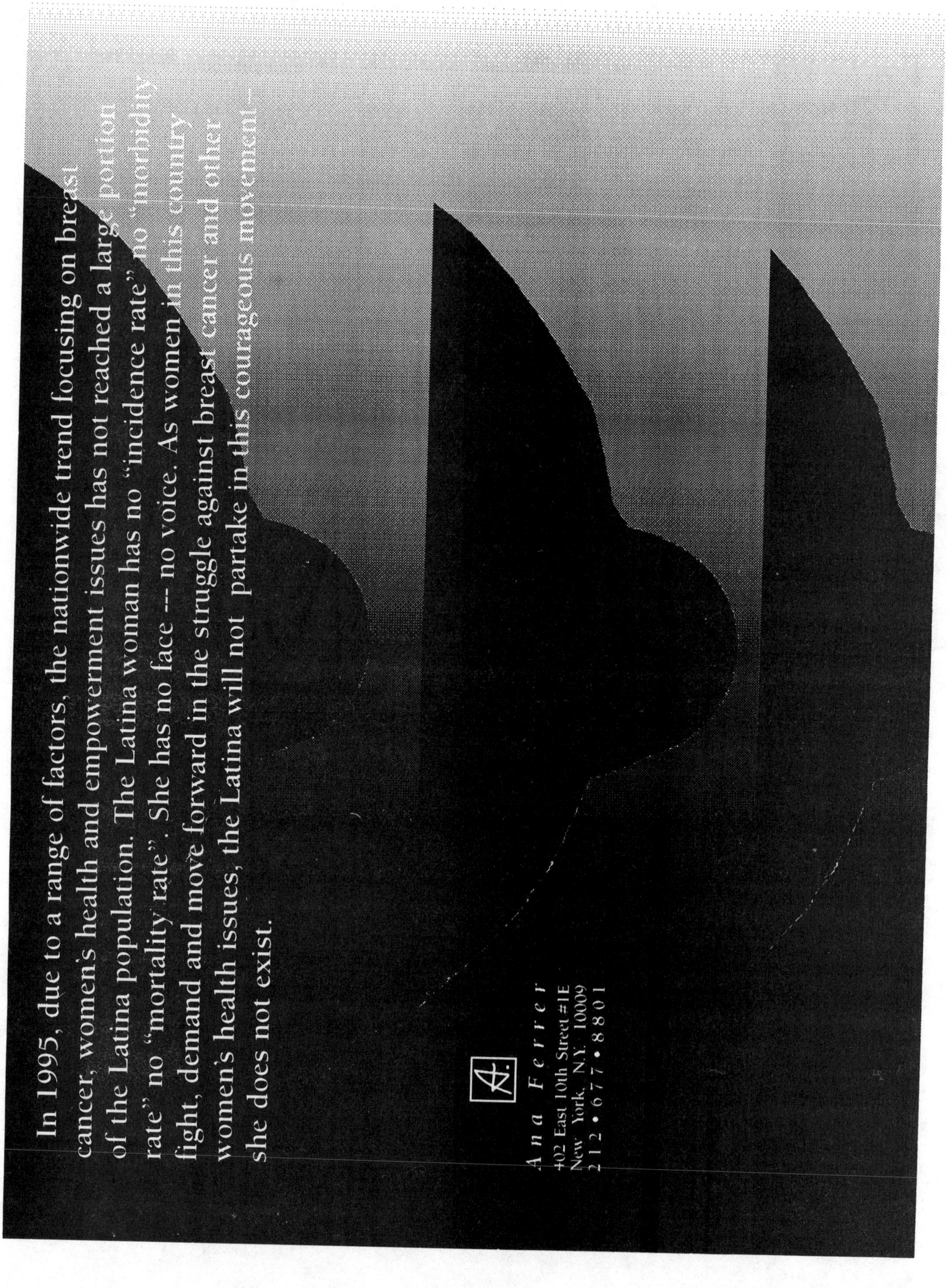

In 1995, due to a range of factors, the nationwide trend focusing on breast cancer, women's health and empowerment issues has not reached a large portion of the Latina population. The Latina woman has no "incidence rate" no "morbidity rate" no "mortality rate". She has no face — no voice. As women in this country fight, demand and move forward in the struggle against breast cancer and other women's health issues, the Latina will not partake in this courageous movement— she does not exist.

*Ana Ferrer*
402 East 10th Street #1E
New York, N.Y. 10009
2 1 2 • 6 7 7 • 8 8 0 1

**ANA FERRER**, NEW YORK, NY, USA

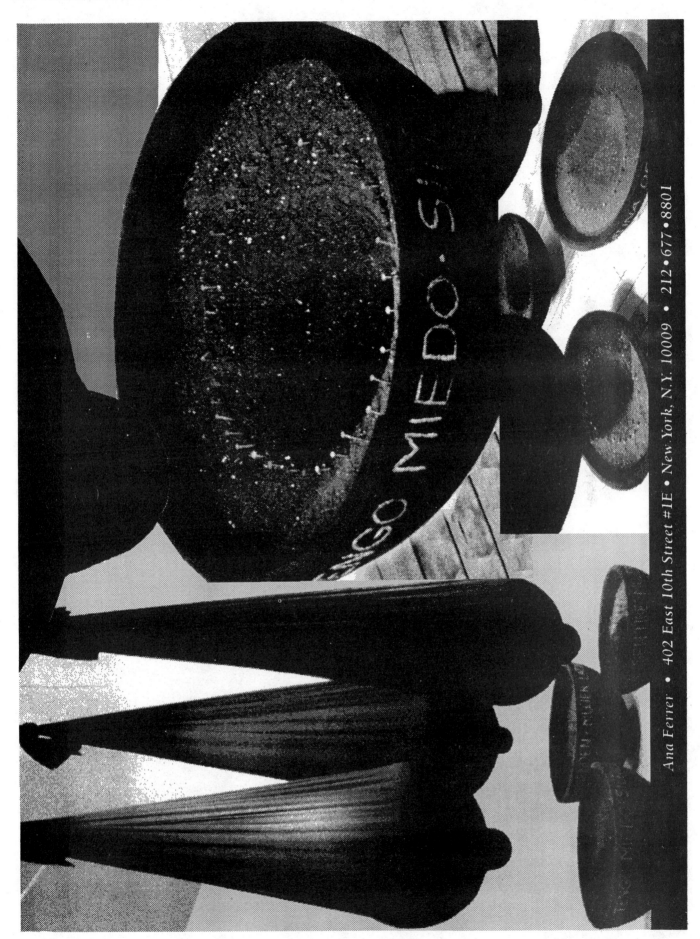

Ana Ferrer • 402 East 10th Street #1E • New York, N.Y. 10009 • 212 • 677 • 8801

ANNE SIDNEY, BROOKLYN, NY, USA

*Things i got to remember not to put in this time capsule
so I don't disgrace myself or embarrass my parents.*
*by Anne Sidney*

1) My big mouth
2) Unseemly grudges
3) Political art
4) My unwaxed Leg and underarm hair
5) My double butt
6) More than 6 grams of fat
7) Dirty words
8) Mean things about men
9) My bushy unwaxed unclipped vagina
10) Beefy man far
11) My unbleached mustache

*Fill in the rest*

13)
14)
15)
16)
17)
18)
19)
21)
22)
23)
24)
25)
26)
27)
28)
29)
30)

LISA DEANNE SMITH, TORONTO, ONT, CANADA

**ADELLE LUTZ**, NEW YORK, NY, USA

wings of light. thought of Tina — the dragonfly sends

→ heaven —

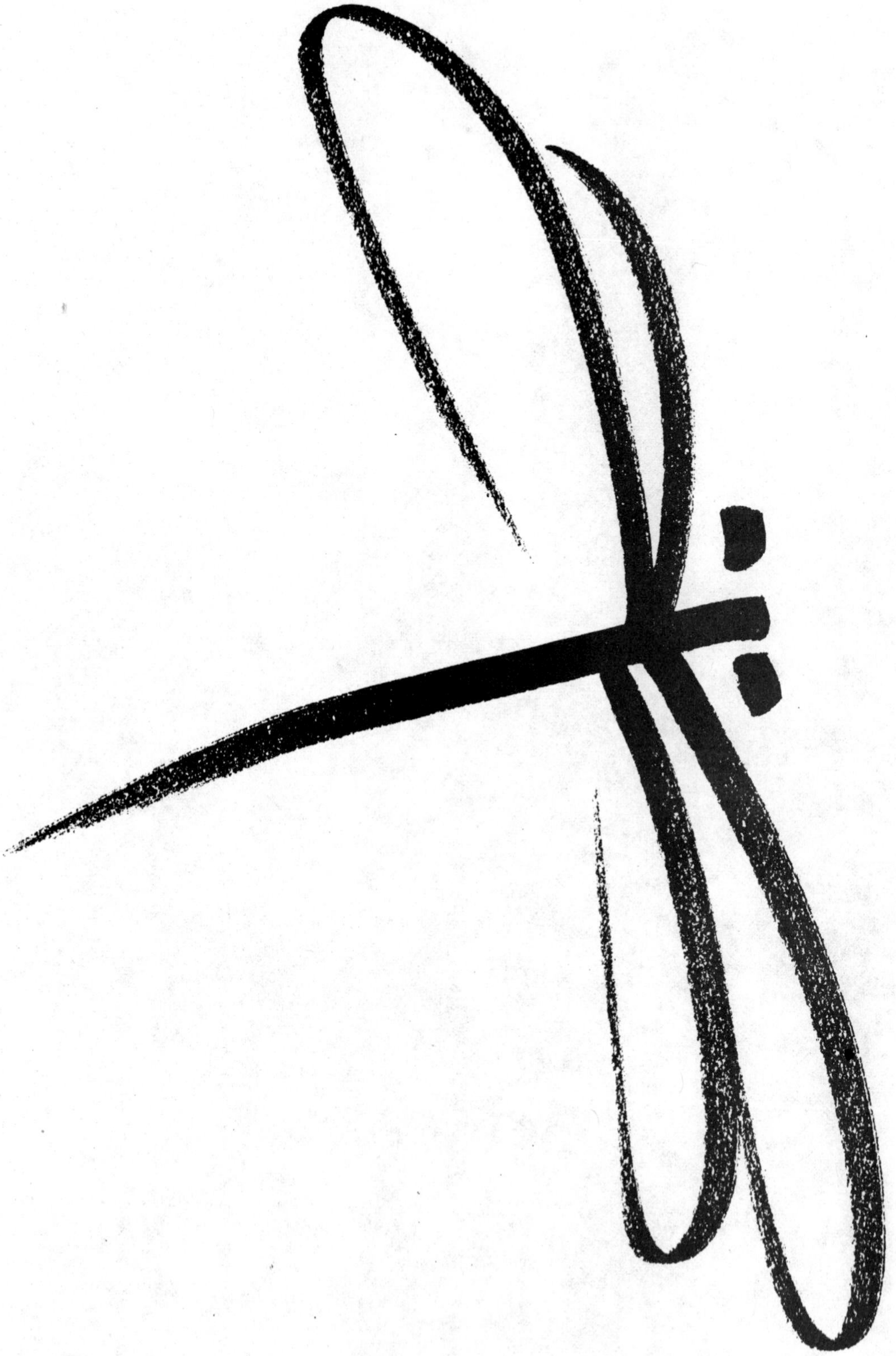

*N.Y.N.Y.*

MARCY BRAFMAN, NEW YORK, NY, USA

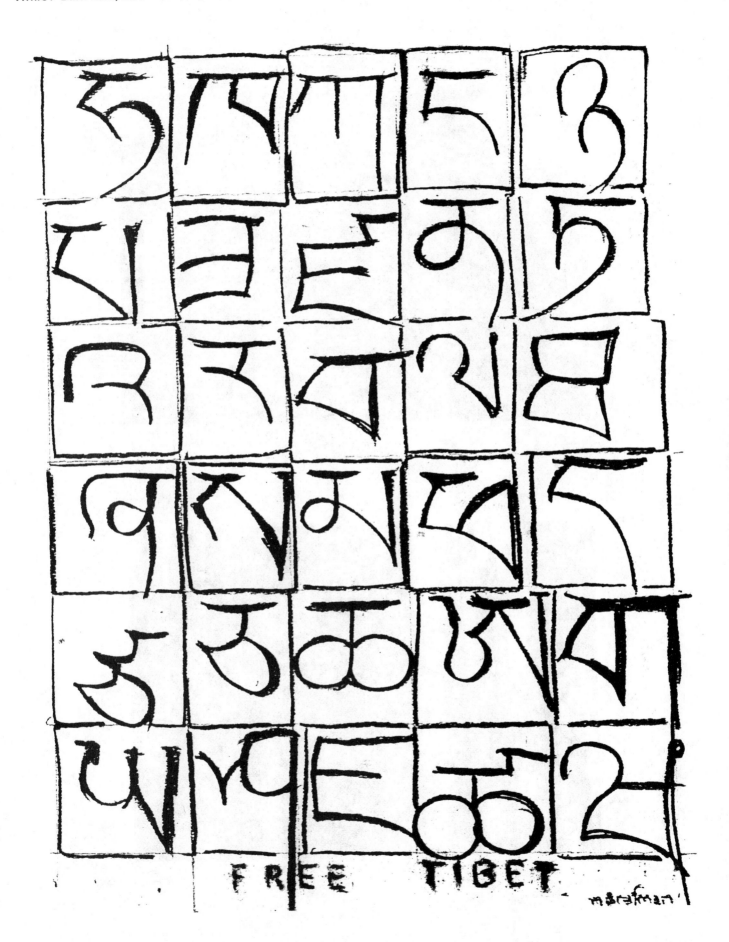

FREE TIBET

m.Brafman

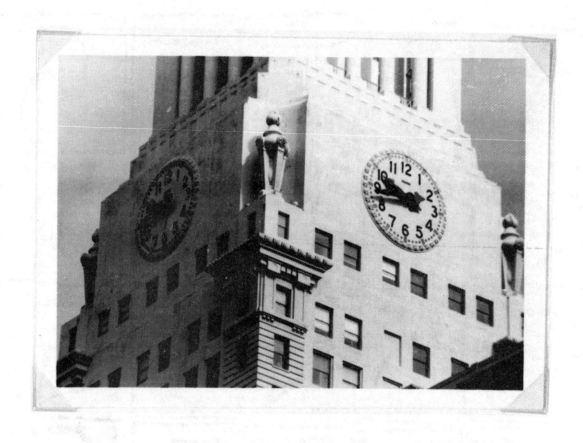

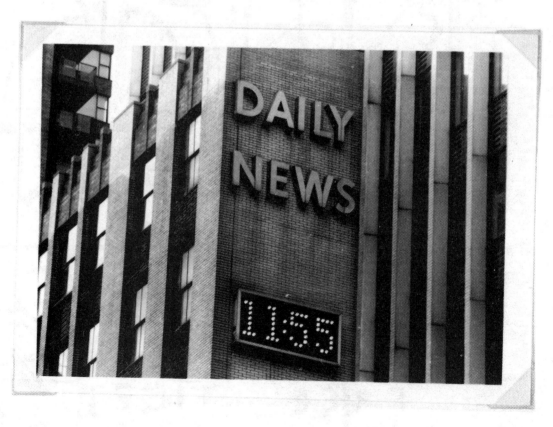

MOYRA DAVEY, HOBOKEN, NJ, USA

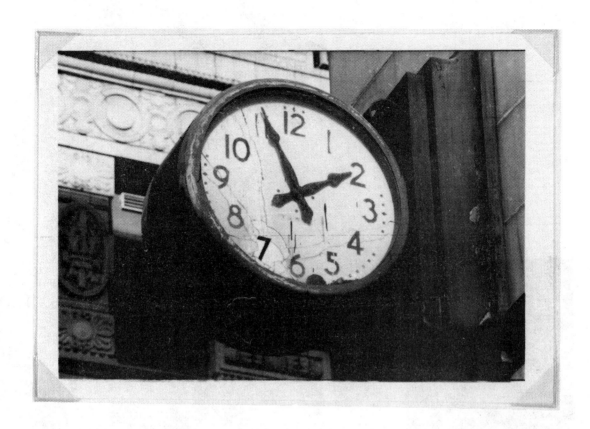

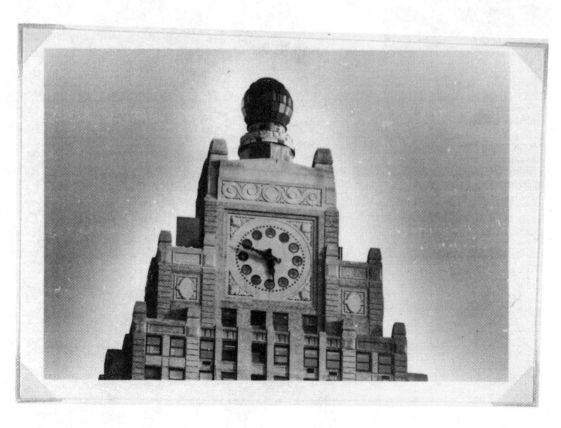

**ALYSON POU**, NEW YORK, NY, USA

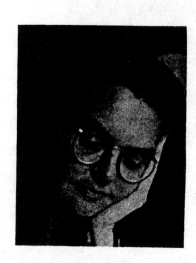

Frances Alyson Pou,
born October 24, 1952,
Memphis Tennessee.

I dedicate these pages and my work
to three generations of women in
my family who fought hard to be
themselves within the rich and violent
cultural boundaries of the Deep South.

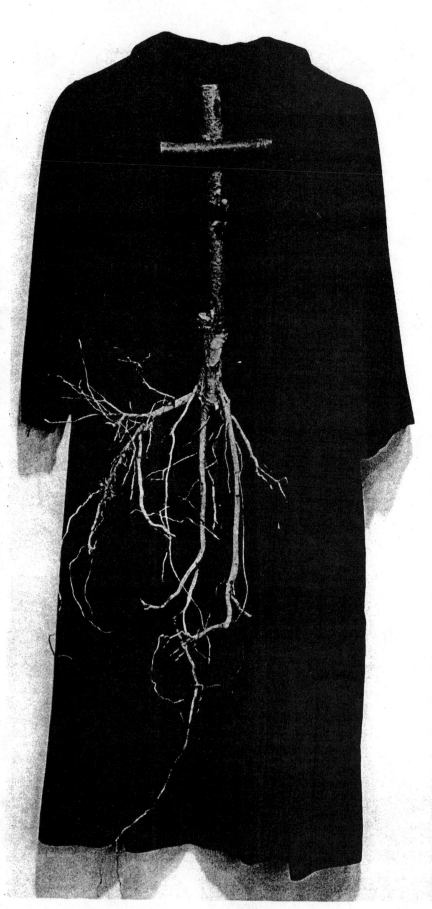

**ALYSON POU,** NEW YORK, NY, USA

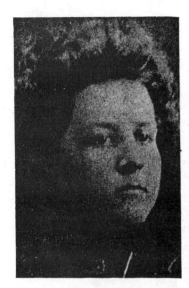

Lottie Gather Wilson, born to Martha Amonetee, April 9, 1884.
"If God had meant for woman-kind to have short hair, he would have made it stop growing." Her hair was so long it reached almost to the floor, and every night she would sit brushing it down and across her lap. 96, 97, 98, 99, 100, one hundred strokes a night every night of her life. By the time my mother was born everybody called Miss Lottie "Big Mama". At 40, days after bearing her eighth child, she broke her hip, took to her bed to recover and never emerged from her bedroom where she ruled her family with an iron fist, a lace bed jacket, and bitter tears. She never again wore street clothes, that is not until her 80th birthday, which was also the same day as her sister's funeral. That evening she returned home, declared she wished to live no longer, folded gardenias into her long hair and died the very next day. "It's the Gather blood that has ruined all the women in this family," said Uncle Lewis.

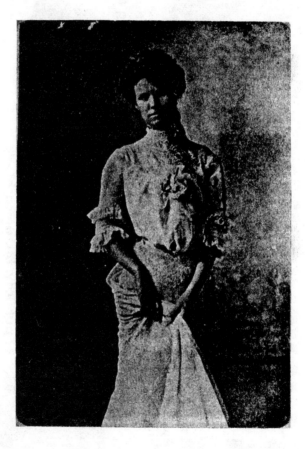

Emma Washington Cartwright, my great grandmother.
She never learned to cook. She single handedly painted the house a different color every year. She had a little woodworking shop out back where she made gigaws and wooden objects that moved in the wind. She often declared these objects fell from the sky and she talked to the air. She also painted large rocks and made piles of them all over her land to keep it from blowing away. Everyone thought she was Crazy, not because of her outdoor decor but because she had absolutely no interest in housekeeping. I was born on the same day that she died, and I know we passed as my eyes opened and hers closed.

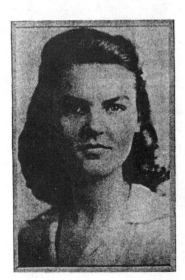

Cary Cartwright Pou.
At 15 my mother could fly a plane and shoot a gun. Her toy designs had been manufactured. At 16 she hitchhiked to California, lived in San Francisco, then moved to Mexico as an ex-patriot and became a road crew surveyor. At 19 she returned home, married my father, and from then on lived within a mile of her parents and cousins.

The first thing Cary heard when she came out from under the anesthesia was Big Daddy telling her "Emma Washington is dead." and " You have a little girl, we'd like you to name her Emma." But she said," No. No, I want to give her a name of her own. A name that doesn't belong to anyone else. I want her to have her own name, her own place in the world."

# TOP TEN WAYS TO TELL IF YOU'RE AN ART WORLD TOKEN:

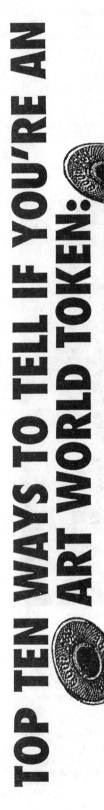

**10.** Your busiest months are February (Black History Month), March (Women's History), April (Asian-American Awareness), June (Stonewall Anniversary) and September (Latino Heritage).

**9.** At openings and parties, the only other people of color are serving drinks.

**8.** Everyone knows your race, gender and sexual preference even when they don't know your work.

**7.** A museum that won't show your work gives you a prominent place in its lecture series.

**6.** Your last show got lots of publicity, but no cash.

**5.** You're asked to do a non-tenure-track teaching position at every art school on the east coast.

**4.** No collector ever buys more than two of your pieces.

**3.** Whenever you open your mouth, it's assumed that you speak for "your people" not just yourself.

**2.** People are always telling you their interracial and gay sexual fantasies.

**1.** A curator who never gave you the time of day before calls you right after a Guerrilla Girls demonstration.

A PUBLIC SERVICE MESSAGE FROM **GUERRILLA GIRLS** CONSCIENCE OF THE ARTWORLD
5 3 2  L a G U A R D I A  P L A C E ,  # 2 3 7 ,  N Y ,  N Y  1 0 0 1 2

GUERILLA GIRLS, NEW YORK, NY, USA

# TRADITIONAL VALUES AND QUALITY RETURN TO THE WHITEY MUSEUM.

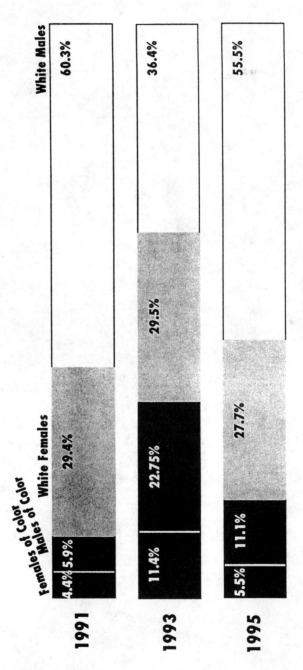

Females of Color
Males of Color
White Females
White Males

1991   4.4%   5.9%   29.4%   60.3%

1993   11.4%   22.75%   29.5%   36.4%

1995   5.5%   11.1%   27.7%   55.5%

BIENNIAL ARTISTS*

A PUBLIC SERVICE MESSAGE FROM **GUERRILLA GIRLS** CONSCIENCE OF THE ARTWORLD
532 LaGUARDIA PLACE, #237, NY, NY 10012

*Film and video artists not included in statistics

**KATIA GOLITSYNA**, MOSCOW, RUSSIA

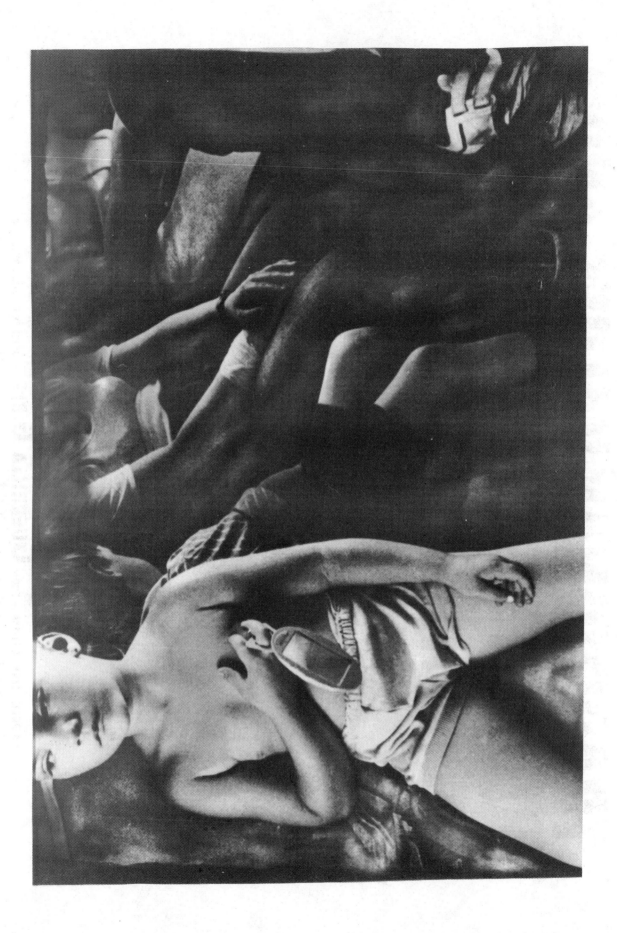

JEAN KAWECKI, UPPER MONTCLAIR, NJ, USA

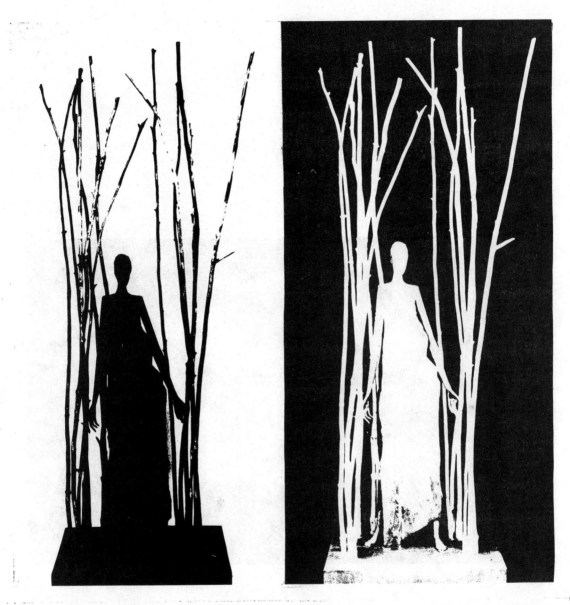

JEAN KAWECKI "Quest" foundstone, metal, wood 72"x 24"x17"

TO ALWAYS SEARCH FOR THE TRUTH    TO KNOW AND UNDERSTAND IT WHEN ONE FINDS IT    TO USE IT WISELY AND TO TRULY SEE

ADRIANA MIRANDA CASEROS, BUENOS AIRES, ARGENTINA

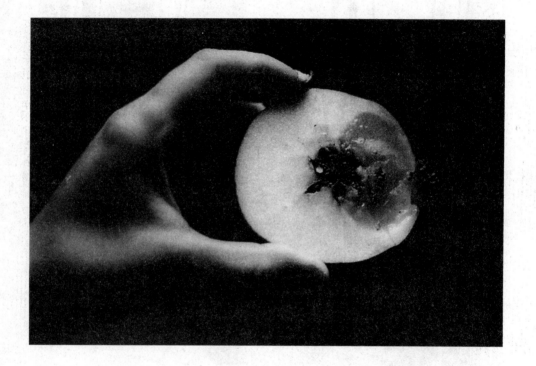

**ADRIANA MIRANDA CASEROS**, BUENOS AIRES, ARGENTINA

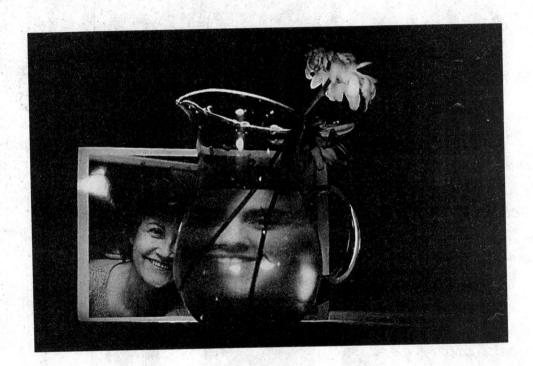

transmigration

ELIZABETH LIDE, ATLANTA, GA, USA

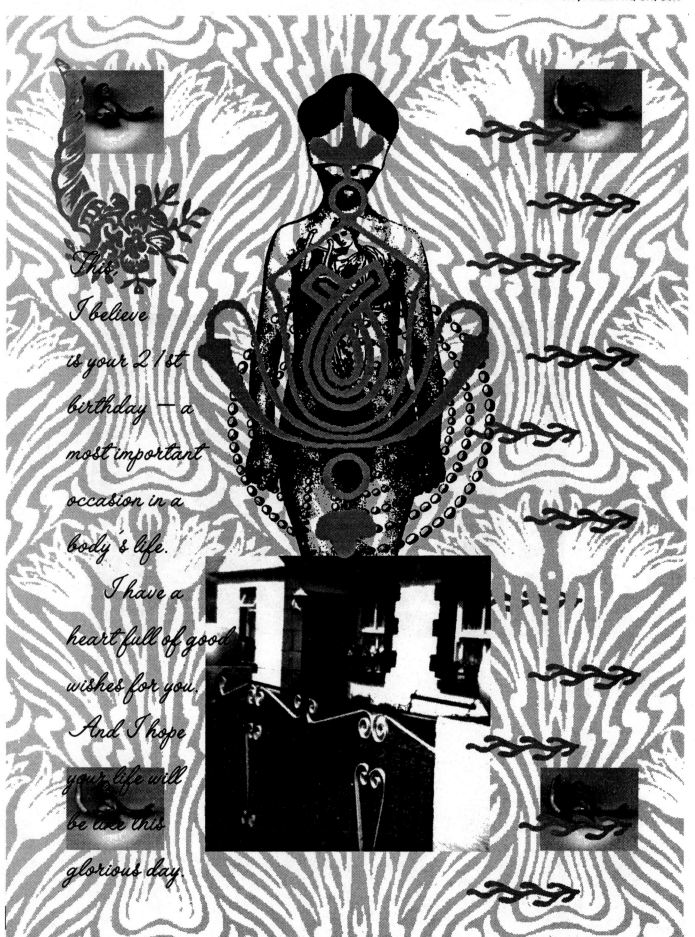

This,

I believe

is your 21st

birthday — a

most important

occasion in a

body's life.

I have a

heart full of good

wishes for you.

And I hope

your life will

be like this

glorious day.

**ELIZABETH LIDE**, ATLANTA, GA, USA

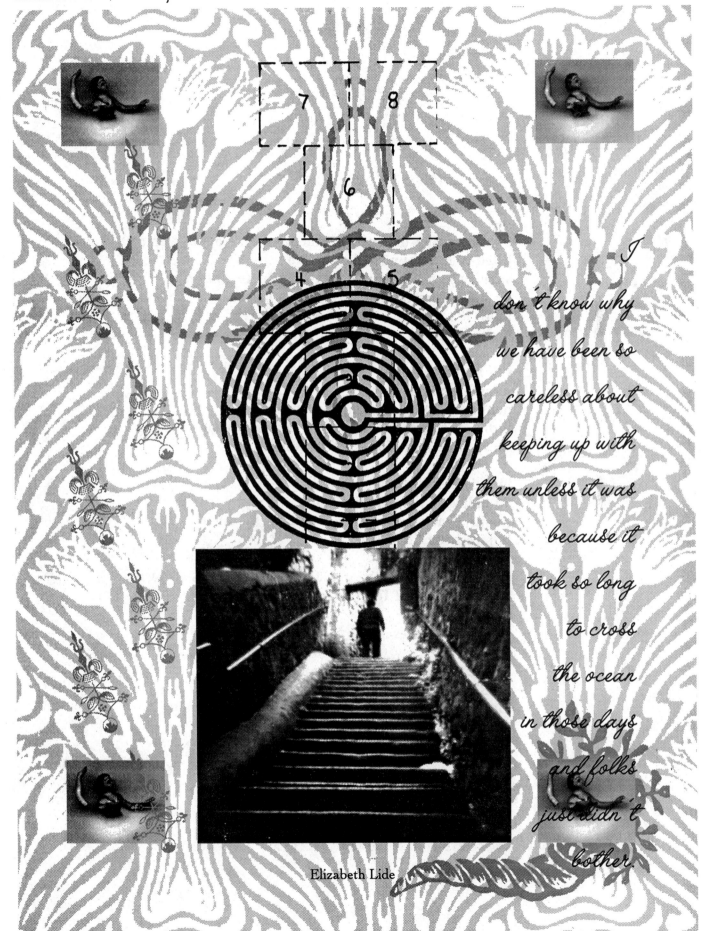

I don´t know why we have been so careless about keeping up with them unless it was because it took so long to cross the ocean in those days and folks just didn´t bother.

Elizabeth Lide

RIA ROERDINK, NYMEGEN, THE NETHERLANDS

a yellow-yellowing curl, it dances a vague dance a smooth dance
lifted over and under the curtain
vaguely seen, rumours enter, the silence scattering
no shape is mentioned, mysterious forgetting
know it's there
it dances

sideways bent lofty seat on trenches
a fanfare plays
drifting erupting, coming out outloud
it dances sidewalk walls, cast voices slip away
sharpening reflections, it's slipping its way

in quietness the beast scattering
all hiding in the dance's flesh
smoke, a new transparency, and it's too silent
in pieces not lifted left

quickly rose under the phantom,through doors and windows
ferocious wave of fire ceasing, surrounded wave glorious sea
named
ending the circles

witches' path, lending an ear an eye
an island of, oh mistaken voices
the legs of dance opening the waves of fire burning
the anger sleeps its covered sleep

KIMBERLY BURLEIGH, CINCINNATI, OH, USA

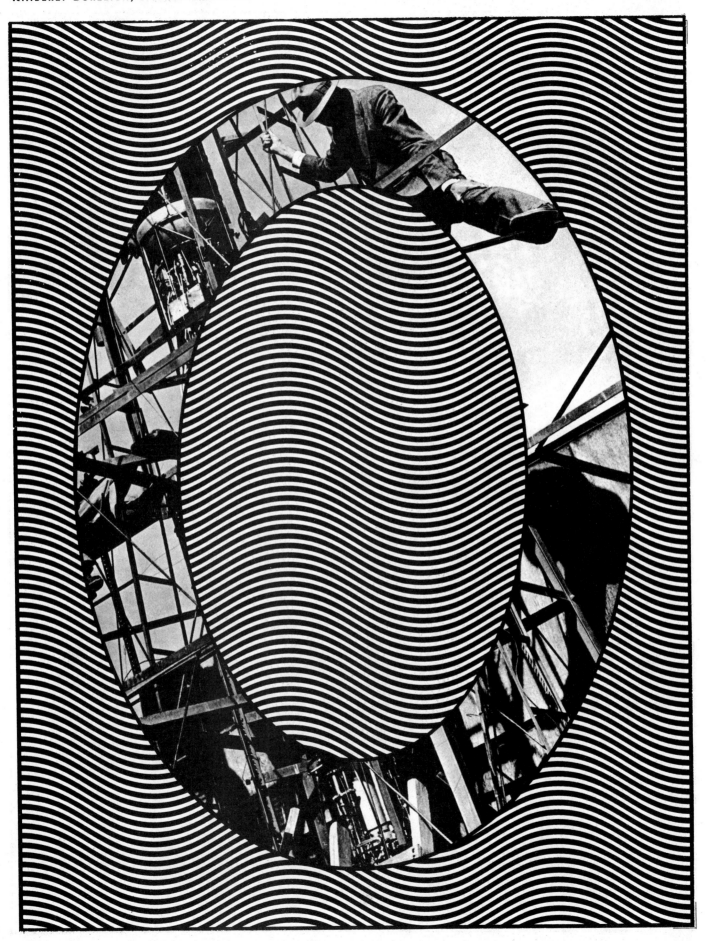

LOUISE EASTMAN, NEW YORK, NY, USA

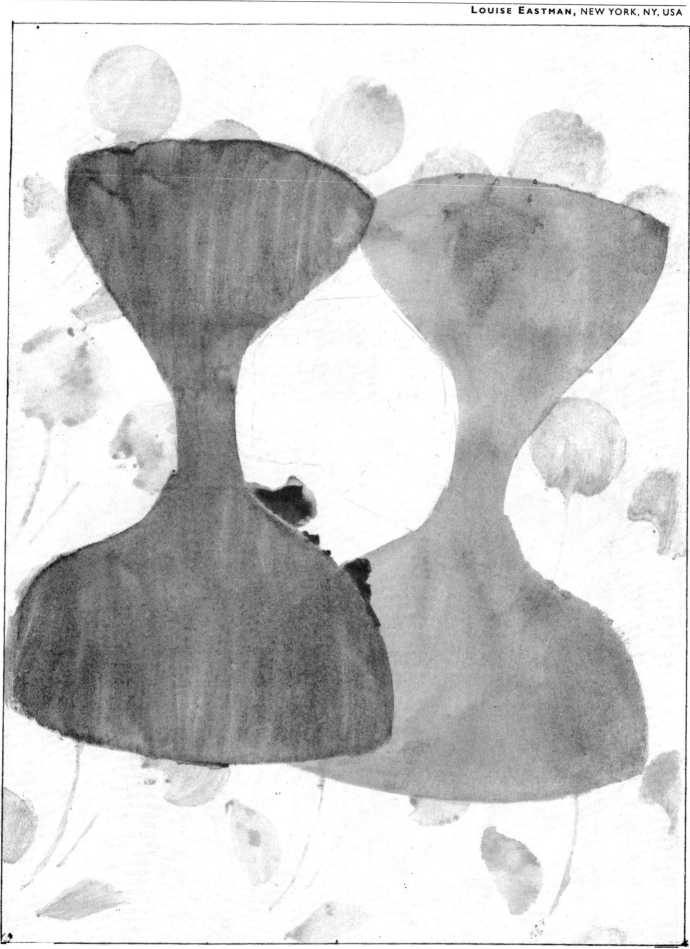

MICHELLE MAROZIK, BROOKLYN, NY, USA

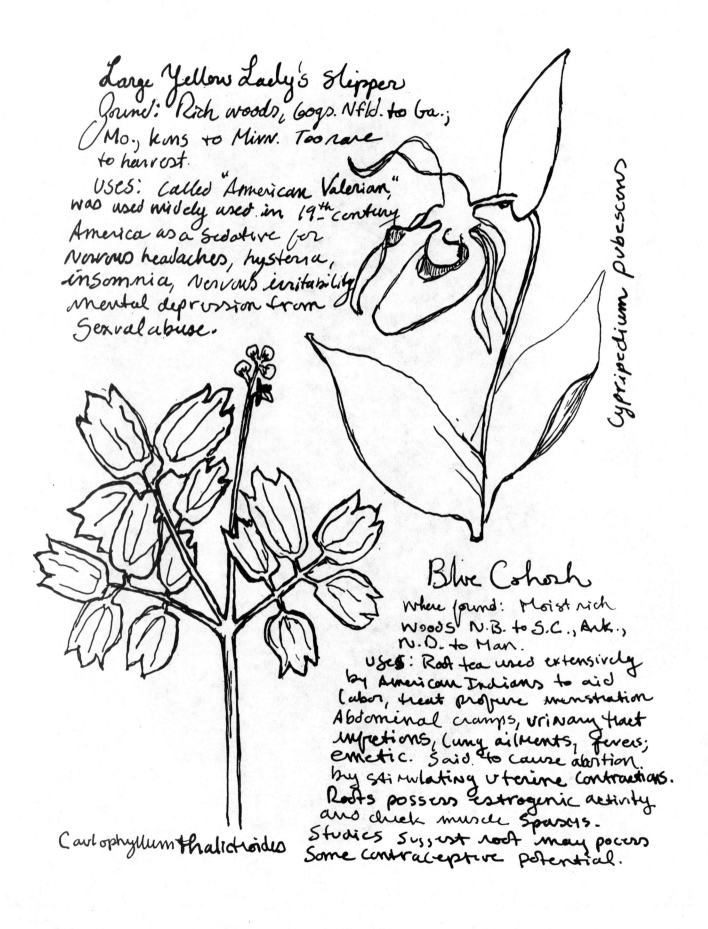

Large Yellow Lady's Slipper
Found: Rich woods, bogs. Nfld. to Ga.;
Mo., kans to Minn. Too rare
to harvest.
USES: Called "American Valerian,"
was used widely used in 19ᵗʰ century
America as a sedative for
Nervous headaches, hysteria,
insomnia, Nervous irritability
mental depression from
sexual abuse.

Cypripedium pubescens

Blue Cohosh
where found: Moist rich
woods N.B. to S.C., Ark.,
N.D. to Man.
USES: Root tea used extensively
by American Indians to aid
labor, treat profuse menstruation
Abdominal cramps, urinary tract
infections, lung ailments, fevers;
emetic. Said to cause abortion
by stimulating uterine contractions.
Roots possess estrogenic activity
and check muscle spasms.
Studies suggest root may possess
some contraceptive potential.

Caulophyllum thalictroides

JOHANNA JACOB, NEW YORK, NY USA

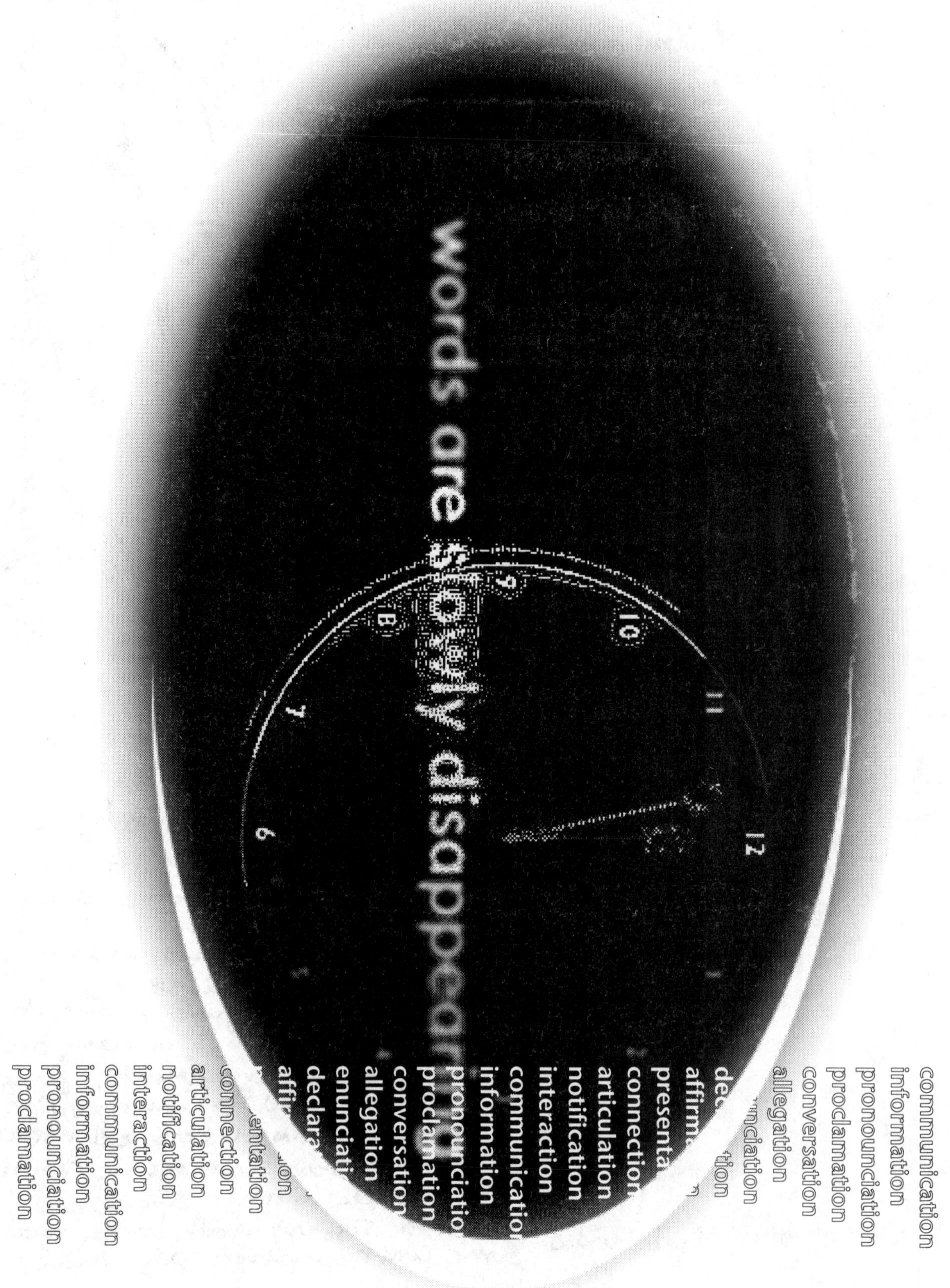
words are slowly disappearing
communication
information
pronounciation
proclamation
conversation
allegation
connection
articulation
notification
interaction
communication
information
pronounciation
proclamation

NANCY MEBANE SHAKIR, MONTCLAIR, NJ, USA

HERS

Sometimes, she glances at it. Surreptitiously.
Relishing the fancy, hand carved curliques of the dark headboard,
Contrasted with the rosy, down comforter.
And if souls could sigh, hers would breathe contentment.

Sometimes she touches it. Polishing it lovingly.
Feeling the heft of the mahogony, admiring the elegance of its
bygone era flambouyancy.
And if souls could fly, hers would soar with joy.

You see, in her long, second half of a century of life,
it is her first time ever, to have such a thing.
Not chosen for her as in childhood.
Not a capitulation to another's taste, as in marriage.

Not a too full single, nor a two empty queen.
But a just right double. Which when necessay can accomodate two .
But is perfect for one.

Sometimes, in the middle of the day, she steals a glimpse
Through the curtained, french doors.
Its rich, brown, furbellowed headboard, its high deep, down mattress
Beckons her. And clandestinely, she slips to it- as to a lover.

And midst the gently mingled, Wood and woman and talc scent,
She slumbers. And if souls do rest, hers does, at last.

**Soledad Arias:** Be oneself, beyond time, reaching those levels of universal images, expanding the limits of consciousness, wandering through unknown realms.

**DOTTY ATTIE,** NEW YORK, NY, USA

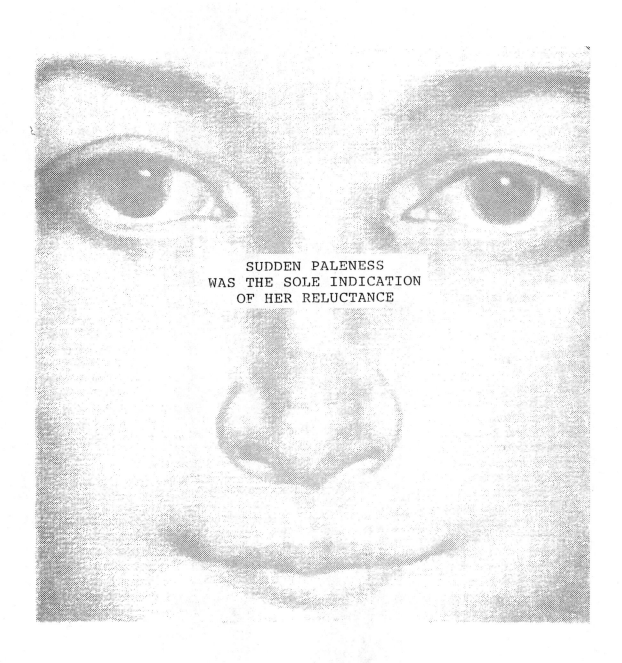

SUDDEN PALENESS
WAS THE SOLE INDICATION
OF HER RELUCTANCE

EMILIE BENES BRZEZINSKI, MCLEAN, VA, USA

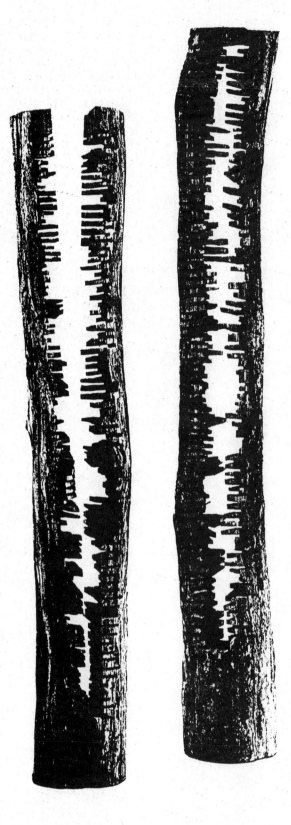

JANET CULBERTSON, SHELTER ISLAND, NY, USA

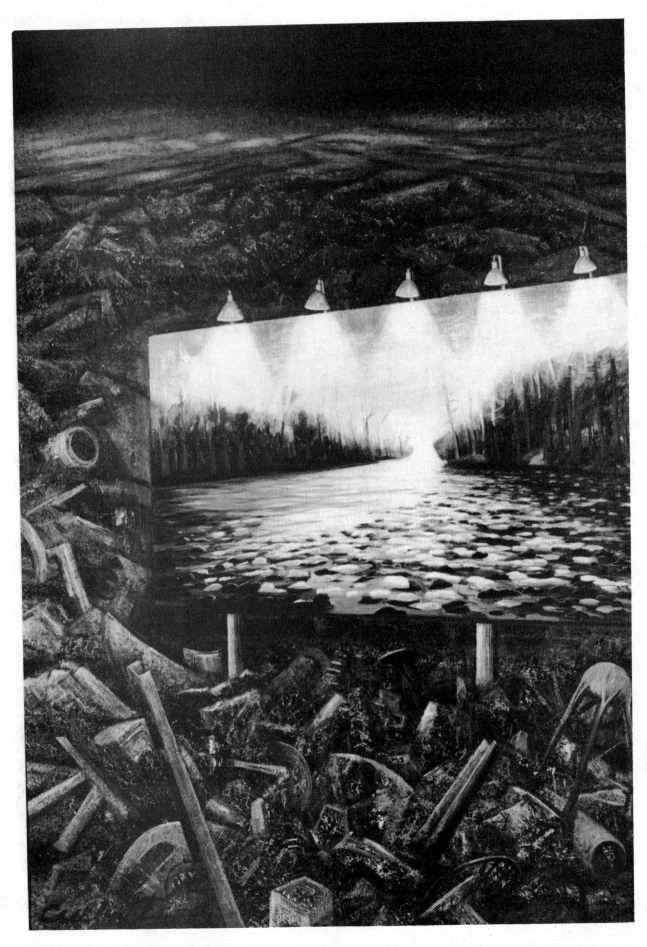

**SUSAN DORY**, SEATTLE, WA, USA

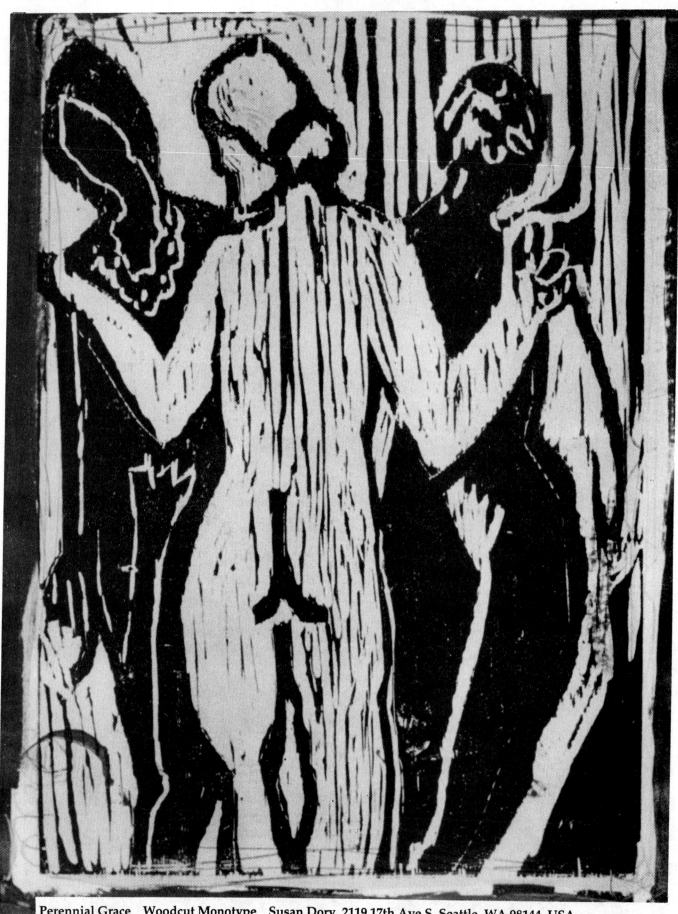

<u>Perennial Grace</u>   Woodcut Monotype   Susan Dory  2119 17th Ave S  Seattle, WA 98144  USA

ASHLEY KING, SAN FRANCISCO, CA, USA

I used to think the truth was some mixture of taboo,
like a love potion.

In the tub, water sucks down the sides of my body.
A small pool of water is trapped in the well of my back.
A smile is an instinct.
I imagine yours.

Certain nerves can be cut that will allow pursuit and lunge,
but no bite.
Once I give it to you;
you can get it again easily.
But it would only seem that I am giving it.
Good to a certain point.
The last drop.
"No, never."
It only resides within the walls of flesh.
Can't, in fact, be pulled down the drain.
But what will become of it?
You told me something complicated in your sleep.
Even repeated it.
But I didn't understand.
You turned over, back
to your dreaming.
And I in my kerchief,
Remember things embedded
showing on the surface of my skin.
Smooth and polished as I can get it.
But eyes looking out
from the animal within.

Ashley King

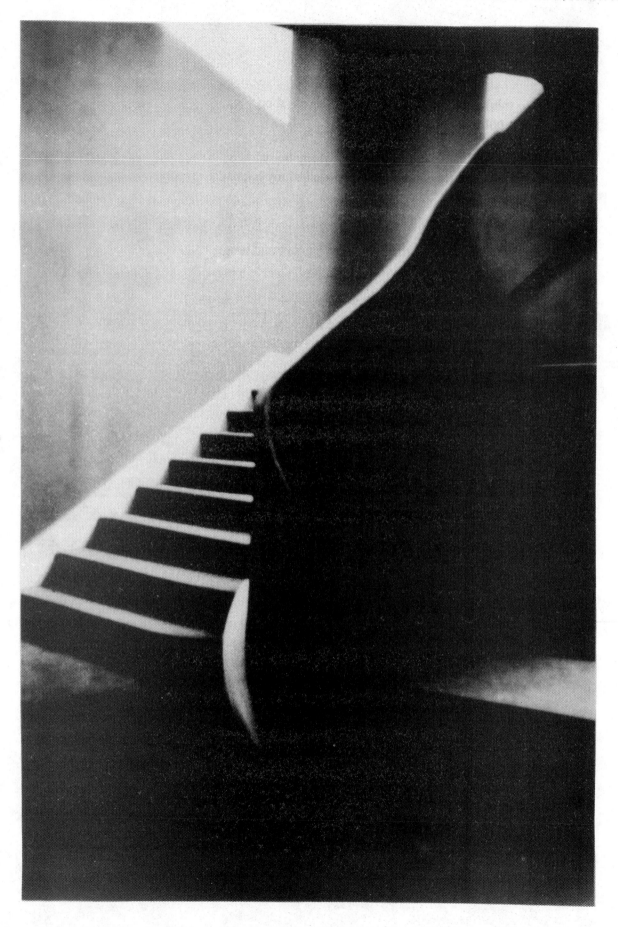

MARIA VELASCO, ISLA VISTA, CA, USA

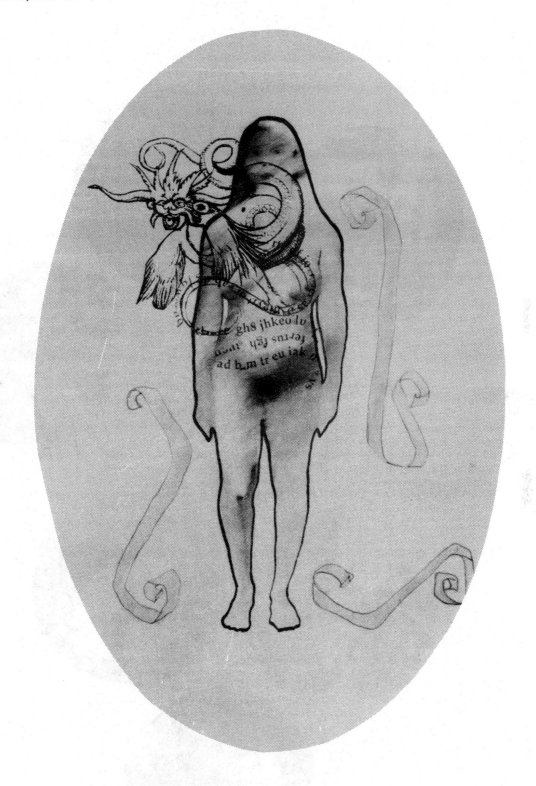

*Sexualidad   Y   Lenguaje*

María Velasco          923 Camino Corto          Isla Vista          Ca 93117          Phone. (805) 685 8712          USA

JULIA PARKER, NEW YORK, NY, USA

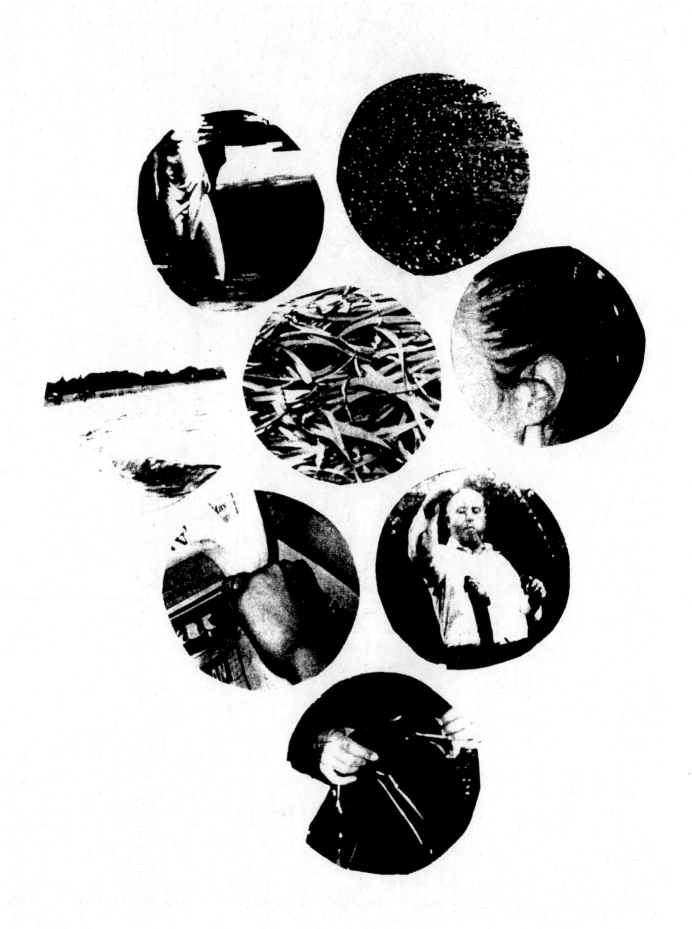

MARCIA HILLIS, BROOKLYN, NY, USA

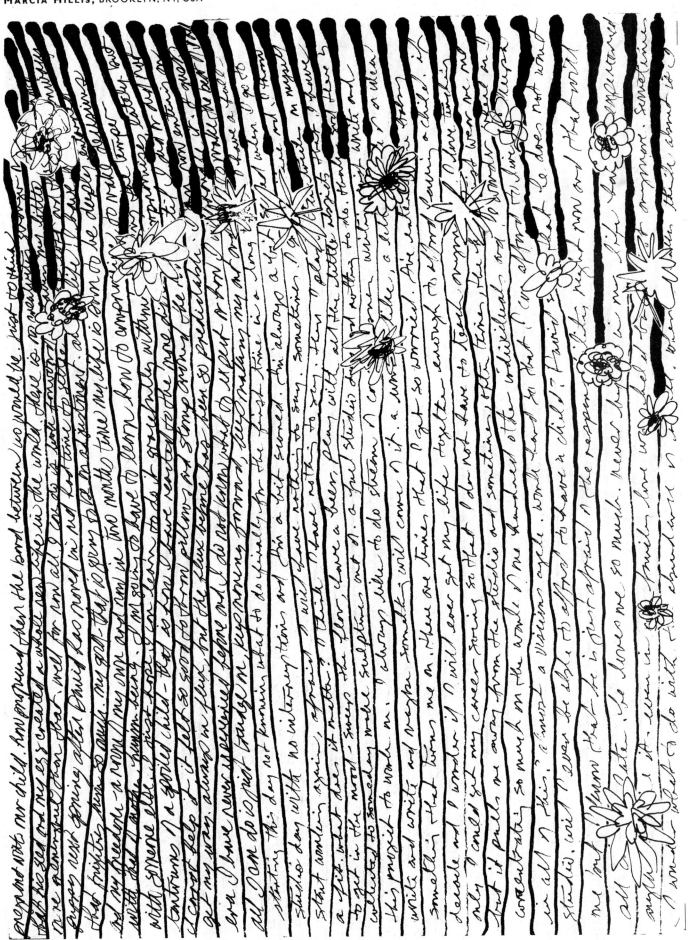

MARCIA HILLIS, BROOKLYN, NY, USA

SUE WILLIAMS, BROOKLYN, NY, USA

## The victim did it.

Some people need to get kicked in the head more than once before they can wake up and smell the sperm sliding down their face.
I myself was a victim of abuse turned sperm sniffer (sometimes I can still smell it on a warm evening). Do victims feel the kick as pain or pleasure? "Fuck off." When the object of my love and affection gives me the boot as hard as he can it hurts quite a bit. Also, a deep feeling of humiliation and rejection (harder please). Yet there is something homey about the feeling: Dear old Dad. Of course I go back for more (home). This is a riot for everyone with their shit together. Well no alternatives came to mind at the time. What can I say? And all these bruises about the face and misshapen lip touching the nose (a turn-off) so everyone knows what you've been up to. Oh, the embarrassment the shameful feeling of worminess.
"Look, an untogether woman."
Even from Dad!
"How could she let that happen?"
No gun.
"How could she do that to herself?"
How did I kick myself in the head?
I am worm, hear me whimper mumble mumble. Fuck you all. Fifteen years of therapy, groups, 12-step programs. I'll never do it again. Then I am attacked and raped by a total stranger (I swear!). Can't he see that I am centered and working on boundary issues? That I have my shit together? Hell — I OWN my OWN SHIT. What gives? Why wasn't I training in combat? Should I go outside again? Well no alternatives came to mind at the time.

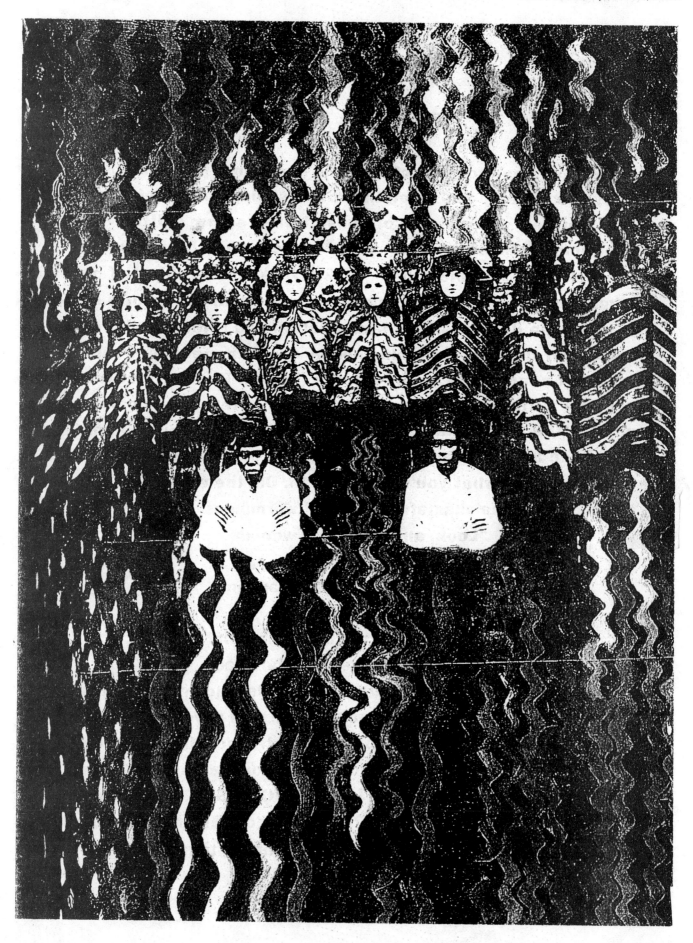

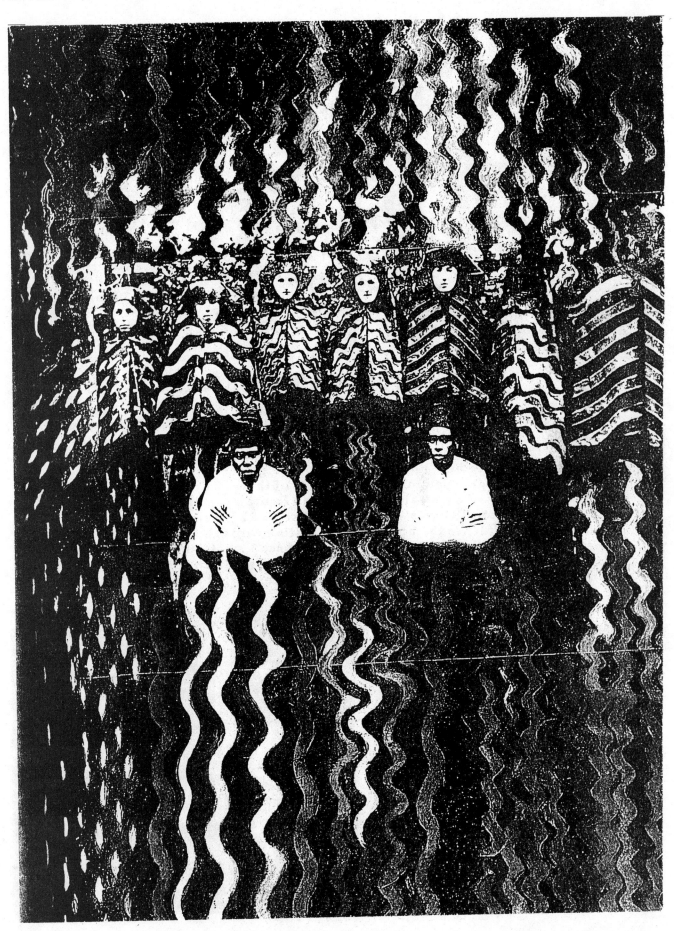

**KATHLEEN LAZIZA**, NEW YORK, NY, USA

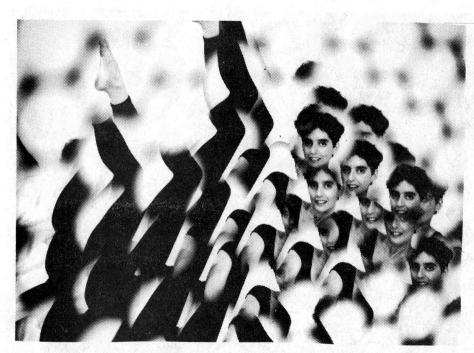

"Warped Crush" inter-active media theater by Laziza Videodance and Lumia Project

Kathleen Laziza is a founder of the Laziza Videodance and Lumia Project - a tour de force art company creating live movement theater and media art. Promote Art Works Inc. - A not for profit organization dedicated to art and technology. @ 123 Smith Street in Brooklyn, NY P.O. Box 154 , Prince St. NYC, NY 10012 -0003 (718) 797-3116 tel/fax

# ARTIST STATEMENT

Art is a passion I have chosen to be the heart of my life. My livelihood with collaborator/partner, William Laziza and our two children Leonardo and Dylan in NYC is a serious roller coaster ride. It takes nerves of steel and a big sense of humor to be here now. My concerns are great. Mostly they involve public safety and education, or rather the lack of them. The political and economic forces weaken my ability to respond to the struggle as I would wish. I am in constant conflict, as a woman, an artist, and a parent. My objectives are to directly influence the upcoming generation through the arts. On a personal note: I'd like to honor the passing of my 3 great dance teachers, Hanya Holm, Erick Hawkins and Alwin Nikolas. I will now carry on their flames as I teach young people about art, movement, light and media.

I look forward to a world wide trend where women create their own political forces - labor organizing, parliamentary bodies, ecological integration, and other structures of power. Women want 100% self-determination. I applaud the women who tirelessly fight for all kinds of freedoms. Women of the world unite!

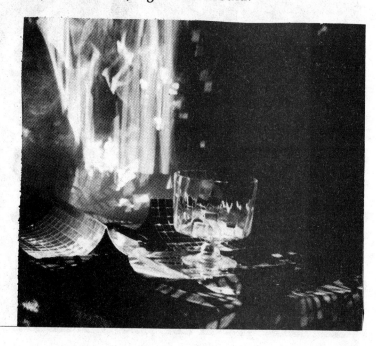

The Crystal Box
A Light Table Installation
by: Kathleen and William Laziza

PHYLLIS BALDINO, BROOKLYN, NY, USA

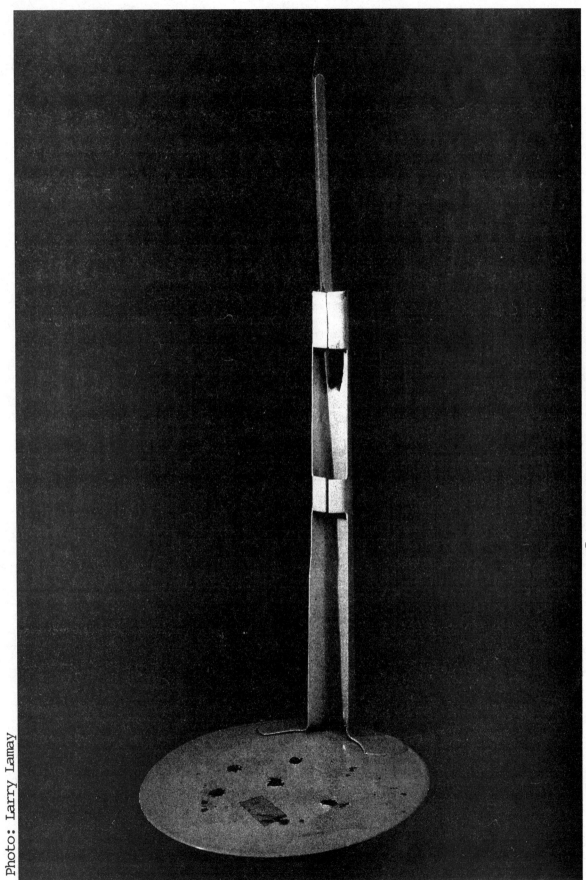

Photo: Larry Lamay

UNKNOWN SERIES (EXCERPTS): "POTATO THING"
VIDEO: 58 SECONDS OBJECT: 11"x4½"x5"

PHYLLIS BALDINO
1994

**Ardele Lister**

**1995**    Director, Producer - *Elemental: Abstract Relations in Space* 7min
- *See Under: Canada-Nationalism (work in progress)*
- *Repentance (work in progress)*

**1991**    Director, Producer– *Behold The Promised Land*
23 min. 1" master ( Des Montages... Travelling Fest., Spain;
W.O.W. Festival, NY; Images Festival, Toronto; Dallas Video Fest.)

**1990**    Editor –*Total Rain*
27 min. 1" master
Written & Directed by Richard Foreman
(PBS-NY, PBS- San Francisco, LA Museum of Modern Art, Museum of
Modern Art)

**1989**    Director, Producer – *It Happens to the Best of us*
23 min. 1" master
(Montreal Film and Video Festival, Three Rivers Festival, Dallas Video Fest.,
Atlanta Fest., Broadcast: "Mixed Signals", New England Cable TV)

**1988**    Director, Producer – *Cancer Scandal: The Policies
and Politics of Failure*
60 min. 1" master
(Produced for and distributed by Patient Rights Legal Action Fund).

**1986**    Producer – *Pee-Wee's Playhouse* (C.B.S.-TV)
"Connect The Dots", "Face Fun"

Director, Producer, Writer –*Zoe's Car*
6 min. 1" master
(1st prize Daniel Wadsworth Memorial Festival, American Film and Video
Festival, Images Fest., NY Film and Video Expo. Broadcast: Cage–TV,
Cincinnati.)

**1985**    Director, Producer, Co–writer – *Hell*
17 min. 1" master
(prizes: JVC Tokyo Video Festival, Three Rivers Arts Festival. Made for TV
Fest., Black Maria Film and Video Fest, Fest. de Films et Video de Femmes)

**1981**    Director, Producer – *Split*
22 min. 3/4" master
(Festival Selections and Prizes:JVC Tokyo Video Festival, Atlanta Film and
Video Festival, US Film and Video Festival, Dallas Video Fest.)

**1980**    Director, Producer, Actress - *Sugar Daddy*
26 min. 3/4" master
*(Collections: Museum of Modern Art, Nat'l Gallery of Canada), Washington
Project for the Arts, 49th Parallel Gallery)*

**1976**    Director, Co–writer – *So Where's My Prince Already?*
20 min. 16mm color . A ReelFeelings Production.
( International Festival of Women and Film, NYC,1976)

Director, Producer –"*The Nightly News from Habitat Forum*"
U.N. Conference on Habitation, Vancouver, Canada

**1974 – 5**    Director, Producer, Host –"*Vancouver Art Gallery*"
30 min. weekly program, broadcast on Cable 10–TV , Vancouver

ARDELE LISTER, BROOKLYN, NY, USA

# Ardele Lister VIDEO

202 - 15th Street
Brooklyn, New York 11215
phone 718-788-4464 fax:908-445-1343 e-mail alister@gandalf.rutgers.edu

"Seeking to understand that which was not articulated (at least in terms of this second wave-feminist outpouring), Lister became the chronicler of the self-deluded; the recorder of internal deception... Highly observant and fearless when it comes to what is within limits to talk about, Lister's work encourages not cynicism but engagement... Ultimately the work discloses the gap between who we think we are and who we turn out to be."- Lisa Steele, Catalogue essay
Shake it Up, Baby: Works of Intervention by Ardele Lister, IMAGES '92

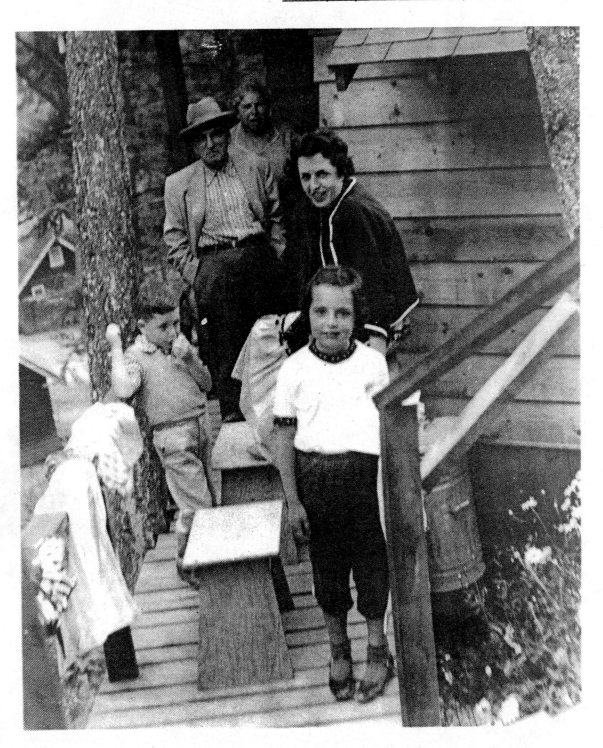

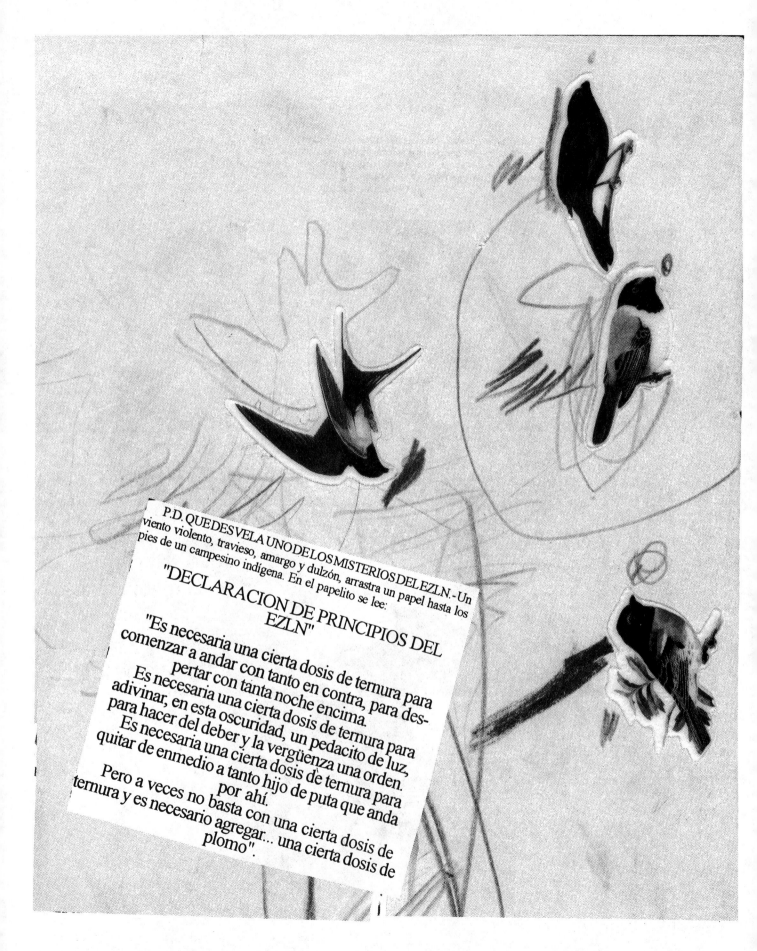

P.D. QUE DESVELA UNO DE LOS MISTERIOS DEL EZLN.- Un viento violento, travieso, amargo y dulzón, arrastra un papel hasta los pies de un campesino indígena. En el papelito se lee:

"DECLARACION DE PRINCIPIOS DEL EZLN"

"Es necesaria una cierta dosis de ternura para comenzar a andar con tanto en contra, para despertar con tanta noche encima.
Es necesaria una cierta dosis de ternura para adivinar, en esta oscuridad, un pedacito de luz, para hacer del deber y la vergüenza una orden.
Es necesaria una cierta dosis de ternura para quitar de enmedio a tanto hijo de puta que anda por ahí.
Pero a veces no basta con una cierta dosis de ternura y es necesario agregar... una cierta dosis de plomo".

GUADALUPE SORDO, SOMEWHERE IN SPAIN

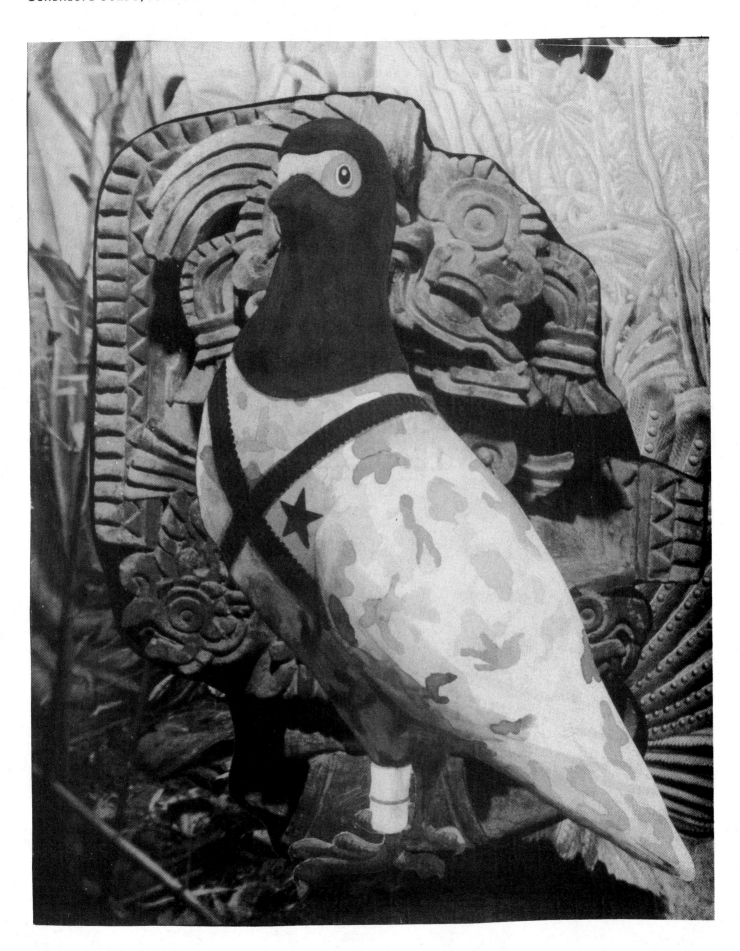

**MARISA GONZÁLEZ**, MADRID, SPAIN

Silence as annulment of space
annulment of space as language of communication
a language of communication based on empty fragment
empty fragments not in the formal but rather in the corporal.

An artificial body like a natural icon,
the artificial body woven by rays of light,
the light modifying the meaning,
light converting the icon-symbol into metaphor,
the metaphor as armament of expression.

Expresion through repetitive fragments.
repetition as a symbol of reproduction,
reproduction between form and meaning.

Dreams are always broken silences
Dreams dreamt are always desires.
Dreams dreamt are always enigmas.
Dreams reflected,
Dreams proyected,
Dreams broken,
are serial silences, unique silences.

# SILENCIOS
# SILENCES

MARISA GONZALEZ
Madrid.

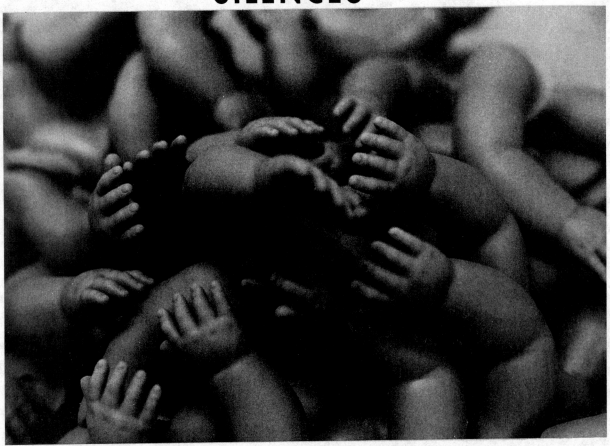

**MARISA GONZÁLEZ**, MADRID, SPAIN

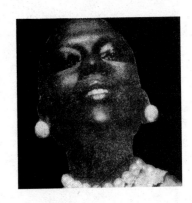

# GLANCES IN TIME

DESIRES          IDENTITY VERTIGOS          TERRITORIES          SILENCES

It is a personal narration based on the conversation between the real me and the ideal me, through multiple glances at the image of a woman alone, the glances in time.

In this symbolic reading, the body speaks in emotional and mental multiplicity. In its vision the images refer to an interactive relation with the "voyeur" responding to a spectator's request for the secret implications of the glance, the memory, the mind, the body, the desire. **M. González**

# MIRADAS EN EL TIEMPO

DESEOS          VERTIGOS DE IDENTIDAD          TERRITORIOS          SILENCIOS

Es una narración personal originada en el discurso entre el yo real y el yo utópico, a través de múltiples miradas de la imagen de una sola mujer, las miradas del tiempo.

En esta lectura simbólica, el cuerpo habla en multiplicidad emocional y mental. En su visión las imágenes apelan a una relación interactiva con el "voyeur", a una demanda del espectador de las implicaciones secretas, de la mirada, la memoria, la mente, el cuerpo, el deseo. **M. González**

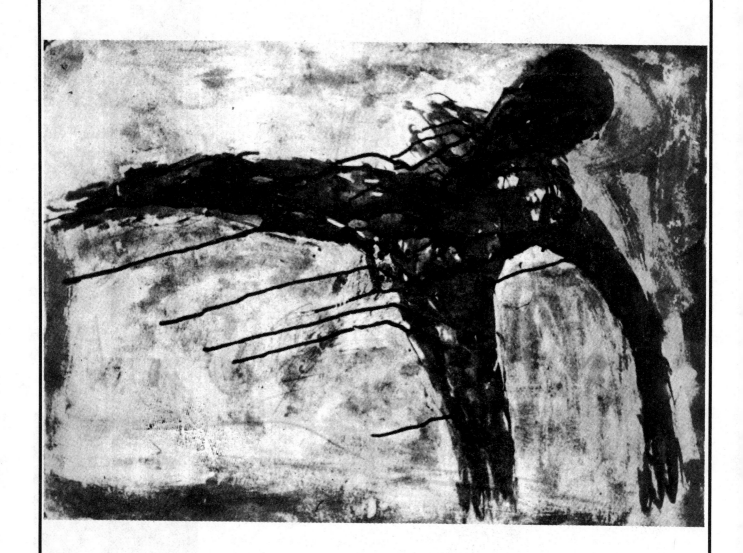

# OPEN SEASON
## Maria Epes

### Acrylic, Menstrual Blood, Oil Pastel, .9mm Luger

### 28 x 40"

MARIA EPES, NEW YORK, NY, USA

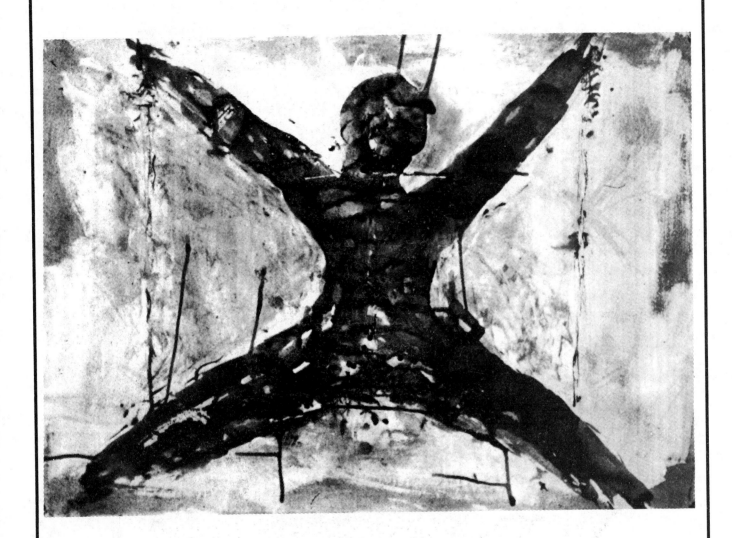

# TARGET PRACTICE
## Maria Epes

Acrylic, Menstrual Blood, Oil Pastel,
.9mm Luger

28 x 40"

RUTH LAXSON, ATLANTA, GA, USA

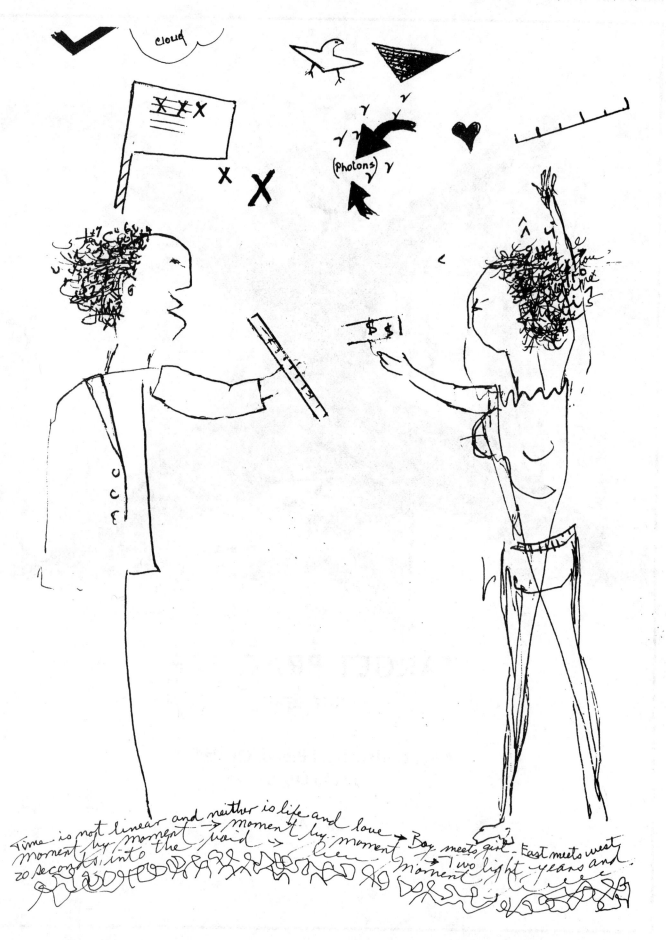

KAY MILLER, BOULDER, CO, USA

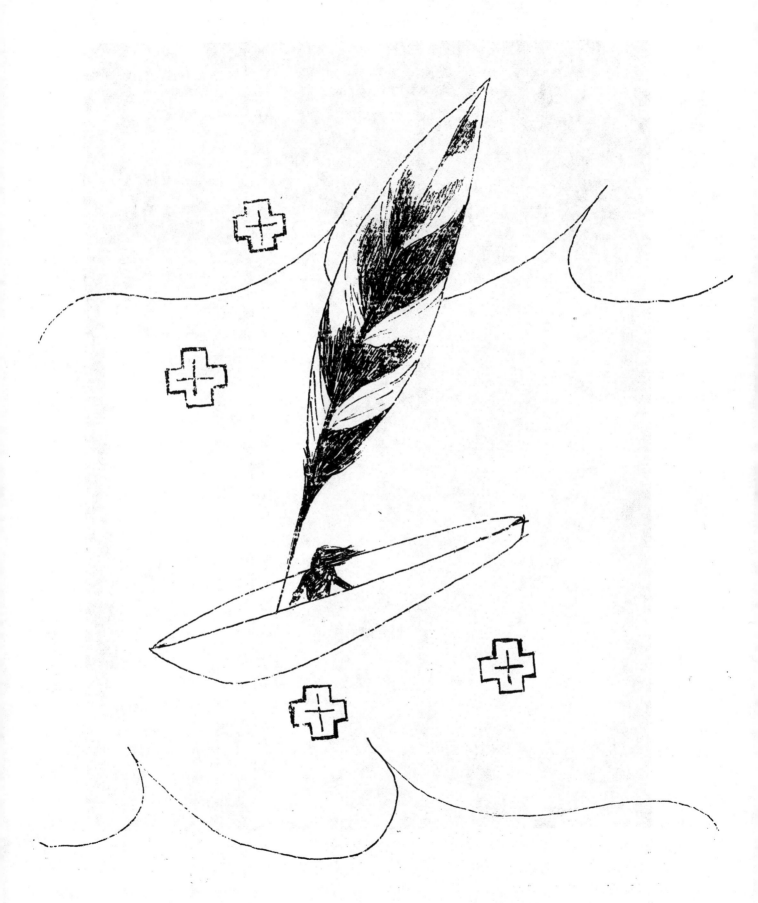

MARIA ELENA GONZÁLEZ, BROOKLYN, NY, USA

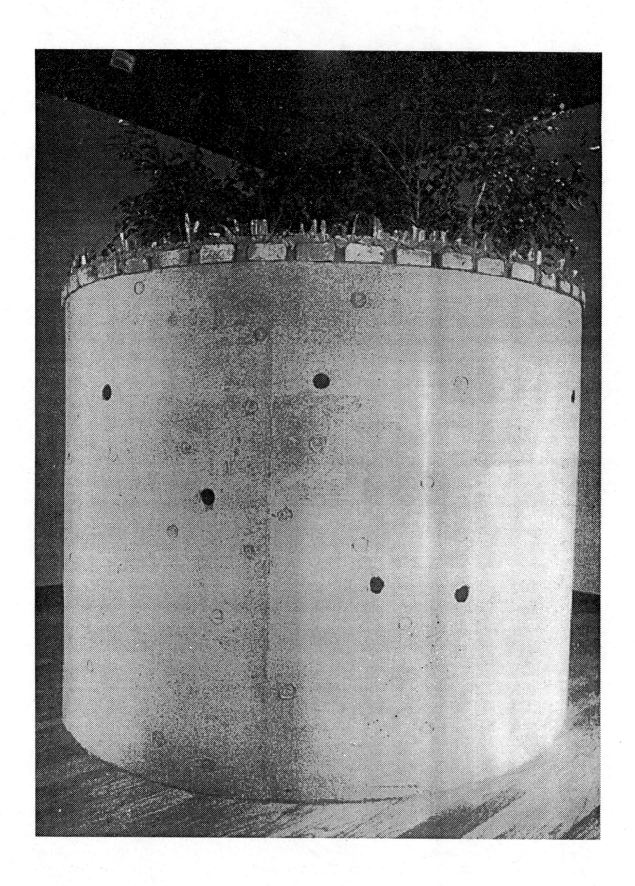

Maria Elena González, BROOKLYN, NY, USA

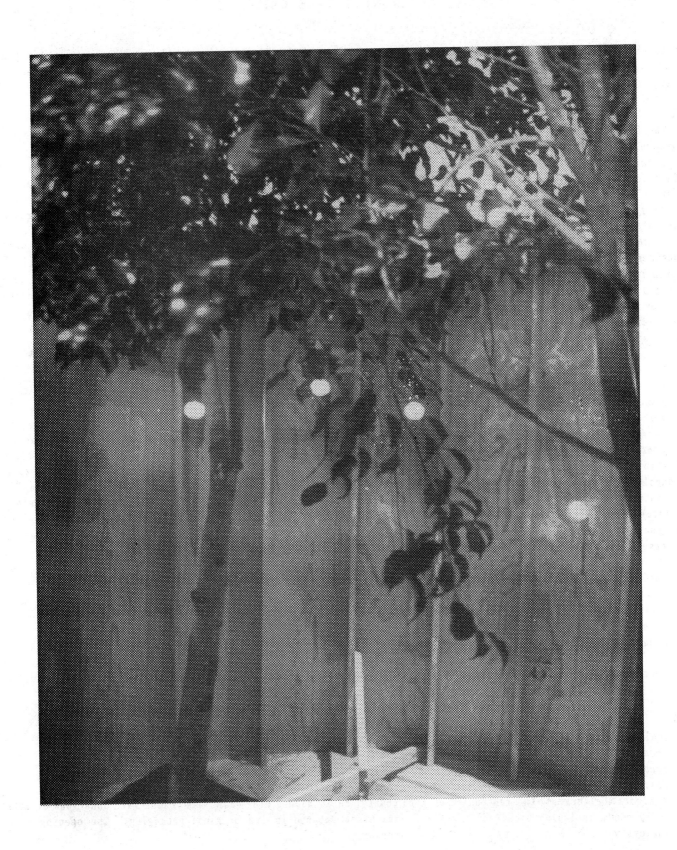

## TEN NOTEWORTHY TIME CAPSULES

Over the past century, the burial of time capsules has been a popular tradition responsible for an estimated 10,000 sealed and dated containers deposited throughout the world. The following 10 time capsules document a range of noteworthy attempts at delivering messages to the future.

### 1.  THE WESTINGHOUSE TIME CAPSULES OF 1939 AND 1964

The first sealed in 1939, the second in 1964; both to be opened in 6939 C.E.

*Sponsor:* Westinghouse Electric & Manufacturing Co.

*Location:* 50 feet below ground in a concrete shaft called the "immortal well" on the former Westinghouse Pavilion site, Flushing Meadows, Queens, NY (former New York World's Fair grounds of 1939 & 1964). A granite marker surrounded by a ring of benches currently marks their location.

*Design:* A torpedo-shaped container (the first made of Cupaloy, a copper alloy; the second made of Kromarc, a stainless steel alloy) preserving objects sealed in glass, tar and inert gas. Weight 800 pounds; length 7.5 feet.

*Contents:* This "800 pound parcel to be delivered in the year 6939," is perhaps the most famous and well documented time capsule. Besides introducing the concept of an encyclopedic "record of World Civilization" preserved for the future, this torpedo-shaped vessel was originally intended to be called a Time Bomb, since when opened, it would trigger a cultural explosion. The impending threat of World War, however, forced Westinghouse to tame the name thus giving birth to the now ubiquitous term Time Capsule. The curious can get a peak inside by visiting the replica TCs originally made for exhibit at the World's Fairs and currently on display in the George Westinghouse Museum, Wilmerding, PA.

### 2.  CRYPT OF CIVILIZATION.

Sealed in 1940; to be opened 8113 C.E.

*Sponsor:* Dr. Thornwell Jacobs, President. Oglethorpe University, Atlanta GA.

*Location:* Cellar of Phoebe Hearst Hall, Oglethorpe University, Atlanta, GA.

*Design:* 2000 cubic foot room cut in granite bedrock. A welded stainless steel door seals off the contents.

*Contents:* Applying state-of-the-art technology in the service of Modernity, Progress and American Manifest Destiny, the Crypt has the distinction of being sealed the longest, while also claiming to house the most encyclopedic selection of natural and man-made artifacts. The contents include Hashish (listed as a "Habit"), miniature renditions of famous works of art and architecture (like the Great Wall of China and Michelangelo's *Pieta*) and the 20th century's own Rosetta Stone: the MUTOSCOPE, a machine designed to teach Futurians the English language. In addition to the usual litany of deposits, microfilm was invented for the Crypt by T.K. Peters (former "motion picture technician" for D.W. Griffith), to preserve "the most essential books of the world containing all of the accumulated knowledge of mankind."

### 3.  OKLAHOMA SESQUICENTENNIAL COMMEMORATIVE TIME CAPSULE

Sealed in 1957; to be opened in 2007 C.E.

*Sponsor:* Oklahoma State.

*Location:* Oklahoma Statehouse grounds, Tulsa, OK.

*Design:* A fully operable, brand new 1957 Plymouth automobile.

*Contents:* The 1957 Plymouth with all of its accessories is to be awarded to the person or their heirs who, in 1957, had most closely estimated the population of Tulsa, OK in the year 2007.

### 4.  TROPICO TIME TUNNEL

Sealed in 1966; to be opened in 2866 C.E.

*Sponsor:* Kern Antelope Historical Society, Kern County, CA.

*Location:* Tropico Gold Mine, Rosamund, CA.

*Design:* 10,000 cubic foot empty mine shaft; entryway sealed off with cement.

*Contents:* Celebrating the centennial of Kern county, an abandoned mine shaft was loaded with donations of 20th century goods including books and a new television set encased in its original packaging. The opening date coincides with the Kern County millennial anniversary.

## 5. OSAKA EXPO'70 DUPLICATE TIME CAPSULES

Sealed in 1970; to be opened in 6970 C.E.

*Sponsor:* Matsushita Electric Industrial Company & Mainichi Newspapers.

*Location:* One buried below the ground, the duplicate above ground. Osaka Castle Park, Osaka, Japan.

*Design:* Duplicate cauldron-shaped containers made of nickel-chrome alloy; interior dimensions: one meter diameter, 500,000 cubic centimeters. Weight: 2.12 metric tons.

*Contents:* Encyclopedic in scope, this time capsule elicited the recommendations of the public and "27 experts" who chose 12,098 objects out of 116,324 suggestions. The placement of the TC above ground serves as a reminder of the existence and location of the buried one. It can be opened, thereby enabling scientific experts to monitor the condition of its contents. Besides traditional items, this TC includes a used diary, insects and plant life.

## 6. ANDY WARHOL TIME CAPSULES

Begun in 1973 or 1974; no set opening date.

*Sponsor:* Andy Warhol, artist.

*Location:* The Andy Warhol Museum, Pittsburgh, PA.

*Design:* 600+ sealed & dated cardboard boxes averaging 18 x 10 x 14 inches.

*Contents:* The contents vary greatly and comprised nearly everything that came across Warhol's desk including personal correspondence, fan mail, junk mail, photos, drawings, clothing, souvenirs, magazines, antiques and collectibles. A changing exhibition of the contents of one TC are on display at all times.

## 7. EL MUERTO QUE TIENE SED [The Dead Man Who Is Thirsty]

Sealed in 1978; to be opened in 6978 C.E.

*Sponsor:* Wolf Vostell, artist.

*Location:* Los Barruecos, Extremadura, Spain. Positioned upon a rock and directed westward.

*Design:* A lead box placed in a cylindrical tank of cement.

*Contents:* The thoughts of the residents of the village of Malpartida, Spain. Outside the cement container is a plaque which reads: "A request to science to open this sculpture after 5000 years. On that date, remove the lead box and analyze the empty interior to visualize its form of energy and thought."

## 8. RICE/TREE/BURIAL PROJECT

Sealed in 1979; to be opened in 2079 C.E.

*Sponsor:* Agnes Denes, artist.

*Location:* Artpark, Lewiston, NY.

*Design:* Metal container buried in the ground.

*Contents:* A set of predictions about life in 2079 C.E., a number of characterizations of the differences between animals and humans and the micro-filmed publications of its designer.

## 9. CAPSULA DE TIEMPO CORDOBA

Completed in 1992, the Cápsula de Tiempo Córdoba remains open.

*Sponsor:* The collaborative Agencia de Viaje, and the Andalucian Pavilion, Expo'92, Sevilla, Spain.

*Location:* Entrance to the Cartujan Monastery on the Expo'92 World's Fair grounds, Sevilla, Spain.

*Design:* A 85 x 2 x .6 meter trench filled with liquid asphalt; with hinged protective grate.

*Contents:* Through workshops and an open invitation to the public advertised in the press, people were asked to put anything they desired into the permeable and preserving liquid asphalt matrix. To date, several thousand people have contributed messages into this viscous wishing well.

## 10. ENVIRONMENTAL TIME CAPSULE

To be sealed in 2000 and opened either in 3000 or 10,000 C.E.

*Sponsor:* Takeharu Etoh, Civil Engineer, Kinki University, Kowake, Higashi-Osaka, Japan.

*Location:* Intended for the polar ice-cap of Mars.

*Design:* Undisclosed.

*Contents:* In the tradition of encyclopedic millennial TCs, the Environmental TC is conceived as "a little globe of the end of the 20th century" containing specimens and information representing environmental and biological conditions of the Earth.

**CLAUDIA LINARES**, NEW YORK, NY, USA

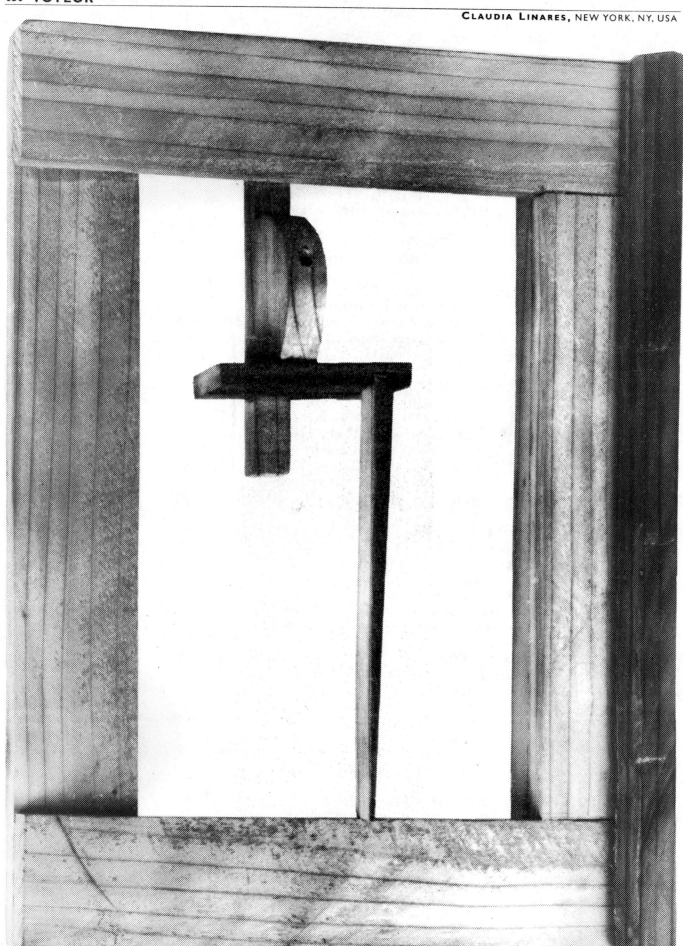

ANN GIORDANO, NEW YORK, NY

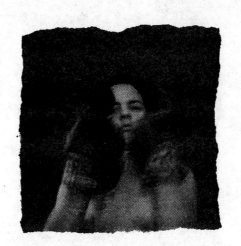

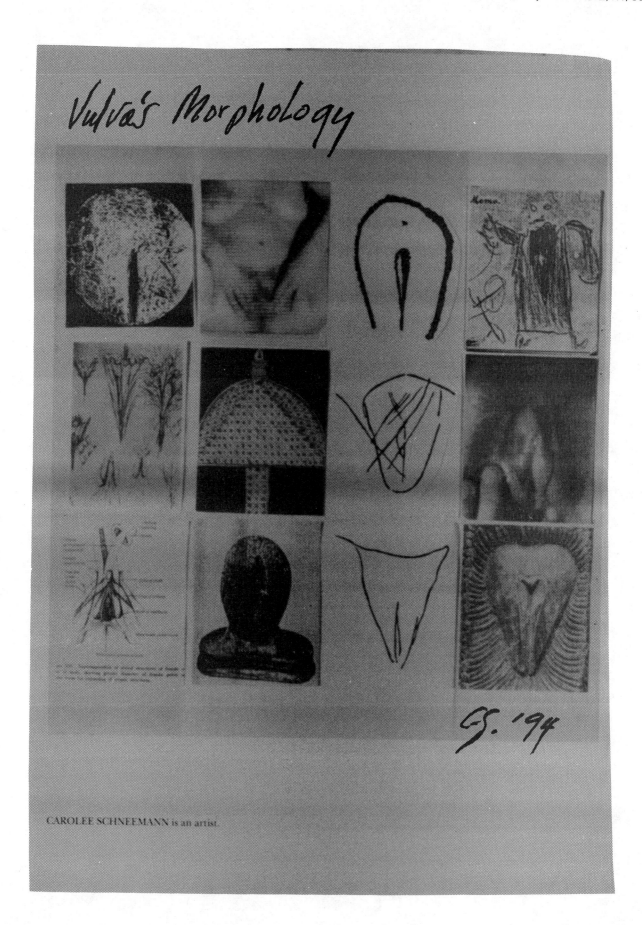

CAROLEE SCHNEEMANN is an artist.

CAROLEE SCHNEEMANN, NEW PALTZ, NY, USA

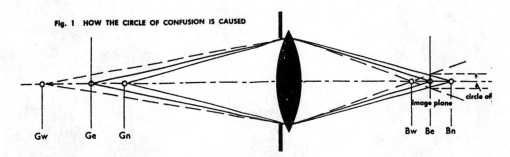

Fig. 1 HOW THE CIRCLE OF CONFUSION IS CAUSED

## VULVA'S SCHOOL

Vulva goes to school and discovers she doesn't exist...

Vulva goes to church and discovers she is obscene...
(quote St. Augustine)

Vulva deciphers Lacan and Baudrillard and discovers she is only a sign, a signification of the void, of absence, of what is not male... (she is given a pen for taking notes...)

Vulva reads biology and understands she is an amalgam of proteins and oxytocin hormones which govern all her desires...

Vulva studies Freud and realizes she will have to transfer clitoral orgasm to her vagina...

Vulva reads Masters and Johnson and understands her vaginal orgasms have not been measured by any instrumentality and that she should only experience clitoral orgasms...

Vulva decodes Feminist Constructivist Semiotics and realizes she has no authentic feelings at all; even her erotic sensations are constructed by patriarchal projections, impositions, and conditioning...

Vulva reads *Off Our Backs* and explores tribadism; then she longs for the other gender's scratching two-day beard, his large hands and insistent cock...

Vulva interprets essentialist Feminist texts and paints her face with her menstrual blood, howling when the moon is full...

Vulva strips naked, fills her mouth and cunt with paint brushes, and runs into the Cedar Bar at midnight to frighten the ghosts of de Kooning, Pollock, Kline...

Vulva reads Gramsci and Marx to examine the privileges of her cultural conditions...

Vulva recognizes her symbols and names on graffitti under the railroad trestle: slit, snatch, enchilada, beaver, muff, coozie, fish and finger pie...

Vulva learns to analyze politics by asking "Is this good for Vulva?"

ELISSE POGOFSKY-HARRIS, OJAI, CA, USA

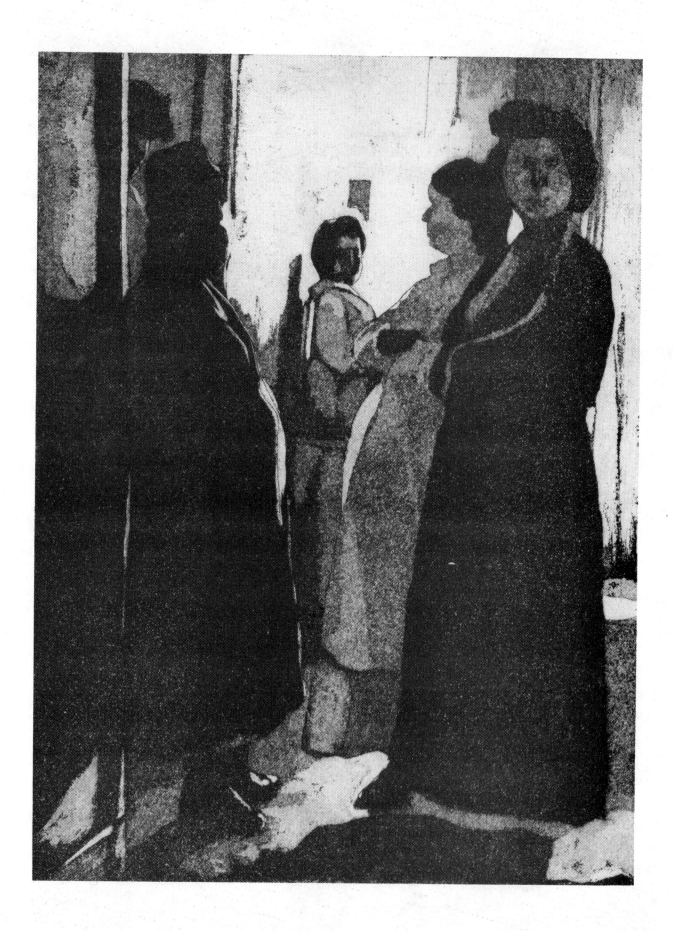

GAIL VACHON, NEW YORK, NY, USA

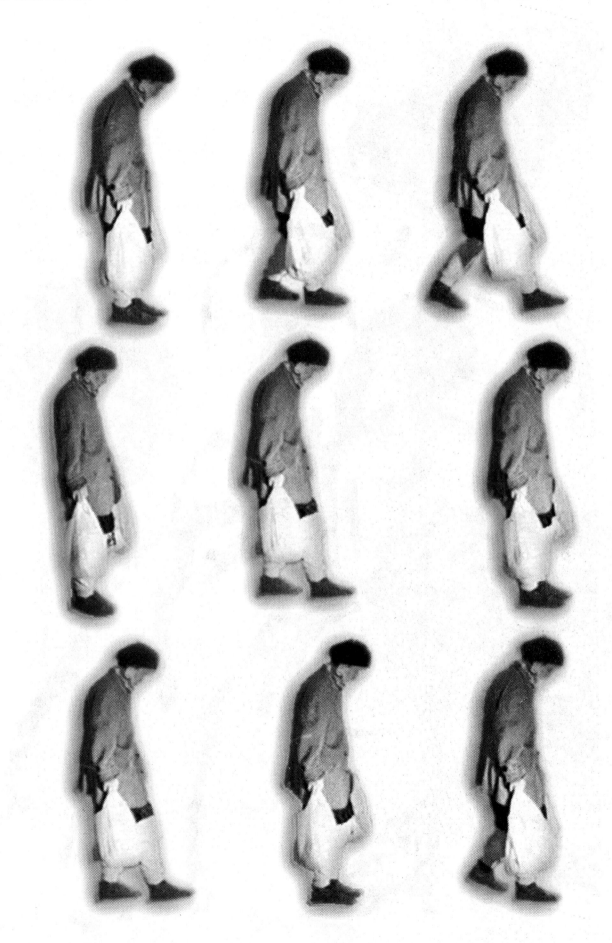

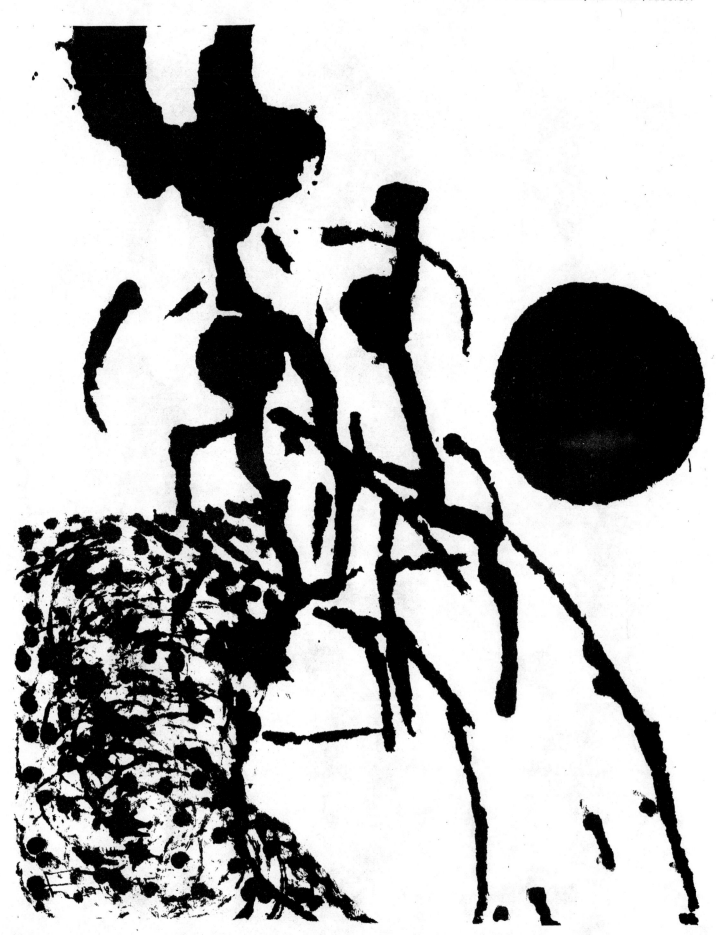

EVERLYN NICODEMUS, ANTWERP, BELGIUM

**EVERLYN NICODEMUS,** ANTWERP, BELGIUM

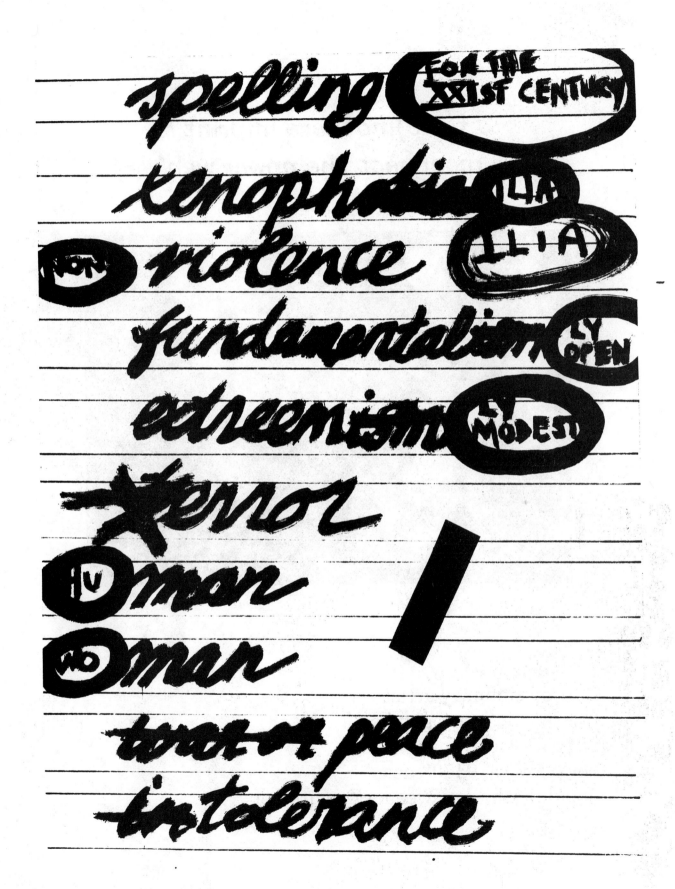

**KATHLEEN SWEENEY,** BERKELEY, CA, USA

# f(ore)mothers imprint
# reconnect the power web

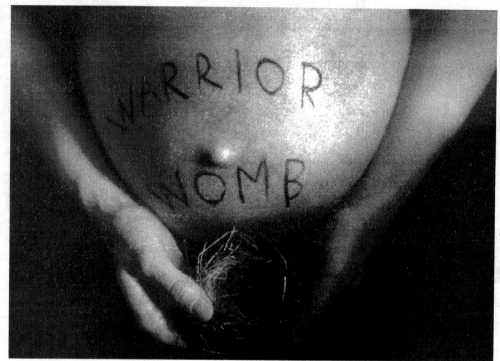

photo: Catherine Allport

kathleen sweeney
interdisciplinary artist
words.video.petroglyphs
2314 mcgee avenue
berkeley, ca  94703 usa
email: kathleen_sweeney@wwire.net

KATHLEEN SWEENEY, BERKELEY, CA, USA

Create-ivity source the deep w(om)b
the main/stream a false stream
a blip scream/screening
girlhate through girlhood.
Electron mindblock to the sacrum
polluted PMS passage toward
cyst-erns of episio/cesari/dural birth.
Mother dance awake umbili/call
to mid/wives with wom(b)en
we all k(no)w
reclaiming/re-calming/re-calling our bodies.
Blood of the month moon
listen to the river
source of matri-lineal trace-back to the
self-sacral marriage/birth.
Listen the drum awake within your
sleepless rite of passage night.
The warriors milk-river the unborn,
double helix ladder to generations,
forward/reward the earth.
Placental natal belly cave
place where words return/begin
speaking cervical circles
long closed
forcep forced
mother of authentic aureoles
singing open the baby home.            (1995)

ELIZABETH SEATON, MONTCLAIR, NJ, USA

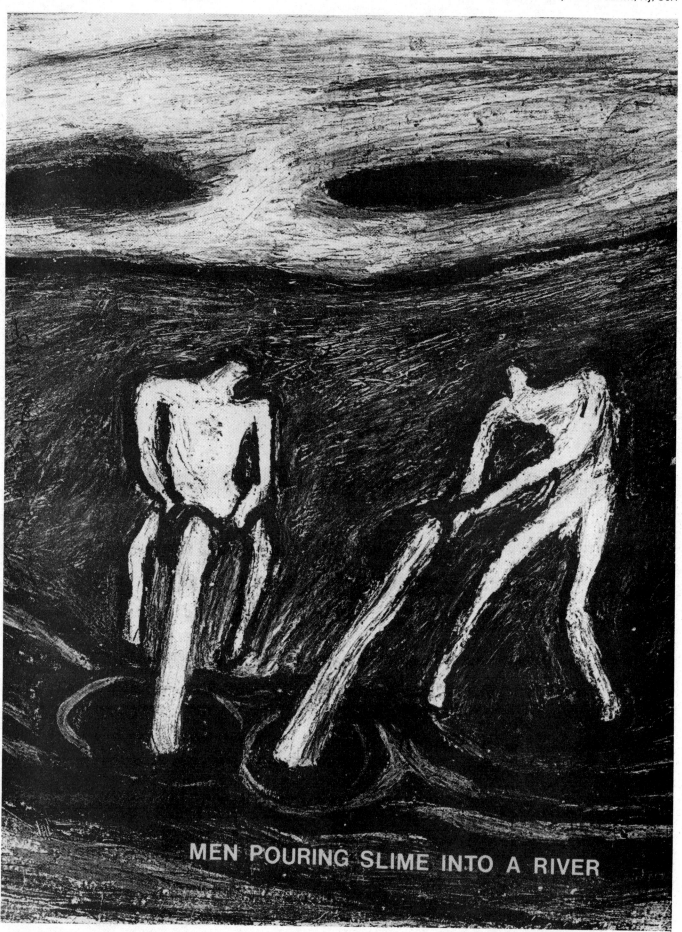

MEN POURING SLIME INTO A RIVER

ELIZABETH SEATON, MONTCLAIR, NJ, USA

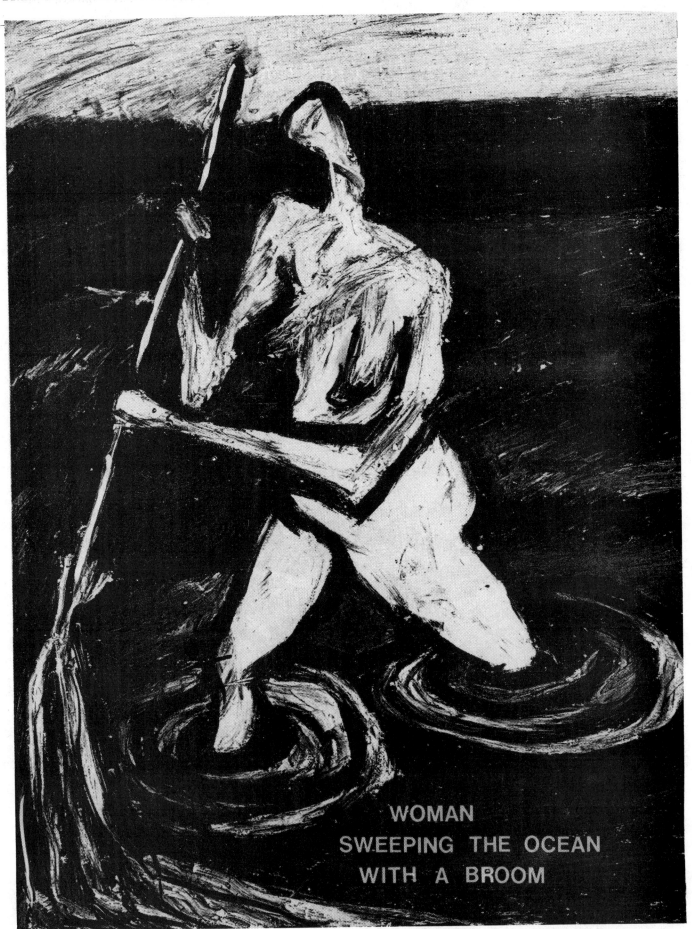

WOMAN
SWEEPING THE OCEAN
WITH A BROOM

Elizabeth Seaton, Montclair, NJ, USA

MARIA CHILF, BUDAPEST, HUNGARY

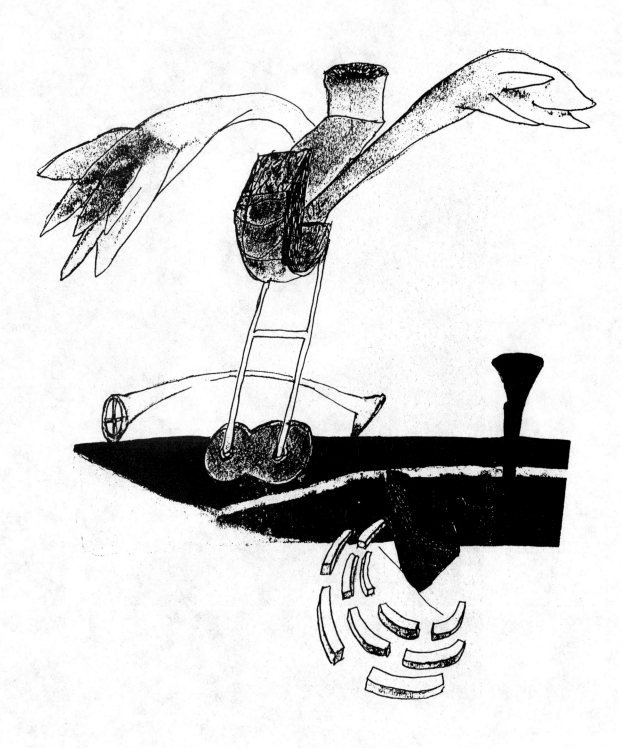

**ALISA DWORSKY**, RANDOLF, VT, USA

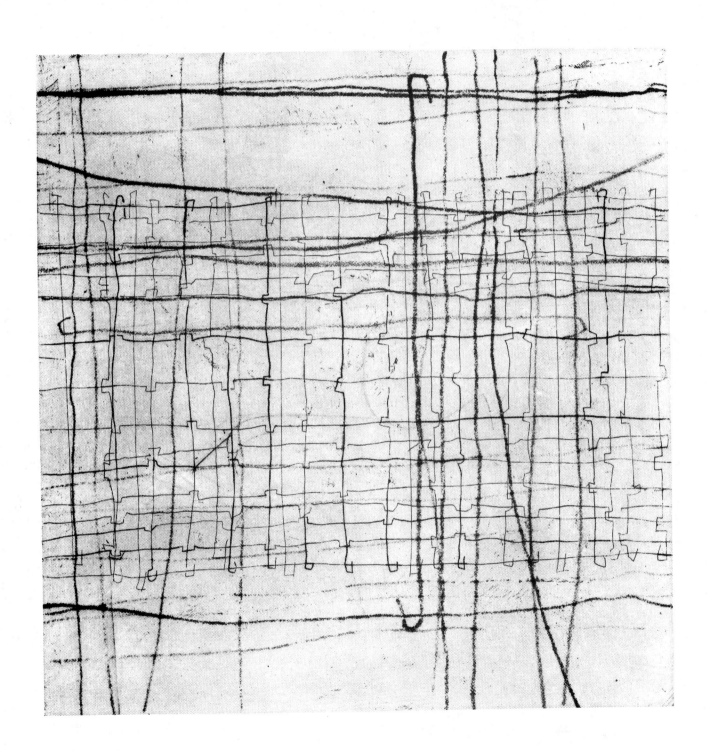

**NATALIE MOORE**, BROOKLYN, NY, USA

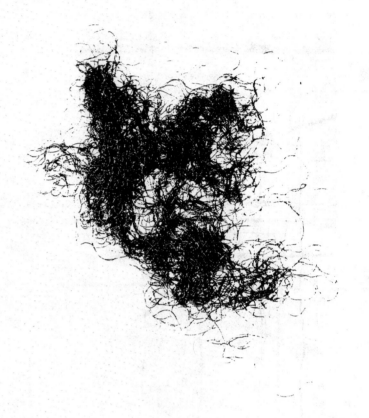

Natalie Moore, BROOKLYN, NY, USA

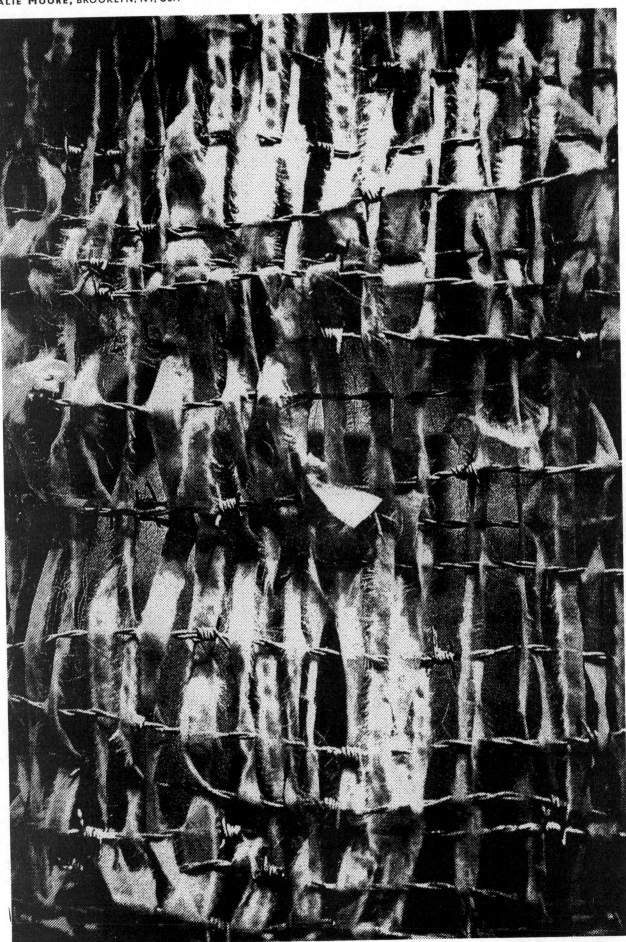

**BARBARA MCGILL BALFOUR**, MONTREAL, QU, CANADA

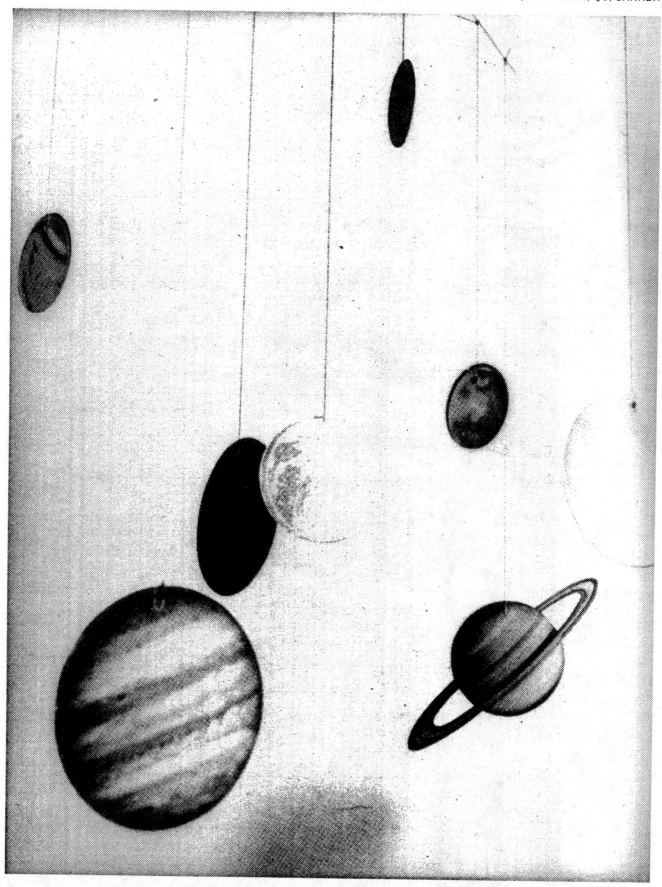

BARBARA McGILL BALFOUR, MONTREAL, QU, CANADA

She thought she must be very self-centered. When she was depressed, it overwhelmed her – all else encased her and she became very small. Like a speck of dust. Or like space garbage. She often imagined herself that way. A helpless particle carried despite herself in an endless orbit around a distant globe.

But in those lovely moments, increasingly present, when she actually felt happy to be alive, she felt full. Full to bursting. Her heart leapt within her ribcage, throwing itself about. She was in rapture, in an exalted state. An outside observer might consider her to be ill. But she knew that this is what she had been waiting for, to feel so much in the present. And even if it didn't last, even knowing it wouldn't, she was on the other side of it.

Barbara McGill Balfour

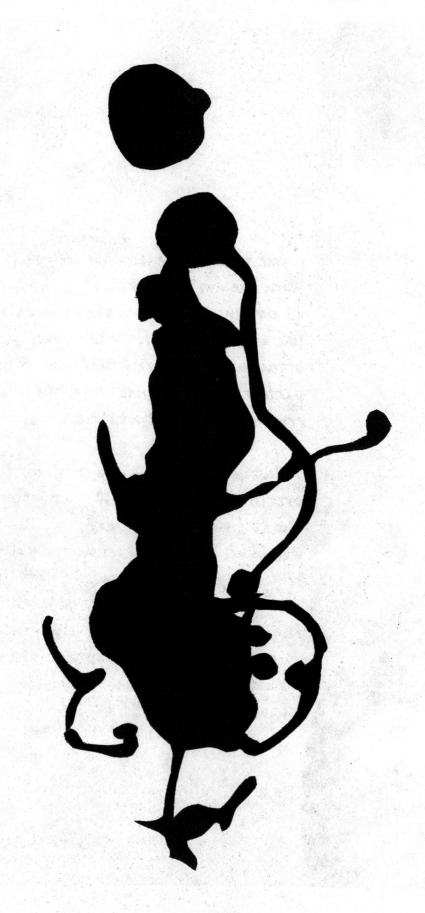

INGRID CALAME, VALENCIA, CA, USA

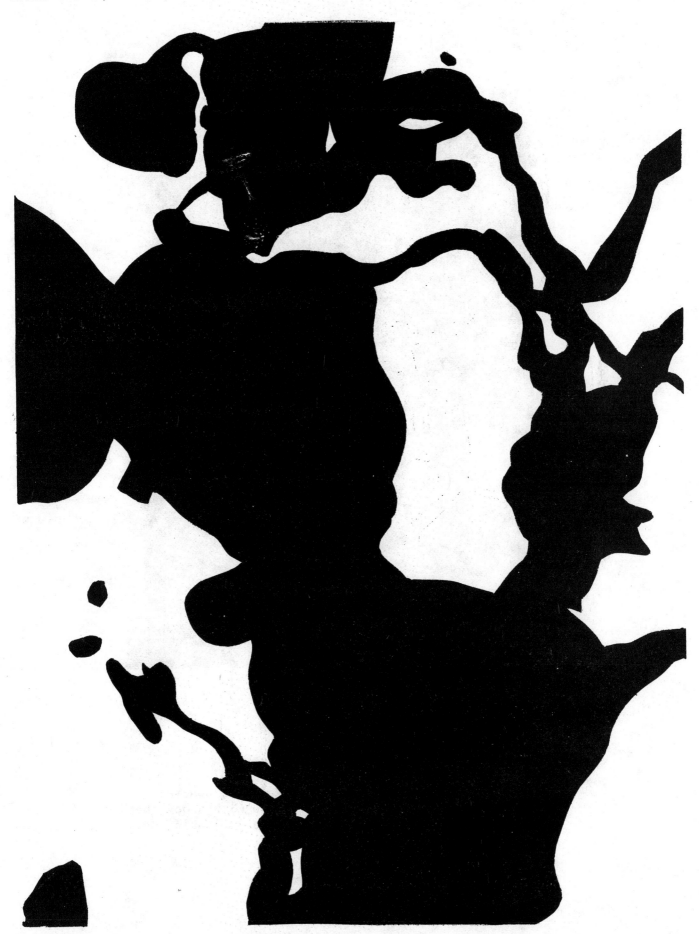

MIRAN FUKUDA, TOKYO, JAPAN

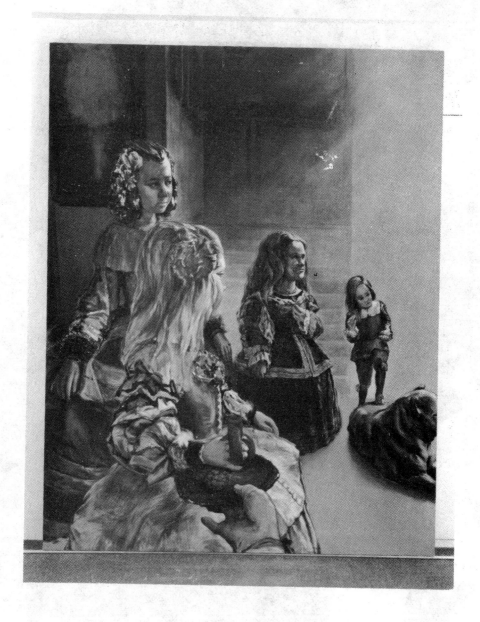

The Princess Margaret, Dona Isabel Velasco, dwarves
Mary Barbora and Nicholasito Pertussato with a dog that
the maid-in-waiting Dona Mary Augustina is looking at.

MIRAN FUKUDA, TOKYO, JAPAN

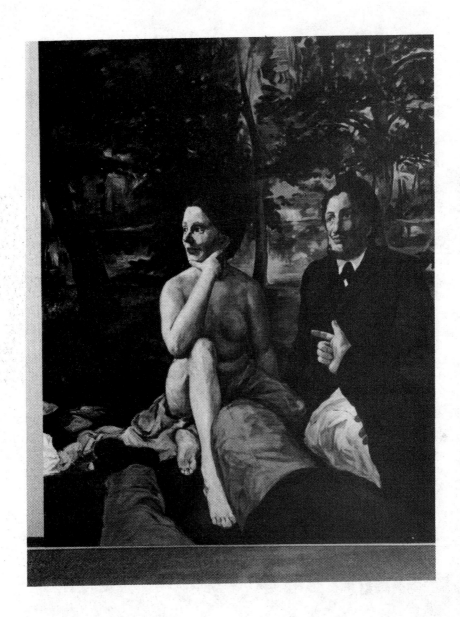

Man and woman on the grass as seen by a man with a hat.

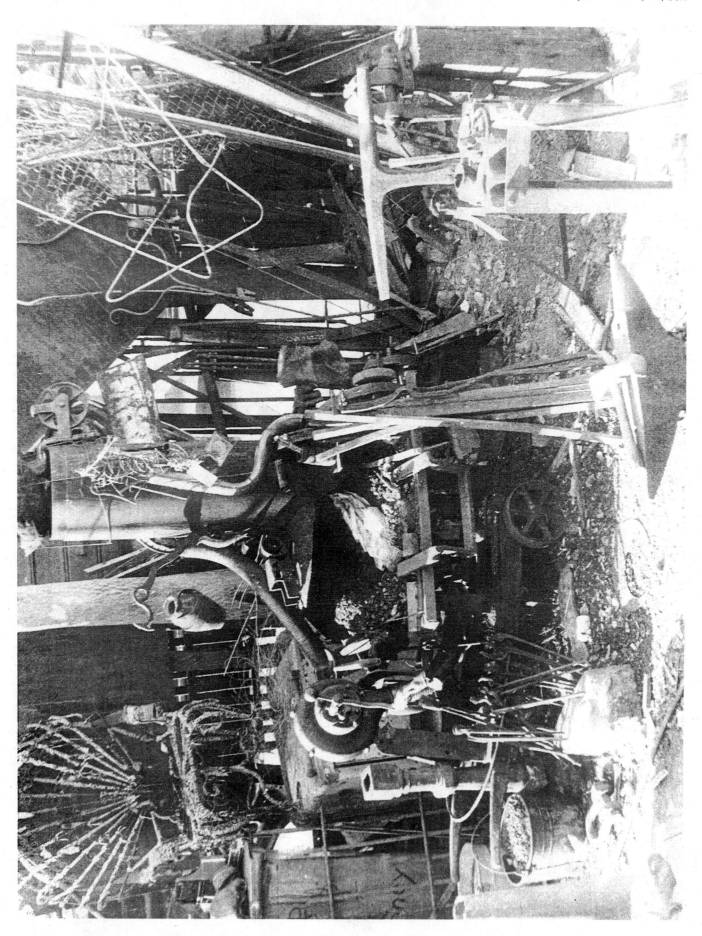

**MARSHA TRATTNER,** NEW YORK, NY, USA

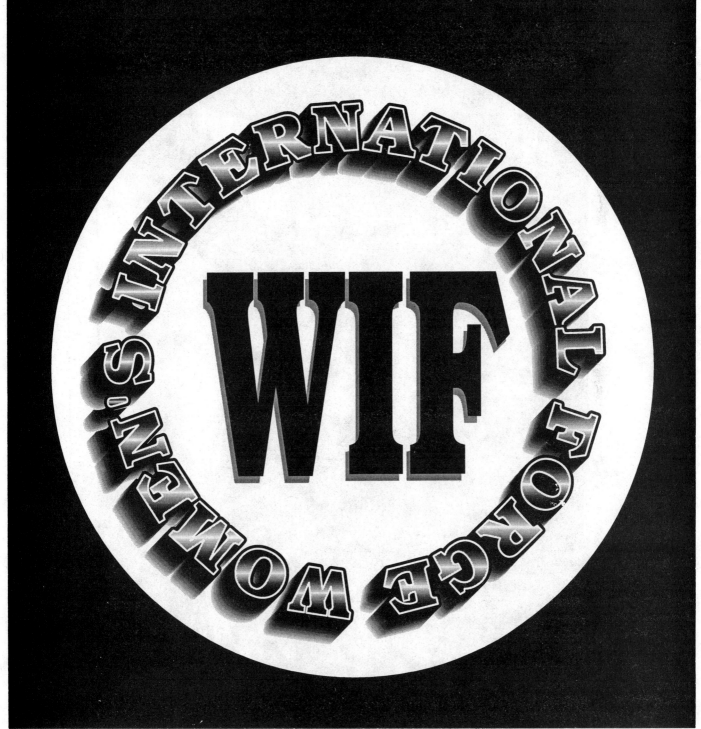

WOMEN'S INTERNATIONAL FORGE 523 EAST 13TH STRRET NEW YORK CITY 10009
TELEPHONE 212 460 9692

# WOMAN about MEN,,,

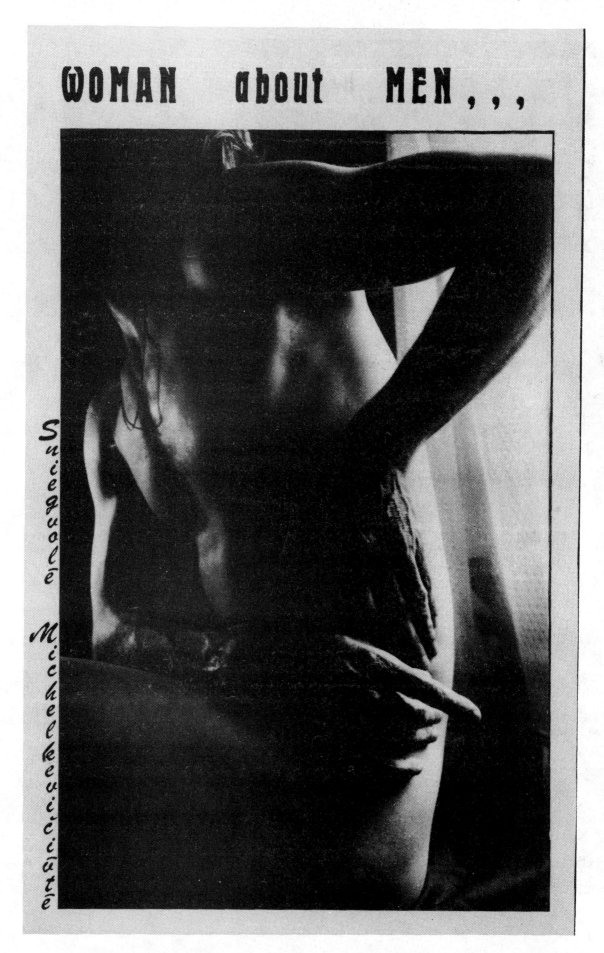

Snlegvolé Michelkevicivté, VILNIUS, LITHUANIA

# Woman about men,,,

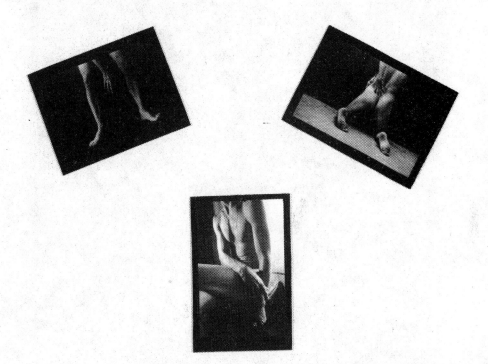

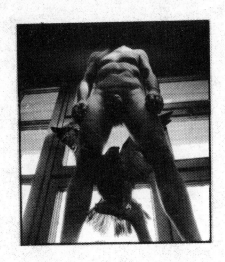

Sniegvolé Michelkevičiūté

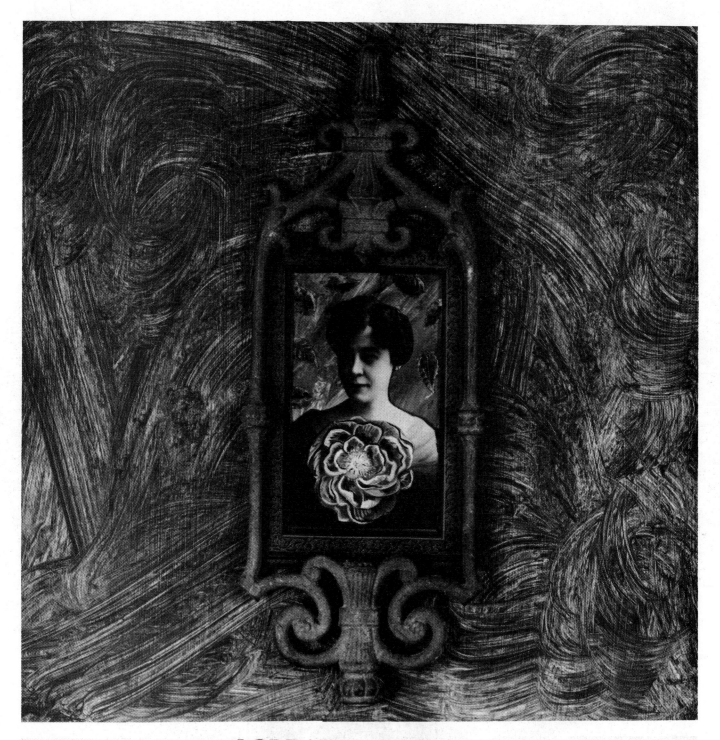

# LORRAINE SERENA

*Woman / Bloom*

voice (805) 684-5908 * fax (805) 684-6990
p. o. box 1315 Carpinteria. CA 93014

MAURA SHEEHAN, NEW YORK, NY, USA

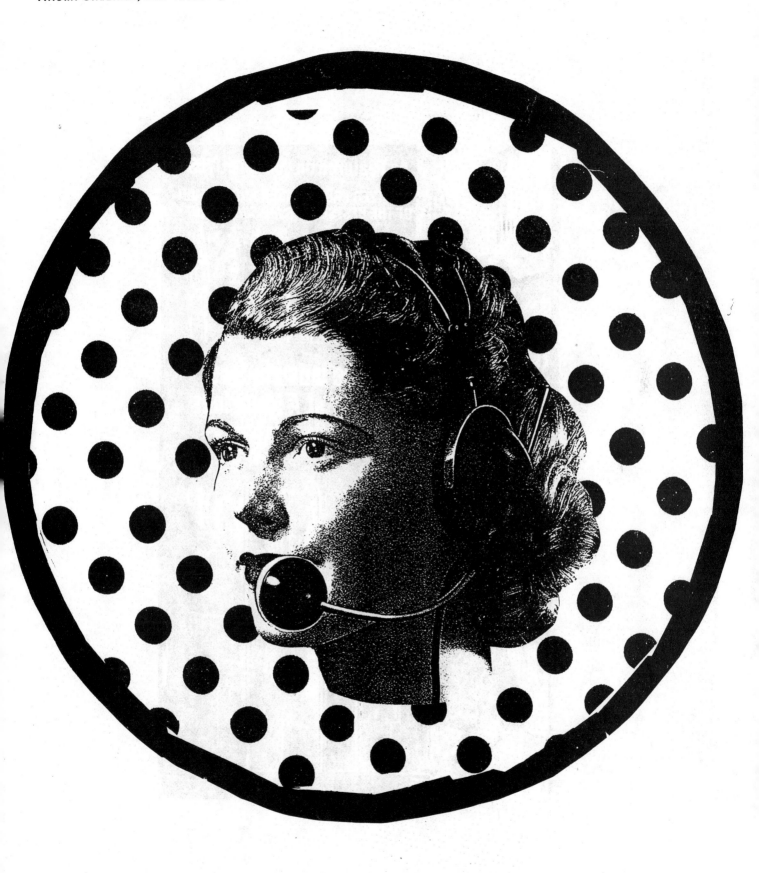

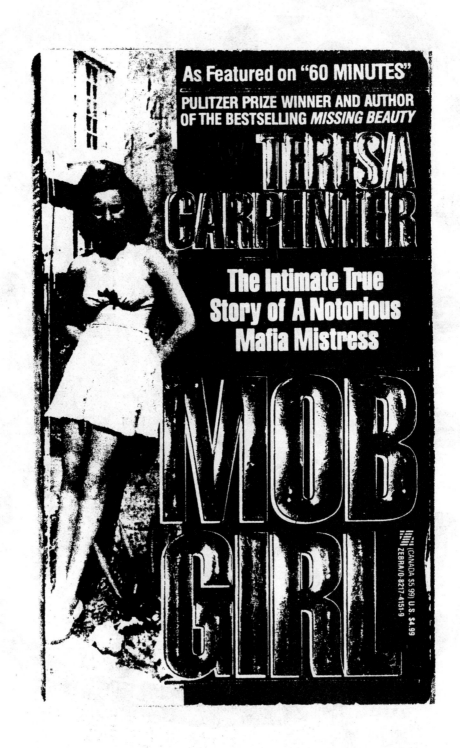

— WOMAN-SEX —  Sketch for "the Mob Girl Show" 95.

MICHELINE GINGRAS, BROOKLYN, NY, USA

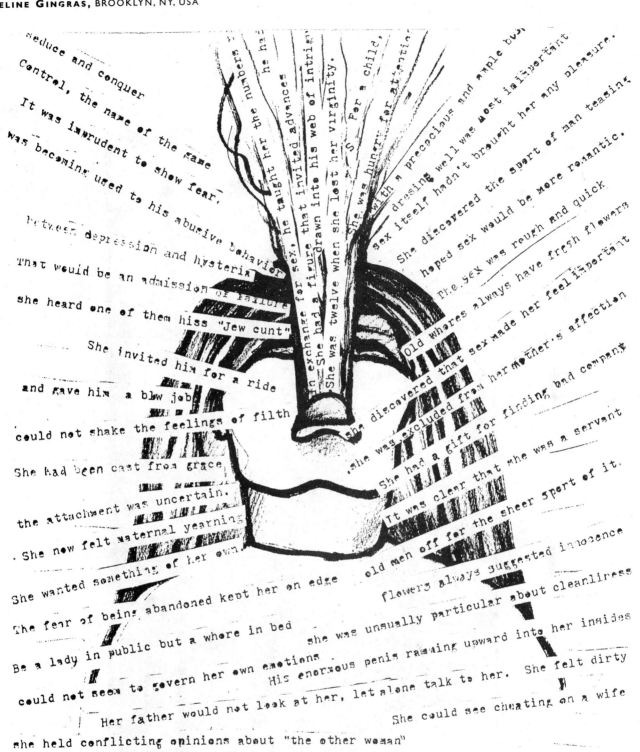

seduce and conquer

Control, the name of the game

It was imprudent to show fear,

was becoming used to his abusive behavior

between depression and hysteria

That would be an admission of failure

she heard one of them hiss "Jew cunt"

She invited him for a ride

and gave him a blow job

could not shake the feelings of filth

She had been cast from grace,

the attachment was uncertain.

. She now felt maternal yearning

She wanted something of her own.

The fear of being abandoned kept her on edge

Be a lady in public but a whore in bed

could not seem to govern her own emotions .

Her father would not look at her, let alone talk to her.

the numbers

he taught her the numbers

he had

in exchange for sex, that invited advances

She had a figure drawn into his web of intrigue

She was twelve when she lost her virginity.

S . For a child,

she was hungry for attention.

with a precocious and ample bust

dressing well was most important

sex itself hadn't brought her any pleasure.

She discovered the sport of man teasing

hoped sex would be more romantic.

The sex was rough and quick

Old whores always have fresh flowers

sex made her feel important

she discovered that sex made her mother's affection

she was excluded from her mother's affection

She had a gift for finding bad company

It was clear that she was a servant

old men off for the sheer sport of it.

flowers always suggested innocence

she was unusually particular about cleanliness

His enormous penis ramming upward into her insides

She felt dirty

She could see cheating on a wife

she held conflicting opinions about "the other woman"

Rather than a rival, she seemed more like a fellow sufferer

Convinced that her husband at last needed her, she felt closer to him

Prostitution was just a set of favors exchanged among "friends

Rule # 1, Think big. # 2: Spend other people's money. # 3. Never appear to
have a care in the world. Men do not want to see that a woman has troubles.

# " he fiLL t'her up and SHe drank IT "

—Canada, Québec - N.Y.

Gingras 95.

# WOMAN WARRIORS

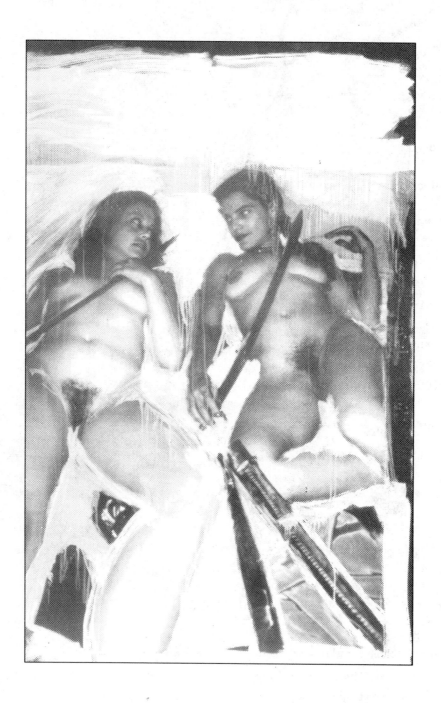

**Suzanne Fiol** *Untitled, 1992, Oil on Cibachrome*

**LAURA FIELDS,** NEW YORK, NY USA

*THE NEW YORK TIMES* **INTERNATIONAL** *SUNDAY, SEPTEMBER 18, 1994*

# Apartheid's Grisly Aftermath: 'Witch Burning'

**By BILL KELLER**
Special to The New York Times
NOBODY, South Africa —

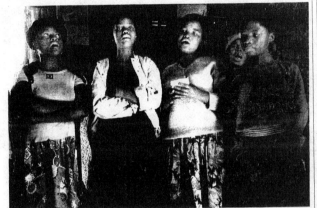

Photographs by Guy Tillim for The New York Times

Braving the anger of mobs in South Africa, Chief Agnes Moloto has created a sanctuary, called Helena, populated entirely by people accused of being witches. Four of those accused sang hymns at a recent service.

**Young militants hardened on defiance turn again to the "necklace."**

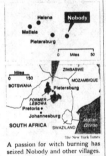

The New York Times

A passion for witch burning has seized Nobody and other villages.

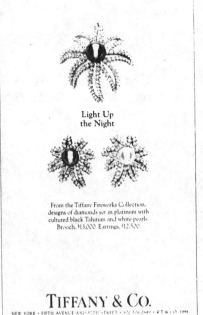

**JENNY MARKETOU,** NEW YORK, NY, USA

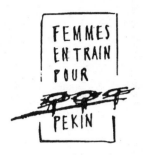

# WOMEN BY TRAIN TO BEIJING

**AALLLL ABBBOARD!!! All women going to Beijing should now board the train! Stand back, the doors are closing, we are about to depart!**

On the 19th of August, 1995, an unusual train will leave Europe, headed for the Chinese capital via Paris, Brussels, Berlin, Warsaw, Moscow, and Siberia. On board, hundreds of women will share a 10,000 km adventure, picking other passengers along the way. Just imagine:

### • TEN DAYS TO TRAIN

for the Non-Governmental Organizations Forum on Women held concurrently in Beijing with the "United Nations' Fourth World Conference on Women for Equality, Development and Peace". The Conference will be held from the 4th to the 15th of September and will evaluate women's status in the world today and over the last ten years. A ten year plan of action for the future will be adopted at the Conference.

The NGO Forum has set itself two objectives: "To influence the document called the Platform for Action that UN members states will adopt in Beijin; and to hold a Forum highlighting women's vision and strategy for the world in the 21st century". The NGO Forum will be held from 30th of August to September 8th, 1995.

### • TEN DAYS TO KEEP OUR OBJECTIVES

on track for this global meeting, our last chance in the 20th century for the women of the world to gather together in such large numbers to exchange our views, to voice our concerns, and to enrich our lives.

### • TEN DAYS IN A TRAIN

for the women of France, or Poland, or Algeria, or Sarajevo, or Malmö or Abidjan, to take the time to discuss the issues which will be debated in Beijing, and also to explore any topic they wish... outside an official context.

### • TEN DAYS AT FULL SPEED

ahead to promote women's interests: to debate, create, meet, collaborate, and share the journey together.

As the NGO Forum is "open to all interested parties", each woman has the right to participate in the World Conference that discusses her status and her future,

The Train for Beijing will pull out of Europe in August 1995! A group of European women spearheaded **Woman by train to Beijing** to help other women attend the Conference. We are already on track preparing the way!

LINDA LINDROTH, NEW HAVEN, CT, USA

# Portrait of the artist **premundane**

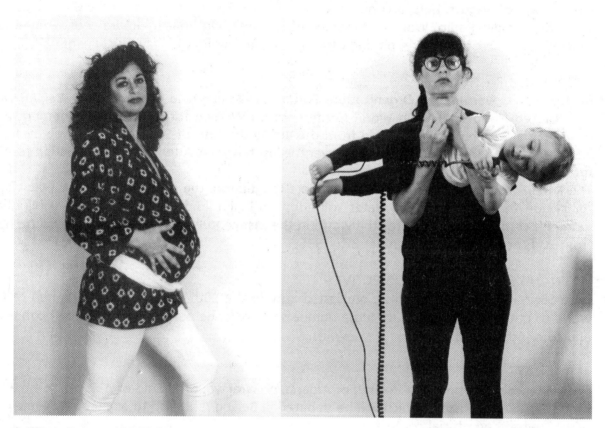

Self-Portrait on my 44th Birthday.

Self-Portrait on my 45th Birthday.

LINDA LINDROTH, NEW HAVEN, CT, USA

Sometime in the early 1970's I sat in the waiting room of my ophthalmologist's Manhattan office with a friend. Across from us sat the diminutive star of the films *Harold and Maude* and *Rosemary's Baby*, Ruth Gordon. I picked up the *Life Magazine* she had been reading and recognized the face of a man I would not soon forget. Milan Vuitch performed an abortion on me in his Washington DC medical office in December, 1967. The magazine article identified Vuitch as a doctor on trial (*United States V. Vuitch*) for performing illegal abortions.

Because I was part of an elite community in 1967—an art student in a northeastern college—I was able to obtain the name of a physician who would presumably perform the operation safely. The code word to make an appointment with Dr. Vuitch was "Sissy Boynton sent me." And early one morning with the boyfriend who some months later would become my first husband, I settled into a seat on the Amtrak to Washington. Dr. Vuitch performed a D & C using only a local anesthetic, without a nurse present. I was 21 years old.

Dr. Vuitch did a competent job—one that allowed me another 23 years to decide to become a mother. The oldest woman in the maternity ward of my local hospital, I was healthy enough and lucky enough to give birth when other women my age were seeing their kids graduate from High School or whose biological clocks had run out. Two years later when I returned to my college for my 25th reunion, I was the mother of the youngest child. There were classmates who had decided not to have children. They had demanding careers. We were the class of 1968. We would change the world, now others want to change it back again.

I do not know what motivated a man like Vuitch to perform illegal abortions in a Washington DC medical building in the 1960's. Perhaps it was because he believed a woman had the right to choose. Perhaps he did it for the money (in my case, the proceeds of the sale of a ten-year old Volkswagen *Microbus* which had once been painted with flowers.) These days when I pass the Women's Health clinic in my town and see the protesters picketing and shouting to women as they enter the building, I am usually accompanied by my almost-5 year old son whose favorite bakery is nearby. He is excited and eager to taste the *chocolate mouse* which is their specialty. We quicken our step, I squeeze his hand.

Linda Lindroth
New Haven, Connecticut
1995

PATRICIA GADEA, MADRID, SPAIN

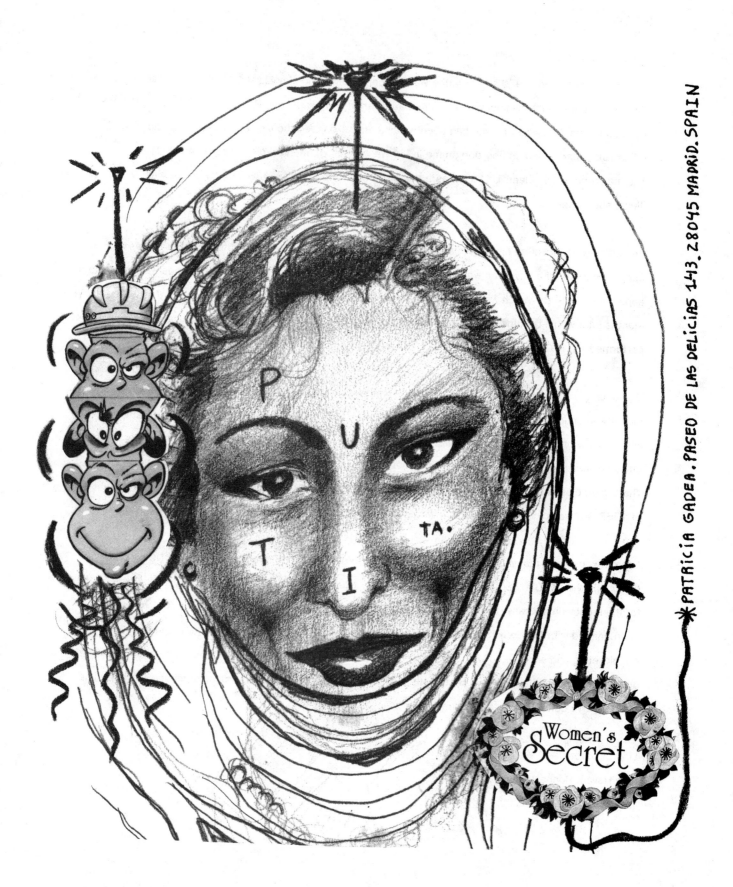

# ONE OF THE MANY THINGS YOU CAN DO WITH THIS TIME CAPSULE:

CONTACT SOMEONE IN IT.

ELISABETH CONDON, BROOKLYN, NY, USA

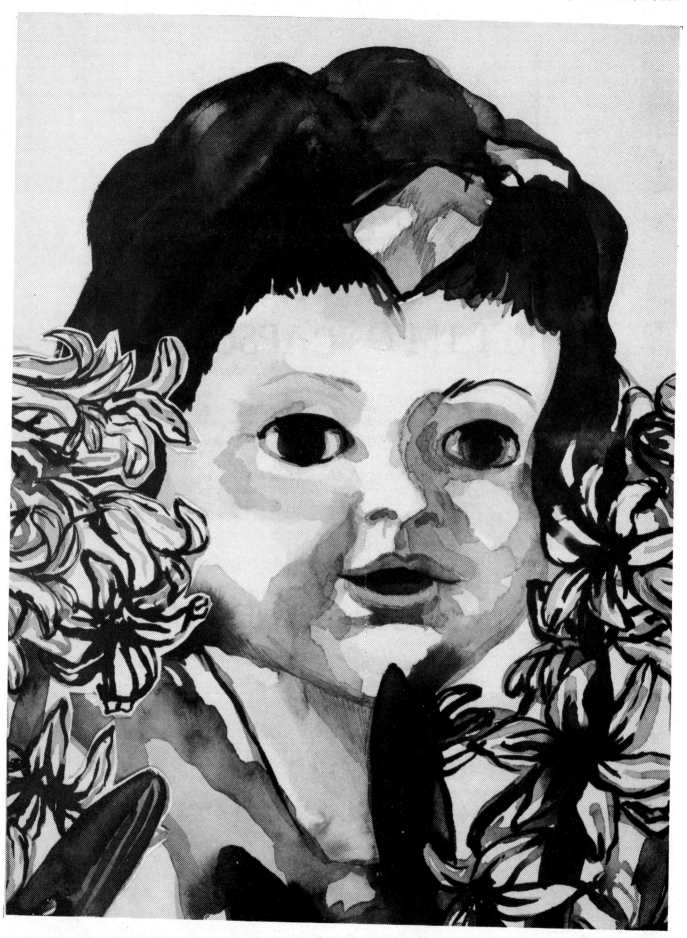

ELISABETH CONDON, BROOKLYN, NY, USA

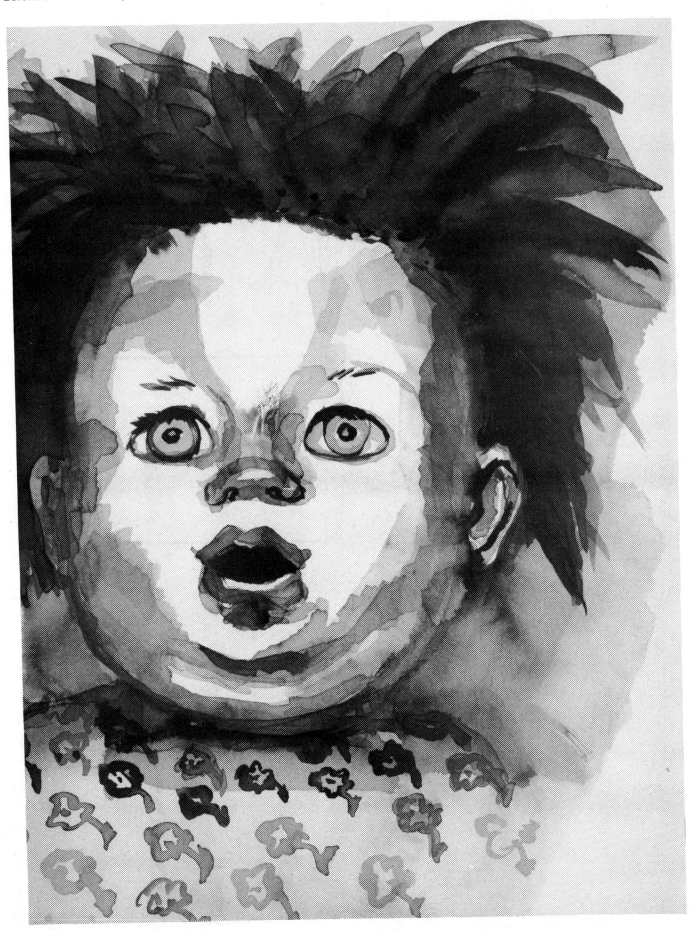

CARA PERLMAN, NEW YORK, NY, USA

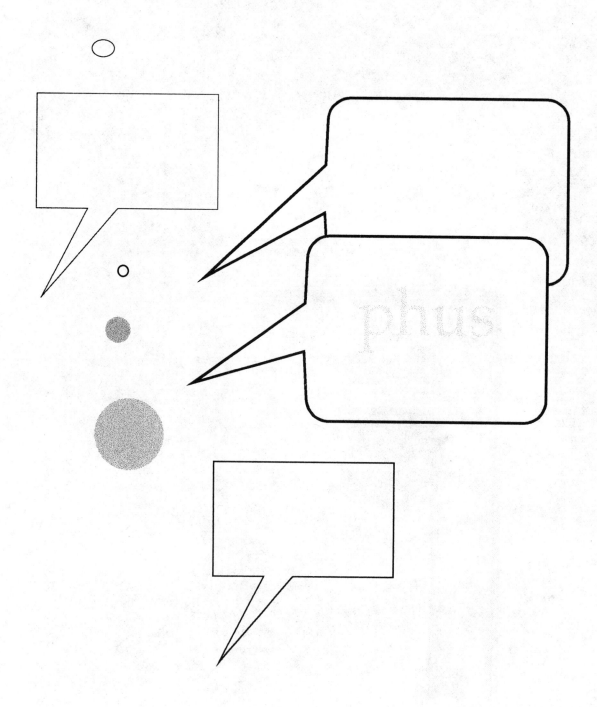

CARA PERLMAN, NEW YORK, NY, USA

CARA PERLMAN
LISPENARD PRODUCTS

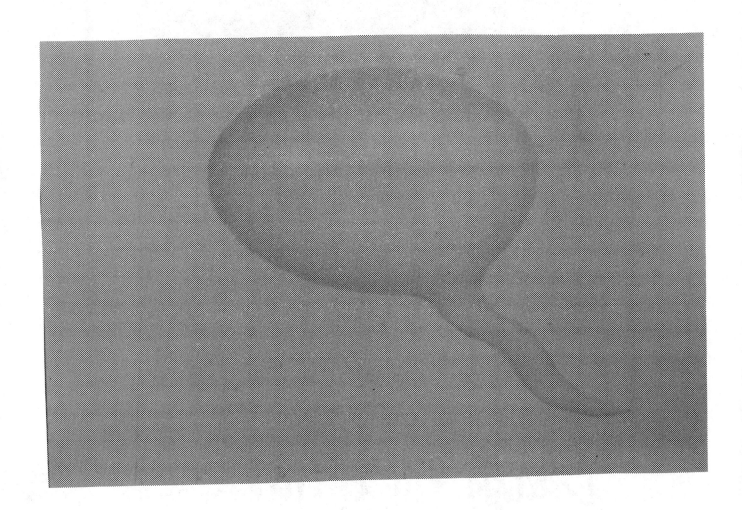

PAULA GOLDMAN, LOS ANGELES, CA, USA

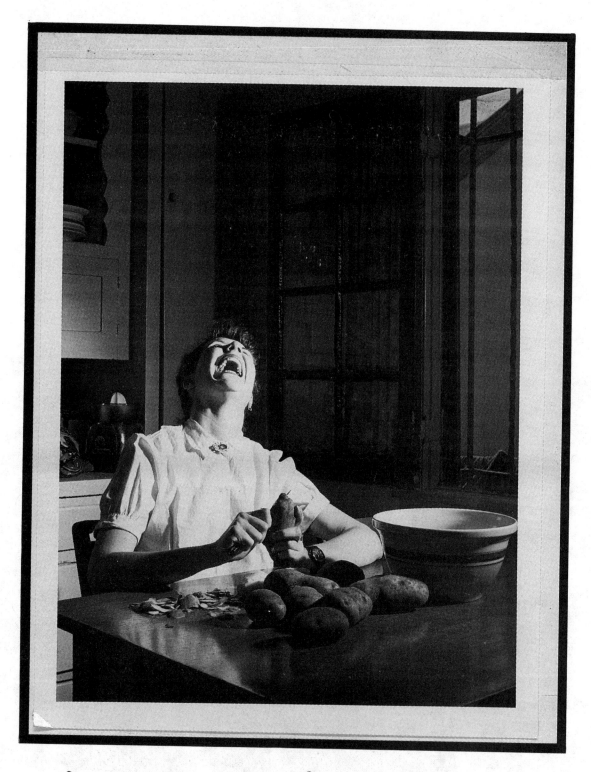

Laugh till it hurts

NANCY GROSSMAN, NEW YORK, NY, USA

WORK: I am fascinated by the physical embodiments of symbolic essences of a person, animal or thing. And I am moved by the human condition in its every day goings on every day. — Nancy Grossman

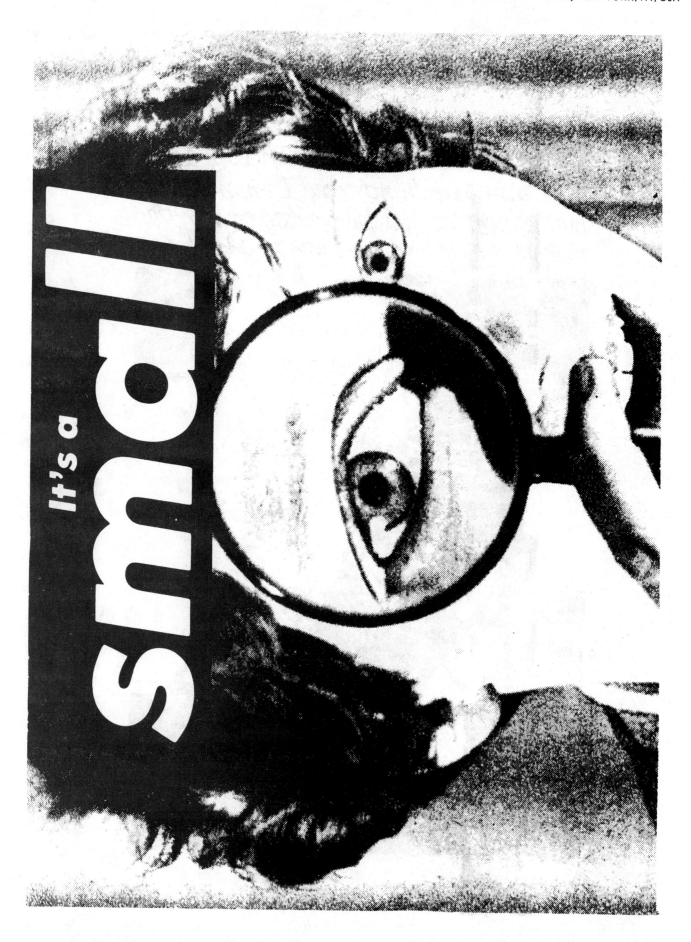

BARBARA KRUGER, NEW YORK, NY, USA

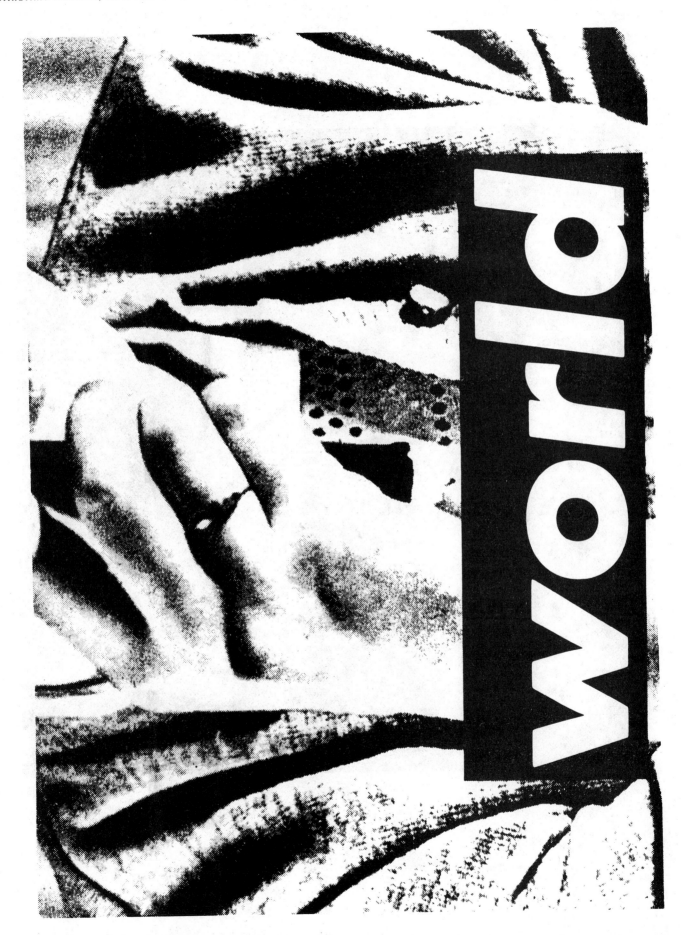

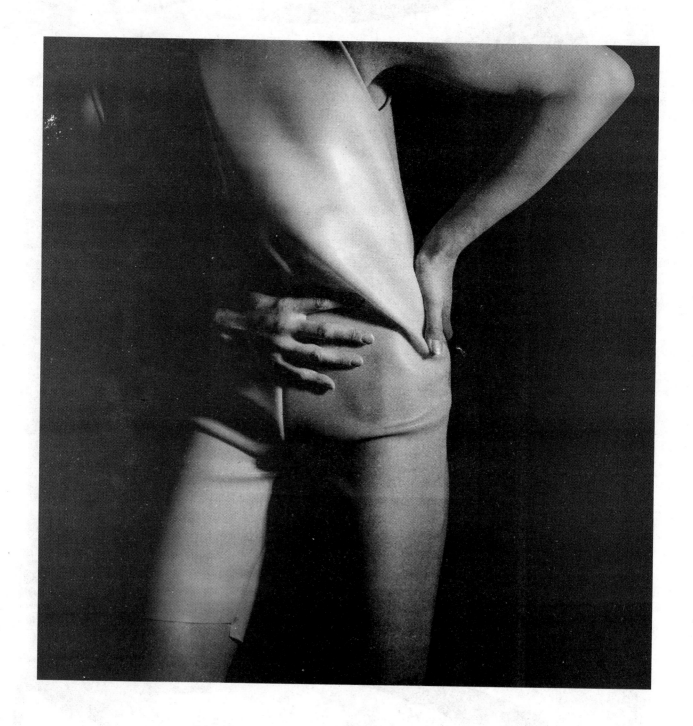

MARGRET WIBMER, AMSTERDAM, THE NETHERLANDS

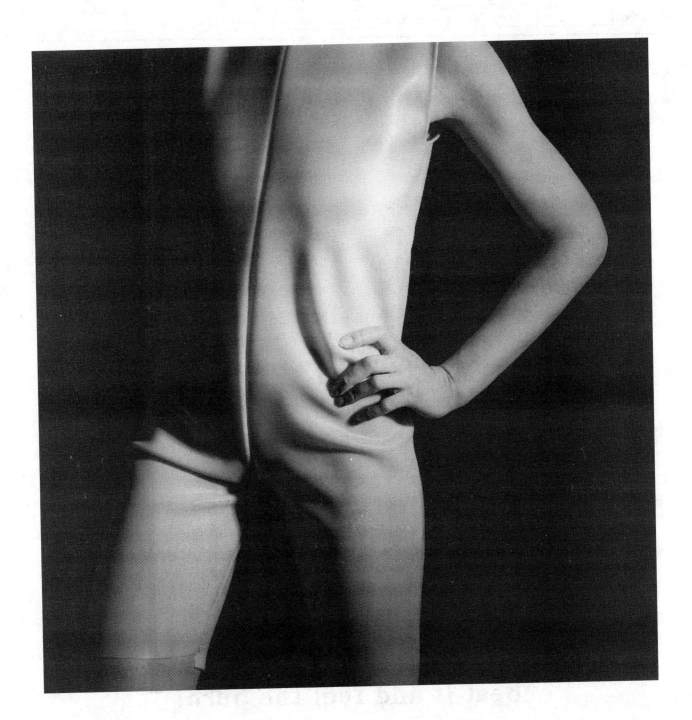

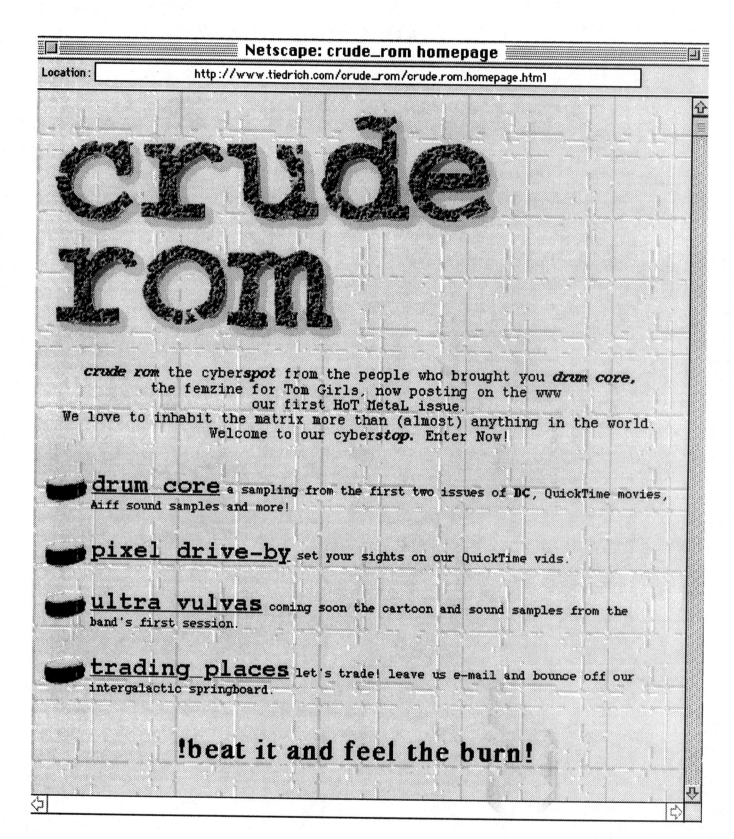

Netscape: crude_rom homepage

Location: http://www.tiedrich.com/crude_rom/crude.rom.homepage.html

# crude rom

*crude rom* the cyber*spot* from the people who brought you *drum core*, the femzine for Tom Girls, now posting on the www our first HoT MetaL issue.
We love to inhabit the matrix more than (almost) anything in the world.
Welcome to our cyber*stop*. Enter Now!

**drum core** a sampling from the first two issues of **DC**, QuickTime movies, Aiff sound samples and more!

**pixel drive-by** set your sights on our QuickTime vids.

**ultra vulvas** coming soon the cartoon and sound samples from the band's first session.

**trading places** let's trade! leave us e-mail and bounce off our intergalactic springboard.

## !beat it and feel the burn!

ELIZABETH SANTEIX, CYBERSPACE

http://www.tiedrich.com/crude_rom/crude.rom.homepage.html

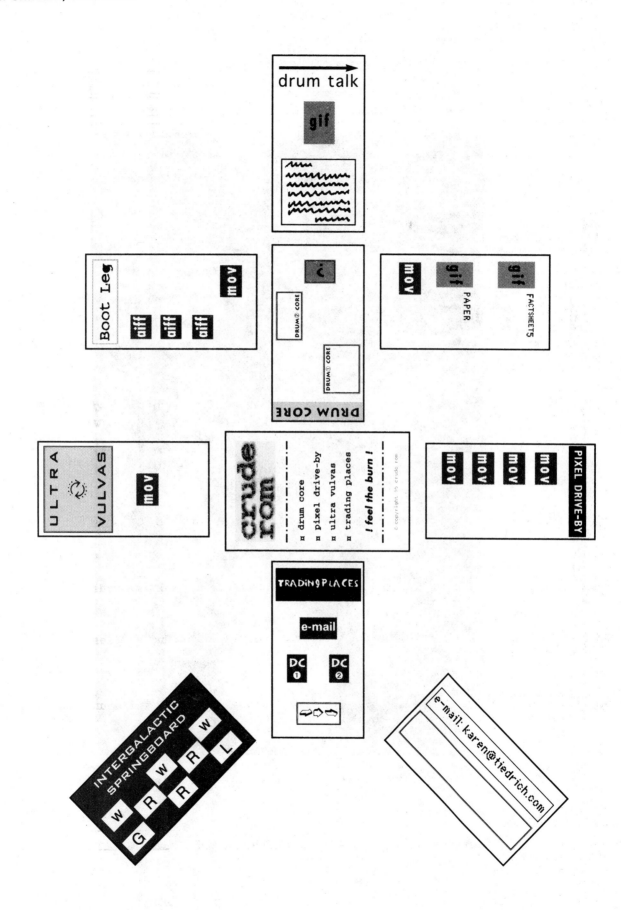

YOUTH CULTURE

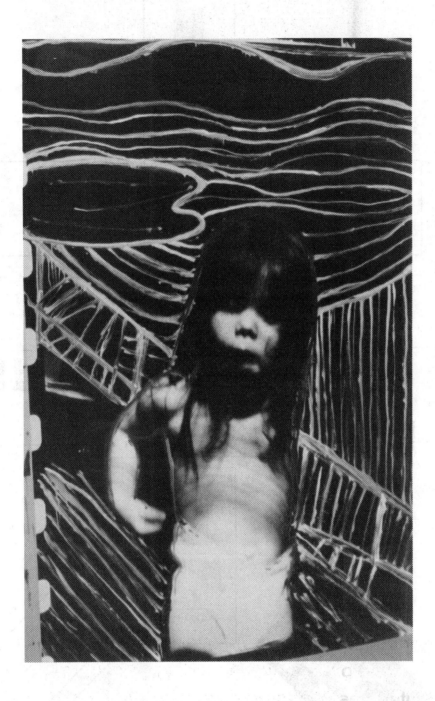

**Suzanne Fiol**  *The Cry at the End of the Millenium,  1995 ,  Oil on Cibachrome.*

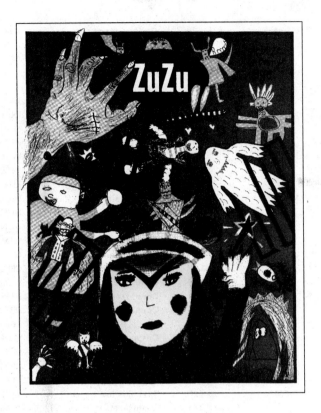

# May 1992 - July 1995

**A three year publishing project featuring the work of artists, writers
and other restless youth age 3 and up.
Distributed free of charge throughout New York City and
additional venues around the world.**

## Beck Underwood – publisher

# ONE OF THE MANY THINGS YOU CAN DO WITH THIS TIME CAPSULE:

## GIVE IT TO A FRIEND.

**DATE DUE**

| | | | |
|---|---|---|---|
| | | | |
| | | | |
| | | | |
| | | | |
| | | | |
| | | | |
| | | | |
| | | | |
| | | | |
| | | | |
| | | | |
| | | | |
| | | | |

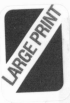
27 DEC 1990

DEMCO